# JUDE AND 2 PETER

# Baker Exegetical Commentary on the New Testament

## ROBERT W. YARBROUGH
## AND ROBERT H. STEIN, EDITORS

Volumes now available

| | |
|---|---|
| Matthew | *David L. Turner* |
| Mark | *Robert H. Stein* |
| Luke | *Darrell L. Bock* |
| John | *Andreas J. Köstenberger* |
| Acts | *Darrell L. Bock* |
| Romans | *Thomas R. Schreiner* |
| 1 Corinthians | *David E. Garland* |
| Philippians | *Moisés Silva* |
| 1 Peter | *Karen H. Jobes* |
| 1–3 John | *Robert W. Yarbrough* |
| Jude and 2 Peter | *Gene L. Green* |
| Revelation | *Grant R. Osborne* |

**Gene L. Green** (PhD, University of Aberdeen) is professor of New Testament at Wheaton College in Illinois. He previously taught New Testament at the Seminario ESEPA in Costa Rica and is the author of two Spanish-language commentaries, *1 Pedro y 2 Pedro* and *1 y 2 Tesalonicenses*. In addition to contributing articles to various books and journals, he is the author of *The Letters to the Thessalonians* (Pillar Commentary Series) and coauthor of *The New Testament in Antiquity*.

# JUDE AND 2 PETER

GENE L. GREEN

Baker Exegetical Commentary on the New Testament

**B** **Baker Academic**
*a division of Baker Publishing Group*
Grand Rapids, Michigan

Published by Baker Academic
a division of Baker Publishing Group
P.O. Box 6287, Grand Rapids, MI 49516-6287
www.bakeracademic.com

Printed in the United States of America

Library of Congress Cataloging-in-Publication Data

Green, Gene L.
    Jude and 2 Peter / Gene L. Green.
       p.  cm.  — (Baker exegetical commentary on the new testament)
    Includes bibliographical references and indexes.
    ISBN 978-0-8010-2672-0 (cloth)
    1. Bible. N.T. Jude—Commentaries. 2. Bible. N.T. Peter, 2nd—Commentaries.  I. Title.
  II. Title: Jude and Second Peter.
    BS2815.53.G74  2008
    227'.9307—dc22                                           2008022211

In memoriam
Rachel Griego (†2005)
Faithful student of Scripture

# Contents

*Series Preface  ix*
*Author's Preface  xi*
*Abbreviations  xiv*
*Transliteration  xx*
*Map  xxii*

**Introduction to Jude  *1***
  I. Epistolary Greeting (1–2)  *43*
 II. Letter Body: An Exhortation to Contend for the Faith (3–23)  *51*
    A. Disclosure of Jude's Purpose for Writing: An Exhortation to the Beloved (3–4)  *52*
    B. A Call to Remember: Predictions about the Heretics and Fulfillment (5–19)  *61*
    C. Exhortations to the Beloved (20–23)  *119*
III. Closing Doxology (24–25)  *130*

**Introduction to 2 Peter  *139***
  I. Epistolary Greeting (1:1–2)  *171*
 II. Letter Body: A Warning against False Teachers (1:3–3:18a)  *178*
    A. Body Opening: God's Call to Glory and Virtue (1:3–11)  *179*
    B. Body Middle: The Apostolic Testimony and the False Teachers (1:12–2:22)  *205*
    C. Body Closing: A Call to Holiness (3:1–18a)  *308*
III. Letter Closing: A Doxology (3:18b)  *344*

*Works Cited  345*
*Index of Subjects  377*
*Index of Authors  384*
*Index of Greek Words  388*
*Index of Scripture and Other Ancient Writings  389*

# Series Preface

The chief concern of the Baker Exegetical Commentary on the New Testament (BECNT) is to provide, within the framework of informed evangelical thought, commentaries that blend scholarly depth with readability, exegetical detail with sensitivity to the whole, and attention to critical problems with theological awareness. We hope thereby to attract the interest of a fairly wide audience, from the scholar who is looking for a thoughtful and independent examination of the text to the motivated lay Christian who craves a solid but accessible exposition.

Nevertheless, a major purpose is to address the needs of pastors and others involved in the preaching and exposition of the Scriptures as the uniquely inspired Word of God. This consideration directly affects the parameters of the series. For example, serious biblical expositors cannot afford to depend on a superficial treatment that avoids the difficult questions, but neither are they interested in encyclopedic commentaries that seek to cover every conceivable issue that may arise. Our aim, therefore, is to focus on those problems that have a direct bearing on the meaning of the text (although selected technical details are treated in the additional notes).

Similarly, a special effort is made to avoid treating exegetical questions for their own sake, that is, in relative isolation from the thrust of the argument as a whole. This effort may involve (at the discretion of the individual contributors) abandoning the verse-by-verse approach in favor of an exposition that focuses on the paragraph as the main unit of thought. In all cases, however, the commentaries will stress the development of the argument and explicitly relate each passage to what precedes and follows it so as to identify its function in context as clearly as possible.

We believe, moreover, that a responsible exegetical commentary must take fully into account the latest scholarly research, regardless of its source. The attempt to do this in the context of a conservative theological tradition presents certain challenges, and in the past the results have not always been commendable. In some cases, evangelicals appear to make use of critical scholarship not for the purpose of genuine interaction but only to dismiss it. In other cases, the interaction glides over into assimilation, theological distinctives are ignored or suppressed, and the end product cannot be differentiated from works that arise from a fundamentally different starting point.

The contributors to this series attempt to avoid these pitfalls. On the one hand, they do not consider traditional opinions to be sacrosanct, and they are certainly committed to do justice to the biblical text whether or not it supports such opinions. On the other hand, they will not quickly abandon a long-standing view, if there is persuasive evidence in its favor, for the sake of fashionable theories. What is more important, the contributors share a belief in the trustworthiness and essential unity of Scripture. They also consider that the historic formulations of Christian doctrine, such as the ecumenical creeds and many of the documents originating in the sixteenth-century Reformation, arose from a legitimate reading of Scripture, thus providing a proper framework for its further interpretation. No doubt, the use of such a starting point sometimes results in the imposition of a foreign construct on the text, but we deny that it must necessarily do so or that the writers who claim to approach the text without prejudices are invulnerable to the same danger.

Accordingly, we do not consider theological assumptions—from which, in any case, no commentator is free—to be obstacles to biblical interpretation. On the contrary, an exegete who hopes to understand the apostle Paul in a theological vacuum might just as easily try to interpret Aristotle without regard for the philosophical framework of his whole work or without having recourse to those subsequent philosophical categories that make possible a meaningful contextualization of his thought. It must be emphasized, however, that the contributors to the present series come from a variety of theological traditions and that they do not all have identical views with regard to the proper implementation of these general principles. In the end, all that really matters is whether the series succeeds in representing the original text accurately, clearly, and meaningfully to the contemporary reader.

Shading has been used to assist the reader in locating the introductory comments for each section. Textual variants in the Greek text are signaled in the author's translation by means of half-brackets around the relevant word or phrase (e.g., ⌜Gerasenes⌝), thereby alerting the reader to turn to the additional notes at the end of each exegetical unit for a discussion of the textual problem. The documentation uses the author-date method, in which the basic reference consists of author's surname + year + page number(s): Fitzmyer 1992: 58. The only exceptions to this system are well-known reference works (e.g., BDAG, LSJ, *TDNT*). Full publication data and a complete set of indexes can be found at the end of the volume.

Robert Yarbrough
Robert H. Stein

# Author's Preface

The Baker Exegetical Commentary on the New Testament is a series designed to engage scholars as well as pastors and others who preach and exposit Scripture. It also invites lay Christians to join in the discussion about the books of the New Testament. Given these goals, writing on Jude and 2 Peter is a daunting task indeed. Among scholars, Jude and 2 Peter have lived on the margins. The critical issues of authorship, audience and environment swirl around any academic discussion of these letters. Jude has been tagged the "Most Neglected" of New Testament books (Rowston 1975). Jack Elliott once called 1 Peter an "Exegetical Stepchild" (J. H. Elliott 1976), leaving us wondering about the family status of 2 Peter. A colleague once commented that these epistles are hardly in the center of the canon. The situation in the church has not been much better. We often hear Jude's doxology (vv. 24–25), and appeals are made to 2 Peter 1:21 in discussions about inspiration. But few sermons locate their foundations in these books and church curricula rarely include discussion of them. Lay Christians may know something about how Jude and 2 Peter are related, but few take them up as texts for a Bible study or reading. These epistles are difficult to interpret and present unique challenges, such as Jude's quotation of 1 Enoch and the predominance of severe language about judgment throughout.

Yet interest in these books is on the rise, and their study is experiencing a revival. A number of commentaries have been published since Bauckham's monumental work (Bauckham 1983),[1] and more are currently in production. At the Annual Meeting of the Society of Biblical Literature, a new consultation was formed called "Methodological Reassessments of the Letters of James, Peter, and Jude." The 2007 meeting focused on 2 Peter and Jude. Moreover, these books by the "Jerusalem Pillars" are moving from the margins toward the center as their canonical significance undergoes reexamination (Nienhuis 2007). This commentary is part of this movement to reassess the message of these books in the hope that they will find a more central place in the life of the church. Their value is much greater than their neglect would suggest. Moving beyond the negative assessments they have received and into a more positive, complete, and nuanced understanding of their message will help us understand more clearly the shape of early Christian faith and our own. The

---

1. Unfortunately, the commentaries by Davids (2006) and Reese (2007) appeared too late to be included in my discussion of these letters.

things that are "hard to understand" (2 Pet. 3:15) are not limited to Paul's writings, but these letters' difficulties do not diminish their value.

The particular concern of this commentary is to read these letters within their cultural and historical contexts. Contextual concerns are not secondary to any communication, whether oral or written. Misunderstanding the appropriate contextual information can distort our understanding of the message being communicated. This task is difficult enough when people live in the same era in a common culture, but when we seek to cross the bridge of time, space, and culture to listen to an ancient author, the task becomes supremely daunting. Reading the letters of Jude and 2 Peter within their contexts is especially problematic due to the difficulty of locating both the authors and the readers. The analysis of Jude and 2 Peter in this commentary seeks to take into account the web of Jewish and Hellenistic culture in which they are embedded. They represent a dialogue with the Jewish heritage as well as the wider philosophical and social realities of life around the eastern Mediterranean. Moreover, this exposition attempts to read the whole of the story and each part in light of the whole. The analysis is detailed, yet the whole situation of the readers is kept in view and the overall thrust of the message remains clearly in sight.

The commentary also addresses difficult interpretive issues in an attempt to move the discussion forward. Questions of authorship, the nature of the relationship between the letters, and the use of pseudepigraphical literature are all given due attention, though without any illusion that all readers will be satisfied with my conclusions. Finally, the theological concerns of the letters are woven together with the contextual and historical discussions. Theology and history can be and should be discussed together and not bifurcated into discrete domains.

As with any work of this type, a cadre of people have contributed to its production in very significant ways. My wife, Deborah, and daughter, Christiana, once again traveled with me to Cambridge, England, where I wrote the major portion of the commentary. Deborah worked as a midwife for the National Health Service and kept our financial foundation firm during our sojourn as well as acting as an ever-constant encourager. Christiana was willing to be uprooted from high school to attend The Leys and embraced her new educational environment with great relish and success. This work never would have been accomplished without the help and sacrifice of these wonderful women.

I must also thank all the staff at Tyndale House in Cambridge who provided great logistic support. Bruce Winter, the former Warden; Elizabeth Magba, the librarian; as well as David Instone-Brewer, David Baker, Tania Raiola, and Fiona Craig labored together to create an environment ideal for research. The final work on this commentary was completed at Wheaton College's Buswell Memorial Library. Thanks go to Lisa Richmond, the librarian, and especially to Greg Morrison for attending to my needs while spending long summer days at Buswell. Wheaton College provided sabbatical leave, and an

Alumni Association Grant helped finance this research effort. Without such generosity this project would not have seen the light of day.

There are a number of people who worked directly with me on the production of this volume, and I owe them many thanks. My assistant, Christopher Hays, labored tirelessly in hunting down literature, checking all the references in the book, doing the first edit, and dialoguing with me about the contents. Out of that work came his first published article (Hays 2004), the promise of good things to come from an excellent scholar. When this project was first under way, Peter Spychalla did a journeyman's job in gathering bibliographic information. I am also very grateful for the editorial labors of Bob Yarbrough, one of the general editors of this series, and Wells Turner of Baker Academic. Their careful eyes, discerning questions, and wise suggestions greatly improved the quality of the book.

While writing this commentary, I had the opportunity to teach a course at Wheaton College on the Petrine Epistles and Jude. Running a bit of a risk, I encouraged the students in their writing for the course by stating that I would include something from the best essay in the commentary. The quality of the essays was quite good, though a bit uneven. However, one stood out head and shoulders above the rest, that of Rachel Griego. Rachel was a psychology major at the college, who loved life and friends and also played the flute quite well. Her essay is a brilliant and insightful piece of research, showing that she was a careful reader of texts, a critical thinker, and a creative writer. As promised, her essay is included in this volume. Most sadly, she did not survive to see the publication of this book. Rachel was killed in an automobile accident in 2005. She is sorely missed by family, friends, and teachers, but her voice and her example live on. Rachel was one of the many students I have seen over the years who come to class with a longing to learn the message of Scripture. She was a model young interpreter who took seriously the careful and sometimes laborious study of the New Testament. She excelled, and serves still as a model of the type of engagement all students of Scripture can and should have. Rachel was quiet in class, but her mind was alive with the texts we read together. This commentary is dedicated to Rachel, a faithful and exemplary student of Scripture.

# Abbreviations

## Bibliographic and General

| | |
|---|---|
| *ABD* | *The Anchor Bible Dictionary*, edited by D. N. Freedman et al., 6 vols. (New York: Doubleday, 1992) |
| AD | *anno Domini*, in the year of our Lord |
| *ANF* | *The Ante-Nicene Fathers*, edited by A. Roberts and J. Donaldson, 10 vols. (1885–87; reprinted, Peabody, MA: Hendrickson, 1994) |
| BC | before Christ |
| BCE | before the common era |
| BDAG | *A Greek-English Lexicon of the New Testament and Other Early Christian Literature*, by W. Bauer, F. W. Danker, W. F. Arndt, and F. W. Gingrich, 3rd ed. (Chicago: University of Chicago Press, 2000) |
| BDF | *A Greek Grammar of the New Testament and Other Early Christian Literature*, by F. Blass and A. Debrunner, translated and revised by R. W. Funk (Chicago: University of Chicago Press, 1961) |
| ca. | *circa*, approximately |
| CE | common era |
| cent. | century |
| cf. | *confer*, compare |
| e.g. | *exempli gratia*, for example |
| Eng. | English |
| *Ep.* | *Epistle(s)* |
| frg(s). | fragment(s) |
| Gk. | Greek |
| *IDBSup* | *Interpreter's Dictionary of the Bible: Supplementary Volume*, edited by K. Crim (Nashville: Abingdon, 1976) |
| intro. | introduction |
| KJV | King James Version |
| l(l). | line(s) |
| lit. | literally |
| LSJ | *A Greek-English Lexicon*, by H. G. Liddell, R. Scott, and H. S. Jones, 9th ed. (Oxford: Clarendon, 1968) |

| | |
|---|---|
| LXX | Septuagint; LXX S, Sinaiticus manuscript of LXX |
| 𝔐 | the reading of the majority of the Byzantine textual witnesses |
| MM | *The Vocabulary of the Greek Testament*, by J. H. Moulton and G. Milligan (London: Hodder & Stoughton, 1930; reprinted, Peabody, MA: Hendrickson, 1997) |
| MS(S) | manuscript(s) |
| NA[27] | *Novum Testamentum Graece*, edited by [E. and E. Nestle,] B. Aland et al., 27th rev. ed. (Stuttgart: Deutsche Bibelgesellschaft, 1993) |
| NASB | New American Standard Bible |
| *NewDocs* | *New Documents Illustrating Early Christianity*, edited by G. H. R. Horsley and S. R. Llewelyn (North Ryde, NSW: Ancient History Documentary Research Centre, Macquarie University, 1981–) |
| *NIDNTT* | *New International Dictionary of New Testament Theology*, edited by C. Brown, 4 vols. (Grand Rapids: Zondervan, 1975–85) |
| *NIDOTTE* | *New International Dictionary of Old Testament Theology and Exegesis*, edited by W. A. VanGemeren, 5 vols. (Grand Rapids: Zondervan, 1997) |
| NIV | New International Version |
| NJB | New Jerusalem Bible |
| NKJV | New King James Version |
| NLT | New Living Translation |
| NRSV | New Revised Standard Version |
| NT | New Testament |
| OCD | *The Oxford Classical Dictionary*, edited by S. Hornblower and A. Spawforth, 3rd ed. (Oxford: Oxford University Press, 1996) |
| ODCC | *The Oxford Dictionary of the Christian Church*, edited by F. L. Cross and E. A. Livingstone, 3rd ed. (Oxford: Oxford University Press, 1997) |
| OG | Old Greek |
| OT | Old Testament |
| OTP | *The Old Testament Pseudepigrapha*, edited by J. H. Charlesworth, 2 vols. (Garden City, NY: Doubleday, 1983–85) |
| par. | parallel(s) |
| PGL | *Patristic Greek Lexicon*, edited by G. W. H. Lampe (Oxford: Clarendon, 1968) |
| RSV | Revised Standard Version |
| Str-B | *Kommentar zum Neuen Testament aus Talmud und Midrasch*, by H. L. Strack and P. Billerbeck, 6 vols. (Munich: Beck, 1922–61) |
| *TDNT* | *Theological Dictionary of the New Testament*, edited by G. Kittel and G. Friedrich, translated and edited by G. W. Bromiley, 10 vols. (Grand Rapids: Eerdmans, 1964–76) |
| Theod. | Theodotion's Greek recension/translation of the Hebrew Bible |
| *TLNT* | *Theological Lexicon of the New Testament*, by C. Spicq, translated and edited by J. D. Ernest, 3 vols. (Peabody, MA: Hendrickson, 1994) |
| TNIV | Today's New International Version |
| UBS[4] | *The Greek New Testament*, edited by B. Aland et al., 4th rev. ed. (Stuttgart: Deutsche Bibelgesellschaft and United Bible Societies, 1994) |
| *v.l.* | *varia lectio*, variant reading |

## Hebrew Bible

| | | | | | |
|---|---|---|---|---|---|
| Gen. | Genesis | 2 Chron. | 2 Chronicles | Dan. | Daniel |
| Exod. | Exodus | Ezra | Ezra | Hos. | Hosea |
| Lev. | Leviticus | Neh. | Nehemiah | Joel | Joel |
| Num. | Numbers | Esth. | Esther | Amos | Amos |
| Deut. | Deuteronomy | Job | Job | Obad. | Obadiah |
| Josh. | Joshua | Ps(s). | Psalms | Jon. | Jonah |
| Judg. | Judges | Prov. | Proverbs | Mic. | Micah |
| Ruth | Ruth | Eccles. | Ecclesiastes | Nah. | Nahum |
| 1 Sam. | 1 Samuel | Song | Song of Songs | Hab. | Habbakuk |
| 2 Sam. | 2 Samuel | Isa. | Isaiah | Zeph. | Zephaniah |
| 1 Kings | 1 Kings | Jer. | Jeremiah | Hag. | Haggai |
| 2 Kings | 2 Kings | Lam. | Lamentations | Zech. | Zechariah |
| 1 Chron. | 1 Chronicles | Ezek. | Ezekiel | Mal. | Malachi |

## Greek Testament

| | | | | | |
|---|---|---|---|---|---|
| Matt. | Matthew | Eph. | Ephesians | Heb. | Hebrews |
| Mark | Mark | Phil. | Philippians | James | James |
| Luke | Luke | Col. | Colossians | 1 Pet. | 1 Peter |
| John | John | 1 Thess. | 1 Thessalonians | 2 Pet. | 2 Peter |
| Acts | Acts | 2 Thess. | 2 Thessalonians | 1 John | 1 John |
| Rom. | Romans | 1 Tim. | 1 Timothy | 2 John | 2 John |
| 1 Cor. | 1 Corinthians | 2 Tim. | 2 Timothy | 3 John | 3 John |
| 2 Cor. | 2 Corinthians | Titus | Titus | Jude | Jude |
| Gal. | Galatians | Philem. | Philemon | Rev. | Revelation |

## Other Jewish and Christian Writings

| | | | |
|---|---|---|---|
| Acts Pet. | Acts of Peter | 1 En. | 1 Enoch (Ethiopic Apocalypse) |
| Add. Esth. | Additions to Esther | | |
| Apoc. Ab. | Apocalypse of Abraham | 2 En. | 2 Enoch (Slavonic Apocalypse) |
| Apoc. El. | Apocalypse of Elijah | | |
| Apoc. Pet. | Apocalypse of Peter | 3 En. | 3 Enoch (Hebrew Apocalypse) |
| As. Mos. | Assumption of Moses | | |
| Ascen. Isa. | Martyrdom and Ascension of Isaiah | 1 Esd. | 1 Esdras |
| | | 2 Esd. | 2 Esdras (4 Ezra) |
| Bar. | Baruch | *Haer.* | Augustine, *Heresies*; Hippolytus, *Refutation of All Heresies*; or Irenaeus, *Against Heresies* |
| 2 Bar. | 2 Baruch (Syriac Apocalypse) | | |
| 4 Bar. | 4 Baruch (Paraleipomena Jeremiou) | | |
| | | Herm. *Mand.* | Shepherd of Hermas, *Mandate* |
| Barn. | Barnabas | | |
| 1–2 Clem. | 1–2 Clement | Herm. *Sim.* | Shepherd of Hermas, *Similitude* |
| Did. | Didache | | |
| Diogn. | Diognetus | Ign. *Eph.* | Ignatius, *Letter to the Ephesians* |
| *Div. Inst.* | Lactantius, *The Divine Institutes* | | |
| | | Ign. *Trall.* | Ignatius, *Letter to the Trallians* |
| *Eccl. Hist.* | Eusebius, *Ecclesiastical History* | | |
| | | Jdt. | Judith |
| | | Jos. Asen. | Joseph and Aseneth |

| | | | |
|---|---|---|---|
| Jub. | Jubilees | Strom. | Clement of Alexandria, Stromata (Miscellanies) |
| L.A.B. | Pseudo-Philo, Liber antiquitatum biblicarum | Sus. | Susanna |
| L.A.E. | Life of Adam and Eve | T. Ab. | Testament of Abraham |
| Let. Aris. | Letter of Aristeas | T. Ash. | Testament of Asher |
| Let. Jer. | Letter of Jeremiah | T. Benj. | Testament of Benjamin |
| 1–4 Macc. | 1–4 Maccabees | T. Dan. | Testament of Dan |
| Mart. Pol. | Martyrdom of Polycarp | T. Iss. | Testament of Issachar |
| Odes Sol. | Odes of Solomon | T. Job | Testament of Job |
| Pan. | Epiphanius, Panarion (Refutation of All Heresies) | T. Jos. | Testament of Joseph |
| | | T. Jud. | Testament of Judah |
| | | T. Levi | Testament of Levi |
| Pol. Phil. | Polycarp, Letter to the Philippians | T. Mos. | Testament of Moses |
| | | T. Naph. | Testament of Naphtali |
| Pr. Azar. | Prayer of Azariah | T. Reu. | Testament of Reuben |
| Ps. Sol. | Psalms of Solomon | T. Sol. | Testament of Solomon |
| Rab. | Rabbah | T. Zeb. | Testament of Zebulun |
| Sib. Or. | Sibylline Oracles | Tob. | Tobit |
| Sir. | Sirach (Ecclesiasticus) | Wis. | Wisdom of Solomon |

## Josephus

| | |
|---|---|
| Ag. Ap. | Against Apion |
| Ant. | Jewish Antiquities |
| J.W. | Jewish War |
| Life | The Life |

## Philo

| | | | |
|---|---|---|---|
| Abraham | On the Life of Abraham | Moses | On the Life of Moses |
| Agriculture | On Agriculture | Names | On the Change of Names |
| Alleg. Interp. | Allegorical Interpretation | | |
| Cherubim | On the Cherubim | Planting | On Planting |
| Confusion | On the Confusion of Tongues | Posterity | On the Posterity of Cain |
| | | QG | Questions and Answers on Genesis |
| Decalogue | On the Decalogue | | |
| Dreams | On Dreams | Rewards | On Rewards and Punishments |
| Drunkenness | On Drunkenness | | |
| Embassy | On the Embassy to Gaius | Sacrifices | On the Sacrifices of Cain and Abel |
| Eternity | On the Eternity of the World | | |
| | | Sobriety | On Sobriety |
| Giants | On Giants | Spec. Laws | On the Special Laws |
| Good Person | That Every Good Person Is Free | Unchangeable | That God Is Unchangeable |
| | | Virtues | On the Virtues |
| Heir | Who Is the Heir? | Worse | That the Worse Attacks the Better |
| Joseph | On the Life of Joseph | | |
| Migr. | On the Migration of Abraham | | |

## Rabbinic Tractates

The abbreviations below are used for the names of the tractates in the Mishnah (indicated by a prefixed *m.*), Tosefta (*t.*), Babylonian Talmud (*b.*), and Jerusalem/Palestinian Talmud (*y.*).

| | | | |
|---|---|---|---|
| B. Bat. | *Baba Batra* | Ber. | *Berakot* |
| B. Meṣiʿa | *Baba Meṣiʿa* | Sanh. | *Sanhedrin* |

## Targums

| | | | |
|---|---|---|---|
| Tg. Isa. | Targum Isaiah | Tg. Onq. | Targum Onqelos |
| Tg. Jon. | Targum Jonathan | Tg. Ps.-J. | Targum Pseudo-Jonathan |
| Tg. Neof. | Targum Neofiti | | |

## Qumran / Dead Sea Scrolls

| | | | |
|---|---|---|---|
| CD | Damascus Document | 4Q'Amram | Visions of Amram (4Q543–548) |
| 1QapGen | Genesis Apocryphon | | |
| 1QH | Thanksgiving Hymns/ Psalms (*Hodayot*) | 4QAstronomical Enoch | 4Q208–211 |
| 1QM | War Scroll (*Milḥamah*) | 4QEnoch | 4Q201–202, 204–207, 212 |
| 1QpHab | Commentary on Habakkuk | 4QFlor | Florilegium (4Q174) |
| 1QS | Rule of the Community (*Serek Hayaḥad*) | 4QPrayer of Enoch/Enosh | 4Q369 |
| 1QSa | Rule of the Congregation (1Q28a) | 4QpsJub | Pseudo-Jubilees (4Q227) |
| | | 11QpsZion | Pseudo-Zion (11Q5) |

## Greek Papyri and Inscriptions

| | |
|---|---|
| *BGU* | *Aegyptische Urkunden aus den Königlichen/Staatlichen Museen zu Berlin, Griechische Urkunden* (Berlin, 1895–) |
| *CPJ* | *Corpus papyrorum judaicarum*, edited by V. Tcherikover, 3 vols. (Cambridge, 1957–64) |
| *CPR* | *Corpus papyrorum Raineri archeducis Austriae* (Vienna, 1895–) |
| *IT* | *Inscriptiones graecae Epiri, Macedoniae, Thraciae, Scythiae*, part 2: *Inscriptiones Macedoniae*, fascicle 1: *Inscriptiones Thessalonicae et viciniae*, edited by Charles Edson (Berlin: de Gruyter, 1972) |
| P.Amh. | *The Amherst Papyri, Being an Account of the Greek Papyri in the Collection of the Right Hon. Lord Amherst of Hackney, F.S.A. at Didlington Hall, Norfolk*, edited by B. P. Grenfell and A. S. Hunt, 2 vols. (London, 1900–1901) |
| P.Berlin | Berlin papyrus 7927, in Fritz Krebs, *Hermes* 30 (1895): 144–50; and in Herwig Maehler, *Zeitschrift für Papyrologie und Epigraphik* 23 (1976): 1–20; cf. *BGU* |
| P.Cair.Zen. | *Zenon Papyri, Catalogue général des antiquités égyptiennes du Musée du Caire*, edited by C. C. Edgar, 5 vols. (Cairo, 1925–40) |
| P.Dura | *The Excavations at Dura-Europos Conducted by Yale University and the French Academy of Inscriptions and Letters*, final report 5.1: *The Parchments and Papyri*, edited by C. B. Welles, R. O. Fink, and J. F. Gilliam (New Haven: Yale University Press, 1959) |
| P.Fay. | *Fayûm Towns and Their Papyri*, edited by B. P. Grenfell, A. S. Hunt, D. G. Hogarth, and J. G. Milne (London: Egypt Exploration Fund, 1900) |

| | |
|---|---|
| P.Oxy. | *The Oxyrhynchus Papyri*, edited by B. P. Grenfell et al., 66 vols. (London: Egypt Exploration Society, 1898–1999) |
| P.Ryl. | *Catalogue of the Greek and Latin Papyri in the John Rylands Library, Manchester*, edited by A. S. Hunt et al., 4 vols. (Manchester, 1911–52) |
| P.Stras. | *Griechische Papyrus der Kaiserlichen Universitäts- und Landesbibliothek zu Strassburg*, edited by F. Preisigke, 9 vols. (Leipzig, 1912–89) |
| P.Tebt. | *The Tebtunis Papyri*, edited by B. P. Grenfell et al., 4 vols. (London: Egypt Exploration Society, 1902–76) |
| SIG | *Sylloge inscriptionum graecarum*, edited by W. Dittenberger, 3rd ed., 4 vols. (Leipzig: Hirzelium, 1915–24) |

## Classical Writers

| | | | |
|---|---|---|---|
| Ag. Cleom. | Plutarch, *Agis and Cleomenes* | Hist. an. | Aristotle, *History of Animals* |
| All. | Heraclitus, *Homeric Allegories* | Il. | Homer, *Iliad* |
| Anab. | Arrian, *Anabasis*; or Xenophon, *Anabasis* | Inst. | Quintilian, *Institutio oratoria* |
| Ann. | Tacitus, *Annals* | Inv. | Cicero, *De inventione rhetorica* |
| Ant. rom. | Dionysius of Halicarnassus, *Roman Antiquities* | Juvenal | *Satires* |
| Art | Horace, *Art of Poetry* | Lives | Diogenes Laertius, *Lives and Opinions of Eminent Philosophers* |
| Athenaeus | *Deipnosophistae* | | |
| Att. | Cicero, *Epistulae ad Atticum* | Lucretius | *De rerum natura* (*On the Nature of Things*) |
| Bell. civ. | Appian, *Civil Wars* | Marcus Aurelius | *Meditations* |
| Cyr. | Xenophon, *Cyropaedia* (*The Education of Cyrus*) | Mem. | Xenophon, *Memorabilia* |
| Demon. | Isocrates, *Ad Demonicum* | Mete. | Aristotle, *Meteorology* |
| Dio Cassius | *Roman History* | Mor. | Plutarch, *Moralia* |
| Diodorus Siculus | *Historical Library* | Nat. | Pliny the Elder, *Natural History* |
| Disc. | Epictetus, *Discourses* | Nat. d. | Cicero, *On the Nature of the Gods* |
| Div. | Cicero, *On Divination* | | |
| Eloc. | Demetrius, *De elocutione* | Od. | Homer, *Odyssey* |
| Ench. | Epictetus, *Enchiridion* (*Handbook*) | Or. | *Oration(s)*, various writers |
| Ep. Men. | Epicurus, *Letter to Menoeceus* | Pausanius | *Description of Greece* |
| Ep. mor. | Seneca, *Epistulae morales* | Pers. | Aeschylus, *Persians* |
| Eth. Nic. | Aristotle, *Nicomachean Ethics* | Pol. | Aristotle, *Politics* |
| | | Polybius | *Universal History* |
| Fam. | Cicero, *Epistulae ad familiares* | Quintus Smyrnaeus | *Posthomerica* |
| Fat. | Cicero, *On Fate* | Res gestae | Augustus, *Res gestae divi Augusti* (*The Deeds of the Divine Augustus*) |
| Hell. | Xenophon, *Hellenica* | | |
| Hercules | Euripedes, *Madness of Hercules* | Sera | Plutarch, *De sera numinis vindicta* |
| Herodotus | *Histories* | Strabo | *Geography* |
| Hipp. | Euripedes, *Hippolytus* | Thucydides | *History of the Peloponnesian War* |
| Hist. | Tacitus, *Historiae* (*Histories*) | | |

# Transliteration

## Greek

| | | | | | | | | | |
|---|---|---|---|---|---|---|---|---|---|
| α | *a* | ζ | *z* | λ | *l* | π | *p* | φ | *ph* |
| β | *b* | η | *ē* | μ | *m* | ρ | *r* | χ | *ch* |
| γ | *g/n* | θ | *th* | ν | *n* | σ/ς | *s* | ψ | *ps* |
| δ | *d* | ι | *i* | ξ | *x* | τ | *t* | ω | *ō* |
| ε | *e* | κ | *k* | ο | *o* | υ | *y/u* | ʽ | *h* |

### Notes on the Transliteration of Greek
1. Accents, lenis (smooth breathing), and *iota* subscript are not shown in transliteration.
2. The transliteration of asper (rough breathing) precedes a vowel or diphthong (e.g., ἁ = *ha*; αἱ = *hai*) and follows ρ (i.e., ῥ = *rh*).
3. *Gamma* is transliterated *n* only when it precedes γ, κ, ξ, or χ.
4. *Upsilon* is transliterated *u* only when it is part of a diphthong (i.e., αυ, ευ, ου, υι).

## Hebrew

| | | | | |
|---|---|---|---|---|
| א | ʾ | ע | ʿ | |
| בּ ב | *b* | פּ פ ף | *p* | |
| ג | *g* | צ ץ | *ṣ* | |
| ד | *d* | ק | *q* | |
| ה | *h* | ר | *r* | |
| ו | *w* | שׂ | *ś* | |
| ז | *z* | שׁ | *š* | |
| ח | *ḥ* | ת | *t* | |
| ט | *ṭ* | | | |
| י | *y* | בָ | *ā* | qāmeṣ |
| כּ כ ך | *k* | בַ | *a* | pataḥ |
| ל | *l* | הַ | *a* | furtive *pataḥ* |
| מ ם | *m* | בֶ | *e* | sĕgôl |
| נ ן | *n* | בֵ | *ē* | ṣērê |
| ס | *s* | בִ | *i* | short *ḥireq* |

| | | | | | |
|---|---|---|---|---|---|
| בִ | ī | long *ḥîreq* written defectively | בֶּי | ê | *sĕgôl yôd* ('בֶ = *êy*) |
| בָ | o | *qāmeṣ ḥāṭûp* | בֵּי | ê | *ṣērê yôd* ('בֵ = *êy*) |
| בוֹ | ô | *ḥôlem* written fully | בִּי | î | *ḥîreq yôd* ('בִ = *îy*) |
| בֹ | ō | *ḥôlem* written defectively | בֲ | ă | *ḥāṭēp pataḥ* |
| בוּ | û | *šûreq* | בֱ | ě | *ḥāṭēp sĕgôl* |
| בֻ | u | short *qibbûṣ* | בֳ | ŏ | *ḥāṭēp qāmeṣ* |
| בֻ | ū | long *qibbûṣ* written defectively | בְ | ĕ | vocal *šĕwā'* |
| בָה | â | final *qāmeṣ hē'* (בָה = *āh*) | | | |

## Notes on the Transliteration of Hebrew

1. Accents are not shown in transliteration.
2. Silent *šĕwā'* is not indicated in transliteration.
3. The spirant forms ב ג ד כ פ ת are usually not specially indicated in transliteration.
4. *Dāgeš forte* is indicated by doubling the consonant. Euphonic *dāgeš* and *dāgeš lene* are not indicated in transliteration.
5. *Maqqēp* is represented by a hyphen.

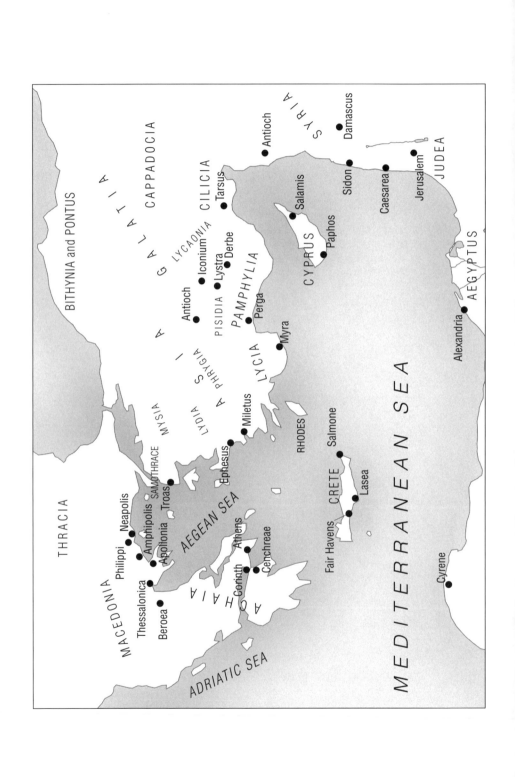

# Introduction to Jude

## Authorship of Jude

According to the normal conventions of ancient Greco-Roman and Semitic letter writing, the Epistle of Jude begins by naming the author "Jude" ('Ιούδας, *Ioudas*).[1] The first line of the letter also includes qualifiers that allowed the readers of the letter to identify him more precisely. He calls himself "a slave of Jesus Christ and brother of James" ('Ιησοῦ Χριστοῦ δοῦλος, ἀδελφὸς δὲ 'Ιακώβου, *Iēsou Christou doulos, adelphos de Iakōbou*). The first reason the author would need to include such additional identification would be to distinguish himself from the many others who went by the name "Jude." In her catalog of names known to us from Palestine, Ilan (2002: 112–25) records 179 occurrences of the name יְהוּדָה (*Yĕhûdâ*, Judah), which is transliterated into Greek as 'Ιούδας.[2] "Jude" was a very common Hebrew name because of its patriarchal (Matt. 1:2–3) and tribal (Matt. 2:6) roots. The author is Jewish since in ancient literature and inscriptions "Jude" never appears as the name of a gentile. 'Ιούδας is variously rendered as Jude, Judas, Judah, and Judea (Luke 1:39), a point that occasionally surprises readers of the English Bible.

In the NT, the name 'Ιούδας appears forty-five times, occasionally as the tribal name Judah (Matt. 2:6; Heb. 7:14; 8:8; Rev. 5:5; 7:5) or the region Judea (Luke 1:39 uses it imprecisely referring to all Palestine, including Galilee). The individuals who bear the name include the patriarch Judah, son of Jacob and father of Perez and Zerah, who appears in the Jesus genealogies (Matt. 1:2–3; Luke 3:33–34) along with Judah the son of Joseph and father of Simeon (Luke 3:30). The most famous 'Ιούδας in the NT is Judas Iscariot (Matt. 10:4; 26:14, 25, 47; 27:3; Mark 3:19; 14:10, 43; Luke 6:16; 22:3, 47, 48; John 6:71; 12:4; 13:2, 26, 29; 18:2–3, 5; Acts 1:16, 25). The others are the revolutionary Judas the Galilean (Acts 5:37; Josephus, *J.W.* 2.17.8 §433; *Ant.* 18.1.1 §§1–10; 18.1.6 §23); Judas of Damascus, in whose house Saul lodged (Acts 9:11); and Judas called Barsabbas, a Jerusalemite prophet in the early church (Acts 15:22, 27, 32). Only these last two are possible candidates for authorship, but it is unlikely that either of them penned the book since the author designates

---

1. Occasionally Aramaic letters began with the name of the recipient (Fitzmyer 1974b: 221–22; and see Weima 1994: 63–73; Taatz 1991: 105–6).

2. Other spellings of the Greek transliteration (some declined) are 'Ιούδης (*Ioudēs*), 'Ιούδα (*Iouda*), 'Ιούδον (*Ioudon*), 'Ιούδατος (*Ioudatos*), 'Ιωύδου (*Iōydou*), 'Ιουδίου (*Ioudiou*), 'Ιοδίου (*Iodiou*), 'Ιουδαῖος (*Ioudaios*), 'Ιεδδοῦν (*Ieddoun*), and possibly 'Ιαύδα (*Iauda*).

himself as "the brother of James." Another of the Twelve is also named Jude, "son of James" (Luke 6:16; John 14:22; Acts 1:13). But this apostle could not be the author of the book since he was a son of someone called James and not his brother.

"Jude . . . the brother of James" is most likely the same person who is named, along with James, as one of the siblings of Jesus (Matt. 13:55; Mark 6:3). The fact that Jude is named at the very end of the list of Jesus's brothers, along with Simon, may indicate that he was the youngest or the next to the youngest male in the family (Jesus's sisters are also mentioned in Mark 6:3, without any indication of their number or names). At various points in the Gospels and Acts, reference is made to Jesus's siblings (Mark 3:32, as his "brothers and sisters"; John 7:3, 5, 10, with a note that they did not believe in Jesus during his ministry; Acts 1:14, gathered with the disciples before Pentecost). Occasionally these family members are said to be in the company of Mary (Matt. 12:46; Acts 1:14), suggesting an earlier death of their father, Joseph. The "brothers of the Lord" were known widely in the early church, alongside the apostles, and appear to have engaged in missionary activity (1 Cor. 9:5).

Since Jude mentions James with no further qualification, we should likely identify this James with "the Lord's brother" who was one of the "pillars" of the Jerusalem church (Gal. 2:9; and see Bauckham 1995a). He was a witness of the resurrection, according to Paul (1 Cor. 15:7), and became the principal leader of the Jerusalem church after Peter "went to another place" (Acts 12:17).[3] James appears as the head of the church both at the time of the Jerusalem Council (Acts 15:13; and see Gal. 2:12) and when Paul returned to Jerusalem after his missionary journeys (Acts 21:18). James had become so prominent a figure in the early church that in the epistle that bears his name he is simply identified as "James, a slave of God and of the Lord Jesus Christ" (James 1:1). Given the prominence of James, the lesser-known Jude could easily secure his own identification by styling himself as the "brother of James." Since honor in the Mediterranean world is shared among members of a family (Neyrey 1993: 3–7; Bartchy 1999; Malina 2001: 37–38), the honor ascribed to James as the leader of the Jerusalem church would enhance the status of Jude in the eyes of his readers. In other words, by identifying himself as the "brother of James," Jude makes a claim to authority that parallels Paul's affirmations of his apostleship (Gal. 1:1), although Jude's familial honor and authority are not identical with apostleship.

Some confusion existed in the early church regarding the identification of Jude. While a number of the fathers understood him to be the brother of the Lord, others also identified him with Jude the apostle. The opinion also circulated that he was the apostle otherwise called Thaddeus (Matt. 10:3;

3. Subsequent to his release from jail, Peter went to the house of Mary, mother of John Mark, where after relating the events of his liberation he said, "Tell these things to James and the brothers" (Acts 12:17). The "brothers" may be the brothers of Jesus (Acts 1:14) and not the larger company of disciples.

Mark 3:18). Still others said Jude was one of the other names of Thomas. In his *Comments on the Epistle of Jude* (1–4), Clement of Alexandria not only states that Jude is the Lord's brother, but also comments on the author's reluctance to identify himself as such: "Jude, who wrote the Catholic Epistle, the brother of the sons of Joseph, and very religious, whilst knowing the near relationship of the Lord, yet did not say that he himself was His brother. But what said he? 'Jude, a servant of Jesus Christ,'—of Him as Lord; but 'the brother of James.' For this is true; he was His brother, (the son) of Joseph." Jerome (*Lives of Illustrious Men* 4) likewise comments that the person who wrote the book is "Jude, the brother of James."

In his discussion of Jesus's siblings, Origen confirms this identification (*Commentary on Matthew* 10.17). On the other hand, Jude is sometimes called "the apostle Jude" (Tertullian, *The Apparel of Women* 1.3; Origen, *On Opposing Powers* 3.2; Augustine, *City of God* 15.23; 18.38). In the Western church, this member of the Twelve (Luke 6:16) was considered to be the same person as the brother of the Lord called by that name (*ODCC* 907). Bede (Hurst 1985: 241), on the other hand, stated that "the apostle Jude, whom Matthew and Mark in their Gospels call Thaddeus, writes against the same perverters of the faith whom both Peter and John condemn in their Letters." The Syrian church forwarded another possibility by occasionally conflating the tradition about Jude with that of Thomas, the supposed author of the Gospel of Thomas. This work begins: "These are the secret sayings that the living Jesus spoke and Didymos Judas Thomas recorded." Eusebius (*Eccl. Hist.* 1.13.10) is aware of this tradition and states, "To these epistles there was added the following account in the Syriac language. 'After the ascension of Jesus, Judas, who was also called Thomas, sent to him Thaddeus, an apostle, one of the Seventy.'"

The name Jude also appears in the lists of bishops of Jerusalem enumerated by Eusebius (*Eccl. Hist.* 4.5.3) and Epiphanius (*Pan.* 66.20.1–2).[4] Epiphanius identifies Jude as the third bishop of Jerusalem, after James and Simeon. The Apostolic Constitutions (7.46) concurs with this identification: "Now concerning those bishops which have been ordained in our lifetime, we let you know that they are these: James the bishop of Jerusalem, the brother of our Lord; upon whose death the second was Simeon the son of Cleopas; after whom the third was Judas the son of James." Eusebius, on the other hand, says the third bishop was Justus, although he concurs that the first two were James and Simeon.

Which of these identifications of the third bishop is accurate is difficult to assess. The names of James, Simon, and Jude are familiar to us as members of the sibling circle of Jesus. But the Apostolic Constitutions' identification of Jude as the "son of James" appears to associate him with James, one of the Twelve (Luke 6:16; Acts 1:13), and Simeon is named as the son of Cleopas. However, since the confusion between Jude the member of the Twelve and Jude the brother of Jesus was common in the early church, we may still assume that the

4. For a discussion of the lists in relation to Jude, see Bauckham 1990: 70–79.

names refer to Jesus's relatives. Moreover, under the Hieronymian (Jerome's) view of Jesus's family (see below), Simeon was known as the son of Cleopas and the cousin of Jesus. In other words, despite the respective identifications in the bishop list of the Apostolic Constitutions, James, Simeon, and Jude may still be identified by the unknown author of this work as Jesus's relatives. Both Epiphanius and Eusebius agree in naming yet another Jude as the last of fifteen Jewish bishops in the city. It is sheer speculation that the fifteenth and final Jewish bishop of Jerusalem was the author of the epistle since no biblical or early church evidence points to such an association. However, the naming of James, Simeon, and Jude as the first bishops of the city is another indication of the way the early church recognized the family of Jesus.

Whichever way the evidence is understood, we cannot draw from it any conclusions regarding the authorship of the epistle. The internal evidence from the NT, however, favors identifying Jude as the brother of Jesus and James, known to us from the Gospels (Matt. 13:55; Mark 6:3).

There was considerable discussion in the early church about the siblings of Jesus and whether they were a product of the union of Joseph and Mary or whether their family line was different. Bauckham (1990: 19–32) summarizes the three views that have found voice in the church, each "known by the names of fourth-century proponents of each, as the Helvidian view (sons of Joseph and Mary), the Epiphanian view (sons of Joseph by his first marriage) and the Hieronymian view (cousins)." In the Hieronymian view, James and Judas should be identified with "James the younger and of Joses," sons of Mary (Mark 15:40), who is "Mary the wife of Clopas" (John 19:25 NRSV), the sister (or more likely, the sister-in-law) of Mary, mother of Jesus. This view also identified Clopas with Alphaeus, father of James, one of the Twelve (Matt. 10:3; Mark 3:18). However, since James and Jude are mentioned in the circle of nuclear family relationships (Matt. 13:55—father/son, mother/son, brothers/sisters), the most accessible reading would be that they were children of this union, and as such half brothers of Jesus. Origen (*Commentary on Matthew* 10.17) mentions the position that came to be known as Epiphanian and explains, "But some say, basing it on a tradition in the Gospel according to Peter, as it is entitled, or 'The Book of James,' that the brethren of Jesus were sons of Joseph by a former wife, whom he married before Mary. Now those who say so wish to preserve the honour of Mary in virginity to the end" (cf. Infancy Gospel of James 9.8). While this view is more likely than the Hieronymian, it is less probable than the Helvidian. At best we can say that it is possible but not probable. But Origen's claim that those who held it did so "to preserve the honour of Mary" should be given full weight. This view is distinctly theological.

The other question that has occupied both ancient and modern commentators is whether Jude is an authentic or pseudepigraphic work. Writing under the name of another was well known and practiced in the ancient world for a variety of reasons, including the desire to gain financial profit, to discredit the opinions of an opponent, to augment the authority of a writing by an unknown author, or to show love for a teacher under whose name one writes (Baum 2001: 42–48). Should Jude be classified as a pseudepigraphic letter?

Serious questions about the book's authenticity were raised in the ancient church. While the letter was accepted widely in the West and in Alexandria, the Syrian churches were slow to acknowledge its canonicity. This is in line with the general tendency of the Alexandrian and Syrian churches. While Alexandria took a "maximalist" approach, allowing a wider variety of books at the beginning and then culling the list, Syria adopted a "minimalist" approach, which meant accepting those twenty-two books that were secure and slowly admitting others (Metzger 1987: 284). The ancient fourth- or fifth-century Syriac version of the NT, known as the Peshitta (or Peshito), excluded Jude along with 2 Peter, 2 and 3 John, and Revelation (Murdock 1851: 495–96). But eventually it was included in the early sixth-century edition of Philoxenus (AD 507/508). Eusebius commented that Jude was one of the "disputed" books (*Eccl. Hist.* 2.23.25; 3.25.3; 6.13.6; 6.14.1), although he recognized that it was read publicly in many churches. Origen (*Commentary on John* 19.6) mentions that doubts existed about the authenticity of Jude, but apparently he did not share them since in his *Commentary on Romans* (3.6) he quotes Jude 6 and classifies the text as "Holy Scripture." He comments that Jude "wrote a letter of few lines, it is true, but filled with the powerful words of heavenly grace" (*Commentary on Matthew* 10.17).

What doubts did arise about the authenticity of Jude can be traced primarily to the epistle's use of 1 Enoch (Jude 14–15). Jerome (*Lives of Illustrious Men* 4), who accepts the book as authentic, says, "Jude, the brother of James, left a short epistle which is reckoned among the seven catholic epistles, and because in it he quotes from the apocryphal book of Enoch it is rejected by many. Nevertheless by age and use it has gained authority and is reckoned among the Holy Scriptures." Didymus of Alexandria (fourth century) likewise accepted Jude despite the sources it used. Over against Jerome's comment about those who rejected Jude, the citation was also read as a confirmation that 1 Enoch should be regarded as Scripture since the canonical book of Jude quotes it. Tertullian interjects a rather lengthy discussion of 1 Enoch in his *On the Apparel of Women*, concluding his argument in favor of its acceptance in the church by saying, "To these considerations is added the fact that Enoch possesses a testimony in the Apostle Jude" (*The Apparel of Women* 1.3). Augustine, on the other hand, later admitted that while Jude is canonical, Enoch should not be accepted by the church. He asks, "Does not the canonical epistle of the Apostle Jude declare that he prophesied?" (*City of God* 18.38). Yet he concludes of Enoch, "But the purity of the canon has not admitted these writings, not because the authority of these men who pleased God is rejected, but because they are not believed to be theirs" (see also 15.23). Whatever doubts were entertained about the authenticity of Jude did not appear to have any other root cause apart from its use of apocryphal sources. Jerome's comment about its antiquity and apparently wide use was enough to secure its authoritative place in the church. No clear voice was raised in antiquity about the possibility that Jude did not write the book, although some confusion did exist about the identity of this Jude.

On the positive side of the ledger, Jude was known and read early in the church and was accepted in the second-century[5] Muratorian Canon and that of Athanasius in the mid-fourth century. The comment in the Muratorian Canon frames Jude over against those books, such as the Epistle to the Laodiceans, "which cannot be received into the catholic church, for it is not fitting that gall be mixed with honey" (66–67). Jude along with two Epistles of John were accepted because they were used in the catholic church (68–69). Clement of Alexandria esteemed Jude highly enough to write a commentary on it, explaining to his gentile audience the meaning of this letter, which exudes the strong flavors of Palestinian Judaism (see below on Jude's place of writing).

Jerome's testimony of the book's early use in the church may possibly be supplemented with the allusions to Jude in other fathers. Bigg and Chaine (Bigg 1901: 306–8; Chaine 1939: 261–62) have assembled lists of references or echoes of Jude in the writings of the fathers, including the second-century Theophilus of Antioch, Athenagoras, Polycarp, and Clement, as well as the Martyrdom of Polycarp, the Didache, Hermas, and the Epistle of Barnabas. The parallels produced are not compelling (Chaine even calls them "vague," and Bigg counts the evidence as "scanty and shadowy"). Many of them could derive from the common liturgical language of the church rather than being evidence of the use of Jude in the church.[6] At best we could say that Jude fits neatly into the conceptual and linguistic frame of the fathers, but this is hardly compelling reason to affirm the book's authenticity.

However, the earliest and strongest testimony of Jude's acceptance comes from 2 Peter. The second chapter of 2 Peter reproduces much of Jude, a phenomenon that can be adequately explained only if we suppose that Peter used Jude (see the introduction on the sources of 2 Peter). The weight of this evidence will vary depending on one's view of the authorship and date of 2 Peter. If Peter truly wrote that book, then we have solid testimony of the

---

5. The date, however, is disputed by some who opt for a fourth-century origin. See "Authorship of 2 Peter" in the introduction to that letter.

6. Compare, e.g., the greeting in Polycarp, *Philippians* ("May mercy and peace from God Almighty and Jesus Christ our Savior be multiplied to you," ἔλεος ὑμῖν καὶ εἰρήνη παρὰ θεοῦ παντοκράτορος Ἰησοῦ Χριστοῦ τοῦ σωτῆρος ἡμῶν πληθυνθείη, *eleos hymin kai eirēnē para theou pantokratoros Iēsou Christou tou sōtēros hēmōn plēthyntheiē*) with that in Jude 2 ("May mercy, peace, and love be multiplied to you," ἔλεος ὑμῖν καὶ εἰρήνη καὶ ἀγάπη πληθυνθείη, *eleos hymin kai eirēnē kai agapē plēthyntheiē*). Or cf. 1 Clem. 65.2 ("through whom [Christ] may there be to him [God] glory, honor, power and majesty, eternal dominion, from the ages into the ages of the ages," δι᾿ οὗ αὐτῷ δόξα, τιμή, κράτος καὶ μεγαλωσύνη, θρόνος αἰώνιος ἀπὸ τῶν αἰώνων εἰς τοὺς αἰῶνας τῶν αἰώνων, *di hou autō doxa, timē, kratos kai megalōsynē, thronos aiōnios apo tōn aiōnōn eis tous aiōnas tōn aiōnōn*) with Jude 25 ("To the only God our Saviour, through Jesus Christ our Lord, be glory, majesty, power, and authority through all the ages and now and into all the ages," μόνῳ θεῷ σωτῆρι ἡμῶν διὰ Ἰησοῦ Χριστοῦ τοῦ κυρίου ἡμῶν δόξα μεγαλωσύνη κράτος καὶ ἐξουσία πρὸ παντὸς τοῦ αἰῶνος καὶ νῦν καὶ εἰς πάντας τοὺς αἰῶνας, *monō theō sōtēri hēmōn dia Iēsou Christou tou kyriou hēmōn doxa, megalōsynē kratos kai exousia pro pantos tou aiōnos kai nyn kai eis pantas tous aiōnas*).

early date and use of Jude. But even if we suppose that 2 Peter is an early second-century document, we would still have strong evidence concerning Jude's early date and use. While the arguments concerning Jude's date and use are not decisive in determining authenticity, they demonstrate that within a significant sector of the church few doubts were entertained about Jude's provenance. Those that did arise can be accounted for by reference to Jude's use of apocryphal literature and the Syrian church's cautious approach to questions of canon.

The contemporary debate about the authorship of Jude revolves around the issues of the Greek style of the epistle, the traces in the letter of a sub-apostolic outlook, and the identification of the heretics whose position the epistle counters. The Greek of Jude's Epistle shows clear evidences of mastery of the language, raising the question of whether a person reared in Galilee could attain this level of linguistic ability in a language that is not his mother tongue, especially if he were not part of the social elite. Oleson (1979: 495) comments that "the relative purity of the Greek prose style of Jude suggests both careful composition and deep Hellenization—although not necessarily Greek racial origin," while Kelly (1969: 233) concludes that "while a Galilean like Jude must have spoken Greek fluently, it is not easy to imagine him handling the language with such art." In his extensive treatment of Jude's literary strategy, J. Charles (1993: 37) says that "Jude shows a normal use of the Greek idiom with bits of artistic flair" and speaks glowingly, along with other commentators, of Jude's "use of very good literary Greek, whether in writing flair or vocabulary." This contemporary assessment agrees with Origen's comment that the book was filled with "powerful words of heavenly grace" (*Commentary on Matthew* 10.17). Jude's composition is replete with vocabulary found nowhere else in the NT (Neyrey 1993: 27; Bauckham 1983: 6), and his style is quite refined.

Over against this assessment of the epistle's style is the enduring question of the linguistic skills of Galileans. Horsley's (1996: 154–75) study of Greek and Hellenization in Galilee leads him to conclude that, as in the rest of the empire, "literacy in Judea and Galilee was concentrated among the political-cultural elite. . . . It seems highly unlikely that many villagers were literate" (158). While we expect Greek to be the common tongue in the gentile city of Sepphoris, "there is much less of an indication that Greek was an everyday language in the rest of Lower Galilee. Pidgin Greek may have been common, but a bilingual situation seems unlikely given evidence now available" (171). Though Nazareth was located near Sepphoris, "we cannot conclude, on the basis of their supposed contact with Sepphoris, that most Galileans had become accustomed to speaking Greek in the first century C.E." (Horsley 1995: 247). Linguistic ability was tied closely to a person's social status. Those of the social elite were the ones adept in Greek. If Horsley's conclusions are correct,[7] then

---

7. Sevenster (1968: 185–86), however, comes to a more positive conclusion saying, "No matter how very superficial and sketchy that knowledge [of Greek] was, many from all layers of

the fine Greek style that J. Charles celebrates becomes distinctly problematic if we argue in favor of authenticity.

In the case of Jude, however, two factors mitigate against this negative assessment. First, we know that Jude, along with the other brothers of Jesus, engaged in itinerant ministry, which presupposes that they either had or acquired fluency in Greek (they hardly traveled with a phrase book, as a modern tourist might do). How they acquired this skill we can only surmise, but that they had gained some mastery of the tongue is hard to deny on historical grounds. Moreover, insufficient weight has been given to the role of secretaries in the composition of letters (see E. Richards 1991; 2004). At times the name of a secretary appears at the end of NT letters (Rom. 16:22; 1 Pet. 5:12), and in other cases we become aware of their presence as Paul steps out to include a final greeting in his own hand (1 Cor. 16:21; Gal. 6:11; Col. 4:18; 2 Thess. 3:17; Philem. 19). But numerous surviving ancient papyri letters show a change in penmanship at the end, indicating that the author took the pen from the secretary and added a final note, with no remark placed in the text of the letter that the pen had changed hands (Weima 1994: 119; Stowers 1986: 60–61; Deissmann 1911: 170–73, 179–80).

Jude, as others during his period, most likely made use of the services of a secretary when he composed the letter. People who did not possess a high degree of literacy "paid professional scribes to draft communication on their behalf. The practice passes undetected in private correspondence" (White 1986: 216). Only in official or legal correspondence was the inclusion of the name of the scribe required. So common was the custom of engaging scribes that such paperwork was done in the streets. In fact, the number of standardized phrases and clichés that fill ancient correspondence, including NT letters, gives evidence of the industry (White 1986: 219, index of conventions on 237). Jude should not be rejected on stylistic grounds since we have no idea how much help he would have received from either a fellow believer or professional scribe. Scribes could take dictation but in other cases would be invested with greater literary responsibilities.

Another objection commonly raised to the authenticity of Jude is the author's reference to the apostolic company as a group in the past. In verses 17–18 Jude calls his readers to "remember the words previously spoken by the apostles of our Lord Jesus Christ." Jude not only implies that he is not a member of the apostolic company but also seems to invest them with a prophetic insight characteristic of those now deceased (cf. 2 Pet. 3:2–3, which is dependent on Jude 17–18). Vielhauer and Strecker (1992: 572) observe: "Only in the post-apostolic generation do 'the apostles of the Lord' become the bearers and the guarantors of apocalyptic tradition" (Jude 17; cf. 5, 18). But Jude hardly relegates the apostles to a previous generation since, in verse 18, he reminds the readers that "they said *to you* that. . . ." The readers themselves lived in

---

society understood it and were able to speak and write it." J. Charles (1993: 69–71) likewise has a more positive assessment of Greek usage in Palestine. For a survey of opinion on the use of Greek in Palestine, see Porter 1994.

the apostles' days, and the apostolic prophecy was for them. Verse 18 implies that the readers heard the apostles' predictions. In these verses, Jude simply wants his readers to recall what they had previously heard and knew, which included the testimony of Scripture (vv. 5–7), the Enoch prophecy (vv. 14–15), and the apostolic predictions (vv. 17–18, and comments on the passage).

Perhaps the more vexing question is the identification of the heretics that Jude seeks to combat. Were these second-century gnostics of some variety, or does the error fit within the frame of problems the church encountered in the first century? If the opponents can be securely identified with some group that was active during the early second century AD, then the case for the authenticity of Jude would be damaged beyond repair. The issue of the heretics' identification will be taken up below, however, and here we simply observe that the type of heresy the epistle addresses fits neatly into the history of the first-century church. The errorists apparently perverted the doctrine of grace as taught by Paul and others and turned it into an excuse for moral license (Jude 4). Paul defended the gospel he preached against this type of perversion of grace (Rom. 6:1, 15). The way that Jude speaks of the faith as sacred tradition that must be held fast and defended (Jude 3) is not unlike Paul's attempt to arrest a heresy in the Thessalonian church by appeal to the received tradition (2 Thess. 2:15 and comments in G. Green 2002: 329–30; 1 Cor. 15:1–8). The deep concern Jude has about the sexual immorality of these heretics (Jude 7–8, 16, 18) and his affirmation that they have denied the Lord by their libertine lifestyle (v. 4) echoes the critique of and warnings against (gentile) lusts, a common topos in the early church (Rom. 1:24; 6:12; 13:13; 2 Cor. 12:21; Eph. 4:3, 19; Titus 1:15; James 1:15; 1 Pet. 1:14; 4:2–3; 1 John 2:16–17). There is, on the other hand, no hint in this epistle of later gnostic cosmology and anthropology, based on the dualism between spirit and matter, nor of its offer of salvation through esoteric knowledge. Jude's perspective is apocalyptic and not gnostic. Given this, his writing fits within the theological matrix of the early church.

The authenticity of Jude will undoubtedly continue to be a subject of debate, but in light of the absence of any compelling arguments to the contrary, we should accept that the letter is a genuine composition written by Jude, albeit likely with some scribal assistance. The issues raised and responses given in Jude stand within the milieu of first-century Christianity, and the weight of early church tradition and internal evidence stand in favor of its authenticity. Where doubts were raised, the concern was with the letter's use of apocryphal literature and not any other consideration.[8] Jude is a representative of non-Pauline Christianity and gives us valuable insight into the character of the early church, most likely within the confines of Palestine.

## Jude and His Circle

Jude's letter is devoid of any precise indication of either the identity of its first readers or of his readers' whereabouts. How, then, do we locate this book

---

8. For a survey of the debate about the book's authorship, see Bauckham 1990: 171–78.

within the matrix of early Christian history? Fuchs and Raymond (1988: 151–52) recognize the difficulties inherent in trying to answer this question and conclude that the best we can do is discuss the cultural milieu of the author and readers. To be sure, localizing the book will depend on the conclusions reached regarding authorship and the heresy he combats. So, for example, if we reckon that the letter was not written by Jude and that the heretics are gnostics, then we may possibly understand the book as part of the matrix of early second-century Christianity in Alexandria, where the gnostic sect of the Carpocratians was becoming established. On the other hand, if we acknowledge that Jude was written by the brother of the Lord himself and that it does not attack a gnostic threat, we may be able to locate it within the matrix of early Jewish Christianity in Palestine. Our reading strategy for this epistle will, in the end, be determined by our answer to this question. Yet at the same time, our reading of the book will be the starting point for placing this piece into the larger puzzle of early Christianity. Whatever hypothesis we construct regarding the social location of Jude and his readers will be modified as we continue to read the epistle within the context of the cultural and theological currents of those early years of the Christian faith.

This species of historical investigation is more than guesswork. Reese (2000: 7) argues that it is essentially no more than that, noting how scholars have variously identified the provenance of the book as anywhere from Antioch to Alexandria and the audience as Jews or gentiles or a mixture of both. According to Reese (2000: 8), the question is of no importance since "even if one could ascertain who the real, original readers of the epistle were, it would still be quite impossible to enter into their minds." For Reese, such endeavors are quixotic. The end result is nothing more than an author and first readers who are merely the contemporary reader's construct. Therefore, "in the case of the epistle of Jude the search for the original readers has been hampered by the lack of available information, but even if real, original readers were to be found, they would be constructs of the commentator rather than real people into whose minds and responses one could enter" (Reese 2000: 8). The role of contemporary readers vis-à-vis texts, authors, and original readers is a hermeneutical issue that goes beyond the scope of this commentary. At this point, I suggest only that the reader-oriented approach that Reese adopts leads, in the end, to historical nihilism and, ultimately, to the breakdown of communication and the possibility of knowing. While we cannot claim certainty in our endeavor to hear faithfully as would a first reader, we are able to work out interpretations to the best possible explanation. This is the case for all human communication, real time or otherwise, yet we are able to carry on speaking/writing and understanding satisfactorily.[9]

---

9. For a summary of the issues involved and the players in the current hermeneutical climate, see Vanhoozer 1998. The present commentary will work within the framework of understanding the role of readers/hearers and authors/readers forwarded by relevance theory as developed by Sperber and Wilson (1995).

Jude has occasionally been located within the sphere of Syrian Christianity, likely around the city of Antioch. Bigg (1901: 321) tentatively sees Jude in these environs, stating, "We may say that no better conjecture can be proposed: but even this is far from certain." His level of uncertainty is reflected in his remark that, in fact, "Jude may have been addressed to almost any community in which Greek was spoken." Grundmann (1974: 19–20) follows a modification of this line, stating that the letter was written for Jewish Christian communities somewhere between Jerusalem and Antioch. Kelly (1969: 234) and Schelkle (1980: 178) are likewise open to either a Syrian or Palestinian origin. M. Green (1987: 56) is somewhat more positive in his conclusion, accepting "somewhere like Antioch as a probable destination," an assessment with which H. Koester (1982: 2.247) concurs. The reasons for this identification vary.

M. Green (1987: 56), on the one hand, observes that the author's knowledge of Pauline teaching argues for this identification as does the mention of the apostles in verse 17, some of whom carried out ministry there. H. Koester (1982: 2.247), on the other hand, opts for a Syrian origin because of the conflation of the traditions about Thomas and Jude. The Gospel of Thomas, as noted above, was ascribed to Didymos Judas Thomas, and Eusebius (*Eccl. Hist.* 1.13.10) mentions an account that came down to him in the Syriac language that speaks of "Jude, who was also called Thomas." H. Koester (1982: 2.247) sees gnostic claims to spirituality behind the critique in Jude 19 and recalls that Thomas was hailed as an authority among gnostics. But any understanding of Jude that traces its roots back to Syria falls hard on the historical evidence that the epistle was excluded from the Syrian canon until the sixth-century edition of Philoxenus. The epistle was not widely used in the region, despite the confused identification of Jude with Thomas.

A more likely location for Jude is within Egyptian or, more precisely, Alexandrian Christianity. The letter was well known in that area, and Clement of Alexandria even penned a commentary on the epistle. Origen, also from Alexandria, knew and accepted the book. Moreover, not a few commentators have identified the heresy that Jude battles as the gnostic teaching of the Carpocratians, who were located in Alexandria. Clement critiques their libertine sexual practices and concludes his diatribe against them by quoting Jude 8 and 16 (*Strom.* 3.2.11).

Gunther (1984) makes an impressive case for an Alexandrian origin and joins ranks with numerous other scholars (Neyrey 1993: 29; Moffatt 1928: 224; Chaine 1939: 288; Paulsen 1992: 45). In Gunther's (1984: 550) view, "Egypt is the most likely land where such errorists would flourish *and* where the authority of Jesus's brothers would be esteemed at the same time among converts from its huge Alexandrian Jewish population." His argument not only links the heretics with Alexandria but also finds within Jude's letter local allusions to the coastal city of Alexandria, where one could see the "wild waves of the sea that toss up their . . . foam" as they crash on the rocky harbor (Jude 13) and experience the arid climate suggested by Jude's reference to the heretics as "clouds without rain" (v. 12). The reference to the judgment that befell the

Israelites who were liberated from Egypt (v. 5) would not be lost on Alexandrian readers (Gunther 1984: 551–52). Jude's penchant for apocryphal literature (vv. 9, 14–15) suggests Alexandria since the city's library was a center of collecting and copying books. Enoch became especially popular among Alexandrian churches. Gunther (1984: 552) also comments on the points of contact between Jude and Egyptian writings, such as the Preaching of Peter, and suggests that the epistle presupposes the teaching and terminology of the Gospel and Letters of John, which were "arguably composed in Alexandria."

While Gunther's case appears strong, the sole argument of weight is the possibility that the epistle counters the Carpocratian error. As we have seen in the section on the heretics Jude opposes (see above on the heresy), this identification is not as certain as would appear from a first reading of ancient commentators on the sect. Clement of Alexandria does indeed bring Jude's teaching to bear in his polemics against them (*Strom.* 3.2.11; and see Clement's *Letter to Theodorus* 1.3, 7), yet Clement himself relegated Jude to a previous time and comments that "of these and other similar sects Jude, I think, spoke prophetically in his letter." Since Clement wrote a commentary on Jude, his quotation of it (likely from memory) in the *Letter to Theodorus* comes as no surprise.

The other strands of Gunther's argument are not strong enough to support his thesis. Allusions to waves and weather need not be read as local references and, even if they did refer to phenomena in the immediate world of the readers, they would fit in any number of places around the Mediterranean. Jewish apocryphal literature was well known elsewhere and can hardly be a marker for Egypt. The exodus story was part of the fabric of Jewish history and significant not only for Jews who lived in Egypt. Moreover, Jude and James were much better known figures in Palestine than in Egypt. The fact that Origen and Clement knew and used the book is simple testimony of the wide circulation of the book, and we can well understand its importance in an area where heresy was rife. The connection between Jude and the Johannine literature is tenuous, and even if such a connection could be established, a stronger case could be made for localizing them and Jude in Asia Minor.[10] There is no compelling reason to locate Jude within the matrix of early second-century Christianity in Alexandria.

A third suggestion is that the epistle finds its roots within the world of Palestinian Christianity of the first century. The weight of the historical evidence in favor of this reading is impressive (Bauckham 1990: 131–33; Gerdmar 2001: 340; J. Charles 1993: 65–81).[11] The simple, unqualified reference to James (v. 1) is most understandable if we suppose that the author wrote to communities where James was well known and recognized. James had become the leader

10. In fact, Fuchs and Raymond (1988: 144) argue that Jude originates from southern Asia Minor or the region northeast of Edessa in Syria.

11. Bauckham (1983: 16) was previously much more tentative about the milieu of Jude, stating that while it is indebted to Palestinian Jewish literature, its destination may be either Syria or Egypt.

of the Jerusalem church, and his influence there was considerable (see above on the authorship of Jude). Wherever the relatives of Jesus are mentioned in the NT they are associated with Palestine, save for 1 Cor. 9:5. While Jude is likely to have engaged in traveling ministry (1 Cor. 9:5), Hegesippus, quoted by Eusebius (*Eccl. Hist.* 3.19.1–3.20.8; 3.32.5–6), relates a story of Domitian's persecution of Jude's grandsons, who were landed peasants apparently within Palestine. They held leadership positions among the churches, a role that began with James (*Eccl. Hist.* 3.20.8). Eusebius (*Eccl. Hist.* 1.7.14)[12] even notes that the later relatives of Jesus were located in Nazareth and the nearby village of Kokhaba.[13] The family had land holdings in Palestine and continued to be known in the region through the passing of generations. The Jerusalem bishop list may well contain the names of Jesus's brothers, depending on our identification of the "Judes" therein (Bauckham 1990: 77). It appears that Jesus's relatives were very important figures "in the mission and leadership of the churches of Palestine in the first century after the death and resurrection of Jesus" (Bauckham 1990: 131).

Jude's midrashic exegesis of the OT also locates the epistle squarely within the sphere of Palestinian Judaism (J. Charles 1993: 71–81; Bauckham 1990: 179–234). Bauckham (1990: 233) notes that "the letter of Jude contains probably the most elaborate passage of formal exegesis in the manner of the Qumran pesharim to be found in the New Testament. . . . Such exegesis must have flourished especially in the early Palestinian church." Likewise, Jude's use of the Testament of Moses (v. 9 and comments) assumes that the readers understood the allusion. This writing was "best known in the Palestinian Jewish Christian circles" (Bauckham 1990: 280), although the same could be said for mixed Jewish and gentile Christian communities in the region. Moreover, if the influences that the epistle combats are not gnostic, then the possibility of locating Jude within the Palestinian sphere is all the more likely. Bauckham also suggests that 2 Peter's use of Jude (see the introduction to 2 Peter) points to a Palestinian origin given "the debt which all early Christian thought owed to the Palestinian Jewish Christianity of the first two decades" (Bauckham 1990: 178).

The argument in favor of understanding Jude as a product of early Palestinian Christianity is, however, difficult to sustain due to the simple fact that the book was written in Greek. The debate about the extent of Greek usage within Palestine is tied, in the first instance, to authorship (see above on authorship). Could a Galilean produce Greek of this caliber? But the related question,

---

12. Eusebius states that the *desposynoi*, as the blood relatives of Jesus were called, came from the Judean (used generally as all Palestine) villages of Nazareth and Kokhaba and went "into the rest of the earth" or "land" (γῆ) and expounded their genealogy along the way. We have no idea regarding the extent of these travels, but the "land" referred to is most likely Palestine, that is, the land around the cities mentioned. However, it is significant that the family territory is located in Palestine.

13. On the location of the town, see Bauckham 1990: 62–66. Various places were known by the name, including a Christian village in Transjordan and a town near Damascus.

and perhaps the more difficult, is whether Palestinian Jewish believers would have been best served by a letter written in Greek rather than in Aramaic. If Horsley (1996: 154–75) is correct in his assertion that Greek was the tongue of the social elite in Galilee[14] as well as elsewhere within Palestine, should we assume that Jude was penned for those who were part of the social elite? This conclusion would not square with what we know of the sociology of early Christianity anywhere in the empire, although some members of the social elite did become Christians both in Palestine and elsewhere (Mark 2:13–17; Luke 8:3; Acts 4:36–37; 5:1; 12:12–17 [Mary]; 13:1 [Manaen]; Fiensy 1995: 226–30; and see Theissen 1982). However, within Palestine we also encounter a sizable population of Hellenistic Jews who had been raised in the Diaspora and whose mother tongue was Greek (see Acts 2:5–11; 6:1, 9; and Moule 1958–59; Fiensy 1995: 234–36).

However, if we assume that Jude's audience was Palestinian Jewish Christians, we are also confronted with the question of whether the heresy he combats would have found inroads among this populace. The heretics promoted a libertine lifestyle with a highly charged sexuality (vv. 4, 6–8, 16). They corrupted the *agapē* meal of the church, treating it like a typical gentile banquet (v. 12). The appeal of the errorists would seemingly have been stronger among a gentile than a Palestinian Jewish population reared on the strict moral codes of Torah and Judaism. But while sexual immorality was not as rife among the Jewish population as among gentiles, it was hardly unknown. Warnings about sexuality outside the bounds of marriage are abundant (see especially Satlow 1995: 119–83; Ilan 1996: 214–21). Although Tacitus stated that Jewish men "are singularly prone to lust, they abstain from intercourse with foreign women; among themselves nothing is unlawful" (*Hist.* 5.5), prostitution was well known, and the snares of temptation were amply discussed. Sirach 9:2–9 warns:

> Do not give yourself to a woman and let her trample down your strength. Do not go near a loose woman, or you will fall into her snares. Do not dally with a singing girl, or you will be caught by her tricks. Do not look intently at a virgin, or you may stumble and incur penalties for her. Do not give yourself to prostitutes, or you may lose your inheritance. Do not look around in the streets of a city, or wander about in its deserted sections. Turn away your eyes from a shapely woman, and do not gaze at beauty belonging to another; many have

14. Rami Arav (2003), director of the Bethsaida excavations project, has similar reservations about the Greek facility of the Jewish population in Galilee for the following reasons: "(1) Greek is not the native language of Galilee. So the population was supposed to 'learn' it somewhere. (2) So far, no single gymnasium was discovered in the entire country. (3) No Roman theaters were built in Galilee before the second century CE. Greek or Roman theaters are a good hallmark for Greek language and culture. You cannot sit in a Greek theater listening to Sophocles and not understanding Greek. You will be bored in 15 minutes. (4) No Greek temple was discovered in Galilee prior to Herod's Roman imperial temples in Caesarea Maritima and Paneas. In my opinion these are the major hallmarks for Greek culture and language, and they all are absent in Galilee."

been seduced by a woman's beauty, and by it passion is kindled like a fire. Never dine with another man's wife, or revel with her at wine; or your heart may turn aside to her, and in blood you may be plunged into destruction. (NRSV)

The communal gathering of the church around the meal threw men and women into a proximity that would be a source of temptation. Osiek and Balch (1997: 59) comment that in the East "women did not ordinarily attend either public or formal domestic dinners with men," although Jewish men and women did gather for a meal during Passover, with the woman always reclining at her husband's side (Corley 1993: 69, 181). Ben Sirah's warning should be viewed in light of this practice. The kind of temptations the recipients of Jude faced were not foreign to Palestine.

The type of moral error promoted by the heretics could also find root in the soil of Palestinian society since not everyone who lived there was Jewish. Cities with significant gentile populations dotted the landscape, such as Caesarea Maritima, Dor, Ptolemais, Caesarea Philippi, Sepphoris, and Sebaste, not to mention the Greek cities of the Decapolis. Tiberias was likewise a seat of Roman power.[15] Given that the extant evidence for Greek usage in these cities is much higher than elsewhere and that the gentile population in these centers was significant, the converts to whom Jude writes likely included a considerable number of gentiles[16] who lived in Palestine and came within the hearing of the gospel (Cornelius and his family and friends represent this group, as we know from Acts 10). Even if the principal adherents to the faith from among the gentiles had been God-fearers, we should not assume that their embrace of the moral, let alone theological, tenets of Scripture was strong. God-fearers were still considered gentiles and acted as such (Levinskaya 1996: 117–26). Some members of the Jewish social elite may well have been among the members of the church that Jude addresses, given their linguistic facilities. Some members of the Hellenistic Jewish populace who had become Messianists may have been part of the group as well.

Jude, James, and other members of Jesus's family were a recognizable and important group within early Palestinian Christianity. They exercised a leadership role within the church and held an authoritative position that paralleled that of the apostolate. Their authority is suggested by Paul's reference to them alongside the apostles who engaged in Christian mission

15. Chancey (2002) surveys the archaeological and textual evidence for gentile presence in and around Galilee. He concludes that the gentile population estimates for Galilee are commonly overstated. There were, however, numerous centers of gentile population and a presence that went beyond an overlay of gentile culture that was part of the imperial governmental mechanism, as even Chancey's evidence demonstrates. Moreover, Chancey's (2002: 108) argument at times appears to be a case of special pleading, such as his suggestion that the temple in Bethsaida is "nothing more than a rectangular public building." See Arav 1999: 85–87, 97–99; 2001: 245–46.

16. Various authors suggest a gentile audience, yet not within the confines of Palestine (Kelly 1969: 234; Bigg 1901: 231). Others propose a mixed community (Grundmann 1974: 19–20; M. Green 1987: 56; Fuchs and Raymond 1988: 144), while Bauckham postulates a "Jewish Christian community in a Gentile society" (Bauckham 1983: 16; 1990: 374).

(1 Cor. 9:5). The most well known of Jesus's brothers, James, became the leader of the Jerusalem church, and other brothers may have been appointed as bishops within that church. Paul singles out James as one of the witnesses of the resurrection of Christ (1 Cor. 15:7). The descendants of Jude held both property and a position of leadership among the churches, both in Galilee and beyond (Eusebius, *Eccl. Hist.* 3.20.8). According to Eusebius (*Eccl. Hist.* 3.11), after James was martyred, the apostles, disciples, and "those who were, humanly speaking, of the family of the Lord" came together to choose James's successor. They selected "Simeon the son of Clopas, . . . a cousin of the Savior."

We should not, however, think of James, Jude, and the others as holding dynastic leadership (Bauckham 1990: 125–30). James identifies himself as a "slave of Jesus Christ" (1:1) as does Jude (v. 1). Eusebius calls Jude the brother of the Lord "according to the flesh" (κατὰ σάρκα, *kata sarka*; *Eccl. Hist.* 3.20.1; and see 1.7.11; 3.11.1). Jesus's relatives are never viewed in Christian history as any more than this, even though the grandsons of Jude were recognized as being of Davidic descent (Eusebius, *Eccl. Hist.* 3.19.1–3.20.1). They made no claims to royalty, even in the face of Domitian's intent to destroy those of the Davidic line. Despite the deference to the family of Jesus, the family maintained a humble socioeconomic status. There was no large estate or inheritance that Jude passed on to his descendants. Eusebius (3.20.5–6) states that when Jude's grandsons were brought in for interrogation before Domitian, "he asked them how much property they had, or how much money they controlled, and they said that all they possessed was nine thousand denarii between them, the half belonging to each, and they stated that they did not possess this in money but that it was the valuation of only thirty-nine plethra of ground on which they paid taxes and lived on it by their own work. They then showed him their hands, adducing as testimony of their labour the hardness of their bodies, and the tough skin which had been embossed on their hands from their incessant work." Domitian recognized them as nothing more than "simple folk" (3.20.7). Evidently the family of Jesus did not find or seek economic or social advancement due to this significant relationship, thus leaving a fine example for generations of leaders to come.

The Epistle of Jude, therefore, brings us into contact with early Palestinian Christianity that was in the process of opening up to the gentile mission. The approach to Scripture that Jude employs provides insight into the hermeneutic of early Christians within Palestine. The moral issues that the epistle addresses help us understand that concerns for proper conduct, especially sexual morality, were not limited to such places as Corinth and Thessalonica. We also have in this letter, along with James, a representative sampling of the role that the family of Jesus played in the church in Palestine down through the first century. Jude's circle includes not only James but Paul as well, insofar as his teaching had been misappropriated for immoral ends. The use of Jude by 2 Peter alerts us to the way that another representative of Palestinian Christianity was part of the same sphere (see the introduction to 2 Peter).

## Date of Writing

The date we ascribe to Jude's letter depends on a number of conclusions reached concerning the origin of the letter. First, is this a genuine or pseudepigraphic document? Second, was the heresy that the letter addresses a second- or first-century phenomenon? Third, was the error a product of a misinterpretation of Pauline teaching? Fourth, was the epistle used by the author of 2 Peter or did Jude use 2 Peter when he composed his letter? Related to this interpretive problem is the question of the authenticity of 2 Peter. Fifth, does the letter reflect the situation of the postapostolic church that recalled the memory of the apostles (v. 17)? Sixth, does the theological character of this letter fit within early Palestinian Christianity, or with its appeal to tradition (v. 3) is it a product of the early catholic period of the second century? Since the answers to these questions have varied significantly among commentators, the range of dates attached to the epistle is a century wide, with the earliest being the mid-50s and the latest in the mid-second century.[17]

The position taken in this commentary (see the respective sections) is that Jude is an authentic composition of the brother of Jesus and that the heresy against which he warns is not second-century gnosticism but antinomianism, which found its theological base in a misinterpretation of the doctrine of grace as taught by Paul and others. The letter appears to have been used by the author of 2 Peter, which is another indicator of its early date, regardless of the conclusions that might be reached regarding that epistle's authenticity. Moreover, the letter does not regard the apostolic era as being in the distant past since the readers heard the apostles themselves (v. 18a and comments). The theological perspectives reflected in the book are precisely those that were current in the first-century church and appear to reflect a Palestinian milieu. Given these conclusions, a date in the middle of the first century appears likely.

The epistle was written after the conversion of Jude and Paul[18] and late enough for the doctrine of grace to be widely circulated and misinterpreted. These factors yield a terminus a quo of approximately the late 40s. We may also take into consideration Jude's age. If he was the youngest or the next to the youngest of Mary and Joseph's children, his birth could have been as late as AD 10. We have no way of knowing when he died, but he may have survived to the early 70s. There appears to be no consciousness of the turmoil surrounding the first revolt and the destruction of Jerusalem (AD 66–70). This factor, in addition to Jude's age, would give us a terminus ad quem of around the mid-60s. If 2 Peter is regarded as authentic, then Peter's martyrdom (AD 64/65) would further support this terminal date. The antinomian situation that Jude addresses is similar, though not identical, to the tendencies that

17. For a summary of the various dates given by commentators, see Bauckham 1990: 168n237.

18. For a discussion of the date of Paul's conversion, see Riesner 1998, who presents evidence that yields either an early (AD 31/32) or late (AD 36/37) date.

Paul corrected in 1 Corinthians (6:12; 10:23; ca. AD 54/55) and the critiques of the gospel of grace that he endured are echoed in Romans (3:8; 6:1; ca. AD 55–58). The errorists' reading of the doctrine of grace was current during the period. These factors all suggest a date for the epistle sometime in the latter part of the 50s or the first half of the 60s of the first century.

## Occasion of Writing

Jude did not write the letter he originally intended. Apparently he had been eager to compose a letter to a church or churches in Palestine in which he was going to reflect on the "common salvation" (v. 3) that he and they held. But Jude found himself constrained to change his tack because he some way or another had heard that there was trouble among the believers. Some teachers whose conduct was ungodly and whose doctrine was a perversion of the teaching on grace had come in from the outside (v. 4). In fact, they had brought in a theological novelty that was not in agreement with the faith that had been handed down to them as a sacred, divine tradition (v. 3b). The false teachers had transformed the teaching on grace into an excuse for licentious or indecent behavior and, in doing that, were effectively denying the only Master and Lord, Jesus Christ.

The error had both a theological and moral component. Jude's Epistle is an impassioned plea for the believers to engage in battle against the incursion of the error, that is, "to contend for the faith that was once and for all handed down to the saints" (v. 3). This letter exhorts the believers facing the error to be built up and stand firm in the faith (vv. 20–21). But the troublers of the church were persuasive in their appeal and some in the church were being swayed by them. Jude, therefore, calls the church to action. On the one hand, they are to show mercy on those who are wavering (v. 22—see the commentary on the textual problems related to this and the following verse). On the other hand, they must also engage in a rescue operation toward those who have succumbed to the temptation: "Snatch some from the fire" (v. 23). Yet in this operation, Jude is quite concerned that the rescuers themselves not become ensnared by the temptation that the heresy presents. Jude's primary focus, therefore, is on the gospel and the community.

The identification of the heretics is a question that has occupied commentators from ancient times. Clement of Alexandria, for example, believed that Jude spoke prophetically of the Carpocratians, a second-century gnostic sect that promoted unrestrained sexual indulgence (*Strom.* 3.2). Our investigation into their identification must begin with the infiltrators' profile as presented in the epistle. But we should also be aware of Jude's rhetorical strategy as he denounces the heretics. Does he present a topos, or standard treatment of the errorists, employing vilifying language that was commonly used to denounce one's opponents or enemies? Since we know these heretics only through Jude's letter, we need to ask whether his representation of them is faithful to the reality of the situation or whether he exaggerates the problem in an attempt to distance the believers from these interlopers. This question has become part of the critical discussion on the errorists, and anyone who teaches or preaches using this text must grapple with the question of Jude's strategy before using it in a contemporary rhetorical context. If, on the other hand, we can truly outline the contours of the heresy from the evidence in the epistle, is it then possible to identify the error promoted by examining sources outside Jude? That is, can we triangulate on their persons or teachings by using other extant evidence from Scripture and the ancient world? Are they the same heretics who had caused problems in the church to which 2 Peter is addressed? Were they gnostics, perhaps even the Carpocratians themselves whom Clement and Irenaeus denounced?

Jude indicates that these heretics had put a new spin on the doctrine of grace by promoting the theology that grace freed a person from moral constraint (v. 4). They knew Christian teaching and were perhaps influenced by Pauline doctrine. The fact that they feasted with the believers in the agape meal indicates that they were recognized by the church as being disciples (v. 12). Jude states that they had denied the Lord (v. 4) but does not indicate, as does 2 Peter, that they had previously been genuine disciples (see the introduction to 2 Peter and comments on 2 Pet. 2:1). Jude does not develop the idea that they held a defective Christology, which suggests that the denial of which Jude speaks is practical. Their conduct was, in effect, a denial of his lordship. In fact, these errorists appear to have rejected any form of authority over their conduct (v. 8a) and were especially bombastic in their rejection of "glories" (v. 8b), a reference to angels. While the mention of these beings may appear strange to contemporary readers who view angels as nothing more than benign supernatural auxiliary workers (or part of ancient myth), Jewish theology understood them to be mediators of divine law (see comments on v. 8 and Acts 7:53; Gal. 3:19). This may be precisely the reason these heretics railed against them. Jude's call to hold to the tradition (v. 4) and to remember the apostolic prophecy (v. 17) may imply that they rejected apostolic authority as well, but this is less certain. For their part, the heretics claimed that their teaching was divinely inspired since it came to them in dreams (v. 8), which were, at that time, a universally recognized form of divine communication. New, inspired revelation was set over against apostolic tradition.

Not a few authors have broadly characterized the error as "antinomianism."[19] Jude portrays the heretics as being not only in error (v. 11b, 13) but also corrupt. Special attention is given to their unbridled sexuality (vv. 4–8, 12, 16, 18). Jude demonstrates a deep concern for those who have been drawn in by the sexual license of these people and gives cautionary instruction to those who would help snatch them from the error (v. 23) lest they too become entangled

19. Kelly (1969: 230) suggests that the essence of antinomianism "is the assumption that the truly spiritual man, in virtue of his privileged relationship with God, is emancipated from the ethical restrictions, obligations and standards (particularly in matters of sex) which bind ordinary mortals."

by the same corrupt practices. The errorists are motivated by avarice (v. 11) and are characterized by prideful verbal excess as they blaspheme angels, slander, grumble, speak arrogantly, and mock (vv. 8–10, 15–16, 18). These people engage in immoral behavior without the slightest shame and act without any self-control (v. 13). They are truly ungodly (vv. 4, 15, 18). What moves them is not the Spirit (v. 19), the source of Christian virtue; instead, they are driven by nothing more than base, animal instincts (v. 10). They are soulish, not spiritual (v. 19), even devoid of rationality in their actions and beset by ignorance (v. 10). At the same time the heretics are intent on persuading others to join with them. By stealth they have infiltrated the members of the church and are likely itinerant preachers, teachers, or prophets (v. 4). They act like friends but are nothing more than flatterers seeking their own advantage as they "shepherd themselves" (v. 12). They came to be recognized as leaders and, like Cain, Balaam, and Korah, were actively influencing others for ill (v. 11). While enjoying the love feast among the believers, they show no fear of God. They are effective in persuading members of the church to follow their ways, though not all who were tempted have fully embraced their error (vv. 22–23). Their persuasive efforts have caused divisions among the believers (v. 19), likely generated by their common struggle about the heretics' case.

Jude is particularly keen not only to unmask the behavior and character of the heretics but also to inform his readers/hearers that destruction awaits such people, as was predicted long ago (v. 4). Their presence, in effect, is a sign that the last times have arrived (v. 18). On the other hand, Jude is confident that God is able to keep the disciples from falling into the heretics' trap and sin (v. 24). They must avail themselves of God's resources of faith and love (vv. 20–21) and mercifully come to the aid of those who are becoming or have been ensnared (vv. 22–23). Yet Jude's confidence in this situation rests in God (vv. 24–25).

The details of the heretics' error will be discussed in greater detail and precision in the body of the commentary. At the outset, however, we need to ask how best to read Jude's polemic against these intruders. The cadences of the denunciation sharply contrast the heretics and the disciples. The repeated introduction of the heretics' error with the expression "these are" or simply "these" (οὗτοί εἰσιν, houtoi eisin, or οὗτοι, houtoi in vv. 8, 10, 12, 16, 19) may be pejorative, yet even if not, it serves to differentiate clearly between "them" and "us." Jude heightens the contrast by prefacing his call to the believers with "but you" (δὲ ὑμᾶς, de hymas or ὑμεῖς δέ, hymeis de in vv. 5, 17, 20). In his polemic, Jude's strategy is to draw the line as sharply as possible between the heretics and the believers in an attempt to minimize the heretics' influence on the church and maximize the disciples' adherence to the received faith.

We can recognize in Jude's rhetorical strategy the use of techniques common to *vituperatio*, the "rhetoric of slander" (Johnson 1989: 420), which was the counterpoint to *laudatio*, the praise of noble character and deeds. As du Toit (1994: 403) observes, "Vilifying your opponent, like praising your addressees, has through the centuries been a useful persuasive weapon from the arsenal of a skilled speaker or writer." *Vituperatio* was a recognized skill that was even taught to students of rhetoric. As Quintilian noted, "From this our pupil will begin to proceed to more important themes, such as the praise of famous men and the denunciation of the wicked" (*Inst.* 2.4.20). Quintilian commented that the purpose of both *laudatio* and *vituperatio* was to "mould the character by the contemplation of virtue and vice." Jude's rhetorical strategy is clearly formative as well. He wants the readers to continue in Christian virtue and avoid the vice of the heretics. He does not intend to persuade the heretics.

In *vituperatio*, a person would employ well-known topoi in the denunciation of others. Johnson (1989: 431) comments on these topoi, saying, "Certain things are conventionally said of all opponents. Their teaching was self-contradictory, or trivial, or it led to bad morals. Their behavior could be criticized in several ways. Either they preached but did not practice (in which case they were hypocrites), or they lived as they taught and their corrupt lives showed how bad their doctrine was (like the Epicureans). Certain standard categories of vice were automatically attributed to any opponent. They were all lovers of pleasure, lovers of money, and lovers of glory"[20] (cf. Jude's categories above). These themes were so well used that they even became part of the syllabus of rhetoric. Jewish rhetoric likewise employed vilification for similar ends. "Since Judaism considered itself to be and was perceived as a form of philosophy," Johnson notes (1989: 434), "it is not surprising to find such polemic well attested in the Jewish literature of the first century." The categories used in Jewish rhetoric were quite similar to the gentile counterparts,[21] even among Palestinian Jews (Johnson 1989: 434–41).

In light of ancient techniques of vilification, how should we read Jude's denunciation of his opponents? Analyzing Jude along with 2 Peter in the light of speech act theory, du Toit (1994: 403) states, "For many a long day the performative dimension of language has been neglected in favour of the propositional. This is also true for NT studies. We have too long neglected the fact that in one way or another each of these writings seeks to persuade its readers/audience in a certain direction. To ask what a NT text is *doing* is at least as important

---

20. Among other examples, Johnson (1989: 430) adduces Dio Chrysostom (of Prusa), who vilifies the sophists, those who make "public declamations for pay in praise of a city or festival." Before his conversion to philosophy, Dio had been one of them. He denounces the sophists, calling them "'ignorant, boastful, self-deceived' (*Or.* 4.33), . . . 'unlearned and deceiving by their words' (4.37), . . . 'evil-spirited' (4.38), . . . 'impious' (11.14), . . . 'liars and deceivers' (12.12), . . . preaching for the sake of gain and glory and only their own benefit (32.30). They are flatterers, charlatans, sophists (23.11) . . . [who] profit nothing (33.4–5), . . . mindless (54.1), . . . boastful and shameless (55.7), . . . deceiving others and themselves (70.10), . . . demagogues (77/78.27)." See especially the texts on 432n47.

21. Johnson (1989: 435) summarizes Philo's critique of the Alexandrians (*Embassy to Gaius*). He vilifies them as "'the promiscuous and unstable rabble of the Alexandrians . . .' (18 §120). He says they were 'more brutal and savage than fierce wild beasts' (19 §131) . . . [and] had 'shameless designs' in their 'frenzy and insane fury' (20 §132). He does not find this a surprise, for, he says, 'Alexandrians are adept at flattery and imposture and hypocrisy, ready enough with fawning words, but causing universal disaster with their loose and unbridled lips' (25 §162)."

as asking what it is *saying*." He concludes, "Ideological literature works with contrasts; it does not seek the neutral middle-field. It creates heroes and villains," and so "in those instances where the vilificatory language has become stereotyped, however, . . . the historical element has disappeared" (du Toit 1994: 411). But du Toit neglects ancient reflection on the issue of moving from standard denunciations to specific accusations. Quintilian, for example, discussed the use of commonplaces in the denunciation of vices "such as adultery, gambling or profligacy," but notes that when a name is attached to them, they "amount to actual accusations" (*Inst.* 2.4.22). He adds, "As a rule, however, the general character of a commonplace is usually given a special turn: for instance we make our adulterer blind, our gambler poor and our profligate far advanced in years" (2.4.22). So while standard denunciations were employed in *vituperatio*, they could become specific when directed at a particular case.

This is precisely what happens in Jude. He does, for example, denounce the heretics for their sexual indulgence, using a commonplace in *vituperatio*, but the specificity is striking. He not only denounces them in general terms for their indecent behavior (vv. 4, 8, 16, 18); he also assembles three ancient texts to support his perspective (vv. 5–7), shows how their seduction was at work in the agape meal of the church (v. 12), and calls the congregation to rescue those who had succumbed to their temptation while "hating even the tunic stained by the flesh" (v. 23). The charge of flattery (v. 16), itself a commonplace in ancient discussions on vice and virtue (see Plutarch, *How to Tell a Flatterer from a Friend*), is woven into the fabric of Jude's denunciation of the heretics as those who are actively persuading the members of the church to follow their cause. Jude points out to the church that these who feast with them are "shepherding themselves" (v. 12) as well as "flattering for their own gain" (v. 16). Given Jude's response, we see that flattery has been an effective mechanism in persuasion (vv. 21–22). The commonplace of denouncing one's opponents for boasting (vv. 16, 18) becomes a concrete accusation as the heretics are charged as those who "slander glories" (vv. 8–10). Jude employs these conventional charges in ways specific to the situation his readers faced.

In the quest to identify the heretics who beset the church, a common assumption is that they were the same people who troubled the church or churches addressed in 2 Peter. Second Peter appears to have been written after Jude, and the second chapter of the epistle lifts many texts dealing with the error straight out of Jude (see the introduction to 2 Peter). This association has led to the conclusion that the heretics denounced in both epistles held the same teachings. While recognizing the differences between 2 Peter and Jude, Kelly (1969: 229) remarks that "the deviations from traditional Christianity attacked in the two pamphlets seem broadly the same, with significant differences of emphasis." Desjardins (1987: 89–90) engages in a joint analysis of the dissidents reflected in 2 Peter and Jude and states, "It is difficult not to conclude that they are addressing, if not the same problem in the same community, then at least remarkably similar tendencies in different communities."

However, the conclusion that both epistles address the same problem because of the clear literary dependency between them is no more warranted than the view that the Synoptic Gospels were addressed to the same audience and responded to the same issues because they drew from common sources. If Mark was used by Matthew and Luke, the authors redacted the material to address particular needs and advance distinct, yet complementary, theological perspectives on the life of Christ. Moreover, Fornberg (1977: 33–59) has underscored the striking differences in the issues that the respective authors of 2 Peter and Jude addressed. While Jude highlights the sexual immorality of the heretics, 2 Peter takes on a group that displayed a defective eschatology (see, e.g., 2 Pet. 3:1–10). Neyrey and Bauckham have both argued strongly that the heretics that Peter refutes are people who had come under the sway of Epicurean teaching that denied both providence and prophecy (see the introduction to 2 Peter; Neyrey 1980b; 1993: 122–28; Bauckham 1983: 154–57). These concerns are not evident in Jude. While the opponents addressed in both epistles have embraced antinomianism (2 Pet. 2:19; Jude 4), the heretics Peter warns against do not claim divine inspiration for their views as do Jude's opponents (Jude 8). Both the foundations and the results of the error are distinct in these two cases. Peter, however, found much useful material in Jude that he skillfully employed in his polemic against the libertine tendencies of his heretics.

Can we identify Jude's opponents with any known sect in early Christianity? In his survey of the critical literature on Jude, Knight (1995: 29) arrives at the sensible conclusion that "healthy pessimism should be maintained about the possibility of being able to identify Jude's opponents with confidence." Not all have been this cautious, however, and some have labeled them "gnostics," likely even the infamous Carpocratian sect. Sidebottom (1967: 75) describes the error as "incipient gnosticism which denied the goodness of the created order and the necessity for observance of the moral law." Kelly (1969: 231) likewise suggests their gnostic outlook since they are "recipients of esoteric revelations (8) and regard themselves as pneumatics (19)." Kelly treats the heresy here as part of the same fabric found in 2 Peter's opponents and so adds their emphasis on true "*gnōsis* (knowledge)" (2 Pet. 1:3, 8, 16) to his reading of Jude. Jude's opponents have a libertine lifestyle like that of later gnostics who, in their disparagement of the body, considered "any actions performed with it as morally indifferent" (1969: 231). Yet Kelly admits that the error is only "incipient" gnosticism, not the full-blown heresy of the second century with its "hierarchies of aeons." They appear to have separated humanity into the natural and spiritual people (v. 19) as did some second-century gnostics (Kelly 1969: 284). Jude 4 might be read as an indicator that the heretics have a defective Christology, while their slandering "glories" (v. 8) could be related in some way to the gnostic view that the world was created through the agency of angels, despite Kelly's disclaimer on this point. Of the gnostic sects known to us, the Carpocratians appear to be the most likely group to be identified with Jude's opponents.

The Carpocratians were a group of heretics discussed frequently in the fathers from the second century onward.[22] Carpocrates, the founder of the sect, lived in Alexandria during the first part of the second century AD and held to a gnostic theology with a decidedly licentious bent. According to Irenaeus, Carpocrates taught that the world was not created directly by God but rather by angels who were inferior to the Father. Jesus, no more than the son of Joseph, had received his soul from God and remembered all the things he had seen concerning the divine. Others could obtain the same stature and likewise "despise those rulers who were the creators of the world" (*Haer.* 1.25.2). The Carpocratians engaged in magic and consulted with "familiar spirits and dream-sending demons" (1.25.3). Their lifestyle was licentious in the extreme; they believed that they had power over all things and had the liberty to do whatever they desired. Clement of Alexandria (*Strom.* 3.2) reveals their belief that the righteousness of God was given to all humans alike and that they preached a radical doctrine of equality with its corollary that no distinction existed between "mine" and "yours." Community use extended even to wives, who were considered common property. This was given expression in their agape feasts, for after eating their fill, they would extinguish the lamps and an orgy would ensue. Clement concludes his exposure of the sect's practices by quoting Jude: "Of these and other similar sects Jude, I think, spoke prophetically in his letter—'In the same way also these dreamers' (for they do not seek to find the truth in the light of day) as far as the words 'and their mouth speaks arrogant things'" (Jude 6, 16). Followers of Carpocrates were identifiable by a brand on the back of the right earlobe.

The points of contact between the error Jude warns against and the Carpocratians are striking, from the denunciation of angels, their appeal to dreams, their participation in the agape meal, to their licentious behavior. The fact that Clement quotes Jude in his critique underscores that ancient opinion likewise saw the connection between the epistle and the error. In the *Clementine Letter* (text and translation in M. Smith 1973), Clement accuses the Carpocratians of being "wandering stars" (Jude 13): "boasting they are free, they have become slaves of servile desires." In doing this, they cast themselves into "the nether world of the darkness" (Jude 13). The interweaving of Jude in the denunciations led Bruce to comment, "It was evidently the predecessors of the Carpocrateans, if not the Carpocrateans themselves, whom Jude denounced so unsparingly for following the precedent of the disobedient angels and the men of Sodom" (Bruce 1974: 18; see Gunther 1984: 554–55).

Although there are similarities between the Carpocratians and Jude's opponents, the striking differences should not be ignored. First, Clement portrays the Carpocratians as a separatist sect who have their own feasts, gathering together with "other enthusiasts for the same wickedness" (*Strom.* 3.2.10).

22. See Irenaeus, *Haer.* 1.25; 2.31–32; Clement of Alexandria, *Strom.* 3.2; Hippolytus, *Haer.* 7.2; Tertullian, *The Soul* 23, 35; *Prescription against Heretics* 3; Epiphanius, *Pan.* 27.1–28.1; 30.14; 32.3–7; Eusebius, *Eccl. Hist.* 4.7.9–11; Augustine, *Haer.* 7.

Jude's opponents, however, are making inroads into a church that has adhered to apostolic tradition (Jude 4, 12). While Clement used Jude in his critique of the Carpocratians, he does not say that Jude wrote specifically to address them but states, "Of these and other similar sects Jude, I think, spoke prophetically in his letter" (*Strom.* 3.2.11). Clement appears to be quoting from memory and is not completely certain if he gets the source of his quotation correct. In any case, he recognizes the book as a received text from another time which, if anything, speaks prophetically of the Carpocratians.

Moreover, the Carpocratians were a gnostic sect, yet Jude evidences no concern about the incursion of the doctrine of dualism between matter and spirit, a characteristic feature of gnosticism. Furthermore, there is no indication that the cosmology of Jude's heretics included the idea of a world created by angels. The fact that they "slandered glories" (v. 8) does not compel us to conclude that they were opposed to world-creating angels. The antinomian character of the heretics is linked with a misreading of the doctrine of grace (Jude 4) and not, as in the Carpocratian heresy, based on notions of equality and common property. While sexual immorality is one of the features of the errorists Jude opposes, we find no traces in the epistle of the type of extreme sexual license so well known among the Carpocratians. The Carpocratian tenet that any disciple could be like Jesus is not echoed in Jude's critique, nor do we find in the epistle a counterpoint to the Carpocratian embrace of magic. It is highly unlikely that Jude addresses this or any other gnostic sect. The distinct features of gnosticism are not under discussion in the epistle (Desjardins 1987), and the texts used to bolster the case for the gnostic background "are scarcely necessary interpretations" (Bauckham 1990: 164). As Bauckham aptly comments, "It seems unlikely that Jude should oppose such extensive deviations from common Christian belief with such obscure hints of disapproval." If Jude is truly a first-century document written by Jude, the brother of James and the brother of the Lord, then the epistle could not have been written to combat the Carpocratians or any other gnostics.

The Carpocratian error does remind us, however, that confusing opinions abounded concerning the nature of the divine, the world, and the human. We would do well not to tame these ancient aberrations just as we should be cautious about taming Jesus, morphing him into a more culturally acceptable figure for twenty-first-century Western palates. He was an itinerant miracle worker who challenged both religious and political powers, claimed divinity and royalty, and was crucified, then resurrected. He is a shocking figure in any generation. Likewise, what heresies were afoot often appear quite exotic by modern standards, and the moral practices that went with them could be outrageous, as a reading of the works by Irenaeus and Clement of Alexandria show us. Following Jude as he refutes the heretics and seeks to rescue the church from their influence will take us into a world of ideas and morality that is strange indeed. But at the same time, the themes that emerge from that ancient milieu are surprisingly familiar and linger with us today as the church seeks to live out its faith in a postmodern world, which has lost all sense of absolutes and embraces hedonism in the extreme. The commentary proper will explore the contours of the heresy sketched above and Jude's response, in detail and on their own terms, ever with the hope of seeing how this message speaks to our confused world and oft-errant church today.

The identity of the errorists cannot be fixed with any precision. Our best hope is to be able to locate them within the fabric of the trends current around the midpoint of the first century. The fundamental tenets of their belief, insofar as these can be deduced from Jude, will receive fuller treatment in the commentary. The heretics were people who had made their way into the church and had received a hearing for their perspectives based on their claims of inspiration and their persuasive power. Their inspired approach to Christianity was set over against the received faith, the apostolic tradition. These people were covetous, arrogant, and dismissive of any form of authority that would place moral restraint on them. Their theological conviction was that grace, as taught by Paul and others, allowed them to indulge their sexuality without restraint. As they gave full play to their baser instincts, they had no place for law.

Jude now calls the church to fight for the traditional faith, to be built up in it, and to come to the aid of those in the community who were being swayed or had fallen into the error. The church had become divided over the heretics, but Jude makes no attempt to negotiate and find a common ground between the established faith and this theological/moral novelty. The finality of the faith that was handed down as sacred tradition was at stake. Jude calls his readers to defend it against those who would warp it beyond recognition.

## Jude and Pseudepigraphic Literature

Woven into the fabric of Jude are a number of references taken from Jewish literature that did not become part of the Jewish or Christian canon. In verse 6 Jude refers to an angelic fall, which was an interpretive tradition based on Gen. 6:1–4 and elaborated extensively in 1 En. 6–12 among other Jewish texts (see comments on Jude 6). In verse 9, Jude brings into his discussion the dispute over the body of Moses between Michael, the archangel, and the devil. This story is not found in the OT but was drawn from a book known as the Assumption, or Testament, of Moses (see comments on Jude 9). The most striking use of extrabiblical literature appears in verses 14–15, where Jude quotes 1 En. 1.9 (see comments on vv. 14–15). That Jude knows, echoes, and even quotes this literature is beyond dispute. The question that all readers of this epistle must ponder is why he makes use of these texts that were not finally received into the canon of Scripture.

A number of interpretive options have been explored through the centuries. One of the earliest was to invest 1 Enoch with canonical authority precisely because Jude used the book. This was the position adopted at the start of the third century AD by Tertullian and Clement of Alexandria, among others. Tertullian's take on the issue appears in *The Apparel of Women* 1.3, where he comments on the general rejection of the book: "I am aware that the Scripture of Enoch, which has assigned this order (of action) to angels, is not received by some, because it is not admitted into the Jewish canon either. I suppose they did not think that, having been published before the deluge, it could have safely survived that world-wide calamity, the abolisher of all things." But Tertullian counters by saying that Noah was the grandson of Enoch and could have preserved the work or even "renewed it, under the Spirit's inspiration, after it had been destroyed by the violence of the deluge" (1.3). Tertullian likewise argues that Enoch spoke about the Lord and that whatever "pertains to us" should not be rejected by us. He then concludes, "To these considerations is added the fact that Enoch possesses a testimony in the apostle Jude" (ibid.). Tertullian also affirms the angelic fall as presented in 1 En. 6–12 and referred to in Jude 6 (*The Veiling of Virgins* 7; *The Apparel of Women* 1.2). He again quotes Enoch, saying that he "predicted" and condemned idolatry (*Idolatry* 4, citing 1 En. 99.6).

Clement of Alexandria takes a similar line when he comments on Jude's use of the Assumption (Testament) of Moses in verse 9: "Here he confirms the Assumption of Moses" (*Fragments from Cassiodorus*, "Comments on the Epistle of Jude"). In the same way, he views Jude's quotation of 1 Enoch as investing that book with authority: "'Enoch also, the seventh from Adam,' he says, 'prophesied of these.' In these words he verifies the prophecy." Clement also refers to the arts that fallen angels taught to humans in *Selections from the Prophets* 53.4, where he makes use of 1 En. 7.1–8.3 (VanderKam and Adler 1996: 45–46). Both Tertullian and Clement considered that if these books were good enough for Jude, then they were good enough for them.

Tertullian and Clement of Alexandria did not stand alone in their positive assessment of these books, which did not become part of either the Jewish or Christian canons. Nickelsburg (2001: 71) traces the reception history of 1 Enoch and, while noting that it was not accepted into the Hebrew canon, observes that "a careful sifting of Jewish writings from the previous centuries attests a substantial and dynamic use of the Enochic corpus." Although the sections that came to comprise 1 Enoch were written between the third century BC and the beginning of the Christian era,[23] the book of Jubilees (mid-second century BC) integrates material from 1 En. 1–36, the Book of the Watchers, and invests it with great authority (Jub. 4.15; 5.1–13; 7.20–39; 8.1–4; 10.1–14). Nickelsburg (2001: 75–76) comments, "What is striking about the *Jubilees* passages is their definition of Enoch's writings as 'testimony,' their statement that Enoch was the first to write a testimony (or testament), and their description of the universal import of this testimony. Enoch is a patriarch whose writings affect

23. The five booklets of 1 Enoch may be dated as follows (VanderKam and Adler 1996: 33):
The Astronomical Book (72–78)—third century BCE
The Book of the Watchers (1–36)—third century BCE
The Epistle of Enoch (91–108)—second century BCE
The Book of Dreams (83–90)—second century BCE
The Book of Parables (37–71)—first century BCE/CE.

*all humanity.* . . . Moses wrote the law and testimony for Israel, but Enoch's commands and predictions are relevant for all." Likewise at Qumran, Cave 4 has yielded eleven MSS that preserve various sections of 1 Enoch. The book was extensively quoted, and nine MSS of the Enochic Book of Giants were also found in the caves (Nickelsburg 2001: 76–78). Moreover, Sir. 16:7 refers to the Enochic story of the giants, and the books of Wisdom, 4 Ezra, Baruch, and the Apocalypse of Abraham all draw from it, as do 2 and 3 Enoch (R. Charles 1913: 2.177–80; Nickelsburg 2001: 68–82). Jude's esteem of 1 Enoch was not out of harmony with the honor ascribed to the book by some circles within Judaism, even though 1 Enoch was not accepted widely.

Although the attestation for the Assumption (Testament) of Moses (see v. 9 and comments) is not as wide as 1 Enoch, this first-century-AD work was known widely enough that Jude merely had to refer to an incident in the book to make his point. He assumed that his readers were well familiar with the story. However, since this book comes from early in the first century AD (Tromp 1993: 116), we should not expect to find a wide witness to its contents much earlier than Jude. The story it records, however, was well known to Jude's readers and beyond (see v. 9 and comments).

Jude's use of 1 Enoch is not unique among NT authors. The book forms the basis of Peter's account of Christ's proclamation to the Spirits (1 Pet. 3:18–22; Dalton 1989), and some have argued that the merger of the Son of Man terminology with the servant theology found in the NT finds its source in 1 Enoch (Nickelsburg 2001: 83–86; R. Charles 1913: 2.180–81). First Enoch also enjoyed considerable acceptance in the early church. The Epistle of Barnabas 16.5 paraphrases parts of 1 En. 89 and prefaces the citation saying, "For the Scripture says" (λέγει γὰρ ἡ γραφή, *legei gar hē graphē*), while the mid-third-century *Ad Novatianum* quotes 1 En. 1.8, introducing the verse with the words "as it is written" (Nickelsburg 2001: 89–90). Moreover, Papias, the Apocalypse of Peter, the Gospel of Peter, Justin Martyr, and Athenagoras all refer to Enoch's story of the Watchers (R. Charles 1913: 2.182; VanderKam and Adler 1996: 36–42, 63–66; Nickelsburg 2001: 87–88). At the end of the second century, Irenaeus (*Haer.* 4.16.2) knows not only the Watchers story but also Enoch's mission to pronounce judgment on them (1 En. 12.4–5; 13.4–7; 15.2; VanderKam and Adler 1996: 42–43, 66; Nickelsburg 2001: 88). Tertullian and Clement of Alexandria's acceptance of 1 Enoch as an authoritative and inspired work was hardly unique during their times.

Yet in the contemporary church, this book is not considered to be authoritative except by the Ethiopian Church and the Church of Jesus Christ of Latter-day Saints, the Mormons. The late date of 1 Enoch makes Tertullian's suggestion that it is an authentic work preserved via Noah more than unlikely. A variation of Tertullian's perspective stated also that the Spirit was capable of renewing Enoch's prophecy, which had been destroyed in the flood. In this case, the book known as 1 Enoch did not come directly from Enoch himself but does reflect what Enoch had previously written. Though one could not trace the true historical line, the contents of the book remained those of

Enoch, as now mediated through the Spirit. But on the basis of this ancient theory, the appearance of the book just a few centuries before the Christian era is difficult to explain.

A second interpretive option is to bring the Epistle of Jude into question precisely because it made use of the Assumption (Testament) of Moses and 1 Enoch. Should Jude be considered authoritative if it bases part of its argument on literature that was widely regarded as pseudepigraphic and noncanonical? The rabbinic denunciation of those who interpreted Gen. 6:1–4 in the way 1 Enoch does was severe (see vv. 14–15 and comments), and some within the early church followed this line of attack. Didymus (*In epistula judae enarratio*) in the fourth century noted that the canonicity of Jude had come into doubt because of the quotation of apocryphal material (Mayor 1907: 35; M. Green 1987: 48–49), although he himself defended the book. At the end of the fourth century, Jerome (*Lives of Illustrious Men* 4) likewise notes that many rejected Jude for this same reason.[24] His opinion of Enoch is that "the book is very explicit and is counted among the Apocrypha. The ancient interpreters have sometime spoken of it. We mention it, however, not as authoritative, but to call it to your attention. . . . I have read about this apocryphal book in the book of a certain person, who used it to confirm his heresy" (*Homily* 45, *Brevium in Ps.* 132:3, cited in Nickelsburg 2001: 94). Jerome did, however, accept Jude due to the book's antiquity. First Enoch was likewise tagged as apocryphal in the late fourth century in the Apostolic Constitutions, which calls this, among other such books, "pernicious and repugnant to the truth" (6.16.3). However, the Apostolic Constitutions does not comment on the meaning of this assessment regarding Jude.

Within the contemporary church, the canonical status of Jude has not been shaken by its use of apocryphal works. As we have already observed, the authorship of Jude is often questioned (see "Authorship of Jude" in the introduction), but not on these grounds. Jude has, however, been slighted in the contemporary church and has even gained the distinction of being identified as the most neglected book in the NT (Rowston 1975). Apart from the doxology (vv. 24–25), Jude is rarely heard from the pulpit, and most Christians have never been engaged in any serious study of the book. If Jude becomes a topic of conversation or discussion, the issue raised is invariably that of its relationship to pseudepigraphic literature. Although the opinion of many during the days of Didymus and Jerome is not echoed in the church, there is a practical marginalization of Jude since it is viewed as a problem more than a source of faith. The neglect is sometimes more than benign.[25]

---

24. "Jude, the brother of James, left a short epistle which is reckoned among the seven Catholic epistles, and because it quotes from the apocryphal book of Enoch it is rejected by many. Nevertheless by age and use it has gained authority and is reckoned among the Holy Scriptures."

25. Since the publication of Bauckham's stellar work on Jude (1983; 1990), Neyrey has contributed a critical commentary (1993) as have Fuchs and Raymond (1988), Paulsen (1992), Vögtle (1994), Schreiner (2003), Senior and Harrington (2003), and Davids (2006). We also await the forthcoming commentary by S. Hafemann and the revision of Bauckham's tome. The days of

A third interpretive option, one that came to dominate reflection on Jude's use of apocryphal books, states that although Jude uses this literature, we will accept Jude but not count the sources from which he drew as authoritative. If 2 Peter was written using Jude, 2 Peter could possibly be the earliest witness of this approach. Although Peter (see the discussion of authorship in the introduction to 2 Peter) used Jude extensively, wherever Jude made explicit use of apocryphal literature, Peter left that material to one side. Augustine held a similar, though not identical, position and reflected rather extensively on the issue in the *City of God* 15.23. His judicious comments are well worth repeating in full:

> We may, however, leave aside the stories contained in those Scriptures which are called "Apocrypha" because their origin is hidden and was not clear to the fathers from whom the authority of the true Scriptures has come down to us by a most certain and known succession. There is, indeed, some truth to be found in these apocryphal Scriptures; but they have no canonical authority because of the many untruths which they contain. We cannot, of course, deny that Enoch, the seventh in descent from Adam, wrote a number of things by divine inspiration, since the apostle Jude says so in a canonical epistle. But it was not for nothing that even these were excluded from the canon of the Scriptures which was preserved in the temple of the Hebrew people by the diligence of the priestly succession. For the accuracy of these books was judged to be suspect by reason of their antiquity; and it was not possible to discover whether they were indeed what Enoch had written, for those who put them forward were not thought to have preserved them with due rigour through a clear succession. Hence, prudent men have rightly decided that we should not believe Enoch to be the author of the works attributed to him, containing tales of giants who did not have human fathers. In the same way, many other works have been put forward by heretics under the names of other prophets, and, more recently, under the names of apostles. But all these have been excluded from canonical authority after diligent examination, and are called Apocrypha. (Dyson 1998: 684)

Augustine also discussed 1 Enoch in *The City of God* 18.38, in which he asks, "Again, is not Enoch, the seventh in descent from Adam, proclaimed as a prophet in the canonical epistle of the apostle Jude?" While not accepting the book of Enoch, he comments, "For some writings are indeed put forward as genuine works of those authors by certain persons who, according to their own inclination, indiscriminately believe whatever they like. But the purity of the canon has not admitted these works, not because the authority of these men, who pleased God, has been rejected, but because the writings in question are believed not to be theirs." To resolve the issue of true things being found in books that are not genuine, Augustine makes a distinction between what is written under the Holy Spirit's inspiration and what is mere human composition.

---

neglect are coming to an end. Part of the resurgence of interest in Jude owes to questions raised about the contours of early Palestinian Christianity.

Augustine, in the end, will not admit Enoch since he does not believe it to be genuine and since it contains material contrary to the gospel (Dyson 1998: 876–77). Augustine's position has held the day through the centuries. He did not fully answer the question at hand, but does affirm that the part of Enoch that Jude quoted is true. Augustine appears to attribute this to the fact that there is some truth in these apocryphal writings and that Enoch left some divine writings. He also wants to affirm divine inspiration and, therefore, religious authority for the parts Jude quotes. So, again, a distinction is made between the question of the origin of the Enochic literature and the authority of certain parts of it. Jude's use of parts acknowledges the authority of those parts.

A popular version of Augustine's view regarding Jude's source says that 1 Enoch may well preserve some authentic tradition from the historic Enoch. The logic runs that the authentic tradition is precisely what Jude quotes. So while the book itself is not considered authentic, the prophecy in 1 En. 1.9 was truly uttered by Enoch. At times this perspective appears as nothing more than special pleading designed to defend Jude's use of 1 En. 1.9. But neither this nor Augustine's view account for Jude's appeal to the Assumption (Testament) of Moses in verse 9. The possibility of the survival of a tradition from before the time of Noah until the compilation of 1 Enoch is remote indeed, even given the care with which ancients preserved ancestral memory. If one appeals to Jude to defend the perspective, the reasoning becomes circular.

In light of the problems left us by Augustine, some variants of his position have been forwarded in recent times. The first takes the perspective that "all truth is God's truth" and affirms that where 1 Enoch speaks something true, we should not be concerned if Jude quotes it. Paul also quotes literature that is noncanonical, and when he does so there is no intent to invest the whole of those authors' writings with any form of authority (Epimenides and Aratus in Acts 17:28; Menander in 1 Cor. 15:33; Epimenides in Titus 1:12). As Chaine (1939: 279) comments, revelation can coexist with the ideas and human conceptions that are not contrary to revelation yet are dependent on the culture and milieu of the author (so also M. Green 1987: 58; J. Charles 1991a: 144; Moo 1996: 273). J. Charles minimizes Jude's statement that Enoch "prophesied" (v. 14), saying, "And if, by way of illustration, a Cretan is to the apostle Paul a 'prophet' (Tit. 1.12), then Enoch, in Jude 14, can 'prophesy'" (1991b: 144).

But the way that Jude introduces the quotation from Enoch is identical to the way prophecies from the OT are presented (see v. 14 and comments). While Titus 1:12 speaks about "one of them, their very own prophet" when quoting Epimenides, Jude invests Enoch with authority that is equal to that of the OT prophets. Enoch's authority is underscored by Jude's identification of him as the "seventh from Adam." Moreover, Enoch and the apostles are the only ones whose words Jude records, preferring to simply summarize the content of his other texts. Words from these two sources are forwarded as authoritative and in both cases give voice to the thematic affirmation that heads up Jude's denunciation of those "who from long ago were marked out for this judgment" (v. 4). As will be argued in the comments on Jude 14–15,

Jude places the testimony of 1 Enoch alongside that of the Torah (vv. 5–6, 11)—in addition to the traditions that emerged surrounding the burial of Moses that were rooted in the Torah (v. 9)—and that of the apostles (vv. 17–18). For Jude, these sources are lined up as the authorities that speak of both the sin and the judgment of the heretics. Jude's use of 1 Enoch, and the Assumption (Testament) of Moses for that matter, is different from Paul's occasional appeal to Greek authors. Jude evokes 1 Enoch as predictive and authoritative revelation.

Despite the weakness of this approach, it does suggest a line of reflection that maintains the authority of what is affirmed in the Enoch quote, the allusion to the contention over Moses's body and the angelic fall, while at the same time not endorsing all that the sources for such material wish to endorse. Jude's use of pseudepigraphic literature is quite judicious, as will be seen in the commentary on the relevant verses (vv. 6, 9, 14–15, among others). That is, Jude eschews the more fanciful aspects of these books and focuses on key canonical themes, using pseudepigraphic literature to underscore his point. In the case of the sin of the angels and the devil's contention over the body of Moses (vv. 6, 9, and comments), Jude highlights the way these figures transgressed proper order. In his quotation from 1 Enoch in vv. 14–15, Jude underscores the canonical affirmation of the judgment of the unrighteous. The lessons learned from the sections of the apocryphal texts from which Jude draws are precisely those that find support elsewhere in texts that were received as canonical.

Moreover, in each case, the incident recorded is tied intimately with some set canonical text. The angelic fall (v. 6) became a very common interpretation of Gen. 6:1–4, and the dispute over the body of Moses (v. 9) was an interpretive tradition that developed due to the rather obscure reference to Moses's death in Deut. 34:5–6, which concludes "but no one knows his burial place to this day" (NRSV). Jude's reference is to the Assumption (Testament) of Moses, but it also evokes the words of Zech. 3:1–2. The quotation of 1 En. 1.9 in vv. 14–15 draws on Deut. 33:2, which was considered prophetic of the day of the Lord: "The LORD came from Sinai. . . . With him were myriads of holy ones; at his right, a host of his own" (NRSV). Jude makes judicious and limited use of references to apocryphal literature and evokes only sources that tie into the canonical text and interpretive traditions surrounding it. Jude's use of apocryphal texts is closer to canonical bedrock than is sometimes acknowledged. Although these observations do not constitute a full solution, they do demonstrate that Jude's practice is not outlandish.

Another contemporary approach to this conundrum has been argued forcefully by J. Charles (1991a: 139–44) and supported by others (M. Green 1987: 57, 192–93; Hillyer 1992: 257; Moo 1996: 272–74): Jude quotes Enoch because his opponents hold the book in high regard. J. Charles (1991a: 144) paraphrases verse 14a in the following way: "For even (your own) Enoch, the seventh from Adam, prophesied of these, saying . . ."; Charles concludes, "Seen as such, vv. 14–15 would be not so much a citation of 1 Enoch due to *Jude's* elevation of the work, as it would be an allusion adapted for Jude's theological and literary end, an allusion which bears authority due to *others'* high regard for Enoch." Yet even J. Charles (1991b: 144n70) admits that while this option is grammatically possible, it remains a conjecture: "While pressing this argument would border on mere conjecture, it is sustained grammatically by the text and allows for a unity of argument throughout the epistle. Furthermore, it does not compromise Jude's view of an authoritative OT canon (e.g., vv. 5, 7, 11) or authoritative apostolic teaching (i.e., the 'received' traditions of vv. 3 and 17)."

But as noted above, the way Jude quotes 1 Enoch marks it as an authoritative work for him since he places it alongside and on a level with canonical and apostolic texts. His preface to the quotation underscores the authority of this particular text. There is no hint that Jude merely regards this text as authoritative for his opponents. Moreover, the letter is directed to the church, not to the opponents themselves. J. Charles's suggestion that καί (*kai*) in verse 14 be translated "even" leads us to believe that only the opponents viewed this book as authoritative. This is a conjecture driven, as he notes, by the concern not to "compromise Jude's view of an authoritative OT canon." J. Charles's conclusion is more theological than historical/exegetical. But this is precisely the tension that has existed from the beginning, because at this point a theological understanding of the entailments of inspiration meet some difficult questions that emerge from historical investigation. One may take the side of historical investigation and simply conclude that Jude was wrong about his source. Or one may take the side of Jude's inspiration and authority, as did Augustine, and work the historical details through as best one can. But even Augustine confessed his lack of full understanding in pondering this issue, speaking of what was "hidden from me" (*City of God* 18.38). We can come only to limited conclusions with the evidence we have. Perhaps we have still not gone beyond Augustine's marvelous wisdom.

## Genre and Structure

Our understanding of the structure of Jude is intertwined with the question of literary genre. Jude comes to us in the form of a Hellenistic letter, complete with the common epistolary opening, which includes the name of the author and an identification of the recipients and is followed by an opening greeting (vv. 1–2). After the body of the letter, Jude inserts a closing doxology (vv. 24–25). The presence of the doxology at the very end is curious since Hellenistic letter closings normally included features such as "a farewell wish, a health wish, secondary greetings, an autograph, an illiteracy formula, the date, and a postscript" (Weima 1994: 55; and see Doty 1973: 14; White 1986: 198–202). Semitic letter closings were somewhat briefer but would likewise contain "a farewell wish and often a signature of the letter sender" (Weima 1994: 76). While variations on these formats were used, Jude opts not to follow any of the normal Hellenistic or Semitic conventions of letter closings. Compare, for example, the way Paul ends his correspondence to Philemon (Philem. 23–25) or the final salutation of the following letter from the mid-first century AD:

> Charitous to her brother Pompeius greeting. I want you to know that I attended to the matter about which you wrote to me. I went to Zoilas, the son of Argaios, and he went to the office of the basiliko-grammateus and he inquired and did not find your name written on the roll. At last, then, come up very quickly to your home. Salute the children of Herennia and Pompeis and Syrion and Thaisous and her children and husband and all my friends. Good-bye.[26]

Numerous authors have observed that Jude's doxology appears to be more suited to a liturgical setting and have therefore suggested that the letter was really an oral discourse that was given an epistolary opening. Was this document originally an early Christian sermon that was styled according to the canons of oral rhetoric? And if the letter was intended for oral address, does its structure follow the contours of ancient rhetoric as taught in the schools?

Duane Watson has argued in favor of a rhetorical approach to understanding Jude. One of the pioneers of this field was George Kennedy, under whose supervision Watson wrote his doctoral dissertation (Kennedy 1984; Watson 1988; and see Neyrey 1993: 23–27).[27] From the time of Alexander the Great's conquests, schools of rhetoric appeared throughout the ancient world. Aristotle, Alexander's teacher, defined "rhetoric" as "the faculty of discovering the possible means of persuading in reference to any subject whatever" (*Rhetoric* 1.2.1). Quintilian, who wrote an extensive handbook on rhetoric during the first century AD, surveyed the various definitions of "rhetoric" known in his day. After some discussion, he sets forth his own definition, which states simply that rhetoric is "the *science of speaking well*. For this definition includes all the virtues of oratory and the character of the orator as well, since no man can speak well who is not good himself" (*Inst.* 2.15.34). Those trained in rhetoric could present public lectures, hold public office, act as legal counsels, and engage in other forms of public service. Anyone who belonged to the social elite was expected to have gained some mastery of rhetoric. Kennedy points out that "grammar and rhetoric furnish local inhabitants with an entry into the new civic life and access to the law courts. A system of formal education came into existence in which young people began the study of Greek grammar around the age of seven; a significant number of boys then entered a rhetorical school at the age of twelve to fourteen. They learned some theory from lectures by their teacher and practiced exercises in declamation in imitation of his examples" (Kennedy 1997: 18–19).

Ancient authors who commented on rhetoric paid considerable attention to the classification and arrangement of oral discourse. Aristotle divided rhetoric

---

26. White 1986: 143. For a representative collection of Hellenistic letters, see Hunt and Edgar 1959: 268–395.

27. For useful summaries of the application of rhetorical criticism to the NT epistles, see Porter and Olbricht 1993; and Porter 1997.

into three categories: deliberative, judicial, and epideictic (*Rhetoric* 1.4–10). Deliberative rhetoric was used in discourses oriented toward the future, whose purpose was to exhort or dissuade. Judicial rhetoric, the rhetoric of the court, was oriented to the past, and its goal was to accuse or defend. Epideictic rhetoric was oriented to the present and sought to praise or blame (1.3.3–4). Aristotle noted that epideictic rhetoric was best suited for written compositions, followed by the forensic style (3.12.6). The fundamental structural elements of oral discourse as discussed in the handbooks included the *exordium*, the *narratio*, the *partitio*, the *probatio*, the *refutatio*, and the *peroratio* (see Watson 1988: 20–21). The *exordium* is the prologue of the discourse, whose purpose "is to prepare our audience in such a way that they will be disposed to lend a ready ear to the rest of our speech" (Quintilian, *Inst.* 4.1.5). The *narratio* is "the nature of the subject on which he [the judge] will have to give judgment: that is the *statement of the facts*" (*Inst.* 4.2.1). The *partitio* presents the problem, or in Quintilian's words, it is "the enumeration in order of our own propositions, those of our adversary or both" (4.5.1). The *probatio* is the proof and, therefore, the most important part of the rhetorical discourse. While other parts may be dispensed with, Quintilian notes that "there can be no suit in which the *proof* is not absolutely necessary" (5.Pr.5). While the proof tries to construct the argument, "the *refutatio* is destructive" (*Inst.* 3.9.5) because it is designed to weaken the opponent's arguments. The *peroratio* becomes the finale of the discourse, of which there are two kinds, "for it may deal either with facts or with the emotional aspect of the case" (*Inst.* 6.1.1).

Watson (1988: 77–78) applies this common schemata for forensic rhetoric to his analysis of Jude and presents the following outline of the epistle (here in abbreviated form):

I. Epistolary Prescript (Quasi-*Exordium*; 1–2)
II. *Exordium* (3)
III. *Narratio* (4)
IV. *Probatio* (5–16)
    A. First Proof (5–10)
    B. Second Proof (11–13)
    C. Third Proof (14–16)
V. *Peroratio* (17–23)
VI. Doxology (Quasi-*Peroratio*; 24–25)

Despite the fact that the taxonomy that Watson employs to analyze Jude is specifically associated with judicial rhetoric, Watson understands the letter as an example of "deliberative rhetoric which relies heavily upon epideictic in its efforts to advise and dissuade" (Watson 1988: 33). Neyrey, on the other hand, argues that the epistle is a true representative of forensic rhetoric (Neyrey 1993: 27).

According to Watson (1988: 25), Jude represents an example of the "middle style" of rhetorical discourse, which Quintilian designates as "intermediate" as opposed to the "plain" or "grand and robust" types (*Inst.* 12.10.58).

In Cicero's view, this style "is fuller and somewhat more robust . . . , but plainer than the grandest style. . . . In this style there is perhaps a minimum of vigour, and a maximum of charm. For it is richer than the unadorned style, but plainer than the ornate and opulent style" (*Orator* 26.91; and 6.21). He comments that this style is marked by "transferred" words or metaphor, "words transferred by resemblance from another thing in order to produce a pleasing effect" (26.92).

Following the rhetorical approach to Jude, J. Charles identifies the letter as a "word of exhortation," a genre that finds its roots in the setting of the synagogue. The "word of exhortation" was a species of synagogue homily that owed aspects of its structure and style to the canons of Greco-Roman rhetoric (J. Charles 1993: 25–30; 1991a: 119).[28] Charles observes that "the 'word of exhortation' as a classification is predicated on a homiletical pattern observable in Hellenistic Jewish and early Christian works. The setting of Acts 13, in which Paul, present in the synagogue at Pisidian Antioch, is invited by the rulers to offer a *logos paraklēseōs* (v. 15), affords an illustration of this type of discourse" (J. Charles 1993: 23; for a summary see J. Charles 1991a).[29] Jude, along with Hebrews and 1 and 2 Peter, should be classified as a "word of exhortation" due to its sermonic character. Charles comments, "The body of Jude (vv. 5–23) is strongly hortatory, as if prepared as a sermon. Furthermore, the doxological conclusion would appear to be more fitting in a sermon. Yet with a formal opening and specific audience addressed, Jude conforms to the ancient epistolary genre" (J. Charles 1993: 20). While he underscores that Jude is a genuine letter, J. Charles (1991a: 115) collapses the distinction between oral address and written communication since an author "could publicly address a congregation when not physically present. If the possibility of a personal visit was precluded, the epistle was in essence the apostle's preaching. Thus it is possible to take note of both the epistolary as well as homiletical character which Jude possesses." While not affirming that Jude can be identified as a "word of exhortation," Bauckham (1983: 3) classifies Jude as an "epistolary sermon." Neyrey (1993: 23–27) and Perkins (1995: 145) both stress the epistolary character of Jude yet assert that in the body of the letter the author employs conventions drawn from rhetoric as identified by Watson.

Should we envision an *oral* setting for the Epistle of Jude? While contemporary commentators acknowledge that Jude is a genuine letter, the question remains whether the epistle should be analyzed in light of the canons of ancient rhetoric. J. Charles is certainly correct when he states, "To the Greeks, reading was to be done aloud, i.e., it was to be *heard*" (J. Charles 1993: 26). Letters such as that of the Jerusalem Council, 1 Thessalonians, and Colossians were read aloud to the gathered believers (Acts 15:30–31; 1 Thess. 5:27; Col. 4:16), in

---

28. J. Charles is especially indebted to Watson 1988 on this point.

29. Wills (1984) likewise traces the contours of the "word of exhortation." For a critique of Wills's position, see C. Black (1988), who questions the existence of the "word of exhortation" genre, contending that the features identified by Wills can be understood entirely within the framework of Greco-Roman rhetoric.

accordance with common practice in the Greco-Roman world (Stirewalt 2003: 14–18; and see Plato, *Letters* 323C;[30] Xenophon, *Hell.* 7.1.39; Diodorus Siculus 15.10.2; 2 Bar. 86; 2 Clem. 19.1; P.Oxy. 2787, 14–15). However, the practice of reading letters orally did not convert these documents into something other than what they were—letters!

Despite the oral conventions surrounding letter reception, ancient writers on epistolary theory distinguished between rhetorical discourse and letters. Seneca (*Ep. mor.* 75.1), for example, wanted his letters to be like conversations: "I prefer that my letters should be just what my conversation would be if you and I were sitting in one another's company or taking walks together—spontaneous and easy." Writing sometime around the beginning of the Christian era, Demetrius quotes Artemon, the editor of Aristotle's letters, as saying, "A letter ought to be written in the same manner as a dialogue, a letter being regarded by him as one of the two sides of a dialogue" (*Eloc.* 223, cited in Malherbe 1988: 17). Cicero likewise compared his letters to conversations (*Att.* 8.14.1; 9.10.1; 12.53). Nonetheless, Demetrius drew a sharp line between the conversational nature of letters and oratory (*Eloc.* 226). Aristotle likewise distinguished between the style of letters and public discourse: "But we must not lose sight of the fact that a different style is suitable to each kind of rhetoric. That of written compositions is not the same as that of debate; nor, in the latter, is that of public speaking the same as that of the law courts" (*Rhetoric* 3.12.1). Since letters were to be more like conversations than formal discourse, analyzing Jude according to the structures of public discourse as outlined in the handbooks on rhetoric appears to be a misguided effort. Demetrius appealed for "a certain degree of freedom in the structure of a letter" and instructed that a letter should not become a treatise couched in an epistolary form (*Eloc.* 228, 229, 231, 234; in Malherbe 1988: 19).

Jude composed a genuine letter and not an oral discourse (see Gerdmar 2001: 92–115). Jude states that his original intention was to *write* to his readers but now finds it necessary to *write* as he exhorts them (v. 3). This is not an oral "word of exhortation" now placed in letter format but rather a "letter of exhortation." As noted above, Jude begins his composition with a common letter opening, signaling to his readers how they are to receive and understand this document. The letter itself contains a strongly hortatory tone as Jude warns his readers against the incursions of the heretics and exhorts them to come to the aid of those who have been taken in by the errorists (vv. 20–23). While this kind of exhortation is not common in contemporary letters, Pseudo-Demetrius, along with Pseudo-Libanius, classified letters into various types, which, among many others, included the "advisory type" and the "vituperative type." Pseudo-Demetrius explains these types, saying:

> It is the advisory type when, by offering our own judgment, we exhort (someone to) something or dissuade (him) from something.

30. "All you three must read this letter, all together if possible, or if not by twos; and as often as you possibly can read it in common."

> It is the vituperative type when we bring to light the badness of someone's character or the offensiveness of (his) action against someone. (Malherbe 1988: 36–37)

Pseudo-Libanius similarly spoke of the "paraenetic style," which was used "to exhort someone by urging him to pursue something or to avoid something" (Malherbe 1988: 69). Letters of exhortation were all too common (Stowers 1986: 91–152). Moreover, Jude salts his correspondence with endearing terminology in the vocative voice ("beloved" in vv. 3, 17, 20), using a convention typical of friendly letters.[31] Exhortation was commonly carried out in the context of friendship. As Stowers (1986: 95) notes, "Paraenesis required some type of positive relationship, e.g., that of parent and child, or friendship. . . . Friends were supposed to care for each other's character development."

The body of Jude's letter begins with a typical epistolary disclosure formula that indicates his purpose for writing (vv. 3–4), although such disclosures normally appeared at the end of a correspondence.[32] At the very end of the body of the letter, Jude urges the readers to adopt responsible behavior, a common epistolary convention of the era (vv. 20–23; for a summary of such expressions, see White 1986: 205). Jude's Epistle fits well within the ancient classification scheme for letters, exhibiting standard letter conventions, so we need not resort to rhetorical theory to explain its contents and structure. In fact, the ancients who wrote on the contours of rhetoric did not appear to see any need for giving detailed instruction about letter structure as they did for oral presentations.[33]

The closing doxology, which for some is a primary marker of the sermonic character of the document, is not outside the normal practice in Christian letters. While final doxologies were not a part of either Greco-Roman or Semitic letters, various NT and early Christian letters include a closing doxology (Rom. 16:25–27;[34] 2 Pet. 3:18; 1 Clem. 65.2; Mart. Pol. 22.3; Diogn. 12.9). The inclusion of the final doxology is a distinctly Christian development within epistolography. Doxologies, along with prayers for the communities addressed,

31. Compare this early-second-century letter: "Claudius Agathas Daimon to most beloved Sarapion, greetings. Since I am going to Thebes, I salute you dearest, sweetest Sarapion and I exhort you also to do the same thing. If you need anything from Thebes, I encourage you to write to me, dearest, and it shall be done" (quoted in Stowers 1986: 61).

32. Compare CPJ 16 (= P.Cair.Zen. I 59018), l. 8: "Therefore, I wrote to you (that you might know)"; P.Cair.Zen. V 59804, l. 10f.: "Therefore, I wrote to you that you would know"; P.Tebt. I 34, l. 13f., "I am writing to you to give these instructions to you." Cited in White 1986: 30–31, 33, 89, and see 204.

33. Malherbe's (1988: 3) comments about the relationship between epistolary theory and rhetoric are worth remembering: "It is thus clear that letter writing was of interest to rhetoricians, but it appears only gradually to have attached itself to their rhetorical systems. The discussion in Demetrius is an excursus, Cicero makes not room for a systematic discussion of it in his works on rhetoric, and the references in Quintilian and Theon are casual."

34. On the textual problems surrounding Rom. 16:25–26, see Schreiner 1998: 816–17; and Metzger 1994: 476–77, 470–73.

were normally used to bring a major division of a letter to a close (Rom. 11:36; Gal. 1:5; Eph. 3:20–21; Phil. 4:20; 1 Tim. 1:17; 2 Tim. 4:18; 1 Pet. 5:10–11).[35]

How, then, should we analyze the structure of Jude? The basic components of a Greco-Roman letter are (1) an introduction, which can contain the author's name, the name of the recipient(s), a greeting (normally χαίρειν, *chairein*, hail!), and occasionally additional greetings or a wish/prayer for the recipient's good health; (2) the body, which begins with some formula; and (3) the conclusion, which can include, as noted previously, "a farewell wish, a health wish, secondary greetings, an autograph, an illiteracy formula, the date, and a postscript" (Weima 1994: 55). We do not have an abundant collection of Semitic letters; those that have survived follow the same three-part structure but with less elaboration (Weima 1994: 63–64). The letter opening would contain the sender's name, the recipient's name, and a greeting. This greeting was commonly שָׁלוֹם (*šālôm*, peace), which functioned as the Greek χαίρειν, or the verbal בָּרַךְ (*bārak*, bless). The greeting could be followed by an extended prayer for the well-being of the recipient. Additional greetings to others might be included in the opening, the body, or as part of the final matter of the letter. Following the body of the correspondence, the letter would close with an additional desire for peace (such as "Be at peace!" or "I have sent this letter for your peace [of mind]"), and occasionally a notation about the scribe who penned the letter and/or the date (Fitzmyer 1974b).

Jude's letter begins with the name and identification of the author, a designation of the addressees, and an elaborate opening greeting in which the author invokes God to multiply mercy, peace, and love for the readers (vv. 1–2). The letter body follows, opening with a vocative address "Beloved" and a disclosure formula indicating the author's purpose in writing (vv. 3–4). After the body of the letter, Jude inserts a doxology (vv. 24–25), which picks up the principal theme of the central exhortation of the letter (vv. 20–23). The praise to God includes the assurance that he is the one who is able to keep them from stumbling and to firmly establish them blameless, over against the incursion and persuasion of the heretics (v. 4). Weima (1994: 55–56, 237–39) has demonstrated that Paul's letter closings, as well as those in Greco-Roman letters, rehearse the themes of the correspondence, and the same can be said of Jude's closing doxology. While the form of Jude's closing is different from common letter closings of the era, its function is the same.

The body of Jude's correspondence is punctuated by a series of rhetorical markers that identify both the readers and the opponents to the gospel. The

---

35. M. Black (1990: 330–31) notes, however, that the form of the doxology in Jude is indebted to the Aramaic Targum on 1 Chron. 29:11. "If the Aramaic Targum is the source of (ἡ) δόξα in the *Pater Noster* doxologies, then δόξα, μεγαλωσύνη at Jude 25 would represent two translation equivalents of רְבוּתָא, and the short form ἡ δόξα καὶ ἡ δύναμις / τὸ κράτος would correspond to Pesh (cf. Targum) רְבוּתָא . . . גְּבוּרְתָא." He translates the Aramaic Targum on 1 Chron. 29:11, which says, "Of thee, O Lord, is the greatness/glory who hast created the world by great might." See the comment on Jude 24–25. See also Deichgräber 1967: 25–40, 99–101; J. K. Elliott 1981.

readers are the "beloved" (ἀγαπητοί, *agapētoi*) whom Jude addresses directly in verses 3, 17, 20. In these last two verses Jude contrasts them with the heretics (vv. 16–17 and 19–20, "These are. . . . But you, beloved"). Jude vilifies the heretics[36] in a series of denunciations that begin with οὗτοι (*houtoi*, these) or οὗτοί εἰσιν (*houtoi eisin*, these are) in verses 8, 10, 12, 16, and 19 (see Cantinat 1973: 1–2; Busto Saiz 1981: 85–87).[37] Each of these denunciations follows a reference to the OT (vv. 5–7, 11), the OT Pseudepigrapha (vv. 9, 14), or an apostolic prophecy (vv. 17–18). Ellis (1978: 225) notes that the denunciations of the heretics are commentaries on these texts, each "marked by a shift in tense," and have a "midrashic character" (followed closely by Bauckham 1983: 4–5; 1990: 150–51; J. Charles 1993: 31–33). Ellis (1978: 226) classifies Jude as "a midrash on the theme of Judgment for which the letter-form provides a convenient dress" and says that in this "the midrash is similar not only to other New Testament commentary on Scripture but also to biblical exposition at Qumran." "Midrash" in this case is understood simply as "an exegesis of Scripture which applies it to the contemporary situation, not with the implication that Jude's midrash bears any close resemblance to the forms of later rabbinic midrashim" (Bauckham 1983: 4; 1990: 150).

Ellis notes that Jude's midrash shares with the Qumran midrashim the belief that the present is the time of eschatological fulfillment. As in the Qumran pesher, which emphasizes the present fulfillment of prophetic hopes, Jude alternates the scriptural quotation with a commentary introduced with the formula "this is" (as 4QFlor), modifies the OT quotation to demonstrate more clearly its application, and refers both to biblical and noncanonical literature (Ellis 1978: 226, and see 159–61). Bauckham notes the differences, however, between Jude's hermeneutic and the Qumran pesharim: "His use of various substitutes for Old Testament texts as citations, and his interpretation of Old Testament material as typology" (Bauckham 1990: 151; 1983: 5). Jude certainly shares with the early church and Qumran the vision that the present is the era of eschatological fulfillment (cf. Luke 4:21; Acts 2:16), but the notion of fulfillment is closely linked with Jude's typological understanding of both the OT and pseudepigraphic literature (vv. 8, 10, 12). On the other hand, he sees the presence of the heretics as a direct fulfillment of both apostolic prophecy (vv. 17–19) and the Enoch prophecy (vv. 14–16).

Ellis's use of the categories of midrash and pesher interpretation are useful but not, in themselves, adequate to explain the way Jude interprets canonical and noncanonical literature. The definition of midrash that Ellis offers, along with Bauckham, is the broadest possible.[38] It does, however, underscore Jude's

36. On the use of *vituperatio*, or vilification, see du Toit 1994; Thurén 1997: 457–62.

37. Busto Saiz (1981: 87) identifies οὗτοί εἰσιν as "el elemento estructural que supla lo que en los escritos apocalípticos es una 'revelación' que a renglón seguido va a ser explicada [the structural element that presents what in apocalyptic writings is a 'revelation' that will be explained in the following line]."

38. Compare Neusner's (1994: 224–25) first definition of midrash as "exegesis," or "studying or re-searching the text to bring out its meaning." In his study of the life of Rabban Yoḥanan

quest to contemporize ancient texts for his readers. The eschatological nature of his exegesis shares features with the Qumran pesharim, but the inclusion of the Enoch and apostolic prophecies as constituents of the prophetic tradition now fulfilled is unique. What these studies on Jude's midrash point out, however, is that the body of the letter is primarily structured around a series of authoritative "texts" and their application to the present realities that Jude addresses. The rhetorical impact of the alternation between "text" and comment highlights that the heretics were entities known by God, who had predicted beforehand both their coming and their doom.

The structure of Jude's Epistle follows the tripartite format of Greco-Roman letters, beginning with an opening greeting (vv. 1–2) and ending with a doxology functioning as the letter closing (vv. 24–25). The body of the letter (vv. 3–23) begins and ends with a call for the recipients to stand firm in the faith that they have received. Jude first presents the call in the disclosure of his purpose (vv. 3–4) and again in the exhortation to keep themselves in the love of God and to come to the aid of those who are in danger of being swept away by the heretics' error (vv. 20–23). Framed within these exhortations are a series of "texts" drawn from the OT, pseudepigraphic literature, and the apostles that either typologically or directly predict the coming and the doom of the heretics (vv. 5–7, 9, 11, 14–15, 17–18). After each authoritative "text," Jude inserts an exposition of the text that highlights its application to and fulfillment in the heretics. Each of these comments is introduced with "these" or "these are" (vv. 8, 10, 12–13, 16, 19). Jude brackets this central section of the body of the letter (vv. 5–19) by introducing the first and the final "texts" with calls to the elect to remember what they already knew about these matters (vv. 5, 17). In light of the forgoing considerations, we may outline Jude in the following manner:

I. Epistolary greeting (1–2)
   A. Author: Jude (1a)
   B. Recipients: The called (1b)
   C. Wish-prayer for mercy, peace, and love (2)
II. Letter body: An exhortation to contend for the faith (3–23)
   A. Disclosure of Jude's purpose for writing: An exhortation to the beloved (3–4)
      1. Original purpose: To write about their common security (3a)
      2. New purpose: To exhort them to contend for the faith (3b)
      3. Reason for the change: The infiltration of godless people (4)
   B. A call to remember: Predictions about the heretics and fulfillment (5–19)
      1. "I want you to remember": Text and comment (5–8)

ben Zakkai, a Galilean contemporary of Jesus, Neusner (1962: 1) comments on the perspective that undergirded rabbinic midrash: "The word of God was like fire, the Jewish sages taught, and like the hammer that breaks the rock into pieces. No word of Scripture could, therefore, fail to yield a particular nuance of light, and, properly understood, none was irrelevant to events at hand."

a. Text: Exodus, angels, and Sodom and Gomorrah (5–7)

b. Comment: These are dreamers who defile the flesh, reject authority, and slander glorious ones (8)

2. Second text and comment (9–10)

a. Text: Michael did not blaspheme the devil (9)

b. Comment: These blaspheme what they do not understand (10)

3. Third text and comment (11–13)

a. Text: The way of Cain, the deception of Balaam, the rebellion of Korah (11)

b. Comment: These are stains in the community meals, clouds without rain, trees without fruit, wild waves of the sea, and wandering stars (12–13)

4. Fourth text and comment (14–16)

a. Text: The prophecy of Enoch (14–15)

b. Comment: These are grumblers, complainers, and boastful flatterers (16)

5. "Remember": Text and comment (17–19)

a. Text: The apostolic prophecy (17–18)

b. Comment: These are people who cause divisions (19)

C. Exhortations to the beloved (20–23)

1. Keep yourselves in the love of God (20–21)

2. Snatch some from the fire; have mercy on others who dispute (22–23)

III. Closing doxology (24–25)

➤ I. Epistolary Greeting (1–2)
  II. Letter Body: An Exhortation to Contend for the Faith (3–23)
  III. Closing Doxology (24–25)

# I. Epistolary Greeting (1–2)

The author constructs the opening of this letter in accordance with the architecture of ancient epistles yet modifies the extant literary conventions by giving them a distinct Christian orientation. The author names himself yet demonstrates his authority as the "slave of Jesus Christ and brother of James" (v. 1). The readers/hearers of the letter are known by their status as the called people of God. Jude also Christianizes the common epistolary greeting of his day. The opening affirms the identity of all parties and also points the reader in the direction of the main concern of the letter. They have been summoned by God and "kept for Christ Jesus," affirmations that serve as counterpoints to the heretics' incursion and persuasion. Before announcing his theme in verse 3, Jude plants his readers on solid ground.

  A. Author: Jude (1a)
  B. Recipients: The called (1b)
  C. Wish-prayer for mercy, peace, and love (2)

## Exegesis and Exposition

¹Jude, a slave of Jesus Christ and brother of James, to the called, ⌜beloved⌝ by God the Father and kept for Christ Jesus. ²May mercy, peace, and love be yours in increasing measure.

## A. Author: Jude (1a)

Jude's objective in composing this letter was to warn the church against the incursion of heretics who had distorted the doctrine of grace and turned it into an excuse for moral license. How Jude heard about this situation is not stated or implied, but we do see that some distance lay between him and those who first read this correspondence. Ancient authors wrote letters to shorten the distance between themselves and their readers, with the letter representing the presence of the absent person. As Seneca wrote in one of his epistles (*Ep. mor.* 40.1), "I never receive a letter from you without being in your company forthwith." The sense of presence was enhanced by the subscript of the correspondence that was frequently added in the hand of the author who, after the body of the letter was written, took the pen from the scribe and added a note in his or her own hand (1 Cor. 16:21; Gal. 6:11; Col. 4:18; 2 Thess. 3:17; Philem. 19). Surviving ancient papyrus letters occasionally show a change in penmanship at the end, indicating the point at which the author took the pen from the amanuensis to add the final words (Deissmann 1911: 170–73, 179–80;

1a

43

Stowers 1986: 60–61). This practice not only authenticated the letter but also served to bring the reader into the author's presence. Seneca comments, "For that which is sweetest when we meet face to face is afforded by the impress of a friend's hand upon his letter—recognition" (*Ep. mor.* 40.1).[1] Jude's letter is a surrogate for his presence as he seeks to correct the error that had invaded the church. The letter and the person could not be separated.

The correspondence begins, as did most ancient letters from the third century BC until the third century AD, by naming and identifying the author and recipients. The common practice was to follow the letter opening with a greeting (in Greek correspondence normally χαίρειν, *chairein*, Greetings! [or] Rejoice!) and a prayer or wish for the good health or well-being of the recipient (White 1986: 200; Doty 1973: 29–31).[2] The author is "Jude" (Ἰούδας, *Ioudas*), an extremely common name among the Jewish people (Ilan 2002: 112–25). If the author had not identified himself more fully, it would be impossible to locate him among the Judes known to us through the NT or other ancient literature and inscriptions from the period. This Jude, however, is the "brother of James" and the half brother of Jesus (see Matt. 13:55; Mark 6:3; and "Authorship of Jude" in the introduction). While he could have said that he was the "brother of the Lord" (note how James was known as such in Gal. 1:19), he styles himself as Ἰησοῦ Χριστοῦ δοῦλος (*Iēsou Christou doulos*, a slave of Jesus Christ). Jude makes no explicit claim regarding his relationship to Jesus beyond the fact that he is Jesus's slave (cf. James 1:1).[3] This identification implies that a radical change in relationship occurred as Jude moved from being one who did not believe (John 7:3, 5; Matt. 13:57; and perhaps Mark 3:21) to gathering with the disciples for prayer (Acts 1:14) and participating in the Christian mission (1 Cor. 9:5).

The fact that Jude's name is qualified by the declaration that he is the "slave of Jesus Christ and brother of James" should perhaps be read within the context of how slaves were named. Slaves would not be identified by the *tria nomina* that every Roman citizen had, but rather were known simply by their *cognomen* along with the name of their master and a description of their function (*TLNT* 1994: 1:380). However, White's study on ancient letters (1986: 200) has pointed out that in legal texts written in letter form and in official

1. Similarly, a young soldier wrote to his father saying, "Now I ask you, my lord and father, write me a letter, telling me first of your welfare, secondly of my brother's and sister's, and enabling me thirdly to make obeisance before your handwriting" (Hunt and Edgar 1959: 1.304–5).

2. For example, the letter cited in the previous note begins, "Apion to Epimachus, his father and lord, very many greetings. Before all else I pray for your health and that you may always be well and prosperous, together with my sister and her daughter and my brother" (Hunt and Edgar 1959: 1.304–5).

3. Clement of Alexandria was the first to comment on this omission: "Jude, who wrote the Catholic Epistle, the brother of the sons of Joseph, and very religious, whilst knowing the near relationship of the Lord, yet did not say that he himself was His brother. But what said he? 'Jude, a servant of Jesus Christ,'—of Him as Lord; but 'the brother of James.' For this is true; he was His brother, (the son) of Joseph" (*Comments on the Epistle of Jude*).

correspondence, the sender's status is emphasized by the use of titles and indicators of position. Is Jude making some claim to authority in this opening address as Paul frequently did in his epistles (e.g., Rom. 1:1; Gal. 1:1)?

Although translators commonly render δοῦλος as "servant" (less frequently "bond-servant"), Spicq (*TLNT* 1:380) vigorously objects: "It is wrong to translate *doulos* as 'servant,' so obscuring its precise signification in the language of the first century." Jude is nothing more than Jesus Christ's δοῦλος, which may be understood within the context of ancient chattel slavery. In the socioeconomic sense, a slave is the property of another, bought and sold as a commodity; as Aristotle declared, "A slave is a living tool, just as a tool is an inanimate slave" (*Eth. Nic.* 1161B; see Varro, *On Agriculture* 1.17.1). A slave is the "unfree," and the fundamental social distinction in ancient society was between status of the "slave" and the "free" (1 Cor. 12:13; Gal. 3:28; Eph. 6:8; Col. 3:11; Rev. 6:15; 13:16; 19:18). As a slave, all rights over his life and property belong to the master, who in Jude's case is Jesus Christ. Jude's high Christology is implicit in this identification.

But Jude's readers, being familiar with biblical narrative in addition to the social fabric of ancient society, would have understood this seeming self-deprecating identification within the frame of divine service. Both in Greek and Jewish thought, the "slave of God" was a person who rendered service to the Deity.[4] In Israel, these persons are leadership figures who proclaim God's message, such as Moses (2 Kings 18:12; 21:8), Joshua (Josh. 24:29; Judg. 2:8), and the prophets (Jer. 25:4; Amos 3:7; see also Sass 1941). Similarly, Paul in the NT commonly designates himself as the "slave of Jesus Christ" (Rom. 1:1; Gal. 1:10; Phil. 1:1) as do James (1:1) and Peter (2 Pet. 1:1). Paul instructed Timothy regarding conduct appropriate for the "slave of the Lord" (2 Tim. 2:24), while in writing to Titus the apostle calls himself the "slave of God" (1:1). Epaphras, the Colossian, shares this status (Col. 4:12) along with John (Rev. 1:1). Jesus employs the image of the slave manager in his discussion of leadership (Luke 12:41–48), evoking understanding of a well-known function of slaves in the Greco-Roman world. As his story reflects, some slaves were invested with authority and held responsible managerial positions under their masters. D. Martin (1990: 56) has argued that "the slave agent of an upper-class person was to be reckoned with. He could keep free citizens waiting on his convenience." The higher the social status of the master, the more weighty the power of the managerial slave. Since Jude is the slave-agent of Jesus Christ, the one who holds the highest status according to Christian thought, we should understand his self-designation as a claim to authority, divine commission,

---

4. In addition to the slave girl's proclamation, "These men are slaves of the Most High God" (NRSV) in Acts 16:17, see Pausanius 10.32.12; Euripides, *Ion* 132, 309. The designation "slave of God," along with its variants, is especially prominent in the LXX ("slave of the Lord" in Josh. 24:30; Judg. 2:8; 2 Kings 18:12; Jon. 1:9; "slave of God" in Dan. 6:21 Theod.; "your slave" in 1 Sam. 3:9–10; 23:10–11; 2 Sam. 7:27–28; 1 Kings 8:28; 18:36; Pss. 18:12 [19:13 Eng.]; 108 [109]:28; 115:7 [116:16]; 118 [119]:23, 125, 140; 142 [143]:12; "my slave" in 1 Kings 11:38; 2 Kings 21:8).

and perhaps even inspiration. Standing behind him is Christ himself. This is not a mere statement of humility.

Jude further identifies himself as the "brother of James." This is most likely the same James who was the brother of Jesus (Matt. 13:55; Mark 6:3), the eventual leader of the Jerusalem church (Acts 15:13; Gal. 2:9, 12), and the named author of one of our NT epistles (see "Authorship of Jude" in the introduction). James was such a prominent figure in the early church that his epistle was sent out with only his name attached, with no further qualification (James 1:1). The first readers of that missive and this one knew full well who he was. Jude, however, was apparently a lesser figure. His status is enhanced by the declaration that he is "brother of James" since the honor of one family member would be ascribed to others (see "Authorship of Jude" in the introduction; Neyrey 1993: 3–7; Bartchy 1999; Malina 2001: 37–38). Since sons were commonly identified by the name of their father (e.g., Matt. 10:2–3; 16:17), Jude's acknowledgment of his relationship with the prominent figure James underscores the claim to authority. No doubt the readers would have understood that this James, as Jude, was the "brother of the Lord" without the fact being mentioned. The relation was well known and the status of the "brothers of the Lord" was recognized, although they did not hold dynastic leadership (Bauckham 1990: 125–33). In this letter opening, Jude does not merely identify who he is but also makes reference to his status, which would increase the weight of the following directives. His weighty words are not those of a person of low honor. They could not be easily dismissed by members of the church who had come under the influence of the heretics.

## B. Recipients: The Called (1b)

**1b**    Jude does not identify where the first readers of this letter lived, so we are left to gather the available pieces of evidence to help us discover both their location and social situation. The first readers were likely located in Palestine and included both gentile believers and those Jewish believers who were identified as Hellenistic or who came from the higher strata of Jewish society (see "Jude and His Circle" in the introduction). Jude does, however, mark out their identity as he writes to those who are "the called" (τοῖς . . . κλητοῖς, *tois . . . klētois*). Greek literature infrequently employs the concept of being called by a deity. For example, Pausanius refers to those summoned by Isis, saying, "No one may enter the shrine except those whom Isis herself has honored by inviting them in dreams" (10.32.13). The literature also contains references to the notion of being called or summoned to a banquet in the name of a god. One invitation to dinner reads, "The god calls you to a banquet being held in the Thoereion tomorrow from the 9th hour" (*NewDocs* 1.5). The concept of being invited to a dinner is represented in both Testaments (1 Kings 1:41, 49; 1 Cor. 10:27; Luke 14:7–14). This banquet custom became one of the images Jesus employed to speak about God's call into his kingdom (Luke 14:15–24; Matt. 22:1–14).

But the dining imagery is not sustained throughout NT usage, which rather finds its principal roots embedded in the OT notion that God is the one who has both chosen and called a people unto himself or who commissions them for divine service. The Servant Songs in Isaiah are especially rich in references to God's gracious call (Isa. 42:6; 43:1; 45:3–4; 48:12; 49:1; 51:2; 54:6), and the notion of God's calling appears also in the Qumran literature (CD 4.4; 1QSa 2.1, 11). The divine call is one of the fundamental tenets of Israel's faith (Wright 1992: 260). As Wright (1992: 457) comments, "The basic Jewish answer to the question, How is the creator dealing with evil within his creation? was of course that he had called Israel." The church now becomes the called by God "to fulfill Israel's vocation on behalf of the world." The theology of God's call becomes dominant in the NT as God is known as "the one who calls" (Rom. 9:11; Gal. 5:8; 1 Thess. 2:12; 5:24; 1 Pet. 1:15; 2:9; 5:10; 2 Pet. 1:3) and his people are "the called" (Rom. 1:1, 6, 7; 8:28; 1 Cor. 1:2, 24; Rev. 17:14), as here in Jude. Jesus likewise takes on the task of calling his own (Matt. 4:21; Mark 2:17). This call, according to God's sovereign choice, is unto salvation and service (Rom. 8:30; 1 Cor. 1:9; Gal. 1:6, 15; Eph. 4:1, 4; Col. 3:15; 1 Tim. 6:12; 2 Tim. 1:9; Heb. 9:15). This constitutes them as the people of God (Rom. 9:6–13; see Dunn 1998: 510).

Although calling comes from God, human agents are employed as men and women are being called through the proclamation of the gospel (2 Thess. 2:14). In the contemporary era characterized by belief in individual initiative and choice, the biblical emphasis on God's call points us back to the source of human hope. For Jude's readers, their identity as the called is the root of his confidence and appeal as he moves the church away from the error of the heretics. The heretics disrupt the community, and their incursions are dividing the members of the church (v. 19; see also "Occasion of Writing" in the introduction). God's call, on the other hand, is corporate and constitutes them together as the people of God (see 1 Pet. 2:9 and J. H. Elliott 1966).

Jude qualifies his readers' status by stating that they, the called, are "beloved by[5] God the Father" (ἐν θεῷ πατρὶ ἠγαπημένοις, *en theō patri ēgapēmenois*). There is no other source for their calling than God's love, which implies his sovereign choice of the church, while the perfect participle ἠγαπημένοις (*ēgapēmenois*, beloved) implies that God's love continues to abide upon them (BDF §342; and see Porter 1989: 256–57). Abraham's call is brought together with God's love for him in Isa. 51:2 LXX: "Look to Abraham your father and to Sarah who bore you, because he was alone when I called him, and blessed him, and loved him, and multiplied him." Similarly, the election of Israel is rooted in God's love for the people: "So says the LORD God who made you and formed you from the womb: You will yet be helped. Do not fear, my servant Jacob, and beloved Israel, whom I chose" (Isa. 44:2 LXX; and see Deut. 4:37; 10:15; Ps. 78:68; Isa. 41:8 LXX).

---

5. ἐν θεῷ πατρί (*en theo patri*, by God the Father), where ἐν plus the dative expresses personal agent; BDF §219.1.

Likewise, the NT brings together the notion of God's love with both his calling (Rom. 9:25; Hos. 2:23 [2:25 MT, LXX]) and election (Matt. 12:18, of Christ; Rom. 11:28; Eph. 1:4; Col. 3:12; 1 Thess. 1:4). God's selection of people is not motivated by their merit (2 Tim. 1:9; cf. Rom. 5:7–8), as if they were elected and called into office due to their virtue, as in a popular election. Perhaps more to the point for Jude's readers, however, is the contrast between the way God deals with his people and the way pagan deities were capricious and needed placating. One could never be sure what to expect from them, since they might, in one moment, do you good but, in the next, do you ill. God's love is steady state, being the root cause of the call that draws men and women together to be his people.

The "called" are also those who are "kept for Christ Jesus" (Ἰησοῦ Χριστῷ τετηρημένοις, *Iēsou Christō tetērēmenois*). The translations vary in their understanding of this clause. Does Jude mean that the elect body is "kept *by* Christ Jesus" (NIV, NLT) or "kept *for* Jesus Christ" (RSV, NRSV, NJB, NASB). While Ἰησοῦ Χριστῷ (*Iēsou Christō*) could be understood as a dative of agent with the passive voice (τετηρημένοις, *tetērēmenois*, have been kept), this use is very rare (BDF §191). The NT speaks of those who are being kept for the eschatological day, whether they are the people of God (John 17:11–12;[6] 1 Thess. 5:23; and 1 Pet. 1:4–5 with "kept" in 1:4) or those destined for judgment (2 Pet. 2:9; 3:7; Jude 6, 13; and see T. Reu. 5.5). Likewise, when Jude exhorts his readers to keep themselves in the love of God (v. 21), the outlook is eschatological: "Eagerly await the mercy of our Lord Jesus Christ unto eternal life." Jude's emphasis therefore appears to be not only on the ground of their calling ("beloved by God") but its goal and end ("for Christ Jesus"), understood as that final eschatological event (cf. 1 Pet. 1:5 NRSV: "for a salvation ready to be revealed in the last time"; 1 Thess. 5:23 NRSV: "at the coming of our Lord Jesus Christ"). They will be kept or preserved from harm for Christ Jesus upon his return (BDAG 1002).

Although the goal of being kept is the focus of Jude's concern, the passive voice here implies divine agency. As the Lord upholds his Servant whom he has loved and chosen, so too these called ones are kept by the God who loves them (Isa. 41:9–10; 42:1). Bauckham (1983: 25) is likely correct in his suggestion that the Servant Songs are the source of Jude's thought ("called: Isa. 41:9; 42:6; 48:12, 15; 49:1; 54:6; loved: 42:1; 43:4; cf. 44:2 LXX; kept: 42:6; 49:8"). Despite the incursion of the errorists who seek to disrupt the faith of the believers, Jude's confidence rests in God's initiative and his preserving power, which will bring to an end what he has begun (Phil. 1:6). What God starts, he finishes. Jude calls the church to be in step with God's intentions (v. 21), but does not regard their preservation as a matter merely in the church's hands.

## C. Wish-Prayer for Mercy, Peace, and Love (2)

2    Jude concludes his opening greeting with a wish-prayer for the believers that expresses his desire that mercy, peace, and love might be theirs more abundantly

---

6. Deiros (1992: 314) suggests that this dominical saying is the source of Jude's thought.

(ἔλεος ὑμῖν καὶ εἰρήνη καὶ ἀγάπη πληθυνθείη, *eleos hymin kai eirēnē kai agapē plēthyntheiē*). Ancient Greek letters commonly included a simple greeting after naming the author and the recipients (as Acts 15:23; 23:26), followed frequently with a wish that the recipient might be in good health. For example, around the middle of the first century AD, Chairas wrote to Dionysios: "Chairas to his dearest Dionysios, many greetings and continued good health" (cf. 3 John 2). Aramaic letters, on the other hand, include an expression of שָׁלוֹם (*šālôm*) "peace, well-being." The desire for peace is sometimes stereotypical and could mean nothing more than the Greek "greetings" (χαίρειν, *chairein*). This simple greeting could be expanded quite extensively, as in the letter that begins, "May the God of Heaven be much concerned for the well-being of our lord (Bagohi) at all times, and may he show you favor before Darius the King and the princes of the palace a thousand times more than now, and may he grant you a long life, and may you be happy and prosperous at all times" (Fitzmyer 1974b: 214–15). Particularly relevant for our understanding of Jude's wish-prayer, however, are those biblical and rabbinic texts that begin "and may your peace be increased" (RSV: Dan. 4:1; 6:25; and see 2 Bar. 78.3).

The opening greeting and the desire for health of the Greek letter are transformed in Christian use, partly under the influence of Semitic letter-writing conventions. The greeting of the Greek letter (χαίρειν, *chairein*) is transformed into a wish-prayer that the recipients might receive "grace" (χάρις, *charis*) from God and Jesus Christ. In Christian correspondence, this desire is usually coupled with the wish-prayer that the recipients also receive "peace" from God (Rom. 1:7; 1 Cor. 1:3; 2 Cor. 1:2; Gal. 1:3; Eph. 1:2; Phil. 1:2; Col. 1:2; 1 Thess. 1:1; 2 Thess. 1:2; Titus 1:4; Philem. 3; 1 Pet. 1:2; 2 Pet. 1:2; Rev. 1:4; 1 Clem. intro.) or "mercy" and "peace" (1 Tim. 1:2; 2 Tim. 1:2; 2 John 3). In Christian hands, the stereotypical greeting and wish for health become wish-prayers offered to God, which entreat him to grant the recipients the fundamental blessings of the gospel.

Jude's greeting, however, varies from the typical Christian wish-prayer in that it does not mention "grace" but "mercy, peace, and love." Since the wish-prayer for "grace" was a commonplace in Christian correspondence, Jude's omission is somewhat striking. Most likely he excludes the wish-prayer for grace since the fundamental problem that he addresses in the epistle is the distorted understanding of grace that the heretics had introduced into the church (v. 4). He does, however, underscore other fundamental blessings given by God. Jude's desire is that "mercy, peace, and love" might abound toward the recipients, the passive voice here implying that God is the one who grants them (2 Pet. 1:2; 1 Clem. intro., "Grace and peace from God Almighty be multiplied to you through Jesus Christ"; Polycarp intro., "Mercy and peace from God Almighty and Jesus Christ our Saviour be multiplied to you"). The Martyrdom of Polycarp (intro.) may be dependent on Jude since the author evokes the Father and the Lord Jesus Christ to make the readers abound in the same blessings expressed in Jude: "Mercy, peace, and love of God the Father and our Lord Jesus Christ be multiplied."

The blessings that Jude emphasizes are woven into the fabric of his epistle and, therefore, this wish-prayer serves as an introduction to the fundamental themes he will take up. While mercy is a present blessing that Jude trusts his readers will possess in abundance, their earnest hope is that the mercy of Jesus Christ will be shown them on his return, resulting in the eternal life of the coming age (v. 21 and comments). Moreover, as God has mercy on the church, so they, too, should have mercy on those who are wavering or who have fallen prey to the heretics' error (vv. 22–23 and comments). Divine mercy is a fundamental theme in the struggle against error.

These believers who are kept for Christ Jesus are also called to keep themselves "in the love of God" (v. 21 and comments), the very one who loved them (v. 1), another thematic note sounded in the opening wish-prayer (cf. v. 12). While the lexeme "peace" does not appear elsewhere in the letter, the concept of "well-being" is very important for this community, whose web of relations was being torn apart. The heretics' error has brought their relation with God to the brink as it perverted the gospel (v. 4) and drew members of the church into the web of sin and judgment (v. 23). Their "peace with God" is at stake (cf. Rom. 5:1). Moreover, the fabric of the divinely called community has been ripped as the errorists have caused divisions (v. 19). Concord within the community has been broken and needs to be restored (cf. Eph. 4:3). Jude's understanding of peace is not the same as contemporary ideas of individual emotional tranquillity ("peace in my heart") but is an interpersonal reality. Their welfare or well-being is relational at its root. Within both Jewish and Christian thought, "peace" is "nearly synonymous [with] messianic salvation" (BDAG 288; Acts 10:36; Rom. 2:10; 5:1; 8:6; 14:17; Eph. 6:15). Jude's opening wish-prayer is not formal or stereotypical but orients his readers to God's abundant blessings, which will preserve and save them in this treacherous moment.

## Additional Note

**1b.** The witnesses strongly favor the reading ἠγαπημένοις (ēgapēmenois, beloved, in 𝔓⁷² ℵ A B Ψ 81) while the variant ἡγιασμένοις (hēgiasmenois, sanctified) is found in the 𝔐 as well as K L P. The variant gave a familiar ring to the letter opening: "sanctified in God the Father."

I. Epistolary Greeting (1–2)
➤ II. Letter Body: An Exhortation to Contend for the Faith (3–23)
III. Closing Doxology (24–25)

# II. Letter Body: An Exhortation to Contend for the Faith (3–23)

Jude's Epistle utilizes the common three-part structure of Greco-Roman letters. It began with a greeting formula (vv. 1–3) and will end with an adapted letter closing that takes the form of a doxology (vv. 24–25). The body of the correspondence (vv. 3–23) opens with an exhortation to the readers regarding the faith they have received (vv. 3–4) and is bracketed at the end with a call regarding the same faith (vv. 20–23). The initial exhortation discloses Jude's purpose for writing: that the readers should contend for the faith handed down to them since certain people had infiltrated the church and brought teachings that lead to immorality (vv. 3–4). The final exhortation urges the readers/hearers to build themselves up on this very faith and to rescue the members of the community who are dangerously influenced by the error of the false teachers (vv. 20–23). Between these poles Jude lays out a series of "texts" that reference the OT, Jewish literature, and apostolic prophecy, each of which predicts the advent and the destruction of the heretics (vv. 5–7, 9, 11, 14–15, 17–18). Following each of these "texts," our author explains how the text applies to and finds its fulfillment in the false teachers. Jude includes a rhetorical marker at the head of each of these applications, stating that "these" heretics are the very people the texts speak about (vv. 8, 10, 12–13, 16, 19). The first and the last texts (vv. 5, 17) bracket the central section of the body of the letter (vv. 5–19) by recalling what the members of the church already know about the subject at hand.

In the body of his letter, Jude inserts a series of rhetorical markers that identify the readers and the heretics. The readers are the "beloved" (vv. 3, 17, 20), who are placed in contrast with the false teachers (vv. 16–17 and 19–20, "These are . . . But you, beloved"). Jude identifies and repeatedly denounces the heretics, marking them as "these" or stating that "these are" (vv. 8, 10, 12, 16, 19). Jude's rhetorical strategy is to distance the readers from the false teachers who have integrated themselves into the church while at the same time drawing them to himself and the wider Christian community, to divine revelation, and to God himself. The heretics are destined for ultimate condemnation, and their demise has been marked from times of old. Jude does not want his readers to have any part with them or their condemnation; he calls the faithful to take action on behalf of those who are being drawn in by their error.

II. Letter Body: An Exhortation to Contend for the Faith (3–23)
➤ A. Disclosure of Jude's Purpose for Writing: An Exhortation to the Beloved (3–4)
   B. A Call to Remember: Predictions about the Heretics and Fulfillment (5–19)
   C. Exhortations to the Beloved (20–23)

# A. Disclosure of Jude's Purpose for Writing: An Exhortation to the Beloved (3–4)

The body of Jude's letter begins with a disclosure formula that outlines his purpose for writing. Though the author has planned to address his readers about the great theme of their "common security" (v. 3a), he is strongly pressed by circumstances to change tack. Outsiders have come among the congregation, promoting an altered doctrine of grace that promotes sexual vice and that, in the end, is a denial of the authority of Christ. Jude urgently calls his readers to take action and enter into the struggle against their teaching, standing by the sacred tradition that was handed down to them and the rest of the people of God. Jude's disclosure of his intent identifies this as a paraenetic letter that calls for action. His goal is not merely to inform but also to exhort his readers to enter into the struggle for the faith against its detractors.

## Exegesis and Exposition

³Beloved, while making every effort to write to you about our common security, I was constrained to write in order to exhort you to contend for the faith that was once and for all handed down to the saints. ⁴For certain men have weaseled their way in, who from long ago were marked out for this judgment, ungodly people, who alter the grace of our God into sexual excess and deny our only Master and Lord, Jesus Christ.

### 1. Original Purpose: To Write about Their Common Security (3a)

3a    The author addresses his readers directly as ἀγαπητοί (*agapētoi*, beloved), the vocative being used as a "general transitional device" to signal the opening of the body of the letter (White 1972: 33). Ἀγαπητοί was the common way a father would address his beloved child (BDAG 7; E. Stauffer, *TDNT* 1:37), but in the hands of the church it became one of the principal forms of direct address in correspondence and, likely, in church gatherings (Rom. 12:19; 1 Cor. 10:14; 2 Cor. 7:1; 12:19; Phil. 2:12; Heb. 6:9; 1 Pet. 2:11; 4:12; 2 Pet. 3:1, 8, 14, 17; 1 John 2:7; 3:2, 21; 4:1, 7, 11; Jude 17, 20). Far from being stereotypical, the address retains its emphasis on the familial bond that exists between members of the Christian community (cf. the variant "beloved brothers and sisters" [see NRSV and its notes] in 1 Cor. 15:58; Phil. 4:1; James 1:16, 19; 2:5). Unsurprisingly, its use in letters peaks in contexts of moral exhortation (see 2 Pet. 3:1, 8, 14, 17). Family letters were one of the most common types of ancient correspondence and are characterized by an interest in the other's welfare (White 1986: 196–97), and the family network, whether natural or Christian, was an appropriate context for moral instruction (Osiek and Balch 1997: 156–73).

Jude also inaugurates the body of his correspondence with a declaration of his purpose for writing (vv. 3–4). Disclosure formulas were a characteristic feature of letter body openings during the Roman period, and these would often include some form of background statement that outlined the author's rationale for writing (White 1972: 33; 1986: 208). In these disclosure statements, περί (peri, concerning) plus the genitive is a common feature, which may serve to signal a reply to a previous correspondence (cf. 1 Cor. 7:1), to introduce the message of the present letter, or to refer back to an issue about which the author had previously written (White 1972: 31; 1986: 208). In Jude's case, the περί construction in verse 3a signals the content of a previous letter: πᾶσαν σπουδὴν ποιούμενος γράφειν ὑμῖν περὶ τῆς κοινῆς ἡμῶν σωτηρίας (pasan spoudēn poioumenos graphein hymin peri tēs koinēs hēmōn sōtērias, while making every effort to write to you about our common security). Reicke (1964: 195), however, suggests that the letter to which Jude refers here is, in fact, the very letter that he wrote (v. 3b). His position is not without merit since writing about their "common security" would be a solid basis for the appeal to "contend for the faith" and may be viewed as the equivalent of "the faith" in verse 3b. However, the use of the περί clause in verse 3a suggests a previous correspondence in contrast with the purpose that now compels Jude to write. Moreover, the grammar is most easily understood if we assume that two letters are in mind. In fact, Jude inserts "to write" two times, the first a present infinitive and the latter an aorist infinitive, which heightens the contrast between what was planned and what was accomplished. Also, the content of Jude is not about the "common security" itself but rather about the defense of the faith (v. 3b).

Jude employs the adverbial participial phrase πᾶσαν σπουδὴν ποιούμενος (pasan spoudēn poioumenos) either to indicate that he had been making diligent plans to write or that he had already begun his composition. The phrase πᾶσαν σπουδήν (pasan spoudēn, all diligence) appears in civic decrees and was used to underscore "extraordinary commitment to civic and religious responsibilities" (BDAG 939–40; for similar expressions, cf. 2 Cor. 7:11; 2 Pet. 1:5). The whole phrase πᾶσαν σπουδὴν ποιούμενος could either indicate that the person was making diligent plans (as in Philo, Embassy 43 §338; Pausanius 7.10.4; Josephus, Ant. 16.7.1 §181) or that the person was engaged in the actual act (as "He now applied himself" in Josephus, J.W. 7.6.4 §190; and see P.Tebt. 1.33.18; 3.769.74). In either case, the phrase is used in the context of the diligent discharge of some civic duty. However, the second interpretation is more likely, given that Jude employs the present participle ποιούμενος, which appears here to indicate coincidental action (Porter 1989: 377–88). Jude has been engaged in a project that is a serious obligation, writing to this church about their "common security." But a new and even more pressing concern has arisen.

The topic that Jude had intended to address concerned their "common security" (περὶ τῆς κοινῆς ἡμῶν σωτηρίας, peri tēs koinēs hēmōn sōtērias).

In the wider sphere of Greek usage, "salvation" could mean simply "bodily health," "well-being," or "safety" (cf. Acts 27:34; Phil. 1:19; Heb. 11:7; MM 622), but within biblical literature the word repeatedly points to God's great redemptive acts or deliverances that he effects on behalf of his people, all the way from the exodus from Egypt (Exod. 14:13; 15:2; Acts 7:25) to the messianic salvation accomplished through Jesus Christ, both as a present reality (Luke 1:69, 77; 19:9; Acts 4:12; Rom. 10:10) and a future hope (Rom. 13:11; 1 Thess. 5:9; 1 Pet. 1:5). It is God's victory over his enemies. God has effected this powerful salvation through the cross of Christ and his resurrection (Rom. 5:10; 1 Cor. 1:18, 21–24) and offered it to all peoples, regardless of their ethnicity or heritage (Acts 13:26, 47; Rom. 1:16). The salvation through the sufferings of the Messiah was predicted by the prophets (1 Pet. 1:10–11) and proclaimed in the gospel message (Eph. 1:13; 2 Thess. 2:13), calling for a response of faith. "Salvation" summarizes God's gracious offer to and hope for humanity. This is the salvation that Jude and his readers share, together with all those who call on the name of the Lord.

But as tempting as it is to read Jude's summary of his intended correspondence completely within this frame, the description of the letter's contents as "our common salvation" or "our common security" (τῆς κοινῆς ἡμῶν σωτηρίας) adopts another well-known concept from their wider world. Amid the struggles against national enemies, concerns for the "common safety" or "security" of a people were paramount (similar to the contemporary idea of "national security"). Those worthy of leadership sought to secure it, and the human cost to obtain it could be high. Philo (*Agriculture* 34 §156) spoke of those "who are dying for the common safety," while in the context of war Diodorus Siculus (37.2.5) says, "They also set up a joint senate of five hundred members, from whose number men worthy to rule the country and capable of providing for the common safety were to be selected for promotion." Xenophon's dictum was that "the safety of all (πάντες γὰρ κοινῆς σωτηρίας, *pantes gar koinēs sōtērias*) is the need of all" (*Anab.* 3.2.32). Isocrates voiced the perspective of the noble leader in the face of war: "Nevertheless I should be ashamed if I showed that I am more concerned about my own reputation than about the public safety" (*De pace* 39).[1] Jude adopts the language of a principal social and political concern of the age and adapted the concept to the setting of the church. He has purposed to write to the church about their "common security" as the people of God who stand against the hostile forces of the age. In this new setting, political thought is recast. We may assume that his work will not be light, casual reading.

## 2. New Purpose: To Exhort Them to Contend for the Faith (3b)

**3b**    Given the scope of Jude's intended composition, the pressure on him to take up a new topic must have been strong. He expresses the constraint he is under:

---

1. See also Isocrates, *Panegyricus* 85.6; *Philippus* 69; Thucydides 2.60.2–7; *SIG* 409; and LSJ 1751. Cf. the Roman concern for "peace and security" echoed in 1 Thess. 5:3.

ἀνάγκην ἔσχον γράψαι ὑμῖν (*anankēn eschon grapsai hymin*, I was constrained to write to you).[2] The expression underscores the fact that he found it necessary and was under compulsion to write to them (BDAG 61). Ἀνάγκην ἔσχον plus the infinitive (here γράψαι) may imply that some kind of orders were received and that the person is under obligation to take action (cf. Luke 23:17; 1 Cor. 7:37; 9:16; 2 Cor. 9:7; Heb. 7:27; Josephus, *Ant.* 16.9.3 §290; *NewDocs* 1:37–39, 45),[3] but occasionally the demand does not come from some personal agent but from circumstances themselves (Luke 14:18; Josephus, *Life* 34 §171). The explanatory clause that begins verse 4 (γάρ, *gar*, for) suggests that the entrance of the heretics was the situation that put the author under strong obligation to act, altering his trajectory in order to counteract this novel trend in the church.

Although Jude likely employed the services of an amanuensis (see "Authorship of Jude" in the introduction and White 1986: 215–16), he is responsible for the composition (cf. 1 Pet. 5:12) and writes ὑμῖν παρακαλῶν ἐπαγωνίζεσθαι τῇ ἅπαξ παραδοθείσῃ τοῖς ἁγίοις πίστει (*hymin parakalōn epagōnizesthai tē hapax paradotheisē tois hagiois pistei*, in order to exhort you to contend for the faith that was once and for all handed down to the saints). In this disclosure statement, Jude lays down his purpose for writing with the adverbial participle παρακαλῶν (*parakalōn,* exhorting; BDF §417). This is one of the principal verbs that NT authors employ in moral instruction (Rom. 12:1; 1 Cor. 1:10; Eph. 4:1; Phil. 4:2; 1 Thess. 3:2; 4:1; 5:11; 2 Thess. 3:12; 1 Pet. 2:11; 5:1), and its presence signals Jude's hortatory aim.[4] He is not content merely to disseminate information about the dangers of the heretics but is calling the church to decisive action (see also vv. 20–23).

As a description of Jude's purpose, παρακαλῶν may also identify the letter that Jude is writing as the "paraenetic" type. On this letter genre, Libanius states, "The paraenetic style is that in which we exhort someone by urging him to pursue something or to avoid something. Paraenesis is divided into two parts, encouragement and dissuasion. Some also call it the advisory style, but do so incorrectly, for paraenesis differs from advice. For paraenesis is hortatory speech that does not admit of counter-statement" (Malherbe 1988: 68–69). Demetrius called this "the advisory type" in which "by offering our own judgment, we exhort (someone to) something or dissuade (him) from something" (Malherbe 1988: 36–37); it is distinguished from admonishment, which would have been directed at the heretics themselves. However, Demetrius also outlines the "vituperative" type, in which someone will "bring to light the badness of

---

2. Although the Greek does not use the passive voice here, the idea of imposed constraint is best expressed in English by the passive.

3. *NewDocs* 1:36–39 includes a transport requisition, in both Latin and Greek, that contains the statement "paying what I have prescribed (*Gk adds:* to those having the obligation to supply them)" (ll. 18–19 in Latin, ll. 42–43 in Greek).

4. Used in the same sense in Jewish (2 Macc. 2:3; 6:12; 7:5, 21; 8:16; 9:26; 12:42; 13:14; 15:8, 17; 3 Macc. 1:4; 5:36; 4 Macc. 8:17; 10:1; 12:6; 16:24) as well as Greek literature (Xenophon, *Mem.* 1.2.55). See MM 484; BDAG 765; *NewDocs* 6:145–46; G. Braumann, *NIDNTT* 1:569.

someone's character or the offensiveness of (his) action against someone" (Malherbe 1988: 36–37). Jude's letter is marked by vituperative language (see "Genre and Structure" in the introduction), mixed with his strong appeals to the church to combat the heretics' incursions.

Jude employs popular athletic imagery in his call to the church "to contend" (ἐπαγωνίζεσθαι, *epagōnizesthai*) for the faith. The metaphor, drawn from competition in the games (the ἀγών, *agōn*, competition; see Pfitzner 1967; BDAG 356), could be employed in the context of warfare (Plutarch, *Fabius Maximus* 23.2.3: "He was contending with Hannibal like a clever athlete"), of progress in virtue (Philo, *Virtues* 26 §142.1: "Not content with his own prowess, he challenges it to a further contest"), or of debate (Philo, *Eternity* 14 §70.1: "Critolaus, in his contention, used also this further kind of argument"). The struggle Jude has in mind is the preservation of the received faith over against the theological/moral novelty of the heretics (v. 3b–4), the growth in that faith and the avoidance of error (vv. 20–21), and the rescue of those who have been drawn into the errorists' snare (vv. 22–23). Jude's call pertains to both the doctrinal and moral issues raised by the heretics. What is at stake is "the faith" (τῇ . . . πίστει, *tē . . . pistei*), here understood as what the church proclaims, the gospel. "Faith" always implies confidence (*TLNT* 3:11; R. Bultmann, *TDNT* 6:177), but here the particular emphasis is on that in which one has confidence. Jude's usage here and in verse 20 is similar to Paul's concept of the gospel as "the faith" that is preached (Gal. 1:23; Acts 6:7; Eph. 4:5) and heard/received (Gal. 3:2, 5) and from which the heretics had departed (1 Tim. 4:1; and 1:19; 6:21). This use of "faith" is hardly evidence of late-date "early catholic" perspectives in Jude (see "Jude and His Circle" in the introduction) but echoes the early and unique Pauline development of the concept of πίστις (see also v. 4).

Jude describes this faith as what was once and for all handed down to the saints. The recipients of this faith or the gospel are "the saints," a common marker of Christian self-identity (Rom. 1:7; 1 Cor. 1:2; 2 Cor. 1:1; Eph. 1:1; Phil. 1:1; Col. 1:2), which views them as people who are consecrated to God (BDAG 10–11). This is not a special sacred group within the church but the church itself. This epithet encircles Jude's readers within the wider believing community.

The faith that they are to contend for is that which is the common property of all the believing community. The faith that they have received was handed down to the saints as a sacred tradition (παραδοθείσῃ, *paradotheisē*). Jesus critiqued many of the "traditions" (παραδόσεις, *paradoseis*) of Judaism insofar as they minimized human obligation before divine revelation (Matt. 15:2–3, 6; Mark 7:3, 5, 8–9), and Paul took a stand against those human traditions that were in contradiction to the gospel (Col. 2:8). But apart from these few pejorative notes, the NT heartily affirms those apostolic teachings handed down as divinely inspired tradition (Rom. 6:17; 1 Cor. 11:2, 23; 15:3; 2 Thess. 3:6). In the Mediterranean world, value was ascribed to what was ancient and part of the tradition handed down from times of old. The new and the novel, on the other hand, was viewed with deep suspicion. Plato, for example, said, "The ancients, who were better than we and lived nearer the gods, handed down the tradition that all the things which are ever said to exist are sprung from one and many and have inherent in them the finite and the infinite" (*Philebus* 16C), while the *mos maiorum*, the customs of the ancestors, "were even more binding in Rome than in Greece" (Ferguson 1993: 160; Neyrey 1993: 54). Even the reforming Augustus hailed the "customs of the ancestors" (*Res gestae* 6).

Likewise within Judaism, the Pharisees highly valued what was handed down from preceding generations (Josephus, *Ant.* 13.10.6 §297; cf. Wis. 14:15). The identity of a group was intimately bound with their faithful adherence to the traditions (Malina and Neyrey 1996: 164–69). The description of the faith as that which is handed down suggests its divine origin, and the finality of that revelation is underscored by Jude's description of the faith as that which was "once and for all" (ἅπαξ, *hapax*) delivered to the saints. The word points to the "perfection and completion" (*TLNT* 1:141) as well as the finality of the faith that they had received (cf. Heb. 6:4; 9:26–28; 1 Pet. 3:18).[5] Jude juxtaposes the final and complete revelation (v. 3) over against the theological novelty that the heretics have introduced into the church by stealth (v. 4).

## 3. Reason for the Change: The Infiltration of Godless People (4)

Jude discloses his motivation for writing the present missive by introducing the situation the church is facing with the explanatory γάρ (*gar*, for, BDAG 189). He employs strong language in denouncing the heretics: παρεισέδυσαν γάρ τινες ἄνθρωποι (*pareisedysan gar tines anthrōpoi*, for certain people have weaseled their way in). Jude impugns the heretics' motives for attaching themselves to the Christian community. The verb παρεισέδυσαν appears in contexts where an author wishes to speak of the way someone or something bad has slipped in unnoticed and suggests ulterior motives (see BDAG 774; MM 492). Josephus (*J.W.* 1.24.1 §468) makes note of a situation where "a large number insinuated themselves into their friendship to spy upon them." Plutarch can speak about the time "when once the love of silver and gold had crept into the city" (*Ag. Cleom.* 3.1) or of "mischievous practices creeping in" (*Mor.* 216B). These men had made their way into the center of the Christian community's life (v. 12) by feigned friendship and flattery (v. 16), and now Jude will unmask them.

In his *vituperatio*, Jude refers to "*certain* people," likely using the indefinite pronoun τινες (*tines*, *certain*) in a derisive manner, along with οὗτοι (*houtoi*, these, vv. 7, 8, 10, 12, 14, 16, 19), an effective technique in English as well (see du Toit 1994: 406). Jude never names the opponents, and their identity is a bit blurred "in order to portray them as negative, shadowy characters" (du Toit 1994: 406). Thurén (1997: 459) has argued, however, that Jude's technique of vilification employs stereotypical denunciations, and we should therefore not

4

---

5. "In AD 54, when the prefect of Egypt, L. Lucius Geta, wrote that his orders and decisions had been formulated 'once,' he means that they always remain binding and must be applied by everyone everywhere just as on the first day" (*TLNT* 1:141–42).

attempt to read each statement as a fact about Jude's opponents. She states, "In the *argumentatio* of Jude 5–16, the author does not give any evidence or specific examples, but merely condemns the behaviour and values of the opponents as shameful" (and see L. Johnson 1989). However, although Jude's characterization of the heretics employs standard elements used in *vituperatio*, he specifies the case and shows the genuine historical contours of the accusations (see "Occasion of Writing" in the introduction).

Jude immediately begins his denunciation of the heretics by marking them out as οἱ πάλαι προγεγραμμένοι εἰς τοῦτο τὸ κρίμα (*hoi palai progegrammenoi eis touto to krima*, the ones who from long ago were marked out for this judgment). "This judgment" Jude has in mind is what he will outline in the rest of the epistle (vv. 5–7, 10–15). His concern is to demonstrate to his readers the final outcome of the heretics' lifestyle and teaching, here presented both as a part of his denunciation and as a deterrent for the believers. Implicit throughout the *vituperatio* is the call to avoid the behavior that characterizes the heretics and that ultimately leads to such disastrous ends. In his outline of the judgment in the following verses, Jude repeatedly makes the point that the coming and doom of such people has been predicted. Prophecy is now fulfilled as the ancient texts typologically prefigure the heretics and their end (vv. 5–7, 11) or directly predict their doom (vv. 14–15; cf. 17–19). Jude's emphasis on prophecy and fulfillment is akin to *pesher* interpretation found in Qumran and throughout the NT (Ellis 1978: 221–36; J. Charles 1993: 31–33).

Jude's use of προγράφω (*prographō*, to write in advance) appears to point to the way their doom was prophetically predicted (cf. the use of the verb in Rom. 15:4). This verb, however, is not commonly employed in the context of predictive prophecy, but in the literature of the era it repeatedly arises in legal contexts. The verb is attached to the concept of making official decrees, either in marriage contracts, deeds of sale, or public notices. The substantives πρόγραμμα and προγραφή (*programma* and *prographē*) are the official decrees or notices themselves (MM 538; LSJ 1473; BDAG 867). Paul picks up the idea of a "public notice" in Gal. 3:1, where he uses the same verb (see *NewDocs* 4:86; Plutarch, *Brutus* 27.6). Jude's emphasis is not simply that the doom of the heretics was predicted, but also that it was decreed and publicly announced. While the predictive sense is not absent entirely, his principal point concerns the official and public condemnation of the heretics. Their judgment was decreed πάλαι (*palai*, long ago; as Matt. 11:21; Luke 10:13; Heb. 1:1; 2 Clem. 11.2). The perspective that predominated during this and previous eras was that the old and the ancient were of superior value and weight to the present. The distant past was idyllic, and what had to do with the ancients was weighty (see the comments on v. 3).[6] To say that the judgment of the heretics was decreed from old was to underscore its weight and solemnity. They will not escape this.

6. In addition to Heb. 1:1, see the perspective of Homer, *Il.* 9.524: "Even in this manner have we heard the fame of men of old that were warriors, when so furious wrath came upon any"; and Aristophanes, *Plutus* 1001: "Once upon a time the Milesians were brave."

Jude first denounces the heretics as people of low character—they are "ungodly" or "impious" (ἀσεβεῖς, *asebeis*). The term and its cognates appear frequently in Jude's *vituperatio* (vv. 4, 15; ἀσέβεια, *asebeia* in vv. 15, 18; ἀσεβέω, *asebeō* in v. 15),[7] although the frequency of the word in this short letter is due largely to the author's quotation of 1 En. 1.9 in vv. 14–15. The term tagged those who did not show reverence for the gods and, as such, reflected a serious religious and social charge since the deities were considered to be protectors and benefactors of the community (W. Günther, *NIDNTT* 2:92; MM 84; BDAG 181). Xenophon (*Cyr.* 8.8.27) denounced the Persians: "For I maintain that I have proved that the Persians of the present day and those living in their dependencies are less reverent toward the gods, less dutiful to their relatives, less upright in their dealings with all men, and less brave in war than they were of old." In classical literature to be "impious" was also to be "unrighteous" (ἀδικία, *adikia*) or a person who did not attend to civic duty. In the LXX it is synonymous with "unjust" and the opposite of "righteous" (Gen. 18:23, 28; Exod. 9:27; 23:7; Deut. 25:1; Ps. 10:5; Prov. 10:16, 20, 24–25, 28, 30, 32; Eccles. 3:16–17; Wis. 4:16). The shifted emphasis to the moral implications of improper attendance on God characterizes Jude's use of the word in his denunciation.

Jude follows the serious charge of impiety with an explanation of the character of their act. They are ones who τὴν τοῦ θεοῦ ἡμῶν χάριτα μετατιθέντες εἰς ἀσέλγειαν (*tēn tou theou hēmōn charita metatithentes eis aselgeian*, alter the grace of our God into sexual excess). Instead of being people who hold to sacred tradition (v. 3b), the heretics altered the meaning of "grace" for the church, reading revelation through the lens of their own corruption and so transforming it into something wholly other. Jude would not countenance the contemporary notion that the meaning of texts is altered with every new reading. As the laws of Isis "are not subject to alterations" (BDAG 642), so too is the faith handed down to the saints (v. 3b). Jude's use of vocabulary may even mark the heretics out as "turncoats" (see Gal. 1:6; 2 Macc. 7:24),[8] although the emphasis here falls on their transformation of apostolic teaching rather than their own defection. The fact, however, that they had manipulated the doctrine of grace does suggest that Jude views the heretics as apostates.

Within Christian vocabulary, "grace" points to God's saving work through Christ Jesus (Rom. 3:24; 5:15; Eph. 2:8; 2 Thess. 2:16) and also includes his continuous activity that enables his people to do his will (Acts 15:40; 2 Cor. 8:1, 7; Gal. 2:9). "Grace" had worked its way deeply into Christian thought (Heb. 12:15; James 4:6; 1 Pet. 1:2, 10; 5:12; 2 Pet. 1:2; 3:18; 2 John 3; Rev. 1:4; 22:21). The pervasive use of "grace" to describe Christian salvation may be

---

7. See the use of ἀσεβής (*asebēs*) in Rom. 4:5; 5:6; 1 Tim. 1:9; 1 Pet. 4:18; 2 Pet. 2:5–6; 3:7; ἀσέβεια (*asebeia*) in Rom. 1:18; 11:26; 2 Tim. 2:16; Titus 2:12; and a variant of ἀσεβέω (*asebeō*) in 2 Pet. 2:6.

8. "Antiochus felt that he was being treated with contempt, and he was suspicious of her reproachful tone. The youngest brother being still alive, Antiochus not only appealed to him in words, but promised with oaths that he would make him rich and enviable if he would *turn from the ways* of his ancestors" (2 Macc. 7:24 NRSV, with emphasis added).

attributable indirectly to Paul, but we cannot conclude that these heretics had directly heard or read his teaching and then misapplied it. The doctrine of grace seems to have been understood by them as giving them license (cf. Rom. 6:1) to engage in sexual excess (ἀσέλγειαν, *aselgeian*; see Mark 7:22; Rom. 13:13; 2 Cor. 12:21; Gal. 5:19; Eph. 4:19; 1 Pet. 4:3; 2 Pet. 2:2, 7, 18; Wis. 14:26). The word is quite common in vice lists and underscores the lack of self-restraint and the sexual indecency of these people (BDAG 141).[9] Jude denounces their sexual immorality at a number of points throughout his letter (vv. 8, 16, 18, 23). Their version of grace was employed in the service of lust.

Jude concludes the opening of his *vituperatio* with the claim that they τὸν μόνον δεσπότην καὶ κύριον ἡμῶν Ἰησοῦν Χριστὸν ἀρνούμενοι (*ton monon despotēn kai kyrion hēmōn Iēsoun Christon arnoumenoi*, deny our only Master and Lord, Jesus Christ). Jude's Christology is very high as he identifies Jesus Christ as "Master" as well as "Lord." "Master" (δεσπότην, *despotēn*) occasionally appears as a christological title (2 Pet. 2:1; God in Luke 2:29; Acts 4:24; Rev. 6:10). In common usage, it referred to the master of slaves (as 1 Tim. 6:1–2; 2 Tim. 2:21; Titus 2:9; 1 Pet. 2:18) but could also be used of rulers. The title underscores their legal control and absolute authority (BDAG 220). But in the LXX it frequently appears as a divine title (Gen. 15:2, 8; Josh. 5:14; Prov. 29:25; Isa. 3:1; 10:33; Jer. 4:10; Tob. 8:17; 2 Macc. 5:17, 20; 15:22; Wis. 8:3; Sir. 36:1). Jude's use of the title highlights the audacity of the heretics' act. What slave or subject would dare repudiate their δεσπότης?

Jude also calls Jesus Christ "Lord" (see Jude 17, 21, 25; Acts 11:17; 15:26; 28:31; Rom. 1:4, 7; 5:1, 11, 21; 1 Thess. 1:3; 5:9; James 1:1; 1 Pet. 1:3; 2 Pet. 1:8), which was another divine title in the LXX, the common translation for Yahweh (Exod. 19:9; 20:2; Isa. 6:3). Likewise in the Greco-Roman world the title was used of divinities (see 1 Cor. 8:5; Deissmann 1911: 353–57) as well as the emperor as part of the fabric of the imperial cult. Jude echoes the Christian version of the *Shema* (Deut. 6:4) in his declaration that Jesus Christ is the "only Master and Lord." The heretics had denied this divine sovereign authority. Jude spotlights the heretics' denial of Christ by employing a verb (ἀρνούμενοι, *arnoumenoi*) that, in the papyri, commonly refers to a verbal denial or repudiation (*TLNT* 1:200; see Philo, *Spec. Laws* 2.46 §255). As such, it is the opposite of "confess" (Matt. 26:70, 72; Mark 14:68, 70; Luke 22:57; John 13:38; 18:25, 27). Jude's use may be influenced by the teaching of Jesus at this point (Matt. 10:32–33; Luke 12:9) and suggests that the heretics had apostatized (cf. 2 Pet. 2:1, where the apostasy of Peter's heretics is clearly noted). The nature of this denial may have been simply practical as in Titus 1:16 ("They deny him by their actions" [NRSV]). Since these heretics continued to banquet with the Christian community, the nature of their denial was likely similar. Their repudiation of Christ came in their actions as they feigned allegiance to Christ and his church.

9. Cf. Philo, *Moses* 1.56 §305: "in the execution by the licentiousness and wantonness of the women, who had caused the ruin of their paramours, of their bodies through lust."

II. Letter Body: An Exhortation to Contend for the Faith (3–23)
    A. Disclosure of Jude's Purpose for Writing: An Exhortation to the Beloved (3–4)
➤  B. A Call to Remember: Predictions about the Heretics and Fulfillment (5–19)
    C. Exhortations to the Beloved (20–23)

# B. A Call to Remember: Predictions about the Heretics and Fulfillment (5–19)

Jude's rhetorical strategy is built around a series of ancient texts (vv. 5–7, 9, 11, 14–15, 17–18) that are subsequently followed by a commentary demonstrating how these "texts" are relevant to the advent of the heretics who had invaded the church (vv. 8, 10, 12–13, 16, 19). Jude builds his denunciation of the heretics by drawing on "texts" from the OT (vv. 5–7, 11), OT Pseudepigrapha (vv. 9, 14), and apostolic prophecy (vv. 17–18). The first "Text and Comment" section (vv. 5–8) recalls the accounts of the judgment on the exodus generation, the fallen angels, and Sodom and Gomorrah. The third likewise harkens back to the OT narrative (vv. 11–13), recounting the judgment on Cain, Balaam, and Korah. The second (vv. 9–10) and fourth (vv. 14–16) "Text and Comment" sections recall Jewish traditions regarding the judgment of the devil and the story of Enoch respectively. The final "Text and Comment" section appeals to the apostolic testimony (vv. 17–19). God's judgments in the past and the prophetic testimony all bear witness to the coming and the doom of the heretics who have invaded the church.

# 1. "I Want You to Remember": Text and Comment (5–8)

In this section, Jude begins his denunciation of the heretics by stringing together three ancient examples of people who sinned and were subsequently judged by God: the Israelites of the exodus generation who did not believe (v. 5a); the angels who did not keep to their proper domain (v. 6a); and the inhabitants of Sodom, Gomorrah, and the surrounding cities who were unfaithful and went after "another kind of flesh" (v. 7a). In each of these examples, which are types prefiguring the heretics who infiltrated the church, Jude's fundamental concern is to show how they transgressed or overstepped divinely established order. Also, Jude shows that whatever their privileged state was, they were subsequently judged for their sin (vv. 5b, 6b, 7b). In each case, the severity of the judgment highlights the gravity of the transgression. Jude ties this summary of the ancient narratives to the situation his readers face in verse 8, introducing the heretics with the characteristic and pejorative "these" or "these are" (cf. vv. 10, 12–13, 16, 19).

Jude's choice of the exodus generation, the fallen angels, and Sodom/Gomorrah as types that prefigure the heretics is not a random selection. Frequently these three groups, as well as various other notable groups, are drawn together in Jewish literature as archetypal examples of sin and judgment. Although Jude is not dependent on any particular ancient exposition of these texts, he apparently knows and echoes this ancient interpretive tradition. For example, Sir. 16:7–10, after an introductory statement about judgment (vv. 5–6), highlights the judgment of giants (v. 7; offspring of fallen angels as discussed in the comments below on v. 6), the Lot/Sodom story (v. 8), the doomed Canaanites (v. 9), and the 600,000 foot soldiers of the exodus generation (v. 10; cf. 48:6; Exod.12:37). Third Maccabees 2:4–7 focuses on God as the Judge who destroyed giants (v. 4), made Sodom "an example to those who should come afterward" (v. 5 NRSV), and judged Pharaoh (vv. 6–7). The string in CD 2.17–3.12 includes the Watchers of the heavens (2.17, who were identified as fallen angels), the giants (2.18–21), and the exodus generation (3.1–12), while T. of Naph. 3.4–5 joins Sodom (v. 4) and the Watchers who were cursed at the flood (v. 5). The list in *m. Sanh.* 10.3 includes the flood generation, the dispersion, Sodom, the wilderness generation, Korah, and the ten tribes. So, too, 2 Pet. 2:4–9's judgment litany includes the angels who sinned (v. 4), the world of Noah's day (v. 5), and Sodom and Gomorrah in Lot's era (vv. 6–8), concluding with the declaration that the Lord knows how to save the godly and judge the wicked. Jude makes his selection with particular reference to the concrete issue that the church faced as he shows how the ancient sinners violated God's order, as do the heretics in the present time.

The unit can be outlined as follows:

a. Text: Exodus, angels, and Sodom and Gomorrah (5–7)
b. Comment: These are dreamers who defile the flesh, reject authority, and slander glorious ones (8)

## Exegesis and Exposition

[5]But I want you to remember, although you know all this, that ⌜Jesus⌝, having ⌜once⌝ delivered the people out of Egypt, later destroyed the ones who did not believe. [6]And the angels who did not keep to their domain but deserted their own dwelling place are kept in eternal chains in the darkness of the netherworld for the judgment of the great day. [7]Likewise Sodom and Gomorrah and the cities around them, in the same way as these, having indulged in unfaithful acts and gone after another kind of flesh stand as an example, suffering the penalty of eternal fire. [8]But in a similar way, too, these dreamers defile the flesh, revolt against lordship, and slander glories.

### a. Text: Exodus, Angels, and Sodom and Gomorrah (5–7)

After the initial disclosure formula concerning the purpose for writing (vv. 3–4), Jude develops his reflection on the divine decree of judgment against the godless heretics (v. 4a). They will come under judgment in the same way as those who did evil in the past (vv. 5–7). Jude prefaces his denunciation by calling the church to bring to mind what they already know: Ὑπομνῆσαι δὲ ὑμᾶς βούλομαι, εἰδότας ὑμᾶς πάντα (*Hypomnēsai de hymas boulomai, eidotas hymas panta*, But I want you to remember, although you know all this). During the Roman era, letter writers commonly inserted in the openings of the letter body statements about what the author wished the reader to know (White 1986: 207),[1] but here the formula is modified according to common conventions of moral instruction. The call to remember what one already knew is heard frequently in moral exhortation (Malherbe 1986: 125), including the NT (see, e.g., 1 Thess. 1:5; 2:1, 2, 5, 11; 3:3–4; 5:2). Dio Chrysostom (*Or.* 17.1–11) commented rather extensively on why it was necessary to remind people of lessons already learned: "However, since I observe that it is not our ignorance of the difference between good and evil that hurts us, so much as it is our failure to heed the dictates of reason on these matters and to be true to our personal opinions, I consider it most salutary to remind men of this without ceasing, and to appeal to their reason to give heed and in their acts to observe what is right and proper" (17.2). For his part, Jude assumes that his readers know the history of God's past judgments and is desirous that they apply the lessons learned from the judgment narratives to the present situa-

5

---

1. "Know that . . . ," or "I want you to know that. . . ."

tion. The use of the reminder formula at the head of the list of past judgments signals that Jude's purpose is not simply to denounce but to exhort. While he underscores that the heretics will be judged in the same way as rebels in the past (v. 8), his ultimate concern is to call the church to contend for the faith handed down to them (v. 3), to keep themselves in the love of God (v. 21), and to engage in a rescue mission extended to those who had come under the errorists' influence (vv. 22–23).

Jude first recalls for his readers the judgment that subsequently came on those who had been delivered from Egypt at the time of the exodus. He reminds them ὅτι Ἰησοῦς ἅπαξ λαὸν ἐκ γῆς Αἰγύπτου σώσας (*hoti Iēsous hapax laon ek gēs Aigyptou sōsas*, that Jesus having once delivered the people out of Egypt). Without quoting any particular text, Jude summarizes the exodus in words that echo the LXX description of the event. Frequently the language used is that God brought out (ἐξάγω, *exagō*) the people (λαόν, *laon*) from the land of Egypt (ἐκ γῆς Αἰγύπτου, *ek gēs Aigyptou*; Exod. 3:10; 7:4; 12:51; 13:3; 32:7, 11; 33:1; Deut. 9:12, 26, 29; 1 Kings 8:51; Jer. 39:21; Bar. 2:11), or redeemed (λυτρόω, *lytroō*) the people from the land of Egypt (Deut. 9:26; 21:8; without "land" in 2 Sam. 7:23; 1 Chron. 17:21). Elsewhere, the Lord is said to have saved (σώζω, *sōzō*) them from Egypt (Ps. 105:21 LXX [106:21 Eng.]; Hos. 13:4). Although Jude has no particular OT text in mind, he echoes the stereotypical descriptions of the exodus.

Jude, however, adapts the language to underscore its applicability to the present situation that his readers face. First, he notes that this deliverance was accomplished "once" (ἅπαξ, *hapax*), a term that does not appear in any LXX reference to the exodus (for the textual problems related to the position of ἅπαξ in the sentence, see the additional note on v. 5). The adverb, used also in verse 3b, points to the exodus as a "decisively unique" event (BDAG 97) that occurred "once and for all" (see Heb. 6:4; 10:2; *TLNT* 1:140–41). The emphasis falls on its finality. This stress serves as a link to Jude's declaration of the gospel as God's final revelation (v. 3b) and at the same time sets up the contrast between the deliverance through the exodus and the subsequent judgment. Those who were once and for all delivered could not suppose that they were immune from judgment. Since the errorists had claimed that grace allowed them to participate in sexual immorality (v. 4b), they would also consider themselves to be immune from judgment. Salvation, despite being the powerful work of God, does not exempt people from judgment if they embrace sin. Jude apparently considered the opponents to be apostates from the faith.

The second way that Jude adapts the traditional language of the exodus is his identification of the one who accomplished this deliverance: Jesus. Repeatedly, the LXX affirms that the "Lord" (κύριος, *kyrios*; Exod. 7:5; 12:51; 13:3, 9, 14, 16; 16:6; 18:1; Deut. 1:27; 26:8; "Lᴏʀᴅ" in NRSV), the "Lord God" (κύριος ὁ θεός, *kyrios ho theos*; Exod. 20:2; 29:46; Num. 15:41; Deut. 5:6, 15; 6:12; 8:14; 13:5, 11; 29:24 [29:25 Eng.]; Dan. 9:15; Bar. 2:11), or simply "God" (θεός, *theos*; Num. 23:22; Deut. 4:20) is the one who brought the people up out of the land of Egypt. The textual history of Jude 5a is very checkered as some MSS state that "the Lord" (ὁ κύριος, *ho kyrios*) saved the people, while others contain the reading "God" (θεός, *theos*). But the strongest MS support (see the additional note on v. 5) favors the reading "Jesus" (Ἰησοῦς, *Iēsous*), with a few witnesses reading "God Christ" (θεὸς Χριστός, *theos Christos*) or "Lord Jesus" (κύριος Ἰησοῦς, *kyrios Iēsous*). "Jesus" is "admittedly . . . the best attested reading among Greek and versional witnesses," according to Metzger along with Wikgren and Osburn (Metzger 1994: 657–58; Wikgren 1967; Osburn 1981). This reading is decidedly the most difficult to understand but "in general, the more difficult reading is to be preferred, particularly when the sense appears on the surface to be erroneous but on more mature consideration proves itself to be correct" (Metzger 1994: 12–13). Moreover, it is very hard to comprehend why an original reading of "Lord" or "God" would have been changed to "Jesus." This difficult reading best accounts for the rise of the other variants, which either reflect the more traditional language of the exodus summaries or seek to clarify the sense.

Nevertheless, the question remains regarding how best to interpret Jude's striking assertion. Paul certainly understands that the preexistent Christ was with Israel in the wilderness (1 Cor. 10:4), and John's Gospel echoes the same belief in his preexistence (John 8:56; 12:41; and see Neyrey 1993: 62) as does Heb. 11:26. The Venerable Bede (AD 672/673–735) follows the reading "Jesus" and comments that Jude "is referring not to Jesus the son of Nun but to our Lord, showing first that he did not have his beginning at his birth from the holy virgin, as the heretics have wished [to assert], but existed as the eternal God for the salvation of all believers. . . . For in Egypt he first so saved the humble who cried out to him from their affliction that he might afterward bring low the proud who murmured against him in the desert" (Hurst 1985: 242–43). Jude draws the parallel between Jesus's agency in the past and present of God's redemptive history, and he makes his case that as judgment came on those formerly delivered, so it will come on those whom Jesus has delivered now. The Savior is also the Judge.

Jude's summary of the judgment that came on the exodus generation states τὸ δεύτερον τοὺς μὴ πιστεύσαντας ἀπώλεσεν (*to deuteron tous mē pisteusantas apōlesen*, later destroyed the ones who did not believe). In time references, τὸ δεύτερον simply refers to what occurs "later" (LSJ 381–82; Herodotus 1.79), but here the sense may be slightly more elevated as Jude places in sharp contrast "two special moments of display of divine power, one in salvation, and the second in destruction" (BDAG 221). The term, however, does not imply "a second occasion" of disbelief for Israel since Jude's concern is only the contrast between exodus deliverance and subsequent judgment (Bauckham 1983: 50).

The judgment on the exodus generation is variously described in the LXX, yet Jude's reference appears to have been drawn from Num. 14:11–12, which uses the same verbs found in Jude 5b: "And the Lord said to Moses, 'How long does this people provoke me? How long will they not believe [οὐ πιστεύουσιν, *ou pisteuousin*] me for all the signs which I have done among them? I will strike them down to death and destroy (ἀπολῶ, *apolō*) them, and I will make you and your father's house into a great nation, even one much greater than this.'" Repeatedly the OT recalls the judgment on the exodus generation (Num. 14:26–35; 26:64–65; Pss. 78:21–31; 106:25–26), as does the NT (1 Cor. 10:5; Heb. 3:16–19), and frequently the root cause of that judgment is identified as unbelief (Num. 14:11; Ps. 78:22 [77:22 LXX]; Heb. 3:18–19). In the OT, faith includes the notion of trust (בָּטַח, *bāṭaḥ*; Jer. 39:18; Hos. 10:13; Hab. 2:18; W. Moberly, *NIDOTTE* 1:644–49) but also faithfulness. God is faithful to his covenant (Deut. 7:9), and his servants are known by their faithfulness (אָמַן, *'āman*; Num. 12:7; 1 Sam. 22:14; Isa. 8:2; Prov. 25:13; W. Moberly, *NIDOTTE* 1:427–33; O. Michel, *NIDNTT* 1:595–96). The failing of Israel is that the nation did not act out of covenant faithfulness to Yahweh (Num. 14:11–12), precisely the point that Jude wishes to make about the heretics. The end result was that they were "destroyed," which in the Exodus narratives meant that they were not allowed to enter the land but died in the wilderness. The NT authors, along with Jude, repeatedly set up the contrast between salvation and destruction (1 Cor. 1:18; 2 Cor. 2:15; 2 Thess. 2:10; James 4:12), with emphasis placed on eternal salvation or ruin (John 3:16; 10:28; 17:12; Rom. 2:12; 1 Cor. 8:11; 15:18; BDAG 115–16). Jude's typological use of the OT suggests that the heretics will meet this very end (see vv. 8, 11).

6     Jude forwards his second example of the divine judgment that came on those who were privileged by God but apostatized. In this case, it is the angels who sinned: ἀγγέλους τε τοὺς μὴ τηρήσαντας τὴν ἑαυτῶν ἀρχὴν ἀλλὰ ἀπολιπόντας τὸ ἴδιον οἰκητήριον (*angelous te tous mē tērēsantas tēn heautōn archēn alla apolipontas to idion oikētērion*, And the angels who did not keep to their domain but deserted their own dwelling place). While the disobedience of the exodus generation is a frequent topic in the OT, the apostasy of the angels to which Jude refers is not found in the Hebrew Scriptures. Jude has in mind a very well-known Jewish interpretation of Gen. 6:1–4 that understood the passage as a reference to angelic sin. The Genesis text reads in part: "When people began to multiply on the face of the ground, and daughters were born to them, the sons of God saw that they were fair; and they took wives for themselves of all that they chose." Judgment came, which limited the human lifespan to 120 years. As a result of this union, "The Nephilim were on the earth in those days—and also afterwards—when the sons of God went in to the daughters of humans, who bore children to them. These were the heroes that were of old, warriors of renown" (NRSV).

Considerable speculation arose within Judaism regarding the identity of these "sons of God" and the offspring of their union with the "daughters of men," who were called the "Nephilim" (see also Num. 13:33) or "giants" (נְפִילִים, *nĕpîlîm*; in the LXX, οἱ γίγαντες, *hoi gigantes*). According to a considerable portion of ancient Jewish literature, these "sons of God" were thought to be fallen angels, although dissenting voices were raised against this interpretation in rabbinic literature. At Gen. 6:2, Tg. Onq. identifies them as "the sons of the great ones" or nobility, and Tg. Neof. calls them "the sons of the judges." Frustration with the prevailing interpretive trend was voiced in Gen. Rab. 26.5 on Gen. 6:2: "R. Simeon b. Yoḥai referred to them as sons of the nobility. R. Simeon b. Yoḥai cursed anyone who called them 'sons of God.'" An explanation was added about why the characters in Gen. 6 were called "sons of God": "Because they lived a long time without suffering and without anguish" (Neusner 1985: 1.282). However, these interpretations of Genesis are mute compared with the strong voices in favor of the angelic interpretation, which was dominant in Jewish literature and made its way into Christian reflection.

The book that contains the most extensive reflection on these fallen angels is 1 Enoch, a work that Jude quotes in verses 14–15 (see comments on vv. 14–15). First Enoch 6–12 recounts the story of the angels who came to earth, took human wives, and engendered evil children, who were the giants. The flood was the judgment that came on the world for this heinous sin (for text and comment, see R. Charles 1893; M. Black 1970; 1985; Nickelsburg 2001). These fallen angels (ἄγγελοι, *angeloi* in 1 En. 6.2; 10.7; 14.4) are most often called "Watchers" in 1 Enoch (οἱ ἐγρήγοροι, *hoi egrēgoroi* in 1 En. 1.5; 10.9, 15; 12.4; 13.10; 14.1, 3; 16.2; for a discussion of the title, see Nickelsburg 2001: 140–41), a title that appears in other Jewish texts to identify the same beings (T. Naph. 3.5; CD 2.18; 4Q227 [4QpsJub] 4; 1QapGen 2.1; Jub. 10.5). First Enoch tells the story in the following way: "And it came to pass, when the children of men had multiplied in those days there were born to them beautiful and comely daughters. And watchers, children of heaven, saw them and desired them, and lusted after them; and they said to another: 'Come, let us choose for ourselves wives from the daughters of earth, and let us beget us children'" (1 En. 6.1–2 from M. Black 1985: 27–28). The judgment on these beings is likewise recounted at various points, among which is 12.3–6:

> And I, Enoch, was standing blessing the Lord of majesty, and the King of the ages, and behold! watchers of the great Holy One were calling me and saying to me: "Enoch, scribe of righteousness, go, declare to the watchers of heaven who have left the high heaven and the holy, eternal Sanctuary and have defiled themselves with women; and they themselves do as the children of earth do, and have taken to themselves wives: (say) 'You have wrought great destruction on the earth; and you shall have no peace or forgiveness.' And inasmuch as they delight in their children, the slaughter of their beloved ones they shall see, and over the destruction of their children they shall lament and make supplication without end: but they shall have neither mercy nor peace." (M. Black 1985: 31–32)

This is the same story told in Jub. 5.1–2 and 2 Bar. 56.10–16, along with CD 2.17–3.1 and even Josephus *Ant.* 1.3.1 §73 (see the additional note on v. 6). Jude is not the only NT author who makes reference to this story. This fall, plus Enoch's commission to proclaim judgment on the Watchers, apparently stands behind 1 Pet. 3:18–22 (Dalton 1989: 143–88; G. Green 1993: 215–27;

J. H. Elliott 2000: 697–705). Second Peter 2:4 follows Jude in his reference to the angelic sin.

Jude's purpose in evoking the story of the angelic fall is to demonstrate that those who hold a privileged position are not exempt from divine judgment if they embrace sin. The apostasy of the angels and the judgment against them is paradigmatic for the present time: as the angels, so these heretics, whom Jude deems to be apostates (v. 8). The link between the heretics and the angelic apostasy is strengthened by the sexual nature of the angels' and the heretics' sin (vv. 4, 8, 16, 18, 23; see Nickelsburg 2001: 272), although Jude refrains from specifying or discussing the sexual nature of the angels' sin; it is implied rather than stated. His rendition of the angelic fall evokes the language of 1 Enoch but falls short of quoting that book directly as he does in vv. 14–15, and his preference is to call them "angels" instead of "Watchers." He does not make any comment on the "giants" that according to the tradition were produced from this union, nor does he refer to Enoch's role in proclaiming judgment over these beings. Jude's use of the tradition, though perplexing to a contemporary reader, is restrained in comparison with other texts that retell this story. He refrains from ascribing the fall of the angels to the temptation of women as does the T. Reu. 5.1–6, and there is no allusion to Enoch's mission to proclaim judgment as in Jub. 4.22 and 1 Enoch. Jude does not understand this fall as the source of sin in the world (cf. Jub. 5.2), nor does he trace the demonic presence in the world back to this sin (cf. Jub. 10.1–5). While evoking the story of the angelic fall, he avoids embracing all of its sometimes fanciful dimensions (see "Jude and Pseudepigraphic Literature" in the introduction).

While 2 Pet. 2:4 speaks simply of the "angels who sinned," Jude gives a more detailed account of their transgression. They are angels τοὺς μὴ τηρήσαντας τὴν ἑαυτῶν ἀρχήν (tous mē tērēsantas tēn heautōn archēn, who did not keep to their domain). The term translated "domain" (ἀρχή, archē) may refer either to an office that one holds or a realm or empire that one inhabits (LSJ 252; BDAG 138). Diodorus Siculus (3.53.1) uses it to speak of the "magistries," while Josephus (Ant. 19.4.6 §273) mentions "the office" someone held. On the other hand, Diodorus (17.24.2) refers to the "ruling house of Caria," and Arrian (Anab. 6.29.1) mentions "his own country." The tradition about the fallen angels, however, underscores the way that these beings did not keep their heavenly realm but came to earth to engage in sin, not that they had given up some office or authority (1 En. 12.4 and 15.3, "left the high heaven"; CD 2.18, "from the heavens fell"; and so 1 En. 15.7; 14.5; 2 Bar. 56.12). They did not stay within their proper realm. In a play on words, Jude affirms their judgment in the latter part of the verse: the angels who "did not keep" (μὴ τηρήσαντας) to their domain "are kept" (τετήρηκεν, tetēreken) for final judgment (cf. v. 13).

In the following clause, Jude echoes but does not quote the language of 1 Enoch concerning the angelic sin: ἀλλὰ ἀπολιπόντας τὸ ἴδιον οἰκητήριον (alla apolipontas to idion oikētērion, but deserted their own dwelling place). In 1 En. 12.4 the author speaks about the Watchers "who left [ἀπολιπόντες, *apolipontes*] the highest heaven" (as 15.3). The verb suggests not only a departure but also an act that is final, an abandonment or desertion (Isa. 55:7; Prov. 2:17; 19:27; Sir. 17:25; *TLNT* 1:183–85). These whose natural place was heaven had deserted their proper abode. Instead of speaking of the angels' realm as "heaven," Jude refers to it as "their own dwelling place." An οἰκητήριον (*oikētērion*) was a dwelling place or habitation but could refer to the dwelling of a deity (cf. Paul's use of the term in 2 Cor. 5:2; see BDAG 695). This was "their own" place or what was appropriate or proper for them (1 Thess. 4:11; BDAG 467). To keep one's proper station in society was a high value during the era when Jude wrote. In a stratified society where status and position were marked by both clothing and positions in banquets and the theater, the accusation that these beings had moved outside their proper sphere or realm would have been understood as a transgression without any further mention of their sin (*OCD* 1440–41; and on markers of social status, see Shelton 1988: 6–10). However, the abbreviated way that Jude refers to their transgression implies, as do the previous and following examples of judgment (vv. 5, 7), that Jude's readers were well acquainted with the traditions regarding the angelic apostasy.

As a result of their transgression, Jude states that the angels εἰς κρίσιν μεγάλης ἡμέρας δεσμοῖς ἀϊδίοις ὑπὸ ζόφον τετήρηκεν (*eis krisin megalēs hēmeras desmois aidiois hypo zophon tetērēken*, are kept in eternal chains in the darkness of the netherworld for the judgment of the great day). The "great day" was a term that could in some contexts refer to the high day of a feast (John 7:37; 19:31), but in the context of judgment indicates that the author has the day of the Lord in mind (Zeph. 1:14; Mal. 4:5; Acts 2:20; Rev. 16:14). This is God's day of judgment (Jer. 30:7) and wrath (Rev. 6:17). In a similar manner, 1 En. 10.6 (M. Black 1985: 30) declares, "And on the day of the great judgment he will be led off to the blazing fire" (καὶ ἐν τῇ ἡμέρᾳ τῆς μεγάλης τῆς κρίσεως ἀπαχθήσεται εἰς τὸν ἐνπυρισμόν, *kai en tē hēmera tēs megalēs tēs kriseōs apachthēsetai eis ton enpyrismon*). The angels are "kept" for that day (τετήρηκεν, *tetērēken*, perfect tense with stative aspect; Porter 1989: 245–90), implying that their doom is sure and that they will not escape the judgment passed on them, as a criminal is "kept" in custody (Matt. 27:36, 54; Acts 12:5; 16:23). Far from enjoying freedom, these fallen angels are fettered with "eternal chains" (δεσμοῖς ἀϊδίοις, *desmois aidiois* [Jude 6]): this binding will not come to an end.

First Enoch 14.5 makes a similar assertion: "From now on you shall no longer ascend to heaven throughout all ages; and it has been ordered to bind you in bonds in the earth for all the days of eternity" (M. Black 1985: 33; ἐν τοῖς δεσμοῖς τῆς γῆς ἐρρέθη δῆσαι ὑμᾶς εἰς πάντας τοὺς αἰῶνας, *en tois desmois tēs gēs errethē dēsai hymas eis pantas tous aiōnas*). The finality of the judgment on the angels is underscored at other points in 1 Enoch's story of the angelic fall (1 En. 10.13; 16.3; 21.10; 22.11). Once again, while Jude echoes the language of 1 Enoch, he does not quote him exactly while expressing the same idea at this point. Though the Enoch tradition locates this binding as on the earth (1 En. 14.5), Jude declares that they are kept "in the darkness of the netherworld" (ὑπὸ ζόφον, *hypo zophon*, under darkness; cf. 2 Pet. 2:4, 17). The exact expression Jude uses to describe the place where the angels are bound was used repeatedly in classical literature as a reference to the dark realm of the underworld (Aeschylus, *Pers.* 839: "As for me, I depart for the darkness beneath the earth"; Euripides, *Hipp.* 1416: "Forever in the nether gloom"; Quintus Smyrnaeus 2.619: "Therefore I will pass into darkness"; and so 2.612; Homer, *Od.* 20.356; 11.55; *Il.* 21.56; Sib. Or. 4.43). This is the place of dread and darkness. Jude could hardly find more graphic terms to describe the final end of the apostate angels. The God who judged them is the one who will bring the heretics who have invaded the church into judgment (v. 4). The eternal darkness is reserved for them as well (v. 13).

7      Jude's third example of sin followed by divine judgment is the story of Sodom and Gomorrah. God revealed to Abraham his forthcoming judgment on these cities, saying, "How great is the outcry against Sodom and Gomorrah and how very grave their sin!" (Gen. 18:20 NRSV). Somewhat surprisingly, the exact nature of the cities' sin is not elaborated. The reader is only made aware of the depravity of the inhabitants of Sodom when the angelic visitors arrive at Lot's house. These soon become the objects of sexual desire by all the male inhabitants of the city, from the youngest to the oldest: "Bring them out to us, so that we may know them" (Gen. 19:5 NRSV). Lot had shown the messengers hospitality and tried to protect his guests by taking the extreme measure of offering the assailants his daughters instead (19:8).[2] Since not even ten righteous people were found in Sodom (18:22–33), God destroyed the city by sulfur and fire along with Gomorrah (19:12–29). Included in the judgment were the surrounding cities of the plain (19:24–25, 28–29), a piece of the story to which Jude refers in the opening of verse 7: ὡς Σόδομα καὶ Γόμορρα καὶ αἱ περὶ αὐτὰς πόλεις (*hōs Sodoma kai Gomorra kai hai peri autas poleis*, Likewise Sodom and Gomorrah and the cities around them). The sin of Sodom and Gomorrah became archetypal in the OT as well as in Jewish and Christian literature (Deut. 32:32; Isa. 1:10; 3:9; Jer. 23:14; 3 Macc. 2:5; 2 Esd. [4 Ezra] 7:106; Matt. 11:23), as did the divine judgment that came on these cities (Isa. 1:9; 13:19; Jer. 49:18; 50:40; Lam. 4:6; Amos 4:11; Zeph. 2:9; 3 Macc. 2:5; 2 Esd. [4 Ezra] 2:8; Matt. 10:15; 11:24; Luke 10:12; 17:29–30; Rom. 9:29; 2 Pet. 2:6). They were therefore set forward as an example to "later generations" (3 Macc. 2:5).

But what was the sin of Sodom and Gomorrah that merited such cataclysmic judgment? The only specific sin mentioned in the Genesis narrative is that the male inhabitants of Sodom desired sexual relationships with the angelic

---

2. Within that oriental context, "a host is responsible for the safety of his guests. If anything happens to his guests while they are under his roof, the host is culpable" (V. Hamilton 1995: 36). Lot was caught on the horns of the dilemma: whether to protect his guests or his daughters. His decision was hardly commendable, albeit somewhat understandable given the moral codes of the era.

messengers, who were identified as men (Gen. 19:5, 8). Male-with-male sexual relationships are condemned in Scripture (Lev. 18:22; 20:13). Yet Jewish comment on this question sometimes speaks only generically of the Sodomites' wickedness along with their arrogance (T. Naph. 4.1; Sir. 16:8–10), their neglect of wisdom (Wis. 10:6–9), or lack of hospitality (Wis. 19:14; cf. Matt. 10:14–15). Other texts highlight the sexual aspect of their sin (T. Levi 14.6; T. Benj. 9.1; Jub. 16.5–9; 20.5–6; cf. 2 Pet. 2:7), while still others underscore that they attempted what was contrary to the order of nature (T. Naph. 3.4). Philo (*Abraham* 26 §133) accuses them of "innumerable iniquities, particularly such as arise from gluttony and lewdness," and says they "multiplied and enlarged every other possible pleasure." Josephus (*J.W.* 4.8.4 §§483–84; *Ant.* 1.11.1 §§194–95) names their sin as "impiety" and "insolence," along with pride and hatred toward foreigners. This tapestry of interpretation is richly textured.

After surveying the ancient comment, Loader (1990: 116–17) concludes: "Often the wickedness is of a generic nature, . . . but it is also often specified: The sexual motif is emphasized in the Testaments and Jubilees, but while it is given prominence in Rabbinic literature, it is subsumed under the social aspect, which is the most prominent in the corpus of literature." Lyons (2002: 235) analyzes the same ancient comment on the Genesis narrative but remarks on the way that "this wicked space in the narrative has been exploited many times in the history of reflection on this text." Whatever summary statements may be drawn concerning ancient understanding of the sin, "Sodom is an exemplar within this process of education in which wickedness itself is not reducible to a single act of sin, but rather indicates a failure to walk in the way. In such a context, the point of judging Sodom is not to demonstrate abhorrence for a particular sin, but to show the consequences of going off the path in any way" (235).[3]

Jude's use of the story of Sodom and Gomorrah underscores these cities' failure to walk in the way, particularly highlighting how they had departed from the natural order of things: τὸν ὅμοιον τρόπον τούτοις ἐκπορνεύσασαι καὶ ἀπελθοῦσαι ὀπίσω σαρκὸς ἑτέρας (*ton homoion tropon toutois ekporneusasai kai apelthousai opisō sarkos heteras*, in the same way as these, having indulged in unfaithful acts and gone after another kind of flesh). Jude links the sin of the angels in verse 6 with that of the inhabitants of Sodom and Gomorrah (the names of the cities standing for their inhabitants), noting that those people sinned τὸν ὅμοιον τρόπον τούτοις, in like manner as "these" angels. Jude employs the accusative τὸν ὅμοιον τρόπον adverbially (BDF §160), using an expression that means the same as ὁμότροπος (*homotropos*), "in the same manner" (LSJ 1228). As the angels abandoned their proper sta-

---

3. Lyons (2002: 235) applauds Robert Hunter's lyrics sung by the late Jerry Garcia of the Grateful Dead: "Just a song of Gomorrah, wondering what they did there, must have been a bad thing, to get shot down for" ("Gomorrah," on *Cats under the Stars*, by the Jerry Garcia Band, April 1978, Arista AB 4160).

tion (v. 6), so too, the inhabitants of Sodom, Gomorrah, and the surrounding cities "indulged in unfaithful acts" (aorist participle ἐκπορνεύσασαι). This verb is found only here in the NT, but appears some forty-one times in the LXX, where it may mean either to indulge in sexual relations (Gen. 38:24; Lev. 19:29; Hos. 2:7; 4:13) or to indulge in acts of unfaithfulness with respect to God (Exod. 34:15; Deut. 31:16; Ezek. 20:30; Hos. 1:2; 4:12; 5:3; Sir. 46:11; see Muraoka 2002: 167). Both the sin of the angels (v. 6) and that of the inhabitants of Sodom and Gomorrah had a sexual component, yet Jude's principal emphasis in verse 6 is on the way the angels abandoned their proper place. This the angels (Watchers) did, according to the tradition, by engaging in sexual relations with humans (1 En. 12.4). The opposite was true of the Sodomites, who left their place and tried to engage in sexual relations with angelic messengers. While Jude notes the sexual component of the sin, he highlights the way such sin is a violation of the order of things. The angels "did not keep" but "deserted," and so also the people of Sodom and Gomorrah indulged in unfaithful acts with respect to God (ἐκπορνεύσασαι, *ekporneusasai*). As noted above (see comments on v. 6), one of the highest values in ancient society was the maintenance of proper order and faithful adherence to one's duty and maintaining one's place in society (see Malina 2001: 104–6). In contemporary Western society, this value is not esteemed as it was in the ancient Mediterranean world. Faithfulness to a prescribed order is often viewed more as an antiquated vice than a virtue.

In the further reflection on the sin of Sodom, Gomorrah, and the surrounding cities, Jude shines the spotlight on the attempt to engage in sexual acts with the angelic messengers: "having gone after another kind of flesh." The "flesh" of the angelic messengers is called "strange" (KJV) in the sense of being of a different kind (BDAG 399, 915), as Judg. 2:12 (Theod.) speaks of going "after other gods" (ἐπορεύθησαν ὀπίσω θεῶν ἑτέρων, *eporeuthēsan opisō theōn heterōn*), which by their nature are other than true gods. Once again, the emphasis falls not simply on the sexual nature of the sin (as the NRSV's rendering "unnatural lust") but also on the way their act contravened the established order of things. Jude's thought in vv. 6–7 is much akin to that found in T. Naph. 3.4–5: "So that you do not become like Sodom, which departed from the order of nature. Likewise the Watchers departed from nature's order." The sexual aspect of their sin is the vehicle by which they had violated the order established by God. The heretics' sin likewise revolves around a rebellion against established order, with their sexual sin being a function of the fundamental problem (v. 8).

As in the two previous examples of sin (vv. 5–6), Jude turns to display the divine judgment that came as a consequence of the cities' sin, holding up to view the moral lesson to be learned: πρόκεινται δεῖγμα πυρὸς αἰωνίου δίκην ὑπέχουσαι (*prokeintai deigma pyros aiōniou dikēn hypechousai*, stand as an example, suffering the penalty of eternal fire). Jude implies that in full view of everyone, God set out or exposed the ancient sinners as an example from which all were to learn. Josephus employs similar language (*J.W.* 6.2.1

§103): "You have a noble example set before you in . . ." (καλόν ὑπόδειγμα πρόκειται, *kalon hypodeigma prokeitai*; and cf. 2 Pet. 2:6). These cities were set before humanity, displayed in public view (BDAG 870) "as a sample of divine retribution" (E. Lee 1961–62: 167). Jude does not state for whom the example is set out, but hurries on to underscore the nature of the judgment. His point appears to be that both the behavior and its consequences serve as an example.

The use of examples in moral exhortation was extremely common in ancient literature since "personal examples . . . were regarded as more persuasive than words" (Malherbe 1986: 135). Examples of both virtue (Heb. 11:4–38; 1 Clem. 9–12) and vice (1 Cor. 10:1–13; 2 Tim. 3:8) fill ancient literature and the NT (Malherbe 1986: 135–36). Examples of blameworthy behavior or vice were employed to instruct in virtue. One needed to know what to avoid as well as what to do. So Plutarch (*Demetrius* 1.6) discusses the issue: "So, I think, we also shall be more eager to observe and imitate the better lives if we are not left without narratives of the blameworthy and the bad." Jude's readers would readily understand the implications for their present situation. They were to avoid the Sodomites' behavior and, in so doing, would avoid its consequences.

The nature of the judgment is sketched in the final words of the verse: πυρὸς αἰωνίου δίκην ὑπέχουσαι (*pyros aiōniou dikēn hypechousai*, suffering the penalty of eternal fire). At this point, Jude switches to a legal register as he lays out the character of the judgment. Ὑπέχουσαι is a forensic term (Josephus, *Ag. Ap.* 2.24 §194; *Ant.* 1.3.8 §99; BDAG 1035; MM 654), often coupled with δίκην (*dikēn*) to mean "undergo punishment" or, as in the papyri, "pay the penalty." This latter term evokes the judicial concept of "punishment meted out as a legal penalty" (BDAG 250). It originally had to do with the verdict in the tribunal but came to signify the execution of the penalty (cf. 2 Macc. 8:11; Wis. 18:11). Jude implies that there has been a divine verdict, which is then executed. The nature of the punishment or penalty is "eternal fire." That the world would be judged by fire was affirmed repeatedly in the OT (Deut. 32:22; Isa. 29:6; 30:27, 30, 33; 33:14; 66:15–16, 24; Joel 2:30; Nah. 1:6; Zeph. 1:18; 3:8; Mal. 4:1), as well as Jewish literature (Sib. Or. 2.196–213; 1 En. 1.6–7; 52.6; Ps. Sol. 15.4; Josephus, *Ant.* 1.2.3 §70) and the NT (Acts 2:19; 2 Thess. 1:8; 2 Pet. 3:7, 10; Rev. 9:17–18; 16:8; 20:9). Jude adds the note that this fire will be "eternal" (cf. 4 Macc. 12:12; T. Zeb. 10.3; Matt. 18:8; 25:41). Jude does not embrace the idea that the people of Sodom and Gomorrah will be eternally annihilated, a notion that would make his statement more accommodating to modern Western sensibilities (see Morgan and Peterson 2004). Rather, the punishment by fire will endure and will not end, according to the perspective found in Jewish literature (1QS 2.15; 5.13; 4 Macc. 10:15). The severity of the punishment underscores the dreadful nature of the sin. As it happened to the inhabitants of the ancient cities, so it will happen to the heretics (v. 7). The arresting power of Jude's rhetoric will be powerful in its persuasion to avoid the errorists' enticement.

## b. Comment: These Are Dreamers Who Defile the Flesh, Reject Authority, and Slander Glorious Ones (8)

**8**     As observed previously in the introduction (see "Genre and Structure"), the body of Jude's Epistle is structured around a series of "texts" drawn from the OT, pseudepigraphic literature, and apostolic preaching (vv. 5–7, 9, 11, 14–15, 17–18), each of which is followed by comments that show their application and fulfillment in the coming of the heretics (vv. 8, 10, 12–13, 16, 19). These comments are introduced by the characteristic "these" or "these are" (likely pejorative; see du Toit 1994: 406; Cantinat 1973: 1–2; Busto Saiz 1981: 85–87), and so the present verse begins: Ὁμοίως μέντοι καὶ οὗτοι ἐνυπνιαζόμενοι (*homoiōs mentoi kai houtoi enypniazomenoi*, But in a similar way, too, these dreamers). Jude compares the sin of the heretics to that of the Israelites who did not believe (v. 5), the fallen angels who left their position (v. 6), and the inhabitants of Sodom and Gomorrah, who were unfaithful (v. 7). Jude employs a typological exegesis of these ancient texts to show their applicability to the present situation (v. 4; J. Charles 1993: 103–18). The correspondence between the sin of these groups and that of the heretics is not one-for-one, so we should not press the typology beyond Jude's intended purpose. In broad outline (ὁμοίως, *homoiōs*, marks similarity and not necessarily identity; see BDAG 707–8) and not in every detail, the ancient sinners prefigure the heretics that have invaded the congregation(s) to which Jude writes. The points of comparison that Jude has in mind are enumerated in the latter part of the verse (see below).

Jude labels the heretics "dreamers" (ἐνυπνιαζόμενοι, participial form of a verb common in the LXX: Gen. 28:12; Deut. 13:2, 4, 6; Jer. 23:25; 34:9 [27:9 Eng.]; Joel 3:1 [2:28 Eng.]). The name does not simply mark them out as people who held outlandish, fanciful, or unrealistic ideas (as in the English, "He's just a dreamer!"). Dreams were commonly considered a source of divine revelation. Jude's opponents apparently claimed such nocturnal inspiration in support of their perspectives. Cicero, who wrote more than a hundred years before Jude, identified forms of divination commonly practiced as those dependent on art ("prophecies of soothsayers, . . . interpreters of prodigies and lightnings, . . . augurs, . . . astrologers, or . . . oracles") and those dependent on nature ("the forewarnings of dreams, or . . . frenzy;" *Div.* 1.6.12; 1.18.34). Dreams had a significant revelatory function in early Christian history as well (Matt. 1:20; 2:12–13, 19–22; Acts 2:17; 16:9–10; 18:9). Since OT times, dreams were considered to be forms of divine communication, as in the narratives of Joseph (Gen. 37:5; 40:5) and Daniel (Dan. 1:17) and the prophecy of Joel (Joel 2:28 [3:1 LXX]), and were placed alongside other forms of divine communication such as prophecy (Deut. 13:1–5; 1 Sam. 28:6, 15). Skepticism about dreams other than those that come from God was voiced within Judaism (Sir. 34:1–7; and see G. Green 2001 on Greco-Roman skepticism).

Jude's identification of the heretics as "dreamers" opens the window on his rhetorical strategy. Since the errorists claimed divine inspiration, Jude made his appeal to established revelation (vv. 3–4) in his attempt to dissuade his readers from their perspectives. In a similar way, Paul hauled the Thessalonian church back to the received tradition in the face of a new and novel revelation (2 Thess. 2:2, 5, 15). All revelation that lays claim to divine agency must come under the evaluative eye of the community (1 Cor. 14:29; 1 Thess. 5:19–22), which shines the light of apostolic tradition on its content (1 John 4:1–3). The subapostolic church recognized this necessity (Did. 11.8–12), as should the contemporary church.

Jude's accusation is tripartite. First, these dreamers σάρκα μὲν μιαίνουσιν (*sarka men miainousin*, defile the flesh).[4] Jude frames his denunciation within the concept of purity, and so it cannot be reduced simply to the charge that they "engage in sexual immorality" without weakening the idea that he forwards. In the LXX, the verb commonly refers to ritual defilement that results in uncleanness (Exod. 20:25; Lev. 5:3; 11:24; 13:3; Num. 5:3; 1 Macc. 1:63; 4 Macc. 7:6), but it could also speak of moral defilement (Gen. 34:5), although the line between cultic and moral defilement was not as hard drawn as Protestant thought presupposes (deSilva 2000: 267). In the ancient world, as in many contemporary societies, purity codes were essential for marking out and maintaining the boundaries of the group to which one belonged. Purity codes then become a way of talking about what is fitting for a group on various occasions.

On the other side, "pollution is a label attached to whatever is out of place with regard to the society's view of an orderly and safe world" (deSilva 2000: 243).[5] So immoral sexual conduct may be viewed as a transgression of the prescribed boundaries and thus constitutes a form of defilement. This language of impurity in relationship to sexual immorality is found repeatedly in Jewish literature (see, e.g., Let. Aris. 141–66; Josephus, *J.W.* 4.5.2 §323; Jub. 7.20–21). Jubilees 16.5–6 develops this idea in a manner similar to Jude as it brings together Sodom and Gomorrah's sexual sin, defilement, and subsequent judgment as a moral example:

> And in that month the Lord executed the judgment of Sodom and Gomorrah and Zeboim and all of the district of Jordan. And he burned them with fire and sulphur and he annihilated them till this day just as (he said), "Behold, I have made known to you all of their deeds that (they were) cruel and great sinners and they were polluting themselves and they were fornicating in their flesh and

4. The elements are marked out by the μέν ... δὲ ... δέ construction, which here "does not emphasize a contrast, but separates one thought from another in a series" (BDAG 630). Cf. verses 22–23, where the elements are placed in contrast by this construction.

5. Similarly, Neusner (1973: 108) states, "Purity therefore, first, serves as an important mode of differentiation and definition for the sects known to us in the first century B.C. and A.D." Malina (2001: 165) adds, "Dirt presumes a system, a set of line markings or definitions. ... Now both defilement and purification presuppose some movement across a symbolic line that marks off the clean from the unclean." On purity/defilement, see Douglas 1966; Neusner 1973; H. Harrington 1993; deSilva 2000; and especially Let. Aris. 144–61 for an explanation of the relationship between ceremonial and moral purity laws. See also Lev. 18.

they were causing pollution upon the earth." And thus the Lord will execute judgment like the judgment of Sodom on places where they act according to the pollution of Sodom. (O. S. Wintermute, *OTP* 2:88)

Jude's point regarding the heretics is that they transgressed proper bounds, as did Israel, the angels, and the Sodom and Gomorrahites, and they had therefore "defiled the flesh." By referring to "flesh," Jude has in mind the body used in sexual acts, a practice in which the heretics had engaged (cf. vv. 7, 23; and 2 Peter's use of Jude's term in 2:10, 18). Once again, however, although Jude does not refrain from denouncing the sexual sin of the heretics, he understands their problem as a transgression of divinely established order and, as such, defilement.

The second accusation Jude levies against the heretics is that κυριότητα δὲ ἀθετοῦσιν (*kyriotēta de athetousin*, they revolt against lordship). Although κυριότης may refer to angelic beings, as is the case in Col. 1:16 and Eph. 1:21 (cf. 2 En. 20.1; 1 En. 61.10; T. Sol. 8.6 [MS D]), here as in 2 Pet. 2:10 it denotes the ruling power of the Lord (κύριος, *kyrios*) himself (see also Did. 4.1; Herm. *Sim.* 5.6.1; BDAG 579; W. Foerster, *TDNT* 3:1096–97; and Carr 1981: 129–32). Jude has already labeled the heretics as those who "deny our only Master and Lord, Jesus Christ" (v. 4), and here the charge is similar (as in Herm. *Sim.* 5.6.1, the "lordship" against which they revolt is that of Christ). Jude charges that his opponents "revolt against" Christ's lordship. In this condemnation, he picks up a verb (*atheteō*) found sixty times in the LXX, which, though it is used to translate seventeen different terms in the Hebrew Scriptures, most commonly stands for "*bāgad*, 'deceive, be unfaithful, betray,' and *pāša*, 'defect, revolt,' with the result that in biblical usage this verb almost always means 'be unfaithful,' to revolt, or to betray, with the sense of 'deceive' or 'scorn'" (*TLNT* 1:40). Once again the question of authority is brought to the fore as Jude accuses these heretics not only of violating established norms but also of revolting against the authority of the Lord himself. As the archetypal examples of sin (vv. 5–7), they have broken faith. As the Lord spoke to his people through Jeremiah, "But as a wife is unfaithful [ἀθετεί, *athetei*] to her husband, so you have been unfaithful [ἠθέτησεν, *ēthetēsen*] to me, house of Israel, says the Lord" (Jer. 3:20 LXX).

The final accusation of this trilogy is that Jude's opponents δόξας δὲ βλασφημοῦσιν (*doxas de blasphēmousin*, they slander glories). Identifying the δόξαι (*doxai*, glories) referred to here and in 2 Pet. 2:10 has been somewhat problematic. Reicke (1964: 167, 201) suggests that they are "dignitaries," that is, civic authority (cf. Diodorus Siculus 15.58.1, which refers to the "glory" or reputation of outstanding citizens), while Bigg identifies them as ecclesiastical authorities (Bigg 1901: 279). M. Green (1987: 182) understands this as a reference to "angelic beings," a line of interpretation followed by Bauckham (1983: 37), Neyrey (1993: 69), and others (Kelly 1969: 263; Schelkle 1980: 157; Sellin 1986: 215; Perkins 1995: 151; Moo 1996: 244). Jude's idea is adopted by the book's oldest interpreter, 2 Peter. In 2 Pet. 2:10–11, the "glories" are angelic beings (although it must be allowed that 2 Peter does not always use the ideas of Jude in the same way as Jude). Clement of Alexandria follows this line: "They 'speak evil of majesty,' that is, of the angels" (*Comments on the Epistle of Jude* [*ANF* 2:573]). The ancient commentator Bede (Hurst 1985: 244), however, took verse 8c as an accusation against "the unbelieving people who blasphemed the majesty of the divine power."

However, the LXX refers to angelic beings as "glories" (Exod. 15:11). The contrast that Jude sets up between the heretics' behavior and that of Michael, who did not blaspheme the devil (vv. 9–10), points in the direction of understanding these "glories" as supernatural beings. This interpretation also finds support, as Bauckham (1983: 57) notes, in the DSS, where angels are called "glories" (1QH 10.8; "and perhaps 11QpsZion [= 11Q5] 22.13"), and in apocalyptic literature (2 En. 22.7; Ascen. Isa. 9.32). Jude's nomenclature is understandable in light of the attribution of "glory" to angels (Rev. 18:1; T. Levi 18.5; Philo, *Spec. Laws* 1.8 §45), an idea "rooted in the OT, where the cherub is the bearer of the divine *kābôd* (Ezek. 9:3; 10:4, 18, 22; cf. also Sir. 49:8)" (J. Charles 1993: 102). We should, however, recognize that "glory" is a term commonly used to refer to "honor" in ancient societies (*TLNT* 1:363–64). To slander those who held the greatest derived (from God) honor would be recognized by all as a heinous social breach. The heretics not only opposed divine authority but also publicly dishonored his supernatural representatives.

The heretics "slandered" the "glories": they "blasphemed" them (βλασφημοῦσιν, *blasphēmousin*). While the verb is most commonly used in Greco-Roman, Jewish, and Christian literature to refer to reviling or defaming the deity (see Matt. 9:3; 26:65; Acts 19:37; Rom. 2:24; see BDAG 178), it could also refer to slanderous and defaming speech against a person (1 Pet. 4:4; Rom. 3:8; Titus 3:2) or, as here, against supernatural beings (cf. 2 Pet. 2:10, 12). Such denigrating speech against supernatural beings is the counterpoint to the heretics' own boasting (vv. 16, 18). While the charge of boasting was a commonplace in *vituperatio*, Jude here molds it to apply to the specific problem that he addresses in the church (see "Occasion of Writing" in the introduction). The heretics' rhetorical strategy was to exalt their own honor and status even at the expense of angelic beings (Neyrey 1993: 69). In both Jewish and Christian theology, angels were regarded as mediators of divine law (Acts 7:53; Gal. 3:19; Heb. 2:2; and possibly Josephus, *Ant.* 15.5.3 §136; 1 En. 93.2) and for this reason became guardians of the divine order. The heretics had rejected this order of things, as had the archetypal heretics that Jude forwards as examples in vv. 5–7. They will allow no voice, no authority, other than their own. Their insolence is beyond measure.

## Additional Notes

**5.** The UBS⁴ and NA²⁷ adopt the reading ὅτι ὁ κύριος ἅπαξ (*hoti ho kyrios hapax*, because the Lord once), which is attested in ℵ and Ψ (without ὁ), as well as C and the uncials 1505, 1611, and 2138. However, the reading ὅτι Ἰησοῦς ἅπαξ (*hoti Iēsous hapax*, because Jesus once) finds support in the uncials 322, 323, 1241, 1739, 1881, and 2298, with the variant reading ἅπαξ πάντα, ὅτι Ἰησοῦς (*hapax panta, hoti lēsous*, all this once, because Jesus) found in A, B, 33, 81, and 2344. A number of the fathers follow the reading "Jesus" (including Origen, Cyril, Jerome, and Bede). Despite the strong attestation for this reading, "a majority of the Committee was of the opinion that the reading was difficult to the point of impossibility" (Metzger 1994: 657). However, even if the interpretive issues loom large, the weightier textual evidence should be followed. The second textual issue, not discussed in the commentary, has to do with the position of ἅπαξ (*hapax*). Should it be read with πάντα (ἅπαξ πάντα, *once and for all*), as in A, B, 33, 81, 2344 (Osburn 1981: 108–10; Metzger 1994: 657–58), or does it stand near the head of the following ὅτι (*hoti*, because) clause as in 322, 323, 1241, 1739, 1881, 2298 (Wikgren 1967: 147–48)? Whether κύριος (*kyrios*) or Ἰησοῦς (*lēsous*) is read as original, the MS evidence is diverse regarding the position of ἅπαξ, as is scholarly opinion. With the evidence being less than clear at this point, internal evidence would favor reading it within the ὅτι clause and so setting up the contrast with the following τὸ δεύτερον (*to deuteron*, later).

**6.** The following texts also tell of the angelic fall.

> And when the children of men began to multiply on the surface of the earth and daughters were born to them, that the angels of the Lord saw in a certain year of that jubilee that they were good to look at. And they took wives for themselves from all those whom they chose. And they bore children for them; and they were the giants. And injustice increased upon the earth, and all flesh corrupted its way; man and cattle and beasts and birds and everything which walks on the earth. And they all corrupted their way and their ordinances, and they began to eat one another. And injustice grew upon the earth and every imagination of the thoughts of all mankind was thus continually evil. (Jub. 5.1–2 [O. S. Wintermute, *OTP* 2:64])

> For he who was in danger to himself was also a danger to the angels. For they possessed freedom in that time in which they were created. And some of them came down and mingled themselves with women. At that time they who acted like this were tormented in chains. But the rest of the multitude of angels, who have no number, restrained themselves. And those living on earth perished together through the waters of the flood. Those are the first black waters. (2 Bar. 56.10–16 [A. F. J. Klijn, *OTP* 1:641])

> For having walked in the stubbornness of their hearts the Watchers of the heavens fell; on account of it they were caught, for they did not follow the precepts of God. And their sons, whose height was like that of cedars and whose bodies were like mountains, fell. All flesh which there was in the dry earth decayed and became as if it had never been, for having realized their desires and failing to keep their creator's precepts, until his wrath flared up against them. Through it, the sons of Noah and their families strayed, through it, they were cut off. (CD 2.17–3.1 [García Martínez 1994: 34])

> For many angels of God now consorted with women and begat sons who were overbearing and disdainful of every virtue, such confidence had they in their strength; in fact the deeds that tradition ascribes to them resemble the audacious exploits told by the Greeks of the giants. (Josephus, *Ant.* 1.3.1 §73 [Loeb])

Other references to this angelic fall can be found in Philo, *QG* 1 §92; T. Reu. 5.6; T. Naph. 3.5; Jub. 4.15, 22.

# 2. Second Text and Comment (9–10)

Jude presents his second section of "text" (v. 9) and comment (v. 10), following the pattern established in the previous section (vv. 5–7 and v. 8). Jude's rhetorical strategy is to denounce the behavior of the heretics as he contrasts them with the figure of the archangel Michael. But Jude also draws the line between the condemnable behavior of the devil and that of the heretics. The sin of the devil that Jude highlights is "slander," precisely what the heretics engaged in as they "slander glories" (v. 8c). The implication is that the judgment that the Lord would bring on the devil for his sin of slander (v. 9b) would likewise come on the heretics who slandered what they did not understand (v. 10). Jude makes use of some typical motifs of *vituperatio* as he denounces his opponents, yet his charges reflect the real situation of these heretics, who like the devil have overstepped the bounds in engaging in immoral behavior.

The unit can be outlined as follows:

a. Text: Michael did not blaspheme the devil (9)
b. Comment: These blaspheme what they do not understand (10)

## Exegesis and Exposition

⁹But Michael the archangel, when disputing with the devil, argued over the body of Moses, did not presume to pronounce the verdict of "slander" but said, "The Lord punish you!" ¹⁰These, on the one hand, slander whatever they do not understand, but on the other, because of everything that they know by instinct as irrational beasts, they are corrupted.

### a. Text: Michael Did Not Blaspheme the Devil (9)

Bede (Hurst 1985: 244–45) commented on this passage in Jude: "It is not entirely obvious from what scriptures Jude took this witness." The story of the dispute between Michael the archangel and the devil over the body of Moses is not part of the OT narrative, as diligent readers of Scripture know. Instead of appealing to the OT, Jude's "text" is a book called the Assumption (Testament) of Moses (known in the early church as Ἀνάληψις Μωϋσέως [*Analēpsis Mōyseōs*] and *Ascensio* or *Assumptio Mosis*; see R. Charles 1897; Nickelsburg 1973; Bauckham 1983: 67–76; Schalit 1989; Bauckham 1990: 235–80; Tromp 1993; Hofmann 2000). Considerable confusion has existed from ancient times regarding whether or not this is the same book referred to as the Testament of Moses (Διαθήκη Μωϋσέως, *Diathēkē Mōyseōs*, or *Testamentum Mosis*).

9

Were these "two distinct works, a single work consisting of two sections, or two separate works which were subsequently joined together" (J. F. Priest, *ABD* 4:920)? Whatever their relationship, the source Jude depended on was known by Clement of Alexandria (*Adumbratio in Epistula Judae*, cited in R. Charles 1897: 107) as well as Gelasius Cyzicenus (*Historia Ecclesiastica* 2.17.17; died ca. 476) as the Assumption (Testament) of Moses or the Ascension of Moses (Origen, *De principiis* 3.2.1).[1] This early-first-century book (Tromp 1993: 116–17) has come down to us in an incomplete Latin MS that does not contain its ending, and this, it appears, is precisely the section to which Jude refers. Our knowledge of the book's ending comes through secondary sources, including Jude. Gelasius, who was familiar with the book, says, "In the book of the Assumption of Moses, the archangel Michael, in a discussion with the devil, says: 'For by his Holy Spirit, all of us have been created,' and further he says: 'God's spirit went forth from his face, and the world came into being'" (Tromp 1993: 272).

Although Gelasius's reference to the book does not mention the dispute over Moses's body, angelic or divine responsibility for his burial is a topic in other ancient texts. Commenting on Moses's death, Philo (*Moses* 2.51 §291) said,

> For when he was already being exalted and stood at the very barrier, ready at the signal to direct his upward flight to heaven, the divine spirit fell upon him and he prophesied with discernment while still alive the story of his own death; told ere the end how the end came; told how he was buried with none present, surely by no mortal hands but by immortal powers; how also he was not laid to rest in the tomb of his forefathers but was given a monument of special dignity which no man has ever seen.

The same tradition appears at a later date in the Armenian Life of Moses: "The angel of the Lord came to Moses and said, 'I know that you have learned many earthly things. Now <the time> has come upon you to return to the earth whence you were taken" (cited in Nickelsburg 1973: 119). So, too, the History of Moses marks Michael's intervention: "Michael, the archangel, buried him and no man knew his tomb and his bones up to the present" (Nickelsburg 1973: 120). Michael's agency in Moses's burial is likewise recorded in Tg. Jon. on Deut. 34:6: "Michael and Gabriel spread forth the golden bed. . . . Metatron, Jophiel, and Uriel, and Jephehya, the wise sages, laid him upon it, and by His Word He conducted him four miles, and buried him in the valley opposite Beth Peor." The supernatural intervention at that time is also echoed in the extant text of the As. Mos. (T. Mos.) 11.5–7, where Joshua says to Moses, "What place will receive you, or what will be the monument on your grave, or who, being human, will dare to carry your body from one place to another?" (Tromp 1993: 21).

---

1. Bauckham (1990: 238), however, proposes "that there were two different versions of the story of the debate over the body of Moses, one in the Testament of Moses and another in the Assumption of Moses." Cf. the discussion in Tromp 1993: 270–81, 115–16, which does not arrive at the same conclusion.

Quarreling between good and evil supernatural powers over the fate of a human being also has its antecedent in 4Q'Amram (4Q543–548) 1.10–14, where the text records a dispute over Amram: "And behold, two were quarreling over me and they said: [. . .] and they entered into a great debate over me. And I asked them: You, why are you [. . . over me? and they replied and said: We] [have received] control and control all the sons of Adam." This particular text may or may not have been the source of the notion of a dispute over Moses's body. But Jude is embedded in a tapestry of tradition that weaves in Zech. 3:1–2 as well. Jude's quotation of the Assumption (Testament) of Moses includes a very clear echo of Zechariah's account of a dispute between the Lord and the devil, in this case over Joshua the high priest. The LXX version of Zech. 3:2 reads, "And the Lord said to the devil, 'The Lord rebuke you, devil, even the Lord who chose Jerusalem rebuke you'" (καὶ εἶπεν κύριος πρὸς τὸν διάβολον Ἐπιτιμήσαι κύριος ἐν σοί, διάβολε, καὶ ἐπιτιμήσαι κύριος ἐν σοὶ ὁ ἐκλεξάμενος τὴν Ιερουσαλημ, *kai eipen kyrios pros ton diabolon Epitimēsai kyrios en soi, diabole, kai epitimēsai kyrios en soi ho eklexamenos tēn Ierousalēm*). In a vision, Zechariah had seen Joshua standing before the Angel of the Lord, with Satan on Joshua's right hand to oppose him (3:1). Here, however, it is the Lord who rebukes Satan with words that are picked up by the Assumption (Testament) of Moses and thereby mediated to Jude (see below). The words of rebuke are now in the archangel Michael's mouth.

The inclusion of Michael the archangel in such a dispute over Moses is hardly surprising considering that he was viewed, both in biblical and extra-biblical literature, as the angel who championed Israel. He is Israel's protector and patron (Dan. 12:1; 1 En. 20.5; 1QM 17.6–8) who fights for their cause (Dan. 10:13, 21) and who executes judgment against Satan (1 En. 54.6; Rev. 12:7–9). According to the T. Ab. 19.4 [A], the patriarch Abraham refused to go with Death until Michael would come and take him (cf. 1.4–7 [A]). In the same way, Tg. Ps.-J. on Deut. 34:6 records that Michael and Gabriel prepared a golden bed for Abraham at his death. So while Jude appears to have quoted the Assumption (Testament) of Moses in verse 9, the traditions that this particular text reflects are part of a larger complex of theology about the roles of Michael and the devil in relation to Israel and the principal characters of the nation, even at the time of their death. Jude's use of the tradition, however, is designed to make a specific point about the character and fate of the heretics he opposes, as we shall see below.

As Jude tells his readers ὁ δὲ Μιχαὴλ ὁ ἀρχάγγελος (*ho de Michaēl ho archangelos*, but Michael the archangel), he sets up the contrast between Michael's behavior and that of the heretics (δὲ, *de* as adversative). Michael appears in the biblical texts of Daniel (10:13, 21; 12:1) and Revelation (12:7). In Daniel he is called "one of the rulers" (10:13: εἷς τῶν ἀρχόντων, *heis tōn archontōn*), "the angel" (10:21: ὁ ἄγγελος, *ho angelos*), or "the great angel" (12:1: ὁ ἄγγελος ὁ μέγας, *ho angelos ho megas*), whereas in Theodotion's translation he is alternatively "your ruler" (10:21: ὁ ἄρχων ὑμῶν, *ho archōn hymōn*) or "the great ruler" (12:1: ὁ ἄρχων ὁ μέγας, *ho archōn ho megas*). Michael's authority over the angels comes into focus in Rev. 12:7's reference to "Michael and his angels." Jude calls Michael an "archangel" (as 1 En. 71.3; 2 Bar. 9.5; T. Ab. 1.3, 6; 2 En. 22.6 [A]; and likely 1 Thess. 4:16), and 1 En. 24.6 says he is "one of the holy and honored angels." In 2 En. 22.6 [B] his title is *archistratig* (captain), which highlights his military role. Michael is often found in the company of the other archangels Gabriel, Raphael, and Phanuel (1 En. 40.9; 54.6; 71.8–9, 13; cf. Tob. 12:15) or Uriel (1 En. 9.1; 20.2; cf. 1QM 9.14–15), and also a larger group that includes Suru'el, Saraqa'el and Remiel (1 En. 20.1–8). Michael was considered the principal of all the angels (Ascen. Isa. 3.16; 9.23 [Latin]). He appears to be the head of this group, and according to 1 En. 20.5–6, he is over humankind and chaos, while 40.9 notes his dominion over human diseases and wounds. His character is marked by mercy and long-suffering (1 En. 40.9), and he is the archangel of righteousness who opens heaven's gates to the righteous (4 Bar. 9.5; for further comment, see Davidson 1992).

The "text" that Jude has in mind has to do with the dispute between Michael and the devil over the body of Moses, as noted above: ὅτε τῷ διαβόλῳ διακρινόμενος διελέγετο περὶ τοῦ Μωϋσέως σώματος (*hote tō diabolō diakrinomenos dielegeto peri tou Mōyseōs sōmatos*, when disputing with the devil argued over the body of Moses). Jude understands the contention between the devil and Michael as a legal dispute (διακρινόμενος, with the name of the disputant in the dative, here τῷ διαβόλῳ, *tō diabolō*; cf. Polybius 2.22.11; BDAG 231; LSJ 399; MM 150, "to have one's case with so-and-so decided") and not simply a quarrel. The severe contention between them is highlighted by the principal verb διελέγετο (*dielegeto*, imperfect), which here, as in Mark 9:34, means "argue" (BDAG 232; MM 150; LSJ 400). Jude does not explore the reason for this pitched dispute over Moses's body. According to Bauckham's reconstruction of the sources, "God sent the archangel Michael to remove the body of Moses to another place and to bury it there, but Samm'el, the devil, opposed him, disputing Moses' right to honourable burial. . . . Michael and the devil engaged in a dispute over the body. The devil slandered Moses, charging him with murder, because he slew the Egyptian and hid his body in the sand [Exod. 2:11–12]" (Bauckham 1990: 239). Given the social importance of an honorable burial during this era, Jude's readers would have understood the importance of the issue. "Correct disposal of the dead was always a crucial element in easing the soul of the deceased into the next world" (*OCD* 431; and Ferguson 1993: 228). However, the direction of Jude's argument does not concern details about the reasons for the dispute over Moses's body. His mention of this incident only serves as a vehicle to discuss Michael's behavior at the time, as is evident in the following clause.

In this dispute, Jude claims that Michael οὐκ ἐτόλμησεν κρίσιν ἐπενεγκεῖν βλασφημίας ἀλλὰ εἶπεν, Ἐπιτιμήσαι σοι κύριος (*ouk etolmēsen krisin epenenkein blasphēmias alla eipen, Epitimēsai soi kyrios*, did not presume to pronounce the verdict of "slander" but said, "The Lord punish you!"). In this dispute over Moses's body, one so great as the archangel Michael did not step beyond his proper place. Jude's claim, taken from his source, is quite similar in language to P.Ryl. 2.144 (cited in MM 638): "Moreover he had the audacity (ἐτόλμησεν, *etolmēsen*) to bring (ἐπαγαγεῖν, *epagagein*) baseless accusations (αἰτίας, *aitias*) of malice against me" (and similarly Josephus, *Ant.* 2.6.7 §130; 4.8.23 §248). In this legal dispute, Michael did not dare or did not have the audacity (οὐκ ἐτόλμησεν, *ouk etolmēsen*; cf. Rom. 15:18; 1 Cor. 6:1; 2 Cor. 10:12; BDAG 1010) to pronounce judgment on the devil (κρίσιν ἐπενεγκεῖν, *krisin epenenkein*). The language here, as in the previous clause, is forensic since ἐπενεγκεῖν (aorist infinitive of ἐπιφέρω, *epipherō*) commonly means "to bring" legal charges against someone (Acts 25:18; Josephus, *Ant.* 2.6.7 §130; 4.8.23 §248; 11.4.9 §117; Polybius 5.41.3; 38.18.2; BDAG 386).

But over and again in Greek literature, what is brought against someone is the "charge" or "accusation" (αἰτία, *aitia*; Matt. 27:37; LSJ 670; BDAG 31) and not the "verdict" or "judgment" (κρίσις, *krisis*; LSJ 997; see Jude 15; Matt. 23:33; Mark 3:29 [A, C², 𝔐]; Heb. 10:27; Rev. 18:10). The verb ἐπιφέρω (*epipherō*), which Jude uses, is not attached to the concept of "verdict" in the literature, and it is precisely this that leads us to Jude's lesson. Jude's point is not that Michael did not dare to bring a "slanderous accusation" (NIV) but that he did not bring the verdict or the judgment itself. This was God's prerogative. Michael did not take it on his own to act as judge in this drama. In other words, he kept his place and did not pronounce the verdict of the sin of "blasphemy" against the devil (BDF §178: the charge against the devil is in the genitive, βλασφημίας, *blasphēmias*). Instead, Michael left judgment to God and so said, "The Lord punish you!" His action is in striking contrast to the devil's, whose misdeed is "slander." While verbal offense may not seem criminal among us (although compare our "defamation of character"), in an honor/shame society, public insult or "slander" would be viewed as an affront to honor and thus a serious action that could result in legal proceedings. Such slander was an offense not only if directed against the Deity (Matt. 26:65–66; John 10:33; Acts 6:11) but also against humans (see 1 Pet. 4:4).[2] The heretics, like the devil, have engaged in blasphemy against superior beings, the "glories" (v. 8), and blaspheme what they do not understand (v. 10).

Michael's words to the devil are likewise framed in legal language: Ἐπιτιμήσαι σοι κύριος (*Epitimēsai soi kyrios*, The Lord punish you!). As noted above, Michael's word to the devil is a near verbatim quotation of Zech. 3:2: ἐπιτιμήσαι κύριος ἐν σοί (*epitimēsai kyrios en soi*). Neyrey (1993: 70) rightly rejects Kee's suggestion (1968) that the rebuke should be understood within the concept of bringing evil powers under submission. Jude's whole argument is salted with legal terminology, and accordingly here he refers to punishment that is meted out to someone and not simply a rebuke (Diodorus Siculus 3.67.2; Josephus, *Ant.* 18.4.6 §107; 3 Macc. 2:24; 1 En. 98.5; see BDAG 384). Michael

---

2. Commenting on the results of drinking too much wine, Athenaeus (2.36) records the comments of one Epicharmus who says, "After the sacrifice, a feast; . . . after the feast, drinking. . . . Yes, but after drinking comes mockery, after mockery filthy insult, after insult a law-suit, after the law-suit a verdict, after the verdict shackles, the stocks, and a fine."

deferred to the Lord and gave way for him to be the executor of judgment and punishment. In the end, Jude's point fits neatly into the structure of his argument up to here (vv. 5–8). The heretics have overstepped the boundaries (v. 8), as had Israel (v. 5), the fallen angels (v. 6), and Sodom and Gomorrah (v. 7). By way of contrast, Michael, who seemed for all the world to be in a place to rightly judge the devil due to his position and the attendant powers ascribed to him as archangel, refrained from doing so, giving way to the Lord as the one who is truly the judge (see Bauckham 1983: 60–61; Perkins 1995: 151; Kraftchick 2002: 44). The arrogance of the heretics is brought into high relief by this claim.

### b. Comment: These Blaspheme What They Do Not Understand (10)

**10**    Jude turns again to apply the lesson of the previous "text" in his denunciation of the heretics: οὗτοι δὲ ὅσα μὲν οὐκ οἴδασιν βλασφημοῦσιν (*houtoi de hosa men ouk oidasin blasphēmousin*, But these, on the one hand, slander whatever they do not understand). As throughout the epistle, Jude applies the lessons of the "text" by introducing its application to the heretics, identifying them with the pejorative "these" (cf. vv. 8, 12, 16, 19, and comments; also J. Charles 1990). Second Peter 2:12 interprets Jude 10 as ἐν οἷς ἀγνοοῦσιν βλασφημοῦντες (*en hois agnoousin blasphēmountes*, slandering that about which they are ignorant). Jude's charge at the head of this verse is twofold: the heretics lack understanding, and they slander even those very things that they do not understand. The charge that someone was ignorant or lacked understanding was a common topos in *vituperatio*.[3] Sirach 50:26 NRSV denounces the Samaritans as "the stupid people that live in Shechem," and in *Against Apion* Josephus rails against Apion for his "shocking ignorance" (2.2 §26; 2.11 §130), calling him an "ignorant fool" (2.4 §37) and "stupid" (2.13 §142). He asks, "Was, then, Apion's mind blinded?" (2.13 §142). In the latter part of verse 10, Jude will compare the heretics to "irrational beasts."

The second charge is that they "slander" what they do not understand. This, too, was a useful accusation in *vituperatio*. Josephus, for example, attacked gentiles as blasphemers (*Ag. Ap.* 1.11 §59) and accused Apion of engaging in "malicious slander" (2.8 §89). As explained above, slander was a serious offense and could make one liable to judicial proceedings because of a person's loss of *dignitas* (B. Winter 2001: 64–65). D. Epstein (1987: 76) remarks on the Roman perspective, "The courts provided an excellent opportunity to avenge wounded honor." Although Jude employs themes common in *vituperatio*, they are given specificity since he has previously charged that the heretics "slander glories" (v. 8). These are the very things (ὅσα, *hosa*, everything that or whatever; BDAG 729.2) that they, in their ignorance, "do not understand." Jude places this unbridled behavior in contrast with the way Michael kept his

---

3. On *vituperatio*, see L. Johnson 1989; du Toit 1994.

proper place, as he demonstrated in the previous verse. On the other hand, the heretics portray the very behavior that the devil exhibited (v. 9b), and Jude likely expects his readers to understand the inference: as the devil would be punished by the Lord (v. 9c), such would be the end of the heretics. Associating someone's behavior with that of the devil was another feature that occasionally appears in *vituperatio* (du Toit 1994: 409).

Jude's accusation continues that, on the other hand, these heretics are governed by nothing higher than base instinct: ὅσα δὲ φυσικῶς ὡς τὰ ἄλογα ζῷα ἐπίστανται, ἐν τούτοις φθείρονται (*hosa de physikōs hōs ta aloga zōa epistantai, en toutois phtheirontai*, but on the other, because of everything that they know by instinct as irrational beasts, they are corrupted). While the heretics are ignorant (v. 10a), whatever understanding of things that they do possess (ἐπίστανται, *epistantai*, they know; BDAG 380) comes through instinct (φυσικῶς, *physikōs*, by instinct; found only here in NT). This is a serious charge since, according to ancient thought, animals are those that are governed by instinct (see the reflection, e.g., in Xenophon, *Cyr.* 2.3.9–10). But instincts were also considered the lower part of human nature, which stood over against rationality. Diogenes Laertius (*Lives* 10.137) spoke of the "prompting of nature and apart from reason [λόγου, *logou*]," the "natural force" (T. Dan 3.4; cf. Josephus, *Ant.* 12.2.12 §99) in humans that, as Plutarch (*Mor.* 706A) said, is the "irrational and 'natural' part of our mind." What was most valued was self-governance by the mind rather than instincts, as the Let. Aris. 222 affirms: "'What is the highest form of sovereignty?' He replied, 'Control of oneself, and not being carried away by one's impulses.'" Jude says the heretics have instinctual knowledge "as irrational animals" (ὡς τὰ ἄλογα ζῷα, *hōs ta aloga zōa*). This is a typical expression used to describe beasts (see Philo, *Alleg. Interp.* 3.9 §30; Josephus, *Ag. Ap.* 2.29 §213; *Ant.* 10.9.2 §162). Plutarch (*Mor.* 493D) comments that "the irrational animals" (τά ἄλογα ζῷα, *ta aloga zōa*) follow "nature," but "in man ungoverned reason is absolute master." The accusation that someone acts out one's irrational nature as an animal was part of *vituperatio* (Philo, *Embassy* 19–20 §§131–32), which Jude's pen pours out as a concrete accusation.

Jude highlights the outcome of being governed by these base instincts in the final clause of the verse: ἐν τούτοις φθείρονται (*en toutois phtheirontai*, because of . . . , they are corrupted). The verb φθείρονται (*phtheirontai*) may mean "are destroyed" in the sense of suffering eternal punishment. This is apparently how 2 Pet. 2:12 understands the claim, in accord with one biblical use of the term (see 1 Cor. 3:17b; Jer. 13:9; cf. Dan. 2:44; 7:14; BDAG 1054). But the verb also commonly appears in contexts where the author wishes to make a point about being corrupted morally (1 Cor. 15:33; 2 Cor. 7:2; 11:3; Eph. 4:22; Rev. 19:2; and LXX: Gen. 6:11; Exod. 10:15; Ezek. 16:52; Hos. 9:9). This understanding appears preferable since ἐν τούτοις (*en toutois*, because of these things) refers back to the previous clause: those things that the heretics know by instinct. Jude uses the preposition ἐν with the dative of cause (BDF §§196, 219.2). His point concerns the cause of their corruption and not the reason for their destruction. This verse focuses on the moral character of the heretics, although the implication is surely that as the devil would be punished for the crime of "slander" (v. 9), so too the heretics (vv. 8, 10). Jude will presently return to comment directly on the condemnation that will come on the errorists, which, to be sure, is one of the major themes of his discourse (see below). For now he shows that the heretics, by acting according to nature, manage to gain only moral corruption for themselves.

# 3. Third Text and Comment (11–13)

In verses 11 through 13, Jude presents his third couplet of ancient "texts" (v. 11) and comments that show the significance of those texts vis-à-vis the heretics who invaded the church (vv. 12–13). Jude, however, varies his presentation here somewhat, not leaving the application of these texts to the present situation exclusively until the comment, as was his practice in the two previous text/comment sections (vv. 5–7 and 9–10). Here Jude draws a straight line between the sins of Cain, Balaam, and Korah and those of the heretics, even before reaching his comments in vv. 12–13: "Woe to them! Because they went the way of Cain, dedicated themselves to the error of Balaam for gain, and perish in the rebellion of Korah" (v. 11).

In his work on rhetoric Quintilian commented that words and ideas should be presented in order (*Inst.* 9.4.23–25), but he notes that just because something comes first in time, it need not come first in order: "Earlier events are sometimes more important and so have to be given a position of climax over the less significant" (9.4.25). In Jude's "texts," the chronological order of Cain, Korah, and Balaam is shifted, thus placing the story of Korah as the climax. The reason for the switch becomes evident if we understand the importance of the Korah narrative. Korah and his followers altered the law and rebelled against Moses. Their judgment was that only they, among all sinners, were swallowed by the earth, going straight to Sheol. What draws these three narratives together is the archetypal nature of their sin, the way these sinners influenced others, and the judgment that they suffered.

When Jude turns to his comment on the "texts" (vv. 11–12), he strings together a series of metaphors that underscore the corrupt nature of the heretics. He likens them to spots, shepherds, clouds, trees, and wandering stars—all rich metaphors prominent in the literature of the era. But Jude brackets the metaphors between two pronouncements of judgment: the woe-oracle in verse 11a and the declaration of their doom in the "nether gloom of darkness" (v. 13). These who are corrupt and influence others in sin shall themselves not escape the most dreadful end. Jude's rhetorical strategy, however, is not simply to denounce the errorists, let alone convince them of their sin. His aim is to dissuade his readers from following their ways and, thus, to avoid their ultimate end.

The unit can be outlined as follows:

a. Text: The way of Cain, the deception of Balaam, the rebellion of Korah (11)
b. Comment: These are stains in the community meals, clouds

> without rain, trees without fruit, wild waves of the sea, and
> wandering stars (12–13)

## Exegesis and Exposition

[11]Woe to them! Because they went the way of Cain, dedicated themselves to the error of Balaam for gain, and have perished in the rebellion of Korah. [12]These who feast together with you without fear are spots in your love-feasts, shepherding themselves. They are clouds without rain driven by the wind; autumn trees without fruit, twice dead, uprooted; [13]wild waves of the sea, tossing up their own shame as foam; wandering stars, for whom the nether gloom of darkness is kept forever.

### a. Text: The Way of Cain, the Deception of Balaam, the Rebellion of Korah (11)

11     In his third pairing of "texts" with comments, Jude reminds his readers of the OT stories of Cain, Balaam, and Korah. These three were the archetypal sinners of old. The heretics have followed their pattern of behavior and will, as a consequence, suffer the judgment that they endure. He begins by sounding a "woe-oracle" against them and shows how they were caught up in the sins of the ancient perpetrators of evil: they went the way of Cain, gave themselves over to Balaam's error, and will be destroyed along with Korah. Jude's exegetical methodology is typological. As observed previously (see "Genre and Structure" in the introduction), Ellis notes that Jude's midrash shares with the Qumran midrashim the belief that the present is the time of eschatological fulfillment (Ellis 1978: 226, 159–61). But as Bauckham (1990: 151; 1983: 5) notes, unlike the Qumran pesharim, Jude uses "various substitutes for Old Testament texts as citations, and his interpretation of Old Testament material as typology." The NT typological interpretation has a distinctly eschatological spin: now, in present events, the ancient types of the OT find their fulfillment (Goppelt 1982: 32–41, 233–37; Buchanan 1987: 118–22; Beale 1994: 313–71). Jude's use of this interpretive methodology hints at the notion that he and his readers are living in the end times. Typology also presupposes an almost organic relationship between the type and its antitype so that what happens to the first entails the second: the sin of ancient sinners is manifest in the behavior of their contemporary counterparts, and so likewise the ancient judgment spills over on them.

    Jude therefore presents this series of "texts" as a "woe-oracle": οὐαὶ αὐτοῖς (*ouai autois*, Woe to them!). On the most basic level, a "woe" is like an animal cry expressing terror or pain in the face of misfortune or misery (*TLNT* 2:442; "woe/alas" in 1 Kings 13:30; Prov. 23:29; Jer. 22:18). But Jude is saying more than that the heretics will suffer miserably. This is a prophetic pronouncement of judgment on those who have forsaken God (Isa. 5:1–30; Jer. 22:13–17; 23:1–4; Amos 6:1–3; Hab. 2:6–20), a form of expression that is conspicuously absent from secular Greek literature (*TLNT* 2:442). The "woe," by extension, echoes the misery that overtakes those who suffer the judgment of God.

The "woes" introduce the ultimate doom that overtakes those who have resisted God's purposes by embracing unrighteousness (Matt. 23:13–36; Luke 11:42–52). The "woe" oracles also appear in extrabiblical literature, and Jude would surely have been familiar with their format from both Scripture and 1 Enoch. Similar to the oracles in 1 Enoch, which contain more woe-oracles than the Hebrew canon itself, Jude begins with the pronouncement of the woe, an identification of those against whom it is directed ("to them"), and an indication of their sin (see Nickelsburg 1977: 310–12; Coughenour 1978).[1] The woe-oracles commonly include a statement of the judgment against those who sin, and Jude does precisely this in the latter part of the verse: "They perish in the rebellion of Korah." Nickelsburg comments on the Enochic woes: "The irreducible common point of these Woes is the relationship: sinner/God; sin/judgment" (1977: 310). The same could be said of Jude. However, Jesus's use of the prophetic woe-oracle is likely the mediating source for this expression of judgment in ecclesiastical use (see Matt. 23:13–36; Luke 11:42–52; Rev. 8:13; 12:12; 18:10, 16, 19). The fact that Jude pronounces such an oracle is evidence of his self-consciousness as one who has taken up the prophetic mantle over against the heretics (cf. Bauckham 1983: 78). His point is clear: the heretics have sinned and will not escape judgment.

The reason for the woe that Jude pronounces on them is threefold. Jude mentions the sins of Cain, Balaam, and Korah, and his economy of expression suggests that he expected his readers to be familiar with both the biblical narrative and the traditions that grew up from that soil (see "Jude and His Circle" in the introduction).

The first reason for the woe of judgment is ὅτι τῇ ὁδῷ τοῦ Κάϊν ἐπορεύθησαν (*hoti tē hodō tou Kain eporeuthēsan*, because they went the way of Cain). The expression πορεύομαι τῇ ὁδῷ (*poreuomai tē hodō*, go in the way) appears frequently in the LXX as a reference to the direction of a person's life or someone's moral conduct, whether good or evil (Pss. 31:8 [32:8 Eng.]; 80:14 [81:13 Eng.]; 100:6 [101:6 Eng.]; Prov. 1:15; 2:13; 28:18; Isa. 2:3; Bar. 4:13; Tob. 1:3). This use is found also in Acts 14:16 and a similar expression in 2 Pet. 2:15. The common phrase does not entail the judgment that subsequently comes on Cain (contra Boobyer 1958: 46–47, who suggests this idea in the translation

---

1. Nickelsburg (1977: 310) notes that the woes in 1 Enoch take on the form of a distich, such as this:
   I   Woe to you who repay your neighbor with evil;
   II  For you will be repaid according to your deeds. (95.5)
He notes that in Enoch's eyes, "it is a world that is out of kilter, a world of unresolved tensions and polarities. Justice is upside down. The sinners are in rebellion against God, and this sin goes unpunished. The righteous are oppressed, and their tribulation is not alleviated, nor are their righteous deeds rewarded. The second half of the Woe announces that the situation will be remedied—in part. The wicked will be judged for their deeds" (311). Jude's perspective, though similar, highlights the imminence of judgment (v. 11c).

"for they go to death in the path of Cain"). We know the reprehensible sin of Cain described in Gen. 4:1–16. Cain slew his brother Abel (4:8) because God had accepted Abel's offering but not Cain's (4:5–6).[2] Does Jude's charge that the heretics "go the way of Cain" imply that they, like Cain, had become murderers? While they were surely corrupt, nothing in Jude suggests that they were violent as well. John, however, compares Cain's murderous deed to hatred of fellow believers (1 John 3:11–15; cf. T. Benj. 7.3–5). But, again, the charge of hatred of the members of the Christian community is not one that finds resonance in other parts of Jude's Epistle.

On the other hand, Jewish and Christian interpretation of the Cain and Abel story highlighted not only Cain's crime of murder but also his self-love (Philo, *Worse* 10 §32; 21 §78), his envy and jealousy (1 Clem. 4.7), his anger and rage (Wis. 10:3), his indulgence in bodily pleasure and vice (Josephus, *Ant.* 1.2.1–2 §§52–66), as well as his desire for gain. Josephus notes that his name means "acquisition" for he "was thoroughly depraved and had an eye only for gain" (Josephus, *Ant.* 1.2.1 §§52–53; so Philo, *Worse* 10 §32). Clearly the Cain story became an interpretive space that longed to be filled!

However, two themes in the tradition appear to be particularly germane to Jude. First, Cain is the "archetypical sinner," as Watson (1988: 59) correctly notes. Jude's purpose is to denounce the heretics in the strongest terms possible. The charge that they "go the way of Cain" identifies them with one who was thought to have laid down the pattern for human sin. But another recurrent theme was that Cain was also an instructor in sin. Josephus (*Ant.* 1.2.1 §61) comments that "he incited to luxury and pillage all whom he met, and became their instructor in wicked practices," a sentiment echoed in Philo (*Posterity* 11 §38): "And if someone bring against you an indictment for impiety, you boldly defend yourselves, asserting that you have been trained under an admirable master and instructor, even Cain, who advised you to honour what was near you rather than the far-off Cause, and that you are bound to attend to his advice both for other reasons and most of all because he proved the strength of his creed by unmistakable deeds in his victory over Abel, the champion of the opposite opinion." Like Cain, the heretics were corrupt and enticed others into their pattern of misdeeds (Jude 19–23). Jude's prophetic woe carries with it a warning to avoid the ways of these who were enticing the church.

The second reason for the woe of judgment is that the heretics τῇ πλάνῃ τοῦ Βαλαὰμ μισθοῦ ἐξεχύθησαν (*tē planē tou Balaam misthou exechythēsan*, dedicated themselves to the error of Balaam for gain). The Balaam story was well known to Jude's readers as were also the traditions that sprang from it. Jude's reflection is based on the story found in Num. 22–24. Balak, the king of Moab, was greatly concerned about Israel's expansion (Num. 22:1–4) and

---

2. The reason for the refusal is not elaborated in the Genesis account. It is unlikely that different offerings, one of grain and the other of blood, were the cause of God's reaction. The Genesis narrative focuses on Cain's reaction rather than on the cause of the offering's rejection. See V. Hamilton 1990: 223–24; Walton 2001: 262–63.

tried to persuade Balaam to curse Israel since, said Balak, "whomever you bless is blessed, and whomever you curse is cursed" (22:6 NRSV). Balak offered him the world for his services: "I will reward you richly" (24:11 NRSV). Despite the promised inducements, Balaam could do nothing more than bless Israel, which he did three times: "If Balak should give me his house full of silver and gold, I would not be able to go beyond the word of the Lord, to do either good or bad of my own will; what the LORD says, that is what I will say" (24:13 NRSV). But the narrative in Num. 22–24 makes no mention of Balaam's transgression, which Jude and other ancient commentators found so heinous. However, the following narrative in Num. 25 tells how the Moabite women sexually enticed Israelite men and led them to sacrifice to their gods. Later, in Num. 31:16, the Moabite tactic was laid down to "Balaam's advice," and Balaam is further charged with at least trying to curse Israel (Deut. 23:3–6; Josh. 24:9–10; Neh. 13:2) and practicing divination (Josh. 13:22). Later tradition knew Balaam as one who was a diviner (Philo, *Moses* 1.48 §§264–65; Josephus, *Ant.* 4.6.2 §104) but especially as a person driven by greed, who provoked the sin of the Israelites with the Moabite women (Philo, *Moses* 1.54–55 §§295–304; Josephus, *Ant.* 4.6.6–9 §§126–40; Tg. Ps.-J. on Num. 24:14, 25; Ps.-Philo, *L.A.B.* 18.13–14). They were used to entice the men "to revere our gods" (Josephus, *Ant.* 4.6.8 §137). As a result, 24,000 of Israel fell in judgment (Num. 25:9). Because of his machinations, Balaam became known as a false teacher (Josephus, *Ant.* 4.6.6 §§126–30; and see Str-B 3:793).

Given this interpretive tradition, Jude understood the importance of the Balaam story for his denunciation of the heretics. These gave themselves over fully or dedicated themselves (ἐξεχύθησαν, *exechythēsan*; BDAG 312; MM 200) to the error of Balaam (cf. 2 Pet. 2:15). The verb itself does not imply the doom that would come on Balaam as Boobyer (1958: 47) suggests, whatever the implications of recalling the story might be. Upon noting Balaam's error, Jude focuses on his avarice. He directs his reader's interpretation of the tradition by underscoring Balaam's greed: he did what he did "for gain" (μισθοῦ, *misthou*). The avarice of the heretics appears as a charge later in the epistle (v. 16 and comments), and as with Balaam, profit was one of their driving forces (cf. 2 Pet. 2:2–3, 14; 1 Thess. 2:5; 1 Tim. 6:5; Titus 1:11; Did. 11.5–6, 12). In the Mediterranean world, itinerant orators who engaged in public declamation entirely for gain were universally condemned (Dio Chrysostom, *Or.* 32.11; Plutarch, *Mor.* 131A). Dio once declared, "Gentlemen, I have come before you not to display my talents as a speaker nor because I want money from you, or expect your praise" (35.1), but noted that greed motivated many people and not only the itinerant orators (17.16). The other aspect of Balaam's error was his agency in enticing others to engage in sexual sin. As noted previously, unbridled sexuality was one of the principal elements of the heresy Jude faced (see vv. 4, 8, 16, 18, 23, and comments there). Jude will take up the theme of "error" (τῇ πλάνῃ, *tē planē*) again in verse 13 (see comments there).

The third reason for pronouncing woe on the heretics was that τῇ ἀντιλογίᾳ τοῦ Κόρε ἀπώλοντο (*tē antilogia tou Kore apōlonto*, they have perished in the rebellion of Korah). Jude, once again, expects that his readers both know the OT narrative and understand the lessons drawn from that passage of Scripture. Numbers 16 recounts the way Korah, along with 250 others, "confronted Moses," opposing his authority and claiming that "all the congregation are holy, every one of them, and the LORD is among them" (Num. 16:2–4 NRSV). A test was set up to bring out the truth of the matter: "The LORD will make known who is his, and who is holy" (16:5 NRSV). When Korah and his followers appeared before the Tent of Meeting, "the earth opened its mouth and swallowed them up, along with their households—everyone who belonged to Korah and all their goods. So they with all that belonged to them went down alive into Sheol; the earth closed over them, and they perished from the midst of the assembly" (16:32–33 NRSV). The sin of Korah and the dramatic judgment that befell him and his followers are recalled again in Numbers (26:9–11; 27:3) and elsewhere (Ps. 106:16–18; Sir. 45:18).

As Bauckham (1983: 83) and Watson (1988: 60) rightly note, in Jewish reflection Korah "became the classic example of the antinomian heretic." Ancient exegesis of the passage connected the rebellion with the law of the tassels in Num. 15:37–41 (as Ps.-Philo, *L.A.B.* 16.1: "At that time did he give him commandment concerning the fringes: and then did Choreb rebel and 200 men with him"; James 1971: 120). While the law prescribed that only the cords on the tassels were to be blue colored, Korah and his followers made both the tassels and the cords blue and, in this way, they altered the message of the Torah. Targum Ps.-J. on Num. 16:1–2 (and Num. Rab. 18.3), however, says Korah's cloak "was entirely" purple and adds that he "arose with boldness and taught a (different) tradition regarding the matter of the purple" (McNamara and Clarke 1995: 233). Similarly, Num. Rab. 18.3 says, "These are things . . . which you have not been commanded, but you are inventing them out of your own mind!" (McNamara and Clarke 1995: 709). Korah was also remembered as having caused strife and division within Israel against Moses and Aaron before the Lord (Tg. Neof. on Num. 16:1–3; 26:9) or against the Lord (Tg. Ps.-J. on Num. 26:9; and see 2 Tim. 2:19 [quoting Num. 16:5]). First Clement 51.1–4 recalls the story in a reflection on "sedition and disagreement" (cf. Num. Rab. 18.2; Josephus, *Ant.* 4.2.2–3 §§14–23). On these two counts Jude could single out Korah as the antitype of the heretics the church faced. They, too, had distorted the message of the gospel (Jude 4) and were opposed to any kind of divinely instituted authority (v. 8).

While Jude may have intended for his readers to draw out these inferences based on their knowledge of the traditions surrounding the Korah story, he directs his readers' interpretation by referring to Korah's rebellion (τῇ ἀντιλογίᾳ, *tē antilogia*) and compares the heretics' judgment to that of Korah and his followers (ἀπώλοντο, *apōlonto*, have perished; cf. v. 5). The fact that Korah and his followers had been swallowed up by the earth alive became the source of considerable comment on this story as this judgment became archetypal (Num. 26:10; Sir. 45:18–19; Ps.-Philo, *L.A.B.* 57.2), so much so that one need only mention the judgment to evoke the whole story (Josephus, *J.W.* 5.13.7

§566; 1 Clem. 51.4). These went straight to Sheol (1 Clem. 51.4). This judgment anticipated that of the last day (Ps.-Philo, *L.A.B.* 16.3), as it apparently does in Jude's reading as well. Previously Jude referred to the destruction of the exodus generation (v. 5), and there, as here, Jude likely understands this temporal judgment as a type of the eternal ruin (Matt. 10:28; 21:41; Mark 1:24; Luke 4:34; Rom. 14:15; James 4:12) that the heretics will face because of their sin. In describing their end, Jude uses the aorist tense in a perfective sense (ἀπώλοντο, *apōlonto*, have perished), indicating that their doom is already a certainty (see Bauckham 1983: 84; Kelly 1969: 268). Their judgment is sure.

## b. Comment: These Are Stains in the Community Meals, Clouds without Rain, Trees without Fruit, Wild Waves of the Sea, and Wandering Stars (12–13)

After presenting his third set of "texts" (v. 11; cf. 5–7, 9), Jude turns to comment on the character of the heretics, marking the transition with his characteristic οὗτοί εἰσιν (*houtoi eisin*, these are; cf. vv. 8, 10, 16, 19, and comments). The previous verse singled out Cain, Balaam, and Korah, men who were notorious sinners and who influenced others in their error according to ancient interpretive traditions that grew from the soil of the biblical narrative. The heretics, who had come in from the outside (v. 4), fully integrated themselves into the Christian community, participating in their common banquet. These people "who feast together with you without fear are spots in your love-feasts" (οἱ ἐν ταῖς ἀγάπαις ὑμῶν σπιλάδες συνευωχούμενοι ἀφόβως, *hoi en tais agapais hymōn spilades syneuōchoumenoi aphobōs*). Banqueting was one of the most important ancient institutions for social bonding. Feasts were held for various reasons such as *koinōnia* (sharing), friendship, or pleasure. Special occasions—such as birthdays, weddings, and funerals—were marked by these meals, but they were also part of the wider fabric of social life. Banquets could be held to accompany sacrifices; as Dio Chrysostom said, "What sacrifice is acceptable to the gods without the participants in the feast?" (*Or.* 3.97; cf. 1 Cor. 10:19–21). Various clubs organized common meals, including those that brought together members of a guild, a funeral society, or a religious or political association. Jewish banquets were well known, with the most prominent being the Passover meal.

12

Meals were occasions for games, entertainment, and philosophical discussion. Drinking wine and the presence of female companions (hetairai) could make these lively events indeed. Satirical accounts of banqueting practices during the period can be found in Juvenal's Fifth Satire (*How Clients Are Entertained*) and Petronius's *Satyricon*, which tells the now-famous story of the banquet of the freedman Trimalchio (for a good summary of banqueting customs, see D. Smith 2003). D. Smith (2003: 9–10) notes: "The act of dining together is considered to create a bond between the diners. In the ancient world this symbolism was carried by various elements of the banquet, such as the sharing of common food or sharing from a common table or dish.

But above all it simply derived from the fact that the diners shared the event together." Inclusion and acceptance were hallmarks of the banquet, despite the fact that positions around the triclinium and the type of food offered clearly delineated people's social class (Luke 14:8–11; Juvenal, *How Clients Are Entertained*). The social bond and the attendant social obligation were strong within these events, and likely for this reason, Jude raises concern about the way the heretics have become fully accepted participants in the Christian feast. A bond was formed in this union, which the heretics were exploiting to their own persuasive end.

For this reason Jude raises the alarm that the heretics participate in the "love-feasts" of the church (ταῖς ἀγάπαις, *tais agapais*), the time when the church celebrates the Lord's Supper (1 Cor. 11:17–34; Matt. 26:17–30; Mark 14:12–26; Luke 22:7–23). The ethical characteristic that marked the early Christian feasts was "love," the principal virtue of the Christian community that reflected the very nature of God himself (John 3:16; Eph. 2:4; 1 John 4:10, 16; 5:1). The virtue of love was so dominant in both the consciousness and experience of the community that, by extension, the sacred meal came to be known as an *agapē*. Jude is the first witness that we have of this use of the term, which became very prevalent in the early church (Jeremias 1966: 116). Jude has in mind the whole Christian feast and not only the Eucharist, for he describes the heretics as those who "feast together" (συνευωχούμενοι, *syneuōchoumenoi*) with the church (BDAG 970; MM 606 cites an invitation; a papyrus in *BGU* 2.596.10 says, "You are also invited to come down and feast along with us"). The virtue of "love" was the highest expression of acceptance by God and the mutual acceptance for fellow members of the community (see *TLNT* 1:8–22 and its bibliography).

The heretics, however, are "spots" (σπιλάδες, *spilades*)[3] in this feast, which should be marked by high virtue and not vice. The term Jude uses has been the subject of some debate since it can mean either "rocks hidden under water," a "reef," or, on the other hand, "that which soils or discolors, [a] spot, stain" (BDAG 938; *TLNT* 3:270–72). The metaphor of the heretics being "reefs" or "projecting rocks" within the community who will do irreparable harm to the unwary would be powerful, and this particular understanding has strong proponents (*TLNT* 3:270–72 and Bauckham 1983: 85–86 present forceful arguments) and surely is the "usual meaning," as Bauckham observes, but it is not the only one.

Jude's first interpreter, 2 Peter, understood σπιλάδες (*spilades*) as moral: he accuses his opponents of being "spots and defects" (2 Pet. 2:13). The word in Peter's hands is changed, however, to σπίλοι (*spiloi*), which is more commonly

---

3. Σπιλάδες (*spilades*) is nominative feminine plural and therefore is not attached to the nominative masculine plural article οἱ (*hoi*). The predicate nominative of the sentence is οἱ . . . συνευωχούμενοι (*hoi . . . syneuōchoumenoi*, the ones who feast with you). Bauckham (1983: 77, 86) and Kelly (1969: 271) rightly note that σπιλάδες is in apposition to οἱ . . . συνευωχούμενοι. Wallace (1996: 331) is incorrect in his assertion that the article οἱ (masculine plural) goes with σπιλάδες (feminine plural) in a *construction ad sensum*.

used in moral contexts (see comments and BDAG 938). Moreover, Jude juxtaposes his accusation against the nature of the feast as an *agapē*, thereby underscoring his moral concerns at this point. He also states that the heretics feast with the believers "without fear" (ἀφόβως, *aphobōs*), which likewise points to their debased character. Jude likely accuses them of being devoid of the fear of God. Proverbs 15:16 LXX says, "Better is a small portion with the fear of the Lord, than great treasures without fear [ἀφοβίας, *aphobias*]" of God (1 Pet. 1:17). But Jude's thought may be that these people do not fear social sanction: they are people without honor. Aristotle noted that the person who does not fear disgrace is shameless (*Eth. Nic.* 3.6.3, quoted below in the comments on v. 13; and see deSilva 1995: 64).

To be sure, in this and the following verse, Jude piles metaphor upon metaphor in his description of the heretics (clouds, trees, waves, stars) so we would not be surprised to find one more at the head of verse 12 (reefs). But Jude does not describe σπιλάδες (*spilades*) in the same way he does the following metaphors, suggesting again that his prime concern is to underscore the moral stain of the heretics. These people exercise influence over the congregation and, as a result, some believers have even had their "garment stained [ἐσπιλωμένον, *espilōmenon*] by the flesh" (v. 23; Neyrey 1993: 74–75). The intimate environment of the symposium was frequently the context of free sexual expression; in the second century AD, the Carpocratians extinguished the lamps and turned the Christian *agapē* into a love-the-one-you're-with orgy (see "Occasion of Writing" in the introduction). Jude's denunciation of the heretics suggests that they, too, had turned this occasion into one where vice reigned, not virtue, although we should not conclude that they went to the extreme of those Alexandrian heretics of a later generation.

In this and the following verse, Jude introduces a series of metaphors whereby he denounces the character of the heretics. First, they are people who are "shepherding themselves" (ἑαυτοὺς ποιμαίνοντες, *heautous poimainontes*). Jude alludes to Ezek. 34:2, 8–10, 18–19, evoking the image of the evil shepherds of Israel who feed themselves. The verb Jude uses is found in Ezek. 34:10 LXX and is relatively frequent in the NT as a reference to the task of leadership within the church (John 21:16, together with "feed" in vv. 15, 17, as in Ezek. 34; Acts 20:28; 1 Pet. 5:2; cf. 1 Cor. 9:7). The concepts of feeding, guidance, protection, as well as governance attach to the image (1 Pet. 5:2; Eph. 4:11–12; BDAG 842). The king "pastors/shepherds" Israel (2 Sam. 5:2; 7:7), and the Lord himself is the great Shepherd of the sheep (Ps. 23:1; Heb. 13:20; 1 Pet. 2:25; 5:4). The leadership within the church is a participation in God's pastoral care for his people, known as his "flock" (Pss. 79:13; 95:7; 100:3; Jer. 13:17; Ezek. 34:31; Acts 20:28–29; 1 Pet. 5:2–3). The use of this pastoral language suggests that these heretics had assumed some form of leadership position in the church. But instead of seeking to benefit the flock, they were "shepherding themselves," using their acquired position to serve their own interests. Jude previously evoked the story of Balaam, who was motivated by avarice (v. 11), and makes the same point regarding the heretics here. These people have not fulfilled the function that they have assumed, a point that Jude underscores in the following metaphors.

Jude's second metaphor of the group is that the heretics are νεφέλαι ἄνυδροι ὑπὸ ἀνέμων παραφερόμεναι (*nephelai anydroi hypo anemōn parapheromenai*, clouds without rain driven by the wind). The image was likely a common one, which appears also in Prov. 25:14 (note that 2 Pet. 2:17 changes the imagery somewhat: "These are springs without water and mists driven by the storm"). Though the clouds from the west would bring rain to Palestine (Luke 12:54), these clouds (in Jude) are devoid of water (ἄνυδροι, *anydroi*) and therefore do not produce rain. The metaphor, spoken within an arid context, would suggest a range of implications: they bring nothing of value, they do not fulfill their promise, they are useless, and they do not satisfy. But Jude doubles the cloud metaphor in his declaration that they are "driven by the wind." Such is the nature of clouds, however, and this suggests that Jude wishes his readers to discover some other implication. The metaphor of being carried away by the wind was sometimes evoked with reference to the influence of false doctrine on a person's life (Eph. 4:14; and the verb in Heb. 13:9; see Plato, *Phaedrus* 265B; Plutarch, *Timoleon* 238 [6.1]). Given the concerns that drive the epistle, Jude likely has this in mind. He implies that the heretics are apostates (see vv. 5–7 and comments) who themselves have come under outside influences. These unseen forces are not identified but only suggested by the imagery.

The third metaphor Jude employs compares the heretics to trees: δένδρα φθινοπωρινὰ ἄκαρπα δὶς ἀποθανόντα ἐκριζωθέντα (*dendra phthinopōrina akarpa dis apothanonta ekrizōthenta*, autumn trees without fruit, twice dead, uprooted). Jude once again multiplies the layers of meaning of the metaphor. While we commonly think of trees as good, the metaphorical use of "trees" in Jude's world classified them as either "good" or "bad" when they stood for people (Matt. 3:10; 7:17–19; 12:33; Luke 3:9; 6:43–44). His reference to them as "autumn" trees suggests the time of the harvest (autumn in the Julian calendar stretching from August eleventh to November tenth), or as Tyndale said, "Trees with out frute at gadring [gathering] time" (quoted in Mayor 1907: 58). Autumn trees hold the promise of fruit, but these are "without fruit" and so, like the rainless clouds, fail in regard to what is expected of them.

But not only are these trees fruitless; they are also "uprooted" (Luke 17:6), an image suggesting that they were blown over by the wind. The notion of "uprooting" could refer to the violent overthrow of a community (Judg. 5:14 KJV; Jer. 1:10; Zeph. 2:4; Dan. 7:8; LXX: 1 Macc. 5:51; 2 Macc. 12:7; Sir. 49:7), but was also a metaphor that could be used in a moral context. Wisdom 4:3–4 says, "But the prolific brood of the ungodly will be of no use, and none of their illegitimate seedlings will strike a deep root or take a firm hold. For even if they put forth boughs for a while, standing insecurely they will be shaken by the wind, and by the violence of the winds they will be uprooted" (NRSV; cf. Sir. 3:9). The uprooting referred to in Wisdom has to do with the judgment that will come on the ungodly, and Jude may well employ this violent metaphor in a similar way, although it may also suggest apostasy as in Herm.

*Mand.* 9.9 and 1 Clem. 6.4. In light of the fact that the "trees" have no fruit
and are uprooted, Jude declares them "twice dead." Bauckham (1983: 88)
suggests that the reference here is to the "second death" (Rev. 2:11; 20:6, 14;
21:8), but the metaphor of being fruitless and uprooted trees points rather to
Jude's desire to demonstrate their absolutely corrupt and useless nature. He
holds out no hope for them.

The fourth metaphor in the series (vv. 12–13) of Jude's denunciations of the          **13**
heretics is that they are κύματα ἄγρια θαλάσσης ἐπαφρίζοντα τὰς ἑαυτῶν
αἰσχύνας (*kymata agria thalassēs epaphrizonta tas heautōn aischynas*, wild
waves of the sea tossing up their own shame as foam). "Wild waves of the
sea" or "wild waves" is a stereotypical description of the sea under stormy
conditions (Sib. Or. 3.778; Wis. 14:1). The untamed and treacherous character
of the sea engendered fear and caution when people approached it. Antipater
of Thessalonica wrote many epigrams that expressed the prevailing attitude,
one of which says: "Approve not the grievous labour of the treacherous ocean
or the heavy toil of perilous seafaring. As a mother is more delightful than
a step-mother, by so much is the earth more desirable than the gray sea." In
another he warned, "Trust not the fatal sea, mariner, not even when at anchor"
(Gow and Page 1968: 2.57, 21). The sea was considered wild and savage (see
Acts 27; 2 Cor. 11:25–26), a notion highlighted by Jude's description of its
"wild waves" (κύματα ἄγρια, *kymata agria*). The Romans took great pride in
conquering lands and building roads, and in the *Res gestae*, Augustus paraded
his conquest of the pirates who plied the sea. But the empire could not tame
the sea itself. "Wild" describes not only the drama of waves tossed up but also
draws attention to their untamable and uncontrollable nature (BDAG 15),
hence touching on a cultural value of the era. The word could describe anything that was wild, such as animals, but one could likewise speak of "savage
cruelty" (3 Macc. 7:5). The word appears in other moral contexts (LSJ 15).
Tacitus quipped, "Tam saeva et infesta virtutibus empora [so savage was the
spirit of the age, so cynical towards virtue]" (*Agricola* 1.4). The barbarians
exhibited traits of savagery, not being governed by *logos* or reason (OCD 233),
and the spectacles held in the amphitheaters of the empire pitted men against
beasts in shows that displayed triumph over the savage world. But the heretics
were as "wild waves of the sea," one with the untamed, wild, and dangerous
things of the world.

Jude once again doubles up the imagery of his metaphor (see v. 12), here
describing the heretics not only as "wild waves" but also as those ἐπαφρίζοντα
τὰς ἑαυτῶν αἰσχύνας (*epaphrizonta tas heautōn aischynas*, tossing up their
own shame as foam). The "foam" of the sea is a metaphor for the shameless
deeds of the heretics. In an honor/shame society, "the fear of disgrace marks the
person of honor, who alone is capable of achieving a life of virtue, and thus of
experiencing happiness" (deSilva 1995: 64). The honorable person recognizes
and lives by the values established within one's community. When a person
transgresses those values, the result is shame. Aristotle said, "Let shame then be

defined as a kind of pain or uneasiness in respect of misdeeds, . . . which seem to tend to bring dishonour; and shamelessness as a contempt and indifference in regard to these same things" (*Rhetoric* 2.6.2; cf. 2.6.13–14). Such failings as lack of courage, injustice, or intemperance regarding one's sexual behavior could all produce shame (2.6.3–8, 13; see Neyrey 1998: 30–31). Therefore, "one who fears disgrace is an honourable man, with a due sense of shame; one who does not fear it is shameless" (ὁ δὲ μὴ φοβούμενος ἀναίσχυντος, *ho de mē phoboumenos anaischyntos*; Aristotle, *Eth. Nic.* 3.6.3). Jude marks the heretics out as people who have no regard for honor and who toss up their shameful deeds as sea foam. They are therefore unbound by moral standards and thus out of control. The shameful acts (cf. Rom. 1:27; Rev. 16:15) of the heretics that Jude has in mind may be sexual in nature (see v. 4 and comments; and Aristotle's category of ἔργων αἰσχρῶν, *disgraceful actions* in *Rhetoric* 2.6.13). The heretics flaunt such deeds rather than having a proper sense of shame (Luke 14:9; Phil. 3:19; Heb. 12:2; Rev. 3:18).

The fifth metaphor of this series of denunciations tags the heretics as ἀστέρες πλανῆται (*asteres planetai*, wandering stars). We know the stars that wander as "planets," the English word derived from the Greek term πλανῆται found here. The combination "wandering stars" was frequently found in the literature to describe these heavenly bodies (Aristotle, *Mete.* 342B, 28, 31; Xenophon, *Mem.* 4.7.5), although sometimes they were known simply as πλανῆται (*planētai*) and distinguished from fixed stars (Plutarch, *Mor.* 604A). Unsurprisingly, the cognate noun πλάνη (*planē*) means "error," a wandering from the truth (as in v. 11; see Wis. 12:24; Matt. 27:64; Rom. 1:27; Eph. 4:14; 1 Thess. 2:3; 2 Thess. 2:11; 2 Pet. 2:18; 3:17; 1 John 4:6). The imagery identifies the heretics as people caught in error. Yet the heretics are not just those who have been deceived but also those out to draw others into their error (as v. 11), and this active sense may also be suggested by Jude's metaphor. The cognate adjective πλάνος (*planos*) points to just such deception (see 2 Cor. 6:8; 1 Tim. 4:1; 2 John 7).

Jude lays bare the consequences of their error/deception in the final part of the verse: οἷς ὁ ζόφος τοῦ σκότους εἰς αἰῶνα τετήρηται (*hois ho zophos tou skotous eis aiōna tetērētai*, for whom the nether gloom of darkness is kept forever). Second Peter 2:17 borrows the phrase almost exactly, leaving out only εἰς αἰῶνα (*eis aiōna*, forever) and not coupling it with the notion that the heretics are "wandering stars." The "nether gloom" (ὁ ζόφος, *ho zophos*) is the place where the fallen angels are bound until the day of judgment (2 Pet. 2:4), the realm of the underworld referenced frequently in ancient literature (Aeschylus, *Pers.* 839: "As for me, I depart for the darkness beneath the earth"; Euripides, *Hipp.* 1416: "Forever in the nether gloom"; Quintus Smyrnaeus 2.619: "Therefore I will pass into darkness"; and so 2.612; Homer, *Od.* 20.356; 11.55; *Il.* 21.56; Sib. Or. 4.43). The addition of the descriptor "darkness" (τοῦ σκότους, *tou skotous*) indicates that this is the place of judgment and torment outside the kingdom (Matt. 8:12; 22:13; 25:30). "Darkness" can, in certain contexts, mean simply the place of the dead, as the funerary inscription: "I live in the darkness; now the earth holds me as a drink from the mute fountain of silence" (*NewDocs* 4:149; Luke 1:79). The "darkness" is also a frequent NT metaphor for moral corruption (Matt. 4:16; 6:23; John 3:19; Acts 26:18; Rom. 2:19; 2 Cor. 6:14; 1 Thess. 5:4–5; 1 Pet. 2:9; 1 John 1:6), with sins being the "deeds of darkness" (Rom. 13:12; Eph. 5:11) and Satan's domain that of "darkness" (Col. 1:13; Eph. 6:12). But here the "darkness" is the place of punishment (cf. Wis. 17:21 [17:20 LXX]; Tob. 4:10; 14:10; 1 En. 17.5–6; 63.6).

The ultimate destiny of the heretics and their punishment in this place will not be temporal but eternal (εἰς αἰῶνα, *eis aiōna*, forever). The NT commonly speaks of "eternal life" (John 4:14; 6:51, 58; 10:28; etc.) but occasionally refers to "eternal judgment" (Matt. 13:40; 18:8; 25:41; Heb. 6:2), the very notion Jude has in mind. As the angels are kept under judgment until the final judgment (v. 6 and comments), so the darkness of the nether gloom is kept (τετήρηται, *tetērētai*, perfect tense with stative aspect, as in Porter 1989: 245–90) for the heretics. Throughout this declaration of judgment, Jude's language echoes both the vocabulary and thought of ancient discourse on judgment.

Reference is sometimes made to 1 En. 18.14–15 as a source of Jude's expression (see Kelly 1969: 274; Bauckham 1983: 89–90; M. Black 1985: 160; BDAG 822; MM 516), but that passage is not similar in vocabulary and speaks rather of the judgment of the Watchers, there called "stars" and not "wandering stars."[4] Key terms and concepts in Jude 13 are absent from the passages in 1 Enoch to which some point as Jude's source. First Enoch 80.6, part of the Ethiopic section known as the "Book of the Luminaries," speaks about a cosmic disruption where "many leaders of the stars shall stray from the commandments (of God)" (M. Black 1985: 69). This may have been the source of Jude's imagery, especially since 80.2 says that "the rain shall be held back" and "the fruits of the trees shall be withheld in their time" (80.3). Jude previously compared the heretics to clouds without water and trees without fruit (v. 12). But even here, both the concepts and language found in this chapter are too remote from Jude's thought and language to be considered the source of his affirmation (contra Bauckham 1983: 90; Osburn 1985). First Enoch 80 is about cosmic disruption; Jude's metaphors point to the worthlessness of the heretics as symbolized by the clouds and trees. Other cosmic imagery in 1 En. 80 finds no parallel in Jude, including the shortening of sinners' years, late sowing, change in work, drought, and the moon's failure to appear. Jude does, however, speak of shepherds, waves, and foam and enriches the other metaphors in various directions that find no counterpart in 1 En. 80. His

---

4. First Enoch 18.14–16: "The angel said to me: 'This place is the end of the heavens and the earth; this has become a prison for the stars and the hosts of heaven. And the stars which rotate in the fire, these are they which transgressed the commandment of the Lord at the beginning of their rising, because they did not come forth at their proper times. And he was wroth with them, and he incarcerated them until the time of the completion of the punishment for their sins, in ten thousand years" (M. Black 1985: 36; 1970: 31). See also 1 En. 21.3–6.

colorful language employs fairly standard and understandable metaphors, as explained above. But whatever his sources may have been, Jude's point is clear: the heretics may embrace error and deceive in the present, but their judgment is sure and it will endure forever. The source of his following "text," however, is undoubtedly 1 Enoch (see vv. 14–15).

# 4. Fourth Text and Comment (14–16)

In these verses, Jude introduces his fourth "text" regarding the coming of the heretics (cf. vv. 5–7, 9, 11), which he then comments on as he did with the previous references to the OT narrative (vv. 8, 10, 12–13). This, however, is the most problematic text-and-comment section of the series since Jude quotes 1 Enoch directly to make his case instead of referring to the OT. He previously referenced traditional material regarding the angelic fall (v. 6), but this is the only place where he quotes a pseudepigraphic text. The way Jude utilizes and comments on this passage is in complete harmony with his purposes up to this point: to show that the coming of the heretics was predicted, as also their corrupt character and final judgment. He does not treat this "text" as any less authoritative than the previous ones (see "Jude and Pseudepigraphic Literature" in the introduction). But Jude also uses the text as an opportunity to continue his *vituperatio* against the heretics as he charges them with acting as victims, who are arrogant flatterers making much of themselves in order to exploit the members of the church. But in the end, they are empty and doomed.

The unit can be outlined as follows:

a. Text: The prophecy of Enoch (14–15)
b. Comment: These are grumblers, complainers, and boastful flatterers (16)

## Exegesis and Exposition

[14]But Enoch also, the seventh from Adam, prophesied about these, saying, "Behold! the Lord will come with his holy myriads [15]to execute judgment against everyone and to convict every person for all their deeds of godlessness that they godlessly committed and for all their hard ⌐words⌐ that godless sinners have spoken against him." [16]These are grumblers and malcontents, living according to the dictates of their own desires, and their mouths speak arrogant things, flattering for their own gain.

### a. Text: The Prophecy of Enoch (14–15)

Jude's fourth "text" section in this epistle is not an allusion to ancient biblical narrative (cf. vv. 5–7, 9, 11) but rather a direct quotation from 1 En. 1.9. Jude cites the full text in this and the following verse: Προεφήτευσεν δὲ καὶ τούτοις ἕβδομος ἀπὸ Ἀδὰμ Ἐνὼχ λέγων, Ἰδοὺ ἦλθεν κύριος ἐν ἁγίαις μυριάσιν αὐτοῦ (*Proephēteusen de kai toutois hebdomos apo Adam Henōch legōn, Idou ēlthen*

14

*kyrios en hagiais myriasin autou*, But Enoch also, the seventh from Adam, prophesied about these, saying, "Behold! the Lord will come with his holy myriads"). The story of Enoch is found in Gen. 5:18, 21–24 (he should not be confused with the son of Cain in Gen. 4:17–18; see V. Hamilton 1990: 246–54). This sparse account of Enoch's life records that he was Jared's son and the father of Methuselah. He is noteworthy as a righteous man who "walked with God" (vv. 22–23; as Noah in Gen. 6:9) but "then he was no more, because God took him" (v. 24 NRSV). Later biblical comment on the Enoch story focused on his faith and the fact that he was taken up by God (Heb. 11:5; cf. Sir. 44:16; 49:14), while Jude emphasizes his prophetic role.

A rather large interpretive tradition developed around the Genesis story as Enoch is featured in three books that bear his name (1, 2, and 3 Enoch) as well as in Jub. 4.16–25; Wis. 4:10–15; and other texts, including some from Qumran (4QEnoch, an Aramaic version of 1 Enoch; as well as 4QPseudo-Jubilees; 4QAstronomical Enoch; 4QPrayer of Enoch; see VanderKam 1984). The best known of these texts is 1 Enoch, which describes the coming judgment of God, ascribing the revelations to Enoch himself (on 1 Enoch, see especially R. Charles 1912; M. Black 1970; 1985; VanderKam 1984; Nickelsburg 2001). This book is preserved for us in various versions, including Aramaic (from Qumran), Greek (a translation of an Aramaic original), and Ethiopic (a translation of a Greek edition). Fragments of 1 Enoch appear in a number of Jewish and Christian Greek texts (M. Black 1970), as well as Latin (R. Charles 1912: 275), Coptic, and Syriac (Nickelsburg 2001: 15). We cannot be certain of the precise date when this book was composed, but it is likely a composite document that drew together strands dating from between the fourth century BC and the beginning of the Christian era (for a summary, see E. Isaac, *OTP* 1:6–7).

In 1 En. 68.1, Noah speaks and identifies the contents of the book as "secret": "And thereafter he (Michael) gave me instructions in all the things that are secret in the book of my great-grandfather Enoch" (cf. 40.2; 65.11; 71.3; this and the following translations from M. Black 1985). "Secret books" were those alleged to have been written by some worthy of the past whose contents were then hidden for generations but are now revealed (Bruce 1974: 3). Enoch was not the author of this pseudepigraphic work, and it is not likely that the book preserves material from that historic personage. At best, we can only hope to identify the milieu in which the various fragments of 1 Enoch were composed and compiled. Given this, Jude's use of the book is problematic for many readers (see "Jude and Pseudepigraphic Literature" in the introduction). However, Jude's use of 1 Enoch aligns with his purpose throughout the epistle: to highlight the sins of the heretics and herald the judgment that will come on them for their deeds and words. Moreover, all the primary motifs in 1 En. 1 find their counterpart and source in Scripture, including the divine theophany, universal judgment, and salvation for the righteous. First Enoch 1.8[1] contrasts this judgment of 1.9 with

---

1. "But with the righteous he will make peace, and he will protect the elect, and mercy shall be upon them. And they shall all belong to God. And he shall show them favour and bless

the mercy shown to the righteous, and 1 En. 1.6–7 depicts the total disintegration of the earth on the day of judgment.[2] The book does not present an independent witness of these events but relies on and interprets scriptural sources.

Jude prefaces the quotation from 1 Enoch with an introductory formula and an identification of the source of his "text": Προεφήτευσεν δὲ καὶ τούτοις ἕβδομος ἀπὸ Ἀδὰμ Ἐνὼχ (*Proephēteusen de kai toutois hebdomos apo Adam Henōch*, But Enoch also, the seventh from Adam, prophesied about these). In the NT, the declaration that someone "prophesied" is an introductory formula used to refer to OT prophets whose prophecies are being fulfilled in the present time (Matt. 11:13—the Law and Prophets; Matt. 15:7 and Mark 7:6—Isaiah; 1 Pet. 1:10—OT prophets; and cf. Jer. 25:13; Acts 2:16; and see Fitzmyer 1960–61: 303). J. Charles (1991a: 144) attempts to show that "prophesied" here may mean something more general than classifying 1 Enoch as a prophetic book: "And if, by way of illustration, a Cretan is to the apostle Paul a 'prophet' (Titus 1.12), then Enoch, in Jude 14, can 'prophesy.'" However, in Titus 1:12 Paul calls Epimenides "*their* very own prophet." Jude, on the other hand, says "Enoch . . . prophesied" and places this "text" together with other authoritative "texts" (vv. 5–7, 9, 11, 17–18) in his quest to outline the heretics' sin and doom. There is no indication here that he simply quotes 1 Enoch because his opponents considered it to be authoritative (contra J. Charles 1991a: 144; Moo 1996: 273). Jude rather identifies the source of the prophecy as Enoch, underscores the significance of that personage ("seventh from Adam," see below), and claims that what was predicted is now fulfilled in the heretics (τούτοις, *toutois*, about these). Nothing in his language or in the context of the book suggests that he viewed this "text" as anything other than authoritative.

Jude's use of this text is not in the same category with Paul's quotations of classic authors (Aratus and Cleanthes in Acts 17:28; Menander in 1 Cor. 15:33; in addition to Titus 1:12). He regards 1 Enoch as a prophecy that predicts present events and binds this "text" with his previous denunciations of the heretics: "But Enoch also" (δὲ καὶ . . . Ἐνώχ, *de kai . . . Henōch*). Charles's suggestion that these words point to his opponents' high regard for his source does not square with the way Jude frames the quotation. Clement of Alexandria commented on this passage, "In these words he [Jude] verifies the prophecy." The prophecy finds its fulfillment in the heretics as it is "about these" (τούτοις, *toutois*; so BDAG 890), noted by Bauckham (1983: 93) as an "odd" use of the dative. Jude may, however, envision the prophecy as being "to them" (Bigg 1901: 336). Under either reading, what was prophesied is now viewed as being fulfilled. The "remote generation" of which Enoch spoke (1 En. 1.2)[3] is Jude's generation.

---

them all, and he will assist all and help us; And light shall appear upon them, and he will make peace with them."

2. "And the lofty mountains shall be shaken; they shall fall and be disintegrated. . . . And the earth shall be rent in sunder, all that is upon the earth shall perish."

3. "And he took up his discourse and said: '[Oracle of Enoch], a righteous man whose eyes were opened by God and who saw a vision of the Holy One in heaven, which the angels showed

Jude attributes the authorship of the prophecy to ἕβδομος ἀπὸ Ἀδὰμ Ἑνὼχ (*hebdomos apo Adam Enōch*, Enoch, the seventh from Adam). In the genealogy of Gen. 5:1–24, Enoch occupies the seventh place starting with Adam (Adam, Seth, Enosh, Kenan, Mahalalel, Jared, Enoch; cf. 1 En. 37.1; 1 Chron. 1:1–3; Luke 3:37–38). The designation "the seventh from Adam" comes from 1 Enoch itself (60.8; 93.3; cf. Jub. 7.39, "the seventh in his generation"). The "seventh" position held particular significance for the Semitic mind (God rested on the seventh day—Gen. 2:2–3; the ark came to rest in the seventh month—Gen. 8:4; the Israelites ate unleavened bread seven days—Exod. 12:15–16; rest on the seventh day—Exod. 20:10–11; seventh generation—Apoc. Ab. 32.1 and Let. Jer. 3; the fever left at the seventh hour—John 4:52; the seventh seal—Rev. 8:1; the seventh angel—Rev. 10:7). Sometimes genealogies were even restructured to highlight the importance of a prominent person (see Sasson 1978 and his article in *IDBSup* 355). Identifying Enoch in this manner highlights the significance of the following words: *no less than* the seventh from Adam spoke against these heretics!

The edition of 1 Enoch from which Jude quoted has been a matter of some debate, some stating that he drew directly from the Greek edition, others arguing for an Aramaic source (see the discussion in Chaine 1939: 321–23; Osburn 1977; Bauckham 1983: 94–96; Dehandschutter 1986; Paulsen 1992: 74–77; Neyrey 1993: 80–81; Vögtle 1994: 72–76). Jude's quotation is quite close to the Greek version of 1 Enoch but diverges from it in significant ways:

| 1 Enoch 1.9 | Jude 14b–15 |
| --- | --- |
| ὅτι <u>ἔρχεται</u> *σὺν* ταῖς μυριάσιν αὐτοῦ καὶ τοῖς <u>ἁγίοις</u> αὐτοῦ, ποιῆσαι κρίσιν κατὰ πάντων, καὶ ἀπολέσει πάντας τοὺς ἀσεβεῖς, καὶ <u>ἐλέγξει</u> πᾶσαν σάρκα περὶ πάντων ἔργων τῆς ἀσεβείας αὐτῶν ὧν ἠσέβησαν καὶ σκληρῶν ὧν ἐλάλησαν λόγων, [καὶ περὶ πάντων ὧν κατελάλησαν] κατ' αὐτοῦ ἁμαρτωλοὶ ἀσεβεῖς. | Ἰδοὺ <u>ἦλθεν</u> κύριος *ἐν* <u>ἁγίαις</u> μυριάσιν αὐτοῦ ποιῆσαι κρίσιν κατὰ πάντων καὶ <u>ἐλέγξαι</u> πᾶσαν *ψυχὴν* περὶ πάντων τῶν ἔργων ἀσεβείας αὐτῶν ὧν ἠσέβησαν καὶ περὶ πάντων τῶν σκληρῶν ὧν ἐλάλησαν κατ' αὐτοῦ ἁμαρτωλοὶ ἀσεβεῖς. |
| *hoti* <u>erchetai</u> *syn* tais myriasin autou kai tois <u>hagiois</u> autou, poiēsai krisin kata pantōn, kai apolesei pantas tous asebeis, kai <u>elenxei</u> pasan *sarka* peri pantōn ergōn tēs asebeias autōn hōn ēsebēsan kai sklērōn hōn elalēsan logōn, [kai peri pantōn hōn katelalēsan] kat' autou hamartōloi asebeis.[4] | *Idou* <u>ēlthen</u> kyrios *en* <u>hagiais</u> myriasin autou poiēsai krisin kata pantōn kai <u>elenxai</u> pasan *psychēn* peri pantōn tōn ergōn asebeias autōn hōn ēsebēsan kai peri pantōn tōn sklērōn hōn elalēsan kat' autou hamartōloi asebeis. |

*Note:* The key to the comparison:
    no correspondence in word or idea
    <u>same word but different form</u>
    *same or similar idea but different word*
    same word and same form
Brackets indicate reconstructed text.

me, and from the words of the [watchers and] holy ones I heard all; and I understood what I saw; not for this generation, but for a generation remote do I speak.' "

4. "Because he comes with his myriads and his holy ones to execute judgment against all, and he will destroy all the ungodly and convict all flesh for all their deeds of ungodliness that they have ungodly committed, and for all the hard words that ungodly sinners have spoken

The considerable amount of duplication of the Greek form of 1 En. 1.9 argues strongly in favor of the position that Jude knew the Greek text very well. The omissions from the original and the transposition of some words may be evidence of the author's reworking of the text or may suggest that he did not have the MS directly in front of him but was quoting from memory. There are clear indications that Jude made conscious modifications of his source since only in Jude's version do we find that "the Lord" is coming, giving the quotation a christological orientation. He understands the passage to refer to Christ's parousia. There are, however, traces of Jude's knowledge of the Aramaic edition. Jude adds the opening "Behold!" (Ἰδού, *Idou*) which is found in the Ethiopic and Latin, an expression that may come from an Aramaic original (M. Black 1985: 108; Osburn 1977: 336). The change from the present ἔρχεται (*erchetai*) to the aorist ἦλθεν (*ēlthen*) reflects the Aramaic (see below). Jude's quotation describes those who will accompany the Lord as "his holy myriads," a reading closer to the Aramaic and Ethiopic of 1 Enoch than the Greek "his myriads and his holy ones." The shortening of the text and the transposition of words are best accounted for by Jude's conscious editing of the Greek text in light of another version he knew or had at hand. The high degree of similarity between the Greek of 1 Enoch and Jude's version points away from the view that Jude composed his own translation from Aramaic (contra Bauckham 1983: 96), although certainty once again eludes us.

Jude has taken a passage that speaks of a divine theophany and has transformed it into a passage that refers to the advent of Christ (Osburn 1977: 334): Ἰδοὺ ἦλθεν κύριος ἐν ἁγίαις μυριάσιν αὐτοῦ (*Idou ēlthen kyrios en hagiais myriasin autou*, Behold! the Lord comes with his holy myriads). Jude refers to Jesus Christ as "Lord" (vv. 4, 17, 21, 25), and it is his coming that is in view. In 1 En. 1.3–4, the one who comes is "the great Holy one, . . . the eternal God," echoing the magnificent theophany passages of the OT that anticipate the majestic advent of Yahweh (Isa. 64:1–3; Mic. 1:2–5; Hab. 3:1–19; cf. Deut. 33:2; Judg. 5:4–5). Jude's high Christology is evident in this passage since Christ is the one whose coming and judgment are anticipated. Jude alters the present "comes" of the Greek of 1 En. 1.9 to the aorist ἦλθεν (*ēlthen*), which here has a future sense (Porter 1989: 232), perhaps representing the Semitic prophetic perfect (M. Black 1985: 108). The Lord will come "with his holy myriads" (ἁγίαις, *hagiais*, "holy" is an adjective modifying μυριάσιν, *myriasin*, "myriads," as RSV). Jude's reference is to the angelic host that accompanies Yahweh in his theophanies, the language being borrowed from the Hebrew text of Deut. 33:2[5] (see also Zech. 14:5; cf. Job 5:1; 15:15; 25:3; Pss. 68:17; 89:5, 7; Dan. 7:10; 2 Bar. 48.10; 2 Esd. [4 Ezra] 8:21).

---

against him" (my own translation, omitting καὶ περὶ πάντων ὧν κατελάλησαν, *kai peri pantōn hōn katelalēsan*, "and concerning all that they spoke against him," a reconstruction of the text suggested by M. Black 1985: 109; Nickelsburg 2001: 143).

5. Deuteronomy 33:3 LXX reads, "with the myriads of Cades, on his right hand angels with him" instead of "With him were myriads of holy ones; at his right, a host of his own" (NRSV), interpreting Hebrew קֹדֶשׁ as a place name instead of a reference to "holy ones."

According to NT theology, the angelic host will accompany Christ upon his return (Matt. 13:41; 25:31; Mark 8:38; 13:27; 1 Thess. 3:13; 2 Thess. 1:7). Jude refers to this angelic company as Christ's "holy myriads," a "myriad" being a group of 10,000 (see Acts 19:19 Gk.), although it may mean a very large number without precise definition of the quantity (BDAG 661). The term refers to the angelic host in various biblical and extrabiblical passages (Dan. 7:10; Heb. 12:22; Rev. 5:11; 1 En. 14.22; 40.1). The composite picture Jude paints, using the Enoch passage, is that the Lord's coming is a divine act that will be awesome in its power and majesty. Myriads of angels will accompany him as he comes to execute universal judgment. Jude arrests the attention of his readers by prefacing the quotation with the demonstrative "Behold!" a word that often calls readers to take notice of divine acts (LXX: Isa. 40:10; Zech. 12:2; 14:1; Mal. 3:1; also 1 Cor. 15:51; 2 Cor. 5:17; Rev. 1:7).

**15**    Jude continues the quotation as he outlines the divine acts of judgment that the Lord will carry out upon his coming: ποιῆσαι κρίσιν κατὰ πάντων καὶ ἐλέγξαι πᾶσαν ψυχήν (*poiēsai krisin kata pantōn kai elenxai pasan psychēn*, to execute judgment against everyone and to convict every person). "Execute judgment" (ποιῆσαι κρίσιν, *poiēsai krisin*) is an expression commonly employed in the LXX (Gen. 18:19, 25; Deut. 10:18; 33:21; Isa. 5:7; 56:1; Jer. 7:5; 1 Macc. 6:22; Sir. 35:18). This divine action (Heb. 12:23; James 4:12) is effected through the Lord Jesus Christ (Acts 10:42; 17:31; Rom. 2:16) who comes to judge (2 Tim. 4:1; 1 Pet. 4:5; Rev. 6:10). The Lord will also "convict" (ἐλέγξαι, *elenxai*), a term that in other contexts means "to show someone his sin and to summon him to repentance" (F. Büchsel, *TDNT* 2:474; see Matt. 18:15; Eph. 5:11; 1 Tim. 5:20; 2 Tim. 4:2; Titus 1:9, 13; 2:15), but in judicial contexts "this rebuke condemns; it is no longer educative" (F. Büchsel, *TDNT* 2:475; 2 Bar. 55.8; 2 Esd. [4 Ezra] 12:31–33; Ps. Sol. 17.25). In the judgment the true character of the heretics will be brought to light (MM 202; John 3:20; 16:8). Jude appears to hold no hope of any redemption for the heretics. In Christ's coming, they will be judged and condemned.

A note sounded throughout the quotation is that this judgment will be universal and comprehensive in nature. "Everyone" will be judged and "every person" convicted. The point is made clearly in 1 En. 1.7, "And the earth shall be rent in sunder, and all that is upon the earth shall perish, And there shall be universal judgment" (including the "Watchers" and their offspring, according to 10.6, 15; see Nickelsburg 2001: 146). Bede is careful to note, correctly, that Jude "does not say against all human beings but against all the wicked, leaving none of them unpunished" (Hurst 1985: 249). Not only will none escape this judgment, but also all deeds and words (πάντων . . . πάντων, *pantōn . . . pantōn*) will be weighed: περὶ πάντων τῶν ἔργων ἀσεβείας αὐτῶν ὧν ἠσέβησαν καὶ περὶ πάντων τῶν σκληρῶν ὧν ἐλάλησαν κατ᾽ αὐτοῦ ἁμαρτωλοὶ ἀσεβεῖς (*peri pantōn tōn ergōn asebeias autōn hōn ēsebēsan kai peri pantōn tōn sklērōn hōn elalēsan kat᾽ autou hamartōloi asebeis*, for all their deeds of godlessness that they godlessly committed and for all their hard words that godless sinners have spoken against him). The prominent vice of those who are subject to the divine judgment is that they are "godless" in their actions. The noun ἀσεβείας (*asebeias*, godlessness), along with its cognate verb (ἠσέβησαν, *ēsebēsan*, godlessly committed) and adjective (ἀσεβεῖς, *asebeis*, godless), point to a lack of reverence toward the Deity (see v. 4 and comments there). To commit godless deeds was "to violate the norms of a proper or professed relation to deity" (BDAG 141), while "deeds of impiety" are those that do not show reverence for God, done by people who are "impious" or "godless." Not showing proper reverence to the Deity was a sharp accusation of antisocial behavior insofar as the Deity was considered to be the patron of the community. As such, this charge was the corollary of nonadherence to civic duty. Xenophon's accusation against the Persians (*Cyr.* 8.8.27) is worth repeating on this point: "For I maintain that I have proved that the Persians of the present day and those living in their dependencies are less reverent toward the gods, less dutiful to their relatives, less upright in their dealings with all men, and less brave in war than they were of old." To be "godless" or to practice "impiety" was the opposite of being "righteous" and practicing "justice" (Gen. 18:23, 28; Exod. 9:27; 23:7; Deut. 25:1; Ps. 10:5 [11:5 Eng.]; Prov. 10:16, 20, 24–25, 28, 30, 32; Eccles. 3:16–17; Wis. 4:16). This accusation recalls Jude's principal charge against the heretics, which opened his accusation against these infiltrators (v. 4) and is also the topic of this "text" and the following apostolic prophecy about the heretics (v. 18). They are truly impious in their actions. Such is their character.

Jude's attention is also turned to the words of the heretics, in this following his source: περὶ πάντων τῶν σκληρῶν ὧν ἐλάλησαν κατ᾽ αὐτοῦ ἁμαρτωλοὶ ἀσεβεῖς (*peri pantōn tōn sklērōn hōn elalēsan kat᾽ autou hamartōloi asebeis*, for all their hard words that godless sinners have spoken against him). The text of 1 En. 1.9 refers to the "hard words" (σκληρῶν . . . λόγων, *sklērōn . . . logōn*; cf. 5.4; 27.2),[6] but Jude omits "words" and uses the adjective σκληρός (*sklēros*) as a substantive (although some Greek MSS add λόγων; see the additional note). "Hard" speech can be that which is difficult to accept (John 6:60) or that which is harsh to the hearer (Gen. 42:7, 30; Tob. 13:14 LXX [Codex Sinaiticus]), with this latter sense in mind here (BDAG 930; *TLNT* 3:258–62). Such speech was considered sinful (Ps. Sol. 4.2), while here the accusation constitutes a charge of "blasphemy" since such words are spoken "against him," the Lord (M. Black 1985: 174). These "godless sinners" will be judged not only for their deeds but also for their words (Mal. 3:13; Matt. 12:36), both of which demonstrate that they did not revere God and had set themselves against him. This is the essence of

---

6. First Enoch 5.4: "But you have changed your works, and have not been steadfast nor done according to his commandments, but you have transgressed against him, and spoken proud and hard words with your impure mouths against his majesty: (you) hard in your heart, you shall have no peace."

First Enoch 27.2: "Here shall all the accursed be gathered together who utter with their lips unseemly speech against the Lord, and speak hard words against his glory."

the sin of the heretics who "deny our only Master and Lord, Jesus Christ" (v. 4 NRSV).

## b. Comment: These Are Grumblers, Complainers, and Boastful Flatterers (16)

16    Jude once again marks the beginning of his comment on the heretics with the pejorative "these" (cf. vv. 8, 10, 12, 16, 19, and comments there). Using 1 En. 1.9, he previously underscored the heretics' character as "godless" or "impious" (v. 15), a charge that is here given concrete definition in this *vituperatio*. The denunciation begins: Οὗτοί εἰσιν γογγυσταὶ μεμψίμοιροι (*houtoi eisin gongystai mempsimoiroi*, These are grumblers and malcontents). The heretics are people who complain bitterly against God and who are unsatisfied with their lot. The charge that they are "grumblers" has an ignoble history in biblical literature. One of the chief charges against the exodus generation (cf. v. 5) was that they were grumblers (Exod. 16:7–9; Num. 17:5–10 [17:20–25 LXX]), giving way to a "wicked murmuring" (Sir. 46:7). This is hardly the same thing as "whining," nor is it a lament in the face of hardship. This "grumbling" (the word is onomatopoeic in Greek [*gongysmon*], capturing the low tones of disgruntled talk) was against Moses (Exod. 15:24; Num. 14:36; 17:5 [17:20 LXX]), or Moses together with Aaron (Exod. 16:2; Num. 14:2; 16:41 [17:6 LXX]), but principally against God, who appointed these leaders (Exod. 16:7–9, 12; Num. 14:27, 29; cf. the grumbling against Jesus in John 6:41, 43, 61; 7:32). The people had opposed God (Num. 14:35) and paid the severest penalty (Num. 14:32; Sir. 46:7–8; 1 Cor. 10:10). In this sin they had put God to the test (Exod. 17:2–3) and refused to believe him (Num. 14:11) or obey him (14:22). Like the wilderness generation, the heretics were "dissatisfied with their lot and therefore with God" (K. H. Rengstorf, *TDNT* 1:737). "Grumbling" was considered a vice in the wider Greco-Roman world as well and was understood as the opposite of thankfulness to the gods. As Marcus Aurelius counseled: "so that you may not die grumbling, but merciful and truly, giving thanks to the gods from the heart" (2.3). "Grumbling" may be understood as the reaction to a sense of having been wronged (one papyrus quoted in MM 130 says, "The gang [of workmen] are murmuring, saying that they are being wronged"; cf. *NewDocs* 4:143–44; Acts 6:1). The heretics unjustly feel like victims and have expressed their discontent.

Jude doubles the impact of this charge by denouncing the heretics as μεμψίμοιροι (*mempsimoiroi*, malcontents). According to Theophrastus (*Characters* 17.1) this "is a species of immoderate complaint about one's allotted circumstances" (BDAG 629; W. Grundmann, *TDNT* 4:571). Such people complain about their lot in life and, within a Christian frame, their complaint would be against God. Truly, "they are dissatisfied with God and they criticize His guidance" (W. Grundmann, *TDNT* 4:574). This kind of discontent is reflected in Isocrates' record of a speech in which it was said, "And yet, although I have been blessed with all these gifts, some in surpassing, others in sufficient measure, I am not content to live on these terms; on the contrary, my old age is so morose and captious and *discontented* that I have oftentimes before this found fault with my nature" (*Panathenaicus* 8, italics added). Likewise, Lucian comments on a proud, gluttonous man who *"grumbles* continually—even if he gets the whole cake or the whole boar to himself" (*Timon* 55, italics added; see 13; Pseudo-Lucian, *The Cynic* 17; Aristotle, *Hist. an.* 608B.10; Plutarch, *De cohibenda ira* 461B). This is not simply an issue of the tongue but also of the character. Jude's heretics are truly the ones who are driven by desire but can find no satisfaction in life.

These dissatisfied heretics are people driven by immoderate desires: κατὰ τὰς ἐπιθυμίας ἑαυτῶν πορευόμενοι (*kata tas epithymias heatōn poreuomenoi,* living according to the dictates of their own desires). Not virtue but rather their own base desires govern their conduct. Previously, in verse 11 (see comments), Jude used the verb of this clause, here found in participial form. He will return to it in verse 18, where the apostolic prophecy "text" makes the same charge that Jude lays out here. Πορευόμενοι (*poreuomenoi*) is a term frequently found in the context of moral instruction where it points to someone's conduct, how a person lives or "walks" (BDAG 853). Some may conduct themselves "according to the purpose of God" (κατὰ τὴν βουλὴν τοῦ θεοῦ, *kata tēn boulēn tou theou*) or "in the fear of God" (Ps. Sol. 18.11). On the other hand, some like Jude's heretics live "according to the dictates of their own desires," resulting in sinful behavior (cf. 1 Pet. 4:3; 2 Pet. 2:10; 3:3). "Desires" are sometimes those that are neutral or positive (Luke 22:15; Phil. 1:23; 1 Thess. 2:17), but more often in the NT the "desires" referred to are sinful (Mark 4:19; Rom. 7:7–8; Gal. 5:16–17; 1 Tim. 6:9; Titus 3:3; 1 Pet. 1:14; 2:11; 1 John 2:16–17). They are the opposite of self-control (Titus 2:12) and are the source of temptation (James 1:14–15) as well as the cause of corruption in the world (2 Pet. 1:4). They are enslaving (Titus 3:3) and characterize those who do not know God (Eph. 2:3; 1 Thess. 4:5; 1 Pet. 1:14). At times these desires are specifically identified as sexual (Matt. 5:28; Rom. 1:24; 1 Thess. 4:5; 1 Pet. 4:3; and Plutarch, *Mor.* 525A–B; Josephus, *Ant.* 4.6.6 §130). This accusation may be part of Jude's denunciation of their unbridled sexuality (see vv. 4–8, 12, 18). The heretics Jude opposes are driven by these lower impulses, looking for satisfaction by yielding to their lusts yet never finding any.

Jude's *vituperatio* against the heretics continues with another denunciation of their speech that vocalizes the core of their character: καὶ τὸ στόμα αὐτῶν λαλεῖ ὑπέρογκα (*kai to stoma autōn lalei hyperonka,* and their mouths speak arrogant things). Jude's words appear to echo As. Mos. (T. Mos.) 7.9, a book he previously referenced (see Jude 9): "Yet their mouths will speak enormous things." The extant Latin version shows clear traces of being a translation from the Greek (J. Priest, *OTP* 1:920).[7] The expression is quite similar to Dan. 7:8, 20 ("a mouth speaking great things")[8] and 1 En. 5.4 ("You have spoken proud

---

7. The Latin reads *os eorum loquetur ingentia.*
8. Στόμα λαλοῦν μεγάλα (*stoma laloun megala*).

and hard words with your impure mouths against his majesty";[9] cf. Jude 15), although these do not appear to be our author's source. The focus is on the heretics' arrogance as evidenced through their boasting.

Aristotle commented on the one who boasts: "The boaster is a man who pretends to creditable qualities that he does not possess, or possesses in a lesser degree than he makes out" (*Eth. Nic.* 1127A). Boasters are vacuous. Plutarch spoke of Socrates' ability to clear out "crack-brained vapourings of folly and elusion—of the ponderous load of silly conceits and noisy boasting" (*Mor.* 1119B), while Arrian (*Anab.* 3.10.2) employs the term: "This grandiloquence looked like confidence in danger rather than arrogance." Jude's point here is not that they spoke "inflated words of flattery" (Neyrey 1993: 79). He rather shines his spotlight on their arrogant speech, which is characteristic of those figures in apocalyptic literature who stand against God. They are all about themselves, not about God. The charge of "arrogance" was common in *vituperatio* (L. Johnson 1989: 430; du Toit 1994: 407–8), although Jude makes the charge specific and frames it in such a way as to echo the condemnation of the apocalyptic figures who opposed God.

Jude's final invective against the heretics exposes their method and motive: θαυμάζοντες πρόσωπα ὠφελείας χάριν (*thaumazontes prosōpa ōpheleias charin*, flattering for their own gain). The expression θαυμάζοντες πρόσωπα is quite common in the LXX, meaning either to rightly favor someone (Gen. 19:21; Deut. 28:50; 2 Kings 5:1; Job 22:8; Isa. 9:15 [9:14 LXX]) or, more commonly, to show undue partiality, of the kind that may pervert justice (Lev. 19:15; Deut. 10:17; 2 Chron. 19:7; Prov. 18:5; Job 13:10; 34:19; Ps. Sol. 2.18). In certain contexts, as here in Jude, the meaning of the phrase appears to be "to flatter" (as in Job 32:21–22; BDAG 888). The connection between flattery and boasting ("Their mouths speak arrogant things") was already made by Aristotle (*Eth. Nic.* 1127A). The arrogant, empty people used flattery "for their own gain." The term ὠφελείας implies an advantage gained (BDAG 1107; see Jude 11), most commonly monetary (Polybius 3.82.8; Josephus, *Ant.* 4.7.29 §274; 12.2.3 §29; see LSJ 2041–42; cf. Neyrey 1993: 82, who emphasizes the advantage gained of "respect, status or honor"). Jude previously denounced the heretics as avaricious (v. 11), and here he returns to that theme.

"Flattery" was a common topic in moral philosophy (see, e.g., Plutarch's *How to Tell a Flatterer from a Friend*). Such people take advantage of good people: "But the fact is, that as bore-worms make their entrance chiefly into the delicate and sweet-scented kinds of wood, so it is ambitious, honest, and promising characters that receive and nourish the flatterer as he hangs upon them" (*Mor.* 49B). Flatterers go after those people who have sufficient means to satisfy their goals (49C; 1 Thess. 2:5–6). The fact that the church to which Jude writes attracted such people because of the profit they thought they could

---

9. Κατελαλέσατε μεγάλους καὶ σκληροὺς λόγους ἐν στόματι ἀκαθαρσίας ὑμῶν κατὰ τῆς μεγαλωσύνης αὐτοῦ, *katelalesate megalous kai sklērous logous en stomati akatharsias hymōn kata tēs megalōsynēs autou*.

derive implies that these were *not* people of extremely modest means. The flatterer's goal is consumption, and such a person uses others while pretending to be their friend. Aristotle (*Eth. Nic.* 1127A) distinguishes between friends and flatterers: "The man who always joins in the pleasures of his companions, if he sets out to be pleasant for no ulterior motive, is Obsequious; if he does so for the sake of getting something by it in the shape of money or money's worth, he is a Flatterer." The flatterer's greed is heard in Eupolis's quip, "And when I catch sight of a man who is rich and thick, I at once get my hooks into him. If this moneybags happens to say anything, I praise him vehemently and express my amazement, pretending to find delight in his words" (Eupolis 236–37). The heretics were in the "business" of religion, yet showed no true piety toward God. They were arrogant and boastful, taking advantage of others for their own profit. Jude's warning in verse 16 echoed the concerns of the era about flatterers and those who would declaim publicly simply for gain (Dio Chrysostom, *Or.* 32.11; Plutarch, *Mor.* 131A). Jude wants the church to have nothing to do with these people whom even the apostles predicted would come (vv. 17–18).

## Additional Note

**15.** Some Greek MSS add λόγων (ℵ, C, 33, 81), although the weight of the evidence favors its exclusion. The thought, however, is understood in the expression τῶν σκληρῶν ὧν ἐλάλησαν . . . ἁμαρτωλοὶ ἀσεβεῖς and, hence, included in my translation: "hard words that godless sinners have spoken."

# 5. "Remember": Text and Comment (17–19)

The present verses bring to a close the cycle of text/comment sections of the book (vv. 5–19), which were introduced with the call to "remember" (v. 5a) and are now brought to conclusion with the same call in verse 17 (μνήσθητε, *mnēsthēte*), thus forming an inclusio (envelope) around this section. Jude's "texts" have ranged through the OT and apocryphal literature. But he now turns to apostolic prophecy about the end and, in doing so, elevates the apostolic word to the level of his other authoritative texts. In contrast with the previous "text" sections (vv. 5–7, 9, 11, 14–15), Jude introduces this apostolic "text" with an appeal that begins by addressing them directly with the familial "Beloved," as he had previously in verse 3 (see comments). Here Jude draws a sharp line between the heretics, introduced with Jude's characteristic "these are" (v. 16), and the church, "But you, beloved." This direct address is repeated in verse 20, at the head of the following section of the letter. With this address, Jude draws his readers once again into his own circle and distances them from the heretics who deny (v. 4b) the one who is "*our* Lord Jesus Christ" (v. 17b).

The unit can be outlined as follows:

a. Text: The apostolic prophecy (17–18)
b. Comment: These are people who cause divisions (19)

## Exegesis and Exposition

[17]But you, beloved, remember the words previously spoken by the apostles of our Lord Jesus Christ, [18]for they said to you, "In the last time mockers will come, who live according to the dictates of their own godless desires." [19]These are people who cause divisions, worldly people, devoid of the Spirit.

### a. Text: The Apostolic Prophecy (17–18)

**17** Jude's final "text" section (vv. 17–18) calls the church to remember what the apostles had predicted concerning the coming of those opposed to the gospel: Ὑμεῖς δέ, ἀγαπητοί, μνήσθητε τῶν ῥημάτων τῶν προειρημένων ὑπὸ τῶν ἀποστόλων τοῦ κυρίου ἡμῶν Ἰησοῦ Χριστοῦ (*Hymeis de, agapētoi, mnēsthēte tōn rhēmatōn tōn proeirēmenōn hypo tōn apostolōn tou kyriou hēmōn Iēsou Christou*, But you, beloved, remember the words previously spoken by the apostles of our Lord Jesus Christ; cf. 2 Pet. 3:2). The call to remember what one already knows was a commonplace in ancient moral instruction (see comments on v. 5a). Isocrates (*Demon.* 9), for example, said, "Nay, if you will but recall your father's principles, you will have from your own house a noble illustration of what I am telling you." Dio Chrysostom likewise underscored the necessity of being reminded of what one knew: "For instance, just as we see physicians and pilots repeating their orders time and again to those under their command, although they were heard the first time—but still they do so when they see them neglectful and unattentive—so too in life it is useful to speak about the same things repeatedly, when the majority know what is their duty, but nevertheless fail to do it" (*Or.* 17.2).

In the context of moral instruction, such reminders become exhortations not simply to call to mind but also to take heed and act. Throughout the text/comment section, Jude's purpose has not been merely to inform his readers of the heretics' error and end, but especially to persuade the "beloved" to have nothing to do with them and their ways, a point made explicit in the following section (vv. 20–23). They are to use what they have known "to contend for the faith" (v. 3), both in their endeavor to build themselves up in the faith (vv. 20–21) and in their rescue mission toward those who are being seduced by the heretics (vv. 22–23). Present engagement against evil is undertaken with a thorough knowledge of divine revelation.

Jude here exhorts them to call to mind τῶν ῥημάτων τῶν προειρημένων ὑπὸ τῶν ἀποστόλων τοῦ κυρίου ἡμῶν Ἰησοῦ Χριστοῦ (*tōn rhēmatōn tōn proeirēmenōn hypo tōn apostolōn tou kyriou hēmōn Iēsou Christou*, the words previously spoken by the apostles of our Lord Jesus Christ; cf. 2 Pet. 3:2–4 and comments). Jude understands these apostolic words as a prophecy given by the apostles, which his readers have heard. He classifies the apostolic message as τῶν ῥημάτων (*tōn rhēmatōn*), which elsewhere refers to a message preached (John 8:20; Acts 2:14; 10:44; Rom. 10:18). But here the context points to a prophetic message (cf. Matt. 26:75; Mark 9:32; 14:72; Luke 1:38; 2:29; 9:45; 18:34; 22:61; 24:8; Acts 11:16; BDAG 905).[1] What marks these "words" as a prophecy is Jude's qualification that they were "previously spoken" (τῶν προειρημένων, *tōn proeirēmenōn*). While the term may mean nothing more than "tell beforehand" (2 Cor. 7:3; 13:2; Gal. 1:9; 5:21; 1 Thess. 4:6; MM 542–43), it is frequently used as here to speak of predictive prophecy, often with the prophet's name designated (Jesus—Matt. 24:25; Mark 13:23; David—Acts 1:16; Heb. 4:7; Isaiah—Rom. 9:29; Paul—1 Thess. 3:4; prophets and the Lord Jesus through apostles—2 Pet. 3:2; and see Josephus, *J.W.* 6.2.1 §109; Appian, *Bell. civ.* 1.71; Herodotus 1.53; BDAG 867). As judgment of the heretics was decreed from ancient times (v. 4 and comments), so also the apostles have prophesied about their coming. In reminding his readers about this prophecy, Jude's point is not to prepare them for what is yet to come but rather to demonstrate that events predicted have now already come to pass. Jude interprets the apostolic oracle as he does his other "texts": *Now* is the

---

1. The Greek term ῥῆμα (*rhēma*) thus covers some of the same semantic range as λόγος (*logos*) in the NT (cf. 1 Pet. 1:23 [λόγος] and 25 [ῥῆμα]). Contrary to popular understanding of the term, ῥῆμα is not distinguished in the NT as some special revelatory word to an individual.

time of fulfillment. This is pesher exegesis applied to the apostolic oracle: Now is the time of fulfillment (on pesher interpretation, see "Genre and Structure" in the introduction).

This prophetic word has come "by the apostles of the Lord Jesus Christ" (ὑπὸ τῶν ἀποστόλων τοῦ κυρίου ἡμῶν Ἰησοῦ Χριστοῦ, *hypo tōn apostolōn tou kyriou hēmōn Iēsou Christou*). The circle of apostles included the Twelve and Paul, but embraced others as well (Acts 14:14; Rom. 16:7; 1 Cor. 15:5b, 7b; 1 Thess. 2:6), although the Twelve and Paul occupied a unique place in the history of salvation as authoritative witnesses of the resurrection of Christ (1 Cor. 9:1). Those whom Jude has in mind are most likely from this more restricted group (Paul and the Twelve). An "apostle" was not merely an ancient "missionary" but rather one who is also sent in the authority of another. Behind NT apostleship is the Jewish institution of the שָׁלִיחַ (*šālîaḥ*), an authoritative messenger who speaks and acts in the authority of another (K. H. Rengstorf, *TDNT* 1:422–23; and see Burton 1920: 364–78). The Mishnah tractate *Berakot* (5.5) captures the significance of the institution: "The one sent by a man is as the man himself" (K. H. Rengstorf, *TDNT* 1:414–20). The apostles were not independent agents but spoke and carried out a mission in the authority and under the authority of another. In this case, the "other" in whose authority they spoke was "the Lord Jesus Christ." Their word was his. The prophetic "text" that follows is invested with nothing less than Christ's authority.

**18**   The prophecy that Jude cites in this verse has no exact parallel elsewhere in the NT, save for 2 Pet. 3:2–3, which, as argued in the introduction to 2 Peter (see "The Relationship between 2 Peter and Jude"), was penned using Jude. A number of NT texts present warnings about the advent of false teachers, some of which couple their coming with the "last days" in a manner similar to Jude 18 (see 1 Tim. 4:1–3; 1 John 2:18, 22; and see Acts 20:29–30; 2 Tim. 3:1–5; 4:3–4). This teaching was echoed later in the church (Did. 16.3) and can even be traced back to the Lord himself (Matt. 24:11, 23–24; Mark 13:5–6, 21–22), although the idea that the end times would be characterized by deception was more widely held (1QpHab 2.5–6; Sib. Or. 2.165–69; and the later Apoc. El. 1.13). It may well be that Jude paraphrases rather than quotes the apostolic prophecy in mind, summarizing and perhaps even modifying the wording (not necessarily the thought) to show its applicability to the present situation. The accusation of ungodliness in verse 18 echoes one of Jude's principal concerns and may be a trace of his redaction of the prophecy. However, in the absence of other concrete evidences concerning his source, we cannot demonstrate with any certainty his method of handling it.

Jude now presents the reason for calling the church to remember the apostolic prophecy: ὅτι ἔλεγον ὑμῖν· [ὅτι] Ἐπ᾽ ἐσχάτου [τοῦ] χρόνου ἔσονται ἐμπαῖκται (*hoti elegon hymin: [hoti] Ep᾽ eschatou [tou] chronou esontai empaiktai*, for they said to you, "In the last time mockers will come"). Jude uses the imperfect ἔλεγον (*elegon*, they were saying), as do other Greek authors when introducing statements or speeches (BDF §329). At the head of the quotation, he notes that the apostles spoke the following "to you" (ὑμῖν, *hymin*). This may mean nothing more than that this was a general prophecy that was for this church as well as every other congregation (cf. 1 Pet. 1:10–12). As Kelly (1969: 282) comments, "When the apostles uttered their message, they addressed it to all generations of Christians, his own correspondents included." However, absent any indication from the context that this was a general word for all (like the Enoch prophecy in v. 14, which is introduced similarly but without "to you"), we should understand the dative pronoun in the simplest way: they had heard the apostolic witness. If the church was located within Palestine (see "Jude and His Circle" in the introduction), it is not unlikely that they would have known members of the Twelve and even Paul, especially given Jude's status as the brother of James and of the Lord.

The apostolic prophecy begins by indicating that the mockers would come "in the last time" (Ἐπ' ἐσχάτου [τοῦ] χρόνου, *Ep' eschatou [tou] chronou*), an expression found only here and in 1 Pet. 1:20 in the NT, although 1 Pet. 1:5 has the similar expression "in the last time" (καιρῷ ἐσχάτῳ, *kairō eschatō*). More commonly, NT authors speak about this era as "the last days" (2 Tim. 3:1; Acts 2:17; Heb. 1:2; James 5:3; 2 Pet. 3:3; following Isa. 2:2; Dan. 2:28–29, 45; 10:14; Hos. 3:5; Mic. 4:1). Jude, as these other NT authors, envisions the "last time" not as an era in the distant future but as a present reality, which has begun with the advent of Christ (see Acts 2:17; 1 Cor. 10:11; Gal. 4:4; Heb. 1:2; 9:26; 1 Pet. 1:20). The "last time" is the era of prophetic fulfillment (2 Bar. 6.8; 41.5; CD 6.11; 1QSa 1.1) and is also considered to be an era when forces of evil will be especially active (1 Tim. 4:1–3; 2 Tim. 3:1–9; T. Iss. 6.1). The presence of the heretics themselves is an indicator that this "last time" has arrived.

The apostolic prophecy indicated that the last time will be marked by the advent of "mockers" (ἐμπαῖκται, *empaiktai*, found only here and in 2 Pet. 3:3 in the NT; see Isa. 3:4 LXX: "Mockers shall rule over them"). "Mockers/ scoffers" frequently appear in the OT (Pss. 1:1; 35:16; Prov. 1:22; 9:7–8; 13:1; 14:6; 19:25, 29). In Kelly's words (1969: 283), a mocker is one "who despises morality and religion, the arrogant and godless libertine." The mockers set themselves strongly against the Lord in the Gospels as they heap ridicule on him and subject him to physical abuse (Matt. 20:19; 27:29, 31, 41; Mark 10:34; 15:20; Luke 22:63; 23:11). "Mocking" is a supreme act of dishonor in an attempt to bring shame on a person (see Herodotus 4.134; Epictetus, *Disc.* 1.4.10). "To mock" is one of many lexical entries attached to the concept of "the disparagement or low estimation of others, or indeed the world, creatures, and even deity, in word, attitude or act" (G. Bertram, *TDNT* 5:630). In 2 Chron. 36:16 the LXX uses the verbal form of the word found here in Jude: "Nevertheless they sneered at his messengers, and set at naught his words, and mocked [ἐμπαίζοντες, *empaizontes*] his prophets."

But when Josephus makes reference to the passage in Chronicles, he uses instead the verb ὕβριζεν (*hybrizen*, treat disgracefully or insult; *Ant.* 10.7.2 §103). Josephus understood the biblical notion of "mocking" within the frame of hubris, behavior whose end was to publicly dishonor another. Aristotle defined hubris as "doing and saying things at which the victim incurs shame, not in order that one may achieve anything other than what is done, but simply to get pleasure from it" (*Rhetoric* 1378B). Hubris could include both verbal and physical assaults on others (*OCD* 732), and in the Roman world "a proud Roman was insulted almost as much by a word as by a deed" (D. Epstein 1987: 36). Ignoring a person or not giving the other proper honor was another way hubris could be shown. Whatever form hubris took, it was universally condemned as a serious social breach that could bring judicial action against the person who caused dishonor. The charge that the heretics were "mockers" was serious indeed since it tags them as people who dishonor others. Jude has no need to detail the content of their mocking (cf. 2 Pet. 3:3–4). The charge, taken from the apostolic prophecy, is enough to demonstrate how degraded the heretics were.

The apostles also predicted that these mockers would be people κατὰ τὰς ἑαυτῶν ἐπιθυμίας πορευόμενοι τῶν ἀσεβειῶν (*kata tas heautōn epithymias poreuomenoi tōn asebeiōn*, who live according to the dictates of their own godless desires). The language of the prophecy is identical with the charge in verse 16 (see comments), which suggests that Jude had the apostolic prophecy in mind when he penned the previous "comment." What drove the heretics was their own base desires and, given this, Jude's readers would have no doubt that these were the very ones whom the apostles have predicted would come. However, the prophecy as quoted by Jude also states that the heretics' desires are rooted in their godlessness (τῶν ἀσεβειῶν, *tōn asebeiōn*, godless), which is a charge that stands at the very head of Jude's warning about the heretics (v. 4) and was the central theme of the Enoch prophecy (v. 15). The apostolic prophecy is again stitched to the preceding text/comment section (vv. 14–16), thus doubling the impact of the charge against the heretics. As noted previously (see vv. 4, 15), the charge of godlessness meant that the heretics were people who did not show due reverence for God (BDAG 141). The evil desires (ἐπιθυμίας, *epithymias*) were rooted in their lack of piety: true religion and right conduct are linked in Jude's mind. The fact that they lived according to no higher values than their own desires was clear evidence of their impiety. To ban God from the center of a person's life is the beginning of evil and moral corruption.

### b. Comment: These Are People Who Cause Divisions (19)

**19**  Jude's final "comment" section begins by accusing the heretics of causing division within the congregation: Οὗτοί εἰσιν οἱ ἀποδιορίζοντες (*Houtoi eisin hoi apodiorizontes*, These are people who cause divisions). Jude introduces the comment with the pejorative "these are" (cf. vv. 8, 10, 12, 16, and comments) and blames the heretics for dividing the congregation. Some within the church have been persuaded by the sophistry of these impious people, and others are wavering (vv. 22–23). While being taken in by the heretics, they are likely also finding themselves at odds with others within the Christian community. Clement of Alexandria comments, "These are people who separate believers from one another, under the influence of their own unbelief" (Bray 2000: 256). Their end was to tear asunder the community instead of building up the believers together (cf. v. 20 and comments).

The term Jude employs to refer to this vice appears only here in the NT. The verb ἀποδιορίζω (*apodiorizō*) appears in Aristotle's discussion about animal classification, where he uses it to mean "mark off by dividing" (*Pol.* 1290B; K. Schmidt, *TDNT* 5:455; BDAG 110; derived from διορίζω, *diorizō*, to define). But the term also could mean "divide" (MM 61), the sense that Jude has in mind since his concern is not merely that the heretics make distinctions between people. Although the word Jude uses is quite rare (much more common in the NT is σχίζειν, *schizein*; σχίσμα, *schisma*; see Mitchell 1991: 68–74), the concern about causing division was expressed often in the early church (Rom. 16:17; 1 Cor. 1:10; 11:18; Gal. 5:20; Titus 3:9–10). Division or separation was one of the outcomes of heresy (1 Tim. 4:1; 1 John 2:18–19) and was one of its central, defining characteristics as in the case in this congregation. Tearing apart the body politic was not considered virtuous either within or outside the Christian community. In an ordered society, where place was established by convention and enforced by law, maintenance of unity within the community was a high social obligation (see 1 Cor. 1:10). The heretics came in to divide a body that should have been unified in both faith and conduct (cf. Eph. 4:1–16).

The second vice in Jude's list (cf. Rom. 1:29–31; Gal. 5:19–21; 1 Pet. 4:3; and the mother of all vice lists in Philo, *Sacrifices* 5 §32) identifies the heretics as ψυχικοί (*psychikoi*). Commenting on 1 Cor. 2:14, Thiselton (2000: 267) rightly remarks that "The difficulty of translating ψυχικός into English is notorious." The term appears in both Paul (1 Cor. 2:14; 15:44, 46) and James (3:15). In common Greek usage, ψυχικός (*psychikos*) was that which pertained to the soul or life as opposed to the σωματικός (*sōmatikos*), which pertained to the body (Josephus, *J.W.* 1.21.13 §430; 4 Macc. 1:32: "Some desires are related to the soul and others to the body"; LSJ 2027–28). However, in Christian hands, ψυχικός is placed in contrast with what is "spiritual" or of the Spirit. The person who is ψυχικός (*psychikos*) is devoid of the Spirit (1 Cor. 2:14) and is entirely earthly (1 Cor. 15:46–49; E. Schweizer, *TDNT* 9:661). James (3:15) likewise talks about the "wisdom" that is "earthly, unspiritual [ψυχική, *psychikē*]." In light of this understanding, Jude's accusation is that the heretics are nothing more than earthly people who are not governed by the Spirit. They are entirely "natural" and belong solely to this world, as "worldly people." In other words, they are not disciples of Christ but simply unregenerate people.

The previous charge is echoed in Jude's subsequent declaration that they are people πνεῦμα μὴ ἔχοντες (*pneuma mē echontes*, devoid of the Spirit). The expression "to have a spirit" (ἔχω πνεῦμα, *echō pneuma*) at times refers to those people who are possessed by an evil spirit (Acts 8:7; 16:16; 19:13), but when the Spirit of God is in mind, it describes Christian existence (Rom. 8:9;

1 Cor. 6:19; 2 Cor. 4:13). To have the Spirit of God is to be a Christian, and not to have the Spirit is to be outside this state of grace. Jude reinforces his previous claim: These people are not even believers! They are nothing more than unregenerate humans, whose lives are lived on a base, even animal and instinctual, level (cf. v. 10). This is the ultimate cause of the heretics' immorality and explains their actions. Their impiety has its roots in the fact that they do not possess the transforming power of the Spirit of God in their lives. Within a Christian context, no accusation could be more devastating.

In this verse, Jude's language and accusation do not presuppose that his opponents were gnostics of the second century who divided the world between those who were "soulish" and those who were "spiritual." Jude's language and viewpoint are fully comprehensible within the frame of mid-first-century Christianity and need not be read in light of later gnostic theology. In verse 19 there is no indication that he is taking up the terminology of some supposed gnostic opponents, turning the table of the accusation on them. Jude's polemic against the heretics does not touch on central tenets of gnostic theology and should not be interpreted within that frame (see "Occasion of Writing" in the introduction). To do so would be anachronistic.

II. Letter Body: An Exhortation to Contend for the Faith (3–23)
   A. Disclosure of Jude's Purpose for Writing: An Exhortation to the Beloved (3–4)
   B. A Call to Remember: Predictions about the Heretics and Fulfillment (5–19)
➤  C. Exhortations to the Beloved (20–23)

# C. Exhortations to the Beloved (20–23)

These words bring us to the final section of the body of Jude's letter. After the extensive litany of texts and comments regarding the coming and corruption of the heretics (vv. 5–19), Jude turns to exhort the believers regarding how they are to resist the incursions of the heretics. The heretics have tried to rend the fabric and faith of the community. Jude counters by calling the believers to community action by building themselves up together in their faith, binding themselves together in God's love, and awaiting Christ's mercy in his coming (vv. 20–21). The heretics have been powerfully persuasive and, as a result, Jude also needs to call the church to redemptive action toward those who have been swayed by the appeal (vv. 22–23). Apostasy is a genuine threat, but even in the face of such ruin, Jude forwards hope if, indeed, the church takes deliberate action. This mission is, however, fraught with danger, so Jude warns the community not to be taken in by the immorality as they engage in this rescue.

The unit can be outlined as follows:

1. Keep yourselves in the love of God (20–21)
2. Snatch some from the fire; have mercy on others who dispute (22–23)

## Exegesis and Exposition

[20]But you, beloved, build yourselves up together upon your exceedingly sacred faith; pray in the Holy Spirit; [21]keep yourselves in the love of God; eagerly await the mercy of our Lord Jesus Christ unto eternal life. [22-23r]Snatch some from the fire. Demonstrate mercy, in fear, toward those who dispute, hating even the tunic stained by the flesh.⌐

## 1. Keep Yourselves in the Love of God (20–21)

Jude begins this final section of the letter by again addressing the members of the church as "beloved": ὑμεῖς δέ, ἀγαπητοί (hymeis de, agapētoi, But you, beloved). As in verse 17, the emphatic "but you" places the believers in sharp contrast with the heretics whom Jude has denounced in verse 19. These infiltrators are devoid of the Spirit and are trying to cause a division in the church by their teaching. Jude exhorts the beloved members of the Christian family (see v. 3 and comments) not to be swayed by their teaching but to build themselves up on the foundation of the faith (v. 20a); pray in the Spirit, which they have as the true people of God (v. 20b); and keep themselves in the love

20

of God (v. 21). The present verse includes two participles (ἐποικοδομοῦντες, *epoikodomountes*, building up; προσευχόμενοι, *proseuchomenoi*, praying), which may have an adverbial function in relation to the imperative τηρήσατε (*tērēsate*, keep) in verse 21. But it is more likely that Jude, like Paul, alternates between participle and imperative (see the additional participle προσδεχόμενοι, *prosdechomenoi*, eagerly await, in v. 21b), considering the participle as an equivalent of the imperative (BDF §468.2; and see D. Daube's appended note, "Participle and Imperative in 1 Peter," in E. G. Selwyn 1946: 467–88).

While the heretics were trying to rend the social fabric of the church, Jude calls the members of the congregation together: ἐποικοδομοῦντες ἑαυτοὺς τῇ ἁγιωτάτῃ ὑμῶν πίστει (*epoikodomountes heautous tē hagiōtatē hymōn pistei*, Build yourselves up together on your most holy faith). Jude uses the same construction metaphor[1] that is known so well from Paul's writings (Rom. 15:2, 20; 1 Cor. 8:1; 10:23; 14:3–5, 12, 26; 2 Cor. 10:8; 12:19; 13:10; 1 Thess. 5:11; Eph. 2:21; 4:12, 16, 29), although it was not used exclusively by him (Acts 9:31; 1 Pet. 2:5, 7). We should not assume that Jude's use of the imagery demonstrates direct dependency on Paul. The construction metaphor did not originate with Paul but was well known in the ancient world, being used especially in discussions about the body politic, though not limited to that context (MM 441–42). Mitchell (1991: 100, 99–111) demonstrates that building imagery became a "*topos* in literature urging unity on divided groups." The metaphor frequently appears in discussions about concord. Aristides, for example, says, "We do not judge that house best established which is built of stones which are as beautiful as possible, but which is dwelled in with the greatest harmony, so also it is fitting to believe that those cities are best inhabited who know how to think harmoniously. Everywhere faction is a terrible, disruptive thing" (*Or.* 23.31; cited in Mitchell 1991: 100). Paul applies it in precisely this way in 1 Corinthians. Jude brings the image to bear in the same way as he calls the church to be built up together instead of allowing itself to be divided by the persuasion of the heretics (cf. v. 19). Jude is not merely exhorting the individual believer to grow in faith but also calls the church to labor together for its corporate growth, which certainly integrates and benefits each particular member (implied in ἑαυτούς, *heautous*, yourselves; see Eph. 4:11–16). Nor is this a function exclusively of the leadership of the church: every member seeks to contribute to the corporate building in the faith (1 Pet. 4:10–11). The early church was not wracked by the rugged individualism and consumer mentality often found in contemporary Western congregations. Community is the soil where faith grows.

The term that Jude employs, ἐποικοδομοῦντες (*epoikodomountes*), is a bit less common than οἰκοδομέω (*oikodomeō*, build), and means "to build on" a foundation or existing structure (found also in 1 Cor. 3:10, 12, 14; Eph. 2:20; Col. 2:7; and see Epictetus, *Disc.* 2.15.8; Plato, *Laws* 736E [of civic structures]; Josephus, *Ant.* 11.4.2 §79; 12.5.4 §253; Philo, *Dreams* 2.2 §8). The foundation

---

1. Compare the literal use in Matt. 21:33; 23:29; Mark 14:58; Luke 12:18; Acts 7:47.

on which one builds is placed in the dative case (Philo, *Confusion* 2 §5; *Giants* 7 §30; Epictetus, *Disc.* 2.15.8), and in the same way Jude sees the foundation on which the church is to be built up as "your exceedingly sacred faith" (τῇ ἁγιωτάτῃ ὑμῶν πίστει, *tē hagiōtatē hymōn pistei*). Jude previously described this foundation as the faith "that was once and for all handed down to the saints" (v. 3 and comments). The heretics had brought in both heterodoxy and heteropraxis; in response, the church is to build on the foundations that were already laid when they received the apostolic tradition.

But instead of identifying the faith as a sacred tradition that was handed down as in verse 3, Jude here describes the faith as "most holy" (ἁγιωτάτῃ, *hagiōtatē*, the adjective ἅγιος, *hagios* in the superlative). One could speak of a temple, as the one in Jerusalem, as "exceedingly holy" (Josephus, *Ant.* 16.4.3 §115; 2 Macc. 5:15; Diodorus Siculus 3.44.2), or contracts made that were "especially sacred" (Plato, *Laws* 729E). That which is "holy" is dedicated or consecrated to God and is used for his service (BDAG 10; Matt. 4:5; 27:53; Acts 7:33; Rom. 1:2; Heb. 9:2; Rev. 21:2). Therefore the faith handed down to the saints is "exceedingly sacred." The believers are to work together to build themselves up on this foundation, which is sacred and inviolable. This is precisely what the heretics are attempting to draw them away from, and for this reason Jude underscores that this is "*your* exceedingly sacred faith." Jude lets the church know that what they have received cannot be dismissed since it is most sacred. Their life as a community is founded on this most excellent foundation.

Jude calls the church also to prayer: ἐν πνεύματι ἁγίῳ προσευχόμενοι (*en pneumati hagiō proseuchomenoi*, pray in the Holy Spirit). Once again, Jude places the position of the believers in sharp contrast with the heretics. The opponents are people who are devoid of the Spirit (v. 19 and comments). On the other hand, what explicitly marks the church is the possession of the Spirit and the communion with God through his agency. Prayer in the Holy Spirit defines the life of those who are the true people of God. The Spirit's presence and assistance in prayer is a theme that surfaces in Paul (Rom. 8:15–16, 26–27; Gal. 4:6; Eph. 6:18), and he notes that such prayer is sometimes expressed in unknown tongues (1 Cor. 14:14–15). Some have suggested that Jude may have in mind speaking in tongues (Bauckham 1983: 113; M. Green 1987: 200), an interpretation of the text that is especially well known in Pentecostal/charismatic circles. In this section, however, Jude's concern is with the corporate life of the church in their struggle against heresy, and given the problems within the Corinthian church regarding speaking in tongues, it is hard to imagine how such a call would contribute to the church's corporate life (see 1 Cor. 14:4). Moreover, Jude places this exhortation over against the claim that the heretics do not have the Spirit. The exhortation implies that the members of the church are the true Christians. Neyrey (1993: 90) makes the interesting suggestion that "praying in the Spirit" is "an act supportive of the tradition," an interpretation that may find support in Jude's previous call for the church to build itself up on the foundation of the received (v. 3) and most sacred faith

(v. 19). However, the apostolic faith and the Holy Spirit, word and Spirit, are the two defining characteristics of true Christian community. The gospel is held and the Spirit is at work in every true Christian church. Jude's call is for them to hold to what makes them a community of Christ.

**21**    In this verse, Jude continues the catena of exhortations to the church that began in verse 20: ἑαυτοὺς ἐν ἀγάπῃ θεοῦ τηρήσατε (*heautous en agapē theou tērēsate*, keep yourselves in the love of God). One of the issues that Jude has consistently raised in this epistle is the way the heretics, like their ancient prototypes, did not keep their proper place but crossed the line to participate in things outside their allotted domain. Certain angels did not remain in their proper domain but engaged in illicit relations (v. 6). These violated God's order, as had the exodus generation (v. 5) and the inhabitants of Sodom and Gomorrah (v. 7 and comments on these verses). The heretics were trying to divert the church down a similar path (v. 4a) by altering the gospel (v. 4b) and persuading members of the congregation to follow their lifestyle (vv. 22–23). Jude therefore calls the church both to "contend for the faith" (v. 3) and to hold on securely to what they have received (v. 21).

Jude previously affirmed that they, as the elect of God, were "kept" for Jesus Christ and his return (v. 1 and comments; John 17:11–12; 1 Thess. 5:23; 1 Pet. 1:4–5). But in the present verse he turns the indicative of their existence into an imperative (Neyrey 1993: 91) as he calls them to "keep" themselves "in the love of God." In the NT, the imperative of ethical action is rooted within the indicative of God's act and is part of God's gracious act (Furnish 1968; G. Green 1979). Furnish (1968: 225) comments on Paul's thought: "God's *claim* is regarded by the apostle as a constitutive part of God's *gift*. The Pauline concept of grace is *inclusive of* the Pauline concept of obedience. . . . The Pauline imperative is not just the result of the indicative but fully integral to it." Jude's framework appears similar.

In the NT, in ethical contexts "to keep" can mean "to obey" (the commandment of God or the law; 1 Tim. 6:14; James 2:10; 1 John 2:3–5; 3:22, 24; 5:3; Rev. 12:17; 14:12), "to hold on to" something (such as "unity" in Eph. 4:3 or "faith" in 2 Tim. 4:7), or to maintain a certain state (purity or being unstained; 1 Tim. 5:22; James 1:27). In the face of the persuasive tactics of the heretics, Jude calls the church to keep themselves "in the love of God." They should not move away from God but remain faithful. Keeping themselves "in the love of God" echoes the thought of verse 1, where Jude identifies the Christians as those who are the beloved of God and kept for Jesus Christ. God's love was the cause of their election (see v. 1 and comments), and now Jude exhorts them to stay within this state of grace. This principal imperative is a powerful call to flee from apostasy.[2]

Before turning to the way the church should deal with those who have been taken in by the heretics (vv. 22–23), Jude adds one final (participial) imperative:

---

2. The interpretation in BDAG 1002 is rather tortured and unlikely: "Keep yourselves from harm by making it possible for God to show his love for you in the future also."

προσδεχόμενοι τὸ ἔλεος τοῦ κυρίου ἡμῶν Ἰησοῦ Χριστοῦ εἰς ζωὴν αἰώνιον (*prosdechomenoi to eleos tou kyriou hēmōn Iēsou Christou eis zōēn aiōnion*, eagerly await the mercy of our Lord Jesus Christ unto eternal life). The verb of this clause in certain contexts may mean to receive or accept (Luke 15:2; Rom. 16:2; Phil. 2:29; Heb. 10:34; 11:35), but it also may be used to refer to the anxious expectation of awaiting someone or something (Luke 12:36; Acts 23:21). The term is apt for eschatological contexts, where what is anticipated is the kingdom of God and the final consummation of all things (Jude 21b; Mark 15:43; Luke 2:25, 38; 12:36–38; Acts 23:21; 24:15; Titus 2:13; BDAG 877; MM 546; W. Grundmann, *TDNT* 2:57–58). Jude exhorts the church not only to maintain their faith but also to anxiously await the coming of "the mercy of our Lord Jesus Christ" (cf. 1 Thess. 1:9–10). The vivid hope of the parousia argues against the view that Jude is a representative of "early catholicism." Eschatological expectation is linked with Christian ethics. Jude reminds the church of the end so that they may live godly lives in the present. Having a lively expectation of final consummation is not escapist but frames and informs life in the present age.

The believers eagerly await τὸ ἔλεος τοῦ κυρίου ἡμῶν Ἰησοῦ Χριστοῦ (*to eleos tou kyriou hēmōn Iēsou Christou*, the mercy of our Lord Jesus Christ). "Mercy" is here viewed as an eschatological blessing that will be given to the believer at the final consummation (Luke 1:78; 2 Tim. 1:16–18; Rom. 9:23; 1 Pet. 1:3; 2 Macc. 2:7; Ps. Sol. 17.45; 1 En. 1.8; 27.4); it is the opposite of judgment, which will befall those who disobey the gospel (James 2:13; cf. Ps. Sol. 14.9–10; 1 En. 27.4). In his coming, God will "set right the evils of the world" (Neyrey 1993: 91), and so the righteous are those who anticipate this mercy (Luke 2:25, 38). The mercy that the church awaits, then, is the counterpoint to the judgment that Jude has shown will come on those who have abandoned their appointed place in God's order (vv. 4, 6, 7, 11, 13, 15).

"Mercy" may be defined as the compassion, clemency, or kindness extended to those who are in need (BDAG 316), shown either by humans to others (Matt. 9:13; 12:7; 23:23; Luke 10:37; James 2:13; 3:17) or by God toward humanity (Jude 2 and comments; Luke 1:50, 58; Rom. 15:9; Gal. 6:16). God's mercy is especially demonstrated in human salvation through Jesus Christ (Eph. 2:4; 1 Tim. 1:2; 2 Tim. 1:2; Titus 3:5; 1 Pet. 1:3; 2 John 3; *TLNT* 1:471–79). The marvel of God's mercy is that it is extended to those who, through sin, were alienated from God (Eph. 2:3–4; Titus 3:3–5). In stark contrast to this divine compassion, Aristotle (*Rhetoric* 1385B [2.8.2]) defines mercy as "a kind of pain excited by the sight of evil, deadly or painful, which befalls one who does not deserve it," and Diogenes Laertius (*Lives* 7.111) similarly says, "Pity [ἔλεον, *eleon*] is grief felt at undeserved suffering." God, however, extends his mercy to those who deserve judgment. While the church awaits the mercy of the Lord Jesus, members of the church are to extend the eschatological blessing of mercy toward those who, in their weakness, have fallen into the snare of the heretics (vv. 22–23 and comments). Once again, the indicative of God's act becomes a call to obedience (see above).

The mercy of the Lord Jesus Christ, shown to them upon his coming, will bring eternal life: εἰς ζωὴν αἰώνιον (*eis zōēn aiōnion*, unto eternal life). "Eternal life" was a fundamental hope within later Judaism. This is the "everlasting renewal of life" (2 Macc. 7:9) given at the resurrection (Dan. 12:2; Ps. Sol. 3.12), which will come in accordance with God's promise (4 Macc. 15:3) and mercy (Ps. Sol. 13.11–12; 14.9–10; 15.13; and see T. Ash. 5.2; 1 En. 40.9; 58.3; R. Bultmann, *TDNT* 2:855–61). The hope of eternal life was linked with the expectation of the coming kingdom of God. We are therefore not surprised to hear questions about eternal life raised in conversations with Jesus (Matt. 19:16; Mark 10:17; Luke 10:25; 18:18; John 5:39). While John is able to speak about eternal life as a present possession of the believer (John 3:15–16, 36; 5:24; 6:47, 54), this life anticipates the final day when the righteous will be raised (John 6:40, 54). Much of the discussion of eternal life in the NT understands it as the future hope of the resurrection (Matt. 19:29; Mark 10:30; Luke 18:30; Rom. 2:7; Titus 1:2; 3:7). This is the final act of salvation and, as such, is in contrast with the final judgment and condemnation of the unrighteous (Matt. 25:46; John 3:36; 10:28; 1 John 3:15; cf. Ps. Sol. 13.11; 15.12–13).

Jude again places the hope of the Christian into contrast with what the unrighteous may expect. Throughout the epistle he has underscored the certainty of judgment for those who have rebelled against God. But these believers should anticipate the mercy of the Lord Jesus Christ, shown supremely in the coming resurrection. Their end is filled with hope and glory. To be sure, Jude's concern is not simply to inform them about a bright future. His call to await this event also implies that in the hope of eternal life, they should continue to avoid the way of the heretics.

## 2. Snatch Some from the Fire; Have Mercy on Others Who Dispute (22–23)

**22–23**     From the standpoint of textual criticism, verses 22–23 are the most difficult of the whole epistle. Osburn (1972: 137) introduced his article on the textual history of these verses by saying: "The text of Jude 22–23, undoubtedly one of the most corrupt passages in New Testament literature, remains a *crux criticorum*. The very ancient, widely diffused, and numerous alterations have caused many to despair of ever being able to ascertain the exact wording of these verses." While some of the textual witnesses contain two clauses (such as the oldest extant MS of the epistle, $\mathfrak{P}^{72}$), others have three clauses (represented by ℵ and other witnesses). Contemporary critical editions of our Greek NT (UBS[4] and NA[27]) closely follow the three-clause reading of ℵ, and in their wake the majority of translations. While some commentators and one major study (Kubo 1981) likewise support a three-clause reading, numerous articles on the textual history of the passage consider the shorter reading of $\mathfrak{P}^{72}$ to represent the original (Birdsall 1963; Osburn 1972; S. Winter 1994), finding support among various commentators as well. Since $\mathfrak{P}^{72}$ is the oldest witness, and since it contains the shorter reading, is supported by other ancient witnesses, and best explains the origins of the others, the present commentary will consider the shorter two-clause reading to be original. See the additional note below for a complete discussion of the problems.

After warning the church to avoid the heretics' error by building themselves up in the faith, praying in the Spirit, keeping themselves in God's love, and expecting the coming mercy of the Lord (vv. 20–21), Jude now instructs them in the way they should deal with those who have, in one way or another, succumbed to the persuasion of the heretics. Following the reading of 𝔓⁷², the exhortation begins: οὓς μὲν ἐκ πυρὸς ἁρπάσατε (hous men ek pyros harpasate, Snatch some from the fire). Jude's thought appears to echo Zech. 3:2, "a brand plucked from the fire" (δαλὸς ἐξεσπασμένος ἐκ πυρός, dalos exespasmenos ek pyros), although the language does not follow the LXX and may reflect knowledge of the Hebrew text (in the LXX, the Hebrew verb נָצַל, nāṣal, deliver/save, is never translated by ἁρπάζω, harpazō, snatch, although the verb Jude uses may mean "deliver," as noted below). The same expression appears in Amos 4:11, but Jude likely has the Zechariah passage in mind since an echo of that text is already found in verse 9 (see comments) and since he again alludes to it in verse 23 (see comments).

The "fire" from which some needed deliverance is that of the final judgment. In both Testaments as well as Jewish literature, divine judgment by fire is a common image (Deut. 32:22; Isa. 29:6; 30:27, 30, 33; 33:14; 66:15–16, 24; Joel 2:30; Nah. 1:6; Zeph. 1:18; 3:8; Mal. 4:1; Acts 2:19; 2 Thess. 1:8; 2 Pet. 3:7, 10; Rev. 9:17–18; 16:8; 20:9; Sib. Or. 2.196–213; 3.80–93; 4.171–82; 5.155–61, 206–13; Ps. Sol. 15.4; 1 En. 1.6–7; 52.6; 1QH 3.19–36; Josephus, *Ant.* 1.2.3 §70; L.A.E. 49.3). Since these people needed to be snatched "from the fire," the implication appears to be that they had succumbed to the persuasion of the heretics and had themselves become liable to the judgment about which Jude has warned throughout this epistle. For Jude, the possibility of apostasy was as real as the hope of redemption for those who have been taken in by the theology and the practices of the heretics.

Jude calls the church to engage in a redemptive act toward those who would face judgment. The church is to "snatch" them (ἁρπάσατε, harpasate) from the fire. The word Jude uses means "to take something forcefully" (Job 24:2, 9; Bar. 4:26; Matt. 11:12; 12:29; 13:19; John 6:15; 10:12, 28–29; Acts 23:10; W. Foerster, *TDNT* 1:472–73; MM 78–79; BDAG 134). In some contexts the word may imply a violent act, but in others it is only forceful. The word may also imply that this forceful snatching happens suddenly (John 6:15; 10:28–29; Acts 23:10; 1 Thess. 4:17) or with speed (Josephus, *Ant.* 6.11.9 §238). The "snatching" may be for the purpose of "rescue," as in Jos. Asen. 12.8 ("For [just] as a little child who is afraid flees to his father, and the father, stretching out his hands, snatches him off the ground, . . . likewise you too, Lord, stretch out your hands upon me as a child-loving father, and snatch me off the earth"). Jude appears to have this sense in mind. He calls the church to forceful and swift action to rescue those who have come under the sway of the heretics' teaching.

As the church is responsible to build itself up on the foundation of faith (v. 20a), so also rapid and drastic measures must be taken to rescue those who have become wayward. Errant members are not to be simply dismissed but also sought out and delivered from the error into which they have fallen. This mutual care for errant members became a key theme in the corporate life of the church (Matt. 18:15–20; 1 Cor. 5:1–5; 1 Thess. 5:14; 2 Thess. 3:6–15) and was not simply the domain of the congregational leadership. In a group-oriented society like that in which Jude and his readers lived, social control over the behavior of the individual was a significant moral force (Malina and Neyrey 1996: 186–87). Hence, to bring the whole church into the attempt to modify the behavior of the individual is a powerful means of persuasion and an effective plan of rescue.

According to the textual reading of $\mathfrak{P}^{72}$ followed in this commentary (see above and the additional note), the following exhortation is διακρινομένους δὲ ἐλεεῖτε ἐν φόβῳ (diakrinomenous de eleeite en phobō, demonstrate mercy, in fear, toward those who dispute). In this second exhortation in this redemptive cycle of instruction, Jude turns his attention to "those who dispute" (διακρινομένους, diakrinomenous). The participle Jude uses to describe these people is from the verb that could mean "to doubt" or "to waver" (Matt. 21:21; Mark 11:23; Rom. 4:20; 14:23; James 1:6; 2:4; and perhaps Acts 10:20; BDAG 231; LSJ 399), a sense not attested in Greek literature before the NT. If this is the meaning of the word here, Jude would have in mind the people who were in the process of being taken in by the persuasive power of the heretics, as opposed to those mentioned in the previous clause who apparently have already succumbed to their ways. But this group has already engaged in immoral behavior (see below). Moreover, Jude has already employed the term (v. 9) in the much more common sense of "to dispute" or "to be at variance with someone" (Polybius 2.22.11; BDAG 231; LSJ 399; MM 150; DeGraaf 2005). The word could even be used of combatants and, in the later church, the participial form became a name for dissident heretics (PGL 354). Since this sense is evident in verse 9, which refers to the Testament of Moses and echoes Zech. 3:2 (see comments), it is likely that Jude means the same thing in the present verse. He echoes Zech. 3 in the previous clause (Zech. 3:2, see above) and in the following (Zech. 3:4, see below).

Who, then, are "those who dispute"? They may be the heretics themselves (S. Winter 1994: 218; Bauckham 1983: 115), but this is unlikely since Jude has spoken of nothing but condemnation for them throughout the epistle. Their doom is sure since they have changed the gospel and denied the Lord. They were even marked out from times of old for this condemnation (v. 4). Throughout the "text/comment" section of the letter (vv. 5–16), Jude has not suggested that these people might be redeemed. But in the present verse, Jude instructs the church to "show mercy" on these who dispute. Such people have engaged in immoral conduct, as the following clause indicates, and therefore likely are those who have been persuaded by the heretics and posture themselves over against the traditional view of the faith. The way Jude tags these people suggests that the church itself has been torn over the heretics' stance and that some who have been persuaded are combative. The heretics themselves have fueled such schism within the church (v. 19). The difficulty with this interpretation is that it becomes difficult to distinguish this group from those who need to be "snatched from the fire" in the previous clause. The attitudes of these two groups differ. The ones spoken of in the present clause appear to have taken a polemic stance; those of the previous clause have fallen and appear to have a more passive posture. Such may be "snatched" from the awaiting judgment.

The approach to the disputers that Jude counsels is both redemptive and cautious. The church is called to "demonstrate mercy" toward them "in fear." Extending mercy to the disputers is truly a divine act since, as noted previously, mercy in the Greek world was the pity one would show to someone who was suffering undeservedly (see v. 21 and comments). "Mercy" was not considered a virtue outside the Christian circle and was even held in suspicion by some and considered to be a weakness (*TLNT* 1:472). The Cynics believed that they should "feel no anger, no rage, no envy, no pity [ἔλεον, *eleon*]" (Epictetus, *Disc.* 3.22.13). Epictetus counseled against it (2.17.26; 4.1.4) and even expressed the opinion, "I am annoyed, says one, at being pitied" (4.6.1–5). But Jude calls the church to act out of mercy toward the heretics' disciples, which would not have been the most natural response toward someone considered now to be in an adversarial position. Enmity would have been naturally met with retaliation and aggression (see the analysis in D. Epstein 1987; 2 Thess. 3:15; comments in G. Green 2002: 356). The LXX commonly talks about living "in the fear of the Lord" (2 Chron. 19:9; 26:5; Ps. 5:8 [5:7 Eng.]; Prov. 14:26; 23:17; Sir. 9:16; 27:3; 40:26; 45:23; Ps. Sol. 17.40) or "of God" (Neh. 5:9; Ps. Sol. 6.5; 18.7–9, 11), although the object of this fear is occasionally implied from the context (Ps. 2:11; Isa. 19:16; Mal. 2:5; Ps. Sol. 17.34). The NT likewise speaks of conducting oneself "in the fear of God" or "of Christ," with the object either stated or implied (2 Cor. 7:1; Eph. 5:21; 1 Pet. 1:17; 3:2). However, in both Testaments "in fear" may be understood as being afraid of adverse circumstances (Isa. 33:7; 1 Cor. 2:3; Heb. 2:15; 1 Pet. 2:18). Since Jude warns about a particular circumstance, that of being tempted (see below), this sense is likely in mind. They should show mercy yet recognize the temptations that could befall them (cf. Gal. 6:1).

Jude adds a warning to those who would engage in such redemptive activity: μισοῦντες καὶ τὸν ἀπὸ τῆς σαρκὸς ἐσπιλωμένον χιτῶνα (*misountes kai ton apo tēs sarkos espilōmenon chitōna*, hating even the tunic stained by the flesh). The idea of having stained clothing, which represents moral defilement, is a thought found also in Zech. 3:4: "The angel said to those who were standing before him, 'Take off his filthy clothes.' And to him he said, 'See, I have taken your guilt away from you, and I will clothe you with festal apparel'" (NRSV). Jude's wording is quite different from either the Hebrew or LXX of this passage, yet it is likely that Jude reflects on this passage since he apparently has knowledge of it (see above and comments on v. 9).

The "tunic" (χιτῶνα, *chitōna*; Matt. 5:40; Luke 6:29; John 19:23; *ADB* 2:236) was the inner garment worn next to the flesh as opposed to the outer toga (ἱμάτιον, *himation*). More than one tunic could be worn at a time (Matt. 10:10; Mark 6:9; 14:63; Luke 3:11; 9:3). This would be the garment most likely to become soiled by the body or, as Jude says, ἀπὸ τῆς σαρκὸς ἐσπιλωμένον (*apo tēs sarkos espilōmenon*). A "stain" (σπίλος, *spilos*) could be a literal stain or spot, such as that caused by dirt or paint (LSJ 1628), but the term could take on a figurative moral sense (Eph. 5:27; 2 Pet. 2:13). In a similar way, the verb could have a literal sense but could also refer to becoming morally defiled (Wis. 15:4; T. Ash. 2.7; James 3:6; LSJ 1628; BDAG 938). "Flesh" may refer to muscular tissue (Luke 24:39; Acts 2:31; Rom. 2:28) or to the body as a whole (Gal. 4:13; Col. 2:1; Heb. 9:10). Paul refers to "flesh" as the fallen aspect of human nature, the domain of sin, in which nothing good can dwell (Rom. 7:18, 25; 8:4–7; Gal. 5:13, 24; Col. 2:23; BDAG 914–16). Although this Pauline sense of "flesh" cannot be reduced to the simple equation that the body is sinful, considerable philosophical and religious discussion was taken up with the question of the relationship between the body ("flesh") and desires and passions or appetites (Plutarch, *Mor.* 1087B–D, 1096C; 4 Macc. 7:18). The "flesh" seeks pleasure (Diogenes Laertius, *Lives* 10.145; Philo, *Unchangeable* 30 §143) and is weak, corrupt, and deceitful (T. Jud. 19.4; T. Zeb. 9.7). The line between the "flesh" as that which desires and seeks pleasure and the Pauline sense is not hard drawn, as is evident in the present verse. Jude previously spoke about the "flesh" in relationship to the sin of the angels, which was considered to be sexual acts, and of the heretics who had "defiled the flesh" (v. 7–8).

Jude likely has this particular fleshly desire in mind here. Sexual immorality was one of the hallmarks of the heretics' praxis (vv. 4–8, 11–12, 16, 18), and here Jude envisions the sexual act as staining the tunic. The "stained tunic" is literal, but it becomes a metaphor for the sinful life of those who have fallen into the sins of the heretics. Jude warns those engaged in this rescue operation not to be taken in but to "hate" the stained tunic, which represents the sin itself (Gal. 6:1). Coming close to the situation of the fallen could ensnare those who did not undertake this operation "in fear." The ones who show mercy should detest the very acts that have ensnared some of the members of the church (John 3:20; Heb. 1:9; Rev. 2:6).

## Additional Note

**22–23.** The text of Jude 22–23 has been handed down in various forms, with the principal distinction between the witnesses being those that contain three clauses (each beginning οὕς μὲν . . . , οὕς δὲ . . . , οὕς δέ, *hous men…, hous de…, hous de*, represented by ℵ A) and those that contain two (which begin οὕς μὲν . . . , οὕς δέ, *hous men . . . , hous de*, represented by B C K L P). Additionally, 𝔓[72], the oldest extant MS that contains Jude (III/IV cent.), has a two-clause reading that is shorter than the other two-clause witnesses and whose second clause does not begin with οὕς δέ, *hous de*, but has only δέ, *de*. The three-clause reading has various supporters (Kubo 1981; M. Green 1987: 201–2; Metzger 1994: 658–59; Vögtle 1994: 102–5; Moo 1996: 286–87), including the critical editions of the Greek NT (UBS[4] and NA[27]). Major translations follow the critical editions in this question. On the other hand, a two-clause reading has found considerable support, with some following the longer two-clause text (Schelkle 1980: 170–71; Albin 1962: 622–26; Kelly 1969: 288–89; Fuchs and Raymond 1988: 178–79) and others the shorter reading in $\mathfrak{P}^{72}$ (Birdsall 1963: 396–99; Osburn 1972; Bauckham 1983: 108–11; Neyrey 1993: 85–86; S. Winter 1994: 215–17; Perkins 1995: 156; Landon 1996: 131–34; Kraftchick 2002: 65–66), a reading that Kubo (1965: 89–92) formerly supported.

The longer, three-clause reading finds minimal support, being found only in ℵ and, with a few variants, in A (καὶ οὓς μὲν ἐλεᾶτε [A ἐλέγχετε] διακρινομένους, οὓς δὲ σῴζετε ἐκ πυρὸς ἁρπάζοντες, οὓς δὲ ἐλεᾶτε [A ἐλεεῖτε] ἐν φόβῳ, *kai hous men eleate* [A *elenchete*] *diakrinomenous, hous de sōzete ek pyros harpazontes, hous de eleate* [A *eleeite*] *en phobō*). The argument that Jude favors groupings of three (as vv. 2, 5–7, 8, 11) does not hold in the face of the stronger support of the witnesses in favor of two clauses. The uncial MSS that contain two clauses (B C K L P S) have a number of variants among them:

| | | |
|---|---|---|
| C | καὶ οὓς μὲν ἐλέγχετε διακρινομένους οὓς δὲ σῴζετε ἐκ πυρὸς ἁρπάζοντες ἐν φόβῳ | *kai hous men elenchete diakrinomenous hous de sōzete ek pyros harpazontes en phobō* |
| K L P S | οὓς μὲν ἐλεεῖτε διακρινομένοι οὓς δὲ ἐν φόβῳ σῴζετε ἐκ πυρὸς ἁρπάζοντες | *hous men eleeite diakrinomenoi hous de en phobō sōzete ek pyros harpazontes* |
| B | καὶ οὓς μὲν ἐλεᾶτε διακρινομένους σῴζετε ἐκ πυρὸς ἁρπάζοντες οὓς δὲ ἐλεᾶτε ἐν φόβῳ | *kai hous men eleate diakrinomenous sōzete ek pyros harpazontes hous de eleate en phobō* |

Apparently B is a conflation of $\mathfrak{P}^{72}$ and C and should not be considered original. The reading of K, L, P, and S appears to be emended from ℵ, which itself arose from the conflated B reading (Osburn 1972: 141–43). The shorter two-clause reading in $\mathfrak{P}^{72}$ appears to be the text that gave rise to the others. The preference in textual criticism is generally to prefer shorter readings, like this one. Moreover, the reading of $\mathfrak{P}^{72}$ commends itself because it is found in the oldest MS of Jude. This reading was followed by Clement of Alexandria (*Strom.* 6.8.65) and finds additional support in various versions (it$^{t}$ syr$^{ph}$ cop$^{sah}$), including the Latin version by Jerome (*Commentary on Ezekiel* 18). Given this wide support, the antiquity of the MS witness, and the multiple variants witnessed in the other texts, the reading of $\mathfrak{P}^{72}$ should be considered original. This short reading is, to be sure, difficult to interpret and translate (S. Winter 1994), so apparently some sought to clarify what Jude had written.

I. Epistolary Greeting (1–2)

II. Letter Body: An Exhortation to Contend for the Faith (3–23)

➤ III. Closing Doxology (24–25)

# III. Closing Doxology (24–25)

Jude concludes his epistle with a doxology instead of the more-common Hellenistic letter-closing conventions, which could include "secondary greetings, health wish, farewell wish, date, illiteracy formula, postscript," usually in that order (Weima 1994: 55).[1] As noted in the introduction (see "Genre and Structure"), Aramaic and Hellenistic letters did not conclude with doxologies. This innovation to the letter genre appears to have Christian origins (Rom. 16:25–27;[2] 2 Pet. 3:18; 1 Clem. 65.2; Mart. Pol. 22.3; Diogn. 12.9), perhaps attributable to Paul (White 1986: 19).[3] In Christian correspondence, doxologies as well as prayers also appear at the end of major divisions in the correspondence (Rom. 11:36; Gal. 1:5; Eph. 3:20–21; Phil. 4:20; 1 Tim. 1:17; 2 Tim. 4:18; 1 Pet. 5:10–11). The use of doxologies in Christian letters reflects the way these documents were used within the church.

As we know, letters were read aloud to the gathered believers during times of corporate worship (Col. 4:16; 1 Thess. 5:27). As the Law was recited aloud in the Jewish synagogue (Luke 4:16; Acts 13:15, 27; 15:21; 2 Cor. 3:14–15; Josephus, *Ag. Ap.* 2.19 §175; Philo, *Moses* 2.39 §§215–16), so Christians read both Scripture (1 Tim. 4:13) and the apostolic correspondence in their assembly.[4] The inclusion of doxologies in letters was, therefore, an understandable development due to the way letters interfaced with the worship service. We should not assume, however, that Christian letters were therefore modeled on oral discourse or that letters were once homilies that were then dressed up as correspondence (see "Genre and Structure" in the introduction). This and the other NT epistles follow, as well as adapt, the epistolary conventions of the era.

In his study of Pauline letter closings, Weima (1994: 135–44) analyzes the Pauline doxologies along with those from other NT letters, including Jude

---

1. See also Doty 1973: 14; White 1986: 198–203; and on Aramaic letter closings, Fitzmyer 1974b: 217.

2. The textual problems of Rom. 16:25–26 are discussed in Metzger 1994: 476–77; Schreiner 1998: 816–17.

3. White (1986: 19) comments: "The Apostle Paul appears to be the Christian leader who was responsible for first introducing Christian elements into the epistolary genre and for adapting existing epistolary conventions to express the special interests of the Christian community. These alterations are more readily comprehended when one recognizes that the letter was a substitute for Paul's apostolic presence with his Christian communities. His use of Christian formulas shows, more exactly, that the setting for which the letter served as a surrogate was the Christian congregation at worship. Namely, it was in his capacity as God's representative that Paul addressed his congregations."

4. In Hellenistic society, it was customary to read letters aloud (Diodorus Siculus 15.10.2). Public reading of discourses of philosophers was practiced as well (Epictetus, *Disc.* 3.23.6).

24–25,[5] and marks out four elements commonly included: (1) the recipient of praise; (2) the elements of praise; (3) the indication of time; and (4) the confirmatory response. The recipient of praise is indicated by the dative (either God or Christ), and this part of the doxology is the most highly elaborated. In Jude's case, God is the recipient, and the elaboration of his attributes is very extensive indeed, comprising all of verse 24 and the first part of verse 25 ("To the one who is able to keep you from stumbling and make you stand in the presence of his glory, blameless and with exceeding joy, to the only God our Savior").

The elements of praise are placed in the nominative case and always include "glory" as well as other common attributions such as "power," "honor," "authority," and "blessing" (in Jude, "glory, majesty, might, and authority"). Every NT doxology marks the time during which the praise is to continue, and the most extensive elaboration of this element is found in Jude ("before all the ages, now, and for all the ages"). The confirmatory response is "Amen," the affirmation of the praise given to God. Weima (1994: 55–56, 237–39) has also demonstrated that Paul's letter closings, as well as those in Greco-Roman letters, rehearse the major themes of the correspondence, and the same is true of Jude's doxology. It reflects the concern that the church stand firm in the faith that they have received (v. 3), acknowledging that God is the one who can keep them (v. 24a). The doxology also looks forward to the final consummation, when the believers will stand blameless before God (v. 24b) instead of being condemned along with the heretics. It also echoes Jude's original intent to write to the church about their "common security" (v. 25a with v. 3). The exaltation of God "through Jesus Christ our Lord" (v. 25b) serves as a counterpoint to the heretics' denial of the Lord Jesus Christ (v. 4). While the form of Jude's closing is different from common letter closings of the era, it serves the same function of taking up the themes that were the major concern of the letter writer.

## Exegesis and Exposition

[24]To the one who is able to keep you from stumbling and make you stand in the presence of his glory, blameless and with exceeding joy, [25]to the only God our Savior be glory, majesty, might, and authority through Jesus Christ our Lord before all the ages, now, and for all the ages. Amen!

The hope that pervades the doxology is astounding in light of the grave situation that Jude faced as he tried to extract the church from the jaws of the heretics. Jude has carefully assembled a most forceful and compelling argument against the heretics and their teaching, charging them with perverting the gospel and denying the Lord (v. 4) and marking out the judgment that

**24**

5. They include Rom. 11:36b; 16:25–27; Gal. 1:5; Eph. 3:20–21; Phil. 4:20; 1 Tim. 1:17; 6:16; 2 Tim. 4:18; Heb. 13:21b; 1 Pet. 4:11; 5:11; Rev. 1:5b–6; 5:13b; 7:12; as well as Jude 24–25.

awaits them as they follow the pattern of sinners in the past (vv. 5–16). He has demonstrated that their coming and their doom were predicted from ancient times (vv. 4, 14), and even the apostles forewarned of their advent (vv. 17–18). In light of this strong condemnation, Jude has called the church to contend for the faith handed down as sacred tradition (v. 3) and exhorted the members of the congregation to engage in an aggressive and compassionate rescue operation toward those who have been seduced by the heretics (vv. 22–23). As a countermeasure against the heretics' attacks, he has called the church to build themselves up on the foundation of faith, to pray, to stand in the love of God, and to keep their eyes on the final consummation of all things (vv. 20–21). Yet in the end he turns his eyes to God, knowing that God is the one who will protect them and purify them so that they will, in the final day, be overwhelmed with joy. Jude does not simply rely on his own powers of persuasion or his readers' ability to act. He is theocentric.

In this doxology he lifts his and the church's eyes to the sovereign Lord and praises him: Τῷ δὲ δυναμένῳ φυλάξαι ὑμᾶς ἀπταίστους (*Tō de dynamenō phylaxai hymas aptaistous*, To the one who is able to keep you from stumbling). As Weima (1994: 136) has noted, the recipient of praise in NT doxologies is placed in the dative case, and so here the doxology is lifted to God (v. 25a), who is titled "the one who is able" (cf. the title in the doxologies of Rom. 16:25; Eph. 3:20). A central tenet of the faith is that God is not impotent but possesses the capability of acting fearfully (Matt. 10:28; James 4:12) and powerfully for the welfare of his people (Rom. 16:25; Eph. 3:20; Heb. 5:7; James 4:12; see 2 Macc. 8:18). This declaration is not simply a statement of potential but especially an exaltation of what God does do. This is realized capacity, and the doxology therefore becomes a call to faith.

With regard to Jude's readers, God is powerfully able "to keep you from stumbling." In some contexts this verb (φυλάσσω, *phylassō*) has to do with keeping prisoners under custody (Luke 8:29; Acts 12:4; 23:35; 28:16), but elsewhere, as here, the more positive sense of "guard" or "protect" is in mind (John 17:12; 2 Thess. 3:3; 2 Tim. 1:12; 2 Pet. 2:5), as shepherds guard their sheep (Luke 2:8) or as someone protects property (Luke 11:21). While the word may be used in the weakened sense of "to watch over" (Acts 22:20), here the term implies that there is some need of protection. In the case of this church, the assault of the heretics is in mind since their end was to divert the church into their immoral ways (cf. the verb in Wis. 14:24). Therefore God is praised for his ability to keep them "from stumbling," as runners who finish a course without tripping (Philo, *Agriculture* 40 §177; Sib. Or. 3.288). Their safety and surety are in mind (Philo, *Drunkenness* 48 §199; Marcus Aurelius 5.9; Let. Aris. 187), and Jude is confident in God's ability to protect them from falling or failing. Although some have been taken in by the heretics (vv. 22–23), God is able to keep them from moral failure, a theme that also appears elsewhere in the NT (Matt. 6:13; 1 Cor. 10:13). Jude does not view the heretics as all-powerful nor does he believe that apostasy is the inevitable outcome of their assault.

Jude also raises praise to God for his powerful ability to make them "stand in the presence of his glory, blameless and with exceeding joy." The notion of "standing" over against the forces of evil (Eph. 6:11, 13–14) or against falling into unbelief (Rom. 11:20) is a common piece of early Christian teaching. The Christian is one who stands firm in the gospel (1 Cor. 15:1) by faith (2 Cor. 1:24). The believer stands in God's grace and will (Col. 4:12; 1 Pet. 5:12). This idea is expressed repeatedly in the NT with special emphasis placed on God's ability to strengthen his people (Rom. 16:25; Eph. 3:17; Col. 1:17; 1 Thess. 3:13; 2 Thess. 2:16–17; 3:3; 1 Pet. 5:10). Being established in the faith was a particular concern of the early church in the face of the assaults believers faced through persecution, doctrinal error, moral temptation, and satanic attack.

But the concern for stability was also voiced more widely during the era. Philo (*Dreams* 2.2 §11) remarked on those who were carried off and were not established in their lives, and Diogenes Laertius (*Lives* 2.136) critiqued people who could never become firm in any teaching. Jude, however, looks beyond the present moment and praises God for his ability to make them stand morally pure before him in judgment. "Before" (κατενώπιον, *katenōpion*) God marks the position of one who stands in God's presence (Lev. 4:17 LXX) as the Judge of a person's life (cf. Eph. 1:4, which also brings together the idea of being "blameless" and "before" God; Luke 1:38; 2 Cor. 2:17; Col. 1:22).[6] Jude's praise anticipates the time when they will stand before τῆς δόξης αὐτοῦ (*tēs doxēs autou*, his glory). Clement of Alexandria interpreted the clause as a reference to angels: "In the presence of His glory: he means in the presence of the angels." But "his glory" should not be confused with the "glories" of verse 8. This is the glory of God (John 11:40; Acts 7:55; Rom. 1:23; 3:7, 23; 5:2; 2 Pet. 1:17; Rev. 15:8), the manifestation of his presence (Exod. 40:34–35; 1 Kings 8:10–11; Ps. 26:8; *TLNT* 1:365–76). Jude's thought and language are quite similar to 1 En. 104.1 and may even echo this passage: "I swear unto you, that in heaven the angels remember you for good before the glory of the Great One, and your names are written before the glory of the Great One [ἐνώπιον τῆς δόξης τοῦ μεγάλου, *enōpion tēs doxēs tou megalou*]" (M. Black 1985: 98).

Jude makes the extraordinary claim that they will be found ἀμώμους (*amōmous*), blameless and without defect (BDAG 56), before God. The term was originally used with reference to sacrificial animals, which had to be flawless (Heb. 9:14), and came also to mean morally blameless (1 Pet. 1:19, where the two senses coalesce; Eph. 1:4; 5:27; Phil. 2:15; Col. 1:22; Rev. 14:5; and Sir. 31:8; 40:19; Philo, *Names* 8 §60; Josephus, *Ant.* 3.12.2 §279; cf. μῶμοι, *mōmoi* in 2 Pet. 2:13). The sense is similar to ἄμεμπτος/ἀμέμπτως (*amemptos/amemptōs*, blameless; Luke 1:6; Phil. 2:15; 3:6; 1 Thess. 5:23; Heb. 8:7). In the final assize, as they stand face-to-face with God himself, they will be found to be without

---

6. A thought more commonly expressed with ἐνώπιον (*enōpion*, before), as in Rom. 12:17; 1 Cor. 1:29; 2 Cor. 8:21; Gal. 1:20; 1 Tim. 5:21; 6:13; 2 Tim. 2:14; 4:1; Heb. 4:13; James 4:10; 1 Pet. 3:4.

moral fault. Jude has a clear view of God's transforming power in the life of the Christian and is assured that they will not be swept away in judgment. While the heretics will be condemned for their dreadful deeds (vv. 4–15), the believers will stand faultless before God. This final evaluation of their lives will result in exceeding joy on their part: ἐν ἀγαλλιάσει (en agalliasei). The word speaks of an unbridled jubilation (Luke 1:44; Acts 2:46; 11:28 [Codex D]) that will be characteristic of the redeemed on the last day (Pss. 96:11–12 [95:11–12 LXX]; 97:8 [96:8 LXX]; Isa. 25:9; 1 Pet. 1:6; 4:13; T. Levi 18.5, 14; 1 En. 104.4, 13). These believers need not fear or dread God's investigation. They will be found blameless and will, in the end, be overwhelmed with joy in his presence.

**25**    In this doxology, praise is further lifted to him as μόνῳ θεῷ σωτῆρι ἡμῶν (monō theō sōtēri hēmōn, to the only God our Savior). In the midst of a pluralistic society, which confesses that there are many gods and many lords (1 Cor. 8:4–6), the confession of the unity of God is truly astounding. The Christian belief in one God is rooted in the OT. The Shema (Deut. 6:4–9; also including 11:13–21; Num. 15:37–41) was repeated twice daily by Jewish men, a practice current during the NT era (Schürer 1979: 454–55). The confession that he is the "only God" is repeated over and again in both the OT (2 Kings 19:15, 19; Ps. 86:10 [85:10 LXX]; Isa. 37:16, 20) and Jewish literature (Pr. Azar. 22; 2 Macc. 7:37; Odes Sol. 7.45) as well as the NT (John 5:44; 17:3; Rom. 3:30; 16:27; Gal. 3:20; 1 Tim. 1:17; 2:5). Although the confession of the unity of God is often framed against the polytheism and idolatry of the ancient world (Isa. 44:6, 8–20; 46:5–13; Jer. 16:20; and Acts 14:15–17; 17:24–31; 19:23–27), Jude's proclamation that he is one becomes the foundation for worship (as Rom. 16:27; 1 Tim. 1:17; 2 Kings 19:15, 19; Pss. 72:18 [71:18 LXX]; 86:10 [85:10 LXX]; Isa. 37:16). As Hilary of Arles commented, "Praise is given to God alone, for he is the only one who deserves our worship" (Bray 2000: 259).

As the "only God," he is the one who is honored and powerful (v. 25b) and able to save (σωτῆρι ἡμῶν, sōtēri hēmōn, our Savior). In both Testaments and in other Jewish literature, the confession that God is the Savior is a central tenet as well (Deut. 32:15; Pss. 24:5; 25:5; 27:9; 62:2, 6; 65:5; 79:9; 95:1 [LXX: Pss. 23:5; 24:5; 26:9; 61:3, 7; 64:6; 78:9; 94:1]; Odes Sol. 2.15; 9.47; Sir. 51:1; Ps. Sol. 3.6; 17.3; Jdt. 9:11; 3 Macc. 6:29, 32; 7:16; Luke 1:47; 1 Tim. 1:1; 2:3; 4:10; Titus 1:3; 2:10; 2 Pet. 3:2). Again, in an environment where saviors abounded, the exclusive claim of Christianity was striking. Zeus could be called "the great savior" (IT, n. 67), and even Augustus was titled "the god and savior, emperor" (Deissmann 1911: 344–45). But again, Jude does not present the fact that God is their Savior as a polemic against the idol or imperial cult but affirms that this One with whom they have to do is not only the Judge of all but *their* Savior. Jude had originally intended to address the issue of their "common security" or salvation (v. 3a), which was threatened by the incursion of the heretics (vv. 3b–4). Now he turns to this topic again in this note of assurance, which is calculated to inspire hope and faith. God is truly their Savior.

The first part of the following phrase, διὰ Ἰησοῦ Χριστοῦ τοῦ κυρίου ἡμῶν (*dia Iēsou Christou tou kyriou hēmōn*, through Jesus Christ our Lord), also appears in the Pauline doxology in Rom. 16:27. The grammar of the doxology may be interpreted in more than one way. Is Jude saying that God is the Savior "through Jesus Christ our Lord" or that glory is given or ascribed to him "through Jesus Christ"? Most likely the latter is the case since the same construction appears in Rom. 16:27, where praise is raised "to the only wise God, through Jesus Christ" (NRSV). Moreover, the NT envisions Christ's mediatorial role in worship (Heb. 13:15; 1 Pet. 2:5; and cf. Rom. 15:16). All praise and honor are acceptable to God only through Christ, a fact that underscores God's transcendence.

In the Greek the doxology lacks a principal verb, and some form of "to be" must be supplied. Doxologies do not merely ascribe to God certain divine attributes, but rather also recognize and exalt aspects of God's person that are inherently his. Therefore, as Weima (1994: 138n1) notes, "The doxologies presuppose, therefore, the indicative ἐστί(ν) [*esti(n)*] rather than the optative εἴη [*eiē*], a fact confirmed by the presence of the indicative in the doxology of 1 Pet. 4:11" (BDF §128.5; G. Kittel, *TDNT* 2:248; contra Deichgräber 1967: 30–32). Where the verb is supplied in the doxology, the indicative rather than the optative mood is used (Rom. 1:25; 2 Cor. 11:31). "Glory" belongs to God, whether or not it is recognized by anyone. His attributes are not relative to culture or time but inherent in his person.

Jude exults in God's δόξα μεγαλωσύνη κράτος καὶ ἐξουσία (*doxa megalōsynē kratos kai exousia*, glory, majesty, might, and authority). The NT doxologies commonly exalt God's "glory" (except for 1 Tim. 6:16 and 1 Pet. 5:11), but only Jude's includes the praise of his "majesty" and "authority." While the exaltation of God's "might" is quite common in other NT doxologies (1 Tim. 6:16; 1 Pet. 4:11; 5:11; Rev. 1:6; 5:13), Jude does not include the common doxological element "honor" (τιμή, *timē* in 1 Tim. 1:17; 6:16; Rev. 5:13; 7:12). Jude's doxology is not a random collection of stereotypical language but rather a carefully selected locus of divine attributes that highlight his grandeur and ruling power. Neyrey is certainly correct in recognizing that God is acknowledged as Patron or Benefactor, with due honor ascribed to him (Neyrey 1993: 96–98), but Jude chooses to highlight specific divine attributes that are in concert with the purposes of his exposition.

God's "glory" (δόξα, *doxa*), already mentioned in verse 24 (see comments), comes from the Hebrew כָּבוֹד (*kābôd*), which "evokes the idea of weight" and "hence esteem or respect, especially power and wealth" (*TLNT* 1:364). The term has to do with God's dignity and the respect, reverence, and honor that are due him, although it may also point to his manifest presence (C. J. Collins, *NIDOTTE* 2:577–87). In this and other doxologies, it becomes the best word to summarize God's exalted position and therefore, in an honor/shame culture, evokes the recognition of his high status. How can one recognize his "honor" and then pervert his ways, as the heretics have done (v. 4)? The notion of God's preeminence is underscored as well by the following attribute, μεγαλωσύνη (*megalōsynē*). This term, used only of God in the NT (Heb. 1:3; 8:1), refers to his "greatness and preeminence," his "majesty" (BDAG 623). In 1 En. 14.16 it is used, in combination with "glory," to describe the grandeur of God's house: "And in every respect it excelled (the other)—in glory and great honor—to the extent that it is impossible for me to recount to you concerning its glory and greatness" (E. Isaac, *OTP* 1:21). "Majesty" shares semantic space with "glory," and this doubling contributes to the impression of God's overwhelming grandeur. These two attributes place in high relief the importance of not turning away from the One who holds the most honorable position. They therefore frame the whole moral argument of the epistle. To dishonor such a one would be unconscionable.

Jude then weaves in two attributes that focus on God's sovereign rule. God's "might" (κράτος, *kratos*) may mean his "power" (Acts 19:20; Eph. 1:19; 6:10; Col. 1:11) as demonstrated in his mighty deeds (Luke 1:51), but here it most likely focuses on his ruling power or sovereignty (Heb. 2:14; Josephus, *Ant.* 10.11.7 §263). Philo (*Spec. Laws* 1.56 §307) links his rule with his position as Benefactor (εὐεργέτης, *euergetēs*). Those who ruled, whether human or divine, were also benefactors. Coupled with this attribute is God's "authority" (ἐξουσία, *exousia*), which is exercised powerfully in his rule and dominion (Dan. 4:17; Luke 12:5; Acts 1:7; Eph. 1:19; 6:10; Col. 1:11; 1 Tim. 6:16; Rev. 1:6; 5:13; Josephus, *Ant.* 5.1.26 §109; 18.6.9 §214). Jude is careful to highlight God's ruling power, which not only points up the folly of perverting his grace (v. 4) but also forms the basis for his authority as the coming judge, a principal theme throughout this letter. God is the honorable one and is in control. The church should honor God and not follow the ways of the heretics. These indicative statements about God's authority and sovereignty have an imperatival illocutionary force. Adoration and ethics clasp hands.

Of all the NT doxologies, Jude's has the most extensive indication of time: πρὸ παντὸς τοῦ αἰῶνος καὶ νῦν καὶ εἰς πάντας τοὺς αἰῶνας (*pro pantos tou aiōnos kai nyn kai eis pantas tous aiōnas*, before all the ages, now, and for all the ages). The attributes of God that Jude has described and praised are not mutable characteristics but are inherently God's throughout all time. In a world of change and decay, this declaration of the immutable nature of God is more than the human mind can comprehend. God's is the "glory, majesty, might, and authority" before time began. The expression "before all the ages" is found only here in the NT (though cf. 1 Cor. 2:7 with Ps. 55:19 [54:20 LXX]; 2 Tim. 1:9; Titus 1:2, which have πρὸ χρόνων αἰωνίων, *pro chronōn aiōnōn*, before the times of the ages). God did not acquire these attributes at some point and therefore become more than he once was, but these were God's from before the ages came into being, before creation. Moreover, what God was before all time he is now: καὶ νῦν καὶ (*kai nyn kai*, both now and), found only here and in 2 Pet. 3:18. This "now" may be a reference to the present moment when Jude writes, but couched as it is between "before time began" and "for all the ages," it likely refers to the present age (νῦν αἰών, *nyn aiōn*, in 1 Tim. 6:17; 2 Tim. 4:10; Titus 2:12), between the creation and the final consummation. What God was before time God is in time. His character will endure throughout eternity: εἰς πάντας τοὺς αἰῶνας (*eis pantas tous aiōnas*, for all the ages).

The eternal duration of God's attributes is usually expressed by εἰς τοὺς αἰῶνας τῶν αἰώνων (*eis tous aiōnas tōn aiōnōn*, unto the ages of the ages; as in Gal. 1:5; Phil. 4:20; 1 Tim. 1:17; 2 Tim. 4:18; Heb. 13:21; 1 Pet. 4:11; Rev. 1:6; 5:13; 7:12), or the simpler εἰς τοὺς αἰῶνας (*eis tous aiōnas*, unto the ages; as in Rom. 11:36; 16:27; 1 Pet. 5:11; and see the other variations in Eph. 3:21; 1 Tim. 6:16). Jude has already mentioned the eternal judgment of the heretics (v. 13), and here the assurance comes that God will be sovereign throughout that never-ending age. What is truly unique about Jude's time reference is that it covers past, present, and future. From ages past (we sing, "O, God our help in ages past"), now in this present (evil) age ("Our shelter from the stormy blast"), and for all the ages ("Our hope for years to come, . . . And our eternal home," Isaac Watts), God's character endures. God is honorable and sovereign from eternity past through eternity future, and in the present, which touches all that has been and all that is to come. Now is never severed from the past and the future, and this is the moment in which Jude and his readers live. The windows are thrown open to see the glory of God, which transcends all others and all time. Awe, reverence, and obedience are the proper responses of worship.

The letter ends with a cymbal crash: Amen! (ἀμήν, *amēn*). The response confirms what has already been stated, in prayers, benedictions, and doxologies, as here. The idea conveyed by this affirmation may be understood as "So be it!" or "It is indeed true!" (Deut. 27:15–26; 1 Kings 1:36; Pss. 41:13 [40:14 LXX]; 72:19 [71:19 LXX]; Jdt. 13:20; 3 Macc. 7:23; 4 Macc. 18:24; Matt. 6:13; Rom. 1:25; 9:5; 16:27; 1 Pet. 4:11; J. H. Elliott 2000: 22). Commonly, NT doxologies end with this affirmation. As the letter is read to the gathered believers, Jude's hope is for the congregation to join in and recite the "Amen!" (1 Cor. 14:16; 1 Chron. 16:36; Neh. 5:13; 1 Esd. 9:47; Tob. 8:8), thereby affirming again their faith in this God and commitment to his way alone.

# Introduction to 2 Peter

## Authorship of 2 Peter

The author of 2 Peter introduces himself in 1:1 as Peter, an apostle of Jesus Christ ("Simeon Peter, slave and apostle of Jesus Christ"). At various points within this letter, he supplements this identification by alluding to incidents in Peter's life, some of which were apparently known to the letter's first readers and which are also familiar to anyone who has read the Gospel narratives. In 1:17–18 he recalls his experience with the Lord Jesus on the Mount of Transfiguration (Matt. 17:1–5; Mark 9:2–7; Luke 9:28–35). The author also betrays a consciousness of his imminent demise due to the prophecy given him by the Lord (1:14), this being most likely a reference to the prophecy recorded in the Gospel of John (21:18–19). The identification of the letter with Peter is underscored in 2 Pet. 3:1, where the author declares this to be the "second letter" he is writing to these recipients, the first most likely being 1 Peter. Finally, the author presents himself as a companion in ministry with Paul, and he places his own teachings on a par with those of the apostle to the gentiles (3:15–16). The author intends that his readers will recognize this letter as an authentic work of the principal apostle, Peter.

However, not a few in both ancient and modern times have questioned the authenticity of the letter. They declare this to be a pseudonymous writing, possibly written during the second century, which placed the name of Peter in the opening greeting and added the personal notes enumerated above as part of the mechanism of pseudepigraphy. As Bauckham (1988c: 3719) states, "The Petrine authorship of 2 Peter has long been disputed, but only since the beginning of this century has the pseudepigraphical character of the work come to be almost universally recognized." Bauckham's 1988 assessment holds true to this day, despite the attempts by a number of scholars to defend the traditional view of Petrine authorship (Bigg 1901; E. Green 1959; J. A. T. Robinson 1976; M. Green 1987; Guthrie 1990; G. Green 1993; Moo 1996; J. Charles 1997; Waltner and J. Charles 1999; Kruger 1999; Schreiner 2003). The arguments forwarded to affirm the authenticity of the letter have not received a favorable hearing, and the failure to convince cannot be fully ascribed to entrenched skepticism. Current literature mirrors the unevenness of the letter's reception in the early church and the ancient concerns voiced about its origin. The contemporary reader must on one hand decide whether the arguments against the book's authenticity are cogent, and on the other whether there is sufficient warrant to affirm that the letter came from Peter.

### 2 Peter in the Early Church

Schelkle (1980: 182) observes that 2 Peter is not mentioned in any second-century document (so Kümmel 1975: 433). Perkins (1995: 160) concurs with this assessment: "The first clear evidence of 2 Peter in early Christian authors does not appear until the third century C.E." Most critical scholars who reject Petrine authorship, however, tend not to engage in detailed analysis of the evidence from the early church, Schelkle's (1980: 182–83) and Bauckham's (1983: 162–63) brief discussions being noteworthy exceptions. On the other hand, Chase (1900: 799–802), Bigg (1901: 199–215), E. Green (1959: 5–10; 1987: 13–17), Picirelli (1988), Guthrie (1990: 805–11), Kruger (1999: 649–56), and Schreiner (2003: 262–64) have presented early evidence, starting from the second century, and have argued for at least a limited use of the book starting in the second century (see also the list of allusions in Mayor 1907: cxv–cxxiii, cxxx–cxxxiv). After examining the earliest evidence from the fathers, even Bauckham, who rejects Petrine authorship, states: "There is better evidence than is sometimes admitted for the fact that 2 Peter existed in the second century" (1983: 162). The evidence in favor of the letter's authenticity, however, is decidedly weaker than that for any other accepted writing but, on the other hand, stronger than for the writings rejected as spurious (J. A. T. Robinson 1976: 188). Was this letter well known and recognized as authentic and authoritative in the earliest years of the church?

If we were to conclude that 2 Peter was prior to Jude, Jude itself would be the earliest witness for the use of this book. Bigg (1901: 216–24) argues precisely this point, but the priority of 2 Peter does not find support in contemporary scholarship (see "The Relationship between 2 Peter and Jude" below). This tide may go out some day in the ebb and flow of academic debate, and if that occurs, new perspectives will come into play regarding the authenticity of 2 Peter (see Moo 1996: 17–18).

Eusebius (ca. 260–ca. 339) records some of the earliest perspectives on the Petrine literature as well as presenting the evaluation of these books in his own day. Of the Petrine Epistles, he accepted only 1 Peter as authentic, and in his list of undisputed books, he observes that "the ancient presbyters used this in their own writings as unquestioned." His assessment of the early reception of 2 Peter was quite different: "The so-called second Epistle we have not received as canonical, but nevertheless it has appeared useful to many, and has been studied with other Scriptures" (*Eccl. Hist.* 3.3.1). But he comments on the books that bear Peter's name, such as the Acts, Gospel, Preaching, and Revelation, and rejects them, "for no orthodox writer of the ancient time or of our own has used their testimonies" (*Eccl. Hist.* 3.3.2). He then positions 2 Peter between these books and the received 1 Peter, concluding, "Now the above are the books bearing the name of Peter, of which I recognize only one as genuine and admitted by the presbyters of old" (*Eccl. Hist.* 3.3.4). He classifies 2 Peter, along with James, Jude, and 2 and 3 John among the "disputed books," which were "nevertheless known to most" (*Eccl. Hist.* 3.25.3). Second Peter keeps good company in Eusebius's list of disputed books since all these documents were finally received into the canon. Eusebius alerts us to the early doubts about 2 Peter but, at the same time, demonstrates the book's presence and use within the second century.

The use of 2 Peter by 1 Clement (ca. 96) and 2 Clement (ca. 140–160) has been the matter of some debate, with Picirelli (1988: 58–65) giving a positive assessment of the evidence, Hagner (1973: 246–48) expressing skepticism about the letter's use by 1 Clement, and Donfried (1974: 90–91, 151) affirming 2 Clement's dependency on the book. Most of the allusions cited by Picirelli are easily attributable to the common language of the early church. However, the way Clement tells the Lot story (1 Clem. 11), placing emphasis on God's ability to save Lot while delivering the unrighteous to punishment, is strikingly similar to 2 Pet. 2:7–10. Bauckham (1983: 284) also presents a detailed examination of the parallel between 1 Clem. 23.3; 2 Clem. 11.2; and 2 Pet. 3:4, which expresses the doubts of the heretics regarding the parousia. He regards the similarity of "ideas and terminology" as evidence that all three writings made use of a common source. The parallels between 2 Pet. 3:4; 1 Clem. 23.3; and 2 Clem. 11.2 are indeed strong[1] but are best accounted for by the assumption that these letters knew 2 Peter rather than postulating an otherwise unknown apocalyptic source (see Gerdmar 2001: 199–203). The reference to the "double-minded" in the quotations does not come directly from 2 Peter (cf. James 1:8; 4:8), but these words aptly describe the wretchedness of those who once knew the Lord and then turned back. Quotations of ancient texts were not made with precision since they served as reminders of what one already knew. In fact, paraphrase was preferred over "rote iteration" (Ferguson 2002: 299). It appears that 1 and 2 Clement assume that the readers knew the story from 2 Peter echoed in these texts. 1 Clement identifies the written source as "Scripture," and 2 Clement calls it "the prophetic word." It is unlikely that some otherwise unknown source would be granted such a high place of honor during this period (cf. 2 Pet. 3:16).

---

1. Second Peter 3:4: "and saying, 'Where is the promise of his coming? Because since the time the fathers died, all things remain as they were from the beginning of creation.'"

First Clement 23.3: "Let this Scripture be far from us in which he says 'Wretched are the double-minded, who doubt in their soul and say, "We have heard these things even in the days of our fathers, and behold we have grown old, and none of these things has happened to us."'"

Second Clement 11.2: "For the prophetic word also says: —'Miserable are the double-minded that doubt in their heart, who say, "These things we heard long ago and in the time of our fathers, but we have waited from day to day, and have seen none of them."'"

Picirelli's catalog of parallels between 2 Peter and the writings of Ignatius, Polycarp, and Hermas (1988: 65–74) do not commend themselves as anything more than similarities reflecting the common language of the early Christian communities. However, the Epistle of Barnabas (written sometime between 70 and 150) contains one striking parallel to 2 Peter, although the rest of the Barnabas citations that Picirelli lists do not merit attention. Speaking of creation and the ages, Barn. 15.4 states, "For a day with him means a thousand years. And he himself is my witness when he says, 'Lo, the day of the Lord shall be as a thousand years.'" The most likely source, or his "witness," is 2 Pet. 3:8. Irenaeus likewise quotes the verse (*Haer.* 5.23.2, "for since 'a day of the Lord is as a thousand years'"; ca. 130–ca. 200). These writers couch the reference to 2 Pet. 3:8 in terms indicating that they regarded the source as authoritative.

The most striking attestation of 2 Peter comes from the apocryphal Apocalypse of Peter (ca. 132–135; see J. A. Robinson and James 1892; Buchholz 1988; Schneemelcher 1991–92: 2.620–38). This book should not be confused with the later gnostic work found at Nag Hammadi, which goes by the same name. Two fragments of the early Christian Apocalypse of Peter in Greek have survived along with the more complete Ethiopic translation. The unknown author of this work was a thoroughgoing apocalypticist who found 2 Peter congenial to his purposes. The Greek (called the Akhmim) text declares, "Many of them shall be false prophets and shall teach ways and diverse doctrines of perdition. And they shall become sons of perdition" (1–2; Schneemelcher 1991–92: 2.633). The first lines of the text echo 2 Pet. 2:1 ("There were false prophets among the people as even there will be false teachers among you, who will bring in heresies of destruction"). As 2 Pet. 1:18, the Apoc. Pet. 4 speaks of going up to the mount, and both documents refer to leaving the way and the way being maligned (2 Pet. 2:2, 15, 21; Apoc. Pet. 22–23; see also Mayor 1907: cxxx–cxxxiv). As Bauckham notes, the use of 2 Peter by the Apocalypse of Peter "is sufficient to rule out a late date for 2 Peter" (1983: 162).

Another early witness to 2 Peter is Clement of Alexandria's *Letter to Theodorus*. The book appears to allude to 2 Pet. 2:19 ("Although they promise them freedom, they themselves are slaves of corruption") in 1.7 ("Boasting that they are free, they have become slaves of servile desires," καὶ καυχώμενοι ἐλευθέρους εἶναι· δοῦλοι γεγόνασιν ἀνδραποδώδων ἐπιθυμιῶν, *kai kauxōmenoi eleutherous einai: douloi gegonasin andrapodōdōn epithymiōn*; M. Smith 1973: 446, 448). If this letter is authentic, it would provide further evidence of Clement's use of the book at the end of the second century. Eusebius (*Eccl. Hist.* 6.14.1) also includes a significant note about the writings of Clement of Alexandria (ca. 150–ca. 215), who, he said, wrote "concise explanations of all the Canonical Scriptures, not passing over even the disputed writings, I mean the Epistle of Jude and the remaining Catholic Epistles." Clement's commentary on 2 Peter has not survived, nor have his writings on the Epistle of Barnabas and the Apocalypse of Peter. Second Peter is not listed in the

Muratorian Fragment, which most likely comes from the second century as well.[2] The surviving fragment, however, is not complete, and conclusions based on the extant text should be held with caution.

The rather weak attestation of the letter during the second century continues on into the third. Origen (ca. 185–ca. 254), in fact, states, "And Peter, on whom the Church of Christ is built, . . . has left one acknowledged epistle, and, it may be, a second also; for it is doubted" (Eusebius, *Eccl. Hist.* 6.25.8; Origen, *Commentary on John* 5.3). Origen does not forward any reasons for this doubt, yet his own assessment is quite positive. In his *Homilies on Joshua*, he says, "Even Peter cries out with trumpets in two of his epistles," and he called the letter "*scriptura*" (*Homilies on Numbers* 6.676). Second Peter finds a place in the early-third-century Sahidic version from Egypt as well as $\mathfrak{P}^{72}$. Methodius (died ca. 311) in his *De resurrectione* explicitly quotes 2 Pet. 3:8 and attributes the words to Peter. In his letter to Cyprian (*Ep.* 75.6), Firmilian of Caesarea refers to 2 Peter's attack on the heretics. The doubts about the letter's genuineness that Origen noted are reflected in the rather weak attestation to this book during the third century.

The debate about the epistle's authenticity intensified during the fourth century. The book found a place in many canons, including those of Laodicea (AD 360), Athanasius (ca. 296–373), Cyril of Jerusalem (ca. 315–387), Mommsen or Cheltenham (AD 359), Apostolic (ca. 350–380), Gregory of Nazianzus (ca. 390), Africa (ca. 393–419), Jerome (ca. 345–420), and Carthage (AD 397). At the very end of the fourth century, Augustine noted his acceptance of 2 Peter. However, precisely during this period Eusebius classified 2 Peter as one of the "disputed" books, which were, however, "known to most" (*Eccl. Hist.* 3.25.3), having been widely circulated. Jerome's comments are some of the most instructive coming from this period. He states, "The apostles James, Peter, John and Jude, have published seven epistles" (*Ep.* 53.9), but in his *Letter to Hebidia* (*Ep.* 120.11), he acknowledges that there were suspicions regarding 2 Peter. Speaking first of Paul, he remarks, "He, therefore, had Titus as an interpreter just as the blessed Peter also had Mark, whose Gospel was composed with Peter narrating and him writing. Further, two epistles also, which are extant as of Peter, are discrepant among themselves in style and character and structure of the words, from which we understand that he used different interpreters as necessary." Jerome is the first to forward this explanation of the stylistic differences between 1 and 2 Peter. His comment names the reason why some in his era were reluctant to accept 2 Peter as authentic. We may assume that doubts about the book's authenticity in earlier centuries were founded on similar concerns, giving rise to the weak early attestation that Eusebius noted. Although stylistic issues may not have been the sole reason for the concern about 2 Peter, this is the only explanation offered by any ancient author.

2. For a summary of the debate regarding whether the Muratorian Fragment comes from the second or fourth century, and a defense of the early date, see Verheyden 2003. The late date has been supported by Sundberg (1973) and Hahneman (1992) and McDonald (1995: 209–20).

The evidence from the early centuries of the church in favor of the authenticity of 2 Peter is not robust, but neither is it sufficiently weak to preclude the possibility of Petrine authorship. The book was used early and widely and, although doubts did exist, the letter was never classified as spurious and eventually found its way into the major canons. Jerome was the sole author to comment on the reason for the reluctance of some to accept the book, citing the stylistic problems. Although apostolicity was the issue that generated Eusebius's doubts, he acknowledged the book's use and, as the evidence shows, its catholicity and antiquity were never questioned. Ancient skepticism about the book did not have the final word. One lesson from antiquity is that acceptance or rejection of the book as authentic should not be a test for orthodoxy.

## Contemporary Assessment of the Authenticity of 2 Peter

The majority in the global church regard 2 Peter as an authentic work of the apostle Peter, although most within the academy have raised their voices against this traditional ascription. As Harrington observes, "Few interpreters today accept the text's claim that 2 Peter was composed directly by the apostle Peter" (Senior and Harrington 2003: 235). They would concur with Kümmel, who states, "*But this letter cannot have been written by Peter*" (1975: 430, emphasis his). This assessment has become canonical, yet the cords of the argument against authenticity are not binding.

Second Peter has been rejected as authentic due to its use of Jude (see "The Relationship between 2 Peter and Jude," below). Kümmel (1975: 431) states the argument succinctly: "Since Jude belongs to the postapostolic age, Peter cannot have written II Pet." However, recent studies of Jude have, in fact, upheld the authenticity of that letter (see "Authorship of Jude" in the introduction to Jude). If Jude was truly written by the half brother of Jesus and the brother of James (Jude 1), then 2 Peter could come from the apostolic period. However, since 2 Peter engages in *imitatio* (μίμησις, *mimēsis*) of Jude (see "The Relationship between 2 Peter and Jude," below), we may rightly ask questions about the social status of the author of 2 Peter in relation to Jude. *Imitatio* was carried out with reference to texts considered canonical (standard texts of ancient literature) and implies a secondary position for the one who copies. This dependence places the author of 2 Peter on a level under Jude, a surprising relationship, given the place of Peter in the early church. However, as suggested below, Jude's place as a member of the family of Jesus gave him a position of special honor within the early church, which would be reflected in Peter's use of his letter.

Since Jerome, the language and style of 2 Peter have been cited as evidence against Petrine authorship. The letter contains a considerable number of hapax legomena and the "list of *hapax legomena* includes enough extremely rare words to show that the author is widely read, and fond of rather literary and poetic, even obscure words" (Bauckham 1983: 136). As Bauckham (1983: 158–59) notes, "The language alone . . . makes it improbable that Peter could have written 2 Peter, while the author's preference for Hellenistic terminology

... can only implausibly be attributed to Peter." Kümmel (1975: 432) notes that language such as "divine power" (1:3), "virtue" (1:3), "knowledge" (1:2, 3, 6, 8; 2:20; 3:18), "participation in the divine nature" (1:4), and "eyewitnesses" (1:16) are Hellenistic concepts (Schelkle 1980: 180). So marked is the Hellenistic influence that it "rule[s] out Peter definitely" (Kümmel 1975: 431). Moreover, the style and conceptual world of 2 Peter are so distinct from that of 1 Peter that we must assume that these books were written by two different hands. Whereas 1 Peter will speak of the "revelation" of Jesus Christ (1:7, 13; 4:13; 5:1), 2 Peter refers to this event as his parousia or "coming" (1:16; 3:4) and "the day of the Lord" (3:10). First Peter describes God's redemption as "the salvation of your souls" (1:9), but 2 Peter prefers to speak of "entry into the eternal kingdom" (1:11; see Kelly 1969: 236). Although 1 Peter cites the OT extensively, OT quotations are scarce in 2 Peter (Schelkle 1980: 181; Kümmel 1975: 430). And although 2 Peter refers to the first letter (3:1), "there is virtually no intersection between the content of 2 Peter and 1 Peter; . . . the two epistles display radically different styles and language" (Kraftchick 2002: 76). Kelly (1969: 236) rejects Jerome's explanation for the differences between 1 and 2 Peter: "His theory that they are to be accounted for by a change of amanuensis fails to explain the altogether different atmosphere of the two writings."

The style and vocabulary of 2 Peter plus the differences between 1 and 2 Peter are not sufficient warrant to reject the authenticity of 2 Peter. We simply do not possess a large enough corpus of Petrine literature to determine what Peter could or could not have written. The same author could in one instance refer to Christ's "revelation" and in another to his "coming." The use of Hellenistic terminology as an argument against authenticity is suspect since, though an author may use terms appearing in that milieu, this does not necessarily mean that he was indebted to the concepts as they were framed in that environment (Gerdmar 2001: 332–34). Many of the texts that betray a decidedly "Hellenistic" viewpoint were also quite at home in a Jewish environment, which was not hermetically sealed against Hellenistic language and thought (see, e.g., the comments on 1:3–4, 16). The way the author of 2 Peter uses the OT is different from 1 Peter, with the latter preferring direct quotations. But 2 Peter is heavily influenced by Jude's summaries of OT narrative, and the author does occasionally allude to OT teaching (2:22; 3:8). Whether or not the author of 2 Peter knows and reflects the content of 1 Peter is a matter of some debate (cf., e.g., Boobyer 1959; Witherington 1985; Gilmore 2002: 91–95). However, 2 Pet. 3:1 acknowledges 1 Peter (see comments) and, as Gilmore (2002: 95) comments, "signaling knowledge of a writing does not necessarily mean that influence or dependence should be expected." Moreover, some of the differences between 1 and 2 Peter can be accounted for by the varied situations they address (M. Green 1987: 20–21; Schreiner 2003: 265). But this explanation cannot account for the sum of the stylistic problems and, as Jerome noted, Peter likely used a different secretary for both letters (1 Pet. 5:12). He may have even written the second letter without aid, although this suggestion is less likely. The stylistic issue is not strong enough to preclude apostolic authorship. Although Bauckham tags 2 Peter as pseudonymous, he does so on grounds other than linguistic, reckoning that this evidence "would be consistent with a secretary hypothesis in which the secretary is not Peter's amanuensis but his agent" (1983: 159). Can we explain the differences between 1 and 2 Peter, in addition to the unique style of 2 Peter, by recurring to the secretary hypothesis?

That Peter was in need of linguistic help was a fact well known in the early church. Thorough knowledge of Greek was not as widespread in Galilee as is sometimes thought (see "Authorship of Jude" in the introduction to Jude), and the ability to write well was not universal by any means. Scribes were commonly employed to aid in the composition of letters at all levels of society (White 1986: 215–16). The ancient witness regarding Peter indicates that he got by with a little help from his friends. Mark was identified as one of Peter's interpreters (Eusebius, *Eccl. Hist.* 3.39.15; Jerome, *Letter to Hebidia* [*Ep.*] 120.11), as was a certain Glaucias (Clement of Alexandria, *Strom.* 7.17). First Peter 5:12 names Silvanus as Peter's amanuensis and not simply the messenger who carries the letter ("through Silvanus I wrote *briefly*"). While we can be certain that Peter needed and used such help, the role that an amanuensis could have played in composition is not examined in the literature with any detail, either by the detractors or defenders of Petrine authorship. E. Richards (1991: 23–67; 2004: 64–80), on the other hand, has demonstrated that the responsibilities of ancient secretaries varied and could be categorized in three different ways. The secretary could take verbatim dictation, with the author dictating the letter either *syllabatim*, syllable by syllable, or viva voce, at the speed of normal speech. To accomplish the latter, the secretary would need to be adept at tachygraphy, or shorthand. This practice was well known, both in Latin and Greek. Suetonius, for example, comments about the emperor Titus, "I have heard from many sources that he used also to write shorthand with great speed and would amuse himself by playful contests with his secretaries" (*Divus Titus* 3.2). Second, an author could speak at the rate of normal speech while the secretary took notes, or the author could give a rough draft to the secretary, who then edited the letter. In both these cases, the secretary became an editor of the final draft. Cicero mentions his secretary Tiro on various occasions and, in a letter to him, remarks, "Without you, I am altogether dumb. Please be ready to render due service to our Muses" (*Fam.* 16.10.2). Elsewhere he notes that his services "are past all reckoning—at home, in the forum, in the City, in my province, in private as in public affairs, in my literary pursuits and performances" (16.4.3; see also 16.11.1). The extent of the editing could be either small or great. Third, the secretary could serve as a composer. Cicero, for example, asked Atticus to write for him and under Cicero's name: "I should like you to write in my name to Basilius and to anyone else you like, even to Servilius, and say whatever you think fit" (*Att.* 11.5; 3.15; 11.2). Philostratus shows awareness that a person or the person's delegate could be responsible for a letter when he mentions "Brutus or the person Brutus employed to write his letters" (Malherbe 1988: 42–43).

Given this broad range of secretarial practices, from taking dictation to editing and beyond to composition, it becomes impossible to say what kind of style Peter could or could not have used. The liberty that could be afforded a secretary as an editor or composer did not mean that the secretary acted as a free agent, since the responsibility for the contents remained that of the author. The custom was to check the secretary's work (Cicero, *Fam.* 5.20). However, at times the secretary might not represent the author accurately, and this could be the source of some pain (E. Richards 1991: 53–56). Jerome's statement, therefore, holds. Peter could have used different secretaries in writing 1 and 2 Peter, and the stylistic features of 2 Peter cannot be invoked as evidence against the letter's authenticity. We may well suppose, however, that Peter approved the contents and, as was the custom, included the final greeting of the letter in his own hand. Surviving ancient Greek letters show the change of hand at the end of the letter but do not commonly signal in the text that the author has taken pen to hand (cf. Gal. 6:11; 2 Thess. 3:17; Deissmann 1911: 170–73, 179–80; Stowers 1986: 60–61; Weima 1994: 119).

According to some critics of Petrine authorship, 2 Peter contains a number of historical references that mitigate against the authenticity of the letter. For example, the expression of the heretics in 3:4, "since the time the fathers died," suggests that the letter was written in response to a problem that arose after the death of the first generation of Christians (cf. 1 Clem. 23.3; 2 Clem. 11.2). Moreover, in 3:2 the author speaks of "your apostles," an expression that views the apostles as a group to which the author does not belong (Schelkle 1980: 181; Kelly 1969: 354). In 3:16, the author refers to a Pauline corpus of letters, which are elevated to the level of "Scripture," another indication that this book was written in the postapostolic age (Richard 2000: 308). But, as will be argued in the commentary proper, the "fathers" of 3:4 was not a common way to speak of the first generation of Christians but was routinely used both within and outside the Jewish community to refer to ancestors. In 3:2 "your apostles" are simply those who spoke the gospel to the readers of the letter, the apostles who preached in Asia Minor (see comments on 3:2). Also, the collection of Paul's letters (3:16 and comments) reflects the common practice of copying and collecting letters, by both authors and recipients. That Paul's letters were regarded as "Scripture" should not surprise us since Paul considered that he was guided by the Spirit and, moreover, he was universally regarded as an "apostle," an authoritative messenger of Christ. Jesus's words were regarded as "Scripture" from early in the life of the church, and the broadening of the concept to include the writings of an apostle is a development that cannot be excluded from this very period (3:16 and comments) .

Earlier discussions of the authorship of 2 Peter identified the heresy against which the author fought as gnosticism. As Käsemann said, "More precisely, we have to do with gnostics. As gnostics, they proclaim the message of redemption under the slogan 'Freedom from the transitory,' to which allusion is made in 2.19" (Käsemann 1982: 171). These knew themselves to be superior to angelic powers (2:10–11), were not subject to ecclesial or civic ordinances or the powers of this age, paid no heed to Christian eschatology (Käsemann 1982: 171–72), and placed special emphasis on esoteric knowledge (*gnōsis*), to which Peter gives his counterpoint (1:5–6; 3:18; and *epignōsis* in 1:2, 3, 8; 2:20; Schelkle 1980: 217–18). Kümmel (1975: 432) concludes, "II Pet is therefore aimed against a movement which bears the essential features of second-century gnosis." But recent discussions on the setting of 2 Peter have not upheld the view that the author is engaged in battle against second-century gnosticism. Absent is any evidence that the opponents embraced gnostic dualism, with its attendant denial of the direct creation of the material world by God and its skepticism regarding the resurrection. The promise of "liberty" that character- ized the heretics is not a marker for gnosticism (see 2:19 and comments) but was rather an offer held out by most philosophies during the era. Moreover, "knowledge" in 2 Peter is always about personal knowledge of God and Jesus Christ (1:2–3, 8; 2:20; 3:18), and at no point does Peter present such knowledge as a counterpoint to a heretical doctrine of *gnōsis* (Bauckham 1983: 156–57). The opponents are indeed difficult to identify, but their doctrine does not betray the characteristics of second-century gnostic thought (see "The Op- ponents in 2 Peter," below).

Käsemann (1982: 169) also forwarded the argument that 2 Peter was an example of early Catholicism and thus was a document representative of the postapostolic era, coming from the middle of the second century (172; Küm- mel 1975: 433). In his critique of the supposed "early Catholic viewpoint" of 2 Peter, Fornberg (1977: 3–4) conveniently summarizes its fundamental features: "The faith as consent to a collection of tenets [*fides quae creditur*], the inspiration of the Scriptures, the idea of the Canon, the theology of the priesthood, the doctrine of the sacraments, the struggle against heresies, and consequently the claim to represent the only true exposition of the Scriptures together with the abandonment of eschatology as the focus of faith." To this list should be added the faded eschatological hope and the emphasis on the ecclesiastical office. But 2 Peter does not hold up the office of the bishop as the antidote to heresy, nor is discussion about the delay of the parousia itself a marker for early Catholic thought. In fact, questions about the delay of the parousia go back to the first century (Matt. 25:1–13; Luke 12:35–40; Heb. 10:36–37; James 5:7–8; see Bauckham 1981). Instead of Christianity being crystallized into nothing more than "orthodox doctrinal tradition" marked by *epignōsis* or *gnōsis* (2 Pet. 1:2; 3:18; so Käsemann 1982: 193), Peter's em- phasis is on the personal knowledge of Jesus Christ and the reception of the gospel (1:2, 8, 12, and comments). Käsemann's argument did not win the day, and contemporary commentators tend not to rally around this flag (for the critique, see especially J. H. Elliott 1969; Marshall 1974; Fornberg 1977: 3–6; Bauckham 1983: 151–53).

Kümmel identified 2 Peter as a "testament of Peter" (1975: 433; Grundmann 1974: 55–56), and Bauckham developed this observation into the mainstay of his argument against the authenticity of the letter (1983: 159–62; 1988b). Bauckham's thesis has convinced numerous scholars and become a mainstay in the discussion of authorship. Kraftchick (2002: 75–76) summarizes the current state of scholarship: "The fictive 'farewell testament' suggests that 2 Peter is pseudonymous, as acknowledged by almost every modern New Testament scholar" (Paulsen 1992: 89–90; Neyrey 1993: 112; Chester and R. P. Martin 1994: 139–40; Vögtle 1994: 161–62; Craddock 1995a: 91–92; Horrell 1998: 136; Richard 2000: 310–11; Senior and Harrington 2003: 236). Second Peter presents itself as a farewell discourse of the apostle (1:12–15; 3:1–2) and the adoption of this testamentary genre marks the letter as pseudepigraphic. The book would therefore come from a "Petrine circle," and its intent was to defend "the apostolic message in the postapostolic age" (Bauckham 1983: 161). The use of the genre was a transparent fiction, according to Bauckham, and so "the pseudepigraphical device is therefore not a fraudulent means of claiming apostolic authority, but embodies a claim to be a faithful mediator of the apostolic message. Recognizing the canonicity of 2 Peter means recognizing the validity of that claim" (161–62). The church, then, eventually recognized the "apostolic content" of the book as it was received into the canon. The letter, however, mixes prophecies about the coming of the heretics (as in 2:1–3) with references to them in the past tense (as 2:10–22), indicating that the pseudepigrapher could not sustain his guise throughout the whole letter.

The question of pseudepigraphy and canon has been given considerable attention (Farkasfalvy 1985–86; Meade 1987; Baum 2001; McDonald and Sanders 2002; Wilder 2004), but the position that a document known to be pseudonymous would have been received into the canon is not entirely secured. Moreover, as argued elsewhere (see "Genre and Structure," below), 2 Peter does not follow the conventions of the testamentary genre and is quite dissimilar to known testaments. However, few have challenged Bauckham's identification of the book as a testament (J. Charles 1997: 45–75), with some affirming that the book is a testament but not for that reason pseudepigraphic (M. Green 1987: 35–36; Moo 1996: 64–65). If the letter only contains testamentary material but does not belong to the genre of "testament," one of the major contemporary arguments against the book's authenticity cannot stand. The combination of the future and past tenses with regard to the heretics, said to be part of the pseudepigrapher's art in the composition of this ostensive testament, will be addressed in the commentary. Here the question may be raised regarding whether a pseudepigrapher would have been so clumsy on this point, especially since he acknowledges that the heretics are feasting with the church (2:13)—a fact known both to the author and readers! As M. Green (1987: 104n1) observes, a similar combination of present and future tenses when speaking of the false teachers appears in 2 Timothy (cf. 1:15; 2:18, 25; 3:5; and 2:16–17; 3:2–9; 4:3–4), and this "combination of future and present is intended to stress the correspondence between prophecy and event. In both cases in 2 Peter where the future is used, it is in immediate juxtaposition to references to the prophets (1:19–2:3; 3:3–4)."

The final argument against Petrine authorship is the use of numerous personal allusions. Kümmel (1975: 433, 430) is of the opinion that "the pseudonymity in II Pet is carried through consistently by means of heavy stress on the Petrine authorship." The letter is replete with references to Peter's life, including the knowledge of his imminent demise (1:12–15), reference to the transfiguration (1:16–18), the note about his first letter (3:1), and the ascription of the letter to Simeon Peter (1:1). But if the author were a pseudepigrapher, we may wonder why certain details from the Gospel narrative were not included, such as the divine call to "listen to him" (Matt. 17:5 and par.), the appearance of Moses and Elijah (Matt. 17:3 and par.), and Peter's desire to put up three tents (Matt. 17:4 and par.; see J. A. T. Robinson 1976: 177). On the other hand, the reference to the "holy mountain" finds no parallel in the Gospel narrative. The inclusion of autobiographical details was commonplace, both in 1 Peter (5:1) and in Paul's letters (1 Cor. 15:8, 32; 2 Cor. 6:3–10; 11:16–28; Gal. 1:11–2:14; etc.). Our author advances his argument by means of these personal allusions (see comments). They are threads in the fabric of his argument and not superfluous. The transfiguration is presented to seal his argument about the coming of the Lord (1:16–17), while the reference to his death (1:14) is included to explain, in part, the urgency of the correspondence. The allusion in 1:14 need not be a reference to the text of John 21:18–19 but could just as well have been a personal reminiscence of the author. Indeed, the note that his demise would come soon argues against such dependency since John includes no similar note. On the other hand, the use of the personal name "Simeon Peter" (1:1) argues in favor of authenticity since it does not appear in 1 Peter (which the author knew, according to 2 Pet. 3:1) and since second-century writers call Peter by this name. Elsewhere in the NT, we hear it for Peter only in Acts 15:14. A pseudepigrapher would have used the more common "Simon Peter."

The contemporary objections to Petrine authorship are not without their weaknesses, and we must not allow the volume of opinion to decide the case (see the discussion on the authorship of the Pastoral Epistles in L. Johnson 2001: 20–90). The verdict of the early church was ambiguous at first, but the problem of literary style in comparison to 1 Peter accounts for the early doubts. The book was used early and, according to early witnesses, used widely. The book is decidedly dissimilar to later literature that went under the name of Peter, such as the Acts of Peter, the Preaching of Peter, the gnostic Apocalypse of Peter, and even the early-second-century Apocalypse of Peter. The concerns raised within the letter fit well within the struggles of the church of the first century, and we may reasonably affirm that Simeon Peter, the apostle, authored the book. The letter stands within the circle of early Christian theology and serves as a witness to the struggles and dangers that the faith faced during its youngest years.

## The Opponents in 2 Peter

The first readers of this letter faced a problem decidedly different from that marked out in 1 Peter. Whereas the recipients of the first Petrine Epistle were facing hostility and social rejection because of their faith (1 Pet. 1:6; 2:12, 15, 20; 3:6, 13–22; 4:1, 12–19), those who first heard and read this letter were facing heretical perspectives, both theological and moral, brought into the community by false teachers (2 Pet. 2:1). These threatened the stability of many. Peter responds to the threat with a sense of urgency (1:5, 10, 15), knowing that the false teachers are trying to draw members of the congregations into their error. They are apostates and are bringing others to the same end. The danger appears to have arisen from within the churches and not from outside the gathered Christian communities.

Those who trouble the faith of the believers have themselves rejected the Lord, who has redeemed them (2:1). According to 2:15, they are apostates from the faith, people who "have wandered off, departing from the straight way and following after the way of Balaam of Beor." In 2:20–22, Peter explains that they have turned back, forsaking the "holy commandment." These had experienced the salvation of the Lord (2:20a, 21a) but have become "entangled again" in the "defilements of the world" (2:20). In 1:9 Peter denounces these people by calling them "blind," having forgotten their "purification" from their "former sins." At no juncture does Peter imply that they have somehow never been disciples or that their apostasy is anything other than a fall from grace.

Peter details the sins of these adversaries of the truth in his *vituperatio*, the vilification of his opponents (on *vituperatio* see "Occasion of Writing" in the introduction to Jude). They have abandoned Christian morality and embraced sexual immorality (2:2, 10, 14, 18), giving themselves over to the inordinate satisfaction of their desires, including drunkenness and gluttony (2:13). They engage in self-indulgent behavior and revelry in the context of the common banquet of the Christians. Although they promise "freedom" (2:19), they are people who live without moral law and are not subject to the divine command (2:21; 3:17). In truth, they are nothing more than "slaves of corruption" (2:19). One of their principal motivations is avarice (2:3, 14), viewing others as a means of gain, people to be exploited for their own ends. The heretics are arrogant in their denial of the Lord and their slander of celestial beings (2:2, 10, 12, 18), a trait especially evident in their strident skepticism (3:3–4). While the accusations against the heretics' avarice, arrogance, and sexual desire are commonplace in *vituperatio*, the way Peter develops these themes suggests that the heretics do indeed manifest these immoral traits (see comments on these verses).

The error of the heretics is doctrinal and not only moral. Peter calls them "false teachers," who have tried to introduce "heresies of destruction" into the congregations (2:1) by using deceptive means (2:3). At the heart of the error is their skepticism regarding the coming of the Lord and the divine judgment on the day of the Lord (3:3–10). Their argument is that future judgment will never occur, and they rest their case on the apparent delay in the Lord's advent (3:4, 9; cf. 2:3). They criticize the apostolic preaching regarding the coming as an invention of the preachers themselves and tag their proclamation as nothing more than "myth." They even place prophetic inspiration in doubt, claiming that the prophets spoke of their own accord and incorrectly interpreted their own visions (1:20–21). This eschatological skepticism translates into an affirmation of liberty that throws off moral restraint (2:19; 3:3–4). Moreover, the heretics have sought support in Paul's Letters, whose message they have twisted (3:15–16). The doctrinal and moral errors of the false teachers are joined at the hip. In fact, at the head of his denunciation Peter declares that the heresy is a denial of the Lord, who has bought them (2:1). At the heart of this denial is the rejection of his sovereignty over their moral lives (2:10).

The false teachers are members of the Christian communities among whom they promote their error. They participate in the banquets of the churches (2:13), and Peter warns the believers about the false teachers who are among them (2:1). Their posture in the congregations is not passive: they seek to gain disciples for their position, especially those who are neophytes in the faith (2:18). They seduce the unstable (2:14) with the promise of freedom to engage in moral corruption, especially sexual immorality (2:18–19). Peter laments that not a few will follow their ways (2:2) and thereby become the means of financial gain for the false teachers (2:3, 14).

We may outline the beliefs of the false teachers via Peter's presentation of their conduct and their teaching, especially their skepticism, although we must keep in mind the character of ancient *vituperatio* and its possible effect on the shaping of our author's denunciation (see the discussion under "Occasion of Writing" in the introduction to Jude). Despite using common critiques of one's opponents, the structure of Peter's presentation suggests that the heretics do indeed exhibit the character here described. Moreover, in the polemic against the false teachers' stance, our author even quotes their opinion (3:4). We must assume that he faithfully represents their teaching to his readers, especially given that the false teachers style themselves as members of the congregations. But who are these teachers?

Second Peter's use of Jude in his denunciation (see "The Relationship between 2 Peter and Jude," below) has led some to the conclusion that the opponents in both cases are the same (Bigg 1901: 216–24; Wand 1934: 131; Kelly 1969: 42–46). Kelly (1969: 229) nuances his position by arguing that although the situation is similar, the problem confronted in 2 Peter is a somewhat later development of the one reflected in Jude. He especially points out how 2 Peter, unlike Jude, engages in a polemic against erroneous teaching regarding the coming of Christ and the interpretation of Scripture. However, although there is literary dependence between the two books, Peter carefully shapes the material adopted from Jude in order to adapt it to his denunciation of the false teachers who have infiltrated the church (see comments on 2 Pet. 2:1–3:3). Peter engages in *imitatio*, which requires that adopters of material adapt it to their own ends instead of slavishly copying, which would have been considered fraud (see "The Relationship between 2 Peter and Jude," below; and the introduction to 2 Pet. 2:1–3). The intertextual relations between the letters do not warrant equating the two heretical groups.

The differences between the situations presented in Jude and 2 Peter argue against identifying the opponents as the same in both letters. The root of the moral problem that Jude combats is a perversion of the doctrine of grace (v. 4). On the other hand, the doctrinal error that is the foundation for the immorality of the opponents in 2 Peter is the negation of the parousia of Christ and future judgment (3:3–10). Second Peter denounces his opponents' erroneous use of the Scriptures (3:15–16) and argues against their prophetic inspiration (1:19–21; 3:3–4), issues that do not arise in Jude's denunciation of the heretics. Although the heretics in Jude base their doctrine in their supposed visions (v. 8) and emphasize their possession of the prophetic Spirit (v. 19), the false teachers in 2 Peter present themselves as false teachers and not prophets (contra Cavallin 1979; see below). Their critique of prophecy and Peter's defense of prophetic inspiration should not be construed as evidence that these heretics claim prophetic inspiration. They do not claim special revelation or endowment with the prophetic Spirit. The opponents whom Jude faces have entered into the congregation(s) from the outside (v. 4), whereas those that Peter denounces are members of the congregations themselves and enjoy the position of teachers among the believers (2:1, 13; see Fornberg 1977: 59; Bauckham 1983: 155; Guthrie 1990: 848, 911–12). Therefore, while the literary relationship between these two letters cannot be denied, we should not assume that once we have identified the opponents in Jude, we have the false teachers in 2 Peter clearly in our sights. The situations are similar yet distinct, and we may suppose that the reason why Peter made such extensive use of Jude was because he recognized these similarities.

Who, then, are the false teachers in 2 Peter? One view from the last century, not entirely out of vogue today, is that the false teachers are gnostics. As noted previously (see "Authorship of 2 Peter," above), this position depends on the conclusion that 2 Peter is a late, second-century document and not an authentic letter of the apostle Peter. In fact, the identification of the heretics as gnostics has been a pillar in the argument against the letter's authenticity since early Christian gnosticism did not arise as a movement until the second century, whatever we might say about the incipient forms that existed in the earlier period. Käsemann (1982: 171; see also Kümmel 1975: 432), for example, states:

> As Gnostics, they proclaim the message of redemption under the slogan "Freedom from the transitory," to which allusion is made in 2.19; they know themselves to be superior to the angelic powers (2.10f.) and also, as the whole chapter gives us to understand, to be exempt from every ordinance of church and civil community, because they are no longer subject to the old aeon and its powers. It is just because they are Gnostics that the primitive Christian eschatology has no longer any meaning for them.

Schelkle (1980: 186, 230–34) points to the emphasis on *gnōsis* (1:5–6; 3:18) and *epignōsis* (1:2–3, 8; 2:20) as further evidence that the author counters the gnostic threat, although he admits that the absence of the characteristic gnostic dualism presupposes a primitive state of that error. Similarly, Caulley (1982) tags them protognostics, and M. Green (1987: 43–44) argues that the error reflects just a few elements that became the gnosticism of the second century. T. Smith (1985: 87) sees the heretics' denial of the Lord (2:1) as "a rejection of the identification of the Old Testament God with the supreme God, as found among many Gnostic groups," and the rejection of the redemptive activity of Christ ("who bought them") as gnostic struggles with the idea of Jesus dying on the cross. Smith goes so far as to suggest that the heretics' beliefs accord best with the teachings of Basilides, who "maintained that the heavens would continue to be formed forever and would therefore never be destroyed" (93).

However, the immutability of the world is a concern that was voiced more broadly than within the domain of gnostic teaching (see, e.g., Philo, *On the Eternity of the World*). Gnostic thought also rested on cosmic dualism, which made it impossible for God, a spiritual being, to create the material world. The denial of the corporeal resurrection of Jesus was also a gnostic marker that finds not even a distant echo in 2 Peter. T. Smith's gnostic interpretation of 2:1 (the heretics "deny the Master who bought them") is better understood as a repudiation of Christ and his moral authority over their lives (see comments). The libertine lifestyle of the heretics does not find its roots in gnostic dualism, which some interpreted as license to do whatever one wished with the body while, at the same time, maintaining the spirit pure. The immoral behavior of the heretics and their followers is instead rooted in their eschatological skepticism and the misinterpretation of the doctrine of freedom, especially as taught by Paul (3:3–4, 15–16). The promise of "freedom" was a near universal motif among philosophical schools and is not an identifier of the gnostic movement (see 2:19 and comments). Moreover, gnostic schools of thought did not promote eschatological skepticism based on a perceived delay in the parousia, as is the case with the false teachers in 2 Peter (3:3–4). Although 2 Peter includes repeated references to "knowledge" (1:2, 3, 5, 6, 8; 2:20; 3:18), we should not assume that the concept identified by the lexemes *gnōsis* and *epignōsis* is the esoteric knowledge of gnosticism. Our author instead is concerned about personal knowledge of God and Jesus Christ (see 1:2–3, 8; 2:20; 3:18; and comments). At no point does Peter forward this concept as a counterpoint to a heretical view of knowledge (Bauckham 1983: 157). The heresy confronted in 2 Peter does not conform to any gnostic system known to us, and therefore it is best to lay aside this identification of the heretics as have many contemporary commentators (Fornberg 1977: 31–32; Neyrey 1980a: 506; Bauckham 1983: 156–57; Desjardins 1987: 93–95; Guthrie 1990: 847–50; Vögtle 1994: 266–72; Knight 1995: 67; Gerdmar 2001: 290; Schreiner 2003: 278–79).

Thiede (1986b: 180) has suggested that the heretics are people who have been influenced by Essene teaching, drawing a line between the Qumran community, the Essene sect, and the heretics in 2 Peter. This reconstruction has little to commend it since the heretics, unlike the Qumran community, embrace eschatological skepticism and a morally libertine lifestyle. Gerdmar likewise tries to understand the heresy within the Jewish matrix and identifies them as *"the people who kept to Balaam's teaching"* (2001: 291–92, with his emphasis), reading Rev. 2:13–14 ("You have some there who hold to the teaching of Balaam" [NRSV]) alongside 2 Pet. 2:1, 13–16 ("They have wandered off, departing from the straight way, following after the way of Balaam of Bosor"). As noted in the comments on 2 Pet. 2:15–16 and Jude 11, Balaam was one of the figures commonly invoked as an archetypal sinner, and the numerous references to him in biblical and extrabiblical literature make the identification of a particular school highly suspect. Somewhat more promising is Cavallin's (1979) view that the dissidents were pseudoprophets. He bases his argument on the keen interest Peter displays toward prophecy and prophets, especially as compared with Jude (2 Pet. 1:19–21; 2:1, 16; 3:2). Cavallin (1979: 269) addresses the problem of Peter's description of them as "false teachers" (2:1) by stating that "the border-line between prophecy and teaching is often rather blurred." This, however, will not do. As noted above, at no time do we hear Peter charging the false teachers with promoting their teaching on the basis of their supposed revelations, nor does he place the teachers' prophetic inspiration over against that of the prophets or apostles (see 1:16–21; 2:1; 3:1–2). Instead, the false teachers are pure empiricists and base their doctrine on sense perceptions (3:4 and comments), having ignored the larger biblical narrative (3:5–7).

One of the most persuasive suggestions forwarded in recent decades regarding the identity of the heretics has been that of Jerome Neyrey (1977; 1980b; 1993: 122–28), who examined the parallels between the teaching of the false teachers and Epicurean philosophy. Not a few have warmly received Neyrey's argument (Bauckham 1983: 156; Perkins 1995: 162; Horrell 1998: 139; Kraftchick 2002: 78; Scaggs 2004: 90), while not all who acknowledge the parallels would identify the false teachers as Epicureans (Schreiner 2003: 279–80). Others have not been persuaded at all (Gerdmar 2001: 290–91; Adams 2005). But Neyrey himself actually holds the identification of the heretics loosely, stating, "It is the hypothesis of this commentary that the opponents were *either* Epicureans, who rejected traditional theodicy, or 'scoffers' (*Apikoros* [*Epikoros*]) who espoused a similar deviant theology" (emphasis mine; Neyrey 1993: 122, and see 128). Epicurean perspectives had wide currency and were even integrated into other systems of belief, including Sadducean and other strains of Jewish theology (Neyrey 1993: 124–25).[3] Epicurean doctrine railed against the notion of divine providence ("They pelt providence," says Plutarch, *Sera* 548C). The gods are not engaged in human affairs, and what occurs does so by chance and not because of divine intervention. The outcome of

---

3. "From both Jewish and Greek sources, we learn that the argument of Epicurus and his followers became a popular doctrine. In its spread, it was no longer formally identified as 'Epicurean' doctrine, but became a generalized popular statement of deviant theology" (Neyrey 1993: 124).

their dogma regarding providence was their denial of any form of divination, which would include prophecy (see Cicero, *On Divination*; G. Green 2001), and they rejected any notion of divine judgment. As Neyrey notes, "Indeed, in literature ranging from Cicero's *Nat. deor.*, Philo's *On Providence*, and Seneca's *De providentia* to Lactantius's *De ira* and Origen's *Contra Celsum*, Epicureans were known in terms of their denial of divine judgment" (Neyrey 1993: 122). This skepticism was buttressed by the apparent delay in judgment, which also brought into question providence: "This procrastination and delay of the Deity . . . destroys belief in providence," says Plutarch (*Sera* 549B). The deity does not trouble himself with human affairs, and so traditional views of theodicy are brought into question: "The delay and procrastination of the deity in punishing the wicked appears to me the most telling argument by far" (*Sera* 548C). The Epicureans upheld a doctrine of freedom of the will (Diogenes Laertius, *Lives* 10.133) and emphasized the importance of the fulfillment of desire. At a later period, the Christian Lactantius argued that Epicurean teaching promoted immoral behavior (*Div. Inst.* 3.17; Neyrey 1993: 123–24). The false teachers, according to 2 Peter, underscore the delay in the parousia (3:9), which includes divine judgment (3:4). Peter counters that God's judgment is not idle: it "will come" (2:3; 3:10). These people promise "freedom" (2:19) yet are immoral. Peter counters by stating that God knows how to keep the wicked for judgment (2:9). The skepticism regarding prophecy is an Epicurean hallmark, which appears likewise as a foundation stone in the heretics' teaching (1:19–21; 3:4).

We should not simply identify the heretics as Epicureans but may, as Neyrey suggests, recognize in their teaching aspects of Epicurean thought that had much wider currency, such as questions regarding theodicy and skepticism about divination, including prophecy (G. Green 2001). If they are Epicureans, we wonder what they are doing within the confines of a Christian gathering that has a decidedly theistic orientation. Lucretius (5.146–49) said, "You cannot, likewise, believe that the holy abodes of the gods are in any region of our world. For the gods' nature is so tenuous and far-removed from our senses that it is scarcely viewed by the mind" (Long and Sedley 1987: 1.139–49). The heretics, on the other hand, are apostates, who have denied the Lord who bought them (2:1). But they remain within the church and even participate in the common banquet of the believers, which includes the memorial that portrays the divine drama of redemption (2:13). We have no evidence that they embrace a doctrine of divine transcendence such as claiming absolutely no intervention by God in the human sphere.

In his comments on 2 Pet. 3:4, Adams (2005: 115) rightly observes, "First, the scoffers make reference to the continuous duration [διαμένει] of the cosmos as an unaltered [οὕτως] physical structure from the day of its creation, to its closed nature, not its freedom from divine activity." In fact, while the false teachers affirm divine creation (3:4), Epicurus flatly denied such a doctrine (Diogenes Laertius, *Lives* 10.73–74). As reflected in Lucretius, Epicurean doctrine postulated a final collapse and regarded change as the very nature of things (Lucretius, 3.338–50). He taught, "All things gradually decay, and go to the reef of destruction, outworn by the ancient lapse of years" (2.1170–74; 5.826–36). We cannot square the false teachers' claim in 3:4, "Because since the time the fathers died, all things remain as they were from the beginning of creation," with Epicurean doctrine.

Regarding ethics, Epicurean doctrine promoted the notion of the satisfaction of desire and did not teach a doctrine of restraint when it came to even sexual desire. Athenaeus (546F) quoted Epicurus as saying, "The pleasure of the stomach is the beginning and root of all good, and it is to this that wisdom and over-refinement actually refer" (see Cicero, *On Ends* 1.29–33, 37–39; Epicurus, *Ep. Men.* 127–32; *Key Doctrines* 3–4, 8–10; see Long and Sedley 1987: 1.112–25). But the characterization of Epicurean ethics as a complete embrace of libertine behavior is a misrepresentation. The philosopher said, "Of all this the beginning and the greatest good is prudence. Therefore prudence is even more precious than philosophy, and it is the natural source of all the remaining virtues: it teaches the impossibility of living pleasurably without living prudently, honourably and justly" (*Ep. Men.* 132). Lactantius's later views about Epicureanism (fourth cent. AD; see above) cannot be taken as proof of Epicurean unbridled embrace of vice under the guise of the virtue of pleasure during this period. Lactantius's critique may even be understood as an example of *vituperatio*, given its attendant accusations. Although the heretics Peter counters did embrace pleasure (2 Pet. 2:13), their arrogance, sexual vice, and revelry are not markers for Epicurean philosophy. While the similarities between Epicurean philosophy and the position of the false teachers in 2 Peter have been discussed since Neyrey's work, little attention has been given to the differences that call into question this identification.

Can we identify the false teachers' doctrine and praxis with any known system of belief? The attempt to place these people within a particular mold is predicated on models in which consistency of belief among members of a school is assumed. While consistency could be true for some groups, it was not the nature of all. There were those who could be tagged "seed-pickers" (Acts 17:18), who snatched up philosophical scraps and joined them together in alliance. In fact, the Eclectic movement that flourished from the second century BC through the first century AD was known for this very practice (Diogenes Laertius, *Lives* 2.12; OCD 502; Dillon and Long 1988). Philo (*Worse* 20–21 §§71–72) rails against the sophists who, in a similar way, join together a diverse array of tenets into an incoherent whole. He says that Balaam "was a sophist, an empty conglomeration of incompatible and discordant notions," and he goes on to charge that "Sophists are bound to find the powers within them at strife, words running counter to ideas and wishes to words, in absolute and utter discord." Philo adds that they are marked by vice, whatever they may say about virtue, and "they entertain all the time sentiments quite at variance with the things they say" (*Worse* 21 §73). Inconsistency in their doctrines and between their doctrine and praxis was their hallmark. We may identify the opponents in 2 Peter as one such group, holding amalgamated beliefs. One stream that fed into the heretics' river was skepticism regarding the possibility of predictive prophecy (not to be confused with the Skeptic movement, which denied that judgments about the nature of things were possible). Since the time of Carneades (ca. 214–129 BC), questions were raised on the validity of divination, in asking whether what apparently occurs by chance can be predicted (see Cicero, *On Divination*; G. Green 2001). Such skepticism did become a piece in Epicurean thought (see Plutarch, *On the Obsolescence of Oracles*) but was not limited to this school. Concerns about prophecy during the period even led to imperial suppression of divination (Judge 1971).

A second stream that fed into their views was the question of the immutability of the world, as argued by Adams (2005). Was the world eternal, or was it subject to decay or destruction? Over against the Stoic doctrine of the creation and subsequent destruction of the world by fire were those who affirmed that the world would not, and indeed could not, be destroyed. Surprisingly, this view is most eloquently argued by Philo in his *On the Eternity of the World*, who appeals to Scripture in support. He cites Moses, who taught that the world "was created and imperishable" (5 §19). Nothing internal or external can dissolve it (5 §§22–24). In this, Philo affirms Plato (6 §§26–27) and proceeds to reflect on whether God will destroy the world. God will not change his mind about what he created and will not change order into disorder (8 §§39–40). He severely critiques the Stoic doctrine of dissolution of the world by fire and its subsequent rebirth (16–17 §§83–88; see Long and Sedley 1987: 1.274–79). He concludes, "Therefore the world is not consumed by conflagration but is indestructible, and if it should be so consumed, another world could not come into existence" (17 §88). The false teachers whom Peter assails appear to hold similar views. The attendant doctrine is the heretics' denial of the notion of divine judgment of the world. Peter's repeated emphasis on divine judgment past and present (2:1–3:13) appears to be a counter to their denial that human immoral action would evoke divine retribution.

A third stream flowing into the heretics' teaching is the promise of freedom (2:19), which, as noted in the comments, is a promise made by many if not most philosophical systems. Freedom was a key concern of the era. Any movement that sought to gain a hearing promised it in some form or another.

A fourth stream is their embrace of immoral conduct, especially sexual immorality and greed. The attempt to make merchandise out of one's followers (2:3 and comments) was a well-known topos in discussions regarding orators and their motives. Sexual enticement is a social problem frequently associated with banquets held in mixed company (2:13–14 and comments). But above all, the heretics are apostates from the faith (2:1, 15, 20–22 and comments), and herein lies the core of their error. These are people who have heard the truth of the gospel but subsequently repudiate the Lord by their teaching and conduct, throwing off divine authority as represented by the "holy commandment" (2:21). They are trying to draw others after them (2:3, 14) and are painfully successful (2:2). For that reason, Peter warns his hearers about the false teachers' final doom and appeals to them to lead lives of holiness and godliness in light of the final dissolution of all things (3:11–13). The end is coming, the world will be dissolved, God will come in judgment. How, then, shall we live?

## The Relationship between 2 Peter and Jude

Any casual reader of 2 Peter and Jude will notice that a good portion of Jude is found also in 2 Peter. Both the language and thought of these letters are paralleled at numerous points, with the principal locus of these correspondences found between Jude and 2 Pet. 2. There are, however, other parallel points between them in 2 Pet. 1 and 3, as shown below. The duplicated material is presented in approximately the same order in both letters. Though the commentary on 2 Peter will discuss the details of these correspondences, the following chart indicates the verses where these correspondences are located:[4]

| 2 Peter | Jude |
| --- | --- |
| 2:1 | 4 |
| 2:2 | 4 |
| 2:3 | 4 |
| 2:4 | 6 |
| 2:6 | 7 |
| 2:9 | 6 |
| 2:10 | 7b, 8 |
| 2:11 | 9 |
| 2:12 | 10 |
| 2:15 | 11 |
| 2:13 | 12a |
| 2:17 | 12b, 13 |
| 2:18 | 16 |
| 3:1–2 | 17 |
| 3:3 | 18 |
| 3:14 | 24 |
| 3:18 | 25 |

Several explanations for these parallels are possible. First, it may be that Jude has borrowed his material from 2 Peter (Spitta 1885: 381–470; Bigg 1901: 216–24; Moo 1996: 16–21), a position that has the firmest hold on the popular consciousness due to Peter's prominence in the early church as an apostle of Jesus Christ. On the other hand, the author of 2 Peter may have borrowed from Jude, an opinion held by the vast majority of contemporary commentators on these letters (Chaine 1939: 18–24; Schelkle 1980: 138–39; Kelly 1969: 226–27; Grundmann 1974: 75–83; Fornberg 1977: 31–59; Sidebottom 1967: 68–69; Bauckham 1983: 141–42; Senior 1987: 232–33; Paulsen 1992: 97–100; Neyrey 1993: 120–22; G. Green 1993: 327–30; Perkins 1995: 178; Gilmore 2002: 83–91; Kraftchick 2002: 79–81; Callan 2004; Scaggs 2004: 84–85). These options do

---

4. For detailed analysis, see especially Mayor 1907: i–xxv; Fornberg 1977: 33–59; Watson 1988: 163–87; Gilmore 2002: 83–91; Callan 2004.

not exhaust the possibilities, however, since both Jude and the author of 2 Peter may have drawn upon a common source (Reicke 1964: 189–90; Spicq 1966: 197; M. Green 1987: 58–64; Osburn 1992: 311) in a manner similar to the integration of the early Christian domestic code into both 1 Peter (2:18–3:7) and the Paulines (Eph. 5:21–6:9; Col. 3:18–4:2) as well as instruction on the state (1 Pet. 2:13–17; Rom. 13:1–7). The most original suggestion comes from Robinson (J. A. T. Robinson 1976: 192–95), who explains these correspondences by postulating that both letters were the composition of the same author.

Robinson's suggestion is by far the least likely and has not found adherents. The differences between the vocabulary and style of these letters argue strongly against this suggestion (Bauckham 1983: 141). Moreover, Jude had sufficient authority in the church to write a letter in his own name. Why would he need to compose a letter in the name of Peter? If we accept the authenticity of 2 Peter, this theory finds no place (see "Authorship of 2 Peter," above). The suggestion that both Jude and 2 Peter used a common source is helpful in that it would not only explain the convergences in vocabulary and thought but also account for their considerable differences. M. Green (1987: 62) notes that if indeed Peter has used Jude, he changed 70 percent of the vocabulary of his source. But we can also account for the differences by assuming that Peter adapted Jude to his own end, and thus there would be no need to postulate an otherwise unknown source. If the differences do not demand the common-source hypothesis, it is best to apply William of Ockham's well-known rule (i.e., the explanation requiring fewest assumptions is best; so Moo 1996: 18). Literary dependency adequately accounts for all the parallels and is even the strongest argument due to the similar ordering of material in 2 Peter and Jude.

The primacy of 2 Peter has to its credit the central position of Peter in the early church, making the letter ascribed to him a likely source for the lesser-known Jude. Bigg contends that the uniform style of 2 Peter argues for this letter being the one that did not borrow from another (1901: 224). Moreover, Jude 17–18 appears to refer to the prophecy of 2 Pet. 3:2–3 (Moo 1996: 18). The heretics in 2 Peter seem to be coming; in Jude they have already arrived. But against these arguments, there is no reason why the author of 2 Peter, whoever he was, could not have used Jude since such borrowing from extant writings and adoption of early Christian tradition was commonplace in apostolic literature. Moreover, as Bauckham (1983: 142) rightly observes, Jude is "a piece of writing whose detailed structure and wording have been composed with such exquisite care, whereas the corresponding parts of 2 Peter, while by no means carelessly composed, are by comparison more loosely structured." Moreover, the concentration of parallels between these two letters in 2 Pet. 2:1–3:3 argues against the priority of 2 Peter, since in this case we would have expected Jude to make wider use of the letter at hand. Why exclude material from 2 Pet. 1 and the bulk of chapter 3? Kelly (1969: 226) also points out: "The tendency in the early Church was in any case towards enlargement rather than curtailment, and not only is 2 Peter a much longer tract but over and over again, . . . its version is found to be more elaborate and verbose than Jude's" (also Gilmore 2002: 83). There is also an attempt on the part of the author of 2 Peter to suppress Jude's use of pseudepigraphic literature (cf. 2 Pet. 2:10–11 and Jude 8–9 and the absence of the 1 Enoch quotation of Jude 14–15). The majority scholarly opinion regarding the priority of Jude rests on good foundations, but we should mind Neyrey's judicious comment: "These studies have all added weight to the hypothesis of Jude's priority by offering convincing interpretations of 2 Peter's use of Jude, but they have by no means proven it" (1993: 122).

In composing his letter, Peter likely has the Epistle of Jude at hand. He repeatedly uses the language of that letter to refute the heretics who have invaded the churches to which he writes. Although the author is the earliest interpreter of Jude, we should not therefore assume that the letters counter identical heresies. Our author has carefully adapted the denunciations found in his source to demonstrate their application to the situation faced by the recipients of this letter (see "The Opponents in 2 Peter," above, and the commentary). The changes he makes from his source dictate classifying this letter in the ancient literary category of "imitation" (μίμησις, mimēsis, imitatio) rather than "theft" (κλοπή, klopē, furtum), or plagiarism, as would be said today.

*Imitatio* allowed borrowed material to be reworked extensively to make it one's own (*priuati iuris,* according to Horace, *Art* 131). "'Theft' involves derivative copying and is condemned," but *imitatio* was "an acceptable, even normal, re-use" (*OCD* 1188; see West and Woodman 1979; Conte 1986). As Horace (*Art* 131–36) continued, "In ground open to all you will win private rights, if you do not linger along the easy and open pathway, if you do not seek to render word for word as a slavish translator, and if in your copying you do not leap into the narrow well, out of which either shame or the laws of your task will keep you from stirring a step." Dionysius of Halicarnassus (*On Literary Composition* 16) commented on authors of prose and poetry who could, on the other hand, imitate features of their source more closely: "But they also borrow many words from earlier writers, in the very form in which they fashioned them." One was expected to "mould oneself on the ancients, choose a good model, and select his best features" (Russell 1979: 2), and this was not considered plagiarism (a category that indeed was current in the ancient world). So Ovid appropriated things from Virgil, "not to pinch them, but to borrow openly, with the intention of being recognized" (Seneca the Elder, *Suasoriae* 3.7; see also Quintilian, *Inst.* 10.2).

Those models one would draw from were regarded as "the books," and due honor is rendered to their authors through this practice of *imitatio*, or μίμησις (*mimēsis*). Authors thus imitated were regarded as occupying a greater place of honor than their imitators. Pseudo-Longinus (*On the Sublime* 13; see also 14) comments on this practice and even notes that it leads to the sublime:

> It is the imitation and emulation of previous great poets and writers. And let this, my dear friend, be an aim to which we steadfastly apply ourselves. For many men are carried away by the spirit of others as if inspired, just as it is related

of the Pythian priestess when she approaches the tripod, where there is a rift in the ground which (they say) exhales divine vapour. By heavenly power thus communicated she is impregnated and straightway delivers oracles in virtue of the afflatus. Similarly from the great natures of the men of old there are borne in upon the souls of those who emulate them (as from sacred caves) what we may describe as effluences, so that even those who seem little likely to be possessed are thereby inspired and succumb to the spell of the others' greatness. Was Herodotus alone a devoted imitator of Homer? No, Stesichorus even before his time, and Archilochus, and above all Plato, who from the great Homeric source drew to himself innumerable tributary streams. And perhaps we should have found it necessary to prove this, point by point, had not Ammonius and his followers selected and recorded the particulars. This proceeding is not plagiarism; it is like taking an impression from beautiful forms or figures or other works of art.

On the other hand, one could also hope to better the models one imitates. As Philodemus stated, "Those who take over a story are better than its previous users, if they make a greater contribution of poetic excellence" (cited in Russell 1979: 5; see Obbink 1995: 266–67; Quintilian, *Inst.* 10.2.14). The best *imitatio* was that which drew from the writings of various authors and not just from a single worthy (Russell 1979: 5).

Peter's intertextual methodology transforms Jude's thought, making it his own to advance his own argument (see the commentary proper on 2 Pet. 2:1–3:3) and offering us an example of *imitatio*. While he uses Jude extensively, he adapts the language and thought to his own ends, making the work at hand his very own. In this process, the new situation before him calls on him to expand on the original. This is not the only source Peter utilizes as he weaves together his tapestry. The way he uses Jude, however, highlights the honor ascribed to Jude since it recognizes him as one worthy of *imitatio*. Jude, as the half brother of the Lord, had considerable honor in the early church along with James. Here we have yet another indication that the relatives of Jesus were indeed highly esteemed from the earliest days of the church (see "Authorship of Jude" in the introduction to Jude; and Bauckham 1990). The intertexual relationship between 2 Peter and Jude is not simply a question of sources and comparative linguistic analysis; it also brings us to the core of the sociology of the early church, especially its structures of honor and authority.

## Genre and Structure

Composing an outline for 2 Peter, or for any NT book for that matter, is not a simple task. Our understanding of how an author has structured his work is bound closely with the genre of literature that he writes, since certain customary formats are associated with this or that genre. Recent discussions on the structure of 2 Peter have brought together these two issues while older and contemporary popular commentaries tend to ignore the question of genre and forward outlines of the book that are thematic and no more, if indeed they present a discussion of the book's structure at all (Bigg 1901; Mayor

1907; Moffatt 1928; Kelly 1969; Mounce 1982; Hillyer 1992; C. Green and Lucas 1995: 5; Horrell 1998: 146). Continental scholars are generally silent about issues of structure, although they occasionally engage the question of 2 Peter's genre (Chaine 1939; Schelkle 1980; Spicq 1966: 193–94, 206; Schrage 1973; Fuchs and Raymond 1988: 24; Paulsen 1992: 90; Vögtle 1994: 122). Recent English commentaries that analyze the genre of 2 Peter along with the book's structure either view it as an example of Greco-Roman rhetoric (Watson 1988: 81–189), as a testament (Bauckham 1983: 131–35), or as a letter (Moo 1996: 26). These approaches are not mutually exclusive. Indeed, Neyrey (1993: 111–18) emphasizes the rhetorical, testamental, and epistolary features of 2 Peter. Decisions about genre and structure will affect our understanding of the author's purposes and the interpretation of particular texts within the book. Moreover, Bauckham and others have linked the question of whether 2 Peter should be considered an example of the testamentary genre with the debate about authorship.

One recent dominant trend in NT studies is the use of rhetorical criticism in the analysis of epistolary structure. Kennedy's book on the topic (1984) laid out the program of reading the NT through the lens of ancient rhetorical theory. Duane Watson (1988) followed the lines laid down, bringing the full force of the rhetorical approach to bear on the interpretation of Jude and 2 Peter. According to Watson's (1988: 85) analysis, 2 Peter may be classified as deliberative rhetoric that is "intended to advise and dissuade the audience with regard to a particular way of thinking and course of action." He also identifies elements of judicial (1:16–2:10; 3:1–13) and epideictic (2:10b–22) rhetoric in the epistle. He does not deny that 2 Peter is a letter and is indebted to Bauckham for the insight that it may also be regarded as a last testament of Peter.

According to Aristotle (*Rhetoric* 1.3.3–4; 1.4–10), deliberative rhetoric was used in discourses that had to do with the future, and its purpose was to exhort or dissuade. Judicial rhetoric, on the other hand, was oriented to the past, and its purpose was to accuse or defend. The context of judicial rhetoric was the tribunal. Epideictic rhetoric concerned the present, and its purpose was to praise or blame. The oral discourse itself commonly comprised the following elements: the *exordium*, the *narratio*, the *partitio*, the *probatio*, and the *peroratio*. The *exordium* is the beginning, or prologue, of the discourse; the *narratio* is the exposition of the events that have occurred; the *partitio* presents the problem; and the *probatio* is the proof and therefore the most important part of the rhetorical discourse. The *peroratio* is added as the finale of the speech.[5] Watson's (1988: 141–42) rhetorical outline of 2 Peter, in abbreviated form, is as follows:

    I. Epistolary prescript (Quasi-*exordium*; 1:1–2)
    II. *Exordium* (1:3–15)

5. For a fuller analysis of the various components of rhetorical discourse, see Aristotle, *Rhetoric* 3.14–19; Cicero, *De inventione rhetorica* 1.1–19; *Partitiones oratoriae* 27.

III. *Probatio* (1:6–3:13)
IV. *Peroratio* (3:14–18)

The *narratio* is missing from the discourse, and the letter includes a long *digressio* in 2:10b–22 as well as a *transitio*, or as Watson calls it, a "secondary *Exordium*," in 3:1–2. He also identifies a "miniature homily" in 1:3–11, included because of the testamentary genre, but its insertion renders the *exordium* "partially faulty" since "it does not relate directly to the refutation of the doctrinal and ethical position of the false teachers in the *probatio*" (Watson 1988: 143). Significant adjustments in the understanding of the structure of rhetorical discourse need to be made to fit 2 Peter into this schema.

The question remains, however, whether NT letters are structured according to the canons developed for *oral* discourse (see the details in "Genre and Structure" in the introduction to Jude). As noted previously, the ancients distinguished between styles appropriate for letters and those used in formal discourse. The editor of Aristotle's letters, Artimon, said, "A letter ought to be written in the same manner as a dialogue, a letter being regarded by him as one of the two sides of a dialogue" (Demetrius, *Eloc.* 223, cited in Malherbe 1988: 17). Aristotle himself differentiated the style of discourse from that of letters: "But we must not lose sight of the fact that a different style is suitable to each kind of Rhetoric. That of written compositions is not the same as that of debate; nor, in the latter, is that of public speaking the same as that of the law courts" (*Rhetoric* 3.12.1). Cicero drew a line between letters and conversations and not letters and oral rhetoric (*Att.* 8.14.1; and 9.10.1; 12.53), and Demetrius likewise distinguished clearly between the conversational style of letters and that of oratory (*Eloc.* 226). He promoted "a certain degree of freedom in the structure of a letter" and taught that letters should not be treatises dressed in a letter form (*Eloc.* 229, 228, 231, 234; in Malherbe 1988: 19). These considerations, among others (see "Genre and Structure" in the introduction to Jude), caution against adopting Watson's rhetorical approach in the analysis of 2 Peter. Second Peter has all the markings of a genuine epistle and should be analyzed according to the canons of ancient epistolography.

One of the most forceful voices in the discussion of the genre and structure of 2 Peter has been that of Richard Bauckham. There is hardly a contemporary commentary that is not indebted to his work. His opening salvo in the discussion on 2 Peter identifies the document as a genuine letter but also a last testament of the apostle Peter (Bauckham 1983: 131–35). A "testament" is a "farewell speech," and this particular genre was in vogue during the period. As R. P. Spittler comments, "The first century B.C. and the first century A.D. were eminently the centuries of the testament" (*OTP* 1:831). Various examples of testamentary literature have been preserved for us (Testaments of the Twelve Patriarchs and the testaments of Job, Abraham, Isaac, Jacob, Moses, and Solomon). Bauckham also catalogs a list of testaments that appear as parts of other ancient works (1 En. 91–104; Tob. 14:3–11; 2 Esd. [4 Ezra] 14:27–36; 2 Bar. 77–86; Jub. 21–22; 35; 36.1–18; Ps.-Philo, *L.A.B.* 19.1–5; 24.1–5; 28.3–4,

5–10; 33; L.A.E. 25–29; Josephus, *Ant.* 4.7.45–47 §§309–19). While admitting that "testament" is not a "well-defined genre," J. H. Charlesworth (*OTP* 1:773) summarizes some salient features of such works: "The ideal figure faces death and causes his relatives and intimate friends to circle around his bed. He occasionally informs them of his fatal flaw and exhorts them to avoid certain temptations; he typically instructs them regarding the way of righteousness and utters blessings and curses. Often he illustrates his words—as the apocalyptic seer in the apocalypses—with descriptions of the future as it has been revealed to him in a dream or vision." So, for example, the Testament of Job follows the sequence also found in the Testaments of the Twelve Patriarchs: it "(1) opens with a deathbed scene; (2) celebrates a virtue; (3) offers moral exhortations; and (4) closes with the death, burial, and lamentation scene" (R. P. Spittler, *OTP* 1:832). The predictive element becomes especially common, as Kolenkow (1975: 57) observes: "The genre serves particularly as a vehicle for literature forecasting the future, written in the name of a patriarch. In this literature, the patriarch receives visions or knowledge of heaven and these make his forecasts of history and descriptions of heaven and judgment strong evidence in the argument for remaining among or joining the righteous."

The contents of the testaments were of two main types: "ethical admonition" and "revelations of the future" (Bauckham 1983: 131). In accordance with this genre, 2 Peter includes a "miniature homily" (1:3–11); the testamentary section, which announces Peter's forthcoming death and his desire to have his teaching remembered (1:12–15); and predictions of the rise of false teachers (2:1–3a; 3:1–4). Bauckham (1983: 132) asserts, "These four passages, but especially 1:12–15, would leave no contemporary reader in doubt that 2 Peter belonged to the genre of 'testament.'" He admits that testaments are usually not found in letter form, although 2 Bar. 78–86 is an example of the combination of letter genre with a testament (1983: 133). Bauckham (1983: 134) concludes that since testaments are always pseudepigraphic, 2 Peter cannot be an authentic work of the apostle Peter: "Second Peter bears so many marks of the testament genre . . . that readers familiar with the genre must have expected it to be fictional, like other examples they knew." Bauckham's analysis has dominated studies on 2 Peter, and authors often refer to his conclusions as assured result (Fuchs and Raymond 1988: 25–26; Paulsen 1992: 90; Neyrey 1993: 112; Perkins 1995: 160, 171; Kraftchick 2002: 73–74; Senior and Harrington 2003: 230).

Bauckham's presentation is not without flaws, although few have sought to address these (see J. Charles 1997: 49–75, whose principal concern is the question of pseudepigraphy in relation to this genre). Although 2 Peter includes a testamentary section (1:12–15), it lacks the common contours of the testamentary genre. There is no deathbed scene and no final account of the "author's" burial. The testaments that have been preserved for us bring us face-to-face with literature whose design is very different from this book. And as J. Charles (1997: 54) notes, "Absent from 2 Peter are apocalyptic dreams and visions and the element of blessings/curses, both of which are salient features of standard testamental genre." In other words, the inclusion of a testamentary section in 2 Peter (1:12–15) does not convert the letter into a testament. As R. P. Spittler observes (*OTP* 1:831), "Some products of the genre of that era were absorbed into other works." Munck (1950) has shown that in Jewish literature (Tob. 14:3–11; 1 En. 91.1–19) and the NT (Acts 20:17–38; 2 Tim. 4:1–18) the "farewell address" feature of testaments appears also in this other, nontestamentary literature.

Stauffer's appendix titled "Valedictions and Farewell Speeches" in his NT theology (1955: 344–47) compares the features of farewell addresses in the "Old Biblical Tradition," including apocryphal literature, and the NT. He identifies characteristics found in both testamental and nontestamental literature, and one could hardly conclude that inclusion of such conventions makes the book in which they are found a testament. For example, 2 Esd. (4 Ezra) 14:8–9 says, "Lay up in your heart the signs that I have shown you, the dreams that you have seen, and the interpretations that you have heard; for you shall be taken up from among humankind, and henceforth you shall live with my Son and with those who are like you, until the times are ended" (NRSV). The announcement of his forthcoming demise does not mean that the book becomes a testament with all of this genre's salient features, any more than Paul's speech to the Ephesian elders (Acts 20:17–38) converts Acts into a testament. The same may be said of 2 Pet. 1:12–15. Bauckham's assertion (1983: 132) that this passage "would leave no contemporary reader in doubt that 2 Peter belonged to the genre of 'testament'" overreaches the evidence. But even Bauckham (1983: 134) admits that major sections of the letter "are not really written within the testamentary genre," a fact suggesting that perhaps another line of analysis would be more fruitful.

Bauckham (1983: 131) echoes Kolenkow's analysis (1975) of the testamentary genre in stating that testaments have two main types of content: ethical admonitions and revelations about the future. Second Peter embraces both these elements. However, the epistle does not link either the author's exhortations or his eschatology with his coming demise. Rather, he roots his appeal in the revelation given him by the Lord at the time of the transfiguration (1:16–18) and the word of prophetic testimony (1:19–21). This is a distinct departure from testamentary literature. Within the testaments there is often a heavenly journey from which the person returns and on the basis of this journey gives revelations about eschatology and ethics (Kolenkow 1975: 57–62). Greek literature also preserves accounts of those who, upon dying, receive revelations about the future (as the myth of Er in Plato, *Republic* 10.13–16 [614B–21D]; or Plutarch, *On Divine Vengeance* 563B–68). Kolenkow (1975: 66–67) draws a bold line between such Persian and Greco-Latin accounts of the experiences of the dying and the accounts of Hellenistic Jewish last words: "Most features mentioned above as characteristic of the genre of last words in Hellenistic Jewish literature are not characteristic of biblical presentations of the patriarchal blessings and would seem to have their closest parallels in foreign literatures. They indeed have their locus in one particular form—the pre-death trip to heaven from which one returns to give others a basis for decision about manner of life." But this kind of journey is absent from 2 Peter, and the encounter with the Lord in the transfiguration appears to take its place. But even this event is not linked with reflections on Peter's demise.

In the farewell or testamentary section of 2 Peter (1:12–15), the principal concern is to remind the readers of "these things." Bauckham (1983: 196) comments that such reminders are "naturally appropriate and recurrent themes of farewell discourses." But the call to "remember" is extremely common in moral exhortation (see Jude 5; 2 Pet. 1:12; 3:1–2; and comments) and is hardly confined to testaments. In Socrates' dialogue with Phaedrus (*Phaedrus* 275C–D), Plato explained why reminders of what is already known are so important: "Then it shows great folly . . . to suppose that one can transmit or acquire clear and certain knowledge of an art through the medium of writing, or that written words can do more than remind the reader of what he already knows on a given subject" (W. Hamilton 1973: 76). Reminders are needed in moral exhortation due to the general belief in the superiority of spoken over written words. Reminders are part of the domain of moral exhortation and not only testaments.

Bauckham (1983: 133) discusses the way the letter genre may be used as a testament since this form for testamentary literature is extremely uncommon. The author of 2 Peter, he states, could have "created" or "invented" it. This combination of genres, the letter and the testament, was not previously known, although the example from 2 Bar. 78–86 may be forwarded as a counterclaim. Second Baruch, written in the second century AD, could hardly serve as a prototype for the author of 2 Peter. Bauckham's argument is interesting in light of his firm assertion that all testaments are pseudepigraphic (1983: 133). If 2 Peter were conceived as a testament, could it not also be that the author "created" this combination for use by a living and authentic author? Bauckham's response is to resort to other evidences that 2 Peter is pseudepigraphic (1983: 134). In the end, if 2 Peter is a testament, that does not necessarily imply that the book is pseudepigraphic. However, the book includes farewell material and does not share the form or many of the characteristic features of ancient testaments. Our understanding of the genre and structure of the book must be found elsewhere.

Numerous authors agree that 2 Peter is a genuine letter and follows the form of ancient Hellenistic correspondence, although many of these view the letter form as merely a frame for the testamentary or rhetorical material (Bauckham 1983: 133; Watson 1988: 85; Kraftchick 2002: 73; Senior and Harrington 2003: 229). Neyrey (1993: 111) stresses the testamentary nature and rhetorical structure of the document to such an extent that he concludes, "In short, the letter form appears to be merely the literary fiction in which the author's remarks are cast." Within the whole debate about genre and structure, little attention has been paid to the contributions of epistolary theory for analyzing 2 Peter. Moo (1996: 26) lays out the structure of 2 Peter according to the canons of ancient epistolography, although he does not discuss the reason to adopt this approach. The formal epistolary characteristics of this document should not be overshadowed by another schema but given their full weight. The author himself classifies his writing as a "letter" (3:1), and we can hardly better his evaluation of the genre.

The contours of Hellenistic and Hellenistic-Jewish letters have already been discussed in the introduction to Jude (see "Genre and Structure"), and the observations about such letters may be applied in the case of 2 Peter as well. As all ancient letters, 2 Pet. 1:1 states the name of the author followed by naming the recipients. He does not identify them beyond indicating that they are "ones who have received a faith of equal honor to ours." Unlike 1 Pet. 1:1, the location(s) of the recipients is not indicated, although 2 Pet. 3:1 remarks that this is the "second letter" the author is writing to his recipients who are, most likely, those named in 1 Pet. 1:1–2. After naming the author and recipients, Hellenistic letters commonly included a greeting (χαίρειν, *chairein*), often followed by a wish-prayer, especially for the recipient's health. Second Peter combines these two conventions in 1:2, joining together the Christian variant χάρις (*charis*, grace) with the Greek translation of the Hebrew greeting שָׁלוֹם (*šālôm*, peace) into a wish-prayer (πληθυνθείη, *plēthyntheiē*, may . . . abound). A greeting in the form of a wish-prayer was also used in letters sent to the Jewish Diaspora (Dan. 6:26 Theod.; 2 Bar. 78.2; *b. Sanh.* 11b; J. H. Elliott 2000: 321). The body of the letter begins in 1:3 and runs up to the final doxology in 3:18b. As in the case of Jude, the letter does not conclude with the usual letter-closing matter, which could include "a farewell wish, a health wish, secondary greetings, an autograph, an illiteracy formula, the date, and a postscript" (Weima 1994: 55).

But while Jude's doxology summarizes the content of the exhortation, as would the normal letter closing of Hellenistic letters, 2 Pet. 3:18b is much briefer and focuses attention on God's eternal honor. It does, however, share many formal traits of other NT doxologies (see 3:18 and comments; Weima 1994: 137). The inclusion of the doxology at the end likely indicates the liturgical use of this document. Reading in the ancient world was commonly done aloud (Acts 8:27–30; 1 Tim. 4:13), and letters were no exception to this general rule. The setting for recitation would have been the gathering of the church (1 Thess. 5:27), although we should not therefore assume that this use makes the letter itself into a homily or "word of exhortation" (see Wills 1984: 289; the response in C. Black 1988; and the comments on Jude under "Genre and Structure" in the introduction to Jude).

The ancient epistolary theorists Pseudo-Demetrius and Pseudo-Libanius discussed the classification of letters (White 1986: 202–3; Malherbe 1988: 30–41, 66–81), and using the taxonomy presented by Demetrius, 2 Peter may be classified as a combination of the advisory and vituperative types. The letter is directed to the church and not to the heretics themselves. In this, 2 Peter's approach is quite similar to that of Jude (see "Genre and Structure" in the introduction to Jude). The letter also has characteristics of Libanius's "paraenetic style," which was used to persuade or dissuade.

This persuasion is carried out in the context of friendship, but it would not do to classify the document simply as a friendly letter since, as Libanius noted, "the friendly style is that in which we exhibit simple friendship only" (Malherbe 1988: 69, 33; Doty 1973: 11). The way 2 Peter takes up the warning about the heretics and the exhortation to the church to avoid their error and continue in the faith fits fully within the framework of ancient epistolary theory.

After the letter opening (1:1–2), the body of the letter begins (1:3–3:17), which itself may be divided into a body opening, body middle, and body closing (White 1972: 9). The body opening (1:3–11) is the place where "the principal occasion for the letter is usually indicated" (White 1972: 33). The body middle is marked by a transitional formula that discloses the purpose for writing (1:12–15) and runs from 1:12 through 2:22. The body closing is introduced by the transitional formula in 3:1–2 that restates the purpose for writing (White 1972: 42–43). The body closing ends in 3:18a, with the final doxology in 3:18b serving as a less-than-elaborate letter closing. Given that 2 Peter is a genuine letter, we may outline it as follows:

I. Epistolary greeting (1:1–2)
  A. Author: Simeon Peter (1:1a)
  B. Recipients: Those who have received a faith of equal honor (1:1b)
  C. Wish-prayer for grace and peace (1:2)
II. Letter Body: A warning against false teachers (1:3–3:18a)
  A. Body opening: God's call to glory and virtue (1:3–11)
    1. Divine power and promises for life and duty (1:3–4)
    2. An urgent appeal to ascend in virtue (1:5–11)
  B. Body middle: The apostolic testimony and the false teachers (1:12–2:22)
    1. A call to remember (1:12–21)
      a. The occasion of remembrance: Peter's farewell (1:12–15)
      b. The content of remembrance (1:16–21)
        i. The transfiguration vision (1:16–18)
        ii. The prophetic word (1:19–21)
    2. The coming and the judgment of the false teachers (2:1–22)
      a. The rise and judgment of the false teachers among you (2:1–3)
      b. Past sinners and their doom (2:4–10a)
        i. The angels (2:4)
        ii. The ancient world (2:5)
        iii. Sodom and Gomorrah (2:6–10a)
      c. "These are"—The vices of the false teachers (2:10b–16)
      d. "These are"—The seduction of the false teachers (2:17–22)
  C. Body closing: A call to holiness (3:1–18a)
    1. A call to remember prophetic and apostolic teaching (3:1–2)
    2. Understand this: The scoffers of the last day (3:3–7)

3. Do not ignore this: One day is as a thousand years (3:8–10)
4. Since all these things will pass away: Living in light of the end (3:11–13)
5. While waiting for these things: Diligence to be found blameless (3:14–18a)

III. Letter closing: A doxology (3:18b)

➤  I. Epistolary Greeting (1:1–2)
    II. Letter Body: A Warning against False Teachers (1:3–3:18a)
    III. Letter Closing: A Doxology (3:18b)

# I. Epistolary Greeting (1:1–2)

The epistolary opening, or *praescriptio*, of 2 Peter is patterned after the style normally found in Hellenistic letters of the era. The name of the author is placed in the first position, followed by the name of the recipient and a greeting, usually χαιρεῖν (*chairein*). Aramaic letters sometimes place the name of the recipient in the primary position (Fitzmyer 1974b: 211), as could Hellenistic letters of petition or other legal correspondence (White 1986: 194–95, 199–200), but 2 Peter follows the order of most of the papyrus letters that have survived from antiquity. The *praescriptio* in 2 Peter, as in other NT correspondence, is quite elaborate and richly theological. Common family letters of the era could include indications of the familial relationship between the author and addressees, in addition to honorific or endearing descriptions such as "lord" or "my own." Julius Victor was of the opinion that "the openings and conclusions of letters should conform with the degree of friendship (you share with the recipient) or with his rank, and should be written according to customary practice" (Malherbe 1988: 65; White 1986: 200). Qualifying descriptions could be quite extensive in the case of legal or official communications, and in the case of the latter, the language could be mixed with warm and familiar terms (White 1986: 200, 59, 61). The highly qualified language of the *praescriptio* in 2 Peter and in other NT letters tends toward the formal and official, while not losing familiarity. The opening greeting in Hellenistic letters was quite brief and was often followed by a wish for the good health of the recipient. In 2 Peter, the greeting "grace and peace" is placed in the form of a wish-prayer, which substitutes for the health wish. While the letter opening would have sounded notes familiar in the day, the content is significantly modified in light of the gospel. The unit can be outlined as follows:

A. Author: Simeon Peter (1:1a)
B. Recipients: Those who have received a faith of equal honor (1:1b)
C. Wish-prayer for grace and peace (1:2)

## Exegesis and Exposition

[1] ⌜Simeon⌝ Peter, a slave and apostle of Jesus Christ, to the ones who have received a faith of equal honor to ours in the righteousness of our God and Savior, Jesus Christ. [2] May grace and peace abound to you in the knowledge of God and Jesus our Lord.

## A. Author: Simeon Peter (1:1a)

**1:1a**    Second Peter begins, as other Hellenistic letters of the period, by naming the author, who in this case identifies himself as Συμεὼν Πέτρος (*Symeōn Petros*), or Simeon Peter. Discussion about whether this book is an authentic composition of the apostle Peter or a pseudepigraphic work has occupied commentators since ancient times (see "Authorship of 2 Peter" in the introduction). Throughout the commentary, the author will be referred to as "Peter," although here he introduces himself as Simeon Peter. A considerable number of Greek MSS read "Simon" (Σίμων, *Simōn*), the more frequent transliteration of the Semitic name שִׁמְעוֹן (*šim'ôn*), instead of "Simeon" (see additional note). Other transliterations of the name also appear in the literature and inscriptions (Σύμων, *Symōn*; Σιμωνίδης, *Simōnidēs*; Σιμωνάθης, *Simōnathēs*). שִׁמְעוֹן was the most popular Palestinian male name of the period. While the transliteration Σίμων (*Simōn*) was a Greek name, it was adopted as the equivalent of biblical Συμεών (*Symeōn*), the name of the son of Joseph (Gen. 29:33). Although the two were used almost interchangeably in Josephus and elsewhere, Συμεών (*Symeōn*) remained the traditional spelling, and Σίμων (*Simōn*) the more Hellenized form (Ilan 2002: 226, 218–35). The only other place where Peter is called Συμεών (*Symeōn*) is in the Palestinian setting of Acts 15:14. The use of this name may, therefore, root the author in that setting, although bilingual people could engage in code switching (cf. Gal. 2:7–8 [Peter] and Gal. 2:9, 11, 14 [Cephas]). We can hardly argue either for or against the authenticity of the letter on the basis of the reading Συμεών (*Symeōn*) since the use of this less-common transliteration for the apostle's name could be viewed as either a mark of authenticity or as part of the pseudepigrapher's art. If this is an authentic epistle of Peter, the use of the name Simeon would be a trace of his bilingualism.

The name Πέτρος (*Petros*, Peter) is the translation of the Aramaic Cephas (כֵּיפָא, *kêpā'*), both of which mean either "rock" or "stone" (John 1:42; Fitzmyer 1981: 112–24; Cullmann 1953: 17–21), although the Aramaic may also mean a "crag" in the rocks. This noun was rarely used as a name, although occurrences of it do appear (Ilan 2002: 436). The Lord himself gave this Aramaic name to Simeon (Mark 3:16; Luke 6:14; cf. Matt. 4:18; 10:2; 16:17–18; Acts 10:5), and though Peter is known best by the Greek form of the name, occasionally he continued to be called Cephas (1 Cor. 1:12; 3:22; 9:5; 15:5; Gal. 1:18; 2:9, 11, 14).[1] In comparison with the simple "Peter," the combination of his given and apostolic name, "Simon Peter," appears rather infrequently (Matt. 16:16; Luke 5:8), with slightly more frequency in John (John 6:68; 13:6, 9, 24, 36; 18:10, 15, 25; 20:2, 6; 21:2, 3, 7; etc.). The combined name "Simeon Peter" recalls the earliest memory of the fisherman who became foundational for the life of the church (Matt. 16:16–18). Both antiquity and authority adhere to the name and by extension to this writing composed under that name.

---

1. The thesis that Peter and Cephas are two different people, as argued by Ehrman (1990), is rather difficult to maintain.

Peter identifies himself as a δοῦλος καὶ ἀπόστολος Ἰησοῦ Χριστοῦ (*doulos kai apostolos Iēsou Christou*, slave and apostle of Jesus Christ). The "servant [δοῦλος, *doulos*] of the Lord" (Josh. 24:30 LXX [24:29 Eng.]; Judg. 2:8; 1 Kings 1:33; 2 Kings 10:23; 18:12; Pss. 36 title; 134:1; 135:1 [LXX: 35:1; 133:1; 134:1]), or less frequently "servant of God" (Neh. 10:30 LXX [10:29 Eng.]; Isa. 42:19 LXX), was a title given to those like Moses, Joshua, and David, who held leadership responsibilities in Israel and carried them out under God's authority. In the same way in the NT, those commissioned by God to give oversight to the churches are called his δοῦλοι (*douloi* as in Rom. 1:1; Phil. 1:1; Col. 4:12; Titus 1:1; James 1:1; Jude 1). The title, so understood, would highlight Peter's authority as an agent of God and not simply his humility and service. Though Peter's self-designation may be read within that frame, throughout the Roman world a δοῦλος (*doulos*) was a slave, who was considered by society to be a "human tool" possessed by a κύριος (*kyrios*, lord). The fundamental social division in that era was between slave and free (1 Cor. 12:13; Eph. 6:8; Col. 3:11), and given the ubiquity of slavery, it is likely that a reader of this Greek letter would have understood the designation within that most accessible context. But as observed in the comments on Jude 1, a "slave" could be the agent of the master and, in this sense, the two frames for understanding "slave of Jesus Christ" coalesce. However, both "slave" and "servant" are problematic translations for the English reader. For those located in the United States, "slave" evokes the racial associations of the antebellum South. In the wider English-speaking world, "servant" implies a voluntary service. Both English glosses have implications that were not attached to the concept of slavery in the ancient world. Peter also identifies himself as an ἀπόστολος Ἰησοῦ Χριστοῦ (*apostolos Iēsou Christou*, apostle of Jesus Christ): a messenger who bears the authority of the one who sent him (see Jude 17 and comments). Given the way Peter uses "slave" as an agent of the divine Master, the title "apostle" underscores his role as one commissioned by God rather than highlighting the contrast between his humility ("slave") and authority ("apostle"). The stress is on his divine commission and authority, an important point in his attempt to uproot the heretical elements from the church. The authority of this letter rests not on Peter's numinous presence in the church but on his role as one whom Christ has sent. Even his name highlights that fact.

## B. Recipients: Those Who Have Received a Faith of Equal Honor (1:1b)

While 1 Pet. 1:1 and the Pauline letters commonly indicate the location of the readers, 2 Peter identifies the first readers/hearers of this correspondence only as people of the faith. Naming the location of one's readers is not a common Hellenistic epistolary convention. Peter does, however, indicate that the recipients are the same as those who received his first correspondence (2 Pet. 3:1), and therefore they are most likely believers located in the provinces of Asia Minor (1 Pet. 1:1; J. H. Elliott 2000: 84–93). Here, however, Peter addresses

1:1b

the letter τοῖς ἰσότιμον ἡμῖν λαχοῦσιν πίστιν (*tois isotimon hēmin lachousin pistin*, to the ones who have received a faith of equal honor to ours). Although the language is quite different, the thought is not far distant from Jude's call "to contend for the faith that was once and for all handed down to the saints" (v. 3). The "faith" that they have received is the gospel itself and not simply the response of assent and trust nor merely the summary of apostolic doctrine (see Jude 3 and comments). It is not the exact equivalent of the "present truth" (2 Pet. 1:12) but a wider concept. This is the faith that the recipients have "received" as their allotted portion.

The verb Peter uses (the participle λαχοῦσιν, *lachousin*; from λαγχάνω, *lanchanō*) was commonly associated with either casting lots (John 19:24), being chosen by lots (Luke 1:9), or as here to speak of receiving what was one's allotted portion or share in something (Acts 1:17). As in Acts 1:17, the verb is found with κλῆρος (*klēros*, lot or portion one is assigned), but this complement is often suppressed. In this latter sense, the verb has to do with that which one receives as one's apportioned share, such as an inheritance or what one receives due to contractual obligations. One inscription, for example, reads, "If I die, I leave my dwelling, which I obtained by the dividing of an inheritance" (P.Dura 16 *b*7, in *TLNT* 2:356). This, then, is the faith apportioned them by God (implied, but not stated),[2] a thought not far distant from Jude's notion of a faith handed down as sacred tradition (Jude 3).

Peter classifies this faith as ἰσότιμον (*isotimon*), a term that has to do with what is of equal honor to something or someone else. So Josephus speaks of Aristobulus, who conferred on his brother Antigonus "honours equal to his own" (*J.W.* 1.3.1 §71). The stress is on equality of dignity and honor (*TLNT* 2:231). Jude notes that the faith for which the church is to contend has been handed down to the saints, thus connecting the readers with the heritage of the larger church (Jude 3); Peter stresses that the faith that God has apportioned these churches is of equal honor to what he and the wider Christian community hold (ἡμῖν, *hēmin*). It holds the same honor as the faith of the eyewitnesses of the life and glory of Christ (1:16–18; 3:2). Peter is anxious to make the church aware of their embeddedness in the wider Christian community (Neyrey 1993: 147). In this affirmation his emphasis becomes the counterpoint to the incursion of those who are bringing destructive heresies into the church (2:1). Moreover, the faith they have received is not a mythic fable (1:16). From the start, he alerts the readers to the status and honor of what they have received, as well as its universal, or "catholic," nature, and this affirmation is an implicit call for them not to abandon what has been granted them by God and what they hold in common with the wider church.

Peter adds that the church has received this equally honorable faith ἐν δικαιοσύνῃ τοῦ θεοῦ ἡμῶν καὶ σωτῆρος Ἰησοῦ Χριστοῦ (*en diakaiosynē tou theou hēmōn kai sōtēros Iēsou Christou*, in the righteousness of our God and

---

2. The use is similar to Sib. Or. 3.580: "Sharing [λαχόντες, *lachontes*] in the righteousness of the law of the Most High."

Savior, Jesus Christ). Second Peter does not emphasize that "righteousness" by which God justifies the ungodly through faith in Jesus Christ (Rom. 1:16–17; 3:21–26), but its moral quality (2 Pet. 2:5, 21; 3:13). The action of apportioning them a faith of equal honor was an act of divine righteousness or justice. God was completely just or impartial in granting them this faith, not preferring one group (the apostles) over another (the recipients of the letter).[3] But here the justice is not that of God the Father but "of our God and Savior, Jesus Christ." One definite article in the Greek (τοῦ, *tou*) governs both "God" and "Savior," which are connected with καί (*kai*, and). The identical grammatical construction appears elsewhere in the epistle where Jesus Christ is called both "Lord and Savior" (1:11; 2:20; 3:2, 18). In a case such as this, "the article is (naturally) omitted with the second of two phrases in apposition connected by καί [*kai*]" (BDF §276.3, although BDF oddly views the present case as an exception to the rule). Here, in a construction identical to Titus 2:13 ("our great God and Savior, Jesus Christ" [NRSV]), our author ascribes to Jesus Christ both the titles "God" and "Savior" (contra Neyrey 1993: 148, who does not address the way that the author uses the same grammatical structure in his comments on 1:11; 2:20; 3:2, 18). This verse is one of the clearest NT declarations of the early church's conviction of the deity of Christ (John 1:1, 18; 20:28; Rom. 9:5; 2 Thess. 1:2; Heb. 1:8–9; 1 John 5:20). The ascription of the divine title to Jesus is hardly evidence for the epistle's late date (Bauckham 1983: 168–69). Jesus Christ is likewise called "Savior," which itself was a divine title both within Judaism and in the wider Roman world (see Jude 25 and comments; 2 Pet. 1:11; 2:20; 3:2, 15, 18), as also the title "Lord," which is likewise ascribed to Jesus Christ (1:2, 8, 11, 14, 16; 2:20; 3:2, 18; and comments). The initiative in allotting them the gospel faith came from Jesus Christ, who is none less than the true God and Savior.

## C. Wish-Prayer for Grace and Peace (1:2)

The *praescriptio* of the letter concludes with a greeting in the form of a wish-prayer: χάρις ὑμῖν καὶ εἰρήνη πληθυνθείη ἐν ἐπιγνώσει τοῦ θεοῦ καὶ Ἰησοῦ τοῦ κυρίου ἡμῶν (*charis hymin kai eirēnē plēthyntheiē en epignōsei tou theou kai Iēsou tou kyriou hēmōn*, May grace and peace abound to you in the knowledge of God and Jesus our Lord). The wish-prayer takes the place of the wish for health commonly found in Hellenistic letters (White 1986: 200–202). In this prayer, instead of expressing the desire that "mercy and peace" might abound to his readers, as does Jude (v. 2), Peter includes the more traditional Christian "grace and peace" (Rom. 1:7; 1 Cor. 1:3; 2 Cor. 1:2; Gal. 1:3; Eph. 1:2; Phil. 1:2; Col. 1:2; 1 Thess. 1:1; 2 Thess. 1:2; Titus 1:4; Philem. 3; Rev. 1:4). The first words of the greeting are identical to 1 Pet. 1:2. "Grace" (χάρις, *charis*) summarizes God's saving work through Christ Jesus (Rom. 3:24; 5:15; Eph.

1:2

---

3. The *Nueva Biblia Española* captures the idea in the translation "gracias a la equidad de nuestro Dios [due to the equity of our God]."

2:8; 2 Thess. 2:16) and embraces the divine enablement given so that his people may do his will (Acts 15:40; 2 Cor. 8:1, 7; Gal. 2:9; 1 Pet. 5:12; see Jude 4 and comments). Cicero defined *gratia*, the Latin equivalent of χάρις (*charis*), as "excessive favor," which would be demonstrated toward the accused in a judicial context, and this favor was granted in direct proportion to the person's *potentia* or social and economic power (Garnsey 1970: 209). In contrast, God's grace abounds to people freely without regard to status and is even given to those who are guilty (Rom. 5:20–21) and God's enemies (Rom. 5:10).

The wish-prayer also expresses Peter's desire that "peace" might abound to his readers, which, as noted on Jude 2, likewise summarizes the content of the messianic salvation. Peter's and other NT authors' concern is not with an experience of "peace" or emotional tranquillity but rather with "peace" with God (Rom. 5:1), which constitutes salvation. In this simplest of Christian greetings, we encounter the core of the gospel. Peter's prayer is that these divine blessings might multiply or increase toward them (BDAG 826; Jude 2; 1 Pet. 1:2; and the verb in Dan. 4:37c LXX; 4:1 and 6:26 Theod.). The epistle demonstrates a particular interest in moral progress of the believers (2 Pet. 1:5–9; 3:18), and this growth and stability in the faith is placed over against the influence of the heretics. Whatever progress they experience is, however, fruit of the divine initiative. The epistle's theme of moral progress is introduced here in the opening wish-prayer.

Although the first part of the wish-prayer follows 1 Pet. 1:2b, here an additional phrase is added: ἐν ἐπιγνώσει τοῦ θεοῦ καὶ Ἰησοῦ τοῦ κυρίου ἡμῶν (*en epignōsei tou theou kai Iēsou tou kyriou hēmōn*, in the knowledge of God and Jesus our Lord). In 2 Peter, two words are used to convey the idea of "knowledge." The first is ἐπίγνωσις (*epignōsis*; here and in 1:3, 8; 2:20), along with its verbal form ἐπιγινώσκω (*epiginōskō*); the other is the uncompounded γνῶσις (*gnōsis*; in 1:5, 6; 3:18) and its corresponding verb γινώσκω (*ginōskō*). The ubiquitous presence of the various forms of "knowledge" and "to know" and the critique of "false knowledge" are not evidence that the epistle combats the gnostic heresy of the second century, since concerns about revelation and true knowledge were part of the fabric of Christian theology from earliest times (contra Schelkle 1980: 230–34; Kelly 1969: 299; M. Green 1987: 42). Peter's opponents were others, most likely those who mixed various philosophic perspectives with Christian teaching (see "The Opponents in 2 Peter" in the introduction). Picirelli (1975: 89–90) has argued that the word γνῶσις (*gnōsis*) is broader than ἐπίγνωσις (*epignōsis*) and means knowledge in the fullest sense, while he affirms that ἐπίγνωσις (*epignōsis*) is used multiple ways in the NT: "(1) to know someone or something for who or what he or it really is; . . . (2) to come to a realization or perception (inwardly) of something; . . . (3) to learn or find out some (outward) fact; . . . (4) a realization or understanding that is already in existence, much like the simple *gnōsis*; . . . (5) to give acknowledgement to someone or something; . . . (6) the equivalent of conversion." In 2 Peter, ἐπίγνωσις (*epignōsis*) has to do with this latter sense of conversion (Picirelli 1975: 93). Neyrey (1993: 149), however, interprets the word within the frame of client-patron relationships and forwards the idea, based on Picirelli's fifth meaning, that the word signifies "acknowledgment" of God, who is the Patron of these believers (cf. Rom. 1:20–21). Neyrey makes a considerable leap from Picirelli's taxonomy and fails to forward any examples of ἐπίγνωσις (*epignōsis*) meaning the honorific acknowledgment of patrons (see the critique of this position in Starr 2000: 35–39).

In the attempt to differentiate these terms, the struggle often observed has roots both in the notion that terms contain a certain meaning and in an undervaluation of the way that lexemes attach to broader concepts. These will vary in meaning given the particular context in which they are used (Sperber and Wilson 1995). In the case of ἐπίγνωσις (*epignōsis*) and γνῶσις (*gnōsis*), either may be used in the context of personal knowledge, and it is that context that is determinative (BDAG 369, 203). This personal knowledge is in mind here, and the genitive τοῦ θεοῦ καὶ Ἰησοῦ τοῦ κυρίου ἡμῶν (*tou theou kai Iēsou tou kyriou hēmōn*, of God and Jesus our Lord) identifies the one known (cf. LXX: Prov. 2:5; Hos. 4:1; 6:6; NT: Eph. 1:17; 4:13; Col. 1:10; 2 Pet. 1:3, 8; 2:20). Given the personal object of knowledge here in 2 Pet. 1:2, Bauer's suggestion that the word may reflect "legal terminology" appears wide of the mark (BDAG 369). In this personal knowledge of God, the great privilege of Christianity, these believers may abound in saving grace and peace. God's benefits are never detached from his person.

The objects of this personal knowledge are "God" and "Jesus our Lord." While verse 1 ascribes the titles "God" and "Savior" to Jesus Christ, here God is differentiated from Jesus, and we should understand Peter's thought to mean "God the Father" (1 Pet. 1:2). Within these verses we find the raw building blocks for trinitarian theology, although the Holy Spirit is not named in this verse (cf. 1 Pet. 1:2). Jesus is called "Lord," which, as noted in the comments on Jude 4, was a divine title both in Hellenistic and Hellenistic-Jewish literature.

## Additional Note

**1:1.** The MS evidence slightly favors the reading Σίμων (*Simōn*, 𝔓72 B Ψ) over Συμεών (*Symeōn*, ℵ A K P) but the testimony of the witnesses is not strong enough to argue for this reading. Likely the scribes sought to harmonize Peter's name in this text with the more common Σίμων (*Simōn*) since Συμεών (*Symeōn*) was used rarely (Acts 15:14).

I. Epistolary Greeting (1:1–2)
➤ II. Letter Body: A Warning against False Teachers (1:3–3:18a)
III. Letter Closing: A Doxology (3:18b)

# II. Letter Body: A Warning against False Teachers (1:3–3:18a)

The body of the correspondence employs many of the conventions of common letters of the era. The section identified as a "testament" in 1:12–15 is in fact a form of disclosure formula commonly included in letters to indicate the author's purpose for writing (White 1986: 30–31, 33, 89, 204). The disclosure formula was shifted to the "introductory part of the body during the Roman period" (White 1986: 207) and served as a transitional device (White 1972: 11). Second Peter includes a second disclosure formula in 3:1–2, at the head of the hortatory section of the correspondence. But this disclosure refers to the author's previous correspondence. References to other correspondence are likewise an ancient epistolary convention (White 1986: 207). Moreover, part of the author's purpose is to make requests of his readers; as White notes, "The most common means of making requests is to employ some form of the polite convention . . . 'therefore you will do well to . . .'" This is precisely the form that the author uses to present his exhortation in 1:19: "You will do well to pay heed." Repeatedly the author addresses his fellow believers as "Beloved" (3:1, 8, 14, 17) in the hortatory section of the letter, and as previously noted (see "Genre and Structure" in the introduction), this is a convention in friendly letters as moral exhortation is carried out in the context of friendship (Stowers 1986: 95). Second Peter also calls for responsible behavior (3:1–2, 8, 11, 14) and urgent action (1:5, 10; 3:14 and cf. 1:15), both recurring features in letters that seek to persuade (White 1986: 205). Stereotypical phrases found in a wide spectrum of ancient letters confront us at every turn (Doty 1973: 12–13). The letter format is much more than "literary fiction" or simply the frame into which the "testament" of Peter is cast. This is not a sermon or a public discourse dressed as a letter but a genuine correspondence in all respects.

II. Letter Body: A Warning against False Teachers (1:3–3:18a)
➤ A. Body Opening: God's Call to Glory and Virtue (1:3–11)
   B. Body Middle: The Apostolic Testimony and the False Teachers (1:12–2:22)
   C. Body Closing: A Call to Holiness (3:1–18a)

# A. Body Opening: God's Call to Glory and Virtue (1:3–11)

Paul's letters commonly included an opening thanksgiving (Rom. 1:8–15; Phil. 1:3–11; Col. 1:3–14; 1 Thess. 1:2–11; Philem. 4–6) or a blessing of God (or בְּרָכָה, *běrākâh*, 2 Cor. 1:3–4; Eph. 1:3–6), whose epistolary function was to introduce the main themes of the letter (O'Brien 1977: 262). In formal public orations, the opening *exordium* of the speech would serve the same purpose. Some, such as Watson (1988: 87), have even argued that the author of 2 Peter structured his letter according to the canons of ancient rhetoric, with 1:3–15 serving as this *exordium* (see "Genre and Structure" in the introduction). But the body opening in Hellenistic letters commonly introduced the main themes of the correspondence, as White (1972: 156) has observed: "Whereas the general function of the body is to impart information to someone at a distance, the body opening performs the specific role of introducing this information. . . . Once this matter of mutual concern has been introduced, the body middle may carry the relevant details forward." The opening of the letter body in 2 Peter is somewhat unusual in that it is neither a thanksgiving nor a blessing, yet it serves this common function of introducing the fundamental themes that the author will subsequently address. In these verses he introduces God's engagement with the readers in salvation (1:3–4) and underscores the necessity of moral growth (1:5–9) in anticipation of entrance into God's eternal kingdom (1:10–11). These themes are placed in juxtaposition to the immoral bent of the heretics who assailed the church as they denied the providential care of God as well as the final judgment. The form that the body opening assumes is that of honorific decrees that extol the virtues of certain benefactors (Danker 1978; Danker 1982: 453–67; Neyrey 1993: 150–51).

Danker (1978: 65) has argued that the opening verses of 2 Peter are "impregnated with terminology used in a broad range of Hellenistic decrees." One such decree that honored Antiochos III said:

> Inasmuch as Great King Antiochos has continued his ancestors' policy of special favor toward all the Greeks, and has brought peace to some and has given aid to many who were in trouble both privately and publicly, and has brought liberty to some who had been enslaved, and during his entire reign has legislated with a view to benefiting mankind, having first rescued our city from slavery he declared it free. (Danker 1978: 67)

The author's adaptation of the common language of such decrees is innovative but suitable for the purpose of extolling the deeds and the subsequent honor that accrues to God, as well as laying out the obligations incumbent on those who are subjects of this one who is their exalted benefactor.

Honorific decrees would begin by naming the celebratory community that offers up honors to a benefactor, a function taken up by the *praescriptio* in 2 Pet. 1:1–2. The following portion of the decree would be "a preamble of varying length, expressed in a circumstantial clause usually introduced by *epeidē* [because, for, since], citing the signal contributions and virtues of the Benefactor" (Danker 1978: 65). Instead of beginning with ἐπειδή (*epeidē*), Peter's preamble (1:3–4) opens with the equivalent Ὡς (*hōs*, because; LSJ 2039), which unfortunately is often left untranslated (NRSV, NIV, TNIV, NJB). This marker of the cause or reason for the honors is followed by a genitive absolute both in public decrees and 2 Peter (BDF §423; Danker 1978: 67; 1982: 455). The preamble to the decree is elliptical in the Greek (1:3–4), a fact not readily discerned in translations that smooth the sense for the English reader. But the moral resolution (Danker 1982: 459) that begins in verse 5 includes the main clause of the sentence and echoes the format of honorific decrees. We should not, therefore, include a period at the end of verse 4 but rather a comma, leaving a construction that is awkward in English but mirrors the tone of the ancient decrees. After the preamble, such decrees included a resolution, which in 2 Peter's adaptation of this genre runs from 1:5 through 1:11. The unit outline is as follows:

1. Divine power and promises for life and duty (1:3–4)
2. An urgent appeal to ascend in virtue (1:5–11)

## Exegesis and Exposition

[3]Because his divine power has given us all things for life and duty through the knowledge of the one who called us in accordance with his own glory and virtue, [4]out of which he has given us honorable and extraordinary promises in order that through these you might become partakers of the divine nature, escaping the corruption that is in the world due to lust. [5]And also for this very reason bring all your energy to bear to add to your faith virtue, and to virtue knowledge, [6]and to knowledge self-control, and to self-control endurance, and to endurance duty, [7]and to duty fraternal love, and to fraternal love—love. [8]For if these things are yours and abound, they will not make you either worthless or unfruitful in the knowledge of our Lord Jesus Christ. [9]But the one who does not possess these things is blind, diseased of the eye, forgetting the purification from his former sins. [10]Therefore instead, brothers and sisters, take pains to confirm your calling and election, for by doing these things you will not ever fall. [11]For in this manner entry into the eternal kingdom of our Lord and Savior Jesus Christ will be generously granted you.

## 1. Divine Power and Promises for Life and Duty (1:3–4)

Peter's solemn decree begins with a declaration of the benefits that God has **1:3** bestowed on his people: Ὡς πάντα ἡμῖν τῆς θείας δυνάμεως αὐτοῦ τὰ πρὸς ζωὴν καὶ εὐσέβειαν δεδωρημένης (*hōs panta hēmin tēs theias dynameōs autou ta pros zōēn kai eusebeian dedōrēmenēs*, Because his divine power has given us all things for life and duty). The source of the benefits is "his divine power" (τῆς θείας δυνάμεως αὐτοῦ, *tēs theias dynameōs autou*), which may be simply a "periphrasis of the term *God*" (Deissmann 1901: 362). Both Deissmann and Danker (1982: 456) point up the use of the phrase in a decree enacted at Stratonikeia: "The statues of the aforementioned Gods, which supply the most illustrious displays of divine power, are set up in the most hallowed council chamber." However, the phrase also appears repeatedly in discussions about the nature of the divine in relationship to human nature. Plato, for example, comments about "some man, in whom human nature [φύσις τις ἀνθρωπίνη, *physis tis anthrōpinē*] was blended with power divine [θείᾳ τινὶ δυνάμει, *theia tini dynamei*]" (*Laws* 3.691E). Dio Chrysostom similarly states, "Again, because men such as these also share in a sort of divine power [θείας τινὸς δυνάμεως, *theias tinos dynameōs*] and purpose . . ." (*Or.* 31.95). Philo (*Worse* 23 §83) merges this discussion of the relationship between the human and the divine into his reflection on the image of God in humans while differentiating human from animal life: "To the faculty which we have in common with the irrational creatures blood has been given as its essence; but to the faculty which streams forth from the fountain of reason breath has been assigned; not moving air, but, as it were, an impression stamped by the divine power [θείας δυάμεως, *theias dynameōs*], to which Moses gives the appropriate title of 'image,' thus indicating that God is the Archetype of rational existence, while man is a copy and likeness." The Letter of Aristeas (155–57) likewise reflects in wonder at the way humans are framed and concludes: "So he exhorts us to remember how the aforesaid parts are maintained and preserved by divine power under his providence" (R. J. H. Shutt, *OTP* 2:23). Peter employs key terms from the discussion of the divine in relationship to the human in the present verse. Power divine makes them what they are, which, according to the following verse, includes divine moral attributes. This transcendent and sovereign power of God, which he exercises on behalf of humans, is the foundation for honoring him, in Peter's view.

Peter states nothing about what God bestows on humanity in general but rather describes what the divine benefactor has given his people (ἡμῖν, *hēmin*, to us): πάντα . . . τὰ πρὸς ζωὴν καὶ εὐσέβειαν (*panta . . . ta pros zōēn kai eusebeian*, all things for life and duty). Peter's way of chronicling the divine benefits follows the common language of the honorific decrees. For example, in 167 BC the assembly of Athens recognized Pharnakes I with the promise to exert every effort to "render him everything that pertains to [πάντα τὰ πρός, *panta ta pros*] glory and remembrance" (Danker 1982: 456). The "life" that comes from God may be "eternal life," that life from God that is the great boon of the gospel of Christ (John 6:68; Acts 5:20; Rom. 6:4; Eph. 4:18; Phil. 2:16; 2 Tim. 1:1). But the term itself need not be interpreted within the frame of eternal salvation since in other contexts it refers to natural human life as opposed to death (Prov. 18:21; Sir. 37:18; Luke 16:25; Acts 8:33; Rom. 8:38; 1 Cor. 3:22; Phil. 1:20; James 4:14). Judges 17:10 Theod. even uses the expression τὰ πρὸς ζωήν (*ta pros zōēn*) in speaking of what pertains to human life. Since reflection on the "divine nature" is a common theme in the discussion about human life, Peter's statement here likely affirms that God is the source of human existence rather than "eternal life" (contra Kelly 1969: 300; Senior and Harrington 2003: 243) or "a godly life" (contra Fornberg 1977: 90; Bauckham 1983: 178; Neyrey 1993: 150).

Fornberg (1977: 90) argues for the ethical sense of "life" here since in 2 Peter nouns coordinated by καί (*kai*, and) "are usually related in meaning," in this case "life and piety." But this is hardly an example of hendiadys (BDF §442.16) any more than were "glory and virtue" in 1:3b. The terms are coordinated only insofar as they both are benefits that issue from the divine power. Peter's thought is that God is the one who frames human existence. In a world of high infant and child mortality, where few people survived beyond their thirties, the value of life was highly esteemed and understood as a divine gift (Shelton 1988: 93–94).

The other benefit received by Peter and his fellow believers is "duty" (εὐσέβειαν, *eusebeian*). This term, equivalent to the Latin *pietas*, should not be understood simply as religious devotion. *Pietas* in the Roman Empire, as well as its Greek equivalent εὐσέβεια (*eusebeia*), had to do with showing reverence and loyalty to those to whom it is due: the gods, parents, relatives, ancestors, social institutions, and fellow citizens. What was prized most highly by the Romans was "dogged determination and an unflinching devotion to duty" (Shelton 1988: 4). The truly pious person demonstrates the high ideal of doing one's duty, which was one of the prime Roman virtues (*OCD* 1182, 1301; BDAG 412; Shelton 1988: 4, 372). As Cicero said, "*Pietas* warns us to keep our obligations to our country or parents or other kin" (*Inv.* 2.66) as well as "justice towards the gods" (*Nat. d.* 1.116). We can hardly imagine that a first-century reader of this letter would have understood the term exclusively as a reference to the faithful discharge of duties toward God although, indeed, this is the primary obligation for which the term is used in the LXX and the NT (cf. Philo and Josephus, who use the term more broadly; W. Foerster, *TDNT* 7:180–81). The divine gift of "duty" is set over against the heretics, who were ἀσεβής (*asebēs*) or impious (2:5–7).

Peter therefore lands on two fundamental values of the era, life and duty, and declares that God supplies to his people all things needful so that one might have them (cf. 1 Tim. 6:17b). What is most essential for self-existence and social existence finds its source in him. Understanding Peter's decree in this way does not diminish any thoughts about the wider issues of redemption such as eternal destiny and moral transformation. These are presented as topics in the following clauses. However, Peter's view of the divine initiative in human life is not separated neatly into sacred and profane since every aspect of existence, both now and for eternity, is bound up with the acts of his divine power or virtue. A Christian sees God's *redemptive* hand in what is most often relegated to "nature" or creation.

God grants his great boon to those who have entered into a personal relationship with him: διὰ τῆς ἐπιγνώσεως τοῦ καλέσαντος ἡμᾶς ἰδίᾳ δόξῃ καὶ ἀρετῇ (*dia tēs epignōseōs tou kalesantos hēmas idia doxē kai aretē*, through the knowledge of the one who called us to his own glory and virtue). The "knowledge" Peter has in mind is the same personal knowledge touched on in verse 2 (see comments), which results in salvation (Picirelli 1975: 90, 93). Yet this knowledge of God is not the mere fruit of human inquiry or speculation but is the result of the divine initiative. The one whom the believers have come to know is "the one who called us." God is known as "the one who calls" in various texts in the NT (Rom. 4:17; 9:12; Gal. 1:6, 15; 5:8; 1 Thess. 2:12; 5:24; 2 Tim. 1:9; 1 Pet. 1:15; 5:10). The call to salvation is always understood as a divine act although a human messenger may be employed (Rom. 8:30; 1 Cor. 1:9; Gal. 1:6, 15; 5:8; Eph. 4:1, 4; Col. 3:15; 1 Tim. 6:12; 2 Tim. 1:9; Heb. 9:15; 1 Pet. 1:15; 2:9; 5:10; 2 Pet. 1:3). The Thessalonian believers, for example, were called by God through the preaching of the gospel (2 Thess. 2:13–14). Jesus assumed this divine privilege of calling (Matt. 4:21; Mark 2:17), which in the OT was attributed to Yahweh (Isa. 41:9; 42:6; 48:12, 15; 51:2), who makes his own those whom he calls. God's call presupposes his election (2 Thess. 2:13–14; Rom. 8:30).

The NT authors do not linger over the reasons for God's election but rather direct attention to the purposes of his calling. Here Peter declares that God has called them "in accordance with his own glory and virtue." The combination found here in 1:3b, "glory and virtue," was fairly common in ancient literature. For example, Pausanias (8.52.6) speaks of someone whose "valour and glory . . . are famed throughout Greece," and Dionysius of Halicarnassus (*Ant. rom.* 5.62.4) honors the brave men who won war "by their own valour; the glory of it would not have been shared [κοινωσόμενοι, *koinōsomenoi*] with anyone else." Such virtues are not limited to men alone. Diodorus Siculus (2.45.2) recalls the story of an Amazon woman: "And since her valour and fame increased, she made war upon people after people of neighboring lands," and hails the goddess Athena's power and the "memorial of her valour and of her well-merited fame" (3.70.5). Ἀρετή (*aretē*) is a way to speak of the acts that invite renown or glory (BDAG 130). In the human sphere, virtuous acts may be those of military conquest. But applied to God, the reference is to his wondrous deeds or manifestations of his power, which are worthy of praise (1 Pet. 2:9; Isa. 42:8, 12, 21; 63:7; Philo, *Spec. Laws* 1.38 §209; *Dreams* 1.43 §256; Josephus, *Ant.* 17.3.2 §54; 17.5.6 §130; Deissmann 1901: 95–96). "Glory" (δόξῃ, *doxē*) is then the honor and praise given to God due to his wondrous deeds (BDAG 257; and comments on Jude 25). The combination of the terms appears in Isa. 42:8, 12 LXX in reference to God.

Peter's statement appears to be that God calls his people "*to* his own glory and virtue," and Spicq (*TLNT* 1:371) concludes, "Actually, the great innovation of the new covenant is that it calls all believers to share the 'eternal glory (of God) in Christ' (1 Pet 5:10)." The thought may be similar to Paul's statement to the Thessalonians that God had called them "into his own kingdom and glory" (1 Thess. 2:12 NRSV) "so that you may obtain the glory of our Lord Jesus Christ" (2 Thess. 2:14 NRSV). However, the expression ἰδίᾳ δόξῃ καὶ ἀρετῇ (*idia doxē kai aretē*, in accordance with his own glory and virtue) echoes ancient honorific decrees. Danker (1982: 457) comments that ἴδιος (*idios*), here in the dative, is "a standard decretal term for describing the intense personal interest that a benefactor takes in a project. In such contexts the adjective functions as a possessive pronoun, serving to focus attention on the primary source of the benefactions, as in the recognition accorded Antiochos I Soter, who effected political stability 'by virtue of his own arete.'" Given this known use and the structuring of 2 Peter around a decretal form, the phrase "points to the instrumental cause of the invitation," and the dative should be understood as instrumental: "in keeping with (in view of) his own reputation and arete" (Danker 1982: 457–58). Peter adopts and adapts common honorific language in order to speak of divine honor held by God as Benefactor (see G. Kittel, *TDNT* 2:233–48).

**1:4**  Having commented on God's "glory and virtue," Peter now states: δι᾽ ὧν τὰ τίμια καὶ μέγιστα ἡμῖν ἐπαγγέλματα δεδώρηται (*di' hōn ta timia kai megista hēmin epangelmata dedōrētai*, out of which he has given us honorable and extraordinary promises). In ancient decrees, the expression δι᾽ ὧν pointed to the personal expenditures of a benefactor (Danker 1978: 69–70). One inscription refers to the expenditures of Zosimos, who conferred benefits "out of his own monies" (Danker 1982: 458).[1] Here Peter declares that God's boon finds its source in his own "glory and virtue." What God has given are "promises" (ἐπαγγέλματα, as in 3:13, a term not distinguished from ἐπαγγελία, *epangelia* in 3:4, 9; J. Schniewind and G. Friedrich, *TDNT* 2:585–86), which are described as being "honorable and extraordinary." Honorific decrees occasionally mention that the honored benefactor had given certain promises that were subsequently fulfilled (Danker 1978: 70; 1982: 458, 479). In one decree, the benefactor Pharnakes said, "I promised to fulfill obligations that had been made earlier." Another from Priene speaks of "those who had been promised an invitation and who had received it." The phase κατ᾽ ἐπαγγελίαν (*kat' epangelian*, according to the promise), similar to Peter's language, is found in honorific inscriptions. The *demos*, or citizens, honored Cassius Lyaios "in accordance with the promise of Epaxion the stonemason" (*New-Docs* 4:147). Promises then, as now, were sometimes no more than words, and so the affirmation that a promise has been fulfilled is truly noteworthy. Cicero even went to some lengths discussing just when a promise was not binding (*De officiis* 3.24.92–3.25.95) and concludes, "Promises are, therefore, sometimes not to be kept."

---

1. Compare the Erastus inscription in Corinth near the theater: "Erastus pro aedilit[at]e s(ua) p(ecunia) stravit [Erastus for his aedileship laid (the pavement) at his own expense]."

In light of the uncertainty of promises, Paul goes to some length to assure the Corinthians of the verity both of his and God's promise (2 Cor. 1:15–22; Rom. 9:8; 15:8; 2 Cor. 7:1; Gal. 3:17, 21; Heb. 4:1; 6:12, 15, 17; 8:6; 9:15; 10:36; 1 John 2:25; as well as Polybius 3.111.10; 18.28.1; J. Schniewind and G. Friedrich, *TDNT* 2:577). While discussion about God's promises sometimes brings into focus those that are fulfilled in the gospel (Acts 2:33; 13:23; Gal. 3:14; Eph. 3:6; 1 Tim. 4:8), 2 Peter was written to assure the church of the surety of God's eschatological promises, which had come under attack by the heretics. The promises Peter has in mind are about Christ's coming (3:4) and the new heaven and new earth (3:13), as well as the believers' entrance into the eternal kingdom (1:11). The apostle strives to assure the church that delay in Christ's return and the coming judgment does not mean that God's promises will not be fulfilled (3:9). Whatever delay there may be is due to God's calculation of time and his mercy (3:8–9).

In the present verse, Peter arrests the heretics' critique of the divine promise by stating that God's promises are τίμια καὶ μέγιστα (*timia kai megista*, honorable and extraordinary). The language again echoes that of honorific decrees, in which nouns often appear with the kind of double qualification that Peter makes about God's promises. The form is not precisely fixed, so we hear of "many and illustrious services," "many and useful things," "many and great contests against the barbarians," and "many and signal services" (Danker 1978: 70; 1982: 458). The first qualifier that Peter uses to describe God's promises is τίμια (*timia*), which may be used to describe what is "valuable" (1 Cor. 3:12; Rev. 17:4; 18:12a, 16; 21:11, 19) or something that is of great worth and precious (a favorite Petrine idea, 1 Pet. 1:19; James 5:7). What was valued in this latter respect was held in high honor (Acts 5:34; Heb. 13:4; cf. τιμή, *timē* in 1 Pet. 1:7; 2 Pet. 1:17; BDAG 1005–6; MM 635). The promises of God are "honorable" because of the character of God (1:3b), and the fact that they are honorable stands as the surety of their fulfillment. These promises are likewise "extraordinary" (μέγιστα, *megista*, is the superlative form of μέγας, *megas*, great, here with an elative sense, that is, meaning "very great" rather than "greatest"). This term, found only here in the NT, survives principally in ancient texts as a description of the gods (MM 393; BDAG 624). However, Peter's use mirrors honorific inscriptions describing the great deeds of benefactors as "many and great" (Danker 1978: 70; 1982: 458). Given the content of the divine promises, which includes Christ's coming and entrance into his eternal kingdom (1:11; 3:4), the description of them as "extraordinary" is hardly hyperbolic and highlights their divine source.

The purpose for giving such promises is outlined in the following clause: ἵνα διὰ τούτων γένησθε θείας κοινωνοὶ φύσεως (*hina dia toutōn genēsthe theias koinōnoi physeōs*, in order that through these you might become partakers of the divine nature). Once again we hear the language found in honorific decrees, which include a purpose clause (frequently beginning with ὅπως, *hopōs*, in order that, but sometimes with ἵνα, *hina*, as in 1:4), which "points to the objective behind giving of the promises" (Danker 1978: 70; 1982: 458).

For example, one inscription from Priene hails the judge Herokrates for his demonstration of zeal, "to the end that the litigants might reach an amicable disposition of their case."

The purpose of God's promises is so that the believers "might become partakers of the divine nature." Peter's affirmation enters into the ancient discussion about the nature of the gods, humans, and the animal world. The question raised was not about humans becoming divine but rather which characteristics and attributes these different classes of beings shared or did not share (see 1:3 and comments). On the one side, Dio Chrysostom is able to say that humans have "this god-given superiority over the other animals of being able to reason and reflect about the gods," and they have received from the divine "intelligence and the capacity for reason, illuminated as they were on every side by the divine and magnificent glories of heaven and the stars, of sun and moon, by night and by day encountering varied and dissimilar experiences" (*Or.* 12.28). The capacity that humans have to see and hear is attributable to the fact that "on every side they were filled with the divine nature through both sight and hearing, and in fact through every sense" (12.29). Diodorus Siculus (5.31.4) comments that philosophers should be present at sacrifices as those who "are experienced in the nature of the divine and who speak, as it were, the language of the gods."

These thoughts about sharing divine characteristics are echoed within Jewish Hellenistic literature as well. Josephus, for example, uses language strikingly similar to 2 Pet. 1:4: "Amenophis, son of Papis, whose wisdom and knowledge of the future were regarded as marks of divinity [θείας δὲ δοκοῦντι μετεσχηκέναι φύσεως, *theias de dokounti meteschēkenai physeōs*]" (*Ag. Ap.* 1.26 §232). Philo commented, "This is the practice, I think, of kings also, who imitate the divine nature" (*Abraham* 28 §144), and he can even speak of the heavenly bodies sharing in the divine nature: "Not that any of the occupants of heaven wander, for sharing as they do in a blessed and divine and happy nature, they are all intrinsically free from any such tendency" (*Decalogue* 21 §104). In his comparative analysis of Josephus, Philo, Plutarch, the Stoics, Paul, and 2 Peter, Starr (2000: 234) concludes, "In all five literary groups we also observed the same *formal* relationship between divine nature and a human sharing in it, that is, between human virtue or character and God's character." Human virtue comes to resemble that of God.

Peter's thought has to do with moral transformation and not divinization or becoming divine men (Holladay 1977), as has sometimes been argued (Wolters 1990: 28–29). Peter's reflection is not principally about becoming "immortal and incorruptible" (Bauckham 1983: 181) but rather about the acquisition of moral character. Josephus reflected on the superiority of the legislation that came through Moses, who showed "that God possesses the very perfection of virtue." Therefore Moses "thought that men should strive to participate [μεταλαμβάνειν, *metalambanein*] in it" (*Ant.* proem 4 §23). In the discussion about the communicable attributes of God, Peter uses the term κοινωνοί (*koinōnoi*), those who share or participate in something (1 Cor. 10:18; 2 Cor.

1:7; 1 Pet. 5:1; BDAG 553), although sometimes other terminology is used, as seen above. Danker (1982: 459) frames Peter's thought: "To share in the divine nature therefore means to participate in the supreme virtues of the Chief Benefactor, with emphasis on righteousness and victory in the face of all that pronounces impermanence for humanity." Peter underscores the moral aspect of participation in the divine nature in the following clause, and in verses 5–7 he outlines the type of character that is exhibited by those who are "partakers of the divine nature."

Peter understands this moral transformation into godlike character to be an escape from moral corruption: ἀποφυγόντες τῆς ἐν τῷ κόσμῳ ἐν ἐπιθυμίᾳ φθορᾶς (apophygontes tēs en tō kosmō en epithymia phthoras, escaping the corruption that is in the world due to lust). The term "corruption" (φθορᾶς) is used repeatedly in the LXX (Ps. 102:4 [103:4 Eng.]; Isa. 24:3; Mic. 2:10; Jon. 2:7; Dan. 3:92 [3:25 Eng.]; Ps. Sol. 4.6) as well as the NT (Rom. 8:21; 1 Cor. 15:42, 50; Gal. 6:8; Col. 2:22; 2 Pet. 2:12) with reference to destruction or decay, and may even refer to death and abortion (*NewDocs* 2:82). If Peter has this sense in mind, his message here would be about the deterioration of the natural world (Rom. 8:21; Col. 2:22) or the destruction brought about by divine judgment (Gal. 6:8; 2 Pet. 2:12). The cause of this ruination of the world, whichever sense is understood, is human "lust." However, φθορά (*phthora*) may also refer to moral "corruption," as in Wis. 14:12 (on the "corruption of life") or 14:25, which locates this amid other vices: "All is a raging riot of blood and murder, theft and deceit, corruption, faithlessness, tumult, perjury" (NRSV). Similarly, in some contexts it may speak of sexual seduction (Aeschines, *Speeches* 1.12; Plutarch, *Mor.* 712C).

Peter takes φθορά in its moral sense in 2:19 (see comments), and in 2:20 he reiterates the thought of the present verse, using nearly identical vocabulary: "escaped [ἀποφυγόντες, apophygontes] the defilements [τα μιάσματα, ta miasmata] of the world [τοῦ κόσμου, tou kosmou]" (see comments). Having spoken of moral "corruption" (φθορᾶς) in 2:19, he varies the vocabulary in 2:20, using the synonym "defilements" (μιάσματα). He is not speaking of the decay of creation, as does Paul in Rom. 8:19–22, but rather understands the "world" as the domain of this moral corruption. This corruption is "in the world" (cf. 2:20, "of the world") because of "lust" (1:4, ἐν ἐπιθυμίᾳ, en epithymia; see Jude 16, 18, and comments).

One of Peter's principal critiques of the heretics who have influenced the church is that they are dominated by "lust" (2:10, 18; 3:3). Neyrey (1993: 156–57) has pointed out that "lusts" were considered one of the four principal vices in moral philosophy. The main or universal passions (παθῶν, pathōn), according to Hecato and Zeno, "constitute four great classes, grief, fear, desire or craving (ἐπιθυμίαν, epithymian), pleasure (ἡδονήν, hēdonēn; cf. 2 Pet. 2:13)" (Diogenes Laertius, *Lives* 7.110). Hierocles, *On Duties*, discusses the causes of human suffering: "Vice brings many of them to their natural end; because of a lack of self-control and lustfulness many diseases are produced, and many mutilations; because of injustice many people have had their hands cut off and received other such mutilations, and many have actually died" (Malherbe 1986: 88). "Lust," according to the Stoic Hierocles (*Elements of Ethics*), is set over against self-control, a thought that can be traced elsewhere. Pseudo-Aristotle, for example, commented, "To self-control [ἐγκρατείας] belongs the ability to strain desire [ἐπιθυμίαν] by reason when it is set on base enjoyments and pleasures [ἡδονάς], and to be resolute, and readiness to endure natural want and pain" (*Virtues and Vices* 1250B.15; cf. 2 Pet. 1:6). Plato even views lust as the cause of moral imprisonment: "Philosophy sees that the most dreadful thing about the imprisonment is the fact that it is caused by the lusts of the flesh, so that the prisoner is the chief assistant in his own imprisonment" (*Phaedo* 82E). The NT likewise denounces sinful desires (Mark 4:19; Rom. 7:7–8; Gal. 5:16–17; 1 Tim. 6:9; Titus 3:3; 1 Pet. 1:14; 2:11), and Peter here considers them the source of moral corruption, which dominates the world and characterizes the heretics. The heretics embody the root cause of the human plight.

## 2. An Urgent Appeal to Ascend in Virtue (1:5–11)

1:5    The previous verses of this section (vv. 3–4) follow the pattern of honorific decrees, which praised the character and the deeds of a benefactor. Peter has adapted this ancient genre to his literary ends in the opening of the letter body, as noted above. After their preamble, such decrees forward a resolution normally prefaced with a purpose clause introduced by ὅπως οὖν (*hopōs oun*). For example, in an honorific decree for the doctor Philistos of the island of Cos, the preamble is followed by the resolution, which begins with a purpose clause: "Therefore, so that all may know that we express appropriate appreciation to those who practice the policy of making us the beneficiaries of their philanthropies, be it resolved to commend Philistos of Kos, son of Nikarchos, and crown him" (Danker 1982: 57, and see 437, 441, 459; 1978: 71). But the inference that Peter draws out in light of the preamble in verses 3–4 has to do with the moral character of the readers of the epistle. Because of God's benefaction, which he previously outlined, the readers should be resolved to adopt a certain course of action. God's bounty begets a moral call.

The author's epistolary purpose eclipses the structure of the decrees while, at the same time, he artfully retains some of the language that framed them: καὶ αὐτὸ τοῦτο δὲ σπουδὴν πᾶσαν παρεισενέγκαντες ἐπιχορηγήσατε ἐν τῇ πίστει ὑμῶν τὴν ἀρετήν, ἐν δὲ τῇ ἀρετῇ τὴν γνῶσιν (*kai auto touto de spoudēn pasan pareisenenkantes epichorēgēsate en tē pistei hymōn aretēn, en de tē aretē tēn gnōsin*, And also for this very reason bring all your energy to bear to add to your faith virtue, and to virtue knowledge). Danker explains this shift in focus from the benefactor to the moral obligation laid on the believers by stating that our author "is about to show how the recipients of God's benefactions become participants in the divine nature and thus themselves become benefactors. In the interest of precision he uses the compound *pareispherō*, which means 'display alongside,' namely alongside the divine generosity" (Danker 1982: 460). Danker's explanation of the meaning of παρεισφέρω (*pareispherō*) overstretches the sense. Peter suggests nothing more than that the readers should "bring in beside" or "introduce" one virtue on top of another (LSJ 1334). Although there is no specific call to engage in benefaction, in Peter's world virtue was closely linked with benefaction. Peter does, however, maintain his emphasis on divine benefaction via completing the inclusio (envelope) in verse 11: God is the one who supplies. After presenting a list of virtues in *Rhetoric* 1366B (see below), Aristotle comments, "The greatest virtues are necessarily those which are most useful to others, since virtue is the faculty of conferring benefits [εἴπερ ἐστὶν ἡ ἀρετὴ δύναμις εὐεργετική, *eiper estin hē aretē dynamis euergetikē*]." Aristotle's subsequent discussion shows the particular social usefulness of justice, courage, liberality, and so forth. Virtue begets dutiful action for the social good.

The clause in verse 5 begins with αὐτὸ τοῦτο (*auto touto*), which functions as an "adverbial accusative" (BDAG 153; Rom. 13:6; 2 Cor. 5:5; Gal. 2:10; Eph. 6:22; Col. 4:8), placed between the conjunction and particle καί . . . δέ (*kai . . . de*, and also; BDAG 213), pointing Peter's readers to the realization that God's character and deeds are not only objects of praise but also moral demands. The indicative and the imperative cannot be separated (see Jude 21 and comments). The adverbial clause that follows makes use of a common expression about the expenditure of significant effort in accomplishing a task: σπουδὴν πᾶσαν παρεισενέγκαντες (*spoudēn pasan pareisenenkantes*, bring all your energy to bear). Josephus (*Ant.* 11.8.4 §324) comments that Sanballat "brought all his energy to bear [πάσαν εἰσενεγκάμενος σπουδήν, *pasan eisenenkamenos spoudēn*] and built the temple," and also notes the way Albinus "bent every effort [πάσαν εἰσενέγκατο σπουδήν, *pasan eisenenkato spoudēn*] and made every provision" to ensure peace in the land (*Ant.* 20.9.2 §204; and see Diodorus Siculus 1.83.8; 18.34.4; Polybius 1.18.11; 21.29.12). The combination πᾶσαν . . . σπουδήν (*pasan . . . spoudēn*) with a compounded form of the verb φέρω (*pherō*; such as εἰσφέρω, *eispherō*; or προσφέρω, *prospherō*) likewise appears frequently in the inscriptions where the great efforts of a benefactor are lauded. In an Athenian inscription, a person from the Society of the Soteriastai received praise for "displaying all enthusiasm and generosity in behalf of the organization" (Danker 1982: 459; see *TLNT* 3:279n14; BDAG 774; Deissmann 1901: 361, 364; 1965: 318n1). Honor accrued to the person who publicly demonstrated such diligence. Peter calls the believers to this kind of concerted and praiseworthy effort in their advancement in moral virtue. This emphasis on diligent action finds remarkable parallel in a first-century inscription from Asia Minor that honors Herostratus by attributing to him a list of virtues: "Being a good man and excelling in faith [πίστει, *pistei*] and virtue [ἀρετῆ, *aretē*] and righteousness [δ(ικ)αιοσύνη, *d(ik)aiosynē*] and duty [εὐσεβείᾳ, *eusebeia*], . . . [he] exerted great effort [τὴν πλείστ(η)ν εἰσενηνεγμένον σπουδήν, *tēn pleist(ē)n eisenēnegmenon spoudēn*]" (Deissmann 1911: 318n1; Danker 1982: 460; J. Charles 1997: 139).

Peter finally includes the principal verb in the imperative ἐπιχορηγήσατε (*epichorēgēsate*), a term that commonly refers to acts of generous benefaction displayed toward individuals or communities. It is particularly apt when used with reference to God's abundant supply (v. 11; 2 Cor. 9:10; Gal. 3:5; cf. Col. 2:19; and note how the uncompounded χορηγέω, *chorēgeō* becomes a term of benefaction in LXX: 1 Kings 4:7; 5:1; Jdt. 12:2; 1 Macc. 14:10; 2 Macc. 3:3; 4:49; 9:16; 3 Macc. 6:30, 40; 7:18; in NT: 2 Cor. 9:10; 1 Pet. 4:11; see also Dionysius of Halicarnassus, *Ant. rom.* 10.54.1; BDAG 386–87). Peter calls his readers to imitate the character of the good person who is a benefactor. They are to make a good and noble investment in the ascendancy of moral virtue. In the ancient world the moral ideal was considered to be within reach only of the educated and the powerful. The Christian faith, on the other hand, calls the lowest to display the character considered the domain of those of noble birth (Shelton 1988: 10–11).

In this and the following verses (vv. 6–7) Peter inserts a list of virtues, one of the many such lists in the NT with the most well known being Paul's "fruit of the Spirit" in Gal. 5:22–26 (see Rom. 5:1–5; 2 Cor. 6:6–7; Eph. 6:14–17; Phil. 4:8; Col. 3:12–14; 1 Tim. 3:2–3; 6:11; Titus 1:7–8; 3:1–2; James 3:17–18; Rev. 2:19; and on the lists see Easton 1932; Vögtle 1936; Wibbing 1959; Kamlah 1964; McEleney 1974; J. Charles 1997: 99–127; 1998). These lists of ethical virtues are counterbalanced with similar catalogs of vices that demonstrate the type of behavior one should avoid (1 Cor. 6:9–10; Gal. 5:19–21; Eph. 5:5; Col. 3:5, 8; 1 Pet. 4:3; Rev. 21:8; 22:15). This form of ethical instruction, while virtually unknown in the contemporary church, was a well-recognized mode of moral teaching in ancient literature. Aristotle commented, for example: "The components of virtue are justice, courage, self-control, magnificence, magnanimity, liberality, gentleness, practical and speculative wisdom" (*Rhetoric* 1366B). Musonius Rufus remarked that Zeus's "commandment and law is that man be just and honest, beneficent, temperate, high-minded, superior to pain, superior to pleasure, free from all envy and malice; to put it briefly, the law of Zeus bids man to be good" (*Fragments* 17; cited in Malherbe 1986: 32). The four cardinal virtues commonly appear together, as Menander notes, "Always divide the actions of those you are going to praise into the virtues (there are four virtues: courage, justice, temperance, and wisdom) and see to what virtues the actions belong and whether some of them, whether in war or in peace, are common to a single virtues" (cited in Malina and Neyrey 1996: 30). These four were distinguished from the subordinate virtues, according to Chrysippus (J. Charles 1997: 116). As does Menander, Quintilian also joins the principal virtues with actions: "At times on the other hand it is well to divide our praises, dealing separately with the various virtues, fortitude, justice, self-control and the rest of them and to assign to each virtue the deeds performed under its influence" (*Inst.* 3.7.15).

Lists of virtues and vices were not considered a wholly adequate form of moral instruction, however. Seneca affirms Posidonius, who says "that not only precept-giving . . . but even persuasion, consolation, and encouragement, are necessary. . . . He remarks that it will also be useful to illustrate each particular virtue. . . . It gives the signs and marks which belong to each virtue and vice, so that by them distinction may be drawn between like things" (Seneca, *Ep. mor.* 95.65). Teaching ethics through vice and virtue catalogs was also embraced within Judaism. Philo, for example, presents an extraordinarily long list of vices in *Sacrifices* 5 §32 and likewise catalogs thirty-three virtues (*Sacrifices* 5 §27), from piety (εὐσέβεια, *eusebeia*) through goodness (ἀγαθότης, *agathotēs*). This mode of moral instruction also appears within the Palestinian setting (1QS 4.9–11).

Virtue lists, whether in Judaism, Christianity, or the wider Greco-Roman world, reflected the worldview of the teachers of virtue (J. Charles 1997: 99–111), although at first sight the list in 2 Peter appears to include only two (faith, love) of the three cardinal virtues of Christianity: faith, hope, and love (vv. 5, 7; Rom. 5:1–5; 1 Cor. 13:13; Gal. 5:5–6; Col. 1:4–5; 1 Thess. 1:3; 5:8; Heb. 10:22–24; 1 Pet. 1:21–22). However, hope was linked intimately with "endurance" (v. 6; 1 Thess. 1:3), and at times faith and love appear in a catalog together with endurance, the fruit of hope (2 Thess. 1:3–4; 1 Tim. 6:11; 2 Tim. 3:10; cf. Rev. 2:2).

Peter presents his virtue list by using a literary device, fashionable during the period, called sorite (or *climax*, ladder; *gradatio*, gradation). As Fischel (1973: 119) describes it, "The sorite is a set of statements which proceed, step by step, through the force of logic or reliance upon a succession of indisputable facts, to a climactic conclusion, each statement picking up the last key word (or key phrase) of the preceding one." So, for example, *m. 'Abot* 1.1 states, "Moses received the Torah from Sinai and delivered it to Joshua, and Joshua to the Elders, and the Elders to the Prophets, and the Prophets delivered it to the Great Men of the Assembly" (cited in Fischel 1973: 119; cf. Homer, *Il.* 2.102–8; Epicharmus, *Fragments* 148). Mishnah *Soṭah* 9.15 includes an ethical sorite, not unlike 2 Pet. 1:5–7, which says, "Eagerness leads to Cleanliness . . . , and Cleanliness . . . to Purity, and Purity . . . to Self-Control . . . , and Self-Control . . . to Holiness, and Holiness . . . to Humility, and Humility . . . to Fear of Sin, and Fear of Sin . . . to Saintliness, and Saintliness . . . to the Holy Spirit, and the Holy Spirit . . . to the Resurrection of the Dead" (Fischel 1973: 133).

In the NT, Paul uses sorites in the virtue list of Rom. 5:3–5 (cf. Wis. 6:17–20; Seneca, *Ep. mor.* 85.2; Cicero, *De legibus* 1.7.23). Such lists are progressive and culminate in the summum bonum of the ethical system embraced by their author, which in the case of 2 Pet. 1:5–7 and Paul is "love." Peter's ethical list is set within the inclusio of knowing God and Christ (1:3–4, 8). The outcome of knowing God and becoming partakers of the divine character (1:4) is progress in moral character. Peter places the virtue list over against the immorality and the enticements of the heretics (2:18), who have themselves committed apostasy (1:9) and seek to carry others away in their error (3:17). Diligence in moral ascendancy is the author's antidote for the moral decline addressed in this correspondence.

The first virtue of Peter's list is "faith" (πίστει, *pistei*). In the NT, "faith" is commonly understood as trust in God (Mark 11:22; Rom. 4:5, 9, 11–13, 16, 19–20; Heb. 6:1; 11:4–33; 1 Pet. 1:21) or the gospel itself (Acts 6:7; Gal. 1:23;

Eph. 4:5; 1 Tim. 2:7; and comments on 2 Pet. 1:1; Jude 3). But when viewed within the frame of moral virtue, πίστις (*pistis*) means "faithfulness" or "reliability" (Matt. 23:23; Rom. 3:3; Gal. 5:22; 2 Thess. 1:4; 2 Tim. 4:7; Titus 2:10; cf. Sir. 1:27; 45:4; BDAG 818). "Faithfulness" was one of the principal ways patronage relationships were described in the Greco-Roman world. Πίστις (*pistis*) and its Latin equivalent, *fides*, both touch the core of this relationship (Calderone 1964; Gruen 1982). A client was received into the *fides* of the socially stronger patron, and so "to be in the *fides*" of someone meant that the person was under the patron's faithful care and protection, whether the client were an individual or a client-state. As Rich (1989: 129) comments, *fides* is virtually synonymous with *clientela*, "and the two words are often bracketed together. 'To be in X's *fides*' in effect means to be his client." On the other side, the client was expected to be faithful to the patron, and the same terms describe the client's end of this relationship. Plautus (*Menaechmi* 571–79) quipped, "What a stupid, irritating practice we have, and one the best people follow most! Everyone wants lots of clients. They don't bother to ask whether they're good men or bad; the last thing that counts is the reliability [*fides*] of the client, and how dependable he is [*clueat*, punning on *cliens*]. If he's poor and no rogue, he's held good for nothing; if he's a rich rogue, he's treated as a solid client" (cited in Wallace-Hadrill 1989: 64; and see also Danker 1978: 72; 1982: 460; Malina and Neyrey 1996: 167–68; Deissmann 1911: 309). Insofar as Peter's fundamental concern is to caution the church against the error of the heretics, placing "faithfulness" at the head of the virtue catalog is a strategic move. They are called to maintain this loyalty to their benefactor (1:3–4, 11), as anyone in ancient society would have understood. To violate loyalty to the one into whose *fides* one had come would be considered a most serious moral breach.

The second in Peter's graded list of virtues is ἀρετήν (*aretēn*), or "virtue," which previously appeared as an aspect of God's character (1:3 and comments). "Virtue" is likewise a social characteristic and marks the person as someone of "consummate excellence or merit within a social context" (BDAG 130; O. Bauernfeind, *TDNT* 1:457–59), whose deeds were worthy of public recognition. The virtue was canonized in both Jewish and Christian circles (2 Macc. 15:12; 3 Macc. 6:1; 4 Macc. 1:2, 10, 30; 10:9; 13:24; Wis. 8:7; Phil. 4:8). The person of "virtue" demonstrates excellence of character, shown in generosity toward others, surpassing what normal constraints of duty demand (Danker 1978: 72; 1982: 318). This character trait was frequently hailed in both literature and inscriptions and is sometimes found in combination with "faith." For example, Herostratus was hailed for his faith, virtue, righteousness, godliness, and diligence (see above; Deissmann 1911: 318; BDAG 130; Danker 1978: 72). Since special emphasis is placed on acts that demonstrate the character, the term should not be understood as simply a recognition of the internal character of the heart. The person marked by "virtue" is engaged socially. Though the heretics have embraced the lowest forms of vice (2 Pet. 2), Peter urges his readers to exert their efforts toward virtuous deeds that would be worthy of praise.

Peter further calls his readers to increase in "knowledge" (γνῶσιν, *gnōsin*), a thematic word in the letter (see 1:6; 3:18) along with its cognate ἐπίγνωσις (*epignōsis* in 1:2–3, 8; 2:20). This is not theoretical knowledge or that of philosophy, which was frequently understood as the foundation of moral character (J. Charles 1997: 141). Nor is it esoteric knowledge of hidden mysteries (see "The Opponents in 2 Peter" in the introduction); rather, it is the personal knowledge of the Lord Jesus Christ (3:18), which results in salvation (1:3 and comments). This "knowledge" stands over against the "ignorance" or animal-like irrationality of the heretics, whose error led to immorality (2:12 and comments). Peter understands that this personal and relational knowledge of God through Christ is essential if one is to progress in moral virtue. Knowing right does not mean doing right, but knowing God results in righteous conduct marked by self-restraint (v. 6a). On the other hand, ignorance of God and lust go hand in hand (1 Pet. 1:14).

In the ladder of virtues that Peter catalogs in these verses, the next rung is 1:6 ἐγκράτειαν (*enkrateian*) or "self-control" (ἐν δὲ τῇ γνώσει τὴν ἐγκράτειαν, *en de tē gnōsei tēn enkrateian*, and to knowledge self-control). The term points to the power or dominion over oneself especially with regard to consumption of food, the tongue, and sexual desire (Acts 24:25; Gal. 5:23; T. Naph. 8.8; also 4 Macc. 5:34; Let. Aris. 277–78; 2 Clem. 15.1; Josephus, *Ant.* 8.8.5 §235; Aristotle, *Eth. Nic.* 7.1.1–7.11.5; verbal form in 1 Cor. 7:9; 9:25). "Self-control" is personal restraint over emotions and desires and as such is the opposite of ἀκρασία (*akrasia*), the absence of power over oneself (cf. the cognates in 1 Cor. 7:9; 2 Tim. 3:3; *TLNT* 1:60–62). The Letter of Aristeas (277–78) records the question, "Why do not the majority of human beings recognize virtue?" The response is, "Because all men . . . have become naturally intemperate, and inclined to pleasures, as a result of which injustice came about and the mass of greed. The virtuous disposition, on the other hand, restrains those who are attracted to the rule of pleasure, and commands them to respect self-control and justice more highly. God directs in these matters" (R. J. H. Shutt, *OTP* 2:31). Socrates gave "self-control" an even more central place: "Should not every man hold self-control to be the foundation of all virtue, and first lay this foundation firmly in his soul? For who without this can learn any good or practice it worthily?" (Xenophon, *Mem.* 1.5.4–5).

The question was whether one would follow passion and desire or pursue virtue. "Self-control" was essential for living the virtuous life. Aristotle therefore said, "The unrestrained man [ἀκρατής, *akratēs*] does things that he knows to be evil, under the influence of passion, whereas the self-restrained man [ἐγκρατής, *enkratēs*], knowing that his desires are evil, refuses to follow them on principle." Therefore, being constrained by conviction rather than passion, "the self-restrained man is the man who abides by the results of his calculations, the unrestrained one who readily abandons the conclusion he has reached" (*Eth. Nic.* 7.1.6). Philo discusses the organs of the body—the eye, the ear, the mouth with its capacity to taste and speak, and sexual organs—and notes how restraint is called for in the use of each. He concludes, "So let us make it our earnest endeavour to bind up each of the openings which we have mentioned with the adamantine chains of self-control" (*Worse* 27 §§101–3). Neyrey (1993: 160) observes that Peter places self-control over against sins of the eyes (2:14), the mouth (2:12–13, 22), and the sexual organs (2:2, 14, 18), which marked the heretics' conduct. Although Peter does not give "self-control" a central place in his list of eight virtues, it plays a significant role in the battle against the profligate behavior that the heretics promote. It stands over against licentiousness (2:7, 18), lust (1:4; 2:10, 18; 3:3), lawlessness (2:8), and unprincipled (2:7; 3:17) and corrupt (1:4; 2:12, 19) behavior. The heretics were given over to what was most base in the human character.

Peter follows on the list of virtues by exhorting his readers/hearers to strive for "endurance": ἐν δὲ τῇ ἐγκρατείᾳ τὴν ὑπομονήν (*en de tē enkrateia tēn hypomonēn*, and to self-control endurance). "Endurance" is the ability "to hold out or bear up in the face of difficulty" (BDAG 1039), not "patience," as the KJV translates the term. In the face of suffering or temptation, the person with "endurance" demonstrates the capacity to remain steadfast and persevere (Luke 21:19; Rom. 5:3–5; 2 Cor. 1:6; 6:4; Col. 1:11; 2 Thess. 1:4; 1 Tim. 6:11; Titus 2:2; Heb. 12:1; James 1:3–4; Rev. 2:2–3). In Jewish reflection, this was the virtue that characterized the persecuted as they faced martyrdom (4 Macc. 1:11; 9:30; 17:4, 23; T. Jos. 10.1; MM 659). Early Christians who faced untold opposition for their faith prized the virtue highly. The capacity to endure was linked to "courage" in classical thought (ἀνδρεία, *andreia*; Plato, *Gorgias* 507B; so Philo, *Names* 36 §197; cf. 1 Cor. 16:13), while Stoicism reflected on it in conjunction with dispassionate resignation to fate (Seneca, *Ep. mor.* 67.10; *TLNT* 3:415). But the source of Christian endurance was hope in God (1 Thess. 1:3; cf. 4 Macc. 17:4). Peter does not have in mind, however, endurance in the midst of persecution or extreme hardship (cf. 2 Thess. 1:4; James 5:11) but rather moral endurance amid the pressures of temptation (cf. 4 Macc. 7:9; 17:12; Rom. 2:7). In light of the tactics of the heretics to draw the church into their error and immorality, the importance of this virtue is evident (cf. 2:1–3, 18–19).

On top of this virtue, Peter exhorts his readers to add "duty" to their character (ἐν δὲ τῇ ὑπομονῇ τὴν εὐσέβειαν, *en de tē hypomonē tēn eusebeian*, and to endurance duty). One of the principal concerns of our author is the development of εὐσέβεια (*eusebeia*) in the lives of his readers. Given the final cataclysmic consummation of all things and the establishment of new heaven and new earth, the believer should be marked by a holy way of life and εὐσέβεια in the present (3:11–13). Peter has previously declared (1:3) that through the divine power the believer has all that is needed for both this life and εὐσέβεια. In the ancient world this virtue was understood as the demonstration of due reverence and loyalty to the gods, parents, relatives, ancestors, social institutions, and fellow citizens (1:3 and comments). In the fabric of the social reality of Peter's readers, the virtue points up the necessity of loyalty to God and to the community in which the readers are embedded. As such, it stands opposite the way the heretics have denied the Lord (2:1) and the way others are abandoning the truth in order to follow them (2:2, 18–22). Given the overarching benefactions that have come from God (1:3–4), the believers are called to fulfill their duty toward him. This is a virtue that the heretics have in no way demonstrated (2:4–10). They will be judged, but the ones who show loyalty to God will be delivered (2:9).

The first of the final two virtues in Peter's catalog is "fraternal love": ἐν δὲ τῇ     **1:7** εὐσεβείᾳ τὴν φιλαδελφίαν (*en de tē eusebeia tēn philadelphian*, and to duty fraternal love). "Fraternal love" describes the love that family members extend to each other and not love toward those outside the family unit (4 Macc. 13:23, 26; 14:1; Philo, *Embassy* 12 §87; Josephus, *Ant.* 4.2.4 §26; Plutarch, *De fraterno amore*), although 2 Macc. 15:14 approaches the NT sense: "This is a man who loves the family of Israel and prays much for the people and the holy city—Jeremiah, the prophet of God" (NRSV; cf. Rom. 12:10; 1 Thess. 4:9; Heb. 13:1; 1 Pet. 1:22; and Mark 3:32–35; Matt. 23:8). The concept was different from φιλανθρωπία (*philanthrōpia*), the affectionate concern for humanity in general (contra Danker 1982: 461; J. Charles 1997: 144; see BDAG 1055–56). Ancient discussion on "fraternal love" stressed the solidarity and collaboration between siblings as well as the harmony or concord between them, although these relationships did not always realize the ideal (Plutarch, *De fraterno amore* 478E–F; 479D; 482E–F; Hierocles, *On Duties* 4.27.202; 4 Macc. 13:19–14:1). A line was drawn between "fraternal love" and friendship, for as Plutarch said, "For most of friendships are in reality shadows and imitations and images of that first friendship which Nature implanted in children toward parents and in brothers toward brothers" (Plutarch, *De fraterno amore* 479D; so Hierocles, *On Duties* 4.27.20). Plutarch as well as Hierocles contended that it would be folly to form friendships with others while not embracing siblings as friends.

This love between natural siblings stamped its impress on the relationship between those who have become brothers and sisters due to their relationship to God the Father through Christ (2 Pet. 1:10; 3:15) and marks the common familial life of those who have received new birth (1 Pet. 1:22; 1 John 4:17). Christian usage is likely indebted to the way Israelites used fraternal language (Deut. 15:2; Hos. 1:2; U. Falkenroth, *NIDNTT* 1:255). As Peter and other NT authors use the term, it is a mark of corporate solidarity. The fabric of the community to which Peter writes is threatened by the heretics' incursion as "many" follow their ways (2:2) after being enticed (2:14, 18). Peace is needed in this community (3:14), where the temptations to be carried away are strong (3:17).

The final virtue in this sorites is the crown jewel of Christian virtue: love (ἐν δὲ τῇ φιλαδελφίᾳ τὴν ἀγάπην, *en de tē philadelphia tēn agapēn*, and to fraternal love—love). This virtue commonly appears alongside faith and hope (Rom. 5:1–5; Gal. 5:5–6; Col. 1:4–5; 1 Thess. 1:3; 5:8; Heb. 10:22–24; 1 Pet. 1:21–22), with love occupying the principal place in this trilogy, according to

Paul (1 Cor. 13:13). It also appears in larger catalogs of virtues (2 Cor. 8:7; Gal. 5:22; Eph. 4:2; 1 Tim. 4:12; 6:11; 2 Tim. 2:22; 3:10; Titus 2:2). This love is extended to other members of the Christian community (1 Pet. 1:22; 4:8; 2 Thess. 1:3), including those in other localities (1 Thess. 4:9–10) or in leadership positions within the church (1 Thess. 5:13). But love was also to be shown to those outside the Christian family (1 Thess. 3:12), despite the hostility often directed at the church by the wider society. Christian love found its source and model in the love that God demonstrated to humanity, even in their hostility against him (Matt. 5:43–48; John 3:16; Rom. 5:6–8; 1 John 4:19). God is love (1 John 4:8), and for that reason those in relationship with him love the ones who are also recipients of his love (1 John 4:7–12). Love is a "cognitive emotion" (M. Elliott 2005: 135–64) that places the welfare of the other in first place (Eph. 4:16; Heb. 6:10). Love is not passive since, as Paul notes, love labors (1 Thess. 1:3), actively seeking to benefit others (1 Thess. 4:10). Although not a common term in inscriptions that honor benefactors (Danker 1982: 461–62), Paul's and John's understanding of the term embraces the notion of benefaction, with the recipients being those in need. Since Peter places this virtue at the culmination of a list that calls the believers to demonstrate the character of benefactors, we suspect that this notion would be implied.

**1:8**  In this and the following verse, Peter contrasts the condition of those who demonstrate and progress in virtue with those who do not display such character. Regarding those who possess these moral qualities, Peter begins with a conditional clause (BDF §418.2): ταῦτα γὰρ ὑμῖν ὑπάρχοντα καὶ πλεονάζοντα (*tauta gar hymin hyparchonta kai pleonazonta*, For if these things are yours and abound). "These things" refer to the virtues of verses 5–7, which Peter expects to be in the possession of the believers (using ὑμῖν as the dative of possession; BDF §189; cf. 1:9). His readers should have these virtues (ὑπάρχοντα; cf. the expression τὰ ὑπάρχοντά τινι, *ta hyparchonta tini*, what belongs to someone; BDAG 1029; see Acts 3:6; 4:37; 28:7; cf. ταῦτα, *tauta*, in 2 Pet. 1:9). Although the catalog in verses 5–7 is presented as an ascending *gradatio*, he expects that the believers demonstrate the plurality of virtues and not simply those basic qualities that began the list.

These virtues should also "abound" (πλεονάζοντα, *pleonazonta*) in their lives, ever increasing in abundance (BDAG 824; MM 517; G. Delling, *TDNT* 6:263–66; W. Bauder and D. Müller, *NIDNTT* 2:130–31; LXX: Num. 26:54; Ps. 70:21 [71:21 Eng.]). The Christian does not abound in sin (Rom. 5:20; Sir. 23:23) but enjoys the abounding grace of God (Rom. 6:1; 2 Cor. 4:15) and should therefore abound in moral character (1 Thess. 3:12; 2 Thess. 1:3; cf. Phil. 4:17). The verb suggests an increase to the point of excess (contemporary youth culture might tag this "extreme" virtue). Peter once again demonstrates his expectation that the best way to arrest the incursion of the heretics and their immoral appeal is for continued growth and increase in moral character (cf. 2 Pet. 3:18). Bede (Hurst 1985: 128) picks up on the polemic sense in his comment, "He has said 'if they prevail,' if by their more powerful strength they prove stronger against the attacks of the vices." Although verse 8 begins as a conditional clause, the sense is imperatival. They *should* have these virtues and abound in them (cf. 1:5, 11).

The result of having and abounding in the virtues listed is that οὐκ ἀργοὺς οὐδὲ ἀκάρπους καθίστησιν εἰς τὴν τοῦ κυρίου ἡμῶν Ἰησοῦ Χριστοῦ ἐπίγνωσιν (*ouk argous oude akarpous kathistēsin eis tēn tou kyriou hēmōn Iēsou Christou epignōsin*, they will not make you either worthless or unfruitful in the knowledge of our Lord Jesus Christ). The effect of virtue on their lives and their relationship with Christ is highly significant. Their personal relationship with Christ was the bedrock of salvation (1:3 and comments), which in the end results in their participation in the moral character of God (1:4). But conversely, moral virtue rebounds to their knowledge of Christ (εἰς, *eis*, in or unto, which introduces the goal; BDAG 290). Possessing virtue and increasing in it will cause them not to be (BDAG 492; Rom. 5:19; James 4:4; cf. 3:6) "worthless" (ἀργούς, *argous*) in this knowledge of Christ.

When describing people, the ἀργοί (*argoi*) are idle folk who are lazy and do not work (Matt. 20:3, 6; 1 Tim. 5:13; Titus 1:12; Sir. 37:11). Comments about the idle in the works of moral philosophers were consistently negative. Speaking on the education of children, Plutarch (*Mor.* 12E) affirmed the Pythagorean allegory: "'Do not sit on a peck measure'; as much as to say that we should avoid idleness [φεύγειν ἀργίαν, *pheugein argian*] and have forethought for providing our daily bread." Dio Chrysostom (*Or.* 17.7; see 17.4) classified idleness as a vice: "Idleness [ἀργίαν], intemperance and, to express it in general terms, all the other vices without exception are injurious to the very men who practice them." Deeds and words could also be considered "idle," without effect or useless (Matt. 12:36; James 2:20; Wis. 14:5; MM 72; BDAG 128; *TLNT* 1:195–98). Peter's point is that having and growing in virtue will make them useful and productive as a συνεργός (*synergos*, one who helps) or εὐεργέτης (*euergetēs*, benefactor; *TLNT* 1:195) instead of being "idle" in the realm of virtue. Moreover, having and possessing Christian virtue will not cause them to be "unfruitful" (ἀκάρπους, *akarpous*) in the knowledge of Christ either. This metaphor of not bearing fruit referred to a life of vice (Jude 12; Matt. 13:22; Mark 4:19; Eph. 5:11) and as such is opposite of a life filled with good deeds (Titus 3:14; also cf. Philostratus, *De gymnastica* 42.14–19; Odes Sol. 11.23; BDAG 35). Being unfruitful is not the same as moral neutrality. Moral growth, therefore, becomes the antidote to vice (Gal. 5:22–23). Those who grow in this way avoid the deplorable condition of the heretics and their disciples (v. 9).

Peter contrasts[2] those who possess and progress in moral virtue (v. 8) with those whose lives do not demonstrate such character: ᾧ γὰρ μὴ πάρεστιν ταῦτα, τυφλός ἐστιν μυωπάζων (*hō gar mē parestin tauta, typhlos estin myōpazōn,* **1:9**

2. Γάρ (*gar*), as a marker of clarification, is sometimes equivalent to δέ (*de*, but); see Rom. 5:7 (BDAG 189.2). Alternatively, the doubling of γάρ (*gar*) at the head of verses 8 and 9 may simply be understood as a means of laying out multiple assertions (BDAG 189.1c).

But the one who does not possess these things is blind, diseased of the eye). As in the previous verse, "these things" (ταῦτα, *tauta*) refers to the virtues listed in verses 5–7. The people Peter has in mind do not possess such virtues (ᾧ γὰρ μὴ πάρεστιν, *hō gar mē parestin*). Τὰ παρόντα (*ta paronta*) were one's possessions (as for Xenophon, *Symposium* 4.42: "For those who are most contented with what they have are least likely to covet what belongs to others"; *Cyr.* 8.4.6; *Anab.* 7.7.36; Heb. 13:5; cf. τὰ ὑπάρχοντά τινι, *ta hyparchonta tini*, what belongs to someone, in the comments on v. 8). The dative ᾧ (*hō*) is, again, a dative of possession (see v. 8). Such virtue is not within the domain of the heretics and their disciples (cf. Wis. 11:21; 12:18), and so Peter classifies such people as "blind, diseased of the eye" (τυφλός ἐστιν μυωπάζων, *typhlos estin myōpazōn*). Both commentators and translators struggle with the way Peter moves from blindness to the less-serious "shortsightedness," leading some to reverse the order: "nearsighted and blind" (NRSV; so NIV, TNIV). Kelly (1969: 308), for example, comments, "The collocation of the adjective and participle (lit., 'is blind, being shortsighted') is curious, especially as the former is stronger than the latter." However, μυωπάζω (*myōpazō*) did not mean the same thing as "myopia" but described a much more serious condition of the eye, which could indeed close it (Pseudo-Zonaras, *Lexicon* 711.11; Suda, *Lexicon* 1065.1). It was the equivalent of the disease of ophthalmia. The malady produced a discharge from the eyes and could even be caused by carrion flies (Pseudo-Zonaras, *Lexicon* 1380.2; Gennadius Scholarius, *Grammatica* 2.467.34). This is not a problem that modern corrective lenses can cure. The "squinting" that the term describes is the experience of a person going blind (contra Mayor 1907: 95–96). The cause is the disease (adverbial participle μυωπάζων, *myōpazōn*), and the effect is blindness. Instead of being "illuminated" (1 Pet. 2:9), those who reject Christian virtue become spiritually blind, a common image in the NT (Matt. 15:14; 23:16–17, 19, 24; John 9:40–41; Rom. 2:19; Rev. 3:17; and the verb in 2 Cor. 4:4; 1 John 2:11; cf. Deut. 28:28–29). Other literature likewise used the metaphor of blindness to describe the inability to comprehend (Lucian, *Vitarum auctio* 18; Josephus, *Ag. Ap.* 2.13 §142; Ps. 146:8 [145:8 LXX: "The Lord gives wisdom to the blind"]). The gospel opens the eyes of a person to the truth of God, but the same person may return to darkness if one embraces sin again. That one will not have the capacity to understand the truth. Such is the case of the heretics to whom Peter refers (2:1; 3:4–5) as well as their disciples (2:17–22). The warning for Peter's readers is clear.

The condition of these people is further qualified by the statement λήθην λαβὼν τοῦ καθαρισμοῦ τῶν πάλαι αὐτοῦ ἁμαρτιῶν (*lēthēn labōn tou katharismou tōn palai autou hamartiōn*, forgetting the purification from his former sins). Although the expression λήθην λαβών (*lēthēn labōn*) commonly refers to a lapse of memory (Josephus, *Ant.* 2.9.1 §202: "Those benefits . . . through lapse of time forgotten"; and 4.8.44 §304), it could also point to a willful act of ignoring something (Josephus, *Ant.* 2.6.9 §163: "I would have you forget the past"; BDAG 584–85). Peter appears to use the expression in this latter sense (cf. 2 Pet. 3:5, 8). The blind person has ignored the "purification" from "his former sins" that have been committed (2:18, 20, 22).

Although Peter speaks about "his" (αὐτοῦ, *autou*; masculine singular), the pronoun may refer to either a man or woman, the masculine pronoun being used when either gender may be in view. The TNIV deals with the problem of grammatical gender specificity in this verse by using the second person ("But if any of you . . . , you are nearsighted and blind, and you have forgotten"), which implies the presence of the heretics and their disciples as part of the readership. This is not warranted since verse 8 uses the second-person plural in speaking to the ones who have not been taken by the error while the present verse refers to anyone engaged in the error in the third person. The NRSV simply leaves αὐτοῦ (*autou*) untranslated, a less-than-satisfactory omission.

Although "purification" (τοῦ καθαρισμοῦ, *tou katharismou*) commonly recalls a religious ritual or ceremonial act (Mark 1:44; Luke 2:22; 5:14; John 2:6; 3:25; 2 Macc. 2:16; Josephus, *Ag. Ap.* 1.31 §282; *m. Tohar., in toto*), the link with "sins" here points to a moral purification (Heb. 1:3; Job 7:21; and the verbal form in Acts 15:9; 2 Cor. 7:1; Eph. 5:26; Titus 2:14; Heb. 9:14; James 4:8; 1 John 1:7, 9). The reference is most likely to their baptism, which, as the Christian rite of initiation/conversion, is viewed as the moment of divine cleansing (Acts 22:16; Rom. 6:1–14; 1 Cor. 6:9–11; Eph. 5:26; Col. 2:11–13; Titus 3:5; Heb. 10:22; Bauckham 1983: 189; deSilva 2000: 304–6). The expectation of early Christians was that the moral change attends conversion. Old ways are left behind while new patterns of morality are embraced. "Purification," understood as a general category, had social entailments as well. The one purified became a member of the community, and conversely, the impure person was separated and excluded (Lev. 15:26, 31; 22:5–7; 1 Macc. 4:43; 2 Cor. 6:17; Eph. 5:5; and Ferguson 1993: 175; J. H. Elliott 1993; Neyrey 1996; Malina 2001: 161–97).

As Peter deals with the issue of apostasy, he recognizes the presence of certain individuals who, though once cleansed from sins and incorporated into Christ and the community through baptism, have returned to their former ways. Such people have ignored their cleansing and, because they have not embraced Christian morality, end up "blind" once again. The problem of apostasy appears again in 2:17–22 (see comments), where Peter brings to light the way some have been taken in by the heretics and have adopted a lifestyle like that which they embraced before conversion. But the heretics themselves are people who had been bought by the Lord but now deny him (2:1 and comments). What awaits such people is not salvation but condemnation (2:3). Apostasy is a genuine and dreadful possibility (see Marshall 1969; J. Charles 1997: 159–74; and cf. Gundry Volf 1990). Peter calls his readers to avoid this diligently by maintaining their life of virtue and holding to the truth, which they have at hand, rather than yielding to the persuasive power of the heretics (1:10–12). Doing this, they will not fall into ruin (1:10).

Peter exhorts his readers to embrace the alternative to the blindness that would be the result of returning to a life of immorality (v. 9): διὸ μᾶλλον,     1:10

ἀδελφοί, σπουδάσατε βεβαίαν ὑμῶν τὴν κλῆσιν καὶ ἐκλογὴν ποιεῖσθαι (*dio mallon, adelphoi, spoudasate bebaian hymōn tēn klēsin kai eklogēn poieisthai*, Therefore instead, brothers and sisters, take pains to confirm your calling and election). Although many translations understand μᾶλλον (*mallon*) as a comparative adverb with the principal verb and translate it "all the more" (as NRSV, "Therefore, brothers and sisters, be all the more eager"), the separation of this adverb from the verb by the vocative ἀδελφοί suggests that it should be read with διό (*dio*, therefore) and translated "instead" or "rather" (NJB, "Instead of this, brothers"). The author draws out a conclusion from the preceding and presents an alternative course of action.

In this strong moral appeal, he addresses the church directly as ἀδελφοί, which includes both men and women. This way of addressing the early Christian communities appears over one hundred times in the NT and opens a revealing window into the self-understanding of the early Christian community. The church is not simply a guild, religious association, or fraternity but is instead a brotherhood/sisterhood (cf. 1 Pet. 2:17; 5:9; also the use within the Jewish community in Exod. 2:11; Hos. 2:1; 2 Macc. 1:1; 1QS 6.10, 22; Rom. 9:3) of those who are members of God's household (Gal. 6:10). Fraternal love predominates (2 Pet. 1:7) among these who together call God their Father (Matt. 6:9; Rom. 8:15; Gal. 4:6; 1 Pet. 1:17; Jude 1). The vocative ἀδελφοί often, unsurprisingly, prefaces moral exhortation (e.g., 1 Thess. 4:1) since the family was the principal place for moral instruction, and obedience of children was expected and commendable (Seneca, *De beneficiis* 3.38.2). The same held within the new kinship relationship that one entered by becoming a disciple.

Peter urges his readers to moral progress by exhorting them to be diligent, conscientious, and even zealous in this endeavor (σπουδάσατε, *spoudasate*, aorist imperative). While this verb may call for swift action (2 Tim. 4:9, 21; Titus 3:12), it commonly refers to the diligent and conscientious activity one does to fulfill obligations (BDAG 939; *TLNT* 3:276–85; Gal. 2:10; Eph. 4:3; 1 Thess. 2:17; 2 Tim. 2:15; Heb. 4:11; 2 Pet. 1:15; 3:14). Honorific inscriptions often praised not only the generosity of benefactors but also the diligence with which they set about to render aid (Danker 1982: 463–64). As Spicq (*TLNT* 3:280) comments, "Whatever the nuance of each particular text, the diligence, care, or effort manifested comes from an initial goodwill, the pursuit of something one cares about, a desire to succeed; and *spoudazō*, in the first century AD, expresses the marks of an attentive benevolence, as thoughtful as it is efficient."

Peter appeals to his readers to adopt the kind of resolve and zeal that are marks of the most noble character. They are to "take pains" in order "to confirm your calling and election" (βεβαίαν ὑμῶν τὴν κλῆσιν καὶ ἐκλογὴν ποιεῖσθαι, *bebaian hymōn tēn klēsin kai eklogēn poieisthai*). Peter understands that salvation is the fruit of divine initiative in both their election and the resultant call to salvation (cf. 2 Thess. 2:13–14). Here Peter first mentions their calling (τὴν κλῆσιν, *tēn klēsin*), which is a frequent theme in the NT and is always understood as a divine activity, although a human messenger may be employed (1:3 and comments; Rom. 8:30; 1 Cor. 1:9; Gal. 1:6, 15; 5:8; Eph. 4:1, 4; Col. 3:15; 1 Tim. 6:12; 2 Tim. 1:9; Heb. 9:15; 1 Pet. 1:15; 2:9; 5:10). In the OT, the "calling" or divine summons is attributed to Yahweh (Isa. 41:9; 42:6; 48:12, 15; 51:2), who takes for himself those whom he calls. Jesus assumes this divine privilege in calling his disciples (Matt. 4:21; Mark 2:17). This calling comes through the proclamation of the gospel (2 Thess. 2:14) and is more than an invitation (cf. 1 Cor. 10:27) but rather a divine summons (Rom. 8:30). While God calls people into his kingdom (Heb. 3:1) and so to an eternal hope (Eph. 1:18; 4:4; Phil. 3:14), the emphasis frequently falls on the moral implications of the divine call (Eph. 4:1; 1 Thess. 2:12; 4:7; 5:23–24; 1 Pet. 1:15; 2:21; 3:9; cf. Gal. 1:6; 5:8). God's election (ἐκλογὴν, *eklogēn*) is the basis for the divine call. Scripture declares that God chose his people Israel as he does the church, and chooses out of love (Pss. 47:4; 78:68; Isa. 42:1; Matt. 12:18; Rom. 11:28; Eph. 1:4; Col. 3:12), grace (Rom. 11:5; 2 Tim. 1:9), or his sovereign purpose (Rom. 9:11; Eph. 1:5).

In the Greek-speaking world, the election or selection of military and political leaders was based on the merit and character of those chosen. But God's love is the root cause of his election, regardless of the character, accomplishments, merits, or virtue of the one called (Rom. 5:7–8; 2 Tim. 1:9). However, God's election is unto a life of holiness (Eph. 1:4). Given the divine initiative in both calling and election, the appeal for diligence "to confirm your calling and election" appears somewhat surprising, especially since making someone "firm" is elsewhere attributed to God (1 Cor 1:8; 2 Cor. 1:21). The word Peter uses (βεβαίαν, *bebaian*) points to what is firm and secure (2 Cor. 1:7; Heb. 6:19; 2 Pet. 1:19) or what is in force over a period of time (Rom. 4:16; Heb. 2:2; 9:17; BDAG 172). The terminology Peter uses also appears in the sense of giving a legal guarantee to confirm something (although most commonly with the verb ἔχω, *echō*, to have, rather than ποιέω, *poieō*, to do; *TLNT* 1:280; MM 107; Deissmann 1901: 104–9). We should understand the exhortation within this frame. The readers can "confirm" or even "ratify" this calling and election by their action, although the giving of such guarantees is usually carried out by the one who gives the promise. The actions Peter has in mind are the exercise of the virtues outlined in verses 5–7. Since election and calling result in a moral life, the confirmation of election comes in the exercise of such virtue (cf. Wis. 6:18).

Peter's conclusion is ταῦτα γὰρ ποιοῦντες οὐ μὴ πταίσητέ ποτε (*tauta gar poiountes ou mē ptaisēte pote*, for by doing these things you will not ever fall). "These things," once again, refers to the virtues of verses 5–7 (cf. "these things" in vv. 8–9). These virtues are not simply what someone has internally but rather are things a person does (ποιοῦντες, *poiountes*). The notion of "doing" virtue rather than simply "being" virtuous is quite common in the NT (John 3:21; Rom. 3:12; 13:3; James 2:13; 1 Pet. 3:11; 1 John 1:6; 2:29; 3:7, 10; Rev. 22:11; and see Acts 9:36; 10:2; 24:17). The promise that Peter holds out is extremely emphatic as he inserts the most decisive negative possible (οὐ μὴ, *ou mē*; BDAG 646) with ποτε (*pote*), which with negatives means "not ever" or "never" (see

1:21; BDAG 856). The person who exercises Christian virtue will never come to the kind of eternal ruin that the heretics and their disciples face.

Although the term that Peter uses to speak about falling (πταίσητε, *ptaisēte*) may refer to falling or stumbling into sin (James 2:10; 3:2), it may also point to eternal ruin (Jude 24 and comments), a sense similar to "falling in battle" (Herodotus 9.101; Diodorus Siculus 15.33.1; Josephus, *Ant.* 7.4.1 §75). Bede (Hurst 1985: 129) comments, "Those who return to their wicked deeds after their calling, when they depart from this life in these [deeds], already make definite to all that they are condemned." The heretics have fallen (2 Pet. 2:1) and are tempting others to sin, with the same result (2:14, 18). The problem Peter faces is apostasy. But he is determined that this will not be his readers' end (3:17) and assures them that it will not be their destiny if they continue to engage in the kind of moral behavior marked out by the gospel. Dedication to a virtuous life is the antidote to both spiritual blindness (2 Pet. 1:9) and eternal ruin (v. 10). Peter's hope for his readers is that the door to Christ's eternal kingdom will be open for them (v. 11). There is, clearly, a choice to be made by his readers between following the corruption of the heretics or the way of the gospel. By implication, if they follow the way of the heretics, they will share their final end.

**1:11**   Peter concludes his reworking of an honorific decree by returning again to underscore the divine benefaction: οὕτως γὰρ πλουσίως ἐπιχορηγηθήσεται ὑμῖν ἡ εἴσοδος εἰς τὴν αἰώνιον βασιλείαν τοῦ κυρίου ἡμῶν καὶ σωτῆρος Ἰησοῦ Χριστοῦ (*houtōs gar plousiōs epichorēgēthēsetai hymin hē eisodos eis tēn aiōnion basileian tou kyriou hēmōn kai sōtēros Iēsou Christou*, For in this manner entry into the eternal kingdom of our Lord and Savior Jesus Christ will be generously granted you). Peter refers back (οὕτως, *houtōs*; Matt. 11:26; Acts 7:8; 1 Cor. 14:25; 1 Thess. 4:17; BDAG 741–42) to the preceding exhortation to confirm their calling and election by diligent progression in moral virtue and the promise that they will never fall while so doing (vv. 5–10). Not only will they not fall into eternal ruin (v. 10b), but they also will actually be granted entrance into Christ's eternal kingdom. Peter uses the verb ἐπιχορηγηθήσεται (*epichorēgēthēsetai*) in the passive voice. The implied agent is God himself, who will provide them entry into the kingdom. This is the same term found in verse 5 (see comments) and here refers to an act of gracious benefaction. In this, Peter returns to the theme of God's benefaction (vv. 3–4), which exceeds all expectations: God richly or generously supplies (πλουσίως, *plousiōs*; 1 Tim. 6:17; Titus 3:6; and see Col. 3:16). Phaus Cyrenesis was praised for his display of duty both toward the deity and toward people "with magnanimity and generosity that exceeded his resources" (μεγαλ[ο]ψύ[χ]ως καὶ πλουσίως ὑπὲρ δ[ύ]ναμιν, *megal[o]psy[ch]ōs kai plousiōs hyper d(y)namin*; MM 521; Danker 1982: 464). God's benefaction is exceedingly generous.

God generously provides "entry" (ἡ εἴσοδος, *hē eisodos*) into the kingdom. The term may refer, as in English, to a place through which one enters (MM 188; Judg. 1:24–25; 2 Kings 11:16; 23:11; Josephus, *J.W.* 5.5.5 §220; *Ant.* 15.10.1

§347). But the word may also refer to the access or entry that someone is granted (1 Sam. 29:6; Ps. 120:8 [121:8 Eng.]; Let. Aris. 120; Philo, *Unchangeable* 28 §132). This is the sense Peter has in mind. The dominant message in the Gospels has to do with entry into the kingdom (Matt. 5:20; 7:21; 18:3; 19:23–24; 23:13; Mark 9:47; 10:15, 23–25; Luke 18:17, 25: John 3:5; Acts 14:22), and Peter echoes this most fundamental theme in Christ's teaching.

Peter's thought in this section, and indeed throughout the epistle, is about inclusion and exclusion. Here he brings to the fore the ultimate and final inclusion. But the future tense of the verb points to the eschatological entry that the church awaits (3:12, 14), the final salvation (3:15). Eschatological issues dominate this letter since the heretics have denied the reality of future judgment (3:3–7). But that final, cataclysmic end will come (3:10–13), just as there will be future salvation. That day will be filled with terror, and one should act now in light of that future judgment (3:11). But the promise is also held out here in 1:11 that those who live according to Christian virtue will be granted entry into that kingdom (cf. Matt. 7:21–27). Peter's teaching on this matter is rooted in that of the Lord himself.

The promise Peter holds out is that God will grant them entry εἰς τὴν αἰώνιον βασιλείαν (*eis tēn aiōnion basileian*, into the eternal kingdom). In Jesus's teaching, as that of Paul, "the kingdom of God" is the rule of God, not a territory, which has begun to be exercised in the present (Matt. 11:12; Mark 1:15; Luke 11:20; Rom. 14:17; 1 Cor. 4:20; Col. 1:13). But the fullness and glory of this kingdom will be revealed in the future, upon Christ's royal return (Matt. 6:10; Mark 9:1; 1 Cor. 6:9; 15:50; Gal. 5:21; 2 Thess. 1:5; 2 Tim. 4:1, 18; cf. 2 Thess. 1:9–10). At that time, God's glory will be revealed (2 Thess. 2:14; Rom. 5:2; 8:17–18; Col. 1:27); though believers have entry into the kingdom, it is a reality from which outsiders are barred (2 Thess. 1:9).

Somewhat surprisingly, this is one of the few NT texts that suggest the notion that the kingdom is eternal (cf. 2 Tim. 4:18; Heb. 1:8; Rev. 1:6; 11:15; and Matt. 6:13 in L W Δ Θ; cf. Dan. 4:3 Theod.; 7:27 LXX), yet the notion of an enduring kingdom arises in the inscriptions that refer, for example, to the "eternal rule" of the Romans (Deissmann 1901: 361–64; Danker 1978: 76; 1982: 465). Although the kingdom's duration is stressed, its finality and immutability are not out of view (Dan. 7:14). This is the kingdom τοῦ κυρίου ἡμῶν καὶ σωτῆρος Ἰησοῦ Χριστοῦ (*tou kyriou hēmōn kai sōtēros Iēsou Christou*, of our Lord and Savior Jesus Christ). Although the NT most commonly speaks of the "kingdom of God," at times the kingdom is referred to as that of Christ (Eph. 5:5; 2 Tim. 4:1; Rev. 11:15; and Luke 22:29–30; John 18:35). Peter presents one of the richest attributions of the kingdom, stating that it is "of our Lord and Savior Jesus Christ." Jesus, the Christ or Messiah, holds the titles of both "Lord and Savior" (the same grammatical construction as in 1:1; see comments). At various points in the letter, Peter calls Jesus "Lord," and this is clearly the preferred title (1:2, 8, 11, 14, 16; 2:20; 3:2, 18), and Peter is able to speak about Christ simply as "the Lord" (2:9, 11; 3:8, 9, 10, 15). Elsewhere Peter refers to Christ as "Lord and Savior" in exactly the same way as here (2:20; 3:18; cf. 3:2). Both titles point to his divinity and were common attributions of the day to both gods and those exalted to divine status in the ruler cult (1:1–2 and comments). The assurance that Peter holds out to his readers is none less than the "Lord and Savior Jesus Christ," who will act on their behalf as the great benefactor and will grant them entrance to his kingdom. These words of assurance conclude the opening section of the letter body and encourage the readers before the stinging denunciation of the heretics begins in full. The believers' lot is salvation. A dreadful end awaits the heretics and their followers.

II. Letter Body: A Warning against False Teachers (1:3–3:18a)
   A. Body Opening: God's Call to Glory and Virtue (1:3–11)
►  B. Body Middle: The Apostolic Testimony and the False Teachers (1:12–2:22)
   C. Body Closing: A Call to Holiness (3:1–18a)

# B. Body Middle: The Apostolic Testimony and the False Teachers (1:12–2:22)

In this section our author begins the body middle of the letter. In the opening (1:12–15), he discloses his purpose for writing (see "Genre and Structure" in the introduction; and White 1972: 51–62, 125–39). The author does not say that he is "writing" to his readers but rather regards this composition as a means to remind them of things that they know (vv. 12–13, 15). He demonstrates a deep desire to have these things before the church both in the present while he is alive (v. 13) and in the future after his death (vv. 12, 15). The letter will serve as the apostle's continued voice in the community well after the time he has passed off the scene; the letter is to be taken up and read publicly again and again (v. 15). The "things" that Peter wants his readers to remember are those referred to in the previous section (vv. 8–10), that is, the moral virtues of verses 5–7. Such values are transcendent for the church. Their importance is underscored by the author's determination to do what he must to ensure the memory of them beyond his death. For Peter, memory is the handmaid of morality.

The body middle continues with reminder of the apostolic (1:16–18) and prophetic testimonies (1:19–21), which serve as a counterpoint to the skepticism of the heretics (3:3). This witness is divinely inspired and stands as a sure word, which the readers should heed. In 2:1 Peter turns to denounce the false teachers who invade the church (2:1–3). He shows that despite the heretics' claim to the contrary, God did certainly judge humanity in the past (2:4–10a). And as God did in the past, so God will do in the future. In 2:10b–16 Peter unveils the heretics' corruption and their ultimate doom and then, in a second volley of denunciations (2:17–22), warns the believers about the false teachers' arrogance and their attempts to win new converts (vv. 17–20). The ultimate concern is to counter apostasy (vv. 20–22).

# 1. A Call to Remember (1:12–21)

This section of the letter is central to Peter's purpose. He must deal with two realities: (1) his absence due to his soon demise (1:13–14) and (2) the advent of those who are spreading false teaching (2:1). He must therefore ensure that his readers continue paying heed to the truth and are not swayed by the error of the heretics. In the opening paragraph (1:12–15), he repeatedly shows the need for them to remember, taking upon himself the task of reminding them (1:12) and refreshing their memory (1:13) so that they will be able to recall the things they know (1:15). His words in this letter will serve as a continual reminder of his teaching, even beyond his death. Yet at the same time, Peter affirms that they already know what they needed to know about the gospel and are established in the truth (1:12). This indicative is an implicit call to stand where they are already theologically established.

The second paragraph of this call (1:16–21) serves as a counterpoint to the theological novelty that the heretics are bringing to those who have already received the faith (1:1). Over against the false teachers' skepticism, Peter lays out the reliability of both the apostolic testimony (1:16–18) and the prophetic witness (1:19–21). Both of these witnesses are divinely inspired and provide a sure foundation for their faith. Their testimony is not contrived (1:16, 20–21) and is therefore reliable. Peter's affirmation in this paragraph stands over against the false teachers' denial of the "Master who bought them" (2:1). He knows that there is a clear danger that as the false teachers themselves had turned away from the true knowledge of the Lord (2:20–22), so too could his readers. His hope is that the divine apostolic and prophetic witness will serve as a sure foundation for them beyond his lifetime.

# a. The Occasion of Remembrance: Peter's Farewell (1:12–15)

Since the publication of Bauckham's commentary on 2 Peter (1983), scholars have underscored the importance of this section as an indicator that this letter is, in fact, a "testament" of Peter. The conclusion that has gone hand in hand with this classification is the dismissal of this composition as a genuine letter of the apostle Peter. The logic is simple: All testaments are pseudepigraphical; 2 Peter is a testament; 2 Peter is therefore pseudepigraphical. Few voices have been raised against Bauckham's view, which has almost come to be regarded as an "assured result" of scholarship, echoed in the majority of publications since 1983. However, Bauckham's view has not gone entirely unchallenged (J. Charles 1997: 49–75). Although this section is surely testamentary since it predicts the forthcoming death of the author and gives moral instruction in light of his demise, we should not thereby conclude that this letter can be classified as a "testament" (see "Genre and Structure" in the introduction). Testamentary material could be included within other literary genres without the literary work becoming no more than a testament (such as Jesus's final discourse in John 13–16). Major elements of the testamentary genre are lacking while the document before us has all the salient features of an ancient letter. In this letter, the "testament" serves to explain the author's purpose for writing and what he hopes to accomplish via this composition in the present and after he has departed from this life.

## Exegesis and Exposition

[12]For this reason I am going to keep reminding you about these things, although you know them and are established in the truth which is present with you. [13]And I consider it the right thing, as long as I am in this temporary dwelling, to rouse you by a reminder, [14]knowing that the laying aside of my temporary dwelling will be soon, just as our Lord Jesus revealed to me. [15]But I shall also act diligently so that, after my departure, you will be able to remember these things on any occasion.

Peter opens the body middle of the letter with an introductory formula that discloses his purpose for writing: Διὸ μελλήσω ἀεὶ ὑμᾶς ὑπομιμνῄσκειν περὶ τούτων καίπερ εἰδότας (*Dio mellēsō aei hymas hypomimnēskein peri toutōn kaiper eidotas*, For this reason I am going to keep reminding you about these things, although you know them). Given the transcendent importance of God's

1:12

act of benefaction and human destiny (vv. 3–11), Peter intends to remind the readers of "these things" (περὶ τούτων, *peri toutōn*)[1] that he has just outlined. The future tense μελλήσω (*mellēsō*) is somewhat rare, found only here and in Matt. 24:6 in the NT. Μέλλω (*mellō*) usually appears with an infinitive, either in the present, aorist, or future, as a periphrasis for the future (LSJ 1099; BDF §356; Mayor 1907: 99). The common classical construction of μέλλω (*mellō*) with the future infinitive has all but vanished, with a few exceptions (Acts 11:28; 24:15; 27:10; 2 Macc. 8:11; BDF §350), and the construction that Peter uses is likely no more than a mishandled version of the classical form (versus Mayor 1907: 99, who suggests that the text of 2 Peter be amended to μελέσω, *melēsō*, "I shall take care"). We may therefore simply translate the opening words: "I am going to remind you."

Peter adds the word ἀεί (*aei*), which is most often understood as "always" or "continually" (2 Cor. 6:10; 1 Pet. 3:15). But here the sense is rather iterative as both the NRSV ("I intend to keep on reminding you") and the NLT ("I plan to keep on reminding you") recognize (BDAG 22; Mark 15:8 [*v.l.*]; Acts 7:51; 2 Cor. 4:11; Heb. 3:10). He plans to keep on reminding them (v. 15, note the inclusio), the letter itself being the means by which he will accomplish this task even after his demise (vv. 13–14). Peter intends the script to be read on various occasions in the future. Tenses in letters are somewhat slippery since the author will often adopt verb tenses that relate to the time when the correspondence is read. So, for example, an aorist indicative "I wrote" (Rom. 15:15; 1 Cor. 9:15; Gal. 6:11) in a letter should be understood from the stance of the reader rather than the author (Trapp 2003: 36–37). This phenomenon explains the futures in verses 12 and 15 as the author looks out at the way the correspondence will be used. We should also remember that the ancients understood how letters "stand in for living speech, and for the living presence of the speakers, each representing its writer to its recipient in his or her inevitable absence" (Trapp 2003: 39). As P. Ovidius Naso wrote to his friend, "Just as once we used to consume long hours in talk, and day gave out before our conversation was over, so now let the written word carry our silent voices to and fro, and let hand and paper play the tongue's role" (Trapp 2003: 67). The juxtaposition of the future function of the letter (vv. 12, 15) and the author's forthcoming demise (vv. 13–14) is poignant indeed.

This communication will serve to "keep reminding you about these things, although you know them" (ὑμᾶς ὑπομιμνῄσκειν περὶ τούτων καίπερ εἰδότας, *hymas hypomimnēskein peri toutōn kaiper eidotas*). As noted in the comments on Jude 5, letter writers commonly inserted a statement about what the author wanted the readers to know, thus presenting a disclosure statement indicating the purpose of the correspondence (White 1986: 207). But Peter, as Jude does, modifies the practice by picking up a thread from moral philosophy

---

1. The author is particularly fond of using the "near" demonstrative pronoun in the neuter plural (these things) as a means to assure coherence in his argument (1:4, 8–10, 12, 15; 2:20; 3:11, 14, 16).

and presenting a reminder as well as an affirmation that the readers already know what the author is reminding them of (cf. 1 John 2:21). As Malherbe (1986: 125) notes, "Since what is advised is already known . . . , the exhorter disavows the need for further instruction (cf. 2 Cor. 9:1; 1 Thess. 4:9; 5:1), but merely reminds his listeners of what they already know (cf. 1 Thess. 2:9; 3:6)." In some detail, Dio Chrysostom explores the reason for reminding people of what they already know, stating that people often fail to act on what they know: "For just as one may see persons who are suffering from ophthalmia [cf. v. 9!] and know that it hurts to put their hand to their eyes, but still are unwilling to refrain from so doing, so likewise in regard to matters in general, the majority, even though they know perfectly well that it is not advantageous to do a certain thing, none the less fall to doing it." He therefore concludes, "Consequently, in my opinion it devolves upon the more thoughtful on all occasions and continually to speak of these matters, in the hope that it may prove possible to make men change their ways and to force them to the better course" (*Or.* 17.3–5). The deference with which Peter approaches his readers should not be mistaken for a lack of forcefulness. His purpose is clear: he is exhorting and will exhort his readers to avoid the error of the heretics, into which some unstable souls have already fallen.

Peter affirms what the readers know but also acknowledges that they are established in the truth: καὶ ἐστηριγμένους ἐν τῇ παρούσῃ ἀληθείᾳ (*kai estērigmenous en tē parousē alētheia*, and are established in the truth which is present with you). On the one hand, this participial clause serves as praise for their adherence to the truth of the gospel, but at the same time it has hortatory force: "You are established, so do not move." Being established (ἐστηριγμένους, *estērigmenous*) was a principal concern of the church as it faced the gale-force winds of persecution and doctrinal error. The verb appears frequently in texts that speak of the dangers of some kind of falling. Sirach states, "When the rich person totters, he is supported by friends" (13:21 NRSV), and Philo (*Dreams* 2.2 §11) comments on those who are not established because they are carried away in various directions. Second Clement 2.6 hails attempts to establish people: "It is great and wonderful to give strength, not to the things which are standing, but to those which are falling." This note is similar to that sounded by Diogenes Laertius's comments on people who fail to become established in any teaching (*Lives* 2.136; *TLNT* 3:291–95; BDAG 945). In the same way, NT authors engage the issue of establishing believers who are in danger of being swayed from their faith due to persecution (Luke 22:32; Acts 14:22; 15:32, 41; 18:23; Rom. 16:25; 1 Thess. 3:13; 2 Thess. 3:3; 1 Pet. 5:10; Rev. 3:2) or, as here, error.

Peter's desire is that his readers continue to be established and firm "in the truth which is present with you" (ἐν τῇ παρούσῃ ἀληθείᾳ, *en tē parousē alētheia*), that is, the truth of the gospel, which they now have (see comments on 1:9 and BDAG 773–74; as Xenophon, *Anab.* 7.7.36: "all the property you possessed"). The "present truth" (KJV) is not what is popular for the moment ("present" in the temporal sense) but what they already have. Peter is addressing the error of the heretics. He will not have his readers moved away from the truth as it has come to them (1:4 and comments). This is the truth of the apostolic (vv. 16–18) and prophetic witness (vv. 18–21), which elsewhere is called the "truth of the gospel" (Gal. 2:5, 14; Eph. 1:13). The Christian message is the "word of truth" (Eph. 1:13; 2 Tim. 2:15; James 1:18), and even the "word of truth of the gospel which is present [παρόντες, *parontes*] with you" (Col. 1:5–6). It is that which the Christian believes (2 Thess. 2:12–13) and does (Eph. 4:24; 2 John 4; 3 John 3–4; cf. 2 Pet. 2:2). The truth is centered in Christ Jesus (John 14:6; 2 Cor. 11:10; Eph. 4:21). Peter will not have his readers moved from this foundation and commends them for being established in this truth that they have received. One may wander from the truth (James 5:19) and engage in unrighteous behavior that is antithetical to the truth (Rom. 1:18; 2:8; 1 Cor. 13:6), but Peter hopes for better things.

1:13    In this and the following verses, Peter lays out his motivation for reminding his readers about "these things" (v. 12). He anticipates his imminent death (vv. 14–15); therefore, while still alive, he will do what he considers right by stirring up their memory. He states: δίκαιον δὲ ἡγοῦμαι, ἐφ᾽ ὅσον εἰμὶ ἐν τούτῳ τῷ σκηνώματι, διεγείρειν ὑμᾶς ἐν ὑπομνήσει (*dikaion de hēgoumai eph᾽ hoson eimi en toutō tō skēnōmati, diegeirein hymas en hypomnēsei*, And I consider it the right thing, as long as I am in this temporary dwelling, to rouse you by a reminder). Peter refers to his own reflective process (ἡγοῦμαι, *hēgoumai*; cf. 2:13; 3:9, 15; 2 Cor. 9:5; Phil. 2:25; BDAG 434) and declares that reminding them is the right or just thing to do (δίκαιον, *dikaion*; Matt. 20:4; Luke 12:57; Eph. 6:1; Phil. 1:7; Diodorus Siculus 12.45.1: δίκαιον γὰρ ἡγοῦντο τοῖς εὐηργετηκόσι, *dikaion gar hēgounto tois euērgetēkosi*, for they considered only fair that the benefactors; BDAG 247), perhaps even thinking here of his obligation before God (Acts 4:19; 2 Thess. 1:6). In the previous verse he laid out what will be done in the future via the letter (note the future tense in v. 12 as well as v. 15), that is, after the time of his demise. But here in verse 13 he speaks about what he will do in the present "as long as I am in this temporary dwelling" (ἐφ᾽ ὅσον εἰμὶ ἐν τούτῳ τῷ σκηνώματι, *eph᾽ hoson eimi en toutō tō skēnōmati*). While ἐφ᾽ ὅσον (*eph᾽ hoson*) means "inasmuch as" in some contexts (Matt 25:40, 45; Rom. 11:13), the temporal sense is in mind here: "as long as" (Matt. 9:15; Rom. 7:1; 1 Cor. 7:39; Gal. 4:1). Peter recognizes that the time of his death is upon him (v. 14), so at the present time he must do what he can.

Our author reflects on his present existence in an interesting way, speaking about life as being a time when he is "in this temporary dwelling." In the LXX the term σκήνωμα (*skēnōma*) refers to a tent (Deut. 33:18; 1 Sam. 4:10; Pss. 14:1 [15:1 Eng.]; 51:7 [52:5 Eng.]; Song 1:8) or booth (2 Macc. 10:6), although this latter idea is usually represented by σκηνοπηγία (*skēnopēgia*). Peter uses the term figuratively (cf. Acts 7:46) in this and the following verse to refer to his body, in a way similar to how some spoke of the body as a σκῆνος (*skēnos*, tent; 2 Cor. 5:1, 4; Wis. 9:15; cf. John 1:14 where the verb σκηνόω [*skēnoō*] is used of the incarnation). The way Peter employs the term is very much like Diogn. 6.8: "The soul dwells immortal in a mortal tabernacle, and Christians sojourn among corruptible things, waiting for the incorruptibility which is in heaven." However, we should not overpress Peter's language to conclude that he viewed the body as nothing more than the temporary dwelling of the soul. His choice of anthropological terms at this point is governed by his desire to stress the transitory nature of his existence and his imminent demise. This is not a discourse about anthropology, which focuses on the relationship between body and soul. However, Peter's use of the demonstrative τούτῳ (*toutō*, this) is noteworthy. Does this suggest that he is verbally "pointing" to his body, or is he differentiating this bodily existence from another form of existence? This latter suggestion appears to be implied by the term that he uses to speak about his body and the manner in which he talks of death in verse 14, which itself suggests continued existence. The demonstrative could additionally serve as a marker for irony (similar to contempt; LSJ 1276): "this (so-called) 'tent.'"

As long as Peter is alive he declares his intent διεγείρειν ὑμᾶς ἐν ὑπομνήσει (*diegeirein hymas en hypomnēsei*, to rouse you by a reminder; cf. 3:1, which repeats nearly the same words). The verb διεγείρειν (*diegeirein*) frequently meant waking someone from sleep (Mark 4:38 [*v.l.*]; Luke 8:24; 3 Macc. 5:15) or, in the passive voice, of awakening (Matt. 1:24 [*v.l.*]; Mark 4:39; Acts 16:10 [*v.l.*]). But it also could be figurative, as when someone aroused courage (2 Macc. 7:21; 15:10), anger (T. Dan 4.2), or desire (Josephus, *J.W.* 2.9.6 §181). Peter's desire is to rouse them by giving them a reminder, a key concern in this letter (1:12, 15; 3:1). As noted in the comments on verse 12, calling people to remember what they already knew was a key theme in moral philosophy (Malherbe 1986: 125). Seneca (*Ep. mor.* 94.21) noted that while "precepts alone are not effective in overthrowing the mind's mistaken beliefs," they do "refresh the memory," as is necessary for proper action. Reminders are part of the fabric of moral instruction (1 Thess. 2:9; 3:4; 4:1; 5:1–2; 2 Thess. 3:5; 3:10), and Peter's purpose in the present (1:13; 3:1) and future (vv. 12, 15) is to remind his readers of the apostolic teaching that they had. Peter even refers to the present correspondence as a reminder of what he has previously written (3:1). His goal reaches far beyond a desire to instill "fond memories." His aim is to exhort them to maintain Christian virtue.

In the present verse, Peter fills out the implication of the clause "as long as I am in this temporary dwelling" (verse 13) and anticipates the following statement about the urgency that presses him to remind his readers of "these things" (v. 15): εἰδὼς ὅτι ταχινή ἐστιν ἡ ἀπόθεσις τοῦ σκηνώματός μου καθὼς καὶ ὁ κύριος ἡμῶν Ἰησοῦς Χριστὸς ἐδήλωσέν μοι (*eidōs hoti tachinē estin hē apothesis tou skēnōmatos mou kathōs kai ho kyrios hēmōn Iēsous Christos edēlōsen moi*, knowing that the laying aside of my temporary dwelling will be soon, just as our Lord Jesus revealed to me). Peter declares that he is aware that the time of his demise is near. This presents the reason (εἰδώς, *eidōs*, adverbial participle) for his declaration in v. 13: "And I consider it the right

**1:14**

thing . . . to rouse your memory." It is only right and fitting that he should do this since his end will arrive shortly.

Peter traces this knowledge of his end to the Lord himself, who "revealed to me" (ἐδήλωσέν μοι, edēlōsen moi) that his death would come "soon" (ταχινή, tachinē; cf. 2:1; Sir. 11:22; Herm. *Sim.* 8.9.4; 9.20.4; BDAG 992; MM 627). M. Green (1987: 89) argues that this adverb refers to the "sudden" nature of Peter's death (as the term is used in Prov. 1:16; Isa. 59:7; Sir. 18:26; Herm. *Sim.* 9.26.6), but this would hardly explain the author's urgency and resolve, so evident in this section. Just when the Lord Jesus revealed this to Peter is not stated, but we do have record in John 21:18–19 of Jesus's prediction about Peter's death: "'But when you grow old, you will stretch out your hands, and someone else will fasten a belt around you and take you where you do not wish to go.' (He said this to indicate the kind of death by which he would glorify God)" (NRSV). Our author may be reflecting on this prediction and, since he is "old" by ancient standards at the time of composition, he concludes that his end will come "soon." The epistle was written after 1 Peter, which was penned from Rome in the early 60s, and the apostle classifies himself in that letter as an "elder" (1 Pet. 5:1). On the other hand, the author may have in mind a prophetic utterance that he attributes to the Lord Jesus since such words were common in the early church (Acts 16:6–7; 21:10–11; 1 Cor. 12–14; 1 Thess. 5:19–22; 2 Thess. 2:2; 1 John 4:1–3). The insertion of the word "just as" or "even" (καί, kai) suggests the possibility that this prophetic word came on top of knowledge Peter already possessed. Two pseudepigraphic books associated with the name of the author relate the Lord's revelation to Peter about his death (Apoc. Pet. 14; Acts Pet. 35; see the discussion in Bauckham 1983: 200–201). Some memory of a revelation appears to have been preserved in the church.

The term that describes the way Peter came to know about his death (ἐδήλωσεν, edēlōsen) could mean simply "to report" some information (1 Cor. 1:11; Col. 1:8) or "to explain or clarify" something (Herm. *Mand.* 4.3.3; *Sim.* 5.4.1; the sense preferred by BDAG 222). But this verb often appears in discussion about forms of divine revelation (LXX: Exod. 6:3; 33:12; 1 Kings 8:36; Dan. 2:23–26, 28–30; 2 Chron. 6:27; Ps. 147:9 [147:20 Eng.]; Diodorus Siculus 18.60.4) and is difficult to distinguish from ἀποκαλύπτειν (apokalyptein; R. Bultmann, *TDNT* 2:61–62). Since the context is about the prediction of someone's death, we should understand the term within the frame of divine revelatory communication.

Despite the acceptance of prophecy in the early church and the widespread use of divination in the ancient world, many voices were raised against divination, which Quintus Cicero, the brother of the famous senator Marcus Tullius, defined as "the foreseeing and foretelling of events considered as happening by chance" (Cicero, *Div.* 1.5.9). For example, Dio Cassius recorded that during Augustus's reign, "the seers were forbidden to prophesy to any person alone or to prophesy regarding death even if others should be present" (56.25.5–6). The most strident voices against divination during the first century were those of the Epicureans, whose views Marcus Cicero had embraced a century earlier (*On Divination*) and against whom Plutarch vigorously defended the oracle at Delphi (*De defectu oraculorum*; *De Pythiae oraculis*; see G. Green 2001). Insofar as the heretics against whom Peter wrote devised a syncretistic mix of Christian faith and Epicurean perspectives (see "The Opponents in 2 Peter" in the introduction), the present declaration about the prediction of Peter's death may be viewed also as a piece of Peter's polemic against their error. Divine prediction does exist, and what has been revealed will come to pass.

Peter speaks of his demise as ἡ ἀπόθεσις τοῦ σκηνώματός μου (*hē apothesis tou skēnōmatos mou*, the laying aside of my temporary dwelling). In the previous verse he referred to his body as a "temporary dwelling" (see comments) that he will soon lay aside. The noun (*apothesis*) that describes this is found in the NT only here and in 1 Pet. 3:21, where it refers to the act of putting off the "filth of the flesh." In the wider circle of Greek literature, it can have a positive sense of laying up in store or preserving something, but more often than not the word is used in more negative contexts, where it points to the act of getting rid of something, the resignation from an office, or even the exposure of children (Aristotle, *Pol.* 1335B; Appian, *Bell. civ.* 1.3.26.12; LSJ 199). The meanings are similar to the semantic range of its verbal form ἀποτίθημι (*apotithēmi*), which may be used to refer to putting away sin, as one would take off clothing, or even putting someone in prison (Matt 14:3; Rom. 13:12; Eph. 4:22, 25; Col. 3:8; Heb. 12:1; James 1:21; 1 Pet. 2:1; BDAG 123–24; LSJ 223). Peter's thought is similar to Paul in 2 Cor. 5:3–4 (see above) and implies the survival of the person after death (compare 2 Cor. 5:8; Phil. 1:23). But the term used for death also suggests that the author is somewhat less than concerned about his demise. It is simply a "putting off" of what is merely a temporary habitation. Again, we should not view this as a comprehensive description of Peter's anthropology (see comments on v. 13).

Peter reiterates his intent to make sure that his readers have available the teaching he has outlined in verses 3–11, especially the catalog of virtues in verses 5–7: σπουδάσω δὲ καὶ ἑκάστοτε ἔχειν ὑμᾶς μετὰ τὴν ἐμὴν ἔξοδον τὴν τούτων μνήμην ποιεῖσθαι (*spoudasō de kai hekastote echein hymas meta tēn emēn exodon tēn toutōn mnēmēn poieisthai*, But I shall also act diligently so that, after my departure, you will be able to remember these things on any occasion). This verse serves as an inclusio for the paragraph that began in verse 12, echoing as it does the thoughts presented previously (vv. 3–11). Peter affirms his intent to act with all diligence in this matter (σπουδάσω, *spoudasō*; see 1:5, 10; 3:14 and comments), and the future tense of the verb suggests that he particularly has in mind the continued presence of this letter in the church (see v. 12 and comments). The inclusion of "But . . . also" (δὲ καί, *de kai*) juxtaposes this future work accomplished through the letter with the way he wants to stir up the readers' memory at the present time (v. 13 and comments). In other words, this composition does double duty, standing for the apostle's presence before the church both now and in the future. The author

1:15

does not see himself divorced from the message of this composition even after his "departure." Authors continue to speak through their texts long after they have passed away, and their texts should never be separated from their person. The extent to which Peter envisions this message as being a useful reminder is indicated by ἑκάστοτε (hekastote), a term familiar in Attic Greek but found less frequently during the Hellenistic period. This adverb does not appear in the LXX, and of the NT writers only Peter uses it. While the word may mean "always," it most commonly reflected an iterative action: "on each occasion" or "at any time" (BDAG 298; LSJ). Peter appears to envision the rehearsal of the letter's contents as it would be picked up and read repeatedly in the assembly (Col. 4:16; 1 Thess. 5:27).

The purpose for Peter's diligent effort is here expressed by the infinitive ἔχειν ὑμᾶς (echein hymas; BDF §490), and the beginning of this clause may be translated "so that you . . . will be able" (see BDAG 421 for ἔχω expressing ability). The letter empowers the readers "to remember these things" (τὴν τούτων μνήμην ποιεῖσθαι, tēn toutōn mnēmēn poieisthai). "These things" refers to the opening discussion in the body of the letter (vv. 3–11), including the grace that God has shown them as Benefactor as recounted in verses 3–4 and the Christian virtues outlined in verses 5–7 (cf. the use of τούτων in v. 4 in reference to God's benefaction and ταῦτα, tauta, in vv. 8–10 with reference to Christian virtues). The centrality of Peter's concern for the church's possession of and ascendancy in divinely empowered moral virtue should not be underestimated, especially in light of the immoral swing of the heretics' error.

Peter weaves this issue together with the dominant theme of "remembrance," especially in this section where he discusses his imminent death (vv. 12–13; 3:1 and comments). In this verse Peter alters the language of memory by speaking of "memory" (μνήμην, mnēmēn), a word fairly common in the LXX but found nowhere else in the NT (Pss. 29:5 [30:4 Eng.]; 144:7 [145:7 Eng.]; Prov. 10:7; Wis. 4:1, 19; 8:13), in combination with the verb ποιέω (poieō). The construction may mean no more than "call to mind" or even "make mention of a thing" (Herodotus 1.15), but could also suggest the more solemn idea of "hold things in remembrance" (P.Fay. 19.10: τῶν πραγμάτων μνήμην ποιεῖσθαι, tōn pragmatōn mnēmēn poieisthai; BDAG 655; TLNT 2:497). Aristotle (Rhetoric 1414A) said, for example, "Homer has increased the reputation of Nireus, though he only mentions him in one passage; he has perpetuated his memory, though he never speaks of him again" (see also Thucydides 2.54.3; cf. Diodorus Siculus 23.15.2; Diogenes Laertius, Lives 10.18; Josephus, Ant. 13.3.1 §63).

To be sure, Peter is not setting up a memorial to himself. The language in this context, where Peter discusses his death, suggests recalling something that had been communicated by those who have passed on. Peter's concern is that "these things" will be available to them after his departure, and these have to do with the moral life. Philo is instructive on this point as he discusses at some length the *moral* role of memory. He speaks of "a virtue-loving tendency" that is "saved from extinction by memories which are a means of keeping alive the flame of noble qualities" (*Migr.* 3 §16). Memory is for remembering the good, and the good memory is "that which is brought to bear upon good things" (Philo, *Agriculture* 30 §133; *Alleg. Interp.* 3.6 §18; *TLNT* 2:498). Peter's aim in leaving this memorial is deeply ethical.

Peter views his death as an "exodus" (τὴν ἐμὴν ἔξοδον, *tēn emēn exodon*, my departure), language that echoes that of the Lord recorded in Luke 9:31, where Jesus speaks about his death in the same fashion. Death as an "exodus" from this life was a known theme within Jewish literature (Wis. 3:2; 7:6; Sir. 38:23; Philo, *Virtues* 12 §77;[2] Josephus, *Ant.* 4.8.2 §189), and may imply continued existence after death. This metaphorical use of "exodus" is quite rare outside Jewish and Christian circles (Epictetus, *Disc.* 4.4.38; W. Michaelis, *TDNT* 5:104; LSJ 596; BDAG 350–51). However, his principal point is simply that he is going to die and that, after he departs, his letter will stand for his presence and serve the church as a continual reminder of the exhortation that he has given.

---

2. In Philo, this language of death does have anthropological importance, for he says in *Virtues* 12 §76: "The body, the shell-like growth which encased him, was being stripped away and the soul laid bare and yearning for its natural removal hence." Due to the broad use of "exodus" for death among those who had differing anthropologies, however, we should not ascribe this understanding of human nature to our author without clearer evidence.

# b. The Content of Remembrance (1:16–21)

In the following two paragraphs, Peter begins to refute the doctrine of the heretics, beginning with a defense of the apostolic doctrine that his readers have received (vv. 16–18) and followed by a defense of prophetic utterances. In order for them to gain converts to their position that denigrated the reality of the eschatological hope and judgment (3:4–5), the false teachers found it necessary to repudiate the apostolic teaching on the coming of the Lord as well as the prophetic testimony of the OT (3:3). In defense of the truth, Peter makes the fundamental point that he and the other apostles, as well as the prophets of old, were commissioned by God and spoke in his authority. The apostles did not present false myths (v. 16), and the prophets did not speak out of their own will (v. 20). The call to the readers to pay heed to the prophetic word (v. 19) is echoed again as a prelude to the explanation of the heretics' denials (3:3), while the eyewitness and earwitness account of the transfiguration by Peter and his associates (vv. 16, 18) shows the credibility of their teaching and implies that it, too, should be heeded. The point is made explicit in 3:3. The particular tenet of the heretics' teaching that Peter counters has to do with the eschatological parousia of Christ (v. 16; 3:3–4). He presents the transfiguration, with its revelation of Christ's kingship, as the guarantee of that final event. The prophets spoke of the final day as well, including the future judgment. Their message continues to be relevant for the present since it is as a "lamp shining in a gloomy place" (v. 19a) as well as for the future until that final day of Christ's return (v. 19b).

The outline of this unit is as follows:

   i. The transfiguration vision (1:16–18)
   ii. The prophetic word (1:19–21)

## Exegesis and Exposition

[16]Now then we were not following sophistic myths when we declared to you the power and parousia of our Lord Jesus Christ, but we were eyewitnesses of that one's majesty. [17]For he received honor and glory from God the Father when such a solemn declaration was made to him by the Magnificent Glory, "This is my beloved Son, in whom I am well pleased." [18]And we heard this declaration brought from heaven when we were with him in the holy mountain. [19]And we have a very sure prophetic word to which you will do well to pay heed, as to a lamp shining in a gloomy place, until the day dawns and the morning star rises in your hearts. [20]Above all know this: that no prophecy of Scripture is of the prophet's own interpretation. [21]You see, prophecy

was never revealed by human will but men spoke from God as they were borne along by the Holy Spirit.

## i. The Transfiguration Vision (1:16–18)

Peter begins this section on the transfiguration vision with a disclaimer that concerns the veracity of the proclamation concerning Christ's advent: Οὐ γὰρ σεσοφισμένοις μύθοις ἐξακολουθήσαντες ἐγνωρίσαμεν ὑμῖν τὴν τοῦ κυρίου ἡμῶν Ἰησοῦ Χριστοῦ δύναμιν καὶ παρουσίαν (*Ou gar sesophismenois mythois exakolouthēsantes egnōrisamen hymin tēn tou kyriou hēmōn Iēsou Christou dynamin kai parousian*, Now then we were not following sophistic myths when we declared to you the power and parousia of our Lord Jesus Christ). The sentence begins with γάρ (*gar*, now then, for) as a marker of clarification that introduces an important point of his argument (BDAG 189). The principal verb of the sentence is "we declared" (ἐγνωρίσαμεν, *egnōrisamen*) while the initial participial clause is adverbial (an awkwardly literal translation would be, "Now then not following sophistic myths, we declared"). He declares that the proclamation that he and others disseminated was not a mere collection of fabricated tales but was based on sound and veracious testimony (vv. 16b–18).

1:16

It appears that the author's affirmation is a reaction to a charge leveled by the heretics, who have denied the veracity of the teaching concerning Christ's coming and the final judgment (3:1–4; cf. 3:12) and who are therefore obligated to negate the apostolic testimony of this theology if they are going to win their case with the church. Here we likely have an echo of the heretics' own *vituperatio* against apostolic theology (on *vituperatio* see "Occasion of Writing" in the introduction to Jude). A standard element in *vituperatio* was to condemn one's opponent for deception and sophistry, precisely the points reflected in our author's defense. As L. Johnson (1989: 430) comments, "Any teacher of whom you disapprove can be called a sophist or charlatan (*sophistēs kai goēs*)." For example, Plutarch condemned the Epicureans by tagging them "sophists and charlatans" (*Mor.* 1124C), and Dio Chrysostom derided the sophists as those whose "speeches were devoid of sense" (*Or.* 54.1). He heaps scorn on such folk in his comment that, on one occasion, "the sophists raised their din, like frogs in a pond when they do not see the water-snake" (*Or.* 8.36). This label was calculated to induce contempt. Sophistry was beguiling and even wicked, according to Josephus (*J.W.* 4.2.3 §103), and Philo condemned sophistry as a form of magic since its goal was to deceive (*Moses* 1.16 §§92–94; cf. 2 Pet. 2:13; BDAG 935; MM 582; B. Winter 2001: 3–4, 59–94). The accusation was that Peter and others were smooth talkers whose aim was to beguile the believers.

So Peter's defense of the apostolic witness begins with the claim that they do not follow "sophistic myths" (σεσοφισμένοις μύθοις, *sesophismenois mythois*). Although "myth" at one time referred to a "narrative" or "story" without regard to its veracity, the term came to be associated with fictive tales that did not reflect the *logos* or truth of history (BDAG 660). Plato (*Timaeus* 26E), for example, made this distinction, saying that a certain story was "no invented fable but genuine history" (τό τε μὴ πλασθέντα μῦθον ἀλλ᾽ ἀληθινὸν λόγον, *to te mē plasthenta mython all' alēthinon logon*). A Greek "myth" (or the Latin *fabula*) could be an entertaining tale or one that helped someone to understand the construction of the social order or the surrounding world, including the gods (*OCD* 1018–19).

But as other NT texts show (1 Tim. 1:4; 4:7; 2 Tim. 4:4; Titus 1:14), the term became highly pejorative and thus was often "synonymous with dupery, illusion, the unreal, as opposed to a veracious account (*logos*), one that is credible (*pistos*), true (*alēthes*)" (*TLNT* 2:530). Such critique of myths or fables is mirrored in Philo's scorn of the "fabled past" and his affirmation of new ideas: "It bids them feed no more on effete fables, which the long course of the ages has handed down for the deception of mortal kind, and thus be filled with false opinions, but rather receive in full and generous measure new, fresh, blessed thoughts from the ever ageless God" (*Sacrifices* 21 §76). The myths are invented (Polybius 3.38.3), and one engaged in historical writing should disregard them (Strabo 5.1.9) since they are not credible (Strabo 11.6.2). They are mere tales (Strabo 9.3.12). While the historian may look for some veracity in the myth (Plutarch, *Theseus* 1.2–3), the patent truth is that they are false and should be regarded as such. As Strabo notes, "For our accounts of other people keep a distinction between the mythical and the historical elements; for the things that are ancient and false and monstrous are called myths, but history wishes for the truth, whether ancient or recent, and contains no monstrous element, or else only rarely" (11.5.3; see also Diodorus Siculus 1.25.4; 4.8.4; 5.23.1–2; Xenophon, *Cynegeticus* 13.5; 2 Clem. 13.3; *TLNT* 2:528–33).

A defense was sometimes raised by the defenders of the gods against the charge that the manifestations of the deity were nothing more than μυθολογία (*mythologia*; *NewDocs* 4:80), and Peter takes a similar tact in his apologetic, for obvious reasons. He affirms that he and the other apostles did not "follow after" (ἐξακολουθήσαντες, *exakolouthēsantes*) such myths, a phrase found elsewhere to describe adherence to what is clearly false (Josephus, *Ant.* proem 4 §22; P.Berlin 7927.8, μυθολογίαις ἐπακολουθοῦσι, *mythologiais epakolouthousi*, they follow mythology). The verb "follow after" implies that one has submitted to some authority with regard to thought or actions (2 Pet. 2:2, 15; T. Naph. 3.3; T. Iss. 6.2; BDAG 344). The heretics' accusation is extremely derogatory and implies that Peter and the rest have capitulated to mere myth and are under its sway as they proclaim the parousia of Christ and the final judgment.

The point under contention between the heretics and Peter is the proclamation of the power and coming of the Lord Jesus Christ (ἐγνωρίσαμεν ὑμῖν τὴν τοῦ κυρίου ἡμῶν Ἰησοῦ Χριστοῦ δύναμιν καὶ παρουσίαν, *egnōrisamen hymin tēn tou kyriou hēmōn Iēsou Christou dynamin kai parousian*, when we declared to you the power and parousia of our Lord Jesus Christ). The switch from the first-person singular in the previous section (1:12–15) to the first-person plural here is significant: Peter presents his case not simply as one who is at the end of his life but also as a person who stands shoulder to shoulder with others. These others are not specified, but Peter simply notes that they have "made known" (ἐγνωρίσαμεν, *egnōrisamen*) the facts of Christ's coming to the church. While the verb sometimes means nothing more than "disclose" facts (Eph. 6:21; Phil. 1:22; 4:6; Col. 4:7, 9), it is often found in the context of disclosing some divine revelation (John 15:15; 17:26; Acts 2:28; Rom. 9:22–23; 16:26; Eph. 1:9; 3:3, 5, 10; Col. 1:27) or, by extension, some apostolic proclamation (1 Cor. 12:3; 15:1; 2 Cor. 8:1; Gal. 1:11; Eph. 6:19), as in the present verse.

How do the author and others make such facts known? Second Peter looks back to the previous correspondence to the church (3:1), which ascribes the evangelization of the church to others and not to the author himself (1 Pet. 1:12). Even 2 Pet. 3:2 distinguishes "your apostles" from the author. The reference in 1:16 may therefore be to the *letter* that Peter penned with the cooperation of Silvanus, his amanuensis (1 Pet. 5:12), since indeed that correspondence introduced the topic of Christ's future "revelation" (1 Pet. 1:5, 7, 13; 4:13; 5:1), albeit with different terminology. But alternatively, the author may simply have in view the way that the gospel proclamation to the church was mediated through "the holy prophets and your apostles" (2 Pet. 3:2 and comments), a more likely explanation of the plural. By using the plural, the author affirms that he stands in the company of those others who make authoritative and inspired proclamation. This is not "Peter versus the heretics" but "the prophets and apostles versus the errorists" (vv. 16–21; 3:2), and so ultimately a contention between the deceivers and the Lord himself (3:2b).

The proclamation in mind is about τὴν . . . δύναμιν καὶ παρουσίαν (*tēn . . . dynamin kai parousian*, the power and parousia) of our Lord Jesus Christ. The construction is a hendiadys[1] (Fornberg 1977: 79; Bauckham 1983: 215; Neyrey 1993: 176) that refers to Christ's "coming in power" or "powerful coming," since Christ's return is often viewed as an event of power (Matt. 24:30; Mark 9:1; 13:26; Luke 21:27; 2 Thess. 1:7; Rev. 4:11; 5:12; 17:13). As Fornberg (1977: 80) notes, "Behind the wording of 2 Pet 1:16 lie the Synoptic prophecies that the Son of Man will return in power and glory (δόξα, 2 Pet 1:17), and the conviction that this power was bestowed on Christ at His Resurrection, Rom 1:4." Our author must emphasize that Christ will come with such divine power since the heretics have denied the final judgment and cataclysmic end (3:10–13). His return will be the moment that ushers in the "day of God," a time when all creation as we know it will be submitted to divine judgment, with the promise of a new heaven and new earth.

The parousia of Christ is his royal and divine advent (παρουσίαν, *parousian*), a term that never refers to the incarnation but rather to his coming at the end of the age (Matt. 24:3, 27, 37, 39; 1 Cor. 15:23; 1 Thess. 2:19; 3:13; 4:15; 5:23; 2 Thess. 2:1; James 5:7–8; 2 Pet. 3:4, 12). Only during the second

1. "The co-ordination of two ideas, one of which is dependent on the other" (BDF §442.16).

century did the church begin to speak of the first "coming" of Christ (Deissmann 1911: 372). In the ancient world a parousia could refer to the coming
of a deity, as Asclepius, the god of healing, would come to the sick who slept
in the *abaton* of his temple, or as Josephus notes, to the "coming" of God to
his people (*Ant.* 3.5.2 §80; 3.8.5 §203; 9.3.3 §55). On the other hand, it could
refer to the advent of a high-status person to a city, especially the emperor.
Third Maccabees 3:17–18 speaks of the parousia of the king Ptolemy. To com-
memorate the parousia of Nero, the city of Corinth issued commemorative
coins inscribed in Latin: *Adventus Aug[usti] Cor[inthi]* (*adventus* is the Latin
equivalent of parousia, "coming"; Deissmann 1911: 368–72; G. Braumann,
*NIDNTT* 2:898–901; A. Oepke, *TDNT* 5:858–71; Wistrand 1987; Kinman
1995: 25–47). Christ's parousia, which is both a divine and royal event, will
occur at the final moment of the present age (1 Cor. 15:23–24) and will bring
with it cataclysmic judgment for the ones who reject the gospel (2 Thess. 1:5–9;
2:1–12). At Christ's coming, the day of the Lord will arrive (2 Pet. 3:10–13
and comments; 1 Thess. 5:2).

As the counter to the charge that Peter and the other apostles had proclaimed a deceptive myth when they announced Christ's powerful advent,
the author states: ἀλλ' ἐπόπται γενηθέντες τῆς ἐκείνου μεγαλειότητος (*all'
epoptai genēthentes tēs ekeinou megaleiotētos*, but we were eyewitnesses of
that one's majesty). The event to which the author was eyewitness was the
transfiguration of Christ (2 Pet. 1:17–18 and comments; Matt. 17:1–5; Mark
9:2–7; Luke 9:28–35), which occurred in the presence of Peter and the sons of
Zebedee, James and John. Peter describes himself and these others as ἐπόπται
(*epoptai*), which are "watchful observers" or, as here, "eyewitnesses" who
have been privileged to observe something (BDAG 387–88; cf. the synonym
αὐτόπται, *autoptai*, eyewitness, in Luke 1:2). While the term *epoptēs* and
related forms in other contexts refer to an "overseer," such as a divinity who
oversees all things (Job 34:23; Esth. 5:1a [Add. Esth. 15:2 Eng.]; 2 Macc. 3:39;
7:35; 12:22; 15:2; 3 Macc. 2:21; 1 Clem. 59.3; Let. Aris. 16), or to the emperor
(see Deissmann 1911: 347 for the inscription: "The Emperor, Caesar, son of
a god, the god Augustus, of every land and sea the overseer"), here the word
has to do with being an observer or even a spectator of events (Aeschylus,
*Prometheus Bound* 301; LSJ 676; W. Michaelis, *TDNT* 5:373), a sense evident
in the verbal form of the word (1 Pet. 2:12; 3:2).

It has often been observed that "eyewitness" is used in a technical sense in
the context of the mystery religions. The initiates in the mysteries who have
obtained the highest rank are called ἐπόπται (*epoptai*, or Latin: *epoptae*),
such as those who have obtained the third and highest rank in the Eleusinian
mysteries (BDAG 387–88; *NewDocs* 2:87; W. Michaelis, *TDNT* 5:374–75; LSJ
676). Plutarch (*Alcibiades* 22.3) singles out Thessalus, who committed the
"crime against the goddesses of Eleusis, Demeter and Cora, by mimicking the
mysteries and showing them forth to his companions in his own house," and
whose misdeed included wearing the robe that the "High Priest wears when
he shows forth the sacred secrets to the initiates [ἐπόπταις, *epoptais*]."

However, the setting of the transfiguration and the way this event is recounted here do not evoke images of initiation into the mysteries. These were always secret affairs and not published, in contrast with the open account of the transfiguration. The author's point has to do with the veracity of the apostolic proclamation about the end and not about secrets to which a select few are privy (note the Plutarch quotation above). Peter, James, and John are not transformed into higher-grade initiates but are simply accredited by being witnesses of this event (see v. 18 and comments; W. Michaelis, *TDNT* 5:375). Although some suggest that there are overtones of the use of the term in the mysteries (Bauckham 1983: 215–26; M. Green 1987: 93; Neyrey 1993: 176; Senior and Harrington 2003: 255–56), that context is too remote for us to conclude that Peter intends his readers to make that connection. In fact, the author guides the interpretation in a direction not related to the mysteries, one that is actually quite contrary to their nature. Peter and his associates witnessed "that one's [Christ's] majesty" (τῆς ἐκείνου μεγαλειότητος, *tēs ekeinou megaleiotētos*), a term found only here, in Luke 9:43 upon one of Christ's healings, and in Acts 19:27 in reference to the goddess Artemis. The term has divine overtones as it refers to God's grandeur and majesty (Josephus, *Ant.* proem 4 §24; *Ag. Ap.* 2.16 §168; BDAG 622; *NewDocs* 2:87; Fornberg 1977: 81), which were evident in the transfiguration. The cognate *megaleios* similarly highlights the greatness and grandeur of God's deeds (Deut. 11:2; Ps. 70:19 [71:19 Eng.]; 2 Macc. 3:34; 3 Macc. 7:22; Odes Sol. 9.49; Sir. 17:8, 10, 13; 18:4; 36:7; 42:21; 43:15; 45:24). Using the word is tantamount to acknowledging Christ's divinity. Peter claims that he and his associates were witnesses of what, in the end, gives their testimony transcendent authority.

The appeal to their eyewitness account of the transfiguration is curious in this context where the author wishes to make a point about the parousia. The underlying assumption is that the one entails the other. What is the nature of this entailment? Bauckham (1983: 216–17) draws attention to the way that veracity of the apostle's testimony about the transfiguration would garner credibility for the proclamation about the parousia. But others suggest a theological connection between the transfiguration and the parousia since the one anticipates the other (Kelly 1969: 318; Neyrey 1993: 173; G. Green 1993: 370). Since the author juxtaposes his eyewitness account with the discrediting *vituperatio* of the heretics, Bauckham is likely correct that confidence in the apostle's testimony is at stake and is here addressed. However, this line does not eliminate what many have seen as the internal theological link between the transfiguration and the parousia, which the author would have expected his readers to understand. The former event anticipated and guaranteed the latter in the Gospel accounts (Matt. 16:27–28; Mark 8:38–9:1; Luke 9:26–27; Boobyer 1942: 43–47; G. Green 1993: 370; Blomberg 1992: 263–64).

Peter begins to explain the nature of the revelation that he and his associates saw (v. 16b): λαβὼν γὰρ παρὰ θεοῦ πατρὸς τιμὴν καὶ δόξαν (*labōn gar para theou patros timēn kai doxan*, for he received honor and glory from God **1:17** the Father). The event Peter has in mind is the transfiguration of Christ (vv. 17b–18), in which God the Father conferred honor on Christ. The ascription of "honor and glory" to someone was quite common in Jewish literature (Philo, *Drunkenness* 18 §75; Josephus, *Ant.* 2.112.1 §267; 10.11.7 §266; 12.2.15 §118; Exod. 28:2, 40; 2 Chron. 32:33; Job 37:22; 40:10; Pss. 8:5 [8:6 LXX]; 29:1 [28:1 LXX]; 96:7 [95:7 LXX]; Dan. 2:37; 4:30; 1 Macc. 14:21; Wis. 8:10; 2 Macc. 5:16) as well as in the NT (Rom. 2:7, 10; 1 Tim. 1:17; Heb. 2:7, 9; 1 Pet. 1:7; Rev. 4:9, 11; 5:12–13; 7:12; 21:26). These are also "the two words which most commonly refer to 'reputation' and 'honor' in Greek literature" (deSilva 1995: 2). Dio Chrysostom (*Or.* 4.116) says in one place that "fame or honour may come to him," while Plutarch (*Mor.* 486B) makes note of those who surpass others in "repute of glory and honor." In the ancient world, one would always hope for "glory and honor" as well as affluence (Dio Chrysostom, *Or.* 44.10), and special note was made of those who were the "grandest in reputation and honour" (Arrian, *Anab.* 8.11.1; cf. Plutarch, *Mor.* 266F–67A; Aristotle, *Rhetoric* 1.5.4; see Danker 1982: 466; BDAG 1005, 257). Insofar as the two terms may be distinguished at all, δόξα (*doxa*) refers to the reputation and fame someone enjoys while τιμή (*timē*) is the honor shown to someone of renown (on the pivotal values of honor and shame, see deSilva 1995; 2000; Neyrey 1998; Malina 2001: 27–57). Peter carefully adds that this honor came from the one who has the highest status and the greatest honor, God the Father. In the author's argument, the surpassing "honor and glory" given to Christ underscores the weight and veracity of the revelation that Peter and his associates received (v. 16). Their testimony was about Christ, and whatever they received from him was of transcendent value due to the honor accorded him. The apostolic testimony is bound with Christ so deeply that an affront against it is best countered by an affirmation of Christ's honor.

The way Christ was honored was through the audible testimony of God the Father at the time of the transfiguration: φωνῆς ἐνεχθείσης αὐτῷ τοιᾶσδε ὑπὸ τῆς μεγαλοπρεποῦς δόξης (*phōnēs enechtheisēs autō toiasde hypo tēs megaloprepous doxēs*, when such a solemn declaration was made to him by the Magnificent Glory). This second clause of the verse, as the first clause, uses a participle rather than a principal verb. Reproducing the construction in English would leave a particularly awkward sentence, and so the first participle (λαβών, *labōn*, receiving) is translated as a finite verb, and the present clause is understood as adverbial. The verb φέρω (*pherō*, bring), here and in the following verse as an aorist passive participle (ἐνεχθείσης), elsewhere in 2 Peter speaks of the way divine revelation is brought to someone (1:18, 21; 2:11; cf. 2 John 10; Diodorus Siculus 13.97.7), a use similar to the idea of "bringing" news or an accusation (John 18:29; Acts 25:7, 18; BDAG 1052). What was brought to Jesus, however, was a φωνή, which may be a simple reference to the divine voice, with all the authority that voice implies (Acts 12:22; and Gen. 3:8; Exod. 9:28; 15:26; Deut. 4:33; 5:25–26; 8:20; Ezek. 10:5; Dan. 9:10; Hag. 1:12; Zech. 6:15; Bar. 1:18, 21; cf. Plutarch, *Mor.* 567F). God spoke to Christ directly instead of through the *bat kôl*, or the "daughter of a voice," which resembled the process of divination (O. Betz, *TDNT* 9:286–90; Bockmuehl 1990: 107–8) and was vastly inferior to revelatory prophecy. But neither did God speak to Christ via prophetic mediation. This divine utterance should not be simply identified with a sound.

The way the voice came and the content of the utterance suggest that this was a solemn "declaration" (BDAG 1071–72). The inclusion of the demonstrative adjective "such" (τοιᾶσδε, *toiasde*) underscores the unusual and unique nature of this declaration (2 Macc. 11:27; 15:12; Josephus, *Ant.* 17.5.8 §142; BDAG 1009). The voice came ὑπὸ τῆς μεγαλοπρεποῦς δόξης (*hypo tēs megaloprepous doxēs*), which is understood as a circumlocution for God himself. He is "the Magnificent Glory." "Glory" is God's radiance and splendor (John 12:41; Acts 7:2, 55; 22:11; Eph. 1:17; Rev. 15:8; 21:11, 23) and here stands for God himself. In the Synoptic accounts of the transfiguration, the voice of God came from the cloud that covered Peter, James, and John (Matt. 17:5; Mark 9:7; Luke 9:34–35), and this cloud, as God's glory, was a manifestation of his presence (Exod. 40:34–35; 1 Kings 8:10–11; Ps. 26:8). Peter describes the "Glory" as "Magnificent," similar to the way Jewish literature could speak of God as "the Great Glory" (ἡ μεγάλη δόξα, *hē megalē doxa*, T. Levi 3.4; 1 En. 102.3; Ascen. Isa. 11.32; cf. Heb. 1:3). The term refers to what is majestic or magnificent (Deut. 33:26; 2 Macc. 8:15; 15:13; 3 Macc. 2:9; 1 En. 32.3; cf. Josephus, *Ant.* 9.8.6 §182; 13.8.2 §242; BDAG 622; *TLNT* 2:458–59). The whole clause is calculated to highlight the transcendence of Christ's words (v. 17b), which in turn bolsters the case of Peter, the apostle of Christ, against the heretics.

The declaration that God made to Jesus is Ὁ υἱός μου ὁ ἀγαπητός μου οὗτός ἐστιν εἰς ὃν ἐγὼ εὐδόκησα (*ho huios mou ho agapētos mou houtos estin eis hon egō eudokēsa*, This is my beloved Son, in whom I am well pleased). The words are taken from the transfiguration declaration of the Father to Christ (Matt. 17:5; Mark 9:7; Luke 9:35), although the affirmation is nearly identical with the divine declaration made at the time of Christ's baptism (Matt. 3:17; Mark 1:11; Luke 3:22). The textual form of the declaration is closest to Matt. 17:5 (Οὗτός ἐστιν ὁ υἱός μου ὁ ἀγαπητός, ἐν ᾧ εὐδόκησα· ἀκούετε αὐτοῦ, *Houtos estin ho huios mou ho agapētos, en hō eudokēsa: akouete autou*, This is my beloved Son, in whom I am well pleased: listen to him). The quotation diverges somewhat from the reading in Matthew, such as the exclusion of the final exhortation (which echoes Deut. 18:15), the change in the word order in the first clause, and the shift from ἐν ᾧ (*en hō*, in whom) to εἰς ὃν ἐγώ (*eis hon egō*, in whom I). The object of the verb εὐδοκέω (*eudokeō*, be well pleased, or take delight) may be expressed by ἐν (*en*) plus the dative (2 Sam. 22:20; Mal. 2:17) as in Matthew, or with εἰς (*eis*) plus the accusative (Justin, *Dialogue with Trypho* 29.1) as in 2 Pet. 1:17, and so the variation from the Matthean version is only of form but not of sense (BDAG 404). However, this formal variation appears also in the Pseudo-Clementine Homilies 3.53, which also notes, as does 2 Pet. 1:18, that the divine voice came "from heaven." This similarity of readings and variations from the textual form of Matt. 17:5 leads Bauckham (1983: 205–10) to the conclusion that in 2 Pet. 1:17 "the author was not dependent on the synoptic Gospels but on independent tradition, which could perhaps be his own knowledge of Peter's preaching, or else the oral traditions current in the Roman church." This may just as well be the author's personal memory and telling of that sacred moment. In either case, we should not suppose that the author is directly dependent on Matthew.

The declaration made to Christ combines allusions to Ps. 2:7 and Isa. 42:1, both of which were understood messianically within Judaism (4QFlor 10–14; Tg. Isa. on 42:1). Psalm 2 is an enthronement psalm, as verse 6 makes clear, "I have set my king on Zion, my holy hill" (NRSV; see also vv. 8–9; cf. 2 Pet. 1:18), so the declaration of Christ's sonship, which evokes the memory of the psalm, points to his messianic rule. The second part of the declaration echoes the Servant Songs of Isaiah: "Here is my servant, whom I uphold, my chosen, in whom my soul delights" (42:1 NRSV). This servant is the one who suffers for the sins of the people as the one on whom the Lord has laid "the iniquity of us all" (Isa. 53:6 NRSV). This combination of allusions points to the very essence of Christ's person and mission as the one who is both the King who rules and the Servant who suffers and dies for human sin. Once again, Peter points to the transcendent authority of Christ as both the King and the Servant. This is his counterpoint to the *vituperatio* that the apostolic proclamation was no more than a myth (v. 16). Christ has been appointed King and Redeemer, and he will surely come in his royal parousia. Peter is particularly interested in Christ's kingship, as is evident in the following verse's reference to the "holy mount," which is an allusion to the "holy hill" in the enthronement Psalm (2:6). The one whom God declared to be King will be enthroned. His coming is sure, whatever the pallid objections of the heretics might be (3:4). They raise their doubts, but God the Father, the Majestic Glory, has spoken!

**1:18**     The author returns to the theme of verse 16b that he and his associates were witnesses of the transfiguration. But while verse 16b highlighted their eyewitness testimony of Christ's majesty, here the declaration is that they were earwitnesses: καὶ ταύτην τὴν φωνὴν ἡμεῖς ἠκούσαμεν ἐξ οὐρανοῦ ἐνεχθεῖσαν σὺν αὐτῷ ὄντες ἐν τῷ ἁγίῳ ὄρει (*kai tautēn tēn phōnēn hēmeis ēkousamen ex ouranou enechtheisan syn autō ontes en tō hagiō orei*, and we heard this declaration brought from heaven when we were with him in the holy mountain). Peter's point is that he is giving veracious testimony of the divine declaration brought to Christ (see v. 17 and comments). Seeing and hearing are the foundation for testimony (Luke 2:20; 7:22), and so apostolic testimony is always about what was experienced through those two senses (Acts 4:20; 22:14–15; 1 John 1:1–3, 5; and John 3:32 of John the Baptist). The value of the information that one has heard directly is deemed greater than the testimony of others (Luke 22:71; John 4:42; Acts 6:11, 14). On the other hand, the NT speaks of the tragedy of those who see and hear but do not understand (Matt. 13:14–15, 17; Mark 4:12; Luke 10:24; Acts 28:26–27) and of the exclusion of those who do not see and hear (John 5:37; see W. Mundle, *NIDNTT* 2:173). Seeing and hearing are what true witnesses of an event have experienced. This is the type of testimony that one expects from a credible witness, whether in a court or elsewhere. Peter and his companions, James and John, are therefore credible witnesses since they did not simply report what others experienced but were "with him" when the heavenly voice spoke. Peter is far from making a point about becoming "initiates" into Christian mysteries (as some understand ἐπόπται, *epoptai*, in v. 16; see comments). Rather, the argument in the present verse, in combination with verse 16, is that the testimony of the apostles is true and reliable and not a "sophistic myth," as the heretics had claimed (v. 16a). At stake is the credibility of Peter's words in the opinion of the church.

The authoritative nature of the declaration made to Christ becomes the topic again as Peter states that the declaration was "from heaven" (ἐξ οὐρανοῦ, *ex ouranou*; cf. Matt. 4:17; Mark 1:11; Luke 3:22; John 12:28; Acts 11:9; Rev. 10:4, 8; 14:13; 18:4). In a number of texts, "heaven" is a circumlocution for "God" (cf. Matt. 4:17 and Mark 1:15; Luke 15:18, 21; Matt. 21:25; John 3:27), and so here, as in the previous verse, our author appeals to the divine source of the declaration. According to rabbinic thought, the "voice from heaven" was heard by Adam (*b. B. Bat.* 58a) and Moses (Num. Rab. 14.19; 19.7), but some Jewish comment considered it inferior to Torah (*b. B. Meṣiʿa* 59b). Peter, however, holds it as the ultimate authority. This repeated emphasis is calculated to drive home the point that none less than God himself is the source of the declaration that Christ received. This is the very testimony that the earwitnesses proclaim.

Special significance is attached to the place of the divine declaration: "in the holy mountain" (ἐν τῷ ἁγίῳ ὄρει, *en tō hagiō orei*). The historical reference is to the mountain where the transfiguration occurred (most likely Mt. Hermon and not Mt. Tabor, the traditional location), which in the Gospels is simply referred to as a "high mountain" (Matt. 17:1, 9; Mark 9:2, 9) or a "mountain" (Luke 9:28, 37). Our author, however, is less concerned about the exact place of the revelation than about the character of the place. The OT and intertestamental authors frequently refer to God's "holy mountain" (Pss. 3:4; 15:1; 43:3; 48:1; 99:9 [LXX: 3:5; 14:1; 42:3; 47:2; 98:9]; Isa. 11:9; 56:7; 57:13; Ezek. 28:14; Joel 2:1; 3:17 [4:17 LXX]; Obad. 16; Zeph. 3:11; Wis. 9:8; 1 Macc. 11:37), and at times this place is specified as Mt. Zion (Zech. 8:3), the mount over which the temple was constructed in Jerusalem. But Peter is hardly implying that the transfiguration occurred at that place. Rather, this affirmation echoes Ps. 2, which was already alluded to in the divine declaration (Ps. 2:7; 2 Pet. 1:17 and comments). Psalm 2:6 states, "I have set my king on Zion, my holy hill" (NRSV). For Peter, the new place where God establishes his King and the new place of revelation is not Jerusalem but the holy mountain. What makes this mountain holy is the presence of God (cf. Exod. 3:5–6). The role of this affirmation in the argument goes back to the *vituperatio* of the heretics. They had classified the apostolic proclamation of Christ's royal parousia as mere myth (v. 16a). But God has declared Christ to be the royal Son (v. 17), and he was installed as such on the "holy mountain," as in Ps. 2:7.

His kingship entails his royal parousia as well as his role as judge: "You shall break them with a rod of iron, and dash them in pieces like a potter's vessel" (Ps. 2:9 NRSV). The King is coming (Matt. 16:28), and the believers rightly anticipate the future entrance into his kingdom (2 Pet. 1:11).

## ii. The Prophetic Word (1:19–21)

**1:19**    Peter recognizes the central role of the apostolic testimony in the battle against the heretics, but the prophets as well need to be heard and heeded. Peter's purpose in writing is to remind his readers of this sure testimony (3:1–2) over against the theological novelty of the heretics, who deny both the royal parousia of Christ and the coming judgment on the day of the Lord (3:3–13). Our author states: καὶ ἔχομεν βεβαιότερον τὸν προφητικὸν λόγον (*kai echomen bebaioteron ton prophētikon logon*, And we have a very sure prophetic word). The adjective that Peter uses to describe the prophetic word is the comparative form of βέβαιος (*bebaios*, reliable, firm, or sure; see 1:10 and comments). At first glance it appears he is stating that the prophetic word is "more sure" than the apostolic testimony of the divine declaration (vv. 16–18). However, the comparative adjective is often used with a superlative sense. The way the authority of the apostolic testimony is paralleled with the prophetic word suggests that the form should be so interpreted (3:2; cf. Luke 11:49; Eph. 2:20; Rev. 18:20; and BDF §§60–61; BDAG 172). This adjective, commonly joined with the verb παρέχομαι (*parechomai*) or as here with ἔχω (*echō*; Heb. 6:19; Thucydides 1.32.1; Appian, *Bell. civ.* 5.19; Diodorus Siculus 2.29.4, who also uses the comparative form with a superlative sense), appears again and again in legal contexts in the sense of "guaranteed security" and therefore "valid." This nuance is likely present here as well (Deissmann 1901: 103–9). As one papyrus states, "The lease may remain guaranteed to us for the period of five years without change" (MM 107). So it comes as little surprise to find this term attached to statements that affirm the reliability of God's Word (Philo, *Moses* 2.3 §14, of Moses's laws, which are "firm [βέβαια, *bebaia*], unshaken, immovable, stamped, as it were, with the seals of nature herself"; Josephus, *Ag. Ap.* 2.16 §156; cf. *J.W.* 4.3.7 §154; *TLNT* 1:280–83; Neyrey 1993: 179–80).

The author understands the importance of "the prophetic word" (τὸν προφητικὸν λόγον, *ton prophētikon logon*) as a stabilizing force in combating the novel claims of the heretics. He counters the skepticism about prophecy (see "The Opponents in 2 Peter" in the introduction) with a reminder of the guarantee stamped on the prophetic word. "The prophetic word" is an expression similar to Paul's "prophetic Scriptures" (Rom. 16:26), and Philo refers to Scripture itself with this very phrase that Peter uses (*Planting* 28 §117; *Alleg. Interp.* 3.14 §43; *Sobriety* 13 §68). In fact, in the following verse (1:20) Peter alters his vocabulary but not the sense as he refers to the "prophecy of Scripture." In the LXX, reference is frequently made to the "word" or "message" of the prophets (Deut. 13:4; 1 Kings 22:13; Jer. 20:1; 23:16; 32:30; 1 Esd. 1:47; Sir. 48:1; Bar. 1:21), and at times this expression refers to a written record

(1 Chron. 29:29; 2 Chron. 9:29; 12:15). It is unlikely that Peter has in mind the word spoken to Christ as recorded in verse 17. He rather refers to either the OT as a whole or to some subset of Scripture that has to do particularly with the final eschatological events as a counter to the heretics' detractions (3:2–4). Verse 20 appears to point to his concern with prophecy as a subset of the whole.

Peter exhorts his readers, therefore, to pay heed to this prophetic word: ᾧ καλῶς ποιεῖτε προσέχοντες (*ho kalōs poieite prosechontes*, to which you will do well to pay heed). The call to "pay heed" or "pay close attention" to instruction was quite common, whether it be to "words" (Deut. 32:46; Prov. 4:20; Jer. 6:19; Sir. 16:24; 1 Macc. 7:11; T. Zeb. 1.2; Josephus, *Ant.* 8.9.1 §241), to the "words of the prophet" (1 Esd. 1:28), or to wisdom (Prov. 5:1). Such attention implies that one will act on the words by embracing and following them. On the other hand, some teaching should be shunned. Plutarch (*Mor.* 362B) exhorted, "It is not worth while to pay attention to the Phrygian writings," and similar exhortations were made about not paying heed to myths (Pseudo-Plutarch, *Pro nobilitate* 21; 1 Tim. 1:4; Titus 1:14; BDAG 880). In particularly difficult and dangerous situations, however, one must pay special attention to sound instruction (Heb. 2:1). Peter tells his readers that if they pay careful attention to the prophetic word, they will "do well," an expression that here refers to doing what is right and correct (Mark 7:37; Acts 10:33; 1 Cor. 7:37–38; Phil. 4:14; James 2:8, 19; 3 John 6; Appian, *Bell. civ.* 3.75; Josephus, *Ant.* 11.6.12 §279; BDF §414.5). Paying heed to the prophets is not simply a good thing to do but indeed the right thing to do. This declaration stands over against the heretics' rejection of the prophetic message that these immoral skeptics have dismissed (2 Pet. 3:2–4) as well as prophetic aberrations of both past and present (2:1, 15–16).

The author strings together a series of rich metaphors that show the place of the prophetic message in the present and the extent to which it will be relevant. This word is like a pottery oil lamp that illuminates a dark space: ὡς λύχνῳ φαίνοντι ἐν αὐχμηρῷ τόπῳ (*hōs lychnō phainonti en auchmērō topō*, as to a lamp shining in a gloomy place). Jesus takes up the image of an oil lamp that shines in speaking about the Baptist (John 5:35), while others see the shining of this small object as a powerful metaphor of God's Word (Ps. 119:105 [118:105 LXX]) or prophetic utterance (2 Esd. [4 Ezra] 12:42 NRSV: "For of all the prophets you alone are left to us, like a cluster of grapes from the vintage, and like a lamp in a dark place, and like a haven for a ship saved from a storm"; for the literal sense see Exod. 25:37; 1 Macc. 4:50; Rev. 18:23).

Peter describes the place where the prophetic word shines with the adjective "gloomy" (αὐχμηρῷ, *auchmērō*; Aristotle, *Colors* 3.793A, "It also makes a difference whether the colour mixed is bright and shining, or on the contrary dark and dull [αὐχμηρὸν καὶ ἀλαμπές, *auchmēron kai alampes*]. Shining is nothing but the continuity and intensity of light"; so the lexicons of Hesychius and Suda). Elsewhere Peter speaks of darkness, using other terminology (2:17), but there the reference is to the nether gloom of the underworld. In this verse the metaphor describes the darkness and gloom of the present age. The Venerable Bede (Hurst 1985: 132) captured the idea well: "For indeed in this world's night, filled with dark temptations, where only with difficulty is anyone found who does not offend, what should we be if we did not have the lamp of the prophetic utterance? But will a lamp always be required? Definitely not. Until the day dawns, he says."

A life dominated by sin is one that is lived in darkness (John 3:19; Rom. 13:12; 2 Cor. 6:14; Eph. 5:11), and such people have their understanding "darkened" (Rom. 1:21; Eph. 4:18) and live in "darkness" (Rom. 2:19). The imagery has deep roots in the OT and Jewish literature (Pss. 74:20; 82:5; 112:4; Prov. 4:18–19; Isa. 2:5; 5:20; 1QM 13.15; 15.9; 1QS 1.9–10; 3.13–4.14; T. Levi 19.1; T. Naph. 2.7–10; T. Benj. 5.3; H. Conzelmann, *TDNT* 7:424–45; H. C. Hahn, *NIDNTT* 1:421–25). Conversion is therefore seen as passing from darkness to light (Acts 26:18; Eph. 5:8; Col. 1:13; 1 Pet. 2:9) or "being enlightened" (Heb. 6:4; 10:32). Peter does not reflect on the psychological category of "inner darkness" but focuses on the "gloomy place," which is his description of his contemporary moral culture. But even in the darkness the lamp illuminates, and this is precisely what the prophetic Scriptures do. Peter does not view the prophetic word as relevant only to times and peoples past but also as a contemporary and therefore relevant light for his readers. The same may be said for us.

The time until which the prophetic word will shine its necessary illumination is ἕως οὗ ἡμέρα διαυγάσῃ καὶ φωσφόρος ἀνατείλῃ ἐν ταῖς καρδίαις ὑμῶν (*heōs hou hēmera diaugasē kai phōsphoros anateilē en tais kardias hymōn*, until the day dawns and the morning star rises in your hearts). When the day comes, there is no more need of the lamp. The "day" that will dawn is most likely the "day of the Lord" (3:10), which is not only a day of salvation to be anticipated (3:12) but also a "day of judgment" (2:9; 3:7). This is the eternal day (3:18). Throughout Scripture the "day" of the Lord is the time of God's coming to judge humanity and execute his wrath (Isa. 13:6, 9; Ezek. 13:5; 30:3; Joel 1:15; 2:1, 11; 3:14; Amos 5:18, 20; Zeph. 1:7, 14; Zech. 14:1; Mal. 4:5; Acts 2:20; 1 Cor. 5:5; 2 Thess. 2:2; 2 Pet. 3:10). But for God's people this will become a day of salvation (Joel 2:21–32; 3:18; Obad. 15–21; Zech. 14:1–21).

Peter also adds that the lamp of the "prophetic word" will shine until "the morning star rises in your hearts." The mention of this star after speaking about the dawn is somewhat curious. A φωσφόρος (*phōsphoros*) is a source of light (*TLNT* 3:492) but here, as elsewhere, it refers to "the morning star," Venus, which precedes and anticipates the dawn (BDAG 1073). Genesis Rabbah 50.10 declared that the morning star was not the same as the dawn. Yet this was not any ordinary "star" since it is, as Euripides (*Ion* 1157–58) notes, "The Daybringer which puts the stars to flight." The coming of the "morning star" heralds the advent of the dawn and, in the end, the two cannot be separated. The anticipated event is the time when the "morning star rises" (ἀνατείλῃ, *anateilē*). In other places this verb refers to the rising of the sun (Judg. 9:33; 2 Sam. 23:4; Eccles. 1:5; Job 9:7; Wis. 5:6), to a light that dawns (Ps. 97:11 [96:11 LXX]), or to a light rising in darkness (Isa. 58:10). But the term becomes a rich metaphor with eschatological coloring in Scripture as it speaks of the rising of the glory of the Lord (Isa. 60:1; cf. Luke 1:78) and messianically of the rising of the sun of righteousness (Mal. 3:20) or the star that rises out of Jacob (Num. 24:17). Peter's reference to both the "day dawning" and the "star rising" are traditional eschatological references that have to do with the advent of God's reign and the coming of his Messiah, the king. The prophetic word, as the apostolic witness (vv. 16–18), stands over against the diminished eschatology of the heretics.

The only fly in this interpretive ointment is Peter's final note that "the morning star" will rise ἐν ταῖς καρδίαις ὑμῶν (*en tais kardias hymōn*, in your hearts). Given that this phrase in both Testaments most commonly refers to deliberations that occur in a person's inner being or mind (Gen. 6:5; Ps. 14:1 [13:1 LXX]; Jer. 5:24; Hag. 1:7; Luke 12:45; Rom. 2:15; etc.), it is difficult not to understand the rising of the star as a psychological event, especially in our age when Western Christianity has been redefined in inward or psychological terms. But this and the previous passage deal with Christ's future advent (cf. 3:4). To speak about some inner rising of the "morning star" in someone's heart is certainly out of place. But the expression may be used in reference to an external source of light that shines in, as Paul speaks of the light of the gospel shining "in our hearts to give the light of the knowledge of the glory of God in the face of Jesus Christ" (2 Cor. 4:6 NRSV). In a similar vein, and using language akin to 2 Pet. 1:19, Philo (*Decalogue* 11 §49) states that those who obey "the divine utterances will live forever as in unclouded light with the laws themselves as stars illuminating their souls [ἀστέρας ἔχοντες ἐν ψυχῇ φωσφοροῦντας, *asteras echontes en psychē phōsphorountas*]." Peter anticipates the full-orbed revelation when Christ, the "morning star," rises (contra Schelkle 1980: 200). This understanding of the metaphor demands that we understand this "rising" as a time when the light will shine, a sense that the verb certainly can bear (see above). Clearly this will have an effect on the inner life of the Christian (Kelly 1969: 321), but the event in mind is not merely existential.

Peter continues the topic of the authority of the prophetic word in the present verse by saying: τοῦτο πρῶτον γινώσκοντες ὅτι πᾶσα προφητεία γραφῆς ἰδίας ἐπιλύσεως οὐ γίνεται (*touto prōton ginōskontes hoti pasa prophēteia graphēs idias epilyseōs ou ginetai*, Above all know this: that no prophecy of Scripture is of the prophet's own interpretation). The opening call, "Above all know this," is repeated in 3:3 in the same form and in a similar context, which juxtaposes the apostolic and prophetic word with the novel teaching of the heretics (3:2–4). In the context of doctrinal controversy, the most important thing (πρῶτον, *prōton*, adverb of degree meaning "in the first place"; cf. Matt. 6:33; Acts 3:26; Rom. 1:16; 2 Cor. 8:5; 1 Tim. 2:1; BDAG 894) to know is the inspired utterances that make up Scripture, including both the prophetic word (vv. 19–20) and the apostolic witness (3:16 and comments, where the author classifies Paul's writings as "Scripture"). Here Peter turns the readers'

1:20

attention to the issue of prophetic inspiration as that which they should keep in mind above all else.

This call to "know" or "understand" (γινώσκοντες, *ginōskontes*, imperatival participle, BDF §468.2) is likely a reminder of something known (see 1:12 and comments) instead of the addition of new information (compare the similar interpretive issue in Rom. 6:6; Eph. 5:5; 2 Tim. 3:1). Seneca (*Ep. mor.* 94.25–26) presents the rationale for keeping certain facts before people:

> People say: "What good does it do to point out the obvious?" A great deal of good; for we sometimes know facts without paying attention to them. Advice is not teaching; it merely engages the attention and rouses us, and concentrates the memory, and keeps it from losing grip. We miss much that is set before our very eyes. Advice is, in fact, a sort of exhortation. The mind often tries not to notice even what lies before our eyes; we must therefore force on it the knowledge of things that are perfectly well known. One might repeat here the saying of Calvus about Atinius: "You all know that bribery has been going on, and everyone knows that you know it." You know that friendship should be scrupulously honoured, and yet you do not hold it in honour. You know that a man does wrong in requiring chastity of his wife while he himself is intriguing with the wives of other men; you know that, as your wife should have no dealings with a lover, neither should you yourself with a mistress; and yet you do not act accordingly. Hence, you must be continually brought to remember these facts; for they should not be in storage, but ready for use. And whatever is wholesome should be often discussed and often brought before the mind, so that it may be not only familiar to us, but also ready to hand. And remember, too, that in this way what is clear often becomes clearer.

We should not assume that Peter's exhortation here in verse 20 implies that the readers have received no teaching previously about the nature of divine inspiration. Given the repeated emphasis on God's Spirit in relation to prophetic utterances in both Testaments, it would be difficult for an early Christian to be unaware of this theology. Moreover, the readers apparently knew 1 Peter, which discusses the matter of prophetic inspiration (2 Pet. 3:2 and 1 Pet. 1:10–11).

Peter wants his readers to understand that "no prophecy of Scripture is of the prophet's own interpretation." "Prophecy" (προφητεία, *prophēteia*) here and in verse 21 refers to the inspired utterances of the ancient prophets, which were written down as Scripture (2 Chron. 32:32; Ezra 5:1; 6:14; Tob. 2:6; Matt. 13:14). That the author has in mind the inscripted prophecies, as opposed to other prophetic utterances (1 Cor. 12:10; 1 Thess. 5:20; 1 Tim. 1:18), is made certain by the qualification "of Scripture" (γραφῆς, *graphēs*), which, though in the singular, here means the whole of the OT (Philo, *Moses* 2.17 §84; Let. Aris. 155; John 20:9; Acts 8:32). "Scripture" is a technical term for the writings that are divinely inspired (Rom. 1:2; 2 Tim. 3:16; G. Schrenk, *TDNT* 1:750–61). Frequently authors note that these writings have come via prophetic agency (Matt. 26:56; Luke 24:27; Rom. 1:2; 16:26). The use of the term "Scripture" implies that the author believes not only in their divine source but also in their authority for the church, so the inclusion of this terminology prefaces what the author is going to say about their divine source. Peter's declaration in this and the following verse is that the utterances of the prophets contained in Scripture are not of human origin (v. 20b) but are the result of the Holy Spirit's activity on the prophets (v. 21).

The clarification that every prophecy of Scripture ἰδίας ἐπιλύσεως οὐ γίνεται (*idias epilyseōs ou ginetai*, is not of the prophet's own interpretation) has been understood as either a statement about the use or interpretation of OT prophecy (as the NRSV: "no prophecy of scripture is a matter of one's own interpretation") or a disclaimer about the origin of prophecy (as the NIV: "no prophecy of Scripture came about by the prophet's own interpretation"). In other words, is Peter countering the heretics' misinterpretation of prophetic Scripture, or is he defending prophetic Scripture against those who doubted its veracity? Kelly (1969: 324), for example, takes the former line of interpretation: "It is distinctly awkward to have to take *one's own* [*idias*] as referring to 'the prophet,' since no such person has actually been mentioned" (emphasis original). Moreover, the misinterpretation of omens was similarly described by Pseudo-Callisthenes (2.1.5), who recorded Stasagoras's complaint about an inadequate interpretation: σὺ σεαυτῇ ἐπέλυσας τὸ σημεῖον (*sy seautē epelysas to sēmeion*, you gave the omen your own interpretation; BDAG 375). This quotation is particularly significant since this author uses the verbal form of Peter's noun ἐπιλύσις (*epilysis*, interpretation or explanation; BDAG 375; MM 241; as in the interpretation of a parable in 2 Esd. [4 Ezra] 12:10). Moreover, Deissmann (1901: 123) has argued forcefully that during the Koine period ἴδιος (*idios*) became a substitute for the genitive of the possessive pronoun.

Given the context of Peter's battle against the heretics' distortion of the message of Scripture and the apostolic writings of Paul (3:2–4, 15–16), this interpretation of the verse has much to commend it. However, Bauckham (1983: 229–30) has shown that the language here is strikingly similar to Philo as he counters the charge that the prophets spoke of their own accord (cf. also John 7:17). For example, Philo (*Spec. Laws* 4.8 §49) declares, "For no pronouncement of a prophet is ever his own [ἴδιον, *idion*]; he is an interpreter [ἑρμηνεύς, *hermēneus*] prompted by Another in all his utterances." Elsewhere he states, "For a prophet (being a spokesman) has no utterance of his own [ἴδιον μὲν οὐδὲν ἀποφθέγγεται], but all his utterances came from elsewhere, the echoes of another's voice" (*Heir* 52 §259; and see *Moses* 1.51 §281; 1.52 §286; *QG* 3 §10). If we understand that a prophet is one who interprets the divine will (BDAG 889–90), then the notion of the prophet as interpreter is not surprising language in the context of a discussion about the divine source of the prophetic word.

If this is the correct understanding of Peter's statement, it is a counter to the heretics' claim that the prophets have spoken of their own accord, at least when it comes to their predictions about the future parousia of Christ and the final judgment. We may then read the doubt they express as recorded in 3:3–4 as a denial of the inspiration of prophecy and not simply a misinterpretation of the prophetic word. Although either interpretation is possible, given the semantics of 1:20 and the context of the book, Peter includes his own interpretative statement in the following verse (1:21), which begins with the explanatory γάρ (*gar*, for). This appears to be decisive in favor of the second reading (inspiration) since a contrast is set up between the prophet undertaking his own interpretation of the divine will (1:20) over against his prophecy being a result of the activity of God, who has moved him (1:21). This is the same kind of contrast that Philo sets out in *Heir* 52 §259 (see above). In his discussion about divine inspiration, Philo goes on to declare, "The wicked may never be the interpreter of God, so that no worthless person is 'God-inspired' in the proper sense." Peter sounds a similar note in the following verse.

**1:21**  This verse, which begins with γάρ as a marker of clarification (BDAG 189; cf. 2:8), explains and expands the thought of the previous verse: οὐ γὰρ θελήματι ἀνθρώπου ἠνέχθη προφητεία ποτέ (*ou gar thelēmati anthrōpou ēnechthē prophēteia pote*, You see, prophecy was never revealed by human will). "Prophecy" is a reference to the prophetic Scripture (v. 20) or the prophetic word (v. 19). Peter again uses a form of the verb φέρω (*pherō*, here as the aorist passive ἠνέχθη, *ēnechthē*) to describe the process of inspiration, just as he did in verses 17–18 (see comments and cf. 2:11). Φέρω (*pherō*) may mean "to bring a thought or idea into circulation" (as an "accusation" or a "teaching," see John 18:29; Acts 25:7, 18; BDAG 1052), and so it sometimes appears in contexts where the topic is divine communication or proclamation. Diodorus Siculus (13.97.7), for example, discusses a revelatory situation: "When the seer heard this, he disclosed that seven of the generals would be slain. Since the omens revealed [φερόντων, *pherontōn*, present participle] victory, the generals forbade any word going out." Peter is emphatic in his statement that prophecy was "never" (οὐ . . . ποτέ, *ou . . . pote*) given by mere human agency or "human will" (θελήματι ἀνθρώπου, *thelēmati anthrōpou*, instrumental dative).

In this and the following verse, the author sets up the classic human/divine dichotomy (cf. Matt. 16:23; Mark 8:33; 12:14; Luke 2:52; Acts 12:22; Rom. 2:29; 1 Cor. 1:25; 2:5, 11; Gal. 1:1; 1 Pet. 4:2; 4 Macc. 1:16–17; 4:13). This contrast occasionally has to do with divine versus human revelation, such as the command of God over against human tradition (Mark 7:8), the Word of God as opposed to the human word (1 Thess. 2:13), or the testimony of God in contrast with human testimony (1 John 5:9). As noted above (v. 20 and comments), Philo set up the same contrast in stating that prophecies were not of the prophet's own making, but the prophet was acted on by Another. He states, "The prophet seems to say something but he does not give his own oracle but is the interpreter of another, who puts things into his mind" (*QG* 3 §10). Peter's previous statement that the prophecies are not the prophet's "own" interpretation (v. 20) is further clarified by stating that they do not come by a mere act of "human will." In fact, the false prophets are those who speak on their own (Jer. 14:13–16; 23:16, 21–22, 26, 31; Ezek. 13:2–9, 17; Bauckham

1983: 234). In such contexts, the human revelation is secondary, inferior, and even unreliable over against the divine, which is primary, truthful, and reliable. Peter wrote during an era when truth was widely considered to be the domain of the divine and not the creation of humans, and so the source of truth among humans was divine revelation. To claim a divine source was to claim veracity. On the other side, to tag something as "human" became a statement that something had its source in a person's own pleasure (Esth. 1:8). The "human will" here is that which is "arbitrary and autonomous" (G. Schrenk, *TDNT* 3:59), but the prophetic word, understood as the interpretation of the divine will, was neither of these.

On the positive side, Peter makes a statement about the agency of the Holy Spirit in moving the prophets to prophesy: ἀλλὰ ὑπὸ πνεύματος ἁγίου φερόμενοι ἐλάλησαν ἀπὸ θεοῦ ἄνθρωποι (*alla hypo pneumatos hagiou pheromenoi elalēsan apo theou anthrōpoi*, but men spoke from God as they were borne along by the Holy Spirit). The role of the Holy Spirit in the inspiration of prophecy is a commonplace in both OT (Num. 11:25–26, 29; 1 Sam. 10:6, 10; 19:20, 23; 2 Sam. 23:2; Neh. 9:30; Isa. 61:1; Joel 2:28 [3:1 LXX]; Zech. 4:6; 7:12) and NT theology (Mark 12:36; Luke 1:67; Acts 1:16; 2:17–18; 19:6; 28:25; Eph. 3:5; 2 Tim. 3:16; Heb. 3:7; 10:15–16; 1 Pet. 1:11). The perspective of both Testaments on the Spirit as the mover in prophetic utterances is echoed in Jewish literature as well (Lam. Rab. prologue 24; Eccles. Rab. 1.1.1; Num. Rab. 13.20; Song Rab. 1.1.9; *b. Ber.* 4b; Str-B 4:435–50). The way that Peter speaks of this process, however, appears unusual at first sight since he says that the prophets were "borne along" (φερόμενοι, *pheromenoi*) by the Spirit.

Bauckham (1983: 233) has argued that the language is similar to Hos. 9:7 LXX and Zeph. 3:4 LXX, which use the word πνευματοφόρος (*pneumatophoros*) to describe the prophets since etymologically the word means "bearing *pneuma* [spirit]" or "borne by *pneuma*," depending whether the Greek accent falls over the penultimate or antepenultimate syllable. However, in both these passages the context is pejorative. The term in Zeph. 3:4 appears in a critique and translates the Hebrew פֹּחֵז (*pāḥaz*, wanton or reckless). Hosea 9:7 speaks of "the prophet that is mad, as a man deranged." However, the verb θεοφορέω (*theophoreō*, lit., "God-bearing" and thus "possessed" or "inspired") as used by Philo to speak of prophetic inspiration comes close to Peter's thought in this verse (*Heir* 14 §69; *Dreams* 1.1 §2 [of dreams]; *Moses* 1.38 §210; 1.51 §283; 2.14 §69; 2.46 §250; 2.48 §264; 2.49 §273). Such a person is "possessed" by the Deity and therefore "inspired." The person so inspired is overtaken by God such that the words spoken by the prophet can be none other than divine (Sawyer 1993: 9–10), an inference that Peter wants his readers to make in this attempt to arrest the critiques of the heretics, who cast doubt over the surety of the prophetic word.

The human side of prophetic speech is not, however, overlooked. These "men spoke from God." The NRSV uses gender-inclusive language here ("but men and women . . . spoke from God"; cf. the gender-neutral rendering in the TNIV: "but prophets, though human, spoke from God"), but the topic from the start of this section has been the prophetic word written in Scripture (vv. 19–20). Insofar as these writings were the production of male prophets, the translation "men" should be maintained. When both genders are clearly intended by the author, recourse to gender-inclusive language preserves the integrity of the author's thought. This clause, however, is a point where gender-inclusive language distorts the author's view, whatever we may conclude about the way ἄνθρωποι (*anthrōpoi*) may be used elsewhere to include both sexes (cf. Eph. 6:7).

But while Peter does note that the prophets spoke, he again emphasizes that their utterances had their source in God and not in themselves. They spoke "from God" (cf. John 3:34; 7:17; 2 Cor. 2:17). Not only were they acted on by God, being borne along by him, but the root source of their message also was God. Peter concludes his defense of apostolic and prophetic authority (vv. 16–21) by claiming divine inspiration to silence the doubts sown by the heretics. This final declaration paves the way for the warning that follows about the false teachers (2:1). As there were false prophets in the past who imitated the true prophets but did not speak for God (vv. 19–21), so now there are false teachers who deny the apostolic teaching, which came from God (vv. 16–18).

# 2. The Coming and the Judgment of the False Teachers (2:1–22)

Having introduced his principal themes in the beginning of the body middle of the letter (1:12–21), Peter now comes to the specifics of the problem at hand. Just as false prophets were among the people of God in ancient times, so false teachers have invaded the church (2:1–3). This theme follows naturally from the preceding section, where the author affirmed the veracity both of apostolic teaching (1:16–18) and the ancient prophetic utterances (1:19–21). The readers are to remember the words of the apostles and prophets over against the false teachers who have invaded their ranks. These heretics are apostates from the faith, and their aim is to draw disciples after themselves. Later in the letter we learn that they have embraced skepticism about the certainty of future judgment and the coming of Christ (see 3:3–4 and "The Opponents in 2 Peter" in the introduction). In the opening section, Peter repeatedly speaks of their final doom (2:1, 3) and then turns to demonstrate from ancient revelation that God certainly did judge humanity in the past (2:4–10a). Whatever delay there may be in judgment does not mean that the final reckoning will not come. As God has done, so he will do. In 2:10b–16 Peter turns the argument to unveiling the heretics' corruption and their certain doom. In a second round of denunciations (2:17–22), he warns the believers about their arrogance and their attempts to gain converts (vv. 17–20), underscoring the problem of apostasy (vv. 20–22).

# a. The Rise and Judgment of the False Teachers among You (2:1–3)

At last Peter identifies the problem that he has been dealing with since the start of this letter and will continue to address down to the very end. False teachers are introducing "heresies of destruction" (2:1). But just as soon as he announces their advent, he signals their doom: "swift destruction" (2:1), "judgment" that does not delay, and "destruction" that "does not slumber" (2:3). The audacity of their teaching is evident—they have denied "the Master who bought them" (2:1). Yet despite their gross error and their ultimate doom, their appeal is persuasive, and their followers are many (2:2). Their disciples follow their immoral behavior despite the fact that they have been exploited by the greed of the false teachers (2:3). In the end, the gospel itself, "the way of truth," is maligned by those outside the community of faith (2:2). The situation is severe and serious.

## Exegesis and Exposition

[1]There were false prophets among the people, as even there will be false teachers among you, who will bring in heresies of destruction and deny the Master who bought them, bringing on themselves swift destruction. [2]And many will follow after their licentious deeds, because of whom the way of truth will be blasphemed. [3]And in greed they will exploit you with pretensions. Their judgment is not delayed for a long time, and their destruction does not slumber.

2:1    For the first time in the letter, Peter directly addresses the problem of the heretics. Up to this moment, the author has laid the groundwork for his denunciation of their teaching and conduct and has apparently answered their charges against the apostolic and prophetic testimony. But not until 2:1 does he turn to name the opponents who were troubling the church. He warns his readers: Ἐγένοντο δὲ καὶ ψευδοπροφῆται ἐν τῷ λαῷ, ὡς καὶ ἐν ὑμῖν ἔσονται ψευδοδιδάσκαλοι (Egenonto de kai pseudoprophētai en tō laō, hōs kai en hymin esontai pseudodidaskaloi, There were false prophets among the people, as even there will be false teachers among you). Peter has just defended prophetic inspiration (1:19–21), which was not only a counter to the heretics' critique but also a prelude to the apostle's charge that the heretics themselves are purveyors of heretical teaching. "False prophets" are those who speak on their own and do not speak for God (see 1:20–21 and comments).

Ancient false prophets are only occasionally spoken of as a group (Luke 6:26), with the NT focus being primarily on contemporary false prophets among the church or those who will come to the church (Matt. 7:15; 24:11, 24; Mark 13:22; Acts 13:6; 1 John 4:1). Revelation even speaks of an eschatological false prophet (Rev. 16:13; 19:20; 20:10). In the LXX, the charge that certain people are "false prophets" is fairly common in Jeremiah (Jer. 6:13; 33:7–8, 11, 16; 34:9; 35:1; 36:1, 8). The epithet is found only once elsewhere (Zech. 13:2), although the idea is surely more widespread. These self-styled prophets were said to have a false spirit (1 Kings 22:22–23; 2 Chron. 18:21–22) and to prophesy lies (Jer. 14:14–15; 23:25–26; 34:15), lying dreams (Jer. 23:32), or lying visions (Ezek. 13:9; 22:28). The identifier marks them as people who do not speak the truth rather than tagging them as those who claim to be prophets but are not (Reiling 1971: 148). The term "false prophet" (ψευδοπροφήτης, *pseudoprophētēs*) is not found in non-Jewish Hellenistic literature, but its use in the LXX of Jeremiah appears to be an adaptation of the term ψευδόμαντις (*pseudomantis*, false prophet). Such people were purveyors of false oracles, and Reiling (1971: 152) concludes that the LXX derivation of "false prophets" from this compound word "was due to the association of prophecy and (pagan) divination." However, 2 Peter does not appear to make a similar association, although Jeremiah's central issue is the false claims of the "false prophets" over against the truth the prophets proclaimed (see 1:20–21 and comments).

The sphere of these ancient "false prophets'" activity is "among the people" (ἐν τῷ λαῷ, *en tō laō*). The "people" are the chosen people of God, Israel (Jude 5 and comments; Matt. 2:6; 15:8; 26:47; Mark 7:6; Luke 1:17; John 11:50; Acts 3:23; 4:10; 7:17; 28:17; Rom. 11:1–2; Heb. 8:10), in contrast to gentiles (Acts 26:17; Rom. 15:10). While this word came to be used of Christians as God's people (Acts 15:14; 18:10; Rom. 9:25; Heb. 4:9; 1 Pet. 2:9–10), our author's attention is turned on ancient Israel. But his interest is more than historical since this group is paralleled with ἐν ὑμῖν (*en hymin*, among you). He includes a typological connection between what occurred in Israel of old and what his readers now experience. The ancient people prefigure the Christian community, as the ancient false prophets are a sign of the coming false teachers. As Goppelt (1982: 158–59) comments, "The reason for comparing old false prophets and new false teachers is not that this forms an ingenious parallel, but that the author sees the former as the types and the latter as the fulfillment—in a typological sense."

The typological link between the ancient and the present is sealed with the statement ὡς καὶ ἐν ὑμῖν ἔσονται ψευδοδιδάσκαλοι (*hōs kai en hymin esontai pseudodidaskaloi*, as even there will be false teachers among you). Ψευδοδιδάσκαλοι (*pseudodidaskaloi*) is a unique term for Peter, found only here in the NT and LXX. However, similar compound terms appear throughout the NT, such as:

ψευδάδελφος (*pseudadelphos*, false brother; 2 Cor. 11:26; Gal. 2:4; translated also as "false believers" in the TNIV) ψευδαπόστολος (*pseudapostolos*, false apostle; 2 Cor. 11:13)

ψευδοδιδάσκαλος/ψευδοδιδασκαλία (*pseudodidaskalos/pseudodidaskalia*, false teacher / false teaching; 2 Pet. 2:1; Pol. *Phil.* 7.2)

ψευδομαρτυρία/ψευδόμαρτυς (*pseudomartyria/pseudomartys*, false witness; Matt. 15:19; 26:59 / Matt. 26:60; 1 Cor. 15:15)

ψευδόχριστος (*pseudochristos*, false christ; Matt. 24:24; Mark 13:22)

Peter's critique of the "false teachers" possibly suggests that he has something more in his sights than their teaching, as the typology with the "false prophets" might indicate. *Pseudo* here "suggests both that the claim of the men concerned is false and also that their teaching is erroneous, so that in every respect they are a perversion of the Christian διδάσκαλος (*didaskalos*, teacher), since they reject the claim of Jesus to domination over their whole lives" (K. H. Rengstorf, *TDNT* 2:160). The early church is in a crisis due to the presence of those who claim divine authority for their teaching and prophecies but whose claims are false according to apostolic evaluation. Mechanisms were put in place to aid the young congregations to differentiate the true from the false in the absence of what we know as the Christian canon (Matt. 7:15–23; 1 Thess. 5:20–22; 2 Thess. 2:2; 1 John 4:1–3; Did. 11; Aune 1983: 222). Many NT epistles were sent precisely for this reason as the apostles sought to warn against error and, at the same time, resolve the tension between the mission that moved them onward and the consolidation of the young congregations.

The author predicts the coming of these false teachers (ἔσονται, *esontai*, there will be; see the future tenses in 2:1–3; 3:3), yet later in the chapter they appear to have already arrived (2:10b–22). They are already feasting with the church (v. 13) and are seeking converts to their way from among the members of the church (vv. 14, 19). They have perverted Pauline teaching (3:15–16) and are ignoring fundamental Christian truth (3:5–7; cf. the same oscillation between present and future in 2 Tim. 2:16–17; 3:2–5, 13; 4:3–4). It may be, as Moo (1996: 92) suggests, that Peter is quoting earlier apostolic prophecies here and in so doing preserves the future tense (cf. Jude 17–18 and comments). Unlike Jude, however, 2 Peter offers the readers no indication that former prophecies are being quoted.

Alternatively, some have argued that the future is part of the mechanism of pseudepigraphy (Kelly 1969: 326; Bauckham 1983: 239; Senior and Harrington 2003: 261): the unknown author writes this pseudepigraphical "testament" of Peter well after the supposed author's death and ascribes a "prediction" of the coming of the heretics to Peter. This explanation is unable to account for the shift to the present tense in the following verses, however, and rests on a foundation no stronger than the supposed ineptitude of the pseudepigrapher.

Another approach is to recognize that, at times, grammatical form and meaning come apart, and this is true for the future indicative as other tenses (Porter 1989: 403–39). While Peter does use the future to refer to coming events, as those that will occur after his own death (1:12, 15) or eschatological events

(1:11; 2:12; 3:10, 12), he may elsewhere use a present (2:3b). The oscillation between the present and the future in the letter in reference to the heretics appears to be rooted in the author's eschatology. The heretics will come in the last days (3:3–4), and their presence in the church is evidence that the last times have come (3:5–7). Peter's thought differs little from the oscillation between present and future in 2 Tim. 2:16–18; 3:1–9, 13; and 4:3–4.

The charge against the false teachers is that they disseminate false teaching within the church: οἵτινες παρεισάξουσιν αἱρέσεις ἀπωλείας (hoitines pareisaxousin haireseis apōleias, who will introduce heresies of destruction). The author first speaks of their method: they will "introduce" (παρεισάξουσιν, pareisaxousin) false teaching. While the majority of the translations suggest that these people use stealth tactics (as the NIV rendering, "They will secretly introduce destructive heresies"), the term does not evoke the concept of secrecy or malicious intent but simply that something will be "brought in" (Polybius 2.7.8; 3.63.2; Diodorus Siculus 12.41.4; Let. Aris. 20; BDAG 774; MM 492). The word is sometimes found in the context of introducing religious belief (Polybius 6.56.12; Diodorus Siculus 1.96.5; Plutarch, Mor. 328D). Peter employs it within this frame. Such introductions were not always welcome, as the charge against Socrates makes clear (he was "tried on the charge of introducing foreign deities"; Plutarch, Mor. 328D), but this does not mean that stealth tactics were employed.

Although Peter's language is similar to Jude 4, a verse on which he is dependent, his thought is not identical to Jude, who says of the heretics, "For certain men have weaseled their way in" (see comments). The heretics Peter seeks to arrest will bring with them "heresies" (αἱρέσεις, haireseis), a noun that originally had to do with a choice made (1 Macc. 8:30) or an inclination. From there it could mean a group, school, or sect differentiated from others (Acts 5:17; 15:5; 24:5; 26:5; 28:22). By extension, it could speak of a faction (1 Cor. 11:19; Gal. 5:20) or the distinct doctrine of a factional group (Philo, Planting 34 §151). In other words, "It thus comes to be the αἵρεσις [hairesis] (teaching) of a particular αἵρεσις [hairesis] (school)" (H. Schlier, TDNT 1:181).[1] Doctrinal and social aspects were tightly bound. But in 2 Pet. 2:1 the author uses it in a pejorative sense: it points to the heretics' heterodox doctrine (Herm. Sim. 9.23.5; Ign. Eph. 6.2; Ign. Trall. 6.1; H. Schlier, TDNT 1:180–84; MM 13–14; BDAG 27–28). The presence of heresy, therefore, is a contradiction both to apostolic teaching and Christian community. In other words, "ἐκκλησία [ekklēsia, church] and αἵρεσις [hairesis, faction/heresy] are material opposites. The latter cannot accept the former; the former excludes the latter" (H. Schlier, TDNT 1:181).

Peter discusses the nature of the heresy in the following verses. Principally, it denied the coming of the Lord and future judgment, and this theological

---

1. The contours of an ancient αἵρεσις (hairesis) included "the gathering of the αἵρεσις [hairesis] from a comprehensive society and therefore its delimitation from other schools; the self-chosen authority of a teacher; the relatively authoritarian and relatively disputable doctrine; and the private character of these features" (H. Schlier, TDNT 1:181).

perspective was joined with a libertine morality (2:14, 18–19; 3:3–9), as well as a rupture with the apostolic and prophetic heritage (1:16–21). The heretics' presence and teaching meant the separation of some from the church, the unstable being taken in by their persuasion (2:14, 18–22). The error had doctrinal, ethical, and social components (see "The Opponents in 2 Peter" in the introduction). Its end is apostasy and, finally, "destruction" (ἀπωλείας, apōleias; cf. 2:1b, 3; 3:7, 16). In the NT this word refers to final and ultimate destruction of those who oppose God and his purposes (Matt. 7:13; Rom. 9:22; Phil. 1:28; 3:19; Heb. 10:39; 2 Pet. 3:7; Rev. 17:8, 11; BDAG 127; A. Oepke, *TDNT* 1:396–97; H. C. Hahn, *NIDNTT* 1:462–66). It is, therefore, the opposite of salvation (Phil. 1:28; Heb. 10:39) and is the result of the execution of God's wrath (Rom. 9:22). Those destined for this end are called "children of destruction" (John 17:12; 2 Thess. 2:3). The final destruction will occur on the day of the Lord (2 Pet. 3:7; see 3:10). Peter warns his readers that it will come swiftly (2:1b) since it does not sleep (2:3). This is where the heresy leads (2:1) because, in the end, the heretics deny the Lord himself (see below). The genitive "of destruction" does not simply mean that the heresies are "destructive" but also that their end is this final doom (objective genitive, not genitive of quality; BDF §163). Wrong belief leads not only to wrong conduct and social rupture but also to eternal separation from God. These heresies are not merely harmful; they also lead to final doom.

Although the heresy that 2 Peter addresses should not be identified with what Jude denounces, they share some similar contours. For that reason, Peter picks up and modifies the language of Jude 4, which outlines the heretics as those who "alter the grace of our God into sexual excess and deny our only Master and Lord, Jesus Christ" (see comments). Our author simply states that the ones who introduce the heresy τὸν ἀγοράσαντα αὐτοὺς δεσπότην ἀρνούμενοι (*ton agorasanta autous despotēn arnoumenoi*, deny the Master who bought them). Peter has dropped the note saying that the heretics "alter the grace of our God into sexual excess" and omits "only . . . Lord, Jesus Christ," and adds that the Master has "bought them." "To deny" Christ (ἀρνούμενοι, *arnoumenoi*; see Jude 4 and comments) is the opposite of "to confess" him (John 1:20; 2 Tim. 2:12; Titus 1:16; 1 John 2:22–23) and thus is saying "no" instead of "amen." It is the renunciation of Christ. In certain contexts, the verb may be a simple denial of some statement or event (Gen. 18:15; Luke 8:45; Acts 4:16; Philo, *Abraham* 22 §112; 36 §206; *Spec. Laws* 2.14 §54); in other contexts it points to a refusal or rejection (Acts 7:35; Josephus, *J.W.* 2.9.2 §171). From here it is a short step to religious refusal or denial (Wis. 12:27; 16:16; Philo, *Spec. Laws* 2.46 §255; Matt. 10:32–33), as in the present verse. Although the verb highlights the verbal aspect of the denial of the Lord, the heretics' conduct included a repudiation of his way (2:15; cf. 1 Tim. 5:8; Titus 1:16).

The accusation that the heretics repudiated Christ is shocking because he is here called the "Master" (δεσπότην, *despotēn*). As noted previously (Jude 4 and comments), the title was used of the master of slaves (1 Tim. 6:1–2) as well as God, and underscores the Master's legal control and authority over the ones subject to him. Peter evokes the imagery of slavery since he notes that this is the Master "who bought them" (τὸν ἀγοράσαντα αὐτούς, *ton agorasanta autous*). The language evokes the image of the manumission of slaves (Deissmann 1911: 322–27). One papyrus, for example, notes the transaction "to buy from Tasarapion her slave Sarapion" (MM 6). The language of commercial transaction in manumission is preserved in the inscriptions from Delphi, where the record of the sale from the slave master to the Pythian Apollo was made. The slave, now freed from former obligations, was consecrated to the deity (1 Cor. 7:22; although no obligation was made to remain at the temple of Apollo as a servant; *TLNT* 1:27). The language of manumission was absorbed into the church as a metaphor of Christian salvation (1 Cor. 6:20; 7:23; Rev. 5:9; 14:3–4; Morris 1965: 53–55).

In the manumission inscriptions, stipulation was made that a person once freed should not be enslaved again, and penalties were prescribed for such injustice (cf. Gal. 2:4; 1 Cor. 7:23). Those redeemed by Christ now belong to Christ (1 Cor. 15:23; Gal. 5:24). Yet the heretics have repudiated the very one who freed them, the Master. The denunciation has shock effect and highlights the audacity of the heretics. As these people have turned from the Master (2:15), they are on a quest to lead others into their error (2:14, 18–22). Such turning is not simply a theoretical but a real possibility, which sets in high relief the urgency with which Peter writes (1:12–15; 3:11–18). He calls his readers not to be swept away by this error (3:18), although some have already succumbed to the heretics' persuasion (2:20–22).

The heretics' dark end is described in the final words of the verse: ἐπάγοντες ἑαυτοῖς ταχινὴν ἀπώλειαν (*epagontes heautois tachinēn apōleian*, bringing on themselves soon-coming destruction). The verb ἐπάγοντες (*epagontes*) may refer to bringing something on others (Acts 5:28; 14:2 [*v.l.*]) or, as here, bringing something on oneself (LXX: Exod. 28:43; Lev. 22:16). In either case, the verb is commonly found in contexts where something bad is brought on someone, even judgment (cf. 2:5; and Gen. 6:17; Ps. 7:11 [7:12 LXX]; Pr. Azar. 5, 8 [= Dan. 3:28, 31 LXX]; Hos. 13:15; Amos 5:9; Ezek. 28:7; BDAG 356). The heretics cannot nor will not be able to cast blame on others since they have subjected themselves to final doom by their denial of the Master. The "destruction" the author speaks of is that final, eschatological ruin (2:1a, 3; 3:7, 16), the final loss of salvation and hope.

While Peter deals with the problem of the delay of the parousia of Christ and the final judgment (3:8–10), noting that the end will come at an unexpected time "as a thief," he holds to the notion that the final judgment is imminent or "soon-coming" (ταχινήν, *tachinēn*; see 1:14 and comments). The term speaks of what will happen soon, and any notion of "suddenness" is only suggested because of the speed of the occurrence (BDAG 992; MM 627; LSJ 1762; cf. the adjective ταχύς, *tachys*, which always refers to that which happens swiftly: James 1:19; Matt. 5:25; 28:7; Luke 15:22; John 11:29; Rev. 2:16; 3:11; 11:14; 22:7, 12, 20; so, too, the adverb ταχέως, *tacheōs*, speedily). The author's affirmation brings into question the view that the letter belongs to a supposed "early catholic" period when the hope of the parousia had faded from view. Peter expects that judgment will come swiftly, even though delay is involved (3:8–10). He is able to hold together the notion of delay and speed in a way that some of Peter's commentators are not. Second Peter is a prime example of "paratactical thinking," which allowed the ancient Hebrew mind to hold seemingly disparate views together in harmony (Caird 1980: 117–21).

**2:2**     The impact of the heretics on the Christian community is twofold: they persuade those in the church to follow their error (2:2a), and since they are associated with the church, their conduct fuels the fires of dissent against the gospel and hinders Christian mission (2:2b). Peter makes the first charge thus: καὶ πολλοὶ ἐξακολουθήσουσιν αὐτῶν ταῖς ἀσελγείαις (*kai polloi exakolouthēsousin autōn tais aselgeiais*, And many will follow after their licentious deeds). Later in the chapter, Peter singles out the persuasive power of the heretics: these people are not passive but are actively seeking disciples. The "unstable people" whom they entice (2:14) and the ones who are persuaded by the errorists (2:18–22) are no small group but "many." The problem of apostasy was one of the principal crises that the early church faced as the fledgling communities reacted to persecution (1 Thess. 3:1–5) and confronted heresy, which as here was linked with an abandonment of Christian morals. Christian as well as Jewish theology even predicted an "apostasy" from the faith before the final consummation (Matt. 24:11–13; 2 Thess. 2:3; 1 Tim. 4:1; 1 En. 93.9; 90.26; 2 Esd. [4 Ezra] 5:1–13; 2 Bar. 41.3; 42.4; G. Green 2002: 307).

Pliny the Younger, who became the governor of Bithynia, exchanged various letters with the emperor Trajan during the early years of the second century. These letters are particularly significant since 1 Peter was written to the Bithynian churches sometime earlier (1 Pet. 1:1), and 2 Peter may have reached them sometime later (2 Pet. 3:1). Pliny queried the emperor about the "Christian problem" and received counsel concerning how to proceed. In one letter dated from about AD 112, Pliny reports not only the progress of the gospel but also accusations against the Christians and the apostasies that have occurred:

> Others who were named by that informer at first confessed themselves Christians, and then denied it; true, they had been of that persuasion but they had quitted it, some three years, others many years, and a few as much as twenty-five years ago. They all worshipped your statue and the images of the gods, and cursed Christ. . . . For this contagious superstition is not confined to the cities only, but has spread through the villages and rural districts; it seems possible, however, to check and cure it. 'Tis certain at least that the temples, which had been almost deserted, begin now to be frequented; and the sacred festivals, after a long intermission, are again revived; while there is a general demand for sacrificial animals, which for some time past have met with but few purchasers. From hence it is easy to imagine what multitudes may be reclaimed from this error, if a door be left open to repentance. (*Ep.* 10.96.6, 9–10)

Although this letter postdates 2 Peter according to our reckoning, it highlights the problem of apostasy, which the churches faced.

Peter notes how those taken in by the heretics "will follow after their licentious deeds." In the Gospels, the concept of discipleship is expressed by a call "to follow" Christ (ἀκολουθέω, *akoloutheō*, in Matt. 4:20, 22; Mark 2:14; John 1:37; 21:22; and elsewhere). The cognate term Peter uses here, "to follow after" (ἐξακολουθήσουσιν, *exakolouthēsousin*), was previously used in 1:16 and points to adherence to what was false (2:15; Josephus, *Ant.* proem 4 §22; P.Berlin 7927.8, μυθολογίαις ἐπακολουθοῦσι, *mythologiais epakolouthousi*, they follow mythology). Those who "follow after" something have submitted to some form of authority in their thought or actions (2 Pet. 2:15; T. Naph. 3.3; T. Iss. 6.2; BDAG 344). As seen from a Christian perspective, this was antidiscipleship.

The ones who have been seduced by the heretics have been drawn in and are following their "licentious deeds" (αὐτῶν ταῖς ἀσελγείαις, *autōn tais aselgeiais*), the plural suggesting that the author has specific acts in mind (cf. 3 Macc. 2:26; Rom. 13:13). The term "licentious," found here and in 2:7, 14 and Jude 4 (see comments), points to some form of "libertine behavior lacking moral restraint" (J. K. Elliott 2000: 722). This is "outrageous conduct" or "indecent behavior" that demonstrates an utter lack of self-restraint (Polybius 1.6.5; 5.28.9; Josephus, *Ant.* 4.6.12 §151; 8.10.2 §252; 20.5.40 §112; LSJ 255) and is sometimes sexual in nature (Mark 7:22; 2 Cor. 12:21; Wis. 14:26; Philo, *Moses* 1.56 §305). This sin characterizes the pagan (Eph. 4:17–19; 1 Pet. 4:3; T. Jud. 23.1–2), and in one vice list Paul classifies it as a work of the flesh (Gal. 5:19). Peter, using typological interpretation, describes the sexual conduct of those in Lot's day as licentious (2 Pet. 2:7), and the heretics bank on this character trait as they make their persuasive appeal (2:18–19). Sexual license is a distinguishing mark of their heresy (2:10, 12, 14; 3:3). In a world where sexual license was the norm and prostitution was a main-street affair (1 Cor. 6:15–20; Epictetus, *Ench.* 33.8; Musonius Rufus, *Fragments* 12; Plutarch, *Conjugalia praecepta* 144C–D), Christian leaders found it necessary to instruct new converts in the need for abstinence in sexual relations outside of marriage (Eph. 4:17–19; 1 Thess. 4:3–8; 1 Pet. 4:3) and to advise believers about the eternal consequences of such actions (1 Cor. 6:9–11; Gal. 5:19–21). The heretics' appeal, on the other hand, resonated with the sexual mores of the street.

The heretics not only fractured the Christian community by persuading some to embrace their lifestyle; their conduct also brought reproach on the gospel: δι' οὓς ἡ ὁδὸς τῆς ἀληθείας βλασφημηθήσεται (*di' hous hē hodos tēs alētheias blasphēmēthēsetai*, because of whom the way of truth will be blasphemed), an expression that may echo Isa. 52:5 LXX (cf. Rom. 2:24). The verb translated "to blaspheme" could refer to slanderous and defaming speech against a person (1 Pet. 4:4; Rom. 3:8; Titus 3:2; cf. 1 Cor. 4:13) or against supernatural beings (2 Pet. 2:10, 12; Jude 8, 10 and comments), but was also used widely in Greco-Roman, Jewish, and Christian literature to speak of reviling or defaming the Deity (2 Kings 19:4, 6, 22; Isa. 52:5; Matt. 9:3; 26:65; Acts 19:37;

26:11; Rom. 2:24; BDAG 178). Such slander brings dishonor and, in the human sphere, results in shame. In his defense of the Jewish faith, Josephus attacks the gentiles as blasphemers (*Ag. Ap.* 1.11 §59) and accuses Apion of engaging in "malicious slander" (2.8 §89; cf. *Ant.* 8.13.8 §§358–59). The conduct of the people of God should be such that it does not cause those outside to slander the name of God (Rom. 2:24; 1 Tim. 6:1; Titus 2:5). If slander is provoked, it should only be the result of the Christians' good conduct (1 Pet. 4:3–4).

The heretics, however, are viewed as part of the Christian community by those on the outside, and the end result is that their conduct brings slander against the "way of truth." Since their conduct has generated such antipathy, we can surmise that they have engaged in behavior that is not even acceptable according to the norms of the wider society (cf. 1 Cor. 5:1). The "way of truth" (ἡ ὁδὸς τῆς ἀληθείας, *he hodos tēs alētheias*) is an expression found elsewhere in biblical and Jewish literature (Gen. 24:48; Ps. 119:30 [118:30 LXX]; Tob. 1:3; Wis. 5:6), but appears only here in the NT. It describes the just and upright life and is equivalent to "the straight way" (2:15) and "the way of righteousness" (2:21). The description of the Christian faith as "the way of truth" underscores how the apostle views it as a lifestyle and not only as a set of beliefs. The irony is that the pagans themselves slander this way, which should be characterized by living according to the truth of the gospel (1:12 and comments).

Slanderous accusations against the gospel were common in the early years of the church. Tacitus (*Annals* 15.44.2–8) called Christianity a "deadly superstition," and the charge laid against the Christians during Nero's persecution was "hatred of the human race." Christians were "hated for their abominations," and their faith was deemed "hideous and shameful." Suetonius (*Nero* 16.2) echoed the sentiment by calling Christianity "a new and wicked superstition." Such slander was unjustified, but the heretics' conduct was provoking antipathy toward the gospel and thereby not only compromising the Christian's already-weak social position but also placing an obstacle in the way of Christian mission. If Christians suffer and the gospel is reproached, it should only be as a result of doing good (1 Pet. 2:15, 19–20; 3:13–17; 4:12–19).

**2:3**   Peter attacks the motives and the methods of the heretics (v. 3a) before he returns to the matter of their destiny (v. 3b). The heretics are driven by their greed and view their potential converts as sources of gain whom they can exploit. In his own *vituperatio* against them, Peter states: καὶ ἐν πλεονεξίᾳ πλαστοῖς λόγοις ὑμᾶς ἐμπορεύσονται (*kai en pleonexia plastois logois hymas emporeusontai*, and in greed they will exploit you with pretensions). Peter accuses the heretics of being motivated by greed (ἐν πλεονεξίᾳ, *en pleonexia*). "Greediness," or "avarice," is the excessive and insatiable desire to obtain more wealth and in this pursuit to be willing to use the other and what belongs to the other to satisfy one's own wants (Sir. 14:9; Philo, *Rewards* 20 §121; Plutarch, *Ag. Cleom.* 3.1; 16.1). Dio Chrysostom devoted a whole discourse (*Or.* 17) to the vice of avarice. He, Plutarch, and others denounced those who engaged in public oratory only to gain what they could from the gathered crowds (Dio

Chrysostom, *Or.* 32.10–11; Plutarch, *Mor.* 131A; cf. 1 Thess. 2:5). Dio once professed, "Gentlemen, I have come before you not to display my talents as a speaker nor because I want money from you, or expect your praise" (*Or.* 35.1; cf. 1 Thess. 2:5–6). This vice is a great evil because it damages both the greedy person and the objects of one's greed (*Or.* 17.6–7), but few people are exempt from it, in Dio's opinion (*Or.* 17.16). In the NT, "avarice" frequently appears in vice lists, often alongside sexual vices (Mark 7:22; Eph. 4:19; 5:3; Col. 3:5; and see Luke 12:15; Rom. 1:29; see BDAG 824; MM 518; *TLNT* 3:117–19; G. Delling, *TDNT* 6:266–74; F. Selter and G. Finkenrath, *NIDNTT* 1:137–39). Later in the chapter, Peter returns to blame the heretics for their adhesion to this vice (2:14–16).

Although the charge of "greed" was a commonplace in *vituperatio* (L. Johnson 1989: 430), the author's development of the theme through the fabric of his accusation suggests that such exploitation was actually going on. Moreover, the topos of orators who declaim merely for gain was more than a caricature since this critique was echoed by numerous ancient authors. The peddling of opinions for gain was a particular vice attributed to the sophists, whom Philo accused of being people "who sell their tenets and arguments like any bit of merchandise in the market, men who forever pit philosophy against philosophy without a blush" (*Moses* 2.39 §212). Philo's language is strikingly similar to Peter's denunciation of the heretics as those who will "exploit" or "make gain" from them (ἐμπορεύσονται, *emporeusontai*; LSJ 548). In negative contexts like this one, the term suggests a "misrepresentation of merchandise" (BDAG 324). That sense is heightened by the statement that they engage in exploitation "with pretensions" (πλαστοῖς λόγοις, *plastois logois*; see Neyrey 1993: 192, whose translation "specious arguments" reflects the sense well). The accusation is that their persuasive talk is not sincere; their motives are cloaked.

The NIV understands these words to mean "stories they have made up." The word πλαστός (*plastos*) tags something as fabricated, made up, or feigned (Euripides, *Bacchanals* 218; Philo, *Dreams* 2.20 §140; Josephus, *Life* 35 §177; 65 §337), such as a "feigned frenzy," a "forged contract," or a "feigned friendship" (H. Braun, *TDNT* 6:262; MM 516; LSJ 1412; BDAG 823). In combination with λόγος (*logos*), the idea suggested is not about fabricating fables (cf. 1:16) but of making a pretense (Herodotus 1.68), or in the plural, "pretensions." Deception is at the heart of their persuasive appeal. Peter's denunciation again echoes Philo's accusation of the sophists as those who not only are corrupt (cf. 2 Pet. 2:2 and comments) and seek to get gain out of others, but who also use deception as a means to their ends (see "The Opponents in 2 Peter" in the introduction; and B. Winter 2002: 80–94).

In the final clauses of the verse, Peter returns to the theme of judgment, which he previously announced in verse 1: οἷς τὸ κρίμα ἔκπαλαι οὐκ ἀργεῖ καὶ ἡ ἀπώλεια αὐτῶν οὐ νυστάζει (*hois to krima ekpalai ouk argei kai hē apōleia autōn ou nystazei*, their judgment is not delayed for a long time, and their destruction does not slumber). Both clauses counter the accusation of the heretics that judgment is delayed and is therefore not coming (3:4), although

Peter does not state that he is challenging their argument. Such an inference was no doubt made by the first readers, who well understood the situation in the church.

Peter begins this double affirmation of coming judgment ("not delayed, . . . does not slumber," meaning "is coming") by pointing out that there has been no delay in the coming condemnation to which the heretics are destined. The verb ἀργεῖ (*argei*) is the opposite of "to work" and has to do with work or some other activity coming to a standstill or ceasing (Ezra 4:24; 2 Macc. 5:25; Eccles. 12:3; Sir. 33:28). By extension, in certain contexts it suggests the idea that work has been delayed (1 Esd. 2:26), and the sense "to delay" or "to come too late" was often in mind (MM 73; BDAG 128). Since the heretics have argued that delay in judgment means that no judgment is coming (3:4, 8–10), Peter is apparently touching on the core of their teaching. He declares that condemnation (τὸ κρίμα, *to krima*) will come not only to the world but also to them (οἷς, *hois*). "Condemnation" is a judicial verdict (Polybius 23.1.12; Rom. 5:16) and here, as in some other texts, not only denotes a negative verdict but also the punishment that follows from that legal decision (Jude 4 and comments; see Mark 12:40; Luke 20:47; Rom. 2:2–3; 3:8; 13:2; Gal. 5:10; 1 Tim. 5:12; James 3:1). The "condemnation" is equivalent to "destruction" in the following clause.

Contrary to the heretics' opinion, their "judgment is not delayed for a long time" (ἔκπαλαι, *ekpalai*). The term means simply "for a long time" (as P.Oxy. 938.3: "although you had been long ago instructed to send twelve baskets of hay thither" [cited in MM 197]; Josephus, *Ant.* 16.8.4 §244: "having long been"; BDAG 307; LSJ 515). The term should not be understood here in 2 Pet. 2:3 as a reference to the way judgment has been established from ancient times but simply as a counter to the heretics' objection that there has been a delay in judgment "for a long time." Peter's declaration is a reworking of Jude 4: οἱ πάλαι προγεγραμμένοι εἰς τοῦτο τὸ κρίμα (*hoi palai progegrammenoi eis touto to krima*, the ones who from long ago were marked out for this judgment). Our author has left to one side the notion of a judgment that was proscribed from ancient times as he hones the affirmation to respond more precisely to the heretics' claims. Though the language is similar (note the substitution of ἔκπαλαι, *ekpalai*, for πάλαι, *palai*), the thought is not exactly the same.

Perhaps more significant than the author's source is the way this counterpoint arrests the widely known Epicurean notion that the delay in divine judgment means that no judgment is coming (see "The Opponents in 2 Peter" in the introduction). In his treatise *De sera numinis vindicta* (*On the Delays of the Divine Vengeance*), Plutarch dialogues with Patrocleas, Timon his brother, and Olympichus. At one point Patrocleas replies, "The delay and procrastination of the Deity in punishing the wicked appears to me the most telling argument by far," and then he quotes Euripides, who said, "Apollo lags; such is the way of Heaven" (548C–D). He also echoes Plato and Hesiod, saying, "But God should be indolent in nothing; least of all does it become him to be so in dealing with the wicked, who are not indolent themselves or 'postponers of their work' of doing wrong; nay, their passions drive them headlong to their crimes." Peter's statement appears to counter the heretics' claim that "the judgment has delayed for a long time." Not so, Peter replies.

The following clause "rhymes" with the thought of the previous as Peter again denies that delay in judgment means no judgment is coming: καὶ ἡ ἀπώλεια αὐτῶν οὐ νυστάζει (*kai hē apōleia autōn ou nystazei*, and their destruction does not slumber). The "destruction" is the final judgment, which Peter has already mentioned twice in 2:1 (see comments) and will again write about in 3:7: "the day of judgment and destruction of ungodly people" (see also 3:16 and comments). This destruction was prefigured in the flood (3:6, where Peter describes that event with the cognate verb ἀπώλετο, *apōleto*), and God desires that none should meet this end (3:9 and comments). The author has already declared that this final destruction will come quickly (2:1b), and here he sets up an inclusio by restating that thought in different terms.

The destruction "does not slumber" (νυστάζει, *nystazei*). While the verb means "to sleep" (2 Sam. 4:6; Ps. 121:3–4 [120:3–4 LXX]; Prov. 6:10; 24:33; Nah. 3:18; Isa. 5:27; 56:10; Jer. 23:31; Sir. 22:10; Ps. Sol. 16.1), it may suggest the idea of becoming drowsy and dozing off (Matt. 25:5). In this metaphor, final destruction is personified and is said not to be dozing or slumbering: it is on its way (BDAG 683). Whatever delay there may be in the advent of judgment (3:4) should not be interpreted as a sign that it has become idle. Peter again affirms the certainty of God's intervention in the final destruction of the impious. We should not assume that Peter has annihilation in mind because he does not develop here or in verse 1 what he means by "destruction" or "eternal ruin." The nature of this destruction becomes a topic later in the epistle (3:5–7, 10–13), although even there he does not discuss the issue of the final state of the ungodly. His argument here is that destruction *will* come, a point he develops in the following verses by showing how in the past God certainly did execute his judgment. As he did then, so he will do in the future.

# b. Past Sinners and Their Doom (2:4–10a)

This section (vv. 4–10a) constitutes one long conditional sentence in which the protasis stretches from verse 4 through verse 8 and begins with "For if God." The apodosis starts in verse 9, "then the Lord." In this section Peter seeks to refute the false teachers introduced in 2:1–3. Their claim is that there is no evidence that God intervenes to judge the world, either in the past or present, and therefore he will not judge humanity in the future. Apparently the opponents bolster their denial of divine judgment by claiming that the righteous will themselves suffer the effects of that judgment. How can God judge the wicked and at the same time preserve the righteous? Peter responds by declaring that God has indeed acted in judgment in the past. He forwards as examples the sinful angels (v. 4), the ancient world of the flood generation (v. 5), and the cities of Sodom and Gomorrah (v. 6), naming these events in chronological order. At the same time, Peter demonstrates that God delivered the righteous during two of these judgments, forwarding the examples of Noah and his family (v. 5) along with Lot (vv. 7–8). He draws his conclusion in verses 9–10. If God kept the righteous and judged the wicked in the past, "then the Lord is able to deliver the devout from trial but keep the unrighteous for the day of judgment" (v. 9). In verse 10a he identifies the current subjects of judgment more specifically as those who indulge in desire and demonstrate condemnable hubris. The heretics will suffer precisely what they deny.

Peter's litany of texts that refer to ancient divine judgment draws principally on Jude 5–8 and stands within the interpretive tradition that has strung together certain archetypal judgment scenes (see the unit introduction to Jude 5–8). Jude's choice, however, is somewhat different from Peter's as he names the exodus generation, the fallen angels, and the Sodom and Gomorrah stories as his types. Jude seeks to show how God judged those who had overstepped their bounds and how whatever privileged state they had before God did not exempt them from divine judgment. Peter, however, strings together these texts for a different purpose, that being to affirm the reality of divine judgment as well as divine preservation. The problems these authors face are not identical and their responses, though similar, are constructed to affirm different points. The outline of this unit is as follows:

   i. The angels (2:4)
   ii. The ancient world (2:5)
   iii. Sodom and Gomorrah (2:6–10a)

# Exegesis and Exposition

[4]For if God did not spare the angels who had sinned but he delivered them over, having sent them to the underworld, keeping them for judgment in ⌜chains⌝ of hell, [5]and if he did not spare the ancient world but kept Noah, a herald of righteousness, and seven others when he brought the flood on the world of the ungodly, [6]and if he condemned the cities of Sodom and Gomorrah ⌜to destruction⌝, having reduced them to ashes and making them an example to the ⌜ungodly⌝ of things to come, [7]and if he rescued righteous Lot, who was oppressed by the licentious way of life of the lawless [8](for that righteous man, residing among them day after day, tormented his righteous soul by the lawless deeds that he saw and heard), [9]then the Lord is able to deliver the devout from trial but keep the unrighteous for the day of judgment, when they will be punished, [10a]but especially the ones who go after flesh because of defiling desire and disdain lordship.

## i. The Angels (2:4)

Second Peter begins the list of ancient examples of sinners whom God judged by referring to the angelic fall: Εἰ γὰρ ὁ θεὸς ἀγγέλων ἁμαρτησάντων οὐκ ἐφείσατο (*Ei gar ho theos angelōn hamartēsantōn ouk epheisato*, For if God did not spare the angels who had sinned). The immediate source of our author's reference is Jude 6, although, as noted in the comments on that verse, discussion about an angelic fall was widespread in both Jewish and Christian literature. Peter has truncated Jude's more-elaborate description of the angelic sin, which says, "And the angels who did not keep to their domain but deserted their own dwelling place" (Jude 6). The verbal similarities between 2 Pet. 2:4 and Jude 6 are relatively few, although the principal referent of an angelic sin and subsequent judgment is present in both. Jude's primary focus, however, is on the angelic apostasy, with special attention given to the way they refused to maintain the divine order. He seeks to demonstrate to the church that their sin was a type of the sin of the heretics who have invaded the church. Peter, on the other hand, is principally interested in the question of the certainty of divine judgment, given that the heretics are denying its inevitability. Therefore, in his discussion of the angels' fall, Peter simply mentions they had "sinned" (ἁμαρτησάντων, *hamartēsantōn*). Apparently the author expected the readers to understand the allusion without any further clarification.

The traditions about an angelic fall grew out of Gen. 6:1–4. The first readers of this letter have to be acquainted with these to interpret the author's reference. As noted previously (Jude 6 and comments), the sources of our knowledge of this interpretive tradition are widespread, with the most extensive reflection being found in 1 En. 6–12, the story of the fall of the "Watchers." There is, however, no direct reference to 1 Enoch either here or elsewhere in 2 Peter (cf. Jude 14–15 and comments). The Genesis text says: "When people began to multiply on the face of the ground, and daughters were born to them, the sons of God saw that they were fair; and they took wives for themselves of

2:4

all that they chose" (Gen. 6:1–2 NRSV). Judgment came as a consequence, which limited the human lifespan to 120 years, although no mention is made in Gen. 6 regarding what became of the "sons of God." The "sons of God" were understood as "angels" or, as in 1 Enoch, "Watchers": "And it came to pass, when the children of men had multiplied in those days there were born to them beautiful and comely daughters. And watchers, children of heaven, saw them and desired them, and lusted after them; and they said to another: 'Come, let us choose for ourselves wives from the daughters of earth, and let us beget us children'" (1 En. 6.1–2; from M. Black 1985: 27–28). The angelic fall was associated with the time of Noah and the flood (see Jude 6 and the unit introduction to Jude 5–8; 2 Pet. 2:5 and comments) and was considered by many ancients to be the root cause of corruption in the world.

Peter's attention is fixed on the fact that "God did not spare" these beings who sinned. To "not spare" someone (οὐκ ἐφείσατο, *ouk epheisato*, with the object in the genitive, ἀγγέλων, *angelōn*) is the opposite of showing mercy and pity and suggests that judgment will come on the one not spared (Deut. 7:16; 13:8 [13:9 LXX]; 19:13, 21; 1 Sam. 15:3; Ps. 78:50 [77:50 LXX]; Jer. 13:14; Ezek. 5:11; 7:4, 9 [7:6, 8 LXX]; Jdt. 2:11; Sir. 16:8; Rom. 11:21; 2 Pet. 2:5; MM 665; LSJ 1920; BDAG 1920). No mercy was extended to the angels after their sin. God did not intervene to exempt them from judgment, but as the following clause shows, he secured their doom. Peter recounts that instead of being extended mercy, the sinful angels met another end: ἀλλὰ σειραῖς ζόφου ταρταρώσας παρέδωκεν εἰς κρίσιν τηρουμένους (*alla seirais zophou tartarōsas paredōken eis krisin tēroumenous*, but he delivered them over, having sent them to the underworld, keeping them for judgment in chains of hell). Peter's thought and some of the language echo Jude 6b: εἰς κρίσιν μεγάλης ἡμέρας δεσμοῖς ἀϊδίοις ὑπὸ ζόφον τετήρηκεν (*eis krisin megalēs hēmeras desmois aidiois hypo zophon tetērēken*, are kept in eternal chains in the darkness of the netherworld for the judgment of the great day). As does Jude, Peter describes how the angels are kept for judgment and that they are bound in chains of the netherworld.

However, Peter notes that instead of sparing the angels who sinned (2:4a), God handed them (implied object) over (παρέδωκεν, *paredōken*). This verb appears in judicial contexts where authors refer to handing over persons to the courts (Matt. 10:17; Mark 13:9), to prison (Luke 21:12; Acts 8:3; 22:4), or as here to a place of eternal punishment (Herm. *Sim.* 9.28.7; 1 En. 97.10; see *NewDocs* 4:165: "Whoever performs any wicked treachery against this tomb, I hand him over to the infernal gods"; 1 Tim. 1:20; BDAG 762; *TLNT* 3:13–23). Peter qualifies that by this divine judicial act they were "sent . . . to the underworld" (ταρταρώσας, *tartarōsas*). This verb, found only here in the NT, refers to being sent to Tartarus, the "deepest region of the underworld, lower even than Hades" (*OCD* 1476). As Zeus says in Homer's *Iliad* (8.13–14), "I shall take and hurl him into murky Tartarus, far, far away, where is the deepest gulf beneath the earth . . . , as far beneath Hades as heaven is above earth." Hesiod (*Theogony* 617–25; 715–25) told the story of the Titans who were consigned

2. The Coming and the Judgment of the False Teachers
b. Past Sinners and Their Doom
**2 Peter 2:4–10a**

to this place of "misty gloom, in a dark place where are the ends of the huge earth" (729–31). Here, according to Hesiod, they were "bound . . . in bitter chains" (718–19; see also Apollodorus, *Library and Epitome* 1.1.2).

The name given to this place of punishment in classical mythology was taken up by Jewish apocalyptic literature and appears to have found its way into the Jewish consciousness in general (Job 41:24; 1 En. 20.2; Philo, *Embassy* 7 §49; 14 §103; Josephus, *Ag. Ap.* 2.33 §240; Sib. Or. 2.303). Jewish thinking modified reflection on the theme, however, as God now becomes the one who consigns the evil to "Tartarus itself and profound darkness" (Philo, *Rewards* 26 §152). "Dark Tartarus" is juxtaposed with Gehenna (Sib. Or. 4.186). A small step was made from seeing this as the place of punishment of the Titans to speaking of it as the place where sinful angels were consigned (Glasson 1961: 62–67). This is precisely the connection made not only in 2 Pet. 2:4 but also in the Sib. Or. 1.98–103: "Watchers . . . were mighty, of great form, but nevertheless they went under the dread house of Tartarus guarded by unbreakable bonds, to make retribution, to Gehenna of terrible, raging, undying fire."

In a manner similar to ancient descriptions of Tartarus, Peter notes the sinful angels are kept (τηρουμένους, *tēroumenous*; see Jude 6 and comments) in chains. When referring to the heretics, Peter notes that God knows how to keep them for judgment as well (2:9, 17; 3:7). The way he kept the angels for this judgment becomes both a type of God's judicial action toward the godless and a guarantee that the future judgment will certainly come. The sinful angels are kept in "chains" (σειραῖς, *seirais*), a synonym for Jude's δεσμοῖς (*desmois*), which are often associated with Tartarus in ancient literature (see above). These are chains "of darkness" or "hell" (ζόφου, *zophou*). The same term appears in Jude 6 (see comments) and, depending on the context, could refer to the darkness of the netherworld or to that world itself (Homer, *Il.* 15.191; 21.56; *Od.* 11.57; BDAG 429). Many of the ancient texts that speak of Tartarus refer to the darkness of that place (see above). But as a descriptor of "chains," it appears to refer to the place itself: "chains of the place of darkness." The composite picture that Peter paints is one in which God is the actor and, in a judicial act, handed over the angels, consigned them to the netherworld, and kept them there, bound in chains for the coming judgment (εἰς κρίσιν, *eis krisin*). There shall be no escape for these who are secured for the final judgment. As these angels are kept for certain judgment, so too are the unrighteous and godless (2:9; 3:7).

## ii. The Ancient World (2:5)

As his second example of ancient sinners who were judged by God, Peter cites those who perished in the flood: καὶ ἀρχαίου κόσμου οὐκ ἐφείσατο ἀλλὰ ὄγδοον Νῶε δικαιοσύνης κήρυκα ἐφύλαξεν κατακλυσμὸν κόσμῳ ἀσεβῶν ἐπάξας (*kai archaiou kosmou ouk epheisato alla ogdoon Nōe dikaiosynēs kēryka ephylaxen kataklysmon kosmō asebōn epaxas*, and if he did not spare the ancient world but kept Noah, a herald of righteousness, and seven others when he brought

**2:5**

the flood on the world of the ungodly). At this point, Peter is not dependent on Jude since Jude does not refer to the flood generation in his catalog of ancient sinners (see Jude 5–7 and comments). However, various lists of ancient archetypal sinners include both the angelic fall and the flood, such as the T. Naph. 3.4–5, which, after recounting the sin of Sodom (cf. 2 Pet. 2:6), says, "Likewise the Watchers departed from nature's order; the Lord pronounced a curse on them at the Flood." Third Maccabees 2:4 similarly comments, "You destroyed men for their wicked deeds in the past, among them giants relying on their own strength and self-confidence, upon whom you brought an immeasurable flood of water." The "giants" were the offspring of the illicit relationship between the sons of God and the daughters of men, according to some Jewish interpretation of Gen. 6:1–4 (see Jude 6 and comments). Third Maccabees 2:5, as 2 Pet. 2:6, continues the catalog with reference to the sin of Sodom (cf. also Sir. 16:7–8). Jubilees puts a finer point on this relationship, pointing to the way the corruption in the world was due to the sin of the angels (5.1–2) and, because of that corruption, the Lord judged the earth via the flood (5.3–5). The Lord commanded that the angels who sinned be "bound in the depths of the earth" (Jub. 5.6; see 2 Pet. 2:4). The story of the Watchers in 1 En. 6–16 also unites the angelic fall with the divine judgment by the flood. Second Peter 2:4–8 stands, as does Jude, within this broad interpretive tradition that connects the angelic fall, human sin, and divine judgment (see Lewis 1978).

First Peter 3:19–20 likewise brings together the angelic fall with the time of Noah (Dalton 1989; J. H. Elliott 2000: 651–69), and Peter possibly echoes this text in the present reflection. Peter makes mention of his previous correspondence (2 Pet. 3:1), and we would expect some common material between these letters. However, in his assessment of the relationship between 2 Peter and other ancient literature, Gilmore (2002: 93) examines the various parallels that commentators have observed between 1 and 2 Peter and concludes, "These similarities do not lend support to the view that the author of 2 Peter was familiar with 1 Peter. The parallels in and of themselves are not so striking as to demand this assumption." He does not, however, discuss the details of the passages under consideration here. Bauckham (1983: 250), over against Dalton (1979: 551–52), similarly states: "There is no good reason for thinking 2 Peter is here dependent on that verse . . . : the only real point of contact between 1 Pet 3:20 and 2 Pet 2:5 is the number eight, and this probably indicates that for some reason Christian tradition was in the habit of specifying that there were eight persons who were saved out of the Flood."

But as already noted, both texts join together the tradition of the angelic fall with the flood as well as mentioning the "eight" who were spared the flood. Moreover, while 1 Pet. 3:20 says that Noah and the others were "saved" (διεσώθησαν, diesōthēsan), 2 Pet. 2:5 remarks that God "kept" or preserved them. Both texts mention the flood (1 Pet. 3:20, δι' ὕδατος, di' hydatos, through water; 2 Pet. 2:5, κατακλυσμὸν, kataklysmon, flood) and characterize the era in which Noah lived as sinful. In 1 Pet. 3:20 the angelic spirits were "disobedient" (ἀπειθήσασιν, apeithēsasin), while 2 Pet. 2:5 comments on the "world

2. The Coming and the Judgment of the False Teachers
b. Past Sinners and Their Doom
**2 Peter 2:4–10a**

of the ungodly" (κόσμῳ ἀσεβῶν, *kosmō asebōn*), thoughts closely connected in Jewish reflection since the fallen angels are seen as responsible for human corruption. Our author's handling of this text from 1 Peter is strikingly similar to the way he adopts and modifies the thought and language of Jude, retelling the story in a way that will further his purposes in arresting the incursion of the heretics. The multiple conceptual similarities between the two texts secure the case.

God did not spare the sinful angels from judgment (v. 4 and comments) "and did not spare the ancient world" (καὶ ἀρχαίου κόσμου οὐκ ἐφείσατο, *kai archaiou kosmou ouk epheisato*). While ἀρχαῖος (*archaios*) may simply refer to what happened some time ago (Acts 15:7), in many other texts it refers to persons or events in the distant past (Pss. 44:1 [43:2 LXX]; 143:5 [142:5 LXX]; Isa. 25:1; 37:26; 43:18; Wis. 8:8; 13:10; Sir. 2:10; 16:7; Matt. 5:21, 33; Luke 9:8, 19; Acts 15:21). The context clarifies that the "ancient world" Peter has in mind is the flood generation, with "world" here referring neither to the cosmos nor the earth but rather to "humanity" that perished in Noah's day (Matt. 18:7; John 4:42; 8:12; 9:5; Rom. 3:19; 5:13; 1 Cor. 1:27–28). Elsewhere Peter comments that this world of humanity is filled with corruption (1:4; 2:20). He will return to the comment on destruction of the ancient world by the flood (3:6). Peter sees this destruction as the type of the future judgment by fire (3:5–7).

Though the ancient world was not spared from judgment, Noah and his family were preserved from disaster: ἀλλὰ ὄγδοον Νῶε δικαιοσύνης κήρυκα ἐφύλαξεν κατακλυσμὸν κόσμῳ ἀσεβῶν ἐπάξας (*alla ogdoon Nōe dikaiosynēs kēryka ephylaxen kataklysmon kosmō asebōn epaxas*, but kept Noah, a herald of righteousness, and seven others when he brought the flood on the world of the ungodly). God "kept" Noah and the others, that is, guarded and preserved them from what spelled doom to the others. God watches over his people to protect them (Jude 24 and comments; 2 Tim. 1:12; LSJ 1961; BDAG 1068) while at the same time bringing judgment on the ungodly. Peter will later call the church to be on guard against being swept away by the heretics' error (3:17), but here his emphasis falls on God's ability to keep Noah and his family as well as rescue Lot (2:7). So too, in the present, "the Lord is able to deliver the devout from trial" (2:9). In the midst of his discussion of past judgment, Peter offers assurance to his readers of deliverance from the coming judgment. As God saved in the past, so he will do in the future.

Those guarded by God at the time of the flood were "Noah and seven others" (ὄγδοον Νῶε, *ogdoon Nōe*), an expression literally translated "as the eighth," which implies the "seven others" (cf. 2 Macc. 5:27, Ιουδας . . . Μακκαβαῖος δέκατος, *Ioudas . . . Makkabaios dekatos*, lit., "Judas Maccabeus tenth," meaning "Judas Maccabeus, with nine others"; BDAG 689; MM 437). Peter comments that Noah was a preacher or "herald of righteousness" (δικαιοσύνης κήρυκα, *dikaiosynēs kēryka*), that righteous or just conduct that conforms to the will of God (1:1 and comments). "Righteousness" or "justice" is an eternal value since the future new creation will be marked by

it (3:13), and the Christian way, in the present age, conforms to it (2:21; cf.
1 Pet. 2:24; 3:14). In Gen. 6:9 Noah is recognized as a "just man" (see Gen.
7:1; Sir. 44:17), yet nowhere in the OT is he described as preacher or herald
(κήρυκα, kēryka) of the message of justice. This title could be used to refer
to those who engaged in religious proclamation (Xenophon, Hell. 2.4.20;
Philostratus, Vitae sophistarum 2.550.21; Epictetus, Disc. 3.22.70; 3.21.13;
1 Tim. 2:7; 2 Tim. 1:11; BDAG 543). But Jewish and Christian literature refers
to Noah's proclamation to sinners of his day and to his own children (Sib.
Or. 1.128–29; Josephus, Ant. 1.3.1 §74; Gen. Rab. 30.7; 1 Clem. 7.6; 9.4; and
the discourses in Sib. Or. 1.147–98; Jub. 7.20–39). Noah himself was a righteous man (Sib. Or. 1.125) and was instructed: "Noah, embolden yourself,
and proclaim repentance to all the peoples, so that all may be saved" (Sib. Or.
1.128–29, 147–98; Jub. 7.34). Although he preached, few were saved, a grim
reminder for Peter's readers, who were tempted by the heretics' persuasion.
The type of righteousness that Peter has in view when he speaks of Noah's
proclamation shares affinities with the reflection on his preaching found in
Jub. 7.20: "And he bore witness to his sons so that they might do justice and
cover the shame of their flesh and bless the one who created them and honor
father and mother, and each one love his neighbor and preserve themselves
from fornication and pollution and from all injustice."

The final clause of the verse presents the counterpoint to God's protection
of Noah and his family: κατακλυσμὸν κόσμῳ ἀσεβῶν ἐπάξας (kataklysmon
kosmō asebōn epaxas, when he brought the flood on the world of the ungodly), an expression that reiterates Gen. 6:17 LXX (ἐπάγω τὸν κατακλυσμὸν
ὕδωρ ἐπὶ τὴν γῆν, epagō ton kataklysmon hydōr epi tēn gēn, I am bringing
a flood of water on the earth; cf. Gen. 7:4; 3 Macc. 2:4b). The verb "bring
on" (ἐπάξας, epaxas) is the same found in 2 Pet. 2:1 and refers to bringing
something, most commonly something bad, on people; it often appears in
contexts where divine judgment is announced (Gen. 6:17; 20:9; Exod. 10:4;
Jer. 19:3; Ezek. 11:8; 2 Macc. 7:38; Bar. 4:9–10, 14, 29; Josephus, Life 4 §18;
Hesiod, Works and Days 242; BDAG 356). The judgment God brought against
the world is described simply as the κατακλυσμόν (kataklysmon), the flood
(Gen. 6:17; 7:6–7, 10, 17; 9:11, 15, 28; 10:1, 32; 11:10; 4 Macc. 15:31–32; Sir.
44:18). The flood destroyed all of humanity (Gen. 6:17; 7:22; Luke 17:27;
Wis. 18:5; Sir. 44:17) and came on the earth because of people's wickedness
(Gen. 6:5–6; Sir. 40:10). Peter states that the flood came on "the world of the
ungodly" (κόσμῳ ἀσεβῶν, kosmōs asebōn), with "world" here denoting not
the cosmos or the earth but rather all humanity (Matt. 18:7; John 4:42; 8:12;
9:5; Rom. 3:19; 5:13; 1 Cor. 1:27–28). The "ungodly" are those who do not
show due reverence for God (see Jude 4 and comments). This was recognized
by all, both Jew and gentile alike, to be a serious offense. The "ungodly" are
not righteous (Gen. 18:23, 25; Exod. 9:27; Pss. 1:6; 11:5 [10:5 LXX]; 58:10
[57:11 LXX]; Prov. 10:30; 28:12; Wis. 4:16), stand guilty before God (Exod.
23:7; Deut. 25:1) as lawless people (Ps. 37:38 [36:38 LXX]), and are sinners
(Ps. 1:1, 5). Within this retelling of the ancient judgment, Peter forwards a dire

warning to those who have embraced the wicked ways of the heretics. As God judged in the past, so he will do in the future. There were no exemptions, save for the ones whom God spared with Noah, who proclaimed righteousness. As it was then, so it will be. Yet the coming judgment will not be by water as in the flood, but by fire (3:5–7).

### iii. Sodom and Gomorrah (2:6–10a)

Peter's third example of ancient judgment is the destruction of Sodom and Gomorrah (v. 6), after which he recounts the deliverance of Lot (vv. 7–8), just as he previously recalled the Noah story, which was also marked by judgment and salvation (v. 5). Continuing the series of conditional clauses begun in verse 4, he states: καὶ πόλεις Σοδόμων καὶ Γομόρρας τεφρώσας καταστροφῇ κατέκρινεν ὑπόδειγμα μελλόντων ἀσεβέσιν τεθεικώς (*kai poleis Sodomōn kai Gomorras tephrōsas katastrophē katekrinen hypodeigma mellontōn asebesin tetheikōs*, and if he condemned the cities of Sodom and Gomorrah to destruction, having reduced them to ashes and making them an example to the ungodly of things to come). Peter returns to Jude as his source (Jude 7 and comments), yet modifying the text of Jude significantly in the direction of his own purposes. Jude 7 reads: "Likewise Sodom and Gomorrah and the cities around them, in the same way as these, having indulged in unfaithful acts and gone after another kind of flesh, stand as an example, suffering the penalty of eternal fire." Second Peter preserves the reference to Sodom and Gomorrah, but instead of commenting on "the cities around them" speaks of the "cities of Sodom and Gomorrah." Peter preserves Jude's note about the way these cities are an "example," but he alters the language that expresses the idea (ὑπόδειγμα, *hypodeigma*, instead of Jude's δεῖγμα, *deigma*). While Jude 7 speaks of the "penalty of eternal fire," 2 Peter simply notes that the cities were "reduced to ashes." Peter shows little interest in the description of the sins of these cities since his primary purpose is to underscore their judgment, which serves as a prototype of future judgment. The way the author adopts and adapts Jude at this point is similar to the way he incorporated the thought of 1 Pet. 3:20 (see v. 5 and comments).

As discussed in the comments on Jude 7, the cities of Sodom and Gomorrah were remembered for the gravity of their inhabitants' sin (Gen. 18:20) and their cataclysmic judgment by fire (Gen. 19:12–29). These cities are frequently mentioned in catalogs of ancient archetypal sinners who met with the judgment of God (see introduction to Jude 5–8), with diverse development of themes surrounding the sin and judgment of the cities. Sometimes the wickedness of the towns is referred to generically, as here in 2 Peter, while elsewhere the specific nature of the sin becomes the topic of reflection, as in the case of Jude. Jewish literature sometimes developed the judgment theme as an "eschatological symbol," as does Peter (Loader 1990: 117). The prototypical motif of the destruction of the cities by fire became an illustration of divine judgment that appears again and again in biblical literature (Deut. 29:22–24; Isa. 34:8–10;

2:6

Ezek. 38:21–23; Amos 1:3–2:3), with the subsequent destruction of the cities of Jericho (Josh. 6:24) and Gibeah (Judg. 20:36–40) echoing the Sodom and Gomorrah story. In each of these cities, fire becomes the instrument of judgment that destroys the inhabitants, although a small group escapes (Fields 1997: 134–42). A remnant is saved, a point stressed by Peter (vv. 7–8) as he looks forward to the final judgment (v. 9).

Instead of speaking of the sulfur and fire that showered these cities, Peter fixes his attention on the outcomes: they were "reduced to ashes" (τεφρώσας, *tephrōsas*, a verb from the term τέφρα, *tephra*, ashes; BDAG 1001; see Sib. Or. 5.124: "Bithynians will bewail their land, reduced to ashes"). Although the biblical account of the cities' destruction does not detail their fate exactly this way, Philo's description is similar to Peter's: "Such . . . were burnt to ashes, when God passed well-deserved sentence on the impious, and the heavens rained instead of water the unquenchable flames of the thunderbolt" (*Drunkenness* 53 §223). As Philo drew the line between the flood and the fire so, too, does Peter (2:5–6; 3:5–7). Although reflecting on the Egyptian plagues, Philo also opens a window into contemporary reflection on God's use of the elements of the universe in the execution of his judgment: "The chastisement was different from the usual kind, for the elements of the universe—earth, fire, air, water—carried out the assault. God's judgment was that the materials which had served to produce the world should serve also to destroy the land of the impious; and to show the mightiness of the sovereignty which He holds, what He shaped in His saving goodness to create the universe He turned into instruments for the perdition of the impious whenever He would" (*Moses* 1.16–17 §96). Peter makes a similar connection between the waters of creation, the waters of judgment, and the judgment by fire in 3:5–7, alerting us again to the way 2 Peter is deeply embedded in the soil of this interpretive history. The approach he takes with his readers strikes familiar and deep cords as he binds together ancient sacred history with the eschatological vision of the end, all in his forceful attempt to secure his reader's adherence to the gospel over against the false teachers.

Peter comments that God "condemned" these cities "to destruction" and did so by reducing them to ashes by fire. The condemnation is a judicial act, the pronouncement of a sentence on the guilty (κατέκρινεν, *katekrinen*; Ps. Sol. 4.2; Matt. 20:18; 27:3; Mark 10:33; 14:64; BDAG 519). The term appears frequently in the context of condemnation by God, the Judge (Matt. 12:41–42; Luke 11:31–32; Rom. 2:1; 8:34; 1 Cor. 11:32; Heb. 11:7). Peter adds that God condemned the cities "to destruction" (καταστροφῇ, *katastrophē*, see the additional note on the textual history surrounding this noun). Peter lifts this word, which points to the utter overthrow and ruin of these cities, from the Sodom and Gomorrah account in Gen. 19:29 (cf. Prov. 1:27; Hos. 8:7; 1 En. 102.10; 3 Macc. 5:47; T. Job 33.4: "The whole world shall pass away and its splendor shall fade. And those who heed it shall share in its overthrow"; BDAG 528). There was no escape and nobody, except Lot (and his family), was rescued (2 Pet. 2:7–8).

Peter's concern, however, is primarily with the typological nature of that dreadful event, which God has made into "an example to the ungodly" (ὑπόδειγμα . . . ἀσεβέσιν τεθεικώς, *hypodeigma . . . asebesin tetheikōs*; the verb τίθημι, *tithēmi*, with ὑπόδειγμα, *hypodeigma*, means "to provide an example"; Josephus, *Ant.* 17.11.2 §313: "Archelaus had also given his future subjects an example"; BDAG 1004). The use of examples in moral instruction was much more common in the ancient Mediterranean world than in contemporary Western culture, whether those examples were positive and to be followed (2 Macc. 6:28; 4 Macc. 17:23; Sir. 44:16; John 13:15; James 5:10) or negative and therefore to be avoided (Heb. 4:11; 2 Pet. 2:6; Jude 7 and comments; BDAG 1037; and Malherbe 1986: 135–36). The "example" was understood as a "specimen" or "sample," and in Peter's view the ancient destruction thus is a sample of the type of doom the ungodly will meet (ἀσεβέσιν, *asebesin*, see the additional note and verse 5 and comments; *TLNT* 3:403). We might say that the doom of Sodom and Gomorrah was just a sample of things to come.

In verse 5, Peter places Noah in relief against the world of the ungodly in his day, and in the present verses he contrasts Lot (vv. 7–8) with the inhabitants of Sodom and Gomorrah (v. 6). Lot, as Noah and seven others, was delivered from divine judgment: καὶ δίκαιον Λὼτ καταπονούμενον ὑπὸ τῆς τῶν ἀθέσμων ἐν ἀσελγείᾳ ἀναστροφῆς ἐρρύσατο (*kai dikaion Lōt kataponoumenon hypo tēs tōn athesmōn en aselgeia anastrophēs errysato*, and rescued righteous Lot, who was oppressed by the licentious way of life of the lawless). Lot's story is juxtaposed with that of Noah in Luke 17:22–37, where both these men are reported to have escaped the judgment of God. The destruction of their day prefigures the final judgment that will come when "the Son of Man is revealed" (Luke 17:30 NRSV). Peter develops this double theme of eschatological judgment and deliverance at the end of this section (v. 9) as well as at the end of his letter (3:1–13). The typology of the Lot story becomes a primary argument in Peter's refutation of the heretics.

Genesis 19:1–26 recounts the story of Lot, the two visitors, and the attempt by the men of Sodom to abuse them. Peter again assumes that his readers are familiar with that narrative. The wickedness of the inhabitants of the city was legendary. Peter's comment about Lot being "righteous" echoes ancient sentiment, although Genesis never states that Lot was "righteous." Wisdom 10:6 reflects not only the thought but also the language with which Peter frames the Lot story: "Wisdom rescued [ἐρρύσατο, *errysato*] a righteous man [δίκαιον, *dikaion*] when the ungodly [ἀσεβῶν, *asebōn*; cf. 2 Pet. 2:6] were perishing; he escaped the fire that descended on the Five Cities" (NRSV; cf. Wis. 19:17; Num. Rab. 10.5: "Lot was more righteous than his wife"; in *Moses* 2.10 §§57–58 Philo describes Lot's virtue). The description of Lot as "righteous" resonates with Peter's thematic concern in this letter. Righteousness characterizes God's saving act in Christ (1:1), and the Christian faith is described as the "way of righteousness" (2:21). "Righteousness" was the subject of Noah's proclamation (2:5) during his own evil days, and "righteousness" will be the primary

2:7

characteristic of life in the eschaton, when God will establish the new heaven and new earth (3:13). The heretics, on the other hand, are people who do unrighteous deeds (2:13), just as Balaam had followed unrighteousness (2:15). The unrighteous are those who are doomed to divine judgment (2:9). The claim that Lot was righteous sets up the promise in verse 9 that "the Lord is able to deliver the devout from trial"—those who are righteous as Lot was will be delivered from eschatological doom, just as Lot was spared the judgment of Sodom.

It is not so evident why Lot is called "righteous," given that he chose to settle in Sodom (Gen. 13:8–13), outside the land of promise, and especially since he offered his daughters to the men who clamored for the celestial visitors to be brought out so that they might "know them" (19:5, 8). The claim that Lot was righteous may be attributed to Abraham's dialogue with the messengers, in which he seeks deliverance for the city if there are a sufficient number of righteous residents (18:22–33). While not enough righteous were found to spare Sodom, Lot himself was delivered, implying that at least he was righteous. Genesis Rabbah highlights his righteous character by commenting that "the whole night Lot prayed for mercy for the Sodomites" (26.5) and noting the way Lot showed the angels honor (50.11). Lot invited the strangers into his home, coming under both his care and his protection. As Fields (1997: 61) notes in his comparison of Lot's hospitality and that of Abraham, "Of particular importance . . . is the offer of protection by the host and ensuing reciprocity by the guest. Protection involves a much deeper commitment on the part of the host and may be more difficult to provide than food and shelter." By comparing the common expressions of hospitality offered by Abraham (Gen. 18:1–8) and Lot (19:1–3) to the messengers, Alexander (1985: 290) concludes, "By caring for the needs of others he resembles Abraham, and since Abraham is commended for his generosity Lot is also therefore to be viewed in a favourable light. Lot's hospitality is a mark of his righteousness." Alexander's appeal is that "we should not judge too harshly a man placed in an extremely dangerous and impossible situation" (1985: 291).

Alexander's assessment, however, has hardly gone unchallenged. Many authors have decried the reprehensible nature of Lot's action and have demonstrated that his character was ambiguous at best, even as it is presented by the Genesis narrative. Lyons (2002: 219–25) contrasts the theme of "Lot the Righteous" with the presentation of "Lot the Wicked," whose hospitality did not rise to the level of Abraham's, who took land outside what was promised, and who did the wicked deed of offering his daughters to the sexually charged citizens. Lyons (2002: 222) summarizes, "But there are difficulties with each position that lead to a less black and white conclusion. The principal flaw with viewing Lot as a wholly righteous man is that it does not deal with the increasingly negative characterization of Lot in the preceding narratives . . . and in his subsequent actions concerning his daughters (19:30–38). In each of these texts Lot is portrayed as selfish and as increasingly absent from the promise made by YHWH to Abraham—he takes the good land around

Sodom outside the land of the promise, Canaan. To suddenly see him now as a paragon of virtue is suspicious to say the least." The problem of ascribing righteousness to Lot is also taken up by Letellier (1995: 184–91), who regards him as a morally ambiguous buffoon.

Genesis offers a composite picture of Lot, who stands out in relief against the righteous Abraham and the unrighteous Sodomites. The offer of his daughters cannot be viewed as a morally acceptable act given that Lot could have offered himself to the men who were looking for a male-with-male sexual relationship. In the end, Lot needed to be rescued by the very heavenly messengers to whom he offered hospitality and protection. Lot's failures are writ large in the narrative; his righteous acts are decidedly pale and mixed with less-than-honorable acts. The early commentator of Genesis Rabbah noted that Lot showed the angels honor (50.11), yet he raised no objection to the idolatry of Sodom as Abraham had (50.4). Peter's concern in the present passage does not take him deep into the moral dilemma of the Lot story. His point is that in the time of divine judgment, God spares the righteous while executing his judgment on the wicked (2 Pet. 2:5–9). There is a moral contrast between the righteous and the unrighteous, but Peter does not explore the ambiguities in the life of Lot or, to a lesser extent, Noah.

Peter notes that Lot was "oppressed" (καταπονούμενον, *kataponoumenon*) by the conduct of the lawless in his city. Sometimes this term is interpreted as a psychological set, that is, as the "distress" that he felt. This understanding of the participle does indeed appear to find support from the next verse (8), which begins with γάρ (*gar*, for; see BDAG 525). However, this verb repeatedly appears where the author speaks of the ill-treatment or oppression that someone suffers (3 Macc. 2:2, 13; T. Levi 6.9; Diodorus Siculus 11.6.3; Josephus, *J.W.* 2.15.1 §313; *Ant.* 7.6.2 §124; Acts 7:24), and as Moulton and Milligan rightly observe, "It is not mental distress that is referred to here—that comes in ver. 8—but the threatened violence of Gen 19.9" (MM 331). Peter's mention of this harassment and oppression suggests that the heretics themselves are acting aggressively and have become an oppressive force among those who have aligned themselves with the righteousness of the gospel.

Lot was oppressed "by the licentious way of life of the lawless" (ὑπὸ τῆς τῶν ἀθέσμων ἐν ἀσελγείᾳ ἀναστροφῆς, *hypo tēs tōn athesmōn en aselgeia anastrophēs*). A person's conduct was frequently viewed as a "way of life," which was conducted according to a person's principles (ἀναστροφῆς, *anastrophēs*, cf. 3:11 and the verb in 2:18). It combined the ideas of being and behaving (*TLNT* 1:111; BDAG 73). This "way of life" could be either good (Tob. 4:14; 2 Macc. 6:23; Let. Aris. 130, 216; 1 Tim. 4:12; Heb. 13:7; James 3:13; Polybius 4.82.1; Epictetus, *Disc.* 1.9.24; 1.22.13) or, as here, evil (Gal. 1:13; Eph. 4:22). The concept of conduct as a "way of life" is given fullest expression in 1 Peter (1 Pet. 1:15, 18; 2:12; 3:1–2, 16; and verb in 2 Pet. 1:17). The present verse forms a link with the language of the first epistle (1 Pet. 3:1). The "way of life" that Peter has in mind here is that of "the lawless" (τῶν ἀθέσμων, *tōn athesmōn*), language that identifies the inhabitants of Sodom as morally lawless, violators of the moral law, and therefore unrighteousness (BDAG 24; MM 12; 3 Macc. 5:12; Philo, *Rewards* 20 §126; Sib. Or. 5.177; Philo, *Moses* 2.37 §198; Josephus, *J.W.* 7.8.1 §264). Such moral lawlessness can sometimes turn into aggression, as here in 2 Peter: "Who is it that has so lawlessly [ἀθέσμως, *athesmōs*] encompassed with outrageous treatment those who from the beginning differed from all nations in their goodwill toward us and often have accepted willingly the worst of human dangers?" (3 Macc. 6:26 NRSV; so Diodorus Siculus 1.14.3). Later in the chapter, Peter underscores the moral lawlessness of the heretics as they aggressively seek disciples, thus drawing a typological line between them and the inhabitants of Sodom (3:17).

Neither here nor in the following verse does Peter discuss the exact nature of the Sodomites' corruption, a subject that is variously interpreted in Jewish literature (see Jude 7 and comments). Loader (1990: 116–17) comments on the rich tapestry of interpretation regarding their sin and concludes, "Often the wickedness is of a generic nature . . . , but it is also often specified: The sexual motif is emphasized in the Testaments and Jubilees, but while it is given prominence in Rabbinic literature, it is subsumed under the social aspect, which is the most prominent in the corpus of literature." However, when Peter turns his focus on their moral character and their aggression, he adds that they conducted themselves ἐν ἀσελγείᾳ (*en aselgeia*, in licentiousness). He also describes the heretics' character by using this term (2:2, 18; see Jude 4 and comments on these verses), which tags them as people who act without moral restraint. In the context of the epistle, it suggests the sexual nature of their sin (2:18–19). Without drawing out the specifics, the author suggests that the Sodomites' sin, as that of the heretics, had a sexual orientation. Peter notes that God "rescued" (ἐρρύσατο, *errysato*) Lot from these people, drawing a parallel between the way he guarded or preserved Noah (v. 5) and will rescue the godly (v. 9 and comments; BDAG 907–8). The verb Peter uses commonly appears in the context of divine rescue or deliverance (Rom. 15:31; 2 Cor. 1:10; Col. 1:13; 1 Thess. 1:10; 2 Thess. 3:2; 2 Tim. 3:11; 4:17–18). Despite the dreadful situation Lot faced in Sodom, God rescued him from the evil oppressors of his day. So too, the believers can hope for divine aid in this conflict with heretics (2:9).

**2:8**  Peter elaborates on Lot's encounters with the inhabitants of Sodom: βλέμματι γὰρ καὶ ἀκοῇ ὁ δίκαιος ἐγκατοικῶν ἐν αὐτοῖς ἡμέραν ἐξ ἡμέρας ψυχὴν δικαίαν ἀνόμοις ἔργοις ἐβασάνιζεν (*blemmati gar kai akoē ho dikaios enkatoikōn en autois hēmeran ex hēmeras psychēn dikaian anomois ergois ebasanizen*, for that righteous man, residing among them day after day, tormented his righteous soul by the lawless deeds that he saw and heard). Lot was deeply entangled in Sodom, so Peter piles comment upon comment to heighten his readers' awareness of Lot's proximity to and awareness of the corruption surrounding him. He became a witness because of what he "saw and heard" (βλέμματι γὰρ καὶ ἀκοῇ, *blemmati . . . kai akoē*, lit., "by seeing and hearing," datives of cause; BDF §196; Matt. 11:4; Luke 10:24). The combination frequently implies moral

2. The Coming and the Judgment of the False Teachers
b. Past Sinners and Their Doom
2 Peter 2:4–10a

perception as well (Deut. 29:4; Isa. 6:9; 21:3; 29:18; Jer. 5:21; Ezek. 12:2; Matt. 13:13–17; Mark 4:12; 8:18; Luke 8:10; Acts 28:26; Rom. 11:8), a nuance that Peter appears to have in mind. He notes that Lot was "residing among them" (ἐγκατοικῶν ἐν αὐτοῖς, *enkatoikōn en autois*; Herodotus 4.204; Josephus, *Ag. Ap.* 1.33 §296), using a verb that places more emphasis on his alien status than κατοικέω (*katoikeō*, reside), which describes Lot's residence in the city in Gen. 19:29 LXX. Lot was among them but not of them. The intensity of Lot's experience is emphasized by the point that he lived among them ἡμέραν ἐξ ἡμέρας (*hēmeran ex hēmeras*, day after day; Gen. 39:10; Esth. 3:7; Tob. 10:1; Sir. 5:7). Lot was not cloistered, nor was he looking in from the outside, but he witnessed their ways continually and intensely.

Because of his close association with the inhabitants of Sodom, Lot faced some form of torment. The torment Lot experienced may be understood as the affliction that comes on a person rather than a mental state (ἐβασάνιζεν, *ebasanizen*, 2 Macc. 1:28; 7:13, 17; 9:6; 4 Macc. 6:10–11; 8:27; Wis. 11:9; 16:4; Matt. 8:6, 29; 14:24; Mark 5:7; Luke 8:28; Rev. 9:5; 11:10; 14:10; 20:10; BDAG 168; MM 104); read this way, verse 8 reiterates the statement of the previous verse about Lot's oppression. The mention of Lot's "righteous soul" (ψυχὴν δικαίαν, *psychēn dikaian*) appears to suggest, however, that our author does have in view Lot's internal reaction of distress. But in a similar turn of phrase that speaks of a harassed soul, T. Ash. 6.5 says, "For when the evil soul departs, it is harassed by the evil spirit which it served through its desires and evil works." The "soul" could signify not merely the inner life of a human but the whole person. In Gen. 2:7, for example, the "soul" identifies the person as a psychosomatic unit (Matt. 16:25–26; Heb. 10:39; 1 Pet. 3:20; Ladd 1993: 499–520). On this reading, the γάρ (*gar*, for) that begins the verse directs the reader to understand the statement as an explanation of the preceding note about the Sodomites' oppression of Lot and not an "essentially affective" torment (BDAG 168). However, the way Peter highlights Lot's perceptions ("seeing and hearing") directs the reader to understand this as a statement about the inner reaction that he experienced rather than the abuse he faced. If Peter has in mind Lot's experience, then the initial γάρ would not be explanatory but simply mark the continuation of his reflection on Lot and the Sodomites. The thought is similar to Hermas, who asks, "Why do you torment yourself [τί σεαυτὸν βασανίζεις]" (*Sim.* 9.9.3; and Epictetus, *Disc.* 2.22.35).

Lot tormented his "righteous soul" as he dwelled among the Sodomites because of their ἀνόμοις ἔργοις (*anomois ergois*), "lawless deeds." The adjective "lawless" could mean "without (the) law" or "against (the) law," but came to be a synonym for "sin" or "iniquity" (see the cognate noun in Rom. 4:7; 2 Cor. 6:14; Titus 2:14; Heb. 1:9; 10:17; W. Gutbrod, *TDNT* 4:1085–87; H.-H. Esser, *NIDNTT* 2:440, 447; BDAG 85–86). These are deeds that violate moral standards (1 Tim. 1:9) and thus are the opposite of righteous deeds (Prov. 21:18). Our author again does not specify what acts are in mind (see Jude 7 on traditions about the nature of the Sodomite sin). He is not specifically thinking about the way the Sodomites wanted to have sex with the visitors but rather refers to something that was happening all the time. The picture is not simply of an individual act but of a way of life (2:7) that produces such actions. The people of Sodom did not just act corruptly on occasion. Their character was marked by lawlessness. Insofar as these prefigure the heretics, Peter highlights the depth of their moral decay.

**2:9**  Verses 9 and 10 form the apodosis of a very long conditional sentence that began in verse 4, "For if God . . . , then the Lord. . . ." Throughout this section, Peter has demonstrated the judgment that God brought on the sinful angels (v. 4), the ancient world of the flood generation (v. 5), and the cities of Sodom and Gomorrah (v. 6), while at the same time recalling the divine deliverance of Noah and his family (v. 5) and Lot (vv. 7–8). If God kept the righteous and judged the wicked in the past, then οἶδεν κύριος εὐσεβεῖς ἐκ πειρασμοῦ ῥύεσθαι, ἀδίκους δὲ εἰς ἡμέραν κρίσεως κολαζομένους τηρεῖν (oiden kyrios eusebeis ek peirasmou rhyesthai, adikous de eis hēmeran kriseōs kolazomenous tērein, then the Lord is able to deliver the devout from trial but keep the unrighteous for the day of judgment, when they will be punished). Peter's declaration that God "knows" (οἶδεν, oiden) how to deliver the devout is not a simple statement about his cognition but rather a declaration of his ability (Matt. 7:11; Luke 11:13; Phil. 4:12; 1 Thess. 4:4; 1 Tim. 3:5; James 4:17; BDAG 694). God's ability to rescue the righteous as he brought judgment on the unrighteous is a key theme in the preceding verses (vv. 5–7) and is now summarized in the present verse.

Those God delivers are the εὐσεβεῖς (eusebeis), the devout who fulfill their obligations before both God and society (see 1:3, 6–7; 3:11 and comments). These are set over against the "unrighteous" (ἀδίκους, adikous, v. 9b) and the "ungodly" (ἀσεβεῖς, asebeis, vv. 5–6), two terms sometimes brought together to describe those whose lives flout divine and human law and convention (Diodorus Siculus 4.2.6: "and punished such men as were unjust and impious"; Josephus, Ant. 8.10.2 §251: "was misled into unjust and impious acts and showed disrespect for the worship of God"). Peter assures the church that God is able "to deliver the devout from trial." He talks about this deliverance by using the same verb found in verse 7 with reference to Lot (ῥύεσθαι, rhyesthai; see comments; BDAG 907), again cementing the typological link between God's past and present deliverance. The verb frequently appears where an author has in mind some divine deliverance, whether from evil people (2 Thess. 3:2), the power of darkness (Col. 1:13), death (2 Cor. 1:10; 2 Tim. 3:11), wrath (1 Thess. 1:10), or evil or "the Evil One" (Matt. 6:13; Luke 11:4 in ℵ[1]). The promise of divine deliverance "from trial" (ἐκ πειρασμοῦ, ek peirasmou) is one of the fundamental building blocks of the Christian faith. As Spicq comments, "It is the faith of the church that 'the Lord knows how to deliver the godly from testing' (2 Pet 2:9), that is, those who seek divine help" (TLNT 3:90). Peter's declaration resonates in the ears of believers who know the Lord's Prayer, "And do not bring us [in]to the time of trial [εἰς πειρασμόν, eis peirasmon], but rescue [ῥῦσαι, rhysai] us from the evil one" (Matt. 6:13 NRSV; cf. 2 Thess.

3:2–3; 2 Tim. 4:17–18). In a world where the gods were considered to be capricious and could do a person harm as well as good, the confidence in God as the Deliverer is striking indeed (*TLNT* 3:86). God brings good, not evil (Sir. 15:11–20; James 1:13–16).

While πειρασμός (*peirasmos*) in some contexts is a "temptation" to sin (1 Cor. 10:13; 1 Tim. 6:9), it may also mean a "trial" that unveils someone's character (Sir. 2:1; 6:7; 27:5, 7; Gal. 4:14; Heb. 3:8; James 1:2; 1 Pet. 1:6; 4:12; Rev. 3:10; BDAG 793; *TLNT* 3:84–90). The typological examples of Noah and Lot (vv. 5, 7) do not highlight their temptations. Peter does, however, make a point about Lot's testing (v. 8 and comments), and we should therefore see the present verse as a declaration of divine deliverance from trials (Bauckham 1983: 253; M. Green 1987: 113–14; Kraftchick 2002: 131). The declaration becomes a promise that Peter holds out as the complement to the exhortation to stand firm in their faith (1:10; 3:17). The "trials" Peter has in mind could be those that the church experiences at the hands of the heretics, but the eschatological reference to the "day of judgment" in the second half of the verse suggests that Peter has eschatological trials in view here as well (cf. Rev. 3:10). This end, however, is not in some distant future but is already at hand (1 Pet. 4:8), with the present testing being part of that final trial the church will endure (1 Pet. 4:12; Rev. 3:10; see Bauckham 1983: 253; Senior and Harrington 2003: 268). We suspect that Peter throughout this section of the letter is responding to the heretics' critique of the belief that divine judgment would certainly sweep all away. Peter presents a strong doctrine of divine immanence. God is involved in the world and acts on behalf of his people to deliver them (see "The Opponents in 2 Peter" in the introduction). Others must face his judgment.

The second part of the verse holds out the warning that God is able to "keep the unrighteous for the day of judgment, when they will be punished." In this second half of verse 9, Peter adopts some of the language of Jude 6, which was already absorbed in verse 4 (see comments). As God has kept the angels bound for the coming judgment day, so he also keeps the unrighteous for that final judicial reckoning. Peter places special stress on the life of righteousness in both this section and the letter as a whole (2:7–8; 1:1; 2:5, 21; 3:13). The "unrighteous" (ἄδικους, *adikous*) are those who do wrong (2:13, 15). These are people whose conduct is the opposite of that of the righteous or the pious (εὐσεβεῖς, *eusebeis*, in v. 9a) and whom Peter tags as the "impious" (ἀσεβεῖς, *asebeis*, in vv. 5–7; 3:7). Peter was not alone in seeing the unrighteous and impious as being fit objects of punishment. Plato notes, for example, various "occasions for wrath and punishment [κολάσεις, *kolaseis*] and reproof," which include "injustice [ἀδικία, *adikia*], and impiety [ἀσέβεια, *asebeia*], and in short all that is opposed to civic virtue" (*Protagoras* 323E; see Pseudo-Aristotle, *Virtues and Vices* 1251A). Paul concurs (Rom. 1:18).

Although Peter presents a general statement about the doom of such people, he has the heretics particularly in mind (2:13–16). As the Lord has kept the sinful angels bound for the final judgment (v. 4; cf. Jude 6 and comments), so he is able "to keep" (τηρεῖν, *tērein*) these unjust people "for the day of judgment" (εἰς ἡμέραν κρίσεως, *eis hēmeran kriseōs*). The declaration that the Lord acts "to keep" them implies that their doom is sure and that they will not escape the judgment (2:4, 17; 3:7; Jude 13; cf. T. Reu. 5.5, "kept for eternal punishment"), as criminals are "kept" in custody (Matt. 27:36, 54; Acts 12:5; 16:23). This affirmation not only counters the heretics' denial of future judgment but also offers assurance to the Christian community. The "day of judgment" (here and in 3:7; LXX: Prov. 6:34; Tob. 1:18 [Codex Sinaiticus]; Ps. Sol. 15.12; 1 En. 22.11; Matt. 10:15; 11:22, 24; 12:36; 1 John 4:17) is that final day that is also called "the day of the Lord" (3:10; cf. Isa. 34:8 "the day of judgment of the Lord") and "the day of God" (2 Pet. 3:12). In the latter part of the letter, Peter elaborates extensively on the character of that day, when God will bring a cataclysmic end to the order of the world as we know it (3:10–13). Whatever delay there may be until it comes can be attributed to God's mercy (3:8–9). But rest assured, as God kept the ancient world for judgment, so he also keeps the present world for that final judgment by fire (3:5–7). Peter asserts God's present sovereignty over the world in the time of delay and assures his readers that just as God keeps the present order for judgment so, too, the unrighteous are kept for the same.

Peter asserts not only that the unrighteous are kept for the day of judgment but also that they are destined "to be punished" (κολαζομένους, *kolazomenous*), a present passive participle as difficult to translate as it is to interpret. Depending on the context, the verb may refer to temporal punishment (1 Esd. 8:24; 1 Macc. 7:7; 3 Macc. 3:26; 7:3, 14; 4 Macc. 2:12; 8:6; Wis. 11:5, 8) or divine punishment (2 Macc. 6:14; Wis. 12:12–15; and see Wis. 3:1–4), even after death (4 Macc. 18:5) or at the final judgment (Matt. 25:46, with the noun κόλασις, *kolasis*, punishment). The present participial form has been interpreted as an indication that this punishment is something that the unrighteous are *currently* experiencing in this life before the final day (Lunn 1998) or in the time between their death and the final judgment (Bigg 1901: 278; Kelly 1969: 335).

The torment of the wicked after death and before the final judgment is a theme found in both Jewish and Christian literature (1 En. 22.1–11; Luke 16:19–31). In a statement that is quite similar to the present verse, 1 En. 22.11 says, "Here their spirits shall be set apart, for this great torment, till the great day of judgment, (the day) of scourgings and torment of the accused everlastingly, *to the end that there be* retribution upon their spirits: there they shall be bound for ever" (M. Black 1985: 38). But the present time is also when God's wrath may be executed on the wicked (Rom. 1:18–23). Ancient ideas of divine jurisprudence included this notion of temporal judgment, as the preceding examples show. Commenting on the use of κολάζω (*kolazō*, punish) in the inscriptions, J. Schneider (*TDNT* 3:815) says, "The sins punished by deity are those against the deity itself, e.g., violations of the sacred cultic laws. The deity smites the offender with sickness and infirmity, or even punished himself and his family with death."

Other commentators, however, note that the present participle may convey a future sense, and so the punishment in view is more likely that which the unrighteous will experience in the future "day of judgment" (Bauckham 1983: 254; M. Green 1987: 114; Kraftchick 2002: 131–32). Since the future participle is rare in the NT and since the time of the participle is relative to that of the main verb with its temporal reference determined from the context (cf. the present participle λυομένων, *lyomenōn*, in 3:11), this is certainly a possible interpretation (BDF §§339, 65; Porter 1989: 377–79). We cannot determine Peter's meaning here solely on lexical or grammatical grounds. The eschatological orientation of the passage, including both the promise of deliverance (v. 9a, see above) and the final judgment of the unrighteous (v. 9b), suggests that Peter has in view the torment that the unrighteous will experience at that time. Moreover, those who are being kept for judgment are viewed as sinful but not tormented in the present time (v. 10). Their doom is sure, and their end is torment that will endure, not annihilation.

Our author's principal point in this verse, however, has to do with God's divine power both to save and to judge, and these two powers are tightly bound. The heretics have denied God's power to judge (3:3–7). Apparently doubts have arisen about God's ability to save as well. If the heretics have absorbed aspects of Epicurean teaching (see "The Opponents in 2 Peter" in the introduction), then their doctrine of divine transcendence precludes both of these. On the other hand, Philo on numerous occasions speaks of the two principal powers of God being his beneficent and his punitive power. He asks, "Cannot you see that the primal and chief powers belonging to the Existent are the beneficent and the punitive [εὐεργέτις καὶ κολαστέριος, *euergetis kai kolasterios*]?" (*Spec. Laws* 1.56 §307), and declares, "The primal and highest Potencies of the Existent, the beneficent and the punitive [δωρητικὴ καὶ κολαστήριος, *dōrētikē kai kolastērios*], are equal" (*Heir* 34 §166; so *Abraham* 25 §129; *Embassy* 1 §6). Peter affirms them both in the face of the heretics' denials.

Peter takes the general statement in verse 9b about the divine judgment leveled against the unrighteous and begins to focus his attention on the heretics: μάλιστα δὲ τοὺς ὀπίσω σαρκὸς ἐν ἐπιθυμίᾳ μιασμοῦ πορευομένους καὶ κυριότητος καταφρονοῦντας (*malista de tous opisō sarkos en epithymia miasmou poreuomenous kai kyriotētos kataphronountas*, but especially the ones who go after flesh because of defiling desire and disdain lordship). In this summary statement, our author draws on Jude 7–8 and 17, but his pattern of borrowing and adaptation is rather complex. Some words are reproduced exactly, but the thought is changed through significant modification of the language.

For example, in Jude 7 we read of those who ἀπελθοῦσαι ὀπίσω σαρκὸς ἑτέρας (*apelthousai opisō sarkos heteras*, have gone after another kind of flesh), a reference to the attempt of the Sodomites to engage in sexual relationships with the angelic messengers. Peter, however, drops the notion of going after "another kind of flesh" and talks rather about the heretics as τοὺς ὀπίσω σαρκὸς . . . πορευομένους (*tous opisō sarkos . . . poreuomenous*, the ones who go after flesh), a reference to the way they follow flesh for sexual gratification

2:10a

(see below). The verb Peter uses here (πορευομένους) and the reference to lust (ἐπιθυμία, *epithymia*) were lifted from Jude 16: κατὰ τὰς ἐπιθυμίας ἑαυτῶν πορευόμενοι (*kata tas epithymias heatōn poreuomenoi*, living according to the dictates of their own desires). Though Jude 8 speaks of those who σάρκα μὲν μιαίνουσιν (*sarka men miainousin*, defile the flesh), Peter refers to those who go after σαρκὸς ἐν ἐπιθυμίᾳ μιασμοῦ (*sarkos en epithymia miasmou*, flesh because of defiling desire). Jude 8 also refers to his heretics' revolt against lordship (κυριότητα δὲ ἀθετοῦσιν, *kyriotēta de athetousin*, they revolt against lordship); Peter's heretics "disdain lordship" (κυριότητος καταφρονοῦντας, *kyriotētos kataphronountas*).

Peter is hardly a slave to Jude's language and thought as he adopts and adapts his source in his quest to warn the church against the heretics who tempt them. The level of modification would have exempted Peter from the charge of theft (see "The Relationship between 2 Peter and Jude" in the introduction to 2 Peter).

Peter sharpens the point about the relevance of the preceding with the introductory words μάλιστα δέ (*malista de*, but especially; Gal. 6:10; Phil. 4:22). The transition could be roughly paraphrased, "This judgment in verse 9 will come upon the unrighteous, *but especially* on the ones described here." That he is turning his attention to the heretics is implied by his reference to their defilement (2:10a and 19) and their going after lust of the flesh (2:10a and 18; 3:3), although this remains a summary statement concerning God's past acts of judgment (2:4–8). Peter tags these people as τοὺς ὀπίσω σαρκὸς . . . πορευομένους (*tous opisō sarkos . . . poreuomenous*, the ones who go after flesh). The expression πορεύομαι ὀπίσω (*poreuomai opisō*, go after) commonly refers to following other gods in the LXX (Deut. 4:3; 6:14; 8:19; 28:14; Judg. 2:12, 17, 19; 1 Kings 11:10) as opposed to following God or the Lord (Deut. 13:5 [13:4 Eng.]; Sir. 46:10; cf. following false messiahs in Luke 21:8). The language may also be used more widely as in warnings about following after strange customs (1 Macc. 1:13–14), after sins (Isa. 65:2; 2 Kings 13:2), or as here, after lusts (Sir. 18:30). This Hebraic notion of following after implies a sense of devotion to something (cf. Jude 7 and comments; BDAG 716). The heretics have pledged their allegiance to nothing higher than the "flesh" (σαρκός, *sarkos*), which the NIV understands in the Pauline sense of the "sinful nature" (so NJB "corrupt human nature"; Rom. 7:18, 25; 8:4–7; Gal. 5:13, 24; Col. 2:23; BDAG 914–16).

Although Paul's concept of "flesh" cannot be equated with the notion that the body is sinful, much discussion in the ancient world was taken up with the question of the relationship between the body ("flesh") and desires and passions or appetites (Plutarch, *Mor.* 1087B, 1096C; 4 Macc. 7:18). The "flesh" seeks pleasure (Diogenes Laertius, *Lives* 10.145; Plutarch, *Mor.* 1098D; Philo, *Unchangeable* 30 §143) and is weak, corrupt, and deceitful (T. Jud. 19.4; T. Zeb. 9.7). The line between the "flesh" as that which desires and seeks pleasure and the Pauline sense is not extremely sharp. However, since Peter speaks of "going after" the "flesh" (σαρκός), he may have in mind the body as an object of sexual desire (BDAG 915). But his use of the term later in the letter suggests that "flesh" is a driving force rather than an object sought or followed (2:18; cf. Jude 8, 23, and comments). The heretics are devoted to the flesh and act out of that allegiance. Peter adds that they are devoted to the flesh ἐν ἐπιθυμίᾳ μιασμοῦ (*en epithymia miasmou*, because of defiling desire). The reason for following the flesh (on this use of ἐν and the dative, see BDF §220.2) is "desire" (2:18; 3:3; Jude 16, 18 and comments), which, as noted previously, is the source of moral corruption that dominates the world and characterizes the heretics (1:4 and comments). The heretics represent archetypal examples of the human plight, from which faith in Christ offers deliverance.

Peter qualifies this "desire" or "lust" as "defiling" (genitive of quality, a Hebrew usage; BDF §165). Though in some contexts the term has to do with cultic defilement (1 Macc. 4:43; Plutarch, *Solon* 12.3), elsewhere moral defilement of the person is in mind, as in the vice list of Wis. 14:26: "confusion over what is good, forgetfulness of favors, defiling of souls, sexual perversion, disorder in marriages, adultery, and debauchery" (NRSV). This is the pollution in the heart that is closely associated with sexual desire (T. Benj. 8.2–3; cf. T. Levi 17.8; BDAG 650; F. Hauck, *TDNT* 4:647). Peter will later return to speak of the escape from the "defilements (τὰ μιάσματα, *ta miasmata*) of the world" (2:20, and comments). Such conduct goes beyond the prescribed boundaries of morality. As Malina (2001: 165) comments, "Now both defilement and purification presuppose some movement across a symbolic line that marks off the clean from the unclean" (see Jude 8 and comments on defilement suggested by the verb μιαίνω, *miaino*, defile). Sexually immoral conduct is a transgression of the prescribed boundaries and thus brings defilement. This language of defilement in relationship to sexual immorality appears in Jewish literature (see, e.g., Let. Aris. 141–66; 1QS 5.13; Josephus, *J.W.* 4.5.2 §323; Jub. 7.20–21).

The heretics also are people who κυριότητος καταφρονοῦντας (*kyriotētos kataphronountas*, disdain lordship; cf. Jude 8 and comments). Although κυριότης may refer to angelic beings, as in Col. 1:16 and Eph. 1:21 (cf. 2 En. 20.1; 1 En. 61.1; T. Sol. 8.6 [MS D]), in such cases the term is found only in the plural. Here, as in Jude 8 (see comments), the author refers to the ruling power of the Lord (κύριος, *kyrios*), who is Jesus Christ (1:2, 8, 11, 14, 16; 2:9, 11, 20; 3:2, 8–10, 15, 18). The heretics are people who "disdain" his ruling authority, a statement that takes up again Peter's previous accusation that the false teachers "deny the Master who bought them" (2:1). Far from being people who honor him, they show contempt for him and consider him of little value (καταφρονοῦντας, *kataphronountas*; Matt. 6:24; 18:10; Luke 16:13; Rom. 2:4; 1 Cor. 11:22; 1 Tim. 4:12; 6:2; BDAG 529).

To "disdain" someone is the opposite of showing honor and often appears in contrast with showing honor (Isocrates, *Archidamus* 6.95: "Instead of being honoured he would be scorned"; Plato, *Greater Hippias* 281C: "as a man not to be despised but held in high repute"; Josephus, *Ant.* 6.5.3 §80). With regard to God or the gods, such dishonor is the equivalent of impiety and a truly audacious act for any mortal (Euripides, *Bacchanals* 199: "Not I condemn the Gods, I, mortal born!"; Josephus, *Ant.* 9.8.5 §173: "He committed as many impieties as did the first [kings] who held God in contempt"; 3.1.4 §16: "by showing at once contempt for God"; 2.15.5 §329; 3.5.3 §85; 4.8.2 §§215, 217; 12.9.1 §357). This is more than an attitude of contempt since it results in disobedience (4 Macc. 4:26; Josephus, *Ant.* 6.7.4 §142: God counted it an outrage that "He should meet with such contempt and disobedience as they would show to no human king"; 2.9.2 §207; 6.7.4 §147; 11.5.1 §130). The heretics are such outrageous characters that they despise and disobey the very one who is worthy of the highest honor.

## Additional Notes

**2:4.** The reading σειραῖς (*seirais*, chains) finds support in 𝔓⁷² along with P and Ψ, while the variant σιροῖς (*sirois*, pit, cave) is attested in ℵ, and the alternative spelling σειροῖς (*seirois*) witnessed in A B C 81. Though the textual evidence does not strongly favor either of these readings, Peter's dependence on Jude 6—which reads δεσμοῖς (*desmois*, chains)—suggests that our author has included the synonym σειραῖς (*seirais*, chains). This reading is probably the most ancient.

**2:6.** The considerable doubt surrounding the reading καταστροφῇ (*katastrophē*, to destruction) is expressed in the critical editions by the inclusion of the word in brackets. Was this word a scribal addition that found its way into ℵ A C² K Ψ, or was it omitted for some reason in 𝔓⁷² B C* among other later MSS? The omission may have been due to "transcriptional oversight" (Metzger 1994: 633), given the juxtaposition in the text of two words that begin with κατ- (καταστροφῇ κατέκρινεν).

**2:6.** The reading ἀσεβέσιν (*asebesin*, the ungodly) is well attested (𝔓⁷², B, P) and is the more likely reading instead of ἀσεβεῖν (*asebein*, act impiously; found in ℵ, A, C, Ψ). The present verse continues the discussion found in 2:5 about the destiny of "the ungodly." We can also understand how the variant ἀσεβεῖν appeared, since the infinitive often follows μέλλω (*mellō*, be about to; here as a participle μελλόντων, *mellontōn*).

# c. "These Are"—The Vices of the False Teachers (2:10b–16)

In 2:10b–16, Peter brings a series of denunciations against the false teachers. He highlights that the heretics are not only in communion with members of the Christian community but also seek to lure others into following their way. In denouncing their sin, Peter focuses on their arrogance, irrationality, dedication to pleasure, enticement of others through sexual desire, and their greed. Their avarice and use of sexual sin as a means to persuade the members of the church suggest the misdeeds of Balaam who, though he could not curse Israel, laid out the means by which they could be tempted to sexual sin. Peter's denunciation of the heretics is highly dependent on Jude 10–12 (see comments). But Peter reworks this material significantly as he tailors it to address the heretics that trouble the churches. Peter's indictment of the heretics will be repeated even more vividly in the following section (2:17–22).

## Exegesis and Exposition

[10b]Audacious and self-willed, they show no fear when blaspheming glories, [11]whereas angels who are greater in strength and power do not bring slanderous judgment against them ⌜before the Lord⌝. [12]But these, as irrational beasts, born in accord with nature to be captured and destroyed, slandering that about which they are ignorant, shall even be destroyed in their destruction, [13]⌜suffering the loss⌝ of the wages of unrighteousness, regarding as pleasure reveling in the daytime, spots and defects reveling in their pleasures when they feast with you. [14]They have eyes full of longing for an ⌜adulteress⌝, and they do not cease from sin, luring unstable people, having hearts trained in greed, cursed children. [15]They have wandered off, departing from the straight way and following after the way of Balaam of ⌜Bosor⌝, the one who loved the wages of unrighteousness, [16]but was accused for his own unlawful deed; a speechless donkey, speaking in a human voice, restrained the prophet's irrationality.

In verses 9 and 10a, Peter began to draw the lessons about God's ancient judgment and salvation, which he had discussed previously (vv. 4–8). Now he turns his *vituperatio* directly against the heretics and charges: Τολμηταὶ αὐθάδεις, δόξας οὐ τρέμουσιν βλασφημοῦντες (*tolmētai authadeis, doxas ou tremousin blasphēmountes*, Audacious and self-willed, they show no fear when reviling glories). Although the first noun used to describe the heretics

**2:10b**

at times identifies those who are courageous and bold (Philo, *Joseph* 38 §222; Thucydides 1.70.3; see the verb τολμάω, *tolmaō*, in Mark 15:43; Rom. 5:7; Phil. 1:14), here it becomes a negative accusation that these people are presumptuous and audacious to the point of being rash (Josephus, *J.W.* 3.10.2 §475; *Ant.* 20.9.1 §199; see the verb τολμάω, *tolmaō*, in Rom. 15:18; 1 Cor. 6:1; 2 Cor. 11:21; Esth. 7:5; Jdt. 14:13; 2 Macc. 4:2; BDAG 1010; G. Fitzer, *TDNT* 8:185). The use of this term was suggested to the author by the presence of the verb in Jude 9 (see comments), where it refers to what Michael, the archangel, did not do ("did not presume to pronounce the judgment of 'slander' but said, 'The Lord punish you!'"). Occasionally "audacious" appears in combination with "self-willed" (αὐθάδεις, *authadeis*; Dionysius of Halicarnassus, *Ant. rom.* 4.28.2; *TLNT* 1:229; BDAG 150), which marks a person as self-centered and arrogant. According to Prov. 21:24 LXX: "An arrogant, self-willed [αὐθάδης, *authadēs*] and boastful person is called a troublemaker," while Titus 1:7 says such people are disqualified from having ecclesiastical oversight. These do what they want, persist in their own opinion, and have no regard for others in their arrogance (*TLNT* 1:229–30). They are hard (Gen. 49:3; Polybius 4.21.3) and contentious (Philo, *Moses* 1.24 §139; see Josephus, *J.W.* 6.2.10 §172), exhibiting a high degree of antisocial behavior due to their arrogance. The accusation was typical in *vituperatio* and appears, for example, in Aelius Aristides' critique of the philosophers in his defense of the sophists (*Platonic Discourses* 307.9–10): "They despise others while being themselves worthy of scorn. They criticize others without examining themselves" (L. Johnson 1989: 430–31). We should not, however, assume that Peter's accusation has no relationship to the "facts on the ground." The heretics have broken with the faith and are mocking fundamental apostolic instruction about the parousia of Christ and the final judgment (3:3). A crisis is looming in the church due to their arrogant dismissal of fundamental tenets of the faith.

As proof of their arrogance, Peter states that the heretics δόξας οὐ τρέμουσιν βλασφημοῦντες (*doxas ou tremousin blasphēmountes*, they show no fear when reviling glories). The source of Peter's thought is Jude 8, parts of which are already incorporated into the previous half of this verse (see 2:10a and comments). Jude 8 simply states δόξας δὲ βλασφημοῦσιν (*doxas de blasphēmousin*, they slander glories), while Peter adds that the heretics do not tremble when they engage in such hubris. Peter omits the legend about Michael's contention with the devil over the body of Moses (Jude 9) but preserves the reference to slandering angels, that is, "glories" (Dan. 7:23–27). There is no reason to think that Peter understands these "glories" in any other way than does Jude. They are not civil or ecclesiastical authorities but rather angelic beings whom the heretics slander (see Jude 8 and comments). For their part, these angels themselves, who are mightier than the heretics, do not engage in arrogant acts (see v. 11 and comments).

The audacity of the heretics is accentuated by the note that they do not tremble or "show fear" (οὐ τρέμουσιν, *ou tremousin*) in their insolence. The verb meant "to tremble," as the earth trembles (Ps. 104:32 [103:32 LXX]; Jer.

4:24) or as a person trembles from cold (1 Esd. 9:6). But one may tremble before God in fear (Isa. 66:2, 5; Dan. 10:11; cf. Mark 5:33; Luke 8:47; BDAG 1014). This psychological aspect is in mind as Peter charges that the heretics show no fear before angels but blaspheme them instead. "Fear" is the common human response in the presence of angels (4 Macc. 4:10; Matt. 28:5; Luke 1:13, 30; Luke 2:9–10; contrast modern popular notions of angelic encounters), but the arrogance of the heretics is such that even angels do not evoke this reaction in them.

The heretics blaspheme or "revile" the "glories." The verb βλασφημοῦντες (*blasphēmountes*) appears repeatedly in Greco-Roman, Jewish, and Christian literature to refer to reviling or defaming the Deity (see Acts 19:37; Matt. 9:3; 26:65; Rom. 2:24; and see BDAG 178), but it could likewise refer to slanderous and defaming speech against a person (1 Pet. 4:4; Rom. 3:8; 1 Cor. 10:30; Titus 3:2) or against supernatural beings (cf. 2 Pet. 2:12; Jude 8). The reason that the heretics have adopted this posture against angelic beings is different from that in Jude. In that letter, the heretics have rejected the divine order of things, of which the angels are guardians. However, the heretics in Peter's sights have denied providence and divine judgment (3:3–4; and "The Opponents in 2 Peter" in the introduction). We may assume that their rejection of angelic authority is linked to the common understanding of the angelic role in the execution of the final judgment (Neyrey 1993: 213; Perkins 1995: 184). These are not the "fallen angels" (contra Bauckham 1983: 261) but those who accompany the Lord in the great assize (Matt. 13:39, 41, 49; 16:27; 24:31; 25:31; 2 Thess. 1:7; Rev. 7:2; 8:2, 6, 13; 9:15). The irony in the heretics' position is that the powerful beings whom they malign never engage in such behavior.

Peter places the conduct of the heretics in stark contrast with that of the angels whom, according to verse 10b, the opponents revile: ὅπου ἄγγελοι ἰσχύϊ καὶ δυνάμει μείζονες ὄντες οὐ φέρουσιν κατ᾽ αὐτῶν παρὰ κυρίῳ βλάσφημον κρίσιν (*hopou angeloi ischyi kai dynamei meizones ontes ou pherousin kat᾽ autōn para kyriō blasphēmon krisin*, whereas angels who are greater in strength and power do not bring slanderous judgment against them before the Lord). While the heretics are so audacious that they show no fear when slandering celestial beings (v. 10b), the angels themselves do not avenge themselves by engaging in such behavior. Peter draws his thought from Jude 9,[1] although he alters the sense in significant ways: "But Michael the archangel, when disputing with the devil, argued over the body of Moses, did not presume to pronounce the judgment of 'slander' but said, 'The Lord punish you!'" (ὁ δὲ Μιχαὴλ ὁ ἀρχάγγελος, ὅτε τῷ διαβόλῳ διακρινόμενος διελέγετο περὶ τοῦ Μωϋσέως σώματος, οὐκ ἐτόλμησεν κρίσιν ἐπενεγκεῖν βλασφημίας ἀλλὰ εἶπεν, Ἐπιτιμήσαι σοι κύριος, *ho de Michaēl ho archangelos, hote tō diabolō diakrinomenos dielegeto peri tou Mōuseōs sōmatos, ouk etolmēsen krisin epenenkein blasphēmias alla eipen, Epitimēsai soi kyrios*). Peter has altogether dropped the reference to the

2:11

---

1. See the comparative analysis of these two texts in Fornberg 1977: 43–54; Neyrey 1990: 208; and the discusssion in Gilmore 2002: 84–85.

apocryphal story of the contention between the archangel Michael and the devil over the body of Moses (see comments on Jude 9). Instead, he substitutes the reference to Michael with the "angels," who themselves are "greater in strength and power." The story has shifted from a specific statement about Michael's actions to a general declaration about the angels' power and what actions they do not engage in.

This switch from Michael to the angels is not as surprising as might appear at first because Michael and the angels are logically linked. Michael frequently appears with the other archangels Gabriel, Raphael, and Phanuel (1 En. 40.9; 54.6; 71.8–9, 13) or Uriel (1 En. 9.1; 20.2; cf. 1QM 9.14–15), and even a larger group including Suru'el, Saraqa'el, and Remiel (1 En. 20.1–8; cf. Tob. 12:15). He was also thought to be the principal of all the angels (Ascen. Isa. 3.16; 9.23 [Latin]; Rev. 12:7). Though the person of the archangel Michael is not emphasized, reference to his power persists in the present verse (cf. Dan. 10:21; 12:1). Moreover, in Peter's handling of his source, the devil fades from view as the heretics themselves are in the adversarial role with angels (v. 10b). Our author is reluctant to integrate the apocryphal traditions as did Jude yet retains some of their significant concepts, while altering even these in notable ways.

The idea of refraining from bringing a legal charge is preserved but instead of "the judgment of 'slander'" (κρίσιν . . . βλασφημίας, krisin . . . blasphēmias, Jude 9 and comments), Peter speaks of a "slanderous judgment" (βλάσφημον κρίσιν, blasphēmon krisin). Instead of Jude's Ἐπιτιμήσαι σοι κύριος (Epitimēsai soi kyrios, "The Lord punish you!"), Peter notes that the powerful angels do not bring a blasphemous charge παρὰ κυρίῳ (para kyriō, before the Lord). Peter's intertextual methodology has truly transformed Jude's thought, making it his own to advance his purposes. What he means is not bound by his source's intent. His mode of adapting his source material is in line with ancient canons of imitatio, which allowed borrowed material to be reworked extensively to make it one's own.[2] As Horace said, "In ground open to all you will win private rights, if you do not linger along the easy and open pathway, if you do not seek to render word for word as a slavish translator, and if in your copying you do not leap into the narrow well, out of which either shame or the laws of your task will keep you from stirring a step" (Art 131–36; see "The Relationship between 2 Peter and Jude" in the introduction to 2 Peter). Peter's omission of the apocryphal tradition is due to his adaptation of Jude to serve his own ends. It need not suggest that the author does not understand his source (Bauckham 1983: 261), that he calculates that his readers would be unfamiliar with the Michael/Moses/devil story (Fornberg 1977: 54), or that he omits the apocryphal source story "to preclude any suggestion that these

---

2. Wisse (1972: 142) misses this methodological point when he says, "The author of 2 Peter certainly took the Epistle of Jude to be an eschatological tract. Thus he could take over the description of the opponents within his own framework. He could not have done this if he believed that his source was denouncing a specific group of heretics." Bauckham's (1983: 261) charge that the author of 2 Peter "misunderstood the point of Jude" outstrips the evidence and does not take into account how imitatio functions.

works should be considered as authoritative Scripture" (Schreiner 2003: 348). Perkins (1995: 184) is likely correct that the omission of the story is "because it is not relevant to the argument of the letter."

The contrast Peter draws between the heretics' audacious slander and the angelic response continues in this subordinate clause, which affirms the angels' higher status: ὅπου ἄγγελοι ἰσχύϊ καὶ δυνάμει μείζονες ὄντες (*hopou angeloi ischyi kai dynamei meizones ontes*, whereas angels who are greater in strength and power; cf. 2 Thess. 1:7, which speaks of the "angels of his power"). The combination of "strength and power" (ἰσχύϊ καὶ δυνάμει, *ischyi kai dynamei*) is a common hendiadys used by Jewish and Christian authors to describe either divine (Deut. 3:24; 1 Chron. 29:11; Wis. 12:17; 1 En. 1.4; Eph. 1:19; Rev. 5:12; 7:12) or human strength and power (Deut. 8:17; 1 Chron. 12:22; Jdt. 5:3; Ps. 32:16 [33:16 Eng.]; Zech. 4:6), especially with reference to military force (compare the contrast between human power and heavenly might in 1 Macc. 3:19). The terms are nearly indistinguishable. Their combination here serves to highlight the exalted status of these angelic beings and their honor.

In a culture that valued honor above all else, power was highly regarded and a marker of one's status and moral character. As Malina and Neyrey (1996: 95) note, "A person endowed with bodily excellence would embody aristocratic ideals that reflect honorable behavior. For example, strength and power are important for athletics and warfare, both aristocratic or elite pursuits." Thus when Aristotle spoke of the need the commonwealth had of good young men, he extolled their virtues both as "bodily excellencies" (ἀρετή, *aretē*), which included "strength, power" (ἰσχὺν δύναμιν), and "moral excellencies," the two being intertwined. Women likewise were to demonstrate both physical and moral excellencies, although the character of these excellencies differed (*Rhetoric* 1.5.6). Likewise, in virtue lists that exalt the honor of God, "strength and power" are noteworthy attributes (Deut. 3:24; Rev. 7:12), and these are sometimes huddled unsurprisingly amid those that we would consider "moral." As Wis. 12:16–18 says, "For your strength is the source of righteousness. . . . Although you are sovereign in strength, you judge with mildness, and with great forbearance you govern us; for you have power to act whenever you choose" (NRSV). Thus Peter's claim that the angels possess "power and strength" exalts their high status as well as their moral excellence. The point is underscored by the note that they are "greater" (μείζονες, *meizones*) in these than the heretics who blaspheme them. The "greater" is the one "superior in importance" (BDAG 624; John 14:28; Heb. 6:13; 1 John 3:20; 4:4).

Despite their exalted status, the angels οὐ φέρουσιν κατ' αὐτῶν παρὰ κυρίῳ βλάσφημον κρίσιν (*ou pherousin kat' autōn para kyriō blasphēmon krisin*, do not bring slanderous judgment against them before the Lord). The "insult" they have received is not avenged. Revenge is the culturally sanctioned response to insults that degrade a person's honor. D. Epstein (1987: 2) notes that a Roman's prestige would suffer "if he showed himself reluctant to respond and retaliate for hostile acts. A Roman, governed by a harsh ethos, simply could not afford to 'turn the other cheek' and expect to maintain his position in society." A common venue to act out revenge was the court system, where the denigration of the opponent's character was the chief end (D. Epstein 1987: 102–4). Humiliating insults were a source of *inimicitiae* and on the streets would have warranted a retaliatory response (D. Epstein 1987: 36–37). To insult angelic beings, as have the heretics (v. 10b), is considered the height of hubris in this Mediterranean context. Aristotle presents one of the most complete descriptions of hubris: "Similarly, he who insults another also slights him; for insult consists in causing injury or annoyance whereby the sufferer is disgraced . . . ; for retaliation is not insult, but punishment. The cause of the pleasure felt by those who insult is the idea that, in ill-treating others, they are more fully showing superiority. Dishonour is characteristic of insult; and one who dishonours another slights him" (*Rhetoric* 2.2.5–6). The angels, though in a superior position and able to enact litigation against their inferiors, show great nobility of character in their restraint by not bringing a "slanderous judgment" against their opponents.

The language Peter uses is legal, the principal verb being oft found in legal contexts (φέρουσιν, *pherousin*, "charge" as in Polybius 1.32.4; see John 18:29; Acts 25:7; BDAG 1052), as likewise the expression "against them" (κατ' αὐτῶν, *kat' autōn*; see John 18:29). In this frame, κρίσιν (*krisin*) is the "legal process of judgment" (BDAG 569). The angels do not engage in denigrating or slanderous judicial proceedings against the heretics (βλάσφημον, *blasphēmon*, see Philo, *Joseph* 41 §247; Josephus, *Life* 32 §158; 62 §320; Wis. 1:6; Sir. 3:16; 2 Macc. 9:28; 10:36; 1 Tim. 1:13; 2 Tim. 3:2; BDAG 178) "before the Lord" (παρὰ κυρίῳ, *para kyriō*; Job 9:2; Ps. Sol. 9.5; Rom. 2:13), the judge of all. The archangels are in position to bring such judicial charges (see 1 En. 9.1–11).

**2:12**  Although the angels do not slanderously condemn the heretics before the Lord for their hubris, these people will indeed be judged. While the heretics have denied the inevitability of future judgment (3:3–10), Peter affirms that they, just as captured beasts, will be slaughtered: οὗτοι δὲ ὡς ἄλογα ζῷα γεγεννημένα φυσικὰ εἰς ἅλωσιν καὶ φθορὰν ἐν οἷς ἀγνοοῦσιν βλασφημοῦντες, ἐν τῇ φθορᾷ αὐτῶν καὶ φθαρήσονται (*houtoi de hōs aloga zōa gegennēmena physika eis halōsin kai phthoran en hois agnoousin blasphēmountes, en tē phthora autōn kai phtharēsontai*, But these, as irrational beasts, born in accord with nature to be captured and destroyed, slandering that about which they are ignorant, shall even be destroyed in their destruction). The source of Peter's thought is Jude 10, from which he draws a number of expressions, such as calling the heretics "irrational beasts" (οὗτοι δὲ . . . ὡς τὰ ἄλογα ζῷα, *houtoi de . . . hōs ta aloga zōa*, but these . . . as irrational beasts) and the comment on how they slander what they do not understand (ὅσα . . . οὐκ οἴδασιν βλασφημοῦσιν, *hosa . . . ouk oidasin blasphēmousin*, slander whatever they do not understand). Peter echoes other parts of Jude 10 yet gives them a somewhat different twist, such as the instinctual knowledge of the beasts (ὅσα δὲ φυσικῶς . . . ἐπίστανται, *hosa de physikōs . . . epistantai*, whatever they know by instinct), which becomes in 2 Pet. 2:12 a note about the nature of the beasts as creatures to be caught and slaughtered. Similarly, the moral corruption Jude 10 mentions (ἐν τούτοις φθείρονται, *en toutois phtheirontai*, by these they are corrupted) is morphed by Peter into a reflection on the heretics' final destruction. Whereas the emphasis in Jude 10 is on the corrupt character of the heretics, Peter's principal concern is with their final destiny. Once again, our author has adopted and adapted his source in a way that speaks directly to the situation at hand. The heretics' denial of future judgment is met by the declaration that they, as captured beasts, are destined to be destroyed.

Peter compares the heretics to animals without reason, whose nature is to be captured and slaughtered. The comparison of a person's nature with that of the animals was a commonplace in ancient *vituperatio* (see Jude 10 and comments). The characteristic that Peter emphasizes is the irrationality of the animals. The expression ἄλογα ζῷα (*aloga zōa*) describes beasts (see Philo, *Alleg. Interp.* 3.9 §30; Josephus, *Ag. Ap.* 2.29 §213; *Ant.* 10.11.6 §262), underscoring their lack of reason. Plutarch (*Mor.* 493D) comments that "the irrational animals" (τὰ ἄλογα ζῷα, *ta aloga zōa*) follow "nature," but by way of contrast, "in man ungoverned reason is absolute master."

Since the sixth/fifth century BC a debate had ensued in philosophical circles about the nature and rights of animals and whether they should be killed or could be rightly ill-treated. The discussion concerning their nature (see Plutarch, *Mor.* 493C–D) centered on the beasts' lack of rationality; Aristotle, later followed by both Epicureans and Stoics, denied them rationality and therefore concluded that justice need not be shown to them. "Epicurean rationale . . . is that justice is owed only where there is a contract, hence only among rational agents" (*OCD* 90). Peter's accusation that the heretics are as "irrational animals" sets the stage for his following statements about the destruction for which they are destined. Moreover, as Griego (2004: 8) observes, "By showing the irrationality of his opponents' views, Peter is able to reassert the honor of Christianity damaged by the false teachers' scoffing."

His second observation about the animals is that they are "born in accord with nature to be captured and destroyed." Peter echoes the axiomatic concept that beasts are born to be destroyed. Plutarch comments, for example, "Furthermore, on learning that Damon and Timotheus . . . had ruined the wives of certain mercenaries, he wrote to Parmenio ordering him, in case the men were convicted, to punish them and put them to death as wild beasts born for the destruction by mankind [ὡς θηρία ἐπὶ καταφθορᾷ τῶν ἀνθρώπων γεγονότα τιμωρησάμενον ἀποκτεῖναι, *hōs thēria epi kataphthora tōn anthrōpōn gegonota timōrēsamenon apokteinai*]" (*Alexander* 22.4.5; so Pliny the Elder, *Nat.* 8.81.219; Juvenal, *Satire* 1.141). They are born for this end, which, according to Peter, is in accord with their nature (φυσικὰ, *physika*; cf. Rom. 1:26–27; BDAG 1069; LSJ 1964). His point is not about their instincts (contra NIV; NRSV; Mayor 1907: 130; contrast Jude 10) but concerns their nature inherited from birth, which makes them objects for capture (εἰς ἅλωσιν, *eis halōsin*; Aristotle, *Hist. an.* 593A, 600A; Epictetus, *Disc.* 4.1.29: "That is why we shall call free only those animals which do not submit to captivity, but escape by dying as soon as they are captured") and destruction (φθορὰν, *phthoran*). Although this latter term is found in 1:4 and 2:19, there it refers to someone's inward depravity (see comments). The thought in 2:12 is about their destruction or death (Xenophon, *Cyr.* 7.5.64, "Of their fidelity they gave the best proof upon the fall [φθορᾷ, *phthora*] of their masters"; scholia on Nicander, *Theriaca* 795, speaks of animals "born to come to an evil end," τὰ ἐπὶ κακῇ φθορᾷ τεχθέντα, *ta epi kakē phthora techthenta*, cited in BDAG 1055). The heretics, as animals, are destined for doom.

The line between the heretics and beasts is further drawn at the end of the verse: ἐν τῇ φθορᾷ αὐτῶν καὶ φθαρήσονται (*en tē phthora autōn kai phtharēsontai*, shall even be destroyed in their destruction). The point is simply that the heretics will share (suffer as) in the destruction of the beasts, who are destined for slaughter. The expression may possibly be translated as the NKJV: they "will utterly perish in their own corruption," reflecting the Semitic idiom φθορᾷ φθαρήσεται (*phthora phtharēsetai*, utterly destroyed; Isa. 24:3; cf. Exod. 18:18; Mic. 2:10; M. Green 1987: 120). However, the inclusion of "their" (αὐτῶν, *autōn*), referring to the animals, precludes this interpretation (NIV; NRSV; Schelkle 1980: 211; Kelly 1969: 339; Schreiner 2003: 350). The topic of the present verse is the destruction of the animals, and these beasts are the immediate and logical antecedent to "their." Bauckham's suggestion (1983: 264) that "their" refers to the evil angels (so he understands "glories" of v. 10b) is unlikely, since that antecedent is too remote. Verse 10b does not speak of evil angels, and even if the reference were to evil angels, no thought of their doom is entertained in this section. While the verb "destroy" may refer to the slaughter of cattle (P.Stras. 1.24.15; MM 667), in 2:12 it points to that "eternal destruction" of the final judgment (1 Cor. 3:17; BDAG 1054). The heretics will be destroyed in the final assize as beasts who are captured and killed. Such is their nature, such is their fate.

In the midst of his comparison between the nature and fate of the animals and the heretics, Peter adds a note, taken from Jude, about the heretics' outlandish slander: ἐν οἷς ἀγνοοῦσιν βλασφημοῦντες (*en hois agnoousin blasphēmountes*, slandering that about which they are ignorant). The sense is the same as the expression in Jude 10: ὅσα . . . οὐκ οἴδασιν βλασφημοῦσιν (*hosa . . . ouk oidasin blasphēmousin*, slander whatever they do not understand). Peter draws a line between the irrationality of the beasts and the heretics' ignorance, a rhetorical point that serves to underscore the justice of their destruction according to ancient philosophical reflection on the nature of beasts (see above). Berating someone as "ignorant" was a common topic in ancient *vituperatio* (see Jude 10 and comments). For example, in *Against Apion* Josephus rails against Apion for his "shocking ignorance" (*Ag. Ap.* 2.2 §26; cf. 2.11 §130), calling him an "ignorant fool" (2.4 §37) and "blind" (2.13 §142). In Peter's view, the heretics are ignorant about the "glories" (v. 10b) whom they slander. This may be a counterpoint to the heretics' claim to insight into the supernatural order. The sin that brings them under judgment, however, is not their ignorance per se but their unwarranted slander of those beings about which they are truly

2. The Coming and the Judgment of the False Teachers
c. "These Are"—The Vices of the False Teachers
**2 Peter 2:10b–16**

ignorant (see v. 10b). These people speak great, bombastic nonsense (2:18), but in the end they are no more well informed than the beasts and hence are proper objects of retribution.

Peter continues his denunciation of the heretics: ἀδικούμενοι μισθὸν ἀδικίας, ἡδονὴν ἡγούμενοι τὴν ἐν ἡμέρᾳ τρυφήν, σπίλοι καὶ μῶμοι ἐντρυφῶντες ἐν ταῖς ἀπάταις αὐτῶν συνευωχούμενοι ὑμῖν (adikoumenoi misthon adikias, hēdonēn hēgoumenoi tēn en hēmera tryphēn, spiloi kai mōmoi entryphōntes en tais apatais autōn syneuōchoumenoi hymin, suffering the loss of the wages of unrighteousness, regarding as pleasure reveling in the daytime, spots and defects reveling in their pleasures when they feast with you). His thought is drawn, in part, from Jude 11 and 12. His reflection on the "reward" or "wages" that the heretics receive (μισθόν, misthon) is rooted in the Balaam story recounted in Jude 11 (τῇ πλάνῃ τοῦ Βαλαὰμ μισθοῦ ἐξεχύθησαν, tē planē tou Balaam misthou exechythēsan, dedicated themselves to the error of Balaam for gain), which is cited more extensively in 2 Pet. 2:15 (see comments). Peter also echoes the denunciation in Jude 12 about οἱ ἐν ταῖς ἀγάπαις ὑμῶν σπιλάδες συνευωχούμενοι ἀφόβως (hoi en tais agapais hymōn spilades syneuōchoumenoi aphobōs, they who fearlessly feast together with you are spots in your love-feasts). While dropping the comment concerning the fearless behavior of the false teachers, Peter preserves the notion that the heretics participate in the Christian feasts (συνευωχούμενοι, syneuōchoumenoi, in both texts). Peter also omits the reference to the participation ἐν ταῖς ἀγάπαις ὑμῶν (en tais agapais hymōn, in your love-feasts) but simply plays on these words by noting the way the heretics revel ἐν ταῖς ἀπάταις αὐτῶν (en tais apatais autōn, in their pleasure). He does, however, include Jude's notion that the false teachers are moral "spots" (σπιλάδες, spilades), but compounds the critique by calling them σπίλοι καὶ μῶμοι (spiloi kai mōmoi, spots and defects). It is unlikely that this subtle engineering of his source is due to our author's lapse in memory as he seeks to recall what he read sometime in Jude but rather suggests that he was engaged in a conscious modification of Jude's thought as he made it his own and applied it to this new situation (see 2:11 and comments).

The first part of verse 13 adds to Peter's thought in verse 11 about the loss that the heretics will endure: ἀδικούμενοι μισθὸν ἀδικίας (adikoumenoi misthon adikias, suffering the loss of the wages of unrighteousness). The verb ἀδικέω (adikeō) commonly suggests "doing wrong" or even "sinning" against God or the law, or in the passive (as here) "to suffer wrong" or "be wronged" (Matt. 20:13; Acts 7:26; 1 Cor. 6:8; Col. 3:25; Philem. 18; Rev. 2:11; 22:11; BDAG 20; G. Schrenk, *TDNT* 1:157–61). The source of the wrongdoing is not expressed here as in Rev. 2:11 ("Whoever conquers will not be harmed by the second death" [NRSV]; cf. Wis. 14:29). Although Peter uses a passive participle, we should hesitate before concluding that God is the one who does this damage since the verb repeatedly refers to some form of wrongdoing that is censurable. Peter's thought appears to be simply that whatever gain they

2:13

obtain from their wickedness will, in the end, be loss for them or lost to them. They cannot hold what they gain. Even the profit of their actions will be lost (cf. Philem. 18), such being the irony of the supposed gain.

By referring to the heretics' μισθὸν ἀδικίας (*misthon adikias*, the wages of unrighteousness), Peter is setting up the comparison between the heretics and Balaam (2:15). They are people who follow "the way of Balaam of Bosor, the one who loved the wages of unrighteousness." The phrase is decidedly Semitic (cf. 2 Macc. 8:33; Wis. 2:22; 10:17; Acts 1:18). Peter makes a point about the heretics' motives: they are out after gain (μισθόν, *misthon*), viewed either as wages or a reward. The avarice of the heretics is a charge previously levied against them (2:2–3). As in the case of Balaam, profit is one of their driving motivations (cf. 2 Pet. 2:2–3, 14–15; 1 Thess. 2:5; 1 Tim. 6:5; Titus 1:11; Did. 11.5–6, 12). Orators who engaged in public declamation merely for gain were universally condemned (Dio Chrysostom, *Or.* 32.11; Plutarch, *Mor.* 131A). Dio once said, "Gentlemen, I have come before you not to display my talents as a speaker nor because I want money from you, or expect your praise" (*Or.* 35.1), but he noted that greed motivated most people, not only orators (17.16). The profit the heretics gain is like that of Judas, who received "the reward of his wickedness" (Acts 1:18; ἐκ μισθοῦ τῆς ἀδικίας, *ek misthou tēs adikias*).

Peter returns to the sin of the heretics in the following participial clause: ἡδονὴν ἡγούμενοι τὴν ἐν ἡμέρᾳ τρυφήν (*hēdonēn hēgoumenoi tēn en hēmera tryphēn*, regarding as pleasure reveling in the daytime). The heretics are those who value not only monetary gain but also pleasure. The pleasure (ἡδονὴν, *hēdonēn*) they pursue is not simply the opposite of pain (though it surely is that, as 4 Macc. 1:20–21, 24, 28) or what is wholesome (Wis. 7:2; 4 Macc. 9:31) but is, rather, the fruit of desire that may even have a "malevolent tendency" (4 Macc. 1:22, 25). It was thought, however, that it could be mastered by self-control (5:23) or reason (1:33; 6:35). Such pleasures are enslaving and spiritually destructive (Luke 8:14; Titus 3:3; James 4:1, 3).

Warnings about the dangers of pleasure were not limited to Jewish and Christian writings. Dio Chrysostom (*Or.* 49.9) quipped, "What race is as knavish and intriguing and traitorous as are pleasures and lusts, by which he must never be overcome?" Lucian (*Icaromenippus* 30) noted how philosophers "spit at wealth and pleasure," although they really "indulge their passions." On the other hand, the Epicureans exalted pleasure as high virtue (hedonism) and therefore promoted the conquest of pleasure over pain. In his *Lives*, Diogenes Laertius cataloged Epicurus's life and philosophy. He included Epicurus's *Letter to Menoeceus*, in which Epicurus declares, "For the end of all our actions is to be free from pain and fear, and, when once we have attained all this, the tempest of the soul is laid. . . . When we are pained because of the absence of pleasure, then, and then only, do we feel the need of pleasure. Wherefore we call pleasure the alpha and omega of a blessed life. Pleasure is our first and kindred good" (*Ep. Men.* 10.128). Epicurus believed that "no pleasure is in itself evil" and that all fears of the mind should be eliminated. Epicurean tenets had wide circulation (see "The Opponents in 2 Peter" in the introduction).

Contrary to Jewish and Christian teaching, these heretics reflected on "pleasure" and sought it in a profligate lifestyle. This kind of debauchery was not what Epicurus himself prescribed but became, in the end, an outcome of his teaching. The later Christian critique of this philosophy underscored the rotted fruits of Epicurus's views, as Lactantius (*Div. Inst.* 3.17) noted: "If any chieftain of pirates or leader of robbers were exhorting his men to acts of violence, what other language could he employ than to say the same things which Epicurus says: that the gods take no notice; that they are not affected with anger or kind feeling; that the punishment of a future state is not to be dreaded, because the souls die after death, and there is no future state of punishment at all." Lactantius charged that Epicurus was "an advocate of most disgraceful pleasure, and said that man was born for its enjoyment." In the same way, what the heretics regarded (ἡγούμενοι, *hēgoumenoi*, with a double accusative; LSJ 763; see 1:13 and comments) as "pleasure" was not the mere absence of pain but reveling or cavorting (τὴν ... τρυφήν, *tēn ... tryphēn*). Such conduct marks the dissolute life that is self-indulgent and totally abandoned to pleasure (Herm. *Sim.* 6.5.5; *Mand.* 6.2.5; 8.3; 12.2.1; BDAG 1018). Though the word may refer simply to what delights (T. Benj. 6.3; Sir. 11:27; 37:29; Song 7:6 [7:7 Eng.]) or to luxury (T. Jos. 3.4; Wis. 19:11; Sir. 14:16; 18:32; Luke 7:25), here, as in Philo, it refers to those who "pursue eagerly luxury and voluptuousness. They applaud the dissolute life" (*Spec. Laws* 2.43 §240). This is the lifestyle of those who have abandoned themselves to luxury and sensual delights (Josephus, *Ant.* 10.10.2 §193; 16.10.1 §301) or, as Cicero commented in *Pro Caelio*, they are "fast bound in the fetters of pleasure" (47).

The scandal of the heretics' lifestyle is that they even engage in such living "in the daytime" (ἐν ἡμέρᾳ, *en hēmera*). The ancients recognized the night as the time of drunkenness and gluttony (Rom. 13:13; 1 Thess. 5:7). John Chrysostom commented, "For it is just as corrupt and wicked men do all things as in the night, escaping the notice of all, and enclosing themselves in darkness. For tell me, does not the adulterer watch for the evening, and the thief for the night? Does not the violator of the tombs carry on all his trade in the night?" (*Homilies on First Thessalonians* 9). Therefore it was particularly scandalous to participate in these activities during the daytime (Isa. 5:11; Eccles. 10:16; T. Mos. 7.4; Acts 2:15) as these heretics are doing. Their lack of public shame is astounding.

As if he has not made his point clearly enough, Peter adds that these people are σπίλοι καὶ μῶμοι ἐντρυφῶντες ἐν ταῖς ἀπάταις αὐτῶν (*spiloi kai mōmoi entryphōntes en tais apatais autōn*, spots and defects reveling in their pleasures). The Christian community is to be without "spot and defect" (3:14; Eph. 5:27). These terms do not refer to physical defect (cf. Lev. 21:17–18, 21; 24:19–20) but bring into focus the immoral life of the heretics. Dionysius of Halicarnassus (*Ant. rom.* 4.24.6) spoke, for example, of those who were "the dregs of humanity from the city" (τοὺς δυσεκκαθάρτους σπίλους ἐκ τῆς πόλεως, *tous dysekkathartous spilous ek tēs poleōs*; see Iamblichus, *Vita Pythagorica* 17.76.2; BDAG 938; MM 584; and comments on Jude 12). If the first term refers to "moral spots," the second, μῶμοι (*mōmoi*), has to do with "moral defects" (Sir. 11:31, 33; 20:24; Philo, *Sobriety* 11; MM 420; BDAG 663), although they are used synonymously. Peter reiterates the comment about their revelry using ἐντρυφῶντες (*entryphōntes*), the verbal form of τρυφή (*tryphē*, pleasure; see above). As its cognate substantive, the verb has to do with engaging in self-indulgent behavior and revelry (Xenophon, *Hell.* 4.1.30; Diodorus Siculus 19.71.3; Philo, *Spec. Laws* 3.5 §27; Tatian, *Address to the Greeks* 12.4; 4 Macc. 8:8; BDAG 341; MM 219). This reveling is driven by their quest for pleasure, which is described as ἐν ταῖς ἀπάταις αὐτῶν (*en tais apatais autōn*). While ἀπάταις (*apatais*) describes a person's deceit, deception, or trickery in other contexts (2 Thess. 2:10), the term sometimes, as here, means "pleasure" according to the second-century lexicographer Moeris; "*apatē*: deceit [πλάνη, *planē*] among the Attics, pleasure [τέρψις] among the Greeks." It was also synonymous with ἡδονή (*hēdonē*; TLNT 1:153–55; A. Oepke, TDNT 1:385; BDAG 99; cf. Mark 4:19; Luke 8:14).

The heretics are completely given over to the satisfaction of their pleasures and revel in the midst of the church's common feast: συνευωχούμενοι ὑμῖν (*syneuōchoumenoi hymin*, when they feast with you). Feasting was a common activity in the Mediterranean world (Slater 1991; for satiric accounts of such events see Juvenal, *Satire 5, How Clients Are Entertained*; Petronius, *Satyricon* 26.6–78.8). The rite we refer to as the Lord's Supper took place within the context of a feast (feasting and religion were closely intertwined; see 1 Cor. 11:17–34). The heretics Peter combats have transformed the Christian celebration into an event marked by cultural practices that are antithetical to authentic Christian feasting. A Greek feast was divided into two parts, the δεῖπνον (*deipnon*, feast or dinner) and the συμπόσιον (*symposion*, the time of drinking together), somewhat analogous to the Roman *cena* and *convivium* (see Cicero, *De senectute* 13.45, who notes that the *convivium* exalts communion among friends over wine drinking). In the latter event, water was mixed with wine in a large vessel (crater) with the strength of the mix dictated by the one who presided over the event (OCD 1461). The march toward inebriation moved forward at a set cadence.

Peter's denunciation of revelry at the time of the Christian feast echoes concerns about such events that go back to the time of Isocrates (436–338 BC), who advised, "If possible avoid drinking-parties altogether, but if ever occasion arises when you must be present, rise and take your leave before you become intoxicated; for when the mind is impaired by wine it is like chariots which have lost their drivers; for just as these plunge along in wild disorder when they miss the hands which should guide them, so the soul stumbles again and again when the intellect is impaired" (*Demon.* 32). These drinking parties were times when sensuality was given free reign (see Ovid, *Amores* [*Love Affairs*] 1.4.1–70; Propertius, *Elegies* 3.8). Unsurprisingly, the "rules of conduct" found inscribed on the walls of the dining room (triclinium) of one house in Pompeii says, "Keep your lascivious looks and bedroom eyes away from another man's wife. Maintain a semblance of decency on your face" (Shelton

1988: 317). Peter's denunciation of the adulterous desires of the heretics in the following verse is well understood within the context of feasting. They approach the Lord's Supper as they would any pagan feast.

The heretics have transformed the communal meal of the Christian community **2:14** into a time to pursue their lustful desires. Peter continues his denunciation of the heretics by exposing their lascivious intent: ὀφθαλμοὺς ἔχοντες μεστοὺς μοιχαλίδος καὶ ἀκαταπαύστους ἁμαρτίας (*ophthalmous echontes mestous moichalidos kai akatapaustous hamartias*, They have eyes full of longing for an adulteress, and they do not cease from sin). Peter's denunciation does not depend on Jude either at this point or in the rest of the verse. We suspect, however, that he echoes the teaching of Jesus about the source of sexual sin: "But I say to you that everyone who looks at a woman with lust has already committed adultery with her in his heart" (Matt. 5:28 NRSV), a logion that became part of the fabric of early Christian teaching (1 John 2:16).

The notion that sexual vice begins with what a person observes was voiced, however, by a larger chorus of ancient moralists. In Plutarch's discussion of compliancy ("For compliancy is excess of shame," *Mor.* 528E), he strikes the contrast with the shameless by using language that is strikingly similar to Peter's: "And so, as the orator said that the shameless man had harlots, not maidens, in his eyes" (*Mor.* 528E–F), a phrase that appears to have been proverbial (Pseudo-Longinus, *On the Sublime* 4.5; the Greek historian Timaeus, *Sicilian History* 4.5). Gellius (*Attic Nights* 3.5.2) recalls Plutarch's comments about the rich man who had "wanton glances, teeming with seduction and voluptuousness," while Plutarch himself recalls a scene from one of Menander's plays when those attending a banquet are exposed to the wiles of a brothel-keeper "who brings a certain very grand courtesan before them. 'Each kept his head down, nibbling at dessert'" (*Mor.* 706B). Profit is the motivation of the one who parades the courtesan: "Yes, the loans at interest are a severe chastiser of incontinence, and to make a man loosen his purse-strings is not a very easy matter" (706B). Peter's description of the heretics as those who are not only lusty but also greedy enticers of the unstable is not far removed from the scenario Plutarch paints. This was hardly a topos limited to Christians (cf. Fornberg 1977: 104).

Banquets (2 Pet. 2:13) were a legendary forum for such sexual enticement. Ovid's *Art of Love* describes the best venues where "women can be caught," including both the theater and banquets, where wine flowed (1.229–52). Ovid vividly describes such seduction at a banquet in his book *Amores* (*Love Affairs*), where the seducer and the lover seek secret means to touch without being discovered by the woman's husband: "When he shall press the couch, you will come yourself with modest mien to recline beside him—in secret give my foot a touch! Keep your eyes on me, to get my nods and the language of my eyes; and catch my stealthy signs, and yourself return them" (1.4.15–20; see the full, passionate account in 1.4). Peter similarly speaks of the heretics as those whose eyes are "full of *adulteress*" (μοιχαλίδος, *moichalidos*; Rom.

7:3; see BDAG 656, "eyes that are full of [desire for] an adulteress"). They see women as objects of sexual desire whom they long to seduce.

Peter's following clause, ἀκαταπαύστους ἀμαρτίας (*akatapaustous hamartias*, they do not cease from sin) should be read in conjunction with his denunciation of the heretics' lust: the "sin" that the heretics unceasingly seek is sexual. The adjective ἀκαταπαύστους (*akatapaustous*) appears rather rarely. At times it is used by historians to speak of civil or social strife (Polybius 4.17.4; Josephus, *J.W.* 7.10.2 §421). In the papyri, however, its use is limited to love charms such as the one that pleads, "Bring Termoutis whom Sophia bore, to Zoel whom Droser bore, with crazed and unceasing, everlasting love, now quickly!" (*NewDocs* 2:45). Peter sees the adulterous "love" of the heretics as a sin that is incessant. This is not the first time that our author highlights the sexual immorality of the heretics, nor will it be the last (2:2, 7, 10, 18).

The heretics are hardly content to keep to themselves but seek to turn others to their way by any means possible: δελεάζοντες ψυχὰς ἀστηρίκτους (*deleazontes psychas astēriktous*, luring unstable people). Peter repeatedly warns of their attempt to persuade others by deceptive means (2:2–3, 18–19; 3:17; and comments). Our author employs a fishing metaphor to describe their tactics (cf. the use of the verb in James 1:14; 2 Pet. 2:18). The heretics lure their catch with bait (δέλεαρ, *delear*), implying that they employ deceptive means to persuade others to their way (see 2:3 and comments; Josephus, *J.W.* 5.3.4 §120; Philo, *Rewards* 4 §25; see also Xenophon, *Mem.* 2.1.4; Isocrates, *De pace* 34; Lucian, *Fisherman* 48). He does not state what bait they use, but when he returns to the thought of the way the heretics entice new believers in 2:18, Peter warns of the way they employ the "licentious desires of the flesh" as bait (see comments). His present discussion about the sexual vice of the heretics suggests that the enticement in mind in 2:14 is sexual as well. Plato commented similarly that pleasure (ἡδονήν, *hēdonēn*; see 2 Pet. 2:13) was "a most mighty lure to evil" (μέγιστον κακοῦ δέλεαρ, *megiston kakou delear*; so Philo, *Good Person* 22 §159).

The heretics cast this lure well as they sought to catch ψυχὰς ἀστηρίκτους (*psychas astēriktous*, unstable people), those "who have only recently escaped from the ones who live in error" (2:18). Peter calls these folk "souls" (ψυχάς, *psychas*), a term that here as elsewhere refers to the whole person and not some component part of a human being (Gen. 2:7; 1 Pet. 1:9, 22; 2:11; 3:20; 4:19; Jude 15). Those enticed are "unstable" or weak and not firmly established in the faith. Such souls can therefore be easily moved with the proper persuasion (see 1:12 and comments). Due to the tremors that the early church experienced through persecution and teaching that was contrary to apostolic tradition, a principal concern of the leadership was the establishment of believers, which, however, was ultimately viewed as a divine act (Acts 14:22; 1 Thess. 3:2, 13; 2 Thess. 2:17; 3:3; 1 Pet. 5:10). Those not firmly established were an easy catch.

Peter returns to the heretics' greed by saying of them καρδίαν γεγυμνασμένην πλεονεξίας ἔχοντες (*kardian gegymnasmenēn pleonxias echontes*, having hearts trained in greed). His language evokes images of the gymnasium, a prominent feature in the cities of the Mediterranean world that had come under Greek influence. These were centers founded for the physical training of young citizens, which then became venues for mental as well as physical education, serving as secondary schools in the community (*OCD* 659–60). The concept of "training" the body was therefore applied to the training of the whole person, especially the moral training someone would receive either via philosophers (Epictetus, *Disc.* 1.26.3) or through the circumstances of life ("I am long trained in the athletics of life," Philo, *Joseph* 5 §26; Isocrates, *Demon.* 21). The king would therefore "train his soul" (Isocrates, *Ad Nicoclem* 10–11; Peter speaks of training the "heart"; cf. 2 Pet. 1:19). The way moral training was undertaken became a common topos (Epictetus, *Disc.* 2.18.27; Josephus, *Ant.* 3.1.4 §15; and Epictetus's tract in *Disc.* 3.12, "Of Training" [Περὶ ἀσκήσεως, *Peri askēseōs*, equivalent of γυμνάζω, *gymnazō*; LSJ 257]); unsurprisingly, *gymnazō* as here is also picked up by other NT authors (1 Tim. 4:7; Heb. 5:14; 12:11). Peter turns the metaphor to highlight the efforts the heretics invest in training themselves in vice rather than virtue, as ones "trained in greed" (Bigg 1901: 283 calls the phrase "semi-poetic"). At the beginning of his *vituperatio* against the heretics, Peter exposes their financial motivation for exploiting members of the church (2:3 and comments). This was a common charge in *vituperatio* (L. Johnson 1989: 430), although in Peter's hand it was not empty rhetoric. The heretics demonstrate a pattern of exploitation that couples sex and money in the same way as Balaam enticed Israel (see 2:15–16 and comments).

In a final salvo before the comparison with Balaam, Peter tags the heretics as κατάρας τέκνα (*kataras tekna*, cursed children). The expression "children of" (here lit., "children of a curse") was a Semitic idiom that classed someone according to some specific characteristic (Eph. 2:3; 5:8; 1 Pet. 1:14; BDAG 995). The idiom makes the charge ring with an elevated, though not un-Greek, style (Deissmann 1901: 161–66). What characterizes the heretics is that a curse is on them. Peter is apparently thinking ahead to the Balaam story (or recalling Jude's account of it), which includes a curse that Balaam could not pronounce (Num. 23:25–26; Deut. 23:5). But here the tables are turned as the heretics are under a curse, most likely that which is pronounced by God (Deut. 11:28–29; 28:15, 45; 29:27; Prov. 3:33; Sir. 41:9–10; Gal. 3:10, 13; Heb. 6:8; James 3:10). Those accursed are under divine judgment. The very verdict that the heretics have denied would ever be pronounced is on them (see "The Opponents in 2 Peter" in the introduction). The irony in this revelation is thick. This is not a simple wish on Peter's part that the heretics be accursed, as if he were invoking a curse formulae (see, e.g., *NewDocs* 2:46), but a recognition of their standing before God.

The heretics combine the sin of sexual immorality and greed plus the entice- **2:15**
ment of others, thus suggesting the archetypal example of Balaam, whose sin becomes the topic of this and the following verse. Peter denounces the heretics

as ones who, having left the path of righteousness, now follow Balaam's way: καταλείποντες εὐθεῖαν ὁδὸν ἐπλανήθησαν, ἐξακολουθήσαντες τῇ ὁδῷ τοῦ Βαλαὰμ τοῦ Βοσόρ, ὃς μισθὸν ἀδικίας ἠγάπησεν (*kataleipontes eutheian hodon eplanēthēsan, exakolouthēsantes tē hodō tou Balaam tou Bosor, hos misthon adikias ēgapēsen,* They have wandered off, departing from the straight way and following after the way of Balaam of Bosor, the one who loved the wages of unrighteousness). In singling out only Balaam, Peter compresses the triple denunciation of Cain, Balaam, and Korah from his source, Jude 11: "Woe to them! Because they went the way of Cain, dedicated themselves to the error of Balaam for gain, and perish in the rebellion of Korah" (see comments). Instead of Jude's "way of Cain" (τῇ ὁδῷ τοῦ Κάϊν, *tē hodō tou Kain*), Peter speaks of "the way of Balaam of Bosor," which the heretics follow (ἐξακολουθήσαντες, *exakolouthēsantes*). The verb is suggested by Jude's charge that the heretics "went (ἐπορεύθησαν, *eporeuthēsan*) the way of Cain." Peter retains the traditional denunciation of Balaam as one motivated by greed (Jude 11: "for gain," μισθοῦ, *misthou*). But instead of emphasizing Balaam's dedication to error, which was motivated by hopes of profit, our author states that he "loved the wages of unrighteousness," as do the heretics he combats (2 Pet. 2:14–15). The heretics Jude faces are committed to "error" (τῇ πλάνῃ, *tē planē,* vv. 11, 13), but Peter makes the point that the heretics themselves are in error or deceived, having wandered off as apostates (ἐπλανήθησαν, *eplanēthēsan*). Although Peter draws on the Balaam story as suggested by Jude, his development of the typology is much fuller as he echoes the wider Balaam traditions.

Peter continues his denunciation of the heretics as he points to their apostasy: καταλείποντες εὐθεῖαν ὁδὸν ἐπλανήθησαν (*kataleipontes eutheian hodon eplanēthēsan,* They have wandered off, departing from the straight way). Peter has already commented on the heretics' apostasy from the faith (2:1 and comments), a point that he here restates by noting that they have "wandered off." Although the verb ἐπλανήθησαν (*eplanēthēsan*) is in the passive voice, the sense is active in this and numerous other texts (Matt. 18:12–13; Mark 12:24, 27; Heb. 3:10; 11:38; James 5:19; 1 Pet. 2:25). The image is of people who wander or animals that go astray (note the literal sense in Matt. 18:12–13; Heb. 11:38), but the verb is also used metaphorically (1 Pet. 2:25; Isa. 53:6; Ps. 119:176 [118:176 LXX]). The heretics' wandering is not due to disorientation or "getting lost" but is rather willful apostasy from God (Deut. 4:19; 13:1–18; 30:17; Wis. 12:24; James 5:19), here described more fully as "departing from the straight way" (Deut. 11:28; Prov. 21:16; Wis. 5:6). This sin is also more than turning aside from truth to error (cf. Plotinus, *Enneads* 6.7.13; LSJ 1411; H. Braun, *TDNT* 6:230–31). The metaphor of God's straight way (εὐθεῖαν ὁδόν, *eutheian hodon*) is quite common in biblical literature (1 Sam. 12:23; Ps. 27:11 [26:11 LXX]; Prov. 2:16; Hos. 14:9 [14:10 LXX]; Dan. 3:27), and its variants appear frequently in Acts (13:10, "right ways of the Lord"; 16:17, "way of salvation"; 18:25, "way of the Lord"; 18:26, "way of God"; or Christianity as "the Way," 19:9, 23; 22:4; 24:14, 22). Living in obedience to God constitutes walking in that way; departing from it is the core of apostasy and rebellion against him (Acts 13:10; Deut. 11:28; Prov. 2:13). In the LXX the expression πορεύομαι τῇ ὁδῷ (*poreuomai tē hodō*, go in the way, as Jude 11) refers to the direction of a person's life or someone's moral conduct, whether good or evil (Pss. 32:8 [31:8 LXX]; 81:13 [80:14 LXX]; 101:6 [100:6 LXX]; Prov. 1:15; 2:13; 28:18; Isa. 2:3; Bar. 4:13; Tob. 1:3; 4:5). Therefore to leave or depart from (καταλείποντες, *kataleipontes*) the "straight way" is to reorient the life away from God and forsake him and his commandments (Jer. 2:17; Bar. 4:1; 1 Macc. 2:21). This verb suggests abandonment and finality (LSJ 898; BDAG 520).

Peter highlights the audacity of the heretics' sin in their abandonment of God's way in favor of the greedy way of Balaam: ἐξακολουθήσαντες τῇ ὁδῷ τοῦ Βαλαὰμ τοῦ Βοσόρ (*exakolouthēsantes tē hodō tou Balaam tou Bosor*, following after the way of Balaam of Bosor; see the additional notes for discussion of the textual problems surrounding Βοσόρ, *Bosor*). In the Gospels, discipleship is summarized by the call "to follow" Christ (ἀκολουθέω, *akoloutheō*, in Matt. 4:20, 22; Mark 2:14; John 1:37; 21:22). Peter has already used the cognate "to follow after" (ἐξακολουθήσουσιν, *exakolouthēsousin*) in 2:2, and *exakolouthēsantes* in 1:16, where the verb means adherring to what is false (see comments; Josephus, *Ant.* proem 4 §22; P.Berlin 7927.8: μυθολογίαις ἐπακολουθοῦσι, *mythologiais epakolouthousi*, they follow mythology). People who "follow after" something submit to some form of authority in their thought or actions (T. Naph. 3.3; T. Iss. 6.2; BDAG 344) and, in the present case, the heretics have committed themselves to "the way of Balaam" as his disciples. Great sinners were considered to be disciples of Balaam. As *m. 'Abot* 5.14 says, the "disciple of Balaam" is one who has "an evil eye, a proud soul, and a haughty spirit." The "way" Balaam traveled when going to curse Israel is a central element in the Balaam story (Num. 22:23, 31, 34). The "way" was not only the road he traveled but also his moral intent, which was not good (Num. 22:32) and therefore brought him into opposition with God.

Peter continues his denunciation of the heretics who follow the way of Balaam by stressing the prophet's greed: ὃς μισθὸν ἀδικίας ἠγάπησεν (*hos misthon adikias ēgapēsen*, the one who loved the wages of unrighteousness). Jude 11 accuses Balaam of greed, and Peter has already denounced the heretics as people who seek the μισθὸν ἀδικίας (*misthon adikias*, the wages of unrighteousness, 2:13 and comments). Balaam had become known as a person who was driven by greed and so provoked the sin of the Israelites with the Moabite women (Philo, *Moses* 1.48 §§266–68; 1.54–55 §§295–304; Josephus, *Ant.* 4.6.6–9 §§126–40; Tg. Ps.-J. on Num. 24:14, 25; 31:8; Ps.-Philo, *L.A.B.* 18.7, 12–14). Balaam had been promised great reward to curse Israel (Num. 22:7, 17) and, although he could not do that, the hope of profit motivated him to find some way to seduce Israel. Rabbinic interpretation found evidence in Num. 22:18 that he was a "covetous soul." The rabbis "understand it as yet another sign of Balaam's greed" (Vermès 1961b: 133). When Balaam thought his hope for gain was lost, he encouraged Balak to entice Israel to sexual sin (Num. 25:1–5; 31:16; Josephus, *Ant.* 4.6.6 §§126–30). The heretics engage in the same practice. Peter's warning against the heretics cannot be more dire. They, too, entice others to sexual sin and are motivated by greed (2:14, 18).

**2:16**   In drawing the line between the heretics and Balaam, Peter goes well beyond Jude's recounting of the Balaam story, recalling contours of the tradition that Jude left to one side: ἔλεγξιν δὲ ἔσχεν ἰδίας παρανομίας· ὑποζύγιον ἄφωνον ἐν ἀνθρώπου φωνῇ φθεγξάμενον ἐκώλυσεν τὴν τοῦ προφήτου παραφρονίαν (*elenxin de eschen idias paranomias; hypozygion aphonon en anthrōpou phōnē phthenxamenon ekōlysen tēn tou prophētou paraphronian*, but was accused for his own unlawful deed; a speechless donkey, speaking in a human voice, restrained the prophet's irrationality). Peter compares the transgression of Balaam with that of the heretics by referencing Balaam's "own [ἰδίας, *idias*] unlawful deed" (cf. 3:17 and comments). The language that Peter uses to describe Balaam's transgression and the subsequent rebuke suggest a legal accusation (ἔλεγξιν δὲ ἔσχεν, *elenxin de eschen*, was accused), which was warranted because of his illegal action (παρανομίας, *paranomias*, unlawful deed). Ἐλέγχω (*elenchō*), the verbal form of the rare ἔλεγξιν, refers to reproof or accusation in legal cases (MM 202; as in P.Amh. II.33[34]: "If any of these who are injuring the revenues is in the future convicted of having acted as advocate in any case, send him to us under arrest"; see Jude 15 and comments). The participial form used as a substantive may mean "the prosecutor" (MM 202). The related noun, ἔλεγχος (*elenchos*, proof, evidence), likewise appears in judicial contexts (P.Stras. I.41[6]: "Then if he has confidence in the proofs of his accusation, he shall enter upon the more serious law suit"; MM 202; BDAG 315; LSJ 530). Peter has in mind more than a mere rebuke but implies that a legal charge was laid against Balaam. The reason for the accusation, indicated by the genitive, which is occasionally used with verbs of accusing (BDF §178; cf. Acts 19:40), is the prophet's "illegal deed" (παρανομίας, *paranomias*). This term, found only here in the NT, points to a violation of law (4 Macc. 2:11, "so that one rebukes her when she breaks the law" [διὰ τὴν παρανομίαν αὐτὴν ἀπελέγχων, *dia tēn paranomian autēn apelenchōn*—note the verb]; 4:19; 5:13; Ps. 37:7 [36:7 LXX]; Ps. Sol. 4.1, 12; 8.9; 17.20; see MM 488, illegality or illegal action; cf. the verbal form in Acts 23:3). Balaam, like the heretics, was in clear violation of (God's) law and was summarily charged or accused for his act of going out against Israel. Not until the next clause do we discover that the one who lays the charge is none other than Balaam's ass.

The account Peter draws on is Num. 22:21–35, where Balaam is restrained from going out to curse Israel by the angel who stands in the way. Balaam's ass sees the angel of the Lord with drawn sword and tries to avoid the encounter with him. Balaam strikes the donkey for its insolence and, in response, "the LORD opened the donkey's mouth, and she said to Balaam, 'What have I done to you to make you beat me these three times?'" (22:28 NIV). After Balaam verbally abuses the beast, she speaks again: "Am I not your donkey on which you have ridden all your life to this day? Have I ever been accustomed to do so to you?" (22:30, cf. RSV). Peter, however, frames the story somewhat differently and ascribes a more critical role to the donkey than merely objecting to Balaam's mistreatment of her: ὑποζύγιον ἄφωνον ἐν ἀνθρώπου φωνῇ φθεγξάμενον ἐκώλυσεν τὴν τοῦ προφήτου παραφρονίαν (*hypozygion aphōnon en anthrōpou phōnē phthenxamenon ekōlusen tēn tou prophētou paraphronian*, a speechless donkey, speaking in a human voice, restrained the prophet's irrationality). Peter sees the ass as the one who levels the accusation against Balaam and thus restrains him. His use of the Balaam story is closer to the targums than to Num. 22:31–35, which identifies the Angel of the Lord as the one who accuses Balaam of acting perversely. Targum Neof. on Num. 22:30 reads, "And the donkey said to Balaam: 'Where are you going, wicked Balaam? You lack understanding! What! If you are not able to curse me who am an unclean beast, and die in this world and who do not enter the world to come, how much less are you able to curse the sons of Abraham, of Isaac and Jacob, on whose account the world was created from the beginning, and for whose merits it is remembered before them?'" Likewise, Tg. Ps.-J. on Num. 22:30 records the donkey's rebuke, "Woe to you Balaam [you are] lacking in knowledge." Josephus (*Ant.* 4.6.3 §§109–10) also ascribes a fuller role to the beast as the one who restrains Balaam from completing his mission.

Peter calls Balaam's ass a ὑποζύγιον ἄφωνον (*hypozygion aphōnon*, speechless donkey) instead of an ὄνος (*onos*, donkey; LXX translation of אָתוֹן, *'ātôn*, she-ass) as in Num. 22:28, 30, another indicator that Peter is not dependent directly on the Numbers passage. This beast of burden (Matt. 21:5) is incapable of human speech (Acts 8:32; Strabo 6.1.9), likely a marker not only of its linguistic incapacity but also its lack of rationality. Philo's comment on the beast highlights this very point: "For the unreasoning animal [ἀλόγου ζῴου, *alogou zōou*] showed a superior power of sight to him who claimed to see not only the world but the world's Maker" (*Moses* 1.49 §272). Animals were generally considered to be lacking in *ratio* (OCD 90–91), although Aristotle, Pliny, and Plutarch all discussed what human characteristics animals possessed. Peter appears to be setting up the deeply ironic contrast between the dumb ass, who speaks rationally, and the prophet Balaam, who is mad or irrational. The beast restrains the prophet by "speaking in a human voice" (ἐν ἀνθρώπου φωνῇ φθεγξάμενον, *en anthrōpou phōnē phthenxamenon*). While animals may make sounds (φθεγξάμενον, *phthenxamenon*; LSJ 1927; Xenophon, *Anab.* 6.1.23; Aristotle, *Hist. an.* 618A), they do not have the capacity for speech (see the discussion in Aristotle, *Hist. an.* 535A–536B). But this ass speaks "in a human voice," a point made twice in Josephus's telling of the Balaam story (φωνὴν ἀνθρωπίνην, *phōnēn anthrōpinēn*; *Ant.* 4.6.3 §§109–10). Stories of animals that spoke circulated among the Greeks as well. Herodotus (2.55) tells of the tale of a dove that "uttered there human speech" (αὐδάξασθαι φωνῇ ἀνθρωπηίῃ, *audaxasthai phōnē anthrōpēiē*), although he deconstructs the story (2.57).[3] Homer (*Il.* 19.404–10) has a similar tale connected with divine

3. "I suppose that these women were called 'doves' by the people of Dedona because they spoke a strange language, and the people thought it like the cries of birds; presently the woman

judgment: "Then from beneath the yoke spoke to him the horse Xanthus, . . . and the goddess, white-armed Hera, gave him speech: 'Yes indeed, still for this time will we save you, mighty Achilles, though the day of doom is near you, nor we be the cause of it, but the mighty god and overpowering Fate." We are left to infer that God likewise gives Balaam's ass the capacity to speak his word of judgment.

Opening its mouth, the donkey ἐκώλυσεν τὴν τοῦ προφήτου παραφρονίαν (*ekōlysen tēn tou prophētou paraphronian*, restrained the prophet's irrationality). In Peter's telling, the ass and not the angel restrained or hindered (ἐκώλυσεν, *ekōlysen*; BDAG 580; Acts 16:6; 27:43; Rom. 1:13; 1 Thess. 2:16; 1 Tim. 4:3) Balaam from carrying out his mission. Balaam is here called a "prophet," which, again, is not the term used in Numbers to describe him. Josephus called him "the best diviner [μάντις, *mantis*] of his day" (*Ant.* 4.6.2 §104) while Philo designated him as a soothsayer (μαντικῆς, *mantikēs*; *Moses* 1.48 §264; and μάντις, *mantis*; *Moses* 1.50 §276), stressing his predictions (*Moses* 1.48 §§264–65). Philo also notes that he possessed the "prophetic spirit" (προφητικοῦ πνεύματος, *prophētikou pneumatos*; 1.50 §277). In Pseudo-Philo, he is an "interpreter of dreams" (*L.A.B.* 18.2) as also in Tg. Ps.-J. on Num. 22:5. In Peter's telling, one who is a spokesman for God as a prophet is countered by the dumb ass, whose mouth God opens. Peter likely has one eye fixed on the heretics, who themselves claim divine authority for their views (2:1). Previously in this paragraph Peter has compared them to "irrational beasts" (2:12), and now in a similar way they are compared with the prophet Balaam's "irrationality" (παραφρονίαν, *paraphronian*). The charge is similar to that found in the targums (Tg. Neof. on Num. 22:30: "You lack understanding"; Tg. Ps.-J. on Num. 22:5: "the son of Beor, who acted foolishly"; Tg. Ps.-J. on Num. 22:30: "[you are] lacking knowledge") and elsewhere (Philo, *Names* 37 §203; *Moses* 1.53 §293). The term Peter uses, found only here in biblical literature, denotes a "state or condition of irrationality, madness, insanity" (BDAG 772; LSJ 1330; cf. the verbal form in 2 Cor. 11:23 and παραφρόνησις, *paraphronēsis*, madness, in Zech. 12:4). Balaam is like a beast, without reason, and therefore deranged. The one who should be able to speak from God lacks rationality. And, as Neyrey (1993: 216) reminds us, "Lack of rationality connotes also ignorance of a rational way of life as well as absence of self-control" (Philo, *Alleg. Interp.* 2.17 §§69–70). The heretics follow in Balaam's way (2 Pet. 2:15). Why should anyone heed them?

## Additional Notes

**2:11.** While a number of MSS and versions omit the phrase παρὰ κυρίῳ/κυρίου (*para kyriō/kyriou*; A, Ψ, 33, 81, 614, 630, 1505, 1881, 2464, 2495, Vulgate, Coptic, Ethiopic), its inclusion is well attested

---

spoke what they could understand, and that is why they say that the dove uttered human speech; as long as she spoke in her foreign language, they thought her voice was like the voice of a bird. For how could a dove utter the speech of men? The tale that the dove was black signifies that the woman was Egyptian."

either with the genitive κυρίου (*kyriou*; $\mathfrak{P}^{72}$, 1241, some Vulgate MSS, some Syriac MSS) or the dative κυρίῳ (*kyriō*; ℵ, B, C, 322, 323, 945, 1175, 1243, 1292, 1739, 1852, 2298, 𝔐). The wide evidence in favor of the prepositional phrase argues for its inclusion, while the dative κυρίῳ (*kyriō*) enjoys stronger attestation than does the genitive. Although the phrase παρὰ κυρίου (*para kyriou*) is the more difficult reading since it suggests that a "blaspheming judgment" could be attributed to God, its inclusion in the uncials ℵ, B, C argues strongly in its favor. See the discussion supporting this reading in Metzger 1994: 633; Kraus 2000.

**2:13.** ἀδικούμενοι (*adikoumenoi*, suffering the loss) is strongly attested ($\mathfrak{P}^{72}$ ℵ B P Ψ), although the alternative κομιούμενοι (*komioumenoi*, receiving) is hardly without witness (ℵ^c A C K 049, along with minuscules). See Metzger 1994: 634. The clause is quite difficult to understand, so much so that some scribes substituted κομιούμενοι (*komioumenoi*, receiving, as KJV, NKJV) for ἀδικούμενοι since it is more commonly linked with μισθός (*misthos*, reward, wages; Lucian, *Phalaris* 2.5; 2 Macc. 8:33: τὸν ἄξιον τῆς δυσσεβίας ἐκομίσατο μισθόν, *ton axion tēs dyssebias ekomisato misthon*, they received the fitting reward for impiety).

**2:14.** Due to the difficulty of the reading μοιχαλίδος (*moichalidos*, adulteress), some witnesses read μοιχείας (*moicheias*, adultery; Ψ and reflected in the Ethiopic, Georgian, and Slavic versions). Others include the rare μοιχαλίας (*moichalias*, adultery; ℵ A 33 Ephraem Syrus). The reading followed here is the most difficult and enjoys strong MSS support ($\mathfrak{P}^{72}$ B C 81 and most minuscules).

**2:15.** Balaam is commonly identified as the son of Beor (Βαλααμ υἱὸς Βεωρ, *Balaam huios Beōr*, in Num. 22:5; 24:3, 15; 31:8; Deut. 23:5; Mic. 6:5; and τὸν Βαλααμ τὸν τοῦ Βεωρ, *ton Balaam ton tou Beōr*, in Josh. 13:22). Unsurprisingly, some MSS and versions attempt to harmonize 2 Pet. 2:15, which reads Βαλαὰμ τοῦ Βοσόρ (*Balaam tou Bosor*), with the common name of Balaam (βεωρ, *Beōr*, in B 453 vg^mss syr^ph cop^sa arm, and so Augustine), but the strong weight of the textual evidence favors the reading Βοσόρ (*Bosor*, in $\mathfrak{P}^{72}$ ℵ² A^c C Ψ plus minuscules, the 𝔐, and it^ar,z vg syr^h cop^bo geo).[4] Clearly Βοσόρ (*Bosor*) is the more difficult reading. A common explanation of Peter's Βαλαὰμ τοῦ Βοσόρ (*Balaam tou Bosor*) is that the author wishes to play on the Hebrew בָּשָׂר (*bāśār*, flesh), styling Balaam as the "son of flesh," thus impugning his character (Bauckham 1983: 267; M. Green 1987: 125; Moo 1996: 128; Schreiner 2003: 354).[5] Later Jewish tradition did play on Balaam's name (*b. Sanh.* 105b says, "Balaam denotes that he corrupted a people [בְּלַע עָם, *bālah 'am*]. The son of Beor [denotes] that he committed bestiality [בְּעִיר, *bĕ'îr*]." However, the particular ascription found in 2:15 would be unparalleled (Bigg 1901: 284). We are left to wonder why *Bosor* would be used instead of *Bāsār*, the transliteration of the Hebrew for "flesh." In either case, would the first readers have any hope of understanding this oblique critique? However, Peter may be referring not to Balaam's father but to the place from which he came. A city called Bosor was located in Syria (not to be confused with Bozrah, located southeast of the Dead Sea), and according to Num. 23:7, Balaam came from Aram, the state around Damascus. Likewise, Num. 22:5 locates Balaam at Pethor "near the river, in his native land," Pethor being situated west of the Euphrates in Aram. Though the descriptions of Aram's location are "noticeably vague, they suggest the general region that included central Syria and extended to the Euphrates" (T. L. Brensinger, *ABD* 5:288). Although no other text identifies Balaam with Bosor, Balaam is associated with this region. What appears to some as "'Peter's' mistake" (Kelly 1969: 343) could, in fact, come from someone who knew the region and the whole Balaam story quite well. Hays (2004), however, takes a different tack. He notes that Balaam's home was Bezer, a city in Aram (Num. 23:7),

---

4. Codex ℵ conflates the original Βοσόρ (*Bosor*) with the patronymic Βεωρ (*Beōr*) and so reads Βεωρσόρ (*Beōorsor*).

5. Zahn 1909: 2.292 suggests the unlikely explanation that Peter's Galilean accent accounts for the change from *Beōr* to *Bosor*.

and this city was called Βοσόρ (*Bosor*) in 1 Macc. 5:25, 36. However, "in the 14th century B.C.E. (the approximate era in which the Balaam events took place) Bezer was an independent Canaanite city kingdom ... and thus could not be Balaam's hometown." Balaam is identified rather with Pethor (Deut. 23:4), a city some 550 km (342 miles) distant from the Canaanite Bezer (Hays 2004: 106). Hays (2004: 105) forwards another suggestion, arguing that "the development of the Balaam traditions in tandem with the Edomite king-lists of Gen 36:32, 1 Chr 1:43, and Job 42:17d (LXX only) reveals a tightly intertwined history that paved the way for the unintentional replacement of Βεώρ with Βοσόρ. The confusion of numerous other names and places associated with the two titles in the Septuagint and Targums witness to a trajectory which culminated in the textual variants of 2 Peter 2.15."

# d. "These Are"—The Seduction of the False Teachers (2:17–22)

This section of the letter presents Peter's second round of denunciations of the heretics (cf. 10b–16). Once again he highlights their doom as well as warning the believers about their arrogance and their attempt to seduce the ones who have only recently become converts (vv. 17–18). The heretics offer "freedom," a state extremely valued across the philosophical spectrum. The vanity of their offer is evident in that the errorists themselves are nothing more than people enslaved by their own corruption (v. 19). The primary focus of the latter part of the section is the problem of apostasy, both that of the heretics themselves and the people whom they seek to entice. Peter reminds his readers that the end of those who turn back is worse than the state in which they began (v. 20). Better never to have known the way than to know it and turn from it (v. 21). To bolster his point, he appeals to two well-known proverbs that highlight the absurdity of the heretics' apostasy. Peter's critique of the heretics' state contrasts sharply with their own aggrandizement.

## Exegesis and Exposition

[17]These are springs without water and mists driven by the storm, for whom the gloom of darkness has been kept. [18]For by uttering grand empty things, they entice with the licentious desires of the flesh those who have only ⌜recently⌝ escaped from the ones who live in error. [19]Although they promise them freedom, they themselves are slaves of corruption. For that by which someone is conquered, to that a person has been enslaved. [20]For if, having escaped the defilements of the world in the knowledge of our Lord and Savior Jesus Christ, they are overcome by them having been entangled again, their last state has become worse than the first. [21]For it would have been better for them not to have known the way of righteousness than, having known it, to turn from the holy commandment that was handed down to them. [22]What the maxim says is true regarding them: The dog returns to its own vomit, and, The sow, having washed, returns to wallowing in the mud.

Peter redoubles his effort in denouncing the heretics, once again drawing on Jude as his source, which he adapts to his own ends. He reintroduces the heretics with the familiar refrain from Jude's preface to his denunciations, "These are" (cf. Jude 8, 10, 16, 19), here specifically drawing on Jude 12–13. Peter states that Οὗτοί εἰσιν πηγαὶ ἄνυδροι καὶ ὁμίχλαι ὑπὸ λαίλαπος ἐλαυνόμεναι, οἷς ὁ ζόφος τοῦ σκότους τετήρηται (*Houtoi eisin pēgai anydroi kai homichlai hypo lailapos elaunomenai, hois ho zophos tou skotous tetērētai*, These are springs without water and mists driven by the storm, for whom the gloom of darkness has been kept). Instead of Jude's "clouds without rain" or water (νεφέλαι ἄνυδροι, *nephelai anydrio*), Peter refers to the heretics as waterless springs (πηγαὶ ἄνυδροι, *pēgai anydroi*). Jude comments that the heretics are as clouds "driven by the wind" (ὑπὸ ἀνέμων παραφερόμεναι, *hypo anemōn parapheromenai*), but Peter alters the thought slightly to speak of the false teachers as "mists driven by the storm" (ὁμίχλαι ὑπὸ λαίλαπος ἐλαυνόμεναι, *homichlai hypo lailapos elaunomenai*). Jude 13 lays out the consequences of the heretics' error: οἷς ὁ ζόφος τοῦ σκότους εἰς αἰῶνα τετήρηται (*hois ho zophos tou skotous eis aiōna tetērētai*, for whom the nether gloom of darkness is kept forever). Second Peter 2:17 borrows the phrase almost exactly, leaving out only εἰς αἰῶνα (*eis aiōna*, forever) and refraining from coupling it with the notion that the heretics are "wild waves of the sea" and "wandering stars." Peter takes pains to preserve some of the central ideas of his source, highlighting the heretics' unproductive and ineffective nature as well as their coming judgment, but reworks the wording in his adaptation for his own readers.

Peter begins his second round of denunciations of the heretics with the rhetorical marker οὗτοί εἰσιν (*houtoi eisin*, These are), which not only signals a new paragraph but also turns attention back to the heretics after the comparison with Balaam in the preceding verses (2:15–16). Peter's first charge is that the heretics are πηγαὶ ἄνυδροι (*pēgai anydroi*, springs without water). For those who walk the length of Palestine and other arid lands, nothing can be more dreadful than a spring without water. Πηγή (*pēgē*) may suggest a "well," as in John 4:6, but this use is rare in comparison with the more common "spring" (Gen. 16:7; 24:13, 16; Num. 33:9; Deut. 8:15; 1 Kings 18:5; Isa. 35:7; James 3:11; Rev. 8:10; 14:7; 16:4). This type of spring is filled with promise but because of drought produces nothing (Jer. 14:3).

The second metaphor Peter invokes to denounce the heretics is that they are ὁμίχλαι ὑπὸ λαίλαπος ἐλαυνόμεναι (*homichlai hypo lailapos elaunomenai*, mists driven by the storm). Aristotle distinguished between "mist" and "clouds": "Mist is the residue of the condensation of air into water." He concluded that "for mist is as it were unproductive cloud" (*Mete.* 346B, 33, 35). The close association between mist and clouds may account for Peter's alteration of his source, which speaks of "clouds" (Jude 12). Peter's metaphor does not suggest that these are pleasant morning mists ("mist" in Wis. 2:4; Sir. 24:3; 43:22); instead, they are mists that produce foreboding darkness (Job 38:9; Joel 2:2; Isa. 29:18; Amos 4:13; Zeph. 1:15), like the classic London fog of a Sherlock Holmes tale. These "mists" are whipped up. The "driving wind" was a common enough expression (Josephus, *Ant.* 5.5.3 §205), but Peter thinks of the mist as being thrashed by a storm or tempest (ὑπὸ λαίλαπος, *hypo lailapos*; as Job 21:18; Wis. 5:14, 23; Mark 4:37; Luke 8:23), or even a whirlwind (as Sir. 48:9, 12; Job 38:1; Jer. 25:32 [32:32 LXX]). Peter's charge may be that the heretics are incapable of producing anything of value through their teachings, despite their grand promises (2:19). They are dry as opposed to God, who gives to thirsty humanity what people need (Ps. 63:1; Isa. 44:3: Jer. 2:13; John 4:13–14; 7:37–39).

However, Peter's meaning may be something other. At times "mist" suggests the transitory nature of human life, which ends in death (Sib. Or. 5.379; Wis. 2:4), and may even be associated with divine judgment (Joel 2:2; Zeph. 1:15). Moreover, death may be described as a "dry spring" as, for example, in a funeral epitaph: "I live in the darkness [τὸ σκότος, to skotos]; now the earth holds me as a drink from the mute fountain [πηγῆς, pēgēs] of silence" (NewDocs 4:149, a "mute fountain" or spring is one that is dry and does not burble). The following clause of 2:17 similarly refers to the "darkness" (τοῦ σκότους, tou skotous) of judgment that awaits the heretics. The metaphors of the first part of the verse ("springs without water and mists driven by the storm") likely refer to the spiritual state of the heretics, which eventuates in their ultimate judgment. These people are dead and destined for doom.

The final clause of the verse graphically depicts the judgment that is reserved for the false teachers: οἷς ὁ ζόφος τοῦ σκότους τετήρηται (hois ho zophos tou skotous tetērētai, for whom the gloom of darkness has been kept). The "gloom" (ὁ ζόφος, ho zophos) is the place where the fallen angels are bound until the day of judgment (2:4 and comments), the realm of the underworld oft described in ancient literature (Aeschylus, Pers. 839, "As for me, I depart for the darkness beneath the earth"; Euripides, Hipp. 1416, "Forever in the nether gloom"; Quintus Smyrnaeus 2.619, "Therefore I will pass into darkness"; and so 2.612; Homer, Od. 20.356; 11.55; Il. 21.56; Sib. Or. 4.43). The description of this "gloom" as "darkness" (τοῦ σκότους, tou skotous) indicates that the place of judgment and torment is outside the kingdom (Matt. 8:12; 22:13; 25:30). "Darkness" may mean simply the place of the dead (see above; Luke 1:79), but here it is the realm of punishment (cf. Wis. 17:21 [17:20 LXX]; Tob. 4:10; 14:10; 1 En. 17.5–6; 63.6). As the angels are kept under judgment until the final judgment (2:4 and comments), so the darkness of the nether gloom is kept (τετήρηται, tetērētai, perfect tense with stative aspect; Porter 1989: 245–90) for the heretics. This will be their final end (cf. 2:4, 9; 3:7). Such people are lost, beyond the limits of salvation. Peter's language echoes both the vocabulary and concepts of ancient discourse on judgment.

Peter returns to the topic of the conduct of the heretics amid the Christian community, which, he explains, is the reason for their coming judgment (the sentence begins with γάρ, gar, which marks the cause or reason for the preceding; BDAG 189). The false teachers are arrogant and seek to entice recent converts into their error through the promise of sexual gratification: ὑπέρογκα γὰρ ματαιότητος φθεγγόμενοι δελεάζουσιν ἐν ἐπιθυμίαις σαρκὸς ἀσελγείαις τοὺς ὀλίγως ἀποφεύγοντας τοὺς ἐν πλάνη ἀναστρεφομένους (hyperonka gar mataiotētos phthengomenoi deleazousin en epithymiais sarkos aselgeiais tous oligōs apopheugontas tous en planē anastrephomenous, For by uttering enormous empty things, they entice with the licentious desires of the flesh those

**2:18**

who have only recently escaped from the ones who live in error). Peter draws on Jude 16, adopting a few words and some significant concepts: Οὗτοί εἰσιν γογγυσταὶ μεμψίμοιροι κατὰ τὰς ἐπιθυμίας ἑαυτῶν πορευόμενοι καὶ τὸ στόμα αὐτῶν λαλεῖ ὑπέρογκα θαυμάζοντες πρόσωπα ὠφελείας χάριν (*houtoi eisin gongystai mempsimoipoi kata tas epithymias heatōn poreuomenoi kai to stoma autōn lalei hyperonka thaumazontes prosōpa ōpheleias charin*, These are grumblers and malcontents, living according to the dictates of their own desires, and their mouths speak arrogant things, flattering for their own gain). In Jude the heretics are characterized as those who are guided by their lustful desires (τὰς ἐπιθυμίας ἑαυτῶν, *tas epithymias heatōn*), whereas Peter notes how the heretics use the licentious desires of the flesh (ἐπιθυμίαις σαρκὸς ἀσελγείαις, *epithymiais sarkos aselgeiais*) as bait to unseat the unstable. Both authors censure the overblown speech of the heretics (ὑπέρογκα, *hyperonka*) and highlight their aggressive attempts to gain converts. Jude comments that the heretics use flattery to gain their end, while Peter tags their persuasive power as both high-sounding speech and sexual bait, which wiggles on the hook. Peter's thought, however, is largely a rehearsal of his previous denunciations of the heretics in 2:10 (τοὺς ὀπίσω σαρκὸς ἐν ἐπιθυμίᾳ μιασμοῦ πορευομένους, *tous opisō sarkos en epithymia miasmou poreuomenous*, the ones who go after flesh because of defiling desire) and 2:14 (δελεάζοντες ψυχὰς ἀστηρίκτους, *deleazontes psychas astēriktous*, luring unstable people). These folk are aggressive in their attempt to persuade others to come their way and use the promise of sex to lure those who are new and still unstable in their faith.

Peter first focuses on the false teachers' arrogant yet empty speech: ὑπέρογκα γὰρ ματαιότητος φθεγγόμενοι (*hyperonka gar mataiotētos phthengomenoi*, For by uttering grand empty things). The adverbial participle is the first indication of the method that the heretics employ to bait the recent converts. They speak or utter (φθεγγόμενοι, *phthengomenoi*; see 2:16; Ps. 94:4 [93:4 LXX]; Job 13:7; Wis. 1:8; BDAG 1054; MM 667; the word is appropriate in a context of extreme or abusive language) "grand things" (ὑπέρογκα, *hyperonka*), which refers to their arrogant and boastful speech (see Jude 16 and comments on the term). This is the speech of those whose boasting is great and whose doom is sure. Euripides recounts Hercules's boast, "Heaven pleases itself: in the teeth of heaven I do the same," to which Theseus replies, "Shut your mouth! Your proud words [μέγα λέγων, *mega legōn*] could bring you worse disaster!" (*Hercules* 1243–44). These heretics' speech suggests that they are filled with overblown pride as they try to impress with great things (1 En. 5.4; As. Mos. [T. Mos.] 7.9; Dan. 7:8, 20; Plutarch, *Mor.* 1119B). But Peter's attack is swift and cutting: he categorizes their boast as nothing, being empty or vain (ματαιότητος, *mataiotētos*; BDAG 621; the genitive functions as an adjective; BDF §165). The term also suggests falsity since there is no reality to their claims (Pss. 38:12 [37:13 LXX]; 144:8, 11 [143:8, 11 LXX]; Philo, *Confusion* 27 §141; and compare the use of similar language in 1 Tim. 1:6; Titus 1:10). There is sound but no substance.

Peter again draws on the metaphor of fishing to describe the false teachers' attempts at persuasion: δελεάζουσιν ἐν ἐπιθυμίαις σαρκὸς ἀσελγείαις τοὺς ὀλίγως ἀποφεύγοντας τοὺς ἐν πλάνῃ ἀναστρεφομένους (*deleazousin en epithymiais sarkos aselgeiais tous oligōs apopheugontas tous en planē anastrephomenous*, they entice with the licentious desires of the flesh those who have only recently escaped from the ones who live in error). In 2:14 Peter spoke of the way the heretics were "luring unstable people" (δελεάζοντες ψυχὰς ἀστηρίκτους, *deleazontes psychas astēriktous*; see comments). In this verse, however, the objects of the heretics' fishing expedition are not called "unstable" but rather those who have "scarcely escaped" (τοὺς ὀλίγως ἀποφεύγοντας, *tous oligōs apopheugontas*). Previously Peter used the language of escape as a descriptor of the divine act of salvation (1:4 and comments; also 2:20; BDAG 125; LSJ 226). They were rescued by God (see 2:5, 9). Peter observes that these have "recently" escaped, using a somewhat rare adverb (ὀλίγως, *oligōs*), which, as the adverbial use of the neuter adjective ὀλίγον (*oligon*), emphasizes a short duration of time (James 4:14; 1 Pet. 1:6; 5:10). The recent converts are, in his eyes, unstable still.

The people from whom the converts escaped, as indicated by the accusative, are τοὺς ἐν πλάνῃ ἀναστρεφομένους (*tous en planē anastrephomenous*, the ones who live in error). As in 2:7, Peter understands a person's conduct and the principles by which one lives as a "way of life" (ἀναστροφῆς, *anastrophēs*; see comments), which he describes using the substantive participle ἀναστρεφομένους (*anastrephomenous*). The heretics' way is marked by error, a theme to which Peter returns at the very end of the letter (3:17). Jude likewise charged Balaam with error (v. 11) and brands his heretics as "wandering stars" (v. 13; see comments). The noun πλάνη (*planē*) means "error," a wandering from the truth (Wis. 12:24; Matt. 27:64; Eph. 4:14; 1 Thess. 2:3; 2 Thess. 2:11; 2 Pet. 2:18; 3:17; 1 John 4:6). But Peter's thought in the present verse is not that the heretics have erred from the truth. Here he lumps the body of the unconverted together as "those who live in error" (Rom. 1:27; Titus 3:3; James 5:20).

The bait the heretics use to catch the recent converts is ἐν ἐπιθυμίαις σαρκὸς ἀσελγείαις (*en epithymiais sarkos aselgeiais*, with the licentious desires of the flesh; instrumental ἐν, *en*, with the dative, BDF §195). Peter weaves together familiar language from Jude and his own letter in the charge that the heretics entice new converts by desires (Jude 16, 18; 2 Pet. 1:4; 2:10; 3:3; and comments) that have their roots in the flesh (Jude 7, 8, 23; 2 Pet. 2:10; and comments) and that may be classified as licentious or sexually immoral (Jude 4; 2 Pet. 2:2, 7; and comments). In the present verse, however, Peter is classifying not the nature of the heretics' sin but the means they employ to gain converts. What they are, however, is what they promise. Sex is at the very heart of the problem. The heretics appear to offer gratification of sexual desire, which is exactly the type of vice that dominated pagan life, according to apostolic critics (Eph. 2:3; 4:19, 22; Col. 3:5; 1 Thess. 4:5; 1 Pet. 1:14; 4:3). The heretics advocate a return to this loose pagan lifestyle, whose ultimate value was gratification of desire. Amazingly, they throw out this bait as they gather with the church, turning the *agapē* meals into times of revelry and lust (2:13–14 and comments). They seek "to dress up vice as virtue" (M. Green 1987: 128). The following verse presents the false teachers' philosophical rationale that allows them to suggest the acceptability of such behavior within the context of the church and the faith.

How can we account for the ability of the heretics to gain a hearing in the church and to find place within that community (2:13), given their emphasis on licentious behavior? We know that during the second century AD the gnostic sect known as the Carpocratians promoted liberty and sexual license.[1] However, as noted previously in the introduction ("The Opponents in 2 Peter"), characteristic features of gnostic thought such as dualism and the creation of the world by a demiurge are apparently not tenets of the false teachers' appeal that Peter counters. But the emergence of the Carpocratians at a relatively early date signals the way that some could understand the faith as compatible with conduct that Jesus and the apostles would classify as vice.

The suggestion that false teachers in 2 Peter had merged Christian with Epicurean thought is surely attractive (see "The Opponents in 2 Peter" in the introduction) since that philosophy not only denied the possibility of future judgment but also elevated desires (ἐπιθυμίαι, *epithymiai*) to the level of virtue, both features that mark the heretics. Epicurus distinguished between natural desires (both those that were necessary and those that were unnecessary) and empty desires. The blessed life is one that satisfies the natural and necessary desires of the flesh. As Epicurus said, "The cry of the flesh is not to be hungry, not to be thirsty, and not to be cold" (*Sententiae Vaticanae* 33). Sexual desires are, therefore, good, according to Epicurus: "As for myself, I cannot conceive of the Good if I eliminate the pleasures of taste, or the pleasures of sex, or the pleasures of listening, or the pleasures of gazing on the motions and forms pleasing to the eye" (Athenaeus 12.546E). But we are pressed hard to imagine how Epicurean thought could have gained any foothold in the church since Epicureans believed that the gods were not involved in any way in human affairs. One could expect nothing from them, neither favors nor judgment. However, the first century was a period in which disparate religious and philosophical traditions could be patched together and juxtaposed without the kind of consistency that we often erroneously presuppose in our attempts to classify movements, whether ancient or modern. Eclecticism was well established during this period (Dillon and Long 1988), and even Paul was labeled as one whose opinions were randomly bound together (Acts 17:18). The trends that the heretics reflect are not difficult to identify but the exact nature of their belief may well defy systemization. Certainly the affirmation of bodily gratification was an appealing notion and, coupled with an exalta-

---

1. Described in Irenaeus, *Haer.* 1.25; 2.31–33; Clement of Alexandria, *Strom.* 3.20; Hippolytus, *Haer.* 70.32–33; Tertullian, *The Soul* 23, 35; Epiphanius, *Pan.* 27; 30.14; 32.3–7; Eusebius, *Eccl. Hist.* 4.7.9–11; Augustine, *Haer.* 7.

tion of freedom (2:19), would put a very attractive, although lurid, spin on the apostolic faith.

Peter presents a summary of the heretics' appeal in the first clause of the verse,    **2:19** which is followed hard by a critique highlighting the irony of their promise: ἐλευθερίαν αὐτοῖς ἐπαγγελλόμενοι, αὐτοὶ δοῦλοι ὑπάρχοντες τῆς φθορᾶς· (*eleutherian autois epangellomenoi, autoi douloi hyparchontes tēs phthoras,* Although they promise them freedom, they themselves are slaves of corruption). This is not the first time Peter echoes the voice of the false teachers (see 2:10b, 12, 18), nor will it be the last (3:3–4). A hallmark of their philosophy is the promise of freedom. We are left to infer what kind of freedom they are offering, a question that generates diverse responses among contemporary commentators. Bauckham (1983: 275; cf. Moo 1996: 143–44; Kraftchick 2002: 143–44) surveys the various ways that "freedom" might be understood, such as "(1) Freedom from moral law. . . . (2) The Gnostic's freedom from the archons or the demiurge. . . . (3) Freedom from φθορά, 'perishability'; . . . Christians were already beyond the power of mortality. . . . (4) Political freedom. . . . (5) Freedom from fear of judgment at the Parousia." The heretics are surely libertine in their ethics, and their apparent distortion of Pauline teaching (3:15–16) possibly suggests that they have turned the apostle's teaching on Christian liberty into a pretext for vice. Paul himself needed to counter this tendency (Gal. 5:13) and emphasized that the person freed from sin who again engages in vice becomes sin's slave (Rom. 6:15–23). The heretics' claim may be plausibly interpreted within this frame. The suggestion that the heretics promote a gnostic form of freedom from the intermediary powers is unlikely since the heresy lacks characteristic contours of gnosticism such as dualism (see "The Opponents in 2 Peter" in the introduction). The notion that the heresy promises freedom from mortality is attractive since φθορά (*phthora*) may indeed refer to decay or death (see 2:12 and comments), but the term may also refer to moral corruption (see 1:4 and comments), and this is certainly the sense here. The present context places emphasis on issues of morality (2:15–16, 18). Moreover, the following verse begins with the explanatory *gar* (γάρ, for; BDAG 189), rephrasing the teaching of the present verse in clear moral, not cosmic, terms: "For if, having escaped the defilements of the world . . . and are overcome by them having been entangled again, their last state has become worse than the first."

Reicke's argument that the heretics are "politically aggressive" and "skillful in exploiting the social unrest prevalent in certain strata of the Roman empire" (1964: 169) is mere conjecture and does not find support from elsewhere in the letter. The view that the heretics promise freedom from the fear of judgment is attractive if we understand the heretics to be people who are influenced by the Epicurean notion that the gods do not intervene in human affairs and that delay in divine vengeance is evidence that there will be no future judgment. This suggestion by Neyrey (1980b: 418–19; 1990: 123) and Bauckham (1983: 275–76) has found considerable acceptance in recent interpretation (Moo 1996: 148–50;

Waltner and J. Charles 1999: 239); earlier commentators forward the position that the false teachers pervert Pauline teaching (Bigg 1901: 286; Hauck 1957: 96; Kelly 1969: 346; Fornberg 1977: 106–7). Kraftchick (2002: 144; Craddock 1995a: 115) opts for the view that "an amalgam of these opinions characterized the opposition's teaching." Schreiner finds both the Pauline perversion view and the Epicurean counterattractive (2003: 359; Horrell 1998: 171).

The promise of freedom, however, was a philosophical commonplace and is not, in and of itself, a marker for any particular school of thought. Epicureans, Stoics, and skeptics alike discussed human freedom and promised the same. One of the highest values of the era was freedom. Great glory was bestowed on the one who could secure it. It was, to be sure, first a political value. When the Romans broke the Macedonian domination of Greece in the second Macedonian war, Flamininus proclaimed freedom for the Greeks at the stadium in Isthmia, outside Corinth (196 BC), and was hailed as "saviour and champion of Greece" (Plutarch, *Titus Flamininus* 10.3–5; 9.5). Freedom also had a social dimension. Throughout the Mediterranean world, the fundamental social distinction was between being a free person, whether freeborn or *liberti*, and being a slave. Given the high value of freedom in the political and social spheres, it is no wonder that the themes of freedom and slavery were worked into the warp and woof of ancient philosophy. The glory of the gospel was, in part, the way Jesus and the apostles engaged this issue and offered a distinctly theocentric and christocentric response regarding the nature of true freedom and the way freedom is obtained and lost (see, e.g., John 8:31–36; Rom. 6:5–23; 1 Cor. 7:20–24; Gal. 5:13; 1 Pet. 2:16).

Given this milieu, we are not surprised that the heretics promise their would-be disciples freedom. Indeed, who at that time did *not* make such an offer? Lucian offered philosophy as the true road to freedom: "For he went on to praise philosophy and the freedom that it gives, and to ridicule the things that are popularly considered blessings—wealth and reputation, dominion and honour, yes and purple and gold" (*Nigrinus* 4). Seneca defined freedom in distinctly Stoic terms: "You ask what this freedom is? It means not fearing either men or gods; it means not craving wickedness or excess; it means possessing supreme power over oneself. And it is a priceless good to be master of oneself" (*Ep. mor.* 75.18). The Stoic Epictetus placed freedom at the very center of what was considered the good: "What sort of thing do you imagine the good to be? Serenity, happiness, freedom from restraint. . . . In what kind of subject matter for life ought one to seek serenity, and freedom from restraint? In that which is slave, or that which is free?" (*Disc.* 3.22.39–40). Epictetus points to his poverty and asks, "Yet what do I lack? Am I not free from pain and fear, am I not free?" (3.22.48; and the discourse on freedom in 4.1).

The Epicureans were hardly outdone on this question. Epicurus was determined to eliminate the notion of determinism (*Ep. Men.* 134, "It would be better to accept the myth about the gods than to be a slave to the determination of the physicists"); in his materialistic philosophy he developed the notion of the random swerve of atoms, which opened the possibility for freedom of the will (noted in Lucretius 2.251–93). Freedom became a principal tenet of Epicurean philosophy: "Freedom is the greatest fruit of self-sufficiency" (*Sententiae Vaticanae* 77; see also 67; and Cicero, *Fat.* 10.23; Diogenes Laertius, *Lives* 10.133 notes his freedom from the fear of death). Skeptics such as Carneades likewise affirmed the free movement of the mind but without resorting to the theory of the swerve of atoms (Cicero, *Fat.* 11.23, differentiates his views from that of Epicurus). Chrysippus held a mediating view (Cicero, *Fat.* 18.41–19.45). The question of the freedom of the will over against fate was bound with the question of freedom for moral action and the question of justice (either in the form of praise and blame or honor and punishment; Cicero, *Fat.* 17.40). "Freedom" was a dominant topos.

The heretics promise freedom, which, within this philosophical frame, includes the ability and not only the license to act. The heretics are on the side of those who hold that a human is free to act, and they likely teach that one should act in accordance with that freedom. While they apparently make appeal to Paul, their notion of freedom is not fully understandable as a perversion of Paul's teaching. Their sanctioning of desire (v. 18) is similar to Epicurean thought but, as noted above, their presence in the church and theism suggest an eclectic system not fully compatible with Epicurean thought. The irony of the offer of freedom, however, is that αὐτοὶ δοῦλοι ὑπάρχοντες τῆς φθορᾶς (*autoi douloi hyparchontes tēs phthoras*, they themselves are slaves of corruption). The "corruption" (φθορᾶς, *phthoras*) to which they are enslaved is moral (see above and comments on 1:4) and, given the licentious nature of the false teachers' conduct, is most likely sexual in nature (the term refers to sexual corruption in Diodorus Siculus 3.59.1; 5.62.1; Plutarch, *Mor.* 712C; Josephus, *Ag. Ap.* 2.24 §202; Philo, *Worse* 27 §102). It should not be understood in this context as mortality (as in 1 Cor. 15:42, 50; Kraftchick 2002: 144 suggests that both senses are in mind, which is unlikely given the strong moral orientation of the present paragraph) or as the final destruction of all things (2:12b; Gal. 6:8). The irony of their promise is the fact that one cannot offer what one does not have. The following verses (2:20–22) describe the apostasy of the heretics, which is evidence of their enslavement, a thought similar to that of Jesus and Paul (John 8:34; Rom. 6:16). The one who is given over to sin is its slave. No slave can promise freedom. Peter hopes that his readers will see the heretics for what they are: mere slaves.

Peter makes his case about the bondage of the false teachers by appealing to what appears to be an aphorism: ᾧ γάρ τις ἥττηται, τούτῳ δεδούλωται (*hō gar tis hēttētai, toutō dedoulōtai*, for that by which someone is conquered, to that a person has been enslaved). Bauckham (1983: 277) notes that the proverb was widely quoted by Christian authors in later centuries; "Adamantius" (*De recta in Deum fide* 58.1) calls it "the saying current among non-Christians." The very form of the statement has a proverbial ring. Peter will again pick up a couple of popular sayings in 2:22. The allusion refers to military conquest, which was the source of numerous slaves in the ancient world (Westermann 1955: 84–90; Bartchy 1973: 45–46). For example, thousands of Jews captured during the First Revolt (AD 66–70) were made slaves and sent to Corinth to try to build a canal across the isthmus. In the battle against sin, the false teachers had yielded and for that reason were defeated (ἥττηται, *hēttētai*; 2:20; Isa. 8:9; 13:15; 30:31; 33:1; 54:17; Jer. 31:1; 2 Macc. 10:24; BDAG 441; MM 282). Having been vanquished by sin, they are now its slaves (John 8:34; Rom. 6:16). As Hilary of Arles commented, "A man is a slave to whatever vice controls him" (cited in Bray 2000: 152).

**2:20**   Peter has warned his readers about the seductive persuasion of the heretics, who hold out a promise of freedom that they cannot deliver. These false teachers have themselves been overcome by corruption and enslaved. Verse 19 suggests that they are apostates from the faith, a point that our author drives hard in this and the following two verses: εἰ γὰρ ἀποφυγόντες τὰ μιάσματα τοῦ κόσμου ἐν ἐπιγνώσει τοῦ κυρίου [ἡμῶν] καὶ σωτῆρος Ἰησοῦ Χριστοῦ, τούτοις δὲ πάλιν ἐμπλακέντες ἡττῶνται, γέγονεν αὐτοῖς τὰ ἔσχατα χείρονα τῶν πρώτων (*ei gar apophygontes ta miasmata tou kosmou en epignōsei tou kyriou [hēmōn] kai sōtēros Iēsou Christou, toutois de palin emplakentes ēttōntai, gegonen autois ta eschata cheirona tōn prōtōn*, For if, having escaped the defilements of the world in the knowledge of our Lord and Savior Jesus Christ, they are overcome by them having been entangled again, their last state has become worse than the first). The subjects of the present verse could, perhaps, be the believers duped by the heretics since both verses 18 and 19 introduce them (v. 18: "those who have only recently escaped from the ones who live in error"; v. 19: "them"). The present verse echoes the language of salvation as "escape" in verse 18 (ἀποφυγόντες), which again suggests that verse 20 addresses the situation of those who are the objects of the heretics' appeal. However, the topic of the paragraph running from verse 17 is the heretics themselves; indeed, Peter's aim throughout this chapter has been to level his *vituperatio* against them (2:1, 12, 17). Moreover, the explanatory γάρ (*gar*, for) at the head of verse 20 suggests that we understand the present verse as elaborating his point about the apostasy of the false teachers mentioned previously. The heretics whom Peter has in mind have been overcome or vanquished, according to verse 19 (ἥττηται, *hēttētai*). Our author uses the same verb in verse 20 to describe their apostasy (ἡττῶνται, *hēttōntai*), lest there be any confusion regarding to whom he refers (contra Bigg 1901: 287; Kelly 1969: 347–48; Schreiner 1998: 360; Scaggs 2004: 128).

Within the first part of the protasis of this conditional sentence, Peter embeds two participial clauses, the first of which says, εἰ γὰρ ἀποφυγόντες τὰ μιάσματα τοῦ κόσμου ἐν ἐπιγνώσει τοῦ κυρίου [ἡμῶν] καὶ σωτῆρος Ἰησοῦ Χριστοῦ (*ei gar apophygontes ta miasmata tou kosmou en epignōsei tou kyriou [hēmōn] kai sōtēros Iēsou Christou*, For if, having escaped the defilements of the world in the knowledge of our Lord and Savior Jesus Christ). As in 1:4 and 2:18, Peter describes salvation as "having escaped" (see comments on 1:4, ἀποφυγόντες τῆς ἐν τῷ κόσμῳ ἐν ἐπιθυμίᾳ φθορᾶς, *apophygontes tēs en tō kosmō en epithymia phthoras*, escaping the corruption that is in the world due to lust; and 2:18, ἀποφεύγοντας τοὺς ἐν πλάνῃ ἀναστρεφομένους, *apopheugontas tous en planē anastrephomenous*, escaped from the ones who live in error). The language of escape was at times connected with the gracious deeds of a benefactor who facilitated escape from disaster (Danker 1982: 459). But the moral context of these verses suggests rather the notion of escape from error and vice, similar to Seneca's comment: "There awaits us, if ever we escape from these low dregs to that sublime and lofty height, peace of mind and, when all error has been driven out, perfect liberty" (*Ep. mor.* 75.18). He goes on to remark, "Some define this class, of which I have been speaking—a class of men who are making progress—as having escaped the diseases of the mind, but not yet the passions, and as still standing upon slippery ground; because no one is beyond the dangers of evil except him who has cleared himself of it wholly." For Seneca, to speak of escape is to recognize continued danger.

Peter knows the danger as well. The heretics have escaped τὰ μιάσματα τοῦ κόσμου (*ta miasmata tou kosmou*, the defilements of the world), language similar to 1:4 yet unduplicated elsewhere in the NT. In 2:10 Peter refers to the heretics as those who go after flesh ἐν ἐπιθυμίᾳ μιασμοῦ (*en epithymia miasmou*, because of defiling desire). The "defilements" in the present verse, as the use of the cognate in 2:10 suggests, are acts that cross the moral boundary. These are deeds that can even be classified as vice or criminal offenses and not simply cultic defilement (Ezek. 33:31; 1 Macc. 13:50; Jdt. 13:16; 1 En. 10.22; Josephus, *J.W.* 2.17.10 §455; Polybius 36.16.6; Polyaenus, *Stratagems in War* 6.7.2; BDAG 650; F. Hauck, *TDNT* 4:646–47). Such immoral deeds are characteristic of the world (τοῦ κόσμου, *tou kosmou*), a thought similar to 1:4 and even 2:18. Peter's view of the surrounding moral culture is hardly positive, but he recognizes that there has been a change in the habits of those who are now the troublers of the church. Such change is not the result of moral progress, as understood in moral philosophy, but rather has come about ἐν ἐπιγνώσει τοῦ κυρίου [ἡμῶν] καὶ σωτῆρος Ἰησοῦ Χριστοῦ (*en epignōsei tou kyriou [hēmōn] kai sōtēros Iēsou Christou*, in the knowledge of our Lord and Savior Jesus Christ). The "knowledge" to which our author refers is that which brings conversion and salvation (see the comments on 1:2, 3, 8, and on the verb in 2:21). As elsewhere, the knowledge is personal. Its object is Jesus Christ (1:2, 3, 8; 3:18), who is here identified as both "Lord and Savior" (see 1:11; 3:2, 18; cf. 3:15). By using language he has already employed and will continue to use to mark salvation, Peter sets up his readers to understand the tragedy of the heretics. They had escaped moral corruption through personal knowledge of none other than the one who is both Lord and Savior, Jesus Christ. Grace and peace (1:2) and all things for "life and duty" (1:3) had been granted them through their knowledge of him. They had obtained entrance into his eternal kingdom (1:11). To this Lord and Savior is ascribed eternal honor (3:18). Given the greatness of the benefactor and his benefaction, their present apostasy is the height of hubris as well as an unfathomable tragedy.

The second clause of the protasis describes the way the heretics have become ensnared and taken captive again by moral corruption: τούτοις δὲ πάλιν ἐμπλακέντες ἥττῶνται (*toutois de palin emplakentes hēttōntai*, they are overcome by them having been entangled again). The dative τούτοις (*toutois*, by these) refers back to τὰ μιάσματα τοῦ κόσμου (*ta miasmata tou kosmou*, the defilements of the world) in the previous clause, that from which they had previously escaped. As in verse 19b, Peter understands the "corruption of the world" as an enticement that overcomes a person (dative of means, BDF §195), and as a result, the person becomes enslaved (ᾧ γάρ τις ἥττηται, τούτῳ δεδούλωται, *hō gar tis hēttētai, toutō dedoulōtai*, for that by which someone is conquered, to that a person has been enslaved; see comments). The notion of yielding to or being overcome by passions is mentioned by Xenophon: "Again, among all the pleasures that prove too strong for many men, who can mention one to which Agesilaus yielded?" (*Agesilaus* 5.1; see Euripides, *Hipp.* 966–69). The verb may suggest that the heretics have succumbed or yielded to corruptions or that such moral corruptions are a power that overcomes them. The repetition of the thought of verse 19b suggests that the latter sense is in mind.

The participial phrase πάλιν ἐμπλακέντες (*palin emplakentes*, having been entangled again) describes the reason the heretics end up being overcome by the corruptions. Πάλιν points to the act of falling back or returning to their previous activities (Rom. 8:15; 1 Cor. 7:5; Gal. 2:18; 5:1; Phil. 2:28; Heb. 5:12; 6:6; James 5:18; BDAG 752). The heretics have become "entangled" again, as a sheep or a hare that becomes entangled in thorns and thistles (Herm. *Sim.* 6.2.6–7; Arrian, *Anab.* 6.22.8). The term is used metaphorically of moral entanglement (Prov. 28:18; 2 Tim. 2:4; Epictetus, *Disc.* 3.22.69; Polybius 24.11.3; Plato, *Laws* 814E) and suggests not only involvement in an activity but also entrapment. Someone cannot enter into corruption without being ensnared and consequently overcome. Peter's description of the heretics' apostasy highlights their engagement in corruptions as well as their defeat by them. This is genuine apostasy, from which there is no escape (Heb. 6:4–8; 10:26; see the comments on Christian apostasy in Pliny the Younger, *Ep.* 10.96). The heretics have turned from "the holy commandment" (2:21) and denied "the Master who bought them" (2:1).

The apodosis or result clause in this conditional sentence is γέγονεν αὐτοῖς τὰ ἔσχατα χείρονα τῶν πρώτων (*gegonen autois ta eschata cheirona tōn prōtōn*, their last state has become worse than the first). The sentence echoes the teaching of Jesus about the person from whom unclean spirits have been driven out and then return (Matt. 12:43–45; Luke 11:24–26; καὶ γίνεται τὰ ἔσχατα τοῦ ἀνθρώπου ἐκείνου χείρονα τῶν πρώτων, *kai ginetai ta eschata tou anthrōpou ekeinou cheirona tōn prōtōn*, and the last state of that person is worse than the first [NRSV]). The statement of Jesus may itself be a traditional proverb (cf. Matt. 27:64, καὶ ἔσται ἡ ἐσχάτη πλάνη χείρων τῆς πρώτης, *kai estai hē eschatē planē cheirōn tēs prōtēs*, and the last deception would be worse than the first [NRSV]). Jesus's teaching was woven into the fabric of early Christian instruction regarding apostasy (Herm. *Sim.* 9.17.5: "Some of them defiled themselves [ἐμίαναν ἑαυτούς, *emianan heautous*] and were cast out from the family of the righteous, and became again what they had been before, or rather even worse"; Mart. Pol. 11.1: "Call for them, for repentance from better to worse is not allowed us"). The reference to defilement, apostasy, and going from better to worse in Hermas is so conceptually similar to 2 Pet. 2:20 that the present epistle likely served as Hermas's source (a parallel not discussed by Gilmore 2002; see the discussion in Bauckham 1983: 277–78).

Peter does not discuss here how the apostates' last state (lit., last things, τὰ ἔσχατα, *ta eschata*) is worse than the first (lit., first things, τῶν πρώτων, *tōn prōtōn*), except in stating that it would have been better not to know the way of righteousness than to know it and turn back (v. 21). This echo of dominical teaching may suggest that demonic forces are at work and that the wickedness of such people has become worse than before their Christ encounter. Leo the Great traced this line as well: "We cannot fathom the depths of God's mercy toward us. Yet we must take care not to be ensnared again by the devil's traps and become entangled once more in the very errors which we have renounced. For the ancient enemy does not stop laying down traps everywhere and doing whatever it takes to corrupt the faith of believers" (*Sermon* 27.3; cited in Bray 2000: 152). But previously Peter has underscored the divine judgment that would come on such people (2:1), the worse state in view being the sentence of damnation. However understood, our author will presently explain the apostates' state in more detail.

Peter continues to develop his readers' understanding of the doom of the heretics, who are genuine apostates from the faith. In the previous verse, he reminded his readers of these people's conversion (v. 20a), their subsequent entanglement in corruption (v. 20b), and their final state, which is worse than their condition before conversion (v. 20c). Peter builds on the last thought of the previous verse ("their last state has become worse than the first") by inserting an explanatory statement, beginning with γάρ (*gar*, for), which has a distinctly proverbial ring: κρεῖττον γὰρ ἦν αὐτοῖς μὴ ἐπεγνωκέναι τὴν ὁδὸν τῆς δικαιοσύνης ἢ ἐπιγνοῦσιν ὑποστρέψαι ἐκ τῆς παραδοθείσης αὐτοῖς ἁγίας ἐντολῆς (*kreitton gar ēn autois mē epegnōkenai tēn hodon tēs dikaiosynēs ē epignousin hypostrepsai ek tēs paradotheisēs autois hagias entolēs*, For it would have been better for them not to have known the way of righteousness than, having known it, to turn from the holy commandment that was handed down to them). Walther Zimmerli (1933) dubbed this kind of proverbial declaration in which something is said to be better than something else a "Tob-Spruch" (from the Hebrew טוֹב, *ṭôb*, better), a form quite common in Jewish literature (Ps. 37:16 [36:16 LXX]; Prov. 3:14; 8:11, 19; 15:16–17; 16:8, 19, 32; 17:1; 19:1; 21:9, 19; 25:7, 24; 27:5; 28:6; Sir. 33:22; 40:18–27; 1 Cor. 7:9; 1 Pet. 3:17; Bryce 1972: 2; Ogden 1977; G. Snyder 1977). Although this kind of proverb appears to reflect a distinctly Semitic orientation, such also appear in Greek literature. Aeschylus in *Prometheus Bound* (750–51) says, "It is better to die once and for all than linger out all my days in misery." In the same text, Io exhorts Prometheus, "Tell me the end of my wandering—what time is set for

2:21

wretched me," to which Prometheus responds in words similar to Peter's, "It would be better not to know than to know, in your case" (622–24). Herodotus employs the same proverbial form, "Bearing in mind how much better it is to be envied than pitied" (3.52.5).[2] We should not conclude that our author draws on a known proverb at this point, however, but the form he employs will ring as a wisdom saying in the ears of his readers/hearers, regardless of their cultural heritage.

In this type of "better . . . than" proverb, "the final element is morally superior to the preceding elements" (Reymond 2001: 91). Our author therefore makes the stunning observation that the superior state would be not to have known the "way" at all than, having known it, to return to the former way of life. In Peter's view, one should not come if one does not expect to stay. Virtue would be to refuse rather than equivocate. In some ways Peter's thought aligns with the dominical teaching in Luke 12:47–48. The greater the knowledge and privilege, the greater the responsibility. The more severe judgment will come on the one who knows.

The "better" part, according to our author, is never to have known the way: κρεῖττον γὰρ ἦν αὐτοῖς μὴ ἐπεγνωκέναι τὴν ὁδὸν τῆς δικαιοσύνης (kreitton gar ēn autois mē epegnōkenai tēn hodon tēs dikaiosynēs, for it would have been better for them not to have known the way of righteousness). Peter has spoken repeatedly about knowing God, and especially knowing the Lord Jesus (1:2, 3, 8; see comments), using the substantive form of the verb in the present verse (ἐπίγνωσις, epignōsis, knowledge). The reference to knowing Christ in verse 20 (ἐν ἐπιγνώσει τοῦ κυρίου [ἡμῶν] καὶ σωτῆρος Ἰησοῦ Χριστοῦ, en epignōsei tou kyriou [hēmōn] kai sōtēros Iēsou Christou, in the knowledge of our Lord and Savior Jesus Christ) leads him to the declaration in verse 21, but he shifts the thought in a significant direction. The heretics have not only known the Lord but have also known "the way of righteousness," implying that knowing the Lord entails embracing a righteous way of life. The ethical dimension of the relationship with Christ cannot be set aside. Peter has previously spoken of the Christian way as the "way of truth" (2:2) and maligned its opposite as "the way of Balaam" (2:15; see comments). In the LXX, the whole expression with the verb ἐπιγινώσκω (epiginōskō, know) appears in Job 24:13, while "way of righteousness" (Prov. 21:16, 21; Wis. 5:6) or the plural "ways of righteousness" (Tob. 1:3; Prov. 8:20; 12:28; 16:17, 31; 17:23; with "truth" in Tob. 1:3 and Wis. 5:6) was a common manner of referring to a person's conduct, the "way" in which one "walks." Peter's statement, however, echoes Matt. 21:32, "For John came to you to show you the way of righteousness, and you did not believe him, but the tax collectors and the prostitutes did. And even after you saw this, you did not repent and believe him" (NIV). His thought also betrays similarities to Job 24:12–13 LXX (L. C. L. Brenton translation):

2. So also Diodorus Siculus 12.16.2: "For it is better to die than to experience such a gross indignity in one's fatherland"; and Demosthenes, *Ep.* 2.21, "Because, if the differences between you and me remain irreconcilable, it were better for me to be dead."

"Why then has he not visited these? Forasmuch as they were upon the earth, and took no notice, and they knew not the way of righteousness, neither have they walked in their appointed paths?"

In both the Matthew and Job passages, the focus is on those who ignore the way of righteousness that was shown to them. Peter takes this thought a step further, commenting on those who did know the Lord (v. 20) and the way of righteousness yet turned away; he thus adapts a common teaching to his ends. Peter equates knowing the Lord with knowing the way of righteousness. They had been converted (the verb means "come to know" as in Col. 1:16; 1 Tim. 4:3, MM 236), but it would have been best had they not.

The second part of Peter's Tob-Spruch says: ἢ ἐπιγνοῦσιν ὑποστρέψαι ἐκ τῆς παραδοθείσης αὐτοῖς ἁγίας ἐντολῆς (ē epignousin hypostrepsai ek tēs paradotheisēs autois hagias entolēs, than, having known it, to turn from the holy commandment that was handed down to them). The heretics had known (ἐπιγνοῦσιν) the way of righteousness (elliptical construction) but had turned back (ὑποστρέψαι). The verb in most contexts suggests a physical turning back or return to something (Luke 1:56; 2:45; Acts 8:25; 13:13; Gal. 1:17) but here has the metaphorical sense of turning away from the "holy commandment." Peter implies that they have returned to their former way of life and thus committed the sin of apostasy. Peter's use of the verb is equivalent to ἐπιστρέφω (epistrephō) in the following verse, which more commonly suggests a change in one's opinion or action (see comments). However, the way Peter uses the verb ὑποστρέψαι is not without parallel. Euripides (Hercules 735–39), for example, says, "Evil has changed sides; he who was once a mighty king is now turning his life backward into the road to Hades. Hail to you! Justice and heavenly retribution." Peter describes an act of anticonversion, the "turning life backward."

The dreadfulness of this return is that the heretics have turned back from τῆς ... ἁγίας ἐντολῆς (tēs ... hagias entolēs, the holy commandment). This is the commandment "of the Lord and Savior given through your apostles," which was proclaimed to them in the gospel (3:2 and comments). The gospel is not simply an offer; it is a demand that must be obeyed, a point lost on the heretics. "Commandment" sometimes stands for the OT law (see Rom. 7:12: "the commandment is holy and just and good"; and Matt. 5:19; 15:3; 19:17; Eph. 6:2; Heb. 9:19) but elsewhere means the "commandment" of Christ (John 13:34; 14:15, 21; 15:10, 12; 1 Cor. 14:37; 2 Pet. 3:2; 1 John 2:7–8; 3:22–24). This could include the love-command of the Lord (John 13:34–35) and also the interpretation of the law given by the Lord (such as the Sermon on the Mount; M. Green 1987: 131). On this reading, the "holy commandment" would be the substance of the initial Christian instruction that new converts receive. This teaching was not mere advice but a sacred demand that was "handed down to them" (παραδοθείσης αὐτοῖς, paradotheisēs autois), a sacred tradition divinely inspired (see Jude 3 and comments). To turn away the divine imperative, and to turn back to their former way, is indeed a state worse than never having heard the sacred command.

**2:22**    After inserting his own proverbial statement (v. 21), Peter concludes his *vitu-peratio* against the apostate heretics with two known proverbs whose truth is made evident by the conduct of the false teachers: συμβέβηκεν αὐτοῖς τὸ τῆς ἀληθοῦς παροιμίας, Κύων ἐπιστρέψας ἐπὶ τὸ ἴδιον ἐξέραμα, καί, ῟Υς λουσαμένη εἰς κυλισμὸν βορβόρου (*symbebēken autois to tēs alēthous paroimias, Kyōn epistrepsas epi to idion exerama, kai, Hys lousamenē eis kylismon borborou*, What the maxim says is true regarding them: The dog returns to its own vomit, and, The sow, having washed, returns to wallowing in the mud). The verb of the opening clause, συμβαίνω (*symbainō*), means "come to pass" and often appears in contexts where the author wishes to focus on the fact that what has been said is indeed true (LSJ 1674.III; BDAG 956). Herodotus (9.101.2), for example, comments, "It happened that the rumor of a victory won by the Greeks with Pausanias was true [συνέβαινε, *synebaine*]," that is, the rumor came to pass and was therefore true. Similarly, Thucydides (2.17.2) states, "And in my opinion, if the oracle proved true [ξυμβῆναι, *xymbēnai*], it was in the opposite sense to what was expected," and Euripides (*Helen* 622) remarks, "This is the meaning of that; her words have turned out to be true." So what has come to pass, or is true with regard to the heretics (αὐτοῖς, *autois*, regarding them; dative of respect; BDF §197), is τὸ τῆς ἀληθοῦς παροιμίας (*to tēs alēthous paroimias*, what the true maxim [says]). The following wisdom statements are classified as maxims or proverbs (BDAG 779–80).

The Greek term παροιμίας (*paroimias*, maxim) appears in the LXX to describe the proverbs of the book by the name (Prov. 1:1), but it was also used more widely of maxims in general (Sir. 8:8;[3] Lucian, *Dialogues of the Dead* 16.2; 18.1;[4] Aristophanes, *Thesmophoriazusae* 528–30).[5] Peter adds that the maxim (he uses the singular although he cites two) is "true" (ἀληθοῦς, *alēthous*). This is a known descriptor for proverbial statements, one that is not unexpected given Peter's note that the maxim is true or has come to pass. Sophocles, for example, commented (*Ajax* 664–65), "Yes, men's proverb is true [ἀλλ' ἔστ' ἀληθὴς ἡ βροτῶν παροιμία, *all' est' alēthēs hē brotōn paroimia*]: the gifts of enemies are not gifts and bring no good" (so Theophrastus, *Characters* 29.6, which both describes the maxim as "true" and refers to the saying as τὸ τῆς παροιμίας, *to tēs paroimias*, what the maxim says). The use of traditional language that emphasizes the veracity of maxims serves to justify Peter's application of these proverbs in his denunciation of the heretics.

The first maxim is drawn from Prov. 26:11: Κύων ἐπιστρέψας ἐπὶ τὸ ἴδιον ἐξέραμα (*Kyōn epistrepsas epi to idion exerama*, The dog returns to its own vomit), although Peter does not quote the LXX verbatim (ὥσπερ κύων ὅταν ἐπέλθῃ ἐπὶ τὸν ἑαυτοῦ ἔμετον, *hōsper kyōn hotan epelthē epi ton heautou emeton*, As when a dog goes to his own vomit). This common and disgusting

---

3. "Do not slight the discourse of the sages, but busy yourself with their maxims" (NRSV).

4. Lucian, 16.2: "This is a novel principle: the man who can no longer derive pleasure from his money is to die"; 18.1: "Why, 'tis the proverb fulfilled! The fawn hath taken the lion."

5. "As the old proverb says, [we] must look beneath every stone, lest it conceal some orator ready to sting us."

habit of dogs is somewhat less revolting for the contemporary reader for whom dogs are beloved pets, but the ancients regarded these beasts as despised and miserable animals, which roamed wild in the streets and, in Jewish circles, were considered unclean (Luke 16:21; O. Michel, *TDNT* 3:1101–4). To call someone a "dog" was a great insult (1 Sam. 17:23; Ps. 22:16, 20; Phil. 3:2), and those so described were considered evil (Matt. 7:6; Rev. 22:15). The heretics were no better than dogs who, having once disgorged the contents of their stomachs, return to eat what they left on the street. Peter's application of the proverb is that the heretics have returned to the evil they left behind and in so doing show themselves to be no more than unclean beasts themselves. Proverbs 26:11 tags this as behavior characteristic of the "fool": "Like a dog that returns to its vomit is a fool who reverts to his folly" (NRSV). Peter concurs.

The second maxim does not come from Proverbs but does seem to have been known: καί, Ὗς λουσαμένη εἰς κυλισμὸν βορβόρου (*kai, Hys lousamenē eis kylismon borborou*, and, The sow, having washed, returns to wallowing in the mud). That sows wallow in mud is common knowledge (Philo, *Spec. Laws* 1.29 §148; *Agriculture* 32 §144; Heraclitus, *All.* 53: "Pigs wash in mud," after which he exclaims Βορβόρῳ χαίρειν, *Borborō chairein*, To delight in mud). But the construction of Peter's maxim is elliptical, leaving the reader to supply some verb such as "return" or "goes back." However, given the syntactical ambiguity, the thought may be that "the sow that washes itself by wallowing in the mire" (MM 381; Sextus Empiricus, *Outlines of Pyrrhonism* 1.56: "Pigs, too, enjoy wallowing in the most stinking mire rather than in clear and clean water"; Clement of Alexandria, *Exhortation to the Greeks* 10.92.4). The immediate context, however, favors the first reading since, as the dog returns, so the sow returns to the filth (cf. the Arabic version of the story of Ahiqar 8.15 in R. Charles 1913: 2.772). The inclusion of the preposition εἰς (*eis*, to) supports this interpretation of the proverb. This is what the apostate heretics have done (v. 21). As with the dog, the sow is unclean (Lev. 11:7; Deut. 14:8), and indeed, the two animals are sometimes classified together (cf. 1 Kings 21:19 [20:19 LXX]; 22:38 LXX). These unclean beasts go right back to uncleanness. Peter emphasizes their return as an illustration of the heretics' conduct. They, once having known the Lord and his holy commandment, have denied the Lord (2:1), have been entangled in the defilements of the world again (2:20), and have turned away after having known the way of righteousness (2:21), forgetting that they had been purified from past sins (1:9). This is genuine apostasy (contra Schreiner 2003: 363–65). Peter holds out no hope for such "beasts."

## Additional Note

**2:18.** Although numerous MSS read ὄντως (*ontōs*, certainly, undoubtedly; ℵ C P 048 1739 𝔐), the reading ὀλίγως (*oligōs*) is that of the Alexandrian and Western families and finds very early testimony in 𝔓⁷² (ℵ² A B Ψ 33 630 1505 2495). It is unlikely that an exchange of a rare word for a common one would have been made.

II. Letter Body: A Warning against False Teachers (1:3–3:18a)
    A. Body Opening: God's Call to Glory and Virtue (1:3–11)
    B. Body Middle: The Apostolic Testimony and the False Teachers (1:12–2:22)
➤   C. Body Closing: A Call to Holiness (3:1–18a)

# C. Body Closing: A Call to Holiness (3:1–18a)

Our author introduces the final section of the letter, the body closing (see "Genre and Structure" in the introduction), with the transitional statement in 3:1–2, which restates his purpose for writing, a characteristic feature of letter body closings (White 1972: 42–43). After these introductory words our author identifies the heretics, noting that they are controlled by desire (v. 3) and that they deny that God will intervene to judge the world (3:3–7). These are the mockers whose presence is a sign of the last days. Peter explains the reason for their skepticism as the apparent lack of divine judgment in the past (v. 4), but at once counters their claim with an appeal to the history of divine judgment (vv. 5–6), which serves as the type of the judgment to come (v. 7). At the same time, our author recounts the reason for God's delay in judging the world (3:8–10), warning that the day of judgment will arrive unexpectedly and cataclysmically. As from the beginning of the letter, Peter's concern is moral, and so in the following section he reminds his readers that the final judgment is also a call to the moral life and a source of hope (3:11–13). Peter concludes the body closing of his letter with a series of exhortations (3:14–18a). The body closing brings us face-to-face with the eschatology of the false teachers, which gave rise to their moral lapse. Their denial of future judgment due to divine delay in judgment in the past has been one of the main evidences forwarded to identify these teachers as people who have embraced aspects of Epicurean thought. However, the skepticism that the heretics evidence is not limited to the Epicureans, and their position appears to be more eclectic than is sometimes recognized.

# 1. A Call to Remember Prophetic and Apostolic Teaching (3:1–2)

In this brief introduction to the body closing, Peter calls his readers to re-member what he has previously written them (3:1) and the prophetic and apostolic witness (v. 2). They know this witness, but the heretics have brought it into question (1:16–21). This is the second major "reminder" of the let-ter (see 1:12–15) as Peter evokes this common topos in moral philosophy of reminding one's hearers/readers of what they already know in order to ensure their moral progress.

## Exegesis and Exposition

¹This is now, beloved, the second letter I am writing to you, in which I rouse your pure understanding by means of a reminder, ²so that you recall the words previously spoken by the holy prophets and the commandment of the Lord and Savior given through your apostles.

Peter addresses the readers/hearers with the vocative "beloved," saying, Ταύτην **3:1** ἤδη, ἀγαπητοί, δευτέραν ὑμῖν γράφω ἐπιστολήν (*Tautēn ēdē, agapētoi, deuteran hymin graphō epistolēn*, This is now, beloved, the second letter I am writing to you). Throughout this section he returns to address them in the same way (3:8, 14, 17) as he makes his appeal to them to heed his teaching and not to succumb to the heretics' appeal to engage in an immoral way of life. The ones normally called "beloved" were children, especially only children (Homer, *Od.* 2.365; 4.817; *Il.* 6.401; Demosthenes, *Speeches* 21.165; Tob. 10:13 LXX; Mark 9:7; 12:6), and indeed, when used outside the context of the family, the family comparison is near at hand (as Aristotle, *Pol.* 2.1262B.23). The use of "beloved" within the early church was a marker of the familial relationship between the disciples of Christ, who call on one Father (Acts 15:25; Rom. 1:7; 1 Cor. 4:17; Eph. 5:1). Since one of the principal contexts of moral exhortation was the family, we are not surprised to find that our author repeatedly appeals to the recipients of the letter as "beloved" (cf. 1 Cor. 4:14; 10:14; 1 Pet. 2:11; 4:12). The address lends force to Peter's appeal and at the same time marks the solidarity of the readers with the author. They are those who are inside, within the circle of the family, and not those separated off, as were the heretics.

The force of Peter's appeal is highlighted by the recollection that this is now the second missive the author is writing to these churches. In the literature on 2 Peter, the weight of discussion about this declaration centers on which let-ter the author refers to (1 Peter, a lost letter, or even Jude?) and the evidences for any relationship between this letter and 1 Peter. As important as these questions are, especially in relationship to debates about authorship, Peter's point is sometimes lost in these interpretive conundrums. The opening words of the sentence, Ταύτην ἤδη (*Tautēn ēdē*, This is now), sometimes appear at the head of numbered sequences (as Gen. 27:36 LXX: "And he said, Rightly was his name called Jacob, for lo! this second time [ἤδη δεύτερον τοῦτο, *ēdē deuteron touto*] has he supplanted me"; John 21:14 NRSV: "This was now the third time [τοῦτο ἤδη τρίτον, *touto ēdē triton*] that Jesus appeared to the disciples after he was raised from the dead"). The emphasis is on the way the second or third in the sequence serves as a confirmation of the previous. The "second" occurrence of some event also appears to hold some particular importance as a confirmation of a previous event (Matt. 26:42; John 4:54; 9:24; Acts 7:13; 10:15; 2 Cor. 13:2; Titus 3:10; Heb. 8:7; 9:28; 10:9; Jude 5 and comments). Euripides remarked about "second thoughts": "Among mortals second thoughts are, I suppose, wiser" (*Hipp.* 436). Peter's comment that this is his second letter confirms the content of the first epistle but, at the same time, highlights the importance of the present teaching. In fact, it elevates the importance of this letter above the first. The expression underscores the weight and authority of the present teaching and thus becomes the basis of the appeal the author makes through the final section of the letter.

There is little doubt that the previous letter is the book known to us as 1 Peter. Oddly enough, J. A. T. Robinson (1976: 195) argues that the first letter written to this audience is Jude. The literary relationship between 2 Peter and Jude is extremely tight since Peter uses Jude as a source and, as Robinson notes, the affinities of the thought between these two letters are stronger than between 1 and 2 Peter. However, no plausible explanation can overcome the simple fact that Jude is not attributed to Peter. How could the readers identify Jude as *Peter's* first letter? Robinson's declaration that the author Jude wrote 2 Peter as well does not convince (1976: 193). M. Green (1987: 134), on the other hand, argues that the previous missive is a lost letter, like Paul's first correspondence with the Corinthian church (1 Cor. 5:9; cf. Col. 4:16). Commenting on the purposes of 1 Peter as declared in 2 Pet. 3:1, he states, "However, it can hardly be said that 1 Peter is primarily a letter of reminder, still less a dissuasive against heresy, which seems to be implied in these two verses." M. Green also argues that the author of 2 Peter had a relationship with the readers (implied in 1:12, 16), whereas the author of 1 Peter is not personally known to the recipients of the letter (1 Pet. 1:12). But in his first letter Peter does indeed remind the readers of what they already know (1 Pet. 1:12; 2:2). Moreover, 2 Pet. 1:12 and 16 do not necessarily imply that Peter had a personal ministry among the readers (see comments).

The interconnectedness of 2 Peter with 1 Peter has been variously assessed. What similarities exist may be accounted for either on the basis of common authorship or the use of 1 Peter by the pseudepigrapher who wrote 2 Peter. Boobyer (1959) presents the case for similarities between the two letters, affirming Bigg's (1901: 232) conclusion that "no document in the New Testament is so like 1 Peter as 2 Peter." On the other hand, Gilmore's (2002: 93) assessment of the evidence for the relationship between the two letters runs in the opposite direction. He states, "Except for the fact that there are other reasons to suspect a relationship with 1 Peter (namely 3:1 which most naturally points back to 1 Peter), little connects these two documents other than the name Peter." Whatever the contemporary assessment of the relationship between 1 and 2 Peter, ancient commentators were struck by the differences between the letters, so much so that the authenticity of 2 Peter was brought into question (see "Authorship of 2 Peter" in the introduction). Patristic comment, however, was limited to stylistic dissimilarities: the ancient commentators did not undertake a comparative analysis of the differences or similarities of perspectives found in these documents.

However we may assess the issue, the author of 2 Peter wishes to underscore the commonality of the two documents: ἐν αἷς διεγείρω ὑμῶν ἐν ὑπομνήσει τὴν εἰλικρινῆ διάνοιαν (en hais diegeirō hymōn en hypomnēsei tēn eilikrinē dianoian, in which I rouse your pure understanding by means of a reminder). He states that both this and the previous correspondence have the same end. Using language almost identical to 2 Pet. 1:13 (διεγείρειν ὑμᾶς ἐν ὑπομνήσει, diegeirein hymas en hypomnēsi, to rouse you by a reminder; see also 1:12), Peter once again employs a common topos of moral philosophy that reminders are necessary to ensure right conduct (see 1:13, 15, and comments). Peter here inserts the direct object τὴν εἰλικρινῆ διάνοιαν (tēn eilikrinē dianoian, pure understanding) in place of the accusative plural ὑμᾶς (hymas, you) of 1:13. His intent is to awaken their "pure understanding," that is, their understanding or way of thinking (BDAG 234; 1 Pet. 1:13) that has not been contaminated by the deceit and corruption of the false teachers (see 2 Pet. 2:14, 18). This understanding is simple, singular, unmixed, and as such sincere (LSJ 486; BDAG 282; Phil. 1:20; Wis. 7:25; T. Benj. 6.5; Plato, Phaedo 66A, 81C; and εἰλικρίνια, eilikrinia, sincerity, in 1 Cor. 5:8; 2 Cor. 2:17). His point is not that he wants their understanding to be "wholesome" (contra Moo 1996: 162; Schreiner 2003: 370; see TLNT 1:420–23). Peter seeks to preserve the singularity and simplicity of their understanding and does not want to see it sullied in any way by the persuasion of the heretics and their error. The question remains, however, how our author can classify this letter and 1 Peter as a reminder that rouses their pure understanding. In the first letter, the author does indeed refer to what was previously received through the gospel messengers (1 Pet. 1:12), a message rooted in the prophetic testimony (1:10–11). Moreover, 1 Peter serves to remind them of previous teaching (1:18). In the following verse (2 Pet. 3:2) Peter identifies what he wants his readers to remember—the words of the prophets and the command of the apostles. To call both 1 and 2 Peter reminders of such teaching is wholly in line with the purposes of both letters.

Since the readers/hearers of this letter face the erroneous ideas of the heretics, who promote their own version of Christian morality and cast doubt on the certainty of future judgment (vv. 3–4), Peter states that his purpose is **3:2** to help them recall the teaching of the OT prophets and the apostles. Peter's language is nearly identical to his source, Jude 17, which exhorts: Ὑμεῖς δέ, ἀγαπητοί, μνήσθητε τῶν ῥημάτων τῶν προειρημένων ὑπὸ τῶν ἀποστόλων τοῦ κυρίου ἡμῶν Ἰησοῦ Χριστοῦ (*Hymeis de, agapētoi, mnēsthēte tōn rhēmatōn tōn proeirēmenōn hypo ton apostolōn tou kyriou hēmōn Iēsou Christou*, But you, beloved, remember the words previously spoken by the apostles of our Lord Jesus Christ; see comments). He does, however, modify the citation, thus making the material his own (a practice known as "imitation" [μίμησις, *mimēsis*] or *imitatio*; see the introduction to 2 Pet. 2:1–3 and "The Relationship between 2 Peter and Jude" in the introduction to 2 Peter) as he adjusts Jude's call in light of the threats facing his readers. Instead of including Jude's exhortation to remember apostolic teaching, Peter states that his purpose is to remind them so that they will recall the prophetic testimony as well as the apostolic teaching. Peter speaks of the "previously spoken words" of the prophets and the "command" given through the apostles, a modification of Jude's "previously spoken words" of the apostles. Peter has already stated that his purpose in writing this missive is to remind the readers of "these things" after his death (1:12–15) and that the teaching the churches have received is well founded on both faithful apostolic testimony (1:16–18) and a sure prophetic word (1:19–21). Those preliminary paragraphs serve as his opening defense against the heretics' dismissal of both the prophetic and apostolic teaching.

As Peter launches this final defense, he writes this reminder: μνησθῆναι τῶν προειρημένων ῥημάτων ὑπὸ τῶν ἁγίων προφητῶν καὶ τῆς τῶν ἀποστόλων ὑμῶν ἐντολῆς τοῦ κυρίου καὶ σωτῆρος (*mnēsthēnai tōn proeirēmenōn rhēmatōn hypo tōn hagiōn prophētōn kai tēs tōn apostolōn hymōn entolēs tou kyriou kai sōtēros*, so that you recall the words previously spoken by the holy prophets and the commandment of the Lord and Savior given through your apostles). The call to remember presupposes that these believers have received the fundamentals of Christian instruction (3:1; 1:12; and comments). This teaching included the OT revelation, which the church regarded as authoritative for its own theology and life (1 Pet. 1:10–11; Rom. 15:4). Here, "words" is a reference to the prophetic Scriptures (Isa. 15:1; 17:1; 40:8; Jer. 1:1; 5:14; Ezek. 33:31–32), which had been "previously spoken." As such, they predict or proclaim beforehand future events (see the use of προλέγω, *prolegō*, to describe prophetic speech in Acts 1:16; Matt. 24:25; Mark 13:23; Rom. 9:29; Josephus, *Ant.* 2.2.4 §17; *J.W.* 6.2.1 §109; Appian, *Bell. civ.* 1.71; Herodotus 1.53; BDAG 867).

Sidebottom (1967: 118) suggests that the "holy prophets" who predicted future events are those of the NT era (Acts 15:32; Eph. 3:5; 4:11) and not OT prophets. But in light of Peter's previous teaching about the veracity of the prophetic message of the OT (1:19–21), which the false teachers have cast in doubt, we should understand these "holy prophets" as messengers known to us through the OT (Luke 1:70; Acts 3:21; Wis. 11:1). Since the false teachers have questioned the reality of future judgment (3:3–10), Peter likely has in mind the multiple prophetic oracles about this future event (as Isa. 2:4; 41:1; Jer. 25:3; Joel 3:2, 12; Mic. 4:3). Alternatively, Bauckham (1983: 287) suggests that

Peter refers to prophecies regarding scoffers who "mock the delayed judgment of God" (as Amos 9:10; Mal. 2:17) and the predictions of divine judgment on them (Isa. 5:18–20; Jer. 5:12–24; Amos 9:10). But Peter has previously defended the veracity and divine inspiration of prophetic teaching in general (1:19–21), and given the close relationship between this passage and the previous section, we should understand the "words previously spoken by the holy prophets" in the same manner here.

He places "the commandment of the Lord and Savior given through your apostles" (τῆς τῶν ἀποστόλων ὑμῶν ἐντολῆς τοῦ κυρίου καὶ σωτῆρος, *tēs tōn apostolōn hymōn entolēs tou kyriou kai sōtēros*) as the foundation stone of the church. The call to remember presupposes that these believers have received the fundamentals of Christian teaching on the same level with the OT prophetic testimony. While the apostles are the spokesmen, "the Lord and Savior," Jesus, is the source of their utterances (see 1:11; 2:20; 3:18; and comments). The "commandment" is the same one referred to in 2:21 (see comments), the "holy commandment" or the substance of apostolic instruction. The reference to "your apostles" is not a sign that this document comes from the subapostolic era (cf. Phil. 2:25; contra Kelly 1969: 354), nor is Peter trying to distinguish between true apostles and false apostles with the pronoun "your" (contra Bigg 1901: 290; Sidebottom 1967: 118). "Your apostles" are simply those who have proclaimed the Christian message to them. Paul was probably one of this company (3:15) and possibly Barnabas also (Acts 14:14). Other "apostles" carried out their ministry in Asia Minor as well. The group of apostles was wider than the Twelve and Paul (Acts 14:14; Rom. 16:7; 1 Cor. 15:5, 7; 2 Cor. 8:23; Gal. 1:19; Eph. 4:11; Phil. 2:25; 1 Thess. 1:1; 2:7; Burton 1920: 363–81). The Letter to the Ephesians declares that the church is "built upon the foundation of the apostles and prophets" (2:20 NRSV), and Peter fully concurs. For the church to maintain its identity, it cannot abandon the prophetic and apostolic testimony.

# 2. Understand This: The Scoffers of the Last Day (3:3–7)

After calling his readers to remember his own testimony, the words of the prophets, and the commandment of the Lord given through the apostles (3:1–2), our author identifies the heretics as those who are controlled by desire (v. 3) and who deny the reality of future judgment since they observe that things remain unchanged since ancient times (v. 4). This is a rare moment, since our author quotes their questions about the promise of the coming, which they understand as linked to the final judgment (see v. 10). As in the previous chapter, Peter's response is that God has indeed judged the world in the past. The reason things continue as they have from the beginning is only because God's word sustains everything (vv. 5, 7). But although God sustained the ancient world, he destroyed it through the flood (v. 6) just as he will usher in judgment by fire for the present heaven and earth (v. 7). This will mean the "destruction of the ungodly" as well. In this section Peter enters into a debate current in his day about the immutability of the world and the possibility of divine judgment. His perspective is not shaped principally by philosophical currents but by the witness of the prophets and the Lord handed down through the apostles. In this clash of ideas and morals, Peter stands on the side of divine revelation.

## Exegesis and Exposition

³Above all know this, that in the last days mockers will come with their mocking, living according to their own desires ⁴and saying, "Where is the promise of his coming? Because since the time the fathers died, all things remain as they were from the beginning of creation." ⁵For they willfully ignore this fact that by the word of God the heavens came into being long ago and the earth is sustained, having been formed out of water and through water, ⁶through which the world at that time was destroyed, being flooded by water. ⁷But by the same word the present heavens and earth have been reserved for fire, being kept for the day of judgment and destruction of ungodly people.

**3:3**   One of the principal goals of our author is to affirm the truth of the prophetic message and emphasize its importance for his readers, since the heretics have brought into doubt the coming of the Lord and the final judgment. Therefore in this passage, as in the defense of prophetic inspiration in 1:20, he begins with the call τοῦτο πρῶτον γινώσκοντες (*touto prōton ginōskontes*, above all know this). Peter has previously stated that, in the midst of doctrinal controversy, the most important thing his readers should know (πρῶτον, *prōton*, adverb of degree meaning "in the first place"; cf. Matt. 6:33; Acts 3:26; Rom. 1:16; 2 Cor. 8:5; 1 Tim. 2:1; BDAG 894) is the inspired prophetic word (2 Pet. 1:19–20). Peter's focus in the present verse, however, is on the presence of the heretics as a sign that the last days have arrived. The readers should be fully aware that their coming was predicted. The call to "know" or "understand" (γινώσκοντες, *ginōskontes*; imperatival participle; BDF §468.2) is likely a reminder of something known (see 1:12 and comments) instead of the addition of new information (compare the similar interpretive issue in Rom. 6:6; Eph. 5:5; 2 Tim. 3:1).

What the readers should recognize above all else is ὅτι ἐλεύσονται ἐπ᾽ ἐσχάτων τῶν ἡμερῶν [ἐν] ἐμπαιγμονῇ ἐμπαῖκται κατὰ τὰς ἰδίας ἐπιθυμίας αὐτῶν πορευόμενοι (*hoti eleusontai ep᾽ eschatōn tōn hēmerōn [en] empaigmonē empaiktai kata tas idias epithymias autōn poreuomenoi*, that in the last days mockers will come with their mocking, living according to their own desires). As in the previous verse, Peter's source is Jude (v. 18), which says, ὅτι ἔλεγον ὑμῖν· [ὅτι] Ἐπ᾽ ἐσχάτου [τοῦ] χρόνου ἔσονται ἐμπαῖκται κατὰ τὰς ἑαυτῶν ἐπιθυμίας πορευόμενοι τῶν ἀσεβειῶν (*hoti elegon hymin: [hoti] Ep᾽ eschatou [tou] chronou esontai empaiktai, kata tas heautōn epithymias poreuomenoi tōn asebeiōn*, for they said to you, "In the last time mockers will come who live according to the dictates of their own godless desires"). According to Jude, these words were an apostolic testimony (v. 17). Peter, on the other hand, does not ascribe these words to the apostles, yet in 3:2 he calls his readers to remember "the words previously spoken by the holy prophets and the commandment of the Lord and Savior given through your apostles," thus implying the apostolic source of the present teaching. In his *imitatio* of Jude, Peter substitutes Jude's ἔσονται (*esontai*, will be) for ἐλεύσονται (*eleusontai*, will come), emphasizes Jude's note about their mocking ([ἐν] ἐμπαιγμονῇ ἐμπαῖκται, *[en] empaigmonē empaiktai*, mockers . . . with their mocking, for Jude's ἐμπαῖκται, *empaiktai*, mockers), and drops Jude's qualification that their desires are "godless" (τῶν ἀσεβειῶν, *tōn asebeiōn*).

Like Jude, Peter recognizes the presence of the heretics as a sign that the last days have arrived (cf. Acts 2:17; 2 Tim. 3:1; Heb. 1:2; James 5:3; Jude 18; and comments). His focus is not on some future time but on his own days. The "last time" was the era of prophetic fulfillment (2 Bar. 6.8; 41.5; CD 6.11; 1QSa 1.1), which was also considered to be an era when forces of evil would be especially active (T. Iss. 6.1; 1 Tim. 4:1–3; 2 Tim. 3:1–9). The heretics are labeled [ἐν] ἐμπαιγμονῇ ἐμπαῖκται ([*en] empaigmonē empaiktai*), "mockers" who come "with their mocking." We frequently meet such mockers in the OT (Pss. 1:1; 35:16; Prov. 1:22; 9:7–8; 13:1; 14:6; 19:25, 29), where they are cast as godless people who engage in a libertine lifestyle. "Mocking" is a supreme act of dishonor in an attempt to bring shame upon a person (see Herodotus 4.134; Epictetus, *Disc.* 1.4.10). As noted previously (Jude 18 and comments), "to mock" is part of a large group of words that stand "for the disparagement or low estimation of others, or indeed the world, creatures, and even deity, in word, attitude or act" (G. Bertram, *TDNT* 5:630). In 2 Chron. 36:16 the LXX uses the verbal form of the word found here in 2 Peter and Jude: "Nevertheless they sneered at his messengers, and set at naught his words, and mocked [ἐμπαίζοντες, *empaizontes*] his prophets." The charge demonstrates how degraded the heretics are. The "mocking" of the heretics is a marker identifying their character. These people are κατὰ τὰς ἰδίας ἐπιθυμίας αὐτῶν πορευόμενοι (*kata tas idias epithymias autōn poreuomenoi*, living according to their own desires), language that also echoes Jude 18 as well as Jude 16. Not virtue but base desires govern the conduct of the heretics.

Peter describes their conduct with the verb πορευόμενοι (*poreuomenoi*), a term frequently found in the context of moral instruction, which refers to how a person lives or "walks" (BDAG 853). Some may conduct themselves "according to the purpose of God" (κατὰ τὴν βουλὴν τοῦ θεοῦ, *kata tēn boulēn tou theou*), "in the fear of God" (Ps. Sol. 18.10), or "according to the dictates of their own desires," resulting in sinful behavior (cf. 2 Pet. 2:10; 3:3; 1 Pet. 4:3). Peter has previously warned against submitting to the control of such desires (1:4; 2:10, 18; and comments). The heretics whom Peter opposes are driven by these lower impulses, looking for satisfaction by yielding to their lusts. The root of their heresy is moral, not intellectual. The doubts about the promise of Christ's coming and the future judgment (2 Pet. 3:4) are framed by reason and experience, but their true source is the base character of the heretics. The doctrinal denial warrants their behavior, but their character and praxis give rise to their skepticism. Heteropraxis begets heterodoxy.

**3:4**   Before refuting the arguments of the false teachers (vv. 5–10), Peter presents their rationale for rejecting the notion of coming judgment. They ask: καὶ λέγοντες, Ποῦ ἐστιν ἡ ἐπαγγελία τῆς παρουσίας αὐτοῦ; (*kai legontes, Pou estin hē epangelia tēs parousias autou?* and saying, "Where is the promise of his coming?"). Throughout biblical history, introducing a question with the words "Where is" was common among those whom we may broadly classify as skeptics (2 Kings 18:34; Pss. 42:3, 10 [41:4, 11 LXX]; 79:10 [78:10 LXX]; 115:2 [113:10 LXX]; Jer. 17:15; Joel 2:17; Mic. 7:10; Mal. 2:17; John 8:19). The form of the question has a familiar ring for anyone who knows Scripture. The question of the false teachers is a demand for evidence regarding "the promise of his coming" (on the advent or παρουσία, *parousia*, of the Lord see 1:16; 3:12; and comments). The heretics have given their own promise of "freedom" (2:19) but at the same time place in doubt the divine promises (3:9; cf. Acts 26:6; Rom. 4:20; 9:8; 15:8; Gal. 3:17, 21; Heb. 10:36). Such promises are firm, according to Paul (2 Cor. 1:20) as well as our author (1:4; 3:9, 13). So fundamental to the divine character are God's promises that the author of Hebrews calls him "the One who promises" (ὁ ἐπαγγειλάμενος, *ho epangeilamenos*; Heb. 10:23; 11:11; 6:13) and affirms that he is faithful to fulfill what is promised. Peter has already extolled God as the great Benefactor who has given "honorable and extraordinary promises," which are the foundation of salvation (1:4 and comments) and on which the hope of final consummation rests (3:13 and comments). But the heretics bring into doubt these promises, which came through divine revelation, basing their skepticism on their own empirical assessment of history: such is the height of their hubris.

To be sure, there is a delay between promise and consummation (see 3:9). Since early in its history, the church has been obliged to present an apologetic to explain the apparent delay in the coming of the Lord (Luke 12:45; Heb. 10:36–37; James 5:7–8), especially in light of various teachings that seem to imply that God will soon bring history to its end (Matt. 10:23; 16:28; 24:34; Mark 9:1; 13:30; John 21:22–23; and cf. Ezek. 12:21–25; and Sir. 16:21–23, which reflect a similar eschatological skepticism). But the heretics question not only the reality of Christ's advent but also the judgment that he will usher in, as is evident from Peter's response in verses 5–10. Peter understands this connection well and stands with the dominical teaching that joins Christ's advent with his judgment of the nations (Matt. 24:29–30; 25:1–46).

The false teachers base their skepticism on the apparent lack of divine intervention in human affairs in the past, beginning with the creation of all things. They argue: ἀφ' ἧς γὰρ οἱ πατέρες ἐκοιμήθησαν, πάντα οὕτως διαμένει ἀπ' ἀρχῆς κτίσεως (aph' hēs gar hoi pateres ekoimēthēsan, panta houtōs diamenei ap' archēs ktiseōs, because since the time the fathers died, all things remain as they were from the beginning of creation).[1] The expression ἀφ' ἧς (aph' hēs) was a common formula that meant simply "since" (1 Macc. 1:11; Acts 24:11; Col. 1:6, 9; BDAG 105). The heretics mark the time since the fathers "fell asleep" (ἐκοιμήθησαν), a well-known euphemism for death in the wider Mediterranean world and not only in the church (Homer, Il. 11.241; Sophocles, Electra 509; Catullus, Poems 5.4–6; 1 Thess. 4:13–15; Matt. 27:52; John 11:11–13; Acts 13:36; 1 Cor. 15:6, 18, 20, 51; MM 350; BDAG 551; LSJ 967; Lattimore 1942: 59, 164–65). The expression communicates the idea "for a long time now," placing the death of the fathers in some distant past. These are the ancestors who have long since passed off the scene (1 En. 99.14; Ps. Sol. 9.10; Josephus, Ant. 13.10.6 §297; Matt. 23:30, 32; Luke 1:55; 6:23, 26; John 4:20; 6:31; Acts 3:13, 25; Heb. 1:1). Their point is that since the distant past, things have continued without change.

The "fathers" has sometimes been taken as a reference to the first generation of Christians who hoped to see Christ's advent but whose hopes were crushed on the wheel of time. This interpretation is especially attractive if the author is identified not as Peter but rather as a second-generation or later Christian writing under his name (see, e.g., Schelkle 1980: 224; Kelly 1969: 355–56; Bauckham 1983: 290–92; Perkins 1995: 189). However, the early church did not refer to the first generation of Christians in this way. "The fathers" was a common enough term for Jewish ancestors, as noted above, but was used in the same way among those who did not share this heritage. As Homer (Od. 8.245) said, "Zeus has

---

1. The argument is similar to 1 Clem. 23.3–4 and 2 Clem. 11.2–4. However, these texts do not show dependence on 2 Pet. 3:4 but rather cite an unknown source. See Hagner 1973: 73–74.

vouchsafed to us from our fathers' days even until now" (see Homer, *Il.* 6.209; John 4:20; O. Hofius, *NIDNTT* 1:615–16; LSJ 1348). Likely the reference is to "ancestors" in general since the heretics are simply making a point about time long past and conditions that have not changed since then.

The heretics affirm that everything continues the same not only since the time of the ancestors but even as far back as creation: πάντα οὕτως διαμένει ἀπ' ἀρχῆς κτίσεως (*panta houtōs diamenei ap' archēs ktiseōs*, "all things remain as they were from the beginning of creation"). "From the beginning of creation" was a common expression (Mark 10:6; 13:19; 1 En. 15.9; Barn. 15.3), which again underscores the heretics' claim that nothing ever changes but everything remains the same (διαμένει; BDAG 233) over the whole course of history. Their doctrine is similar to the claims of Epicurus: "But, in truth, the universal whole always was such as it now is, and always will be such. For there is nothing into which it can change; for there is nothing beyond this universal whole which can penetrate into it, and produce any change in it" (*Letter to Herodotus* 38; Lucretius 1.225–37). This is a claim of permanence (LSJ 403; MM 152) over against philosophical notions of change and mutability. In the famous Epicurean inscription, Diogenes of Oenoanda stated: "Since the first bodies ["also called elements," frg. 6] cannot be broken up by anyone, whether he is god or man, one is left to conclude that these things are absolutely indestructible, beyond the reach of necessity. For if they were destroyed, in accordance with necessity, into the nonexistent, all things would have perished" (frg. 8; cf. 2 Pet. 3:10–11). The heretics' argument is that God has not intervened in human history, empirical evidence showing that all things continue without change. Since there have been no changes, no divine intervention in the past, no judgment, one should expect conditions to continue as they are into the future. The promises of God have not come to pass in the past, nor will they come to pass in the future. This is the foundation of their skepticism and mocking of the apostolic teaching regarding the promises of God (2 Pet. 2:3). Peter will reject this position vigorously in the following verses.

**3:5**  In verses 5–7, Peter refutes the affirmation of the heretics found in 3:4b: "Because since the time the fathers died, all things remain as they were from the beginning of creation." In the following paragraph (vv. 8–10), he argues against the heretics' question posed in 3:4a: "Where is the promise of his coming?" Bauckham (1983: 296) notes that the structure of these verses is chiastic: A (3:4a), B (3:4b), B′ (3:5–7), A′ (3:8–10). The apostle begins his refutation by denouncing the willful ignorance of the heretics: λανθάνει γὰρ αὐτοὺς τοῦτο θέλοντας (*lanthanei gar autous touto thelontas*, for they[2] willfully ignore this fact). The verb λανθάνω (*lanthanō*) most commonly refers to not taking notice of something or something escaping a person's notice (Mark 7:24; Luke 8:47; Acts 26:26; Heb. 13:2; Wis. 1:8; 10:8; 17:3; BDAG 586; MM 370). In just a few verses (3:8), Peter will call his readers to avoid being counted among those who ignore the divine perspective on time. However, in the present verse Peter does

---

2. Translation *ad sensum*. The verb λανθάνει (*lanthanei*, ignore) is singular.

not tag the false teachers simply as those who have failed to take note of some fundamental truths. Rather, they are people who have ignored or willfully passed over them (see the same use of the verb in Homer, *Il.* 9.537; Aeschylus, *Agamemnon* 39). Lest there be any doubt among his readers about his intent, Peter adds the present participle of θέλω (*thelō*), θέλοντας (*thelontas*), which suggests the idea "willingly" or even "gladly" (LSJ 479; G. Schrenk, *TDNT* 3:46; as Homer, *Od.* 3.272: "and her, willing as she was willing, he led to his own house"; 2 Tim. 3:12; Heb. 13:18). The accusation underscores the heretics' intent. Their ignorance is not merely an unfortunate circumstance. They are marked as those who have willfully passed over the fundamental truths from Scripture that Peter now elaborates. Faced with these facts, they have turned their backs.

The heretics ignore this truth from Scripture: ὅτι οὐρανοὶ ἦσαν ἔκπαλαι καὶ γῆ ἐξ ὕδατος καὶ δι' ὕδατος συνεστῶσα τῷ τοῦ θεοῦ λόγῳ (*hoti ouranoi ēsan ekpalai kai gē ex hydatos kai di' hydatos synestōsa tō tou theou logō*, that by the word of God the heavens came into being long ago and the earth is sustained, having been formed out of water and through water). The apostle looks back to the creation of the heavens and, in this verse, the verb ἦσαν (*ēsan*, were) implies this act ("came into being"; cf. John 17:5). Peter notes that this event occurred "long ago," using the adverb ἔκπαλαι (*ekpalai*), a term he used in 2:3 but whose sense in the present verse is "long ago" and not "for a long time" (BDAG 307; MM 197; cf. Plutarch, *Nicias* 9.3; *Themistocles* 30.1). The creation of the heavens and the earth by the "word of God" is a fundamental and oft-repeated theme (Gen. 1:3–30; Pss. 33:6 [32:6 LXX]; 148:5; Wis. 9:1; Sir. 48:3; 2 Esd. [4 Ezra] 6:38, 43; John 1:1–3; Heb. 11:3).

But Peter's concern is not simply with God's creation of the heavens via his word. He turns his attention to the earth (γῆ, *gē*, feminine singular), which exists or is sustained (συνεστῶσα, *synestōsa*, a perfect participle in the feminine singular; cf. Let. Aris. 154; W. Kasch, *TDNT* 7:897; BDAG 973; MM 608) by this very same divine word. The verb, here used as a participle modifying "earth," suggests "a condition of coherence": the earth endures or is held together by this very word. Paul makes a similar declaration by using the same verb in Col. 1:17, "in him all things hold together" (NRSV), there echoing a relatively common thought regarding the way divine agency assures the continued existence of all things (Plato, *Republic* 7.530A; Ps.-Aristotle, *De mundo* 6.2; Philo, *Heir* 12 §58; Aristides, *Or.* 1.3–5). The notion of God's sustaining power is given prominent voice in Sir. 43:5–26. Speaking of the stars, the author says, "On the orders of the Holy One they stand in their appointed places; they never relax in their watches" (43:5). He concludes, "By his word all things hold together [NRSV]" (ἐν λόγῳ αὐτοῦ σύγκειται τὰ πάντα, *en logō autou synkeitai ta panta* [43:26]). Peter's affirmation echoes that of Heb. 1:3 ("He sustains all things by his powerful word" [NRSV]) and anticipates his claim in 3:7 that "by the same word the present heavens and earth have been reserved for fire." The heretics have rejected divine revelation by asserting that all things have remained the same from creation. Peter, in part, concedes their point. The heavens came into being and the earth is sustained by God, in fact, by the word of God. Things have indeed continued the same from creation until the present. But this stability, as the creation, is due to divine agency. And that same agency, the word of God, sustains the present world for the future judgment (3:7). The heretics have diminished God's word, questioning his promises (3:4).

Although Peter places his emphasis on the way the word of God sustains the earth, he notes, parenthetically, that the creation of the earth was ἐξ ὕδατος καὶ δι' ὕδατος (ex hydatos kai di' hydatos, having been formed out of water and through water; elliptical construction). He alludes to Gen. 1:6–10 and appears to be cognizant of the traditions based on this text. Genesis 1:9 records the divine command, "Let the waters under the sky be gathered together into one place, and let the dry land appear" (NRSV). The separation of the waters as part of the act of creation of the earth echoes throughout subsequent accounts of creation. Second Esdras (4 Ezra) 6:42 states, "On the third day you commanded the waters to be gathered together in a seventh part of the earth; six parts you dried up and kept so that some of them might be planted and cultivated and be of service before you" (NRSV). Likewise, 2 En. 47.5 says, "And the earth he solidified above the waters, and the waters he based upon the unfixed things," which itself appears to allude to the telling of creation in Ps. 24:2 (23:2 LXX): "He has founded it upon the seas, and established it upon the rivers" (RSV). Jubilees 2.5–7 recounts the same story: the waters "turned aside from upon the surface of the earth into one place outside of this firmament. And dry land appeared" (2.7).[3] On the other hand, Peter speaks of the earth as coming "out of water and through water," language that does not appear to find parallel in the literature. However, the notion that land would appear as the waters were separated and gathered is the most common note in this tradition, and this thought is likely what Peter has in mind. The point that Peter makes, however, is linked with his purpose. The earth came out of water, but the water turned and destroyed the earth (3:6). God, the sustainer of the earth, is also the judge of the earth.

**3:6**    Over against the opinion of the false teachers, Peter has shown that God is not only the creator but also actively sustains the world. The present verse advances his argument one step further as he reminds his readers that God has already judged the world in the past by means of the cataclysmic flood. By recalling the flood, our author cuts the heart out of the heretics' claim that "all things remain as they were from the beginning of creation" (3:4b) and at the same time lays the foundation for his assertion in the following verse that God will indeed judge the world in the future, just as he has done in the past. The apostle asserts, δι' ὧν ὁ τότε κόσμος ὕδατι κατακλυσθεὶς ἀπώλετο (di' hōn hō tote

---

3. The Nag Hammadi library contains a text that postdates 2 Peter, titled "On the Origin of the World." The same themes are echoed: "And when that spirit appeared, the ruler set apart the watery substance. And what was dry was divided into another place. And from matter, he made for himself an abode, and he called it 'heaven' and from matter, the ruler made a footstool, and he called it 'earth'" (100.10–14).

*kosmos hydati kataklystheis apōleto*, through which the world at that time was destroyed, being flooded by water). Peter has previously reminded his readers of the judgment of God in the flood (2:5 and comments). There he identified the world that was destroyed by the flood as the ἀρχαίου κόσμου (*archaiou kosmou*, ancient world), but in the present verse he calls it ὁ τότε κόσμος (*hō tote kosmos*, the world at that time). This adjectival use of τότε (*tote*) was a well-known way of referring to those things or those people who existed in the distant past (LSJ 1808; BDAG 1012). Given the rather sparse description of the flood, we may assume that Peter's readers are well acquainted with the narrative found in Gen. 7, especially the way the flood came and destroyed all living creatures, including humanity, save for Noah and those with him (Gen. 7:21, 23). The topic of the flood was also taken up in the first letter (1 Pet. 3:18–22) but for different ends. There the emphasis was on the flood as a type of the waters of baptism (3:21). Peter's end here is to show that the flood is an example of God's intervention to judge the world. In 2 Pet. 2:5 our author refers to that destruction by saying that God οὐκ ἐφείσατο (*ouk epheisato*, did not spare) the ancient world, but in the present verse Peter notes that the world ἀπώλετο (*apōleto*, was destroyed), a verb that is the antonym of "salvation" (see Jude 5, 11, and comments). Peter previously warned of the destruction that will come on the heretics (2 Pet. 2:1, 3; 3:16; and comments) and in this section again advises his readers that the day of destruction is coming (3:7). Although the language is somewhat different, Peter's thought is similar to 3 Macc. 2:4: "You destroyed men for their wicked deeds in the past, among them giants relying on their own strength and self-confidence, upon whom you brought an immeasurable flood of water."

The destruction of the ancient world is a type of that greater destruction to come when God judges the world. As noted previously, the flood generation of people were archetypal sinners, and so the flood itself became the pattern for future divine judgment. But in the present verse Peter turns his readers' attention to the way that the very waters out of which and through which the world was created (2 Pet. 3:5) became the agency for the destruction of the world of that time (δι᾽ ὧν, *di᾽ hōn*, through which). God reversed his creative act as the waters that brought forth the world also brought that world to its end. Peter's language is somewhat redundant: he not only comments that the ancient world was destroyed through the waters but also that it came to its end ὕδατι κατακλυσθείς (*hydati kataklystheis*, being flooded by water; cf. Wis. 10:4). Previously Peter has referred to the flood by using the substantive form of this verb κατακλυσμόν (*kataklysmon*, flood; 2:5 and comments). This additional comment about the waters clarifies for his readers how the ancient destruction occurred.

Peter now arrives at his conclusion, contradicting the opinion of the false teachers who have denied the coming judgment. God will judge the present world just as he destroyed the former or ancient world (3:6). Peter refers to three worlds in this letter: the antediluvian (3:6), the present (3:7), and the world

**3:7**

to come (3:13). Just as the first world was brought into being and sustained by the word of God (3:5), so also the present world is sustained by that very same word (3:7). But as the first world was destroyed (3:6), so too the second will end in a cataclysmic divine judgment (3:7, 10–12), after which God will usher in the world to come (3:13). Peter, however, not only takes up the topic of past and future judgment but also affirms, as he has done previously (3:5), that God's providence keeps the world for that very judgment. He sees no tension between the affirmation of divine providence and divine judgment. Peter declares: οἱ δὲ νῦν οὐρανοὶ καὶ ἡ γῆ τῷ αὐτῷ λόγῳ τεθησαυρισμένοι εἰσὶν πυρὶ τηρούμενοι εἰς ἡμέραν κρίσεως καὶ ἀπωλείας τῶν ἀσεβῶν ἀνθρώπων (*hoi de nyn ouranoi kai hē gē tō autō logō tethēsaurismenoi eisin pyri tēroumenoi eis hēmeran kriseōs kai apōleias tōn asebōn anthrōpōn*, but by the same word the present heavens and earth have been reserved for fire, being kept for the day of judgment and destruction of ungodly people). With these words, Peter not only contradicts the heresy that has made its way into the churches; he also motivates the believers to maintain a holy way of life (3:11).

Peter explains that "the same word" (τῷ αὐτῷ λόγῳ, *tō autō logō*) that sustained the ancient world (3:5) is the very divine word by which "the present heavens and earth have been reserved." The verb, here in a periphrastic participial construction (τεθησαυρισμένοι εἰσίν, *tethēsaurismenoi eisin*, perfect passive participle), commonly appears in contexts where the author speaks of guarding or preserving treasure (Matt. 6:19–20; Luke 12:21; 1 Cor. 16:2; 2 Cor. 12:14; 4 Macc. 4:3; Philo, *Sacrifices* 16 §62; *Unchangeable* 34 §156). But Peter employs the term to refer to the ad hoc concept of the divine preservation of the created order for the coming judgment. In his hands it becomes synonymous with "keep" (τηρέω, *tēreō*, in 2:4, 9, 17; and 3:7b). God is not only able to keep the righteous for salvation but also to keep the ungodly for their final doom and to keep that doom for the ungodly (cf. Jude 6, 13 and comments; T. Reu. 5.5; Josephus, *Ant.* 1.3.7 §96). As prisoners awaiting the execution of the judgment pronounced upon them, so the present world is reserved for that final day. Divine providence extends down to judgment.

The means of judgment will be "fire" (πυρί, *pyri*) and not water, as in the flood (cf. 3:6). Previously Peter spoke of the judgment of Sodom and Gomorrah, which were turned to ash (2:6 and comments; Jude 7), and that judgment by fire presaged the one to come. The judgment of the world by fire is an archetypal theme in the OT (Deut. 32:22; Isa. 29:6; 30:27, 30, 33; 33:14; 66:15–16, 24; Joel 2:30; Nah. 1:6; Zeph. 1:18; 3:8; Mal. 4:1) as well as the NT (2 Pet. 3:10 and comments; Acts 2:19; 2 Thess. 1:8; Rev. 9:17–18; 16:8; 20:9) and Jewish literature (Sib. Or. 2.196–213; 3.80–93; 4.171–82; 5.155–61, 206–13; Ps. Sol. 15.4; 1 En. 1.6–7; 52.6; 1QH 11.19–36; Josephus, *Ant.* 1.2.3 §70). The first-century-AD L.A.E. 49.3 joins together the judgment by flood and fire in a way similar to Peter's discourse: "Our Lord will bring over your race the wrath of his judgment, first by water and then by fire; by these two the Lord will judge the whole human race."

The Stoics also spoke of the judgment of the world by fire, but the roots of Peter's declaration are markedly Judeo-Christian. The Stoic doctrine of judgment was that "periodically the universe was dissolved and renewed by means of a conflagration (ἐκπύρωσις) in which everything returned to its most basic element, fire, before reconstituting itself" (Bauckham 1983: 300; see Diogenes Laertius, *Lives* 7.134; Cicero, *Nat. d.* 2.118). According to Heraclitus (*All.* 20–26), the world was made from fire, and that fire was transformed into air, the air became water, water was turned into earth, and then earth to fire. The fire is identified with the divine and is therefore present in all things (Diogenes Laertius, *Lives* 7.137). Ovid likewise proclaimed a destruction by fire, saying of Jupiter, "He remembered also that 'twas in the fates that a time would come when sea and land, the unkindled palace of the sky and the beleaguered structure of the universe should be destroyed by fire." But he also contemplated a destruction by water (*Metamorphoses* 1.253–61). Peter's cosmology would have sounded a familiar note, regardless of the cultural matrix of his audience (Riesner 1984; Thiede 1986a). His cosmology, however, is different from Stoic doctrine since God is transcendent and the creative word of God brings the world into being. The same God will bring in the new order of heaven and earth. Peter does not share Stoic cyclicism but understands that there are three worlds: the past, the present, and the future. God is the one who creates, sustains, judges, and then re-creates without any suggestion that the process is anything other than linear.

Peter reiterates the doctrine that the present order is being kept by God for judgment, but now expands his thought to embrace the consequences for humanity: τηρούμενοι εἰς ἡμέραν κρίσεως καὶ ἀπωλείας τῶν ἀσεβῶν ἀνθρώπων (*tēroumenoi eis hēmeran kriseōs kai apōleias tōn asebōn anthrōpōn*, being kept for the day of judgment and destruction of ungodly people). The "day of judgment" (2:9; 1:19 and comments) is also called "the day of the Lord" (3:10) and "the day of God" (3:12), the very day that is marked by the advent of the Lord Jesus (2 Cor. 1:14; 1 Thess. 5:2; 2 Thess. 2:2). That "day" will bring the "destruction" (2 Pet. 2:1, 3 and comments; 3:16) on those who reject that way of God, those who are here described as "ungodly people" (2:5–6 and comments). The judgment of the world has personal consequences.

# 3. Do Not Ignore This: One Day Is as a Thousand Years (3:8–10)

Although our author has refuted the heretics who claim that all things have continued without change since creation and that therefore there will be no future judgment (vv. 3–7), he must now explain to his readers why there has been an apparent delay in judgment. Peter gives his own interpretation to the phenomena that the heretics rally around. First, he states that God's perception of time must be set over against human calculation since a long time for humans is but a short span for God (v. 8). Indeed, one cannot speculate on when God will intervene since the "day of the Lord" will come at an unexpected moment, like the coming of a thief (v. 10a). Whatever delay in judgment there may be is not rooted in the inability of God to intervene in human affairs but is an expression of the mercy of God, who desires salvation for humans and not their destruction (v. 9). But at the end of this brief paragraph, he again affirms, as he did in verse 7, that judgment will indeed come (v. 10). The end will be a time when both heaven and earth will suffer destruction and when all the deeds of humanity will be exposed.

## Exegesis and Exposition

⁸But do not let this one thing escape your notice, beloved, that with the Lord one day is as a thousand years and a thousand years as one day. ⁹The Lord is not slow to fulfill the promise, as some count slowness, but he is patient toward you, not willing for anyone to perish but all to come to repentance. ¹⁰But the day of the Lord will come ⌜as a thief⌝ in which the heavens will pass away with a roar and the elements will be destroyed by burning, even the earth and the works that are ⌜discovered⌝ in it.

**3:8**   Peter now responds to the question that the false teachers have raised in order to sow doubt in the minds of many regarding the coming day of judgment. They have forwarded their position by asking, "Where is the promise of his coming? Because since the time the fathers died, all things remain as they were from the beginning of creation" (3:4). According to the heretics, the apparent delay in the coming of the Lord argues strongly against the reality of this event with its attendant judgment. Peter responds: Ἕν δὲ τοῦτο μὴ λανθανέτω ὑμᾶς, ἀγαπητοί, ὅτι μία ἡμέρα παρὰ κυρίῳ ὡς χίλια ἔτη καὶ χίλια ἔτη ὡς ἡμέρα μία (*Hen de touto mē lanthanetō hymas, agapētoi, hoti mia hēmera para kyriō hōs chilia etē kai chilia etē hōs hēmera mia*, But do not let this one thing escape your notice, beloved, that with the Lord one day is as a thousand years and a thousand years as one day). Peter addresses his readers as "Beloved" (see 3:1 and comments; and 3:14, 15, 17), which not only marks a transition in his argument but also draws the readers into the circle with himself while arguing that they should not be like the heretics, who have willfully neglected the facts about God's creation, providence, and judgment (3:5). The contrast between the believers and the heretics is marked by the use of the same verb in this verse and in verse 5. What the heretics have ignored, the recipients of the letter should not let escape their notice (μὴ λανθανέτω, mē lanthanetō; see 3:5 and comments on the verb). The contrast with the heretics is further emphasized by the inclusion of the emphatic "But . . . you" (δὲ . . . ὑμᾶς, de . . . hymas; here translated in conjunction with the verb, "not escape your notice"). The believers are informed by biblical teaching while the heretics rely only on their perceptions (3:4). Theology should guide the church and not specious historical argument.

The second part of the verse alludes to Ps. 90:4 [89:4 LXX], which in the LXX states: "For a thousand years in your sight are as the yesterday that is past, and as a watch in the night" (ὅτι χίλια ἔτη ἐν ὀφθαλμοῖς σου ὡς ἡ ἡμέρα ἡ ἐχθές, ἥτις διῆλθεν, καὶ φυλακὴ ἐν νυκτί, hoti chilia etē en ophthalmois sou hōs hē hēmera hē echthes, hētis diēlthen, kai phylakē en nykti; on the source of Peter's thought, see especially the extensive discussion in Bauckham 1981; 1983: 306–10). The psalm speaks of the judgment of God that comes upon humanity (vv. 3, 5–11) and the transitory nature of life (v. 10 NRSV: "The days of our life are seventy years, or perhaps eighty, if we are strong; even then their span is only toil and trouble; they are soon gone, and we fly away") in contrast with the eternal nature of God (v. 4). Peter's use of the psalm is consonant with its purpose to encourage right conduct in light of the transitoriness of life (Ps. 90:12; cf. 2 Pet. 3:11).

Psalm 90 was the impetus for the development in Jewish thought that "one day" was a way to speak figuratively of "a thousand years" (Jub. 4.30: "For a thousand years are like one day in the testimony of heaven"; 2 En. 33.1–2; Gen. Rab. 19.8; 22.1), that is, "one day" is to God as "a thousand years" according to human calculation. After the first century, the same math appeared in the theology of the church, so that the six days of creation represented six thousand years in human history. For example, Barn. 15.4 interpreted Gen. 2:2 accordingly: "Notice, children, what is the meaning of 'He made an end in six days'? He means this: that the Lord will make an end of everything in six thousand years, for a day with him means a thousand years. And he himself is my witness when he says, 'Lo, the day of the Lord shall be as a thousand years (ἡ γὰρ ἡμέρα παρ' αὐτῷ σημαίνει χίλια ἔτη).' So then, children, in six days, that is in six thousand years, everything will be completed." The form of the citation in Barnabas is close to 2 Pet. 3:8 and may have been influenced by this letter instead of being a direct citation from Ps. 90:4 (see also Irenaeus, Haer. 5.23.2; 5.28.3).

However, we should not interpret 2 Pet. 3:8 along these lines. Peter does not forward an interpretive key by which we may understand certain "days" in

God's plan as if they represent "a thousand years," or even understand references to "a thousand years" as if this period means "one day" (Rev. 20:2–7). Peter includes the comment taken from Psalm 90:4 [89:4 LXX] to explain his declaration in the following verse ("The Lord is not slow to fulfill the promise, as some count slowness"). His argument is simply that the divine perspective on time is not the same as the human perspective. A period that may appear prolonged by human standards is actually brief according to divine calculation. A similar thought appears in 2 Bar. 48.12–13, which contrasts the brevity of human existence ("For we are born in a short time, and in a short time we return") with the divine perspective on time ("With you, however, the hours are like the times, and the days like generations"; cf. Sir. 18:9–10). Peter does not relativize time but simply affirms that the criteria for "rapid" and "slow" are different for humans and God (contra Käsemann 1982: 193–94). On the basis of his affirmation, Peter constructs the argument of the following verse.

3:9 Peter affirms οὐ βραδύνει κύριος τῆς ἐπαγγελίας (*ou bradynei kyrios tēs epangelias*, The Lord is not slow to fulfill the promise) as a response to the opinion of the false teachers, which is echoed in the second clause of the verse: ὥς τινες βραδύτητα ἡγοῦνται (*hōs tines bradytēta hēgountai*, as some count slowness). His argument builds on the previous verse, in which our author has declared that God's estimation of time spans is not the same as human reckoning. The first clause of the verse may be translated, as Danker suggests, "The Lord of the promise does not delay" (BDAG 183), although the translations prefer to render the genitive τῆς ἐπαγγελίας (*tēs epangelias*) as "about his promise" (NRSV) or "in keeping his promise" (NIV) instead of a genitive of quality or definition. The idea, however, is likely that the Lord does not "delay from the promise" in the sense of delaying its fulfillment (genitive with verbs of restraint; BDF §180.5). The "promise" Peter has in mind is that of Christ's coming (3:4 and comments) with its attendant judgment (3:7, 10, 12) and promise of the new world (3:13).

The topos of divine delay, whether in judgment or for salvation, appears with regularity in the OT and Jewish literature. Deuteronomy 7:10 LXX affirms God's swift judgment, saying that he "will not delay [οὐχὶ βραδυνεῖ] with those that hate him; he will recompense them to their face" (cf. Hab. 2:3, which, in the version of Aquila, uses the same verb instead of χρονίσῃ, *chronisē*, delay, of the LXX; and 1QpHab 7.5–14). Isaiah 46:13 LXX assures the same with regard to divine deliverance: "I will not delay [οὐ βραδυνῶ] the salvation which is from me." God's judgment hastens, according to 2 Bar. 20.1–6: "I shall show you my strong judgment and my unexplorable ways. . . . With regard to the course of times, . . . they will come and will not tarry" (A. F. J. Klijn, *OTP* 1:627). Likewise, Sir. 35:19 LXX [35:22 Eng.] affirms that God's judgment will come swiftly: καὶ ὁ κύριος οὐ μὴ βραδύνῃ οὐδὲ μὴ μακροθυμήσῃ ἐπ' αὐτοῖς (*kai ho kyrios ou mē bradynē oude mē makrothymēsē ep' autois*, indeed the Lord will not delay, neither will he be patient with them). The entire section of Sir. 35:14–26 concerns the certainty of judgment: God will not take a bribe, he is impartial in his judgment, and he will judge the unrighteous. Peter is concerned precisely about this issue: God's judgment will indeed come. But in contrast with 2 Pet. 3:9b, Sirach declares that God will not show mercy by turning aside from judgment. Peter emphasizes that the delay in judgment is due to divine mercy.

The present verse also resonates with current philosophical debate regarding the certainty of divine judgment. At the heart of Epicurean philosophy was the notion that the gods, if indeed they existed at all, are not providentially engaged in the workings of the world. Since theirs is an ideal existence of unsullied bliss, they do not become entangled in human affairs. Humans cannot expect anything whatsoever from them, including answers to prayers or demonstrations of divine displeasure. The gods are beyond this world, not present, and not perceptible. Lucretius (5.146–52) questioned divine intervention into human affairs: "Another thing it is impossible that you should believe, I mean that any holy abode of the gods exists in any part of the universe. For the nature of the gods, being thin and far removed from our senses, is hardly seen by the mind's intelligence; and since it eludes the touch and impact of the hands, it cannot possibly touch anything that we can touch: for that cannot touch which may not be touched itself." The Epicureans likewise denied the reality of predictive prophecy, and their struggle with the Stoics over this issue is laid out in full in Cicero's *On Divination*, a fictive debate between Marcus Cicero and his brother Quintus. At the end of the first century AD, the Epicurean critique of divination was pitched to a level that called for a response from Plutarch, the senior priest of Apollo at Delphi. In his polemic, he echoes the Epicurean argument that "either . . . the prophetic priestess does not come near to the region in which is the godhead, or else . . . the spirit has been completely quenched and her powers have forsaken her" (*De Pythiae oraculis* 402B).

This debate was part of the wider fabric of skepticism regarding predictive prophecy current during the first century (G. Green 2001). Since the gods were removed from the world, there was therefore neither divine providence nor any divine judgment, past or future. Paul debated with the Epicureans as well as the Stoics in Athens (Acts 17:18), and in his speech before the Areopagus he leveled part of his polemic against the Epicureans' view of judgment, saying that God "has fixed a day on which he will have the world judged in righteousness by a man whom he has appointed" (17:31 NRSV). Plutarch likewise engaged the Epicureans over this issue, and from this polemic we become aware that the delay in divine judgment was a key argument in the denial of the reality of judgment: "The delay [βραδύτης, *bradytēs*] and procrastination of the Deity in punishing the wicked appears to me the most telling argument by far" (*The Delay of Divine Judgment*, in *Mor.* 548C). According to Plutarch, this delay (βραδύτης, *bradytēs*) "destroys belief in providence" (*Mor.* 549B). Neyrey (1980a: 414; 1993: 239) points out these parallels between the heretics' argument and Epicurean thought but is reluctant to identify the heretics as Epicureans (see Senior and Harrington 2003: 289).

It is hard to imagine, however, how those who embrace Epicurean philosophy can sit at table in the church, which is decidedly theistic. On the other hand, we must recognize that Epicurean philosophical tenets were common currency in the first century, and aspects of their philosophy found their way into the warp and woof of common discussion (M. Lee 2002: 186–256). In the end, the question about the delay in divine judgment is not a marker to identify specifically who these heretics are since, as noted above, this was a common topos both within Judaism (see "The Opponents in 2 Peter" in the introduction) and in the wider Mediterranean world. The heretics appear to have an eclectic admixture of beliefs, not all of which can be melded into a harmonious whole. The question about delay voiced by the heretics is part of the general fabric of reflection on divine judgment current during the era.

In response to the skepticism of the false teachers, Peter explains the true reason for the divine delay in judgment: ἀλλὰ μακροθυμεῖ εἰς ὑμᾶς, μὴ βουλόμενός τινας ἀπολέσθαι ἀλλὰ πάντας εἰς μετάνοιαν χωρῆσαι (*alla makrothymei eis hymas, mē boulomenos tinas apolesthai alla pantas eis metanoian chōrēsai*, but he is patient toward you, not willing for anyone to perish but all to come to repentance). According to our author, the delay in judgment does not argue against its reality but is rather evidence that God "is patient toward you" (μακροθυμεῖ εἰς ὑμᾶς, *makrothymei eis hymas*). The patience of God toward sinners is a theme that occurs repeatedly in biblical literature (Exod. 34:6–7; Num. 14:18; Pss. 86:15; 103:8; Joel 2:13; Nah. 1:3) as well as Jewish reflection (2 Esd. [4 Ezra] 7:132–34; 2 Bar. 24.1–2; 85.8–9). Such patience is perplexing, especially in light of the way God endures those who act wickedly while his people perish (2 Esd. [4 Ezra] 3:28–33). Although some regard this patience as a sign of divine weakness (2 Bar. 21.19–21), Peter views it as the mercy of God toward humanity (3:9c). But this patience should not be confused with tolerance toward sin, because God's patience will come to an end in the terrible day of judgment (3:10; Ps. 7:12–16; Acts 17:30–31). Somewhat surprisingly, Peter notes that God is patient "toward you." With these words, which will be read publicly during the gatherings of the believers, Peter stretches out the hand to those who are tempted to follow or who have begun to follow the way of the false teachers (2:14, 18).

The reason God delays his judgment is that he is "not willing for anyone to perish but all to come to repentance": he does not wish that anyone "perish" (ἀπολέσθαι, *apolysethai*) eternally (John 3:16; 10:28; 17:12; Rom. 2:12; 1 Cor. 1:18; 15:17–19; see Jude 5, 11; 2 Pet. 3:6; and comments). The same divine desire for salvation of humanity is expressed in 1 Tim. 2:4, which says that God "desires everyone to be saved and to come to the knowledge of the truth" (NRSV). This does not imply that Peter believes in universal salvation, as the following verse makes clear. Rather, God wants "all to come to repentance." This explanation of the divine delay in judgment finds parallel in the OT (Joel 2:12–13; Jon. 4:2) as well as other Jewish literature (Wis. 11:23; 12:10; 2 Esd. [4 Ezra] 4:38–39; Philo, *Alleg. Interp.* 3.34 §106; and cf. Plutarch, *The Delay of Divine Judgment*, in *Mor.* 551C–52D; Neyrey 1980b:

423–25). This "repentance" (μετάνοιαν, *metanoian*) is not simply a change of opinion (this was one of the uses of the term; *NewDocs* 4:160) nor does it mean to do penance. Rather, it is the act of abandoning deeds associated with sin (Heb. 6:1), turning to God (Acts 20:21), and doing works that provide evidence of "repentance" (Matt. 3:8; Luke 3:8; Acts 26:20) as illustrated in 1 Thess. 1:9–10.

"But the day of the Lord will come" (Ἥξει δὲ ἡμέρα κυρίου, *Hēxei de hēmera kyriou*), says Peter, despite its apparent delay (v. 9). "The day of the Lord" is the eschatological moment when God will appear, judge the inhabitants of the earth, and pour out his wrath against the unrepentant because of their sin (Isa. 13:6, 9; Ezek. 13:5; 30:3; Joel 1:15; 2:1, 11; 3:14; Amos 5:18, 20; Zeph. 1:7, 14; Zech. 14:1; Mal. 4:5; Acts 2:20; 1 Cor. 5:5; 1 Thess. 5:2; 2 Thess. 2:2). Although this will also be a day of salvation for God's people (Joel 2:21–32; 3:18; Obad. 15–21; Zech. 14:1–21), Peter's focus is on the terror of that event. In the epistles, this time is sometimes known as "the day of the Lord Jesus" (1 Cor. 1:8; 2 Cor. 1:14; and see Phil. 1:6, 10; 2:16), when he comes to execute the divine judgment (2 Thess. 1:6–10). This day will come at an unexpected moment, ὡς κλέπτης (*hōs kleptēs*, as a thief). Jesus taught that it is impossible to know when that day will come (Matt. 24:36; Mark 13:32–37; Acts 1:7); for that reason, believers should be ready for it at all times (2 Pet. 3:10–11; 1 Thess. 5:4–6).

**3:10**

The assertion that the coming will be "as a thief in the night" finds its roots in the teaching of Jesus (Matt. 24:43–44; Luke 12:39–40), which was then incorporated into the instruction given to the church about the end (1 Thess. 5:2; Rev. 3:3; 16:15). Peter, however, omits the note about the thief coming "in the night" (see the first additional note on 3:10). We need not assume that Peter draws directly from Paul (3:15–16; cf. Neyrey 1993: 242) given the common knowledge of this dominical teaching. The unexpected end calls for vigilance (1 Thess. 5:1–11).

Peter describes cataclysmic judgment on that day: ἐν ᾗ οἱ οὐρανοὶ ῥοιζηδὸν παρελεύσονται στοιχεῖα δὲ καυσούμενα λυθήσεται καὶ γῆ καὶ τὰ ἐν αὐτῇ ἔργα εὑρεθήσεται (*en hē hoi ouranoi rhoizedon pareleusontai stoicheia de kausoumena lythēsetai kai gē kai ta en autē erga eurethēsetai*, in which the heavens will pass away with a roar and the elements will be destroyed by burning, even the earth and the works that are discovered in it). Peter describes the event again in verse 12, and the horror of this cosmic conflagration defies comprehension. The heavens and the earth, created and sustained by God (3:5–7), will be destroyed by him before the new heavens and earth are ushered in (3:13). At the time of the "day of the Lord" (ἐν ᾗ, *en hē*, in which), οἱ οὐρανοὶ ῥοιζηδὸν παρελεύσονται (*hoi ouranoi rhoizēdon pareleusontai*, the heavens will pass away with a roar). This was a basic element in the church's expectation regarding the end of the present world (Matt. 5:18; 24:35; Mark 13:31; Luke 16:17; 21:33; Rev. 20:11; 21:1) and has its roots in OT and Jewish teaching (Isa. 34:4; 51:6; 1 En. 91.16; cf. T. Job 33.4: "The whole world will pass away and its splendor shall fade. And those who heed it shall share in its overthrow"; and Did. 10.6). In verse 12 Peter notes that the heavens will be set ablaze, but in verse 10 he focuses attention on the sound of the fury, the type of "roar" generated by something "passing with great force and rapidity" (BDAG 907). Although the term Peter uses is rare (ῥοιζηδόν, *rhoizēdon*), found only here in biblical literature, he may have in mind the "thunder" that accompanies the judgment of God (1 Sam. 2:10; 7:10; Job 40:9; Isa. 29:6; 33:3; Jer. 25:30; Joel 3:16). On the other hand, he may be thinking of nothing other than the sound generated by intense fire (3:7, 12).

Peter also warns that in the execution of divine judgment on the day of the Lord, στοιχεῖα δὲ καυσούμενα λυθήσεται (*stoicheia de kausoumena lythēsetai*, the elements will be destroyed by burning). Ancient literature used the term στοιχεῖα (*stoicheia*, elements; see also v. 12) in various ways, referring to celestial bodies such as the sun and stars (Diogenes Laertius, *Lives* 6.102), the elements from which the world is made (earth, air, fire, and water; Wis. 7:17; 19:18; 4 Macc. 12:13; Aristotle, *Metaphysics* 998A.20–30; Plutarch, *Mor.* 875C; Philo, *Cherubim* 2.35 §127), or supernatural powers that control the world (Gal. 4:3; Col. 2:8, 20). In 3:12 these "elements" are placed in contrast with "the heavens," and they should therefore be understood as the totality of the material of the world. Moreover, 3:7 refers to the construction of the cosmos as simply "the heavens and the earth," corresponding to the "the heavens and the elements" in the present verse. In the final clause of verse 10 Peter identifies the elements with "the earth." The repeated affirmations in the biblical literature regarding the final destruction of the earth by fire (here καυσούμενα, *kausomena*, by burning) favors this interpretation (Isa. 66:16; Mic. 1:4; Nah. 1:6; Zeph. 1:18; Mal. 3:2, 19 LXX [4:1 Eng.]; Acts 2:19; 2 Thess. 1:7–8; 2 Pet. 3:7 and comments; 3:12; Rev. 9:18; 18:8; cf. Sib. Or. 3.75–92, which speaks of the destruction of the world by fire when a woman, Cleopatra, rules the world; BDAG 946; G. Delling, *TDNT* 7:670–87). Once again, though Peter's readers are likely familiar with Stoic doctrine concerning a coming conflagration, Peter's thought is more likely indebted to the biblical, Jewish, and Christian traditions regarding the end (see 3:7 and comments).

The final clause of the verse expands on the anterior affirmations. What shall be destroyed by burning is καὶ γῆ καὶ τὰ ἐν αὐτῇ ἔργα εὑρεθήσεται (*kai gē kai ta en autē erga eurethēsetai*, even the earth and the works that are discovered in it). The verb εὑρεθήσεται in this context, as in verse 14, suggests a judicial inquiry through which God will discover the deeds of humanity and will execute his judgment on the basis of what he finds (see Exod. 22:8 [22:7 LXX]; Deut. 22:22, 28; Ezra 10:18; Jer. 50:24 [27:24 LXX]; Luke 23:4; John 18:38; 19:4; Acts 13:28; 23:9; Rev. 14:5). The passive voice of the verb here suggests the divine agency in this inquiry. The verse becomes part of the fabric of early Christian teaching that God will judge τὰ ἔργα (*ta erga*, the works) of each, which will become manifest in the final judgment (Mark 4:22; John 3:21; 1 Cor. 3:13; 14:25; Eph. 5:13). The false teachers have sown doubt about the reality of final judgment. Peter faces off against them, declaring that nothing and no one will escape God's wrath save for those who embrace the salvation of God (2 Pet. 3:15). "The works" of those who do evil will be discovered.

## Additional Notes

**3:10.** Unsurprisingly, some MSS and versions include the words "in the night" (ἐν νυκτί, *en nykti*, in C 𝔐 vg^mss sy^h; cf. 1 Thess. 5:2), although they are absent from the principal witnesses (𝔓⁷² ℵ A B Ψ).

**3:10.** The reading εὑρεθήσεται (*heurethēsetai*, will be discovered) enjoys strong textual support (ℵ B P), although 𝔓⁷² adds λυόμενα (*lyomena*, "will be found *dissolved*"). Various other readings appear in the scribal attempt to clarify the sense although none has strong early witness. The reading as here presented and in the critical texts is indeed the more difficult one. See the commentary.

# 4. Since All These Things Will Pass Away: Living in Light of the End (3:11–13)

Peter has previously explained the reason for the divine delay in judgment. The delay is relative to God's perception versus human perception of time and, in fact, whatever delay there is grows out of divine mercy (3:8–9). But the fierce and fiery judgment day will indeed come and with it the destruction of all things (3:10). In the present section, Peter turns from his counter to the heretics' claims and, in the minds and hearts of his readers, sows a different perspective regarding the end. The final judgment is a call to live a holy and dutiful life (3:11), knowing that the end will bring not only destruction but also a new order in God's creation—a new heaven and new earth—which will be characterized by righteousness (3:12–13). Peter joins together eschatology and ethics as a counter to the heretics' dissolution of the two.

## Exegesis and Exposition

[11]Since all these things will be destroyed ⌜in this way⌝, what kind of people ought ⌜you⌝ to be, living in a holy and dutiful way, [12]expecting and hastening the coming of the day of God, because of which the heavens will be destroyed by fire and the elements will be melted by burning. [13]But according to his promise we await new heavens and a new earth, in which dwells righteousness.

3:11  Our author does not engage in speculation about the timing of forthcoming eschatological events. He rather sees the final events of the world described above as motivation for Christian conduct. As in other passages of the NT, Christian ethics are rooted within eschatology (Mark 13:32–37; Rom. 13:12; 1 Cor. 15:58; Eph. 5:11–13; Phil. 4:5; Col. 4:5; 1 Thess. 5:1–11; 2 Tim. 4:1–2; James 5:8–9; 1 Pet. 1:13–17; 4:7; 1 John 2:28). The false teachers have tried to refute the reality of coming judgment, and their speculation has formed the foundation of their immoral teaching. They understand the delay in judgment as an excuse to embrace an immoral lifestyle. Peter, on the other hand, affirms the terrible reality of coming judgment, and this then becomes a fundamental motivation in his ethics. He begins by briefly echoing his previous teaching (2 Pet. 3:7, 10): τούτων οὕτως πάντων λυομένων (*toutōn houtōs pantōn lyomenōn*, Since all these things will be destroyed in this way). The verb λύω (here as a present participle used adverbially, understood as a future event in accordance with v. 10) could be used to describe the destruction of a building

(Josephus, *J. W.* 6.1.4 §32; Sib. Or. 3.409; John 2:19) or a ship (Acts 27:41), but here, as in verse 10, it summarizes the events of the final judgment, when the world as he knows it will be destroyed.

Despite the final assize, hope comes (3:13), and the preceding warning of future judgment calls for right conduct: ποταποὺς δεῖ ὑπάρχειν [ὑμᾶς] ἐν ἁγίαις ἀναστροφαῖς καὶ εὐσεβείαις (*potapous dei hyparchein [hymas] en hagiais anastrophais kai eusebeias*, what kind of people ought you to be, living in a holy and dutiful way?). Although Peter asks a question that begins with the interrogative ποταπούς ("what kind of," suggesting a question of moral character, as in Luke 7:39, not simply of kind, as in Sus. 54; Matt. 8:27; Mark 13:1; Luke 1:29; BDAG 856), the sentence has imperatival force: "You ought to live in a holy and dutiful way!" Peter regards such conduct not as an option but as a necessity, marked in this clause by the term δεῖ (*dei*, it is necessary; BDAG 214). Whereas a modern might *suggest* a course of action to another, Peter understands how necessity governs human conduct.

In ancient literature, a person's conduct was regularly referred to as "a way of life" (ἀναστροφή, *anastrophē*; see 2:7 and comments). Although not reflected in the translation, ἀναστροφαῖς is in the plural. The plural was sometimes employed when an author wished to speak of abstract concepts such as "conduct" (Mayor 1907: 161). Peter describes the conduct that should mark the believers in anticipation of the end as holy (ἁγίαις; see 2:21 and comments), not immoral like that of the false teachers (2:12–14, 18–22), and as devoted in duty to God (εὐσεβείαις; see 1:3, 6–7, and comments). Peter has already described such behavior in the first chapter of this letter (1:3–11 and comments). Just as eschatological skepticism has led to immorality, so eschatological expectation leads to holy conduct marked by devotion in duty to God.

The attitude of the believers regarding the "day of the Lord" should be different from that of the false teachers, who have denied its reality and questioned the coming judgment (3:4). The last day, with its attendant judgment, will indeed come and bring with it cosmic destruction (3:7, 10–12). But it also carries the promise of the coming of a new heaven and new earth and the inauguration of a truly just society (3:13). Therefore, in contrast with the false teachers, Peter calls his readers to προσδοκῶντας καὶ σπεύδοντας τὴν παρουσίαν τῆς τοῦ θεοῦ ἡμέρας (*prosdokōntas kai speudontas tēn parousian tēs tou theou hēmeras*, expecting and hastening the coming of the day of God). The verb προσδοκάω (*prosdokaō*, here used as a present participle) does not mean simply "hope for," as if the coming of the day were some unsure future event, but rather suggests firm expectation or sure hope with expectation of fulfillment (cf. Matt. 11:3; Luke 1:21; 8:40; Acts 3:5; 10:24; 28:6; and in an eschatological context, Matt. 24:50; Luke 12:46; and see 2 Pet. 3:13–14, where the verb is repeated).

The second verb, σπεύδω (*speudō*), which also is in the form of a present participle (σπεύδοντας, *speudontas*), is not intransitive here ("to be in a hurry" or "make haste"), but with the direct object τὴν παρουσίαν (*tēn parousian*, the coming, the object of the previous verb as well) is instead transitive, "to

**3:12**

hasten" something. Because God retards his judgment due to his desire that sinners should repent (3:9), this repentance will accelerate "the coming of the day of God" (cf. Matt. 6:10; 24:14; Acts 3:19–21). A number of Jewish texts similarly speak of the way God will hasten the end (Isa. 60:22; Sir. 36:7 LXX [36:10 Eng.]; 2 Esd. [4 Ezra] 4:26; 2 Bar. 20.1–2; 83.1). Although God is the one who effects the acceleration, he brings it to pass with reference to human repentance, a thought later reflected in some rabbinic literature (*b. Sanh.* 97b, 98a; *b. Yoma* 86b; Str-B 1:163–65). What the believers expect and hasten is "the coming of the day of God." The παρουσία (*parousia*, parousia) is commonly the advent of Christ (1:16 and comments; 1 Cor. 15:23; 1 Thess. 2:19; 4:15; 2 Thess. 2:1; 1 John 2:28), but here the expectation is the coming of the "day of God," the same event described as "the day of the Lord" in 3:10 (cf. Rev. 16:14).

Peter again declares that this "day" will be marked by terrible destruction: δι' ἣν οὐρανοὶ πυρούμενοι λυθήσονται καὶ στοιχεῖα καυσούμενα τήκεται (*di' hēn ouranoi pyroumenoi lythēsontai kai stoicheia kausoumena tēketai*, because of which the heavens will be destroyed by fire and the elements will be melted by burning). Peter has already spoken of the destruction (see v. 10, where the same verb, λύω, *lyō*, describes the event) of the heavens by fire (3:7, 10) and of the way the "elements" would be consumed in that conflagration (3:10 and comments). These "elements," the apostle adds, "will be melted" (τήκεται, *tēketai*, present passive describing a future event; cf. Mic. 1:4; 1 En. 1.6; T. Levi 4.1; 2 Esd. [4 Ezra] 8:23; and 2 Clem. 16.3) because of the intense heat of the final judgment. Although this will be the end of the present heaven and earth, the believers hold a glorious hope, as Peter explains in the next verse. The end is not for fear but for hope.

**3:13** In spite of the destructive forces of the divine judgment (3:7, 10–12), the Christian hope is the renovation of creation and not its annihilation. As the ancient world destroyed by the flood (2:5; 3:6) gave way to the present order, so also the present world will suffer divine judgment (3:7), but in turn God will usher in the new creation. Peter declares this hope: καινοὺς δὲ οὐρανοὺς καὶ γῆν καινὴν κατὰ τὸ ἐπάγγελμα αὐτοῦ προσδοκῶμεν (*kainous de ouranous kai gēn kainēn kata to epangelma autou prosdokōmen*, But according to his promise we await new heavens and a new earth). As in the previous verse, Peter affirms that he and the believers (note the first-person plural) expect (προσδοκῶμεν, *prosdokōmen*) a reality beyond the final judgment because of τὸ ἐπάγγελμα αὐτοῦ (*to epangelma autou*, his promise), the very promise that the heretics have put in doubt (3:4 and comments). Peter places the churches in solidarity with himself and the prophetic witness regarding this expectation.

The "promise" that Peter has in mind is specifically that of Isa. 65:17, repeated in 66:22: "For I am about to create new heavens and a new earth; the former things shall not be remembered or come to mind" (NRSV). The hope of a new creation was vivid especially in Jewish apocalyptic thought (1 En. 72.1; 91.16; 2 Bar. 32.6; Jub. 1.29; Sib. Or. 5.211–12; Tg. Jon. on Mic. 7:14) and within the primitive church as well (Rom. 8:19–21; Rev. 21:1; cf. Rev. 20:11). The created order is not eternal but is subject to upheaval and change, as evidenced by the coming judgment; yet this should bring hope rather than despair since God the Creator will inaugurate a new order. The same perspective on the end is found in 2 Bar. 57.2: "The belief in the coming judgment was brought about, and the hope of the world which will be renewed was built at that time, and the promise of the life that will come later was planted." Peter resonates with the eschatological hope that destruction is followed by renewal.

The expectation of a new order was not simply a hope that revolved around the destiny of the material world; within Jewish reflection this hope also embraced the moral order (see, e.g., 1 En. 45.4–5). The new heaven and new earth, in contrast with the present world filled with evil deeds (see 3:10b), will be one ἐν οἷς δικαιοσύνη κατοικεῖ (*en hois dikaiosynē katoikei*, in which dwells righteousness). The expectation of a new world where injustice would be excluded was an element in prophetic proclamation (Isa. 9:7; 11:4–5; 32:16–19; 60:21). This was one of the "sure promises" that God gave through the prophets (2 Pet. 1:4). Peter knows God as one who acts in justice (1:1 and comments) and calls humans, by means of his messengers, to live according to the dictates of justice (2:5). The reaction of humanity has been to reject this call (2:5–7), as the situation of the first readers of this letter amply illustrates. The false teachers have rejected Christian morality, which Peter calls "the way of righteousness" (2:21). These people and their followers will be excluded from the "new heavens and a new earth" because in these only "dwells righteousness." The NT authors are not reluctant to speak of the terrible separation and exclusion of the unjust from the eternal reign of God (1 Cor. 6:9–10; Rev. 21:27; 22:15), a teaching that was common among Jewish authors (2 Bar. 44.12; 1 En. 5.8–9; 10.16, 20–22; 38.2; 91.18–19; 2 En. 65.8; Ps. Sol. 17.25, 36). In that new world, there will be no sin, no injustice. All will be just and will act in justice toward their fellows.

## Additional Notes

**3:11.** The reading οὕτως (*houtōs*, in this way) is found in 𝔓⁷² B 614 1739 while the alternative οὖν (*oun*, therefore) appears in א A Ψ 048. While the MS evidence is not decisive in either direction, the reading οὖν (*oun*) is the easier to understand, lending support to the idea that it may have been a scribal addition.

**3:11.** While ὑμᾶς (*hymas*, you) is the variant that has the support among many Greek MSS (A C K P Ψ 33 81 614) and early versions (vg syr cop arm), the alternative ἡμᾶς (*hēmas*, we) appears in א 104 209 241 630. The papyri (𝔓⁷², ⁷⁴) as well as B, however, include no pronoun at this point. The decision is difficult and left the editors of the critical texts (UBS⁴, NA²⁷) uncertain about which reading was original, leading them to enclose the reading ὑμᾶς (*hymas*) in brackets.

# 5. While Waiting for These Things: Diligence to Be Found Blameless (3:14–18a)

In bringing the letter to a close, Peter gives his readers a series of exhortations, calling them to "be diligent" in their moral life (v. 14), to regard the delay in judgment as a sign of salvation (v. 15), to be on their guard against succumbing to the heretics and thereby falling away (v. 17), and finally to grow in knowledge and grace (v. 18a). This is the life they are to lead as they await the final consummation, which includes both judgment and promise (vv. 11–13). In the midst of these summary exhortations, Peter turns once again to counter the heretics, noting the way they twist Paul's writings and the "other Scriptures," a move that spells their own destruction (vv. 15b–16). To be sure, there are things Paul wrote that are difficult to comprehend (v. 16b). But Peter does not see the heretics' lack of comprehension as their principal problem. While they try to evoke Paul's writings in support of their views, Peter distances them from Paul while drawing Paul into his own circle. Their perversion of God's revelation brings with it dire consequences. Peter hopes better things for his readers.

## Exegesis and Exposition

¹⁴Therefore, beloved, as you await these things, be diligent to be found by him without spot or blemish in peace. ¹⁵And consider the forbearance of our Lord as salvation, just as even our beloved brother Paul, according to the wisdom that was given to him, wrote to you, ¹⁶as he also writes in all his letters, speaking in them concerning these matters, in which there are some things hard to understand, which the ignorant and unstable twist as even the other Scriptures to their own destruction. ¹⁷Therefore you, beloved, since you know these things beforehand, be on your guard so that you do not fall from your own firm position, being carried away by the error of the lawless. ¹⁸ªBut grow in grace and in the knowledge of our Lord and Savior Jesus Christ.

**3:14**    In the final verses of this letter, Peter concludes his argument with a series of exhortations that encourage his readers to continue in the way of truth and not abandon it by being carried away by the seductive arguments of the false teachers. In 3:14 his point of departure is the eschatological events just described, the final judgment (3:10–12) and the new creation (3:13). In light of these ultimate events, the apostle exhorts his readers: Διό, ἀγαπητοί, ταῦτα προσδοκῶντες σπουδάσατε ἄσπιλοι καὶ ἀμώμητοι αὐτῷ εὑρεθῆναι ἐν εἰρήνῃ

(*Dio, agapētoi, tauta prosdokōntes spoudasate aspiloi kai amōmētoi autō heurethēnai en eirēnē*, Therefore, beloved, as you await these things, be diligent to be found by him without spot and blemish in peace). The expectation of the consummation ("as you await these things," using the same verb found in vv. 12–13, προσδοκάω, *prosdokaō*, here as an adverbial participle) forms the basis of his moral exhortation. Eschatology is not a topic of speculation for Peter, nor an excuse to escape from responsibility, but rather a motivation to preserve the moral life. Human deeds will be judged by God (3:10), who will establish a new order into which only the just shall enter (3:13).

The "beloved" (see 1:17; 3:1, 8, 14, 15; and comments) should "be diligent" (σπουδάσατε, *spoudasate*, a favorite term Peter uses to express the urgency of the exhortation; see 1:10, 15, and comments) "to be found" blameless by him. As in 3:10, the verb εὑρίσκω (*heuriskō*, here as an infinitive in the aorist passive) refers to God's judicial inquiry into the deeds of humanity, an experience through which even the believer must pass (for the judicial use of the term, see John 18:38; 19:4, 6; Acts 13:28; 24:20; Gal. 2:17; Phil. 3:9; 1 Pet. 1:7; 2:22; Rev. 3:2). Before the One who examines them (αὐτῷ, *autō*, by him), and not simply before human eyes (cf. 1 John 2:28), they should be ἄσπιλοι (*aspiloi*), "without spot," without moral defect (1 Tim. 6:14; James 1:27; cf. 1 Pet. 1:19). Moreover, they should be found to be ἀμώμητοι (*amōmētoi*), "without blemish" or blameless (see Jude 24 and comments, where the cognate ἄμωμος appears). Peter's hope is that they will stand before God without moral fault; this in contrast with the false teachers, who are "spots and defects" (σπίλοι καὶ μῶμοι, *spiloi kai mōmoi*, 2:13). In 3:14 Peter employs the negative form of these terms (ἄσπιλοι καὶ ἀμώμητοι, *aspiloi kai amōmētoi*) to emphasize his call that the believers should in no wise adopt the conduct of the heretics. The believers' deportment should be such that they will not be found guilty before the Judge, thus imitating the example of the Lord, who was "a lamb without defect or blemish" (1 Pet. 1:19 NRSV, ἀμνοῦ ἀμώμου καὶ ἀσπίλου, *amnou amōmou kai aspilou*). This striking parallel is one point of contact between 2 Peter and the first letter (2 Pet. 3:1; contra Gilmore 2002: 92). Although the false teachers and their followers will be excluded from the new heaven and new earth, the faithful will stand before God "in peace" (ἐν εἰρήνῃ, *en eirēnē*). This "peace" is not some form of emotional tranquillity but rather the objective condition of being reconciled with God (Rom. 5:1) and being found acceptable before him (1 Pet. 1:2; 5:14; 2 Pet. 1:2; and comments).

3:15   The false teachers are of the opinion that the delay in the advent of the day of the Lord is evidence that places in doubt the reality of the coming judgment and serves as the license to engage in immoral behavior. In 3:9 Peter has argued that God delays the coming of that day in order to offer humanity the opportunity to repent. Now he returns to affirm the same by teaching καὶ τὴν τοῦ κυρίου ἡμῶν μακροθυμίαν σωτηρίαν ἡγεῖσθε (*kai tēn tou kyriou hēmōn makrothymian sōtērian hēgeisthe*, And consider the forbearance of our Lord as salvation). Obviously Peter and the false teachers evaluate the empirical evidence differently (compare 2:13 and 3:9, the evaluation of the false teachers, with 1:13 and 3:15, Peter's perspective). Peter calls his readers to align themselves with his own perspective, that is, "consider" (ἡγεῖσθε; as Acts 26:2; 2 Cor. 9:5; Phil. 2:25; 2 Thess. 3:15; James 1:2; BDAG 434) or think about these things in a way that differs from the thinking of the heretics (2:13; 3:9, which use the same verb). Peter urges them to properly evaluate "the forbearance of our Lord" (μακροθυμίαν, *makrothymian*; see the verbal form of the term in 3:9 and comments), which is God's patience toward sinful humans and not his procrastination (Rom. 2:4; 9:22; 1 Pet. 3:20; and cf. Artemidorus Daldianus, *The Interpretation of Dreams*, 4.11; 2.25, where the term is used of procrastination; J. Horst, *TDNT* 4:374–87). God delays his vengeance (cf. the prophet's call in Jer. 15:15 LXX, "Do not bear long with them"), desiring the σωτηρίαν (*sōtērian*, salvation) of those who sin (cf. Rom. 2:4; see Jude 3 and comments). In the present context salvation includes rescue from the coming wrath of God (3:10–12) and entrance into his new righteous world (3:13).

In the second part of this verse and 3:16, Peter makes mention of the apostle Paul and his letters, which the false teachers as well as the recipients of this letter have read. The reason Peter needs to mention Paul's letters is because the false teachers have distorted their message and have used those epistles to support their heresy (3:16b). It is possible that the heretics identify themselves as followers of Paul, the apostle of liberty, although we should remember that the promise of "freedom" was a commonplace in ancient philosophical reflection (2:19 and comments). Due to the false teachers' appeal to Paul, Peter seeks to show the complete harmony between himself and the apostle to the gentiles, not only with respect to his teaching but also in their personal relationship. Therefore our author says, καθὼς καὶ ὁ ἀγαπητὸς ἡμῶν ἀδελφὸς Παῦλος κατὰ τὴν δοθεῖσαν αὐτῷ σοφίαν ἔγραψεν ὑμῖν (*kathōs kai ho agapētos hēmōn adelphos Paulos kata tēn dotheisan autō sophian egrapsen hymin*, just as even our beloved brother Paul, according to the wisdom that was given to him, wrote to you). Although at one time Paul rebuked Peter publicly (Gal. 2:11–21), he recognized Peter's divinely given ministry (Gal. 2:7–10). According to Acts, Peter not only defended his own mission to the gentiles during the Jerusalem Council but also affirmed the gospel that Paul preached among the gentiles (Acts 15:7–12). Although the relationship between Paul and Peter has been a topic of considerable debate, especially since the time of Baur and the Tübingen School (Harris 1975), here there is no evidence of a breach between them. Our author calls Paul "our beloved brother." With the adjective "beloved" (ἀγαπητός, *agapētos*; 1 Pet. 2:11; 4:12; 2 Pet. 1:17; 3:1, 8, 14, 17; and comments), Peter expresses his profound love for and solidarity with Paul. Paul is not only a "brother" (ἀδελφός, *adelphos*) in the faith (2 Pet. 1:10 and comments) but also his colleague in the service of the gospel (cf. 2 Cor. 1:1; 8:18, 22, 23; Eph. 6:21; Col. 1:1; 4:7; 1 Thess. 3:2; Philem. 1; 1 Pet. 5:12; where the concept "brother" is narrowed to "companion in ministry").

Paul wrote (ἔγραψεν, *egrapsen*) to congregations in Asia Minor, some of which likely are recipients of this letter and of 1 Peter (2 Pet. 3:1; 1 Pet. 1:1), and he spoke to them of themes that Peter touches on in this letter (implied in Peter's opening comment καθὼς καί, *kathōs kai*, just as even [3:15]; and in 3:16, "speaking in them concerning these matters"). It is impossible to determine with any certainty which letters our author has in mind on the basis of a comparison between the Pauline corpus and 2 Peter (as Bauckham 1983: 320 correctly notes). But the location of the readers in Asia Minor suggests that some may know letters such as Galatians, Ephesians (especially if this missive is a circular letter; note the textual problem in Eph. 1:1), Colossians, and the lost correspondence to the Laodiceans (Col. 4:16). Peter displays profound respect for Paul, recognizing that he wrote κατὰ τὴν δοθεῖσαν αὐτῷ σοφίαν (*kata tēn dotheisan autō sophian*, according to the wisdom that was given to him; cf. 1 Cor. 3:10; Gal. 2:9; and others given divine wisdom, such as Solomon [Matt. 12:42; Luke 11:31] and Stephen [Acts 6:10]; cf. Exod. 36:1–2; 1 Kings 4:29; Prov. 2:6; Wis. 7:7, 15; Sir. 43:33; Luke 21:15). Divine wisdom is not simply savvy but in biblical literature is intimately tied with right conduct. Peter's affirmation of the wisdom that God granted Paul marks Paul's writings as inspired and not simply of human origin, a point confirmed in the following verse. The Paulines note that the apostle proclaims "in all wisdom" (Col. 1:28) and that the wisdom with which he speaks is not merely human (1 Cor. 2:3–5) but rather divine (2:6–7). This wisdom is the gospel, the proclamation of salvation through Jesus Christ (1:18–31). Peter's acknowledgment of Paul's divine inspiration is consonant with Paul's own affirmations.

Peter continues his reflection on the Pauline letters: ὡς καὶ ἐν πάσαις ἐπιστολαῖς λαλῶν ἐν αὐταῖς περὶ τούτων (*hōs kai en pasais epistolais lalōn en autais peri toutōn*, as he also writes in all his letters, speaking in them concerning these matters). In the previous verse, Peter spoke of the communications that Paul sent to the churches in Asia Minor (he "wrote to you"), while in the present verse Peter focuses his attention on the content of "all his letters." We are aware that in the first century the Pauline letters circulated among the churches (Col. 4:16), but the present verse implies that the churches have collected his writings and that at the time when Peter pens this missive, some form of the Pauline corpus was already in existence. E. Richards (1991: 2–7; 2004: 211–23) has demonstrated how common the practice of copying and collecting letters was, both by the authors themselves and the recipients, so that we cannot assume that the existence of a "Pauline corpus" is a sign that 2 Peter comes to us from the postapostolic era (see "Authorship of 2 Peter" in the introduction). In these writings, which the author knows, the apostle to the gentiles spoke "concerning these matters" (περὶ τούτων, *peri toutōn*), the "matters" that the church expects (3:14), such as the coming judgment (3:12) and the new creation (3:13; see below). With these words, Peter affirms the unity between the theology that he teaches and that of Paul, while at the same time negating the claim of the false teachers, who appear to claim solidarity with Paul as they appeal to his teaching (which, Peter will note, they distorted).

**3:16**

Instead of being faithful to Paul and his presentation of the gospel, the false teachers have distorted his message. Peter admits that in Paul's letters (ἐν αἷς, *en hais*, in which) there are "some things hard to understand" (ἐστιν δυσνόητά τινα, *estin dysnoēta tina*). The term δυσνόητα appears in a number of texts in the context of an oracle, vision, or some theme that is hard to understand (Diogenes Laertius, *Lives* 9.13; Lucian, *Alexander the False Prophet* 54; Herm. *Sim.* 9.14.4). Yet Peter does not affirm that everything within Paul's writings is hard to understand but rather only "some things" (τινα, *tina*). However, the problem of the false teachers is not the difficulty of interpreting the message that God gave Paul. Rather, the heretics have distorted his teaching: ἃ οἱ ἀμαθεῖς καὶ ἀστήρικτοι στρεβλοῦσιν (*ha hoi amatheis kai astēriktoi streblousin*, which the ignorant and unstable twist). Those "ignorant" (ἀμαθεῖς, *amatheis*; cf. Josephus, *Ant.* 12.4.6 §191; Plutarch, *Mor.* 25C; Epictetus, *Ench.* 48.3) of the fundamental teaching of the church are the false teachers themselves (2:12; 3:5). On the other hand, the "unstable" (ἀστήρικτοι, *astēriktoi*) are the weak or not stable morally, the disciples of the false teachers (according to 2:14). This double description suggests that Peter has in mind both the heretics and those from the church who have succumbed to their teaching. These people "twist" (στρεβλοῦσιν, *streblousin*) Paul's teaching, wrenching and distorting it in such a way that the true is turned into the false (BDAG 948; MM 593). From Paul's own writings we are aware that some in his audience distorted his preaching concerning grace (Rom. 3:8), misunderstanding various declarations (e.g., Rom. 3:21–27; 4:15; 5:20; 8:1; 1 Cor. 6:12; Gal. 5:13) as support of antinomianism (cf. Jude 4). Others also perverted his teaching regarding eschatological events (2 Thess. 2:2–3; 2 Tim. 2:17–18). The Pauline doctrines that the "ignorant and unstable" have distorted have to do with precisely these two points (2:19; 3:4).

The false teachers and those who follow them do not solely target Paul's teaching. They twist his teaching ὡς καὶ τὰς λοιπὰς γραφάς (*hōs kai tas loipas graphas*, as even the other Scriptures). During Peter's era, the term "Scriptures" referred specifically to the divinely inspired writings of the OT (2 Pet. 1:20–21 and comments; Luke 24:27, 32, 45; John 5:39; Rom. 1:2; 1 Cor. 15:3–4; Gal. 3:8, 22; 1 Tim. 5:18; 2 Tim. 3:16; 1 Pet. 2:6). But early in the life of the church, the concept of "Scripture" was expanded to include the teachings of Jesus (1 Tim. 5:18; cf. Matt. 10:10; Luke 10:7). In the present verse, Peter takes one step further in the development of the canon, calling the writings of the OT "the other Scriptures." Peter here implies that Paul's letters are classified as "Scripture" as well (the term "other," λοιπάς, *loipas*, denotes those apart from which the author or speaker is referring to; see Matt. 25:11; Acts 2:37; Rom. 1:13; 1 Cor. 9:5; 2 Cor. 12:13; Phil. 4:3). If we regard 2 Peter as an authentic work of the apostle, then this categorization of Paul's writings as "Scripture" is an ad hoc broadening of the concept communicated via this lexeme. To say that Peter could not have engaged in such concept broadening is not defensible, even at this early date and considering the authoritative nature of the apostolate as the messengers commissioned by the Lord himself (see

K. H. Rengstorf, *TDNT* 1:407–45). The early church fathers did not lavishly use the introductory formulas that would tag NT writings as Scripture. But such ascriptions were certainly not absent (see the discussion in Hill 2004 and the note on 2 Pet. 3:16 in "2 Peter in the Early Church" in the introduction). When, for example, 2 Clement (2.4; 13.4) makes this kind of ascription, "the nonchalant, incidental character of these formulae indicates no consciousness on the author's part that he is making a radical innovation" (Hagner 1973: 277). The evidence regarding how the church of the second half of the first century regarded the apostolic writings is scant, deducible only from later sources. Dating 2 Peter as a document written in the early second century on the basis of 3:16 outstrips the evidence (see "Authorship of 2 Peter" in the introduction).

In the final clause, Peter underscores the seriousness of distorting the teaching of the Scriptures, whether that of Paul, Jesus, or the OT. The heretics and those who follow them distort this teaching πρὸς τὴν ἰδίαν αὐτῶν ἀπώλειαν (*pros tēn idian autōn apōleian*, to their own destruction; see the comments on 2:1, 3; 3:7 regarding ἀπώλεια, *apōleia*). The result of their error, which includes their embrace of immorality on the basis of their distorted teaching, is condemnation before God. The problem of the false teachers is not that they have poorly understood portions of divine revelation but that they use their twisted interpretation to justify their immorality (e.g., 2:19; 3:3–4; and comments). Twisted teaching and twisted practice go hand in hand. Heretical teaching has led to moral decadence.

Before the final doxology of the letter, Peter gives his last call that his readers not fall into the error of the false teachers. As in the previous verses, his love and pastoral concern are evident as he once again addresses them as those who are "beloved" (3:1, 8, 14, and comments). He exhorts, Ὑμεῖς οὖν, ἀγαπητοί, προγινώσκοντες φυλάσσεσθε (*Hymeis oun, agapētoi, proginōskontes phylassesthe*, Therefore you, beloved, since you know these things beforehand, be on your guard). Peter once again speaks of the heretics' error, which is rooted partly in a distortion of the teachings of Scripture (v. 16b). In the present verse he highlights the sharp contrast between the heretics and their disciples and the readers of this letter, addressing his audience with the emphatic Ὑμεῖς (*Hymeis*, you) and drawing them into the circle with himself by calling them "beloved."

**3:17**

From the use of the participle προγινώσκοντες (*proginōskontes*, since you know these things beforehand), we might infer that the false teachers have not yet arrived at the churches that receive Peter's letter. Bigg (1901: 303) takes a different tack, translating the participle as "knowing this first," placing the present as of primary importance. However, the verb was not employed in this way (see, e.g., Josephus, *Ant.* 2.5.6 §86), and Peter indeed uses the phrase πρῶτον γινώσκω (*prōton ginōskō*) to express this idea (1:20; 3:3). Bauckham (1983: 337, 317–18; and also Richard 2000: 391; Kraftchick 2002: 175–76; Senior and Harrington 2003: 296), on the other hand, suggests that the word is part of the fabric of fiction in the testamentary genre. The unknown author of this letter put this prophecy in the mouth of Peter after his death. But as noted previously, although Peter sometimes uses the future tense to speak of the false teachers (see 2:1–3; 3:3; and comments), the heretics are already promoting their error, seducing the unstable (2:14, 18), and participating in the common meal of the churches (2:13). The previous verse (3:16) even speaks of the heretics as those who are already twisting the Pauline teaching as well as the other Scriptures. We should not understand προγινώσκοντες (*proginōskontes*) as a reference to a future advent of the heretics, regardless of whether we identify the author as Peter or some other person writing under his name. Rather, since the recipients of this letter have not yet succumbed to the error and since they already have in hand the apostolic argument against the error via this letter as well as the prophetic and apostolic teaching regarding the coming error (3:2–3), they are advised in advance and can guard themselves from the heresy (Moo 1996: 213; Schreiner 2003: 399–400). The exhortation φυλάσσεσθε (*phylassesthe*) does not mean here "to protect" (as in 2:5 and Jude 24) but rather "to guard against" or "to avoid" (Luke 12:15; Acts 21:25; 2 Tim. 4:15; BDAG 1068). They are to be on their guard against the error of the false teachers lest they succumb to the error (3:17b).

The reason Peter concludes with this strong exhortation to be on their guard is ἵνα μὴ τῇ τῶν ἀθέσμων πλάνῃ συναπαχθέντες ἐκπέσητε τοῦ ἰδίου στηριγμοῦ (*hina mē tē tōn athesmōn planē synapachthentes ekpesēte tou idiou stērigmou*, so that you do not fall from your own firm position, being carried away by the error of the lawless). The problem Peter faces is not only doctrinal but also social. It is quite easy to be "carried away" (συναπαχθέντες) by the opinion of others, as the case of Barnabas in Antioch illustrates (Gal. 2:13, where the same verb appears). The appeal of the false teachers, along with their false teaching, holds a powerful appeal but places the readers in moral danger. These teachers are identified as "the lawless" (τῶν ἀθέσμων), just as our author has tagged the wicked of Sodom earlier in this letter (2:7 and comments). The heretics refuse to subject themselves to any moral law and thus are prefigured by those who did evil in that ancient city.

Peter identifies the heresy of the teachers as πλάνη, which may suggest that their teaching is not only false but also deceptive (Eph. 4:14; 1 Thess. 2:3; 1 John 4:6; so Kelly 1969: 374; Bauckham 1983: 337). The accusation that a teacher promoted "error" appeared in ancient *vituperatio* against philosophers (Malherbe 1970: 214). But Peter previously spoke about "those who live in error" (2:18 and comment), placing emphasis on the conduct that accompanies false teaching. The heretics are not of the church but outside it, and their teaching is linked with their conduct as "the lawless." Peter's appeal is that his readers do not "fall" (ἐκπέσητε) from their "firm position." Peter warns against the sin of apostasy (cf. Gal. 5:4, where the term is used the same way as here, and 2 Pet. 1:10 and comments). The heretics have already persuaded the unstable (2:14; 3:16, ἀστήρικτοι, *astēriktoi*, see comments), but the readers should hold on to and not fall from their "own firm position" (τοῦ ἰδίου στηριγμοῦ, *tou idiou stērigmou*; see the verbal form in 1:12 and comments; 1 Pet. 5:10). Peter's earnest desire is that they stay firm in the teaching that is founded on the prophetic and apostolic revelation, and not follow after the deceptive and corrupting error of the false teachers and thereby come into ruin.

The apostle recognizes that the best antidote against apostasy is a Christian life that is growing. Therefore, in this the final exhortation of the section (3:14–18a) and of the letter, Peter urges αὐξάνετε δὲ ἐν χάριτι καὶ γνώσει τοῦ κυρίου ἡμῶν καὶ σωτῆρος Ἰησοῦ Χριστοῦ (*auxanete de en chariti kai gnōsei tou kyriou hēmōn kai sōtēros Iēsou Christou*, but grow in grace and in the knowledge of our Lord and Savior Jesus Christ). Peter does not suggest that this growth is solely for neophytes in the faith but for all the congregation (Col. 1:10), although the verb αὐξάνω (*auxanō*) does appear in the context of the growth of children, either literally or figuratively (Luke 1:80; 2:40; 1 Pet. 2:2; cf. Col. 1:10). The term was more widely used of various forms of growth or increase, even "in power" or "strengthen" (LSJ 277). From the beginning of this letter, our author has emphasized the necessity of moral growth (1:5–7 and comments). But in the present verse, the focus is on their increase "in grace and in the knowledge of our Lord and Savior Jesus Christ." Increase in "grace" (ἐν χάριτι, *en chariti*) suggests advances in the appropriation or experience of the benefits of salvation (1 Pet. 1:10; 3:7; 4:10; 5:5, 12; see 2 Pet. 1:2; Jude 4; and comments), although Kelly (1969: 375) argues that this is growth in favor with God (cf. 1 Pet. 2:19–20). The increase in "knowledge" (γνώσει, *gnōsei*) is not theoretical but rather personal knowledge (see 1:2, 5–6, and comments), whose object is "our Lord and Savior Jesus Christ" (1:1, 11; 2:20; 3:2; and comments). Such knowledge, which marked the believers' conversion, also continues and increases throughout the life of the Christian. Along with grace, such knowledge is the strongest antidote against the destructive lures of the false teachers.

I. Epistolary Greeting (1:1–2)

II. Letter Body: A Warning against False Teachers (1:3–3:18a)

➤ III. Letter Closing: A Doxology (3:18b)

# III. Letter Closing: A Doxology (3:18b)

The body closing of the letter came to its conclusion in 3:18a. The final doxology in 3:18b serves as a less-than-elaborate letter closing, which ascribes honor to Jesus Christ throughout eternity.

## Exegesis and Exposition

[18b]To him be the glory both now and into the day of eternity. ⌜Amen⌝.

**3:18b**　Peter concludes his letter with a doxology to Jesus Christ (see "Genre and Structure" in the introduction to 2 Peter): αὐτῷ ἡ δόξα καὶ νῦν καὶ εἰς ἡμέραν αἰῶνος. ἀμήν (*autō hē doxa kai nyn kai eis hēmeran aiōnos. amēn*, To him be the glory both now and into the day of eternity. Amen). The majority of the doxologies in the NT are dedicated to God the Father. This doxology is one of the very few dedicated specifically to Jesus Christ (see 2 Tim. 4:18; Rev. 1:5–6). Its presence at the end of this letter provides evidence of Peter's high Christology. His high Christology is suggested in the first part of this verse as well as at the beginning of this letter, where he ascribes to Christ the divine titles "God," "Savior," and "Lord" (1:1–2 and comments; cf. Jude 25). This "glory" (δόξα, *doxa*; see 1:3, 17, and comments) is his "now" (νῦν, *nyn*), and therefore all should honor him with their conduct and faithfulness at the present time (not as the false teachers; see their regard for celestial beings in 2:10). The honor ascribed to him now will endure "into the day of eternity" (εἰς ἡμέραν αἰῶνος; cf. Sir. 18:10). The "day" that Peter and his readers anticipate will signal the destruction of the present order (3:10, 12) and will also inaugurate a new era that will last throughout eternity (1:19; 3:13). With his vision fixed on that hope, he utters the final "amen" (see Jude 25 and comments). Peter frames the readers' present existence and situation in the light of the honor that is ascribed to Christ, thus placing the final call to stand firm in the faith on a foundation that lasts through eternity.

## Additional Note

**3:18.** Although the final ἀμήν (*amēn*) does not appear in B 1241 1243, its inclusion in 𝔓[72] ℵ A C P Ψ 33 as well as 𝔐 argues strongly in favor of its inclusion.

# Works Cited

**Abbott, E. A.**
1882     "On the Second Epistle of St. Peter. I. Had the Author Read Josephus? II. Had the Author Read St. Jude? III. Was the Author Saint Peter?" *Expositor* 2/3:49–63, 139–53, 204–19.
1903     *Contrast, or, A Prophet and a Forger.* London: Black.

**ABD**     *The Anchor Bible Dictionary.* Edited by D. N. Freedman et al. 6 vols. New York: Doubleday, 1992.

**Adams, E.**
2005     "Where is the Promise of His Coming? The Complaint of the Scoffers in 2 Peter 3.4." *New Testament Studies* 51:106–22.

**Albin, C. A.**
1962     *Judasbrevet: Traditionen, Texten, Tolkningen.* Stockholm: Natur och Kultur.

**Aleith, E.**
1937     *Paulusverständnis in der alten Kirche.* Beihefte zur Zeitschrift für Religions- und Geistesgeschichte 18. Berlin: Töpelmann.

**Aletti, J.**
1990     "La Seconde Épître de Pierre et le canon du Nouveau Testament." Pp. 239–53 in *Le canon des Écritures: Études historiques, exégétiques et systématiques.* Edited by Jean Noël Aletti and Christoph Theobald. Paris: Cerf.

**Alexander, T. D.**
1985     "Lot's Hospitality: A Clue to His Righteousness." *Journal of Biblical Literature* 104:289–91.

**Allen, J. S.**
1998     "A New Possibility for the Three-Clause Format of Jude 22–3." *New Testament Studies* 44:133–43.

**Allmen, D. von.**
1966     "L'apocalyptique Juive et le retard de la parousie en 2 Pierre 3:1–13." *Revue de théologie et de philosophie* 16:255–74.

**ANF**     *The Ante-Nicene Fathers.* Edited by A. Roberts and J. Donaldson. 10 vols. 1885–87. Reprinted, Peabody, MA: Hendrickson, 1994.

**Arav, R.**
1999     "New Testament Archaeology and the Case of Bethsaida." Pp. 75–99 in *Das Ende der Tage und die Gegenwart des Heils.* Edited by Michael Becker and Wolfgang Fenske. Leiden: Brill.
2001     "Bethsaida." *Israel Exploration Journal* 51:239–46.
2003     Greek in Galilee. Personal communication.

**Argyle, A. W.**
1973     "Greek among the Jews of Palestine in New Testament Times." *New Testament Studies* 20:87–89.

**Arichea, D. C., and H. Hatton**
1993     *A Handbook on the Letter from Jude and the Second Letter from Peter.* United Bible Societies Handbook Series. New York: United Bible Societies.

**Aubineau, M.**
1959     "La thème du 'bourbier' dans la littérature grecque profane et chrétienne." *Recherches de science religieuse* 33:185–214.

**Auer, J.**
1984    "Die Bedeutung der Verklärung Christi für das Leben des Christen und für die Kirche Christi." Pp. 146–76 in *Die Mysterien des Lebens Jesu und die christliche Existenz.* Edited by Leo Scheffczyk. Aschaffenburg: Pattloch.

**Aune, D. E.**
1983    *Prophecy in Early Christianity and the Ancient Mediterranean World.* Grand Rapids: Eerdmans.

**Austin, B. R.**
1968    *Clouds without Water.* Nashville: Broadman.

**Austin, M. R.**
1985    "Salvation and the Divinity of Jesus." *Expository Times* 96:271–75.

**Baasland, E.**
1982    "2 Peters brev og urkristelig profeti: Eksegese av 2, Pet. 1,12–21." *Tidsskrift for Teologi og Kirke* 53:19–35.

**Bagatti, B.**
1971    *The Church from the Circumcision: History and Archaeology of the Judaeo-Christians.* Studium Biblicum Franciscanum: Smaller Series 2. Jerusalem: Franciscan Print.

**Baird, J. A., J. D. Thompson, and D. N. Freedman**
1991    *A Critical Concordance to I, II, III John, Jude.* The Computer Bible 33. Wooster, OH: Biblical Research Associates.

**Balz, H., and W. Schrage**
1973    *Die "katholischen" Briefe: Die Briefe des Jakobus, Petrus, Johannes und Judas.* Das Neue Testament Deutsch. Göttingen: Vandenhoeck & Ruprecht.

**Bammel, E.**
1988    *Jesu Nachfolger: Nachfolgeüberlieferungen in der Zeit des frühen Christentums.* Heidelberg: Schneider.

**Bandstra, A. J.**
1997    "Onward Christian Soldiers—Praying in Love, with Mercy: Preaching on the Epistle of Jude." *Calvin Theological Journal* 32:136–39.

**Barclay, J. M. G.**
1996    *Jews in the Mediterranean Diaspora: From Alexander to Trajan (323 BCE–117 CE).* Edinburgh: T&T Clark.

**Barclay, W.**
1976a   *The Letters of James and Peter.* Daily Study Bible Series. Philadelphia: Westminster.
1976b   *The Letters of John and Jude.* Daily Study Bible Series. Philadelphia: Westminster.

**Barnard, L. W.**
1957    "The Judgment in 2 Peter 3." *Expository Times* 68:302.

**Barnett, A. E.**
1941    *Paul Becomes a Literary Influence.* Chicago: University of Chicago Press.
1957a   "The Epistle of Jude: Introduction and Exegesis." Vol. 12 / pp. 315–43 in *The Interpreter's Bible.* Edited by G. A. Buttrick. Nashville: Abingdon.
1957b   "The Second Epistle of Peter: Introduction and Exegesis." Vol. 12 / pp. 161–206 in *The Interpreter's Bible.* Edited by G. A. Buttrick. Nashville: Abingdon.

**Barns, T.**
1904    "The Catholic Epistles of Themison." *Expositor* 6:369–93.

**Barrett, C. K.**
1956    "The Apostles in and after the New Testament." *Svensk exegetisk årsbok* 21:30–49.
1974    "Pauline Controversies in the Post-Pauline Period." *New Testament Studies* 20:229–45.

**Bartchy, S. S.**
1973    *First-Century Slavery and 1 Corinthians 7:21.* Missoula, MT: Society of Biblical Literature.
1999    "Undermining Ancient Patriarchy: The Apostle Paul's Vision of a Society of Siblings." *Biblical Theology Bulletin* 29:68–78.

**Barth, M.**
1979    "Der gute Jude Paulus." Pp. 107–37 in *Richte unsere Füsse auf den Weg des Friedens: Helmut Gollwitzer zum 70. Geburtstag.* Edited by A. Baudis et al. Munich: Kaiser.

**Barth, M. (ed.)**
1977    *Paulus—Apostat oder Apostel? Jüdische und christliche Antworten.* Regensburg, Germany: Pustet.

**Baskin, J. R.**
1983    "Origen on Balaam: The Dilemma of the Unworthy Prophet." *Vigiliae christianae* 37:22–35.

**Bauckham, R. J.**
1981    "The Delay of the Parousia." *Tyndale Bulletin* 31:3–36.
1982    "2 Peter: A Supplementary Bibliography." *Journal of the Evangelical Theological Society* 25:91–93.
1983    *Jude, 2 Peter.* Word Biblical Commentary. Waco: Word.
1988a   "James, 1 and 2 Peter, Jude." Pp. 303–17 in *It Is Written: Scripture Citing Scripture;*

*Essays in Honour of Barnabas Lindars.* Edited by D. A. Carson and H. G. M. Williamson. Cambridge: Cambridge University Press.

1988b "The Letter of Jude: An Account of Research." *Aufstieg und Niedergang der römischen Welt* 2.25.5:3791–3826. New York: de Gruyter.

1988c "2 Peter: An Account of Research." *Aufstieg und Niedergang der römischen Welt* 2.25.5:3713–52. New York: de Gruyter.

1988d "Pseudo-Apostolic Letters." *Journal of Biblical Literature* 107:469–94.

1990 *Jude and the Relatives of Jesus in the Early Church.* Edinburgh: T&T Clark.

1992 "The Martyrdom of Peter in Early Christian Literature." *Aufstieg und Niedergang der römischen Welt* 2.26.1:539–95. New York: de Gruyter.

1995b "James and the Jerusalem Church." Pp. 415–80 in *The Book of Acts in Its Palestinian Setting.* Edited by Richard J. Bauckham. The Book of Acts in Its First Century Setting 4. Grand Rapids: Eerdmans/Carlisle, UK: Paternoster.

1997 "James, 1 Peter, Jude and 2 Peter." Pp. 153–66 in *Vision for the Church: Studies in Early Christian Ecclesiology in Honour of J. P. M. Sweet.* Edited by M. Bockmuehl and M. B. Thompson. Edinburgh: T&T Clark.

**Bauckham, R. J. (ed.)**

1995a *The Book of Acts in Its Palestinian Setting.* The Book of Acts in Its First Century Setting 4. Grand Rapids: Eerdmans/Carlisle, UK: Paternoster.

**Baudis, A., et al. (eds.)**

1979 *Richte unsere Füsse auf den Weg des Friedens: Helmut Gollwitzer zum 70. Geburtstag.* Munich: Kaiser.

**Baum, A. D.**

2001 *Pseudepigraphie und literarische Fälschung im frühen Christentum.* Wissenschaftliche Untersuchungen zum Neuen Testament—2. Reihe. Tübingen: Mohr-Siebeck.

**Bärsch, C. E.**

1995 "Der Jude als Antichrist in der NS-Ideologie: Die kollektive Identität der Deutschen und der Antisemitismus unter religionspolitologischer Perspektive." *Zeitschrift für Religions- und Geistesgeschichte* 47:160–88.

**BDAG** *A Greek-English Lexicon of the New Testament and Other Early Christian Literature.* By W. Bauer, F. W. Danker, W. F. Arndt, and F. W. Gingrich. 3rd edition. Chicago: University of Chicago Press, 2000.

**BDF** *A Greek Grammar of the New Testament and Other Early Christian Literature.* By F. Blass and A. Debrunner. Translated and revised by R. W. Funk. Chicago: University of Chicago Press, 1961.

**Beale, G. K.**

1994 *The Right Doctrine from the Wrong Texts? Essays on the Use of the Old Testament in the New.* Grand Rapids: Baker Academic.

**Beare, F. W.**

1970 *The First Epistle of Peter.* Oxford: Blackwell.

**Beck, J. T.**

1995 *Petrusbriefe: Ein Kommentar.* Giessen: Brunnen.

**Ben-Chorin, S.**

1984 "Der Jude des Cusanus." *Zeitschrift für Religions- und Geistesgeschichte* 36:55–59.

1994 "Der Jude Petrus—ein Christ? Im Dickicht der Legenden." Pp. 41–49 in *Petrus, der Fels des Anstosses.* Edited by R. Niemann. Stuttgart: Kreuz.

**Berger, K.**

1970 "Hartherzigkeit und Gottes Gesetz, die Vorgeschichte des antijüdischen Vorwurfs in Mc 10,5." *Zeitschrift für die neutestamentliche Wissenschaft* 61:1–47.

1986 "Streit um Gottes Vorsehung: Zur Position der Gegner im 2 Petrusbrief." Pp. 121–35 in *Tradition and Re-interpretation in Jewish and Early Christian Literature: Essays in Honour of Jürgen C. H. Lebram.* Edited by J. W. van Henten. Leiden: Brill.

1994 *Theologiegeschichte des Urchristentums: Theologie des Neuen Testaments.* Tübingen: Francke.

**Best, E.**

1960 "Spiritual Sacrifice: General Priesthood in the New Testament." *Interpretation* 14:273–99.

1970 "1 Peter and the Gospel Tradition." *New Testament Studies* 16:95–113.

1971 *1 Peter.* New Century Bible. Grand Rapids: Eerdmans / London: Marshall, Morgan & Scott.

**Bénétreau, S.**

1994 *Le deuxieme epître de Pierre; L'epître de Jude.* Commentaire évangélique de la Bible 16. Vaux-sur-Seine, France: Faculté de Théologie Évangélique.

**BGU**  *Aegyptische Urkunden aus den Königlichen/Staatlichen Museen zu Berlin, Griechische Urkunden.* Berlin, 1895–.

**Bieder, W. J.**
1950  "Judas 22f.: Οὓς δὲ ἐλεᾶτε ἐν φόβῳ." *Theologische Zeitschrift* 6:75–77.

**Bigg, C.**
1901  *A Critical and Exegetical Commentary on the Epistles of St. Peter and St. Jude.* International Critical Commentary. Edinburgh: T&T Clark.

**Bijker, T.**
1992  *Als het anders gaat dan u denkt: De eerste brief van Petrus.* Kampen: Kok.

**Birdsall, J. N.**
1963  "Text of Jude in 𝔓⁷²." *Journal of Theological Studies* 14:394–99.

**Bishop, E. F. F.**
1958  *Apostles of Palestine: The Local Background to the New Testament Church.* London: Lutterworth.

**Black, C. C.**
1988  "The Rhetorical Form of the Hellenistic Jewish and Early Christian Sermon: A Response to L. Willis." *Harvard Theological Review* 81:1–18.

**Black, D. A., K. G. L. Barnwell, and S. H. Levinsohn**
1992  *Linguistics and New Testament Interpretation: Essays on Discourse Analysis.* Nashville: Broadman.

**Black, M.**
1964  "Critical and Exegetical Notes on Three New Testament Texts, Hebrews Xi. 11, Jude 5, James i. 27." Pp. 39–45 in *Apophoreta: Festschrift für Ernst Haenchen.* Edited by W. Eltester and F. H. Kettler. Berlin: Töpelmann.

1970  *Apocalypsis Henochi Graece.* Pseudepigrapha veteris testamenti graece. Leiden: Brill.

1973  "The Maranatha Invocation and Jude 14, 15 (I Enoch 1:9)." Pp. 189–96 in *Christ and Spirit in the New Testament: Studies in Honor of Charles Francis Digby Moule.* Edited by B. Lindars and S. S. Smalley. Cambridge: Cambridge University Press.

1985  *The Book of Enoch or 1 Enoch: A New English Edition.* Studia in veteris testamenti pseudepigrapha. Leiden: Brill.

1990  "The Doxology to the Pater Noster with a Note on Matthew 6.13B." Pp. 327–38 in *A Tribute to Geza Vermès: Essays on Jewish and Christian Literature and History.* Edited by P. R. Davies and R. T. White. Sheffield: Sheffield Academic Press.

**Blakely, W. A.**
1964  "Manuscript Relationships as Indicated by the Epistles of Jude and II Peter." PhD diss., Emory University.

**Blank, J.**
1973  "The Person and Office of Peter in the New Testament." Pp. 42–55 in *Truth and Certainty.* Edited by E. Schillebeeckx and B. M. F. van Iersel. Concilium 83. New York: Herder & Herder.

1977  "Paulus—Jude und Völkerapostel: Als Frage an Juden und Christen." Pp. 147–72 in *Paulus—Apostat oder Apostel? Jüdische und christliche Antworten.* Edited by M. Barth. Regensburg, Germany: Pustet.

**Blomberg, C. L.**
1992  *Matthew.* New American Commentary. Nashville: Broadman.

**Blum, E. A.**
1981a  "Jude." Pp. 381–96 in *The Expositor's Bible Commentary.* Edited by F. E. Gaebelein. Grand Rapids: Zondervan.

1981b  "2 Peter." Pp. 255–89 in *The Expositor's Bible Commentary.* Edited by F. E. Gaebelein. Grand Rapids: Zondervan.

**Bockmuehl, M.**
1990  *Revelation and Mystery in Ancient Judaism and Pauline Christianity.* Wissenschaftliche Untersuchungen zum Neuen Testament. Tübingen: Mohr (Siebeck).

**Bockmuehl, M., and M. B. Thompson.**
1997  *A Vision for the Church: Studies in Early Christian Ecclesiology in Honour of J. P. M. Sweet.* Edinburgh: T&T Clark.

**Boehmer, J.**
1923  "Tag und Morgenstern? Zu II Petr 1.19." *Zeitschrift für die neutestamentliche Wissenschaft* 22:228–33.

**Boismard, M. É.**
1957  "N. B. on II Petr. ii,18." *Revue biblique* 64:401.

1961  *Quatre hymnes baptismale dans la première épître de Pierre.* Lectio divina. Paris: Cerf.

**Bonaventura, M.**
1969  "La predizione del martirio di S. Pietro nel 'Quo Vadis?' e nela 2 Pe 1,14." Pp. 565–86 in *Miscellanea in honorem Card. Greg P. Agagianian.* Edited by Paolo Marella. Rome: Pontificia Universitas Urbaniana.

**Bonus, A.**
1920–21  "2 Peter III.10." *Expository Times* 32:280–81.

**Boobyer, G. H.**
1908    "II Peter." Pp. 1031–34 in *A Commentary on the Bible*. Edited by A. S. Peake. London: Hodder & Stoughton.
1942    *St. Mark and the Transfiguration Story*. Edinburgh: T&T Clark.
1958    "The Verbs in Jude 11." *New Testament Studies* 5:45–47.
1959    "The Indebtedness of 2 Peter to 1 Peter." Pp. 34–53 in *New Testament Essays: Studies in Memory of Thomas Walter Manson, 1893–1958*. Edited by A. J. B. Higgins. Manchester: University of Manchester Press.
1962    "II Peter." Pp. 1031–34 in *Peakes's Commentary on the Bible*. Edited by M. Black and H. H. Rowley. London: Nelson.

**Bornemann, W.**
1919–20    "Der erste Petrusbrief, eine Taufrede des Silvanus?" *Zeitschrift für die neutestamentliche Wissenschaft* 19:143–65.

**Botermann, H.**
1996    *Das Judenedikt des Kaisers Claudius: Römischer Staat und Christiani im 1. Jahrhundert*. Stuttgart: Steiner.

**Bouchat, R. A.**
1992    "Dating the Second Epistle of Peter." PhD diss., Baylor University.

**Bowman, J. W.**
1963    *The Letter to the Hebrews, the Letter of James, the First and Second Letters of Peter*. Richmond, VA: John Knox.

**Boys-Smith, E. P.**
1896–97    "'Interpretation' or 'Revealment': 2 Pet. i.20. II." *Expository Times* 8:331–32.

**Bratcher, R. G.**
1984    *A Translator's Guide to the Letters from James, Peter, and Jude*. New York: United Bible Societies.

**Bray, G. (ed.)**
2000    *James, 1–2 Peter, 1–3 John, Jude*. Ancient Christian Commentary on Scripture. Downers Grove, IL: InterVarsity.

**Bretscher, P. G.**
1968    "Exodus 4:22–23 and the Voice from Heaven." *Journal of Biblical Literature* 87:301–11.

**Brown, R. E., K. Donfried, and J. Reumann (eds.)**
1973    *Peter in the New Testament: A Collaborative Assessment by Protestant and Roman Catholic Scholars*. Minneapolis: Augsburg/New York: Paulist.

**Bruce, F. F.**
1974    *The "Secret" Gospel of Mark*. London: Athlone.

**Bryce, G. E.**
1972    "'Better'-Proverbs: An Historical and Structural Study." Vol. 2 / pp. 343–54 in *Society of Biblical Literature Seminar Papers*. Edited by L. C. McGaughy. Missoula, MT: Society of Biblical Literature.

**Buchanan, G. W.**
1987    *Typology and the Gospel*. Lanham, MD: University Press of America.

**Buchholz, D. D.**
1988    *Your Eyes Will Be Opened: A Study of the Greek (Ethiopic) Apocalypse of Peter*. Society of Biblical Literature Dissertation Series. Atlanta: Scholars.

**Buis, H.**
1961    "The Significance of II Timothy 3:16 and II Peter 1:21." *Review of Religion* 14:43–49.

**Burton, E. D. W.**
1920    *A Critical and Exegetical Commentary on the Epistle to the Galatians*. International Critical Commentary. Edinburgh: T&T Clark.

**Busto Saiz, J. R.**
1981    "La carta de Judas a la luz de algunos escritos judíos." *Estudios bíblicos* 39:83–105.

**Buttrick, G. A. (ed.)**
1957    *The Interpreter's Bible*. 12 vols. Nashville: Abingdon.

**Caird, G. B.**
1980    *The Language and Imagery of the Bible*. London: Duckworth.

**Calderone, S.**
1964    *Pistis-Fides: Ricerche di storia e diritto internazionale nell'antichità*. Messina: Università Deligi Studi.

**Callan, T.**
2001a    "The Christology of the Second Letter of Peter." *Biblica* 82:253–63.
2001b    "The Soteriology of the Second Letter of Peter." *Biblica* 82:549–59.
2004    "Use of the Letter of Jude by the Second Letter of Peter." *Biblica* 85:42–64.

**Calvin, J.**
1855    *Commentaries on the Catholic Epistles*. Translated by J. Owen. Edinburgh: Calvin Translation Society.
1963    *The Epistle of Paul the Apostle to the Hebrews and the First and Second Epistles of Peter*. Translated by W. B. Johnston. Grand Rapids: Eerdmans.

**Cantinat, J.**
1973    *Les épîtres de Saint Jacques et de Saint Jude*. Sources bibliques. Paris: Gabalda.

Caragounis, C. C.
1990    *Peter and the Rock*. Berlin: de Gruyter.
1998    "From Obscurity to Prominence: The Development of the Roman Church between Romans and I Clement." Pp. 245–79 in *Judaism and Christianity in First-Century Rome*. Edited by K. P. Donfried and P. Richardson. Grand Rapids: Eerdmans.

Carr, W.
1981    *Principalities and Powers: The Background, Meaning and Development of the Pauline Phrase* Hai Archai kai hai Exousiai. Society for New Testament Studies Monograph Series. Cambridge: Cambridge University Press.

Carrez, M., P. Dornier, and M. Dumais, et al.
1984    *Les lettres de Paul, de Jacques et de Jude*. Paris: Desclée de Brouwer.

Carson, D. A., and H. G. M. Williamson (eds.)
1988    *It Is Written: Scripture Citing Scripture; Essays in Honour of Barnabas Lindars*. Cambridge: Cambridge University Press.

Carston, R.
1988    "Implicature, Explicature and Truth-Theoretic Semantics." Pp. 155–81 in *Mental Representation: The Interface between Language and Reality*. Edited by R. M. Kempson. Cambridge: Cambridge University Press.

Caulley, T. S.
1982    "The False Teachers in 2 Peter." *Studia biblica et theologica* 12:27–42.
1983    "The Idea of Inspiration in 2 Peter 1:16–21." PhD diss., University of Tübingen.
1984    "The Idea of Inspiration in 2 Peter 1:16–21." *Theologische Literaturzeitung* 109:76–77.

Cavallin, H. C. C.
1979    "The False Teachers of 2 Peter as Pseudo-Prophets." *Novum Testamentum* 21:263–70.

Cazeaux, J.
1991    "Liberté ou mémoire? La rhétorique dans la seconde Épître de Pierre." *Studia Philonica Annual* 3:222–55.

Cedar, P. A.
1984    *James; I, II Peter; Jude*. Communicator's Commentary 11. Waco: Word.

Chadwick, H.
1966    *Early Christian Thought and the Classical Tradition*. New York: Oxford University Press.

Chaine, J.
1937    "Cosmogonie aquatique et conflagratio finale d'apres la secunda petri." *Revue biblique* 46:207–16.
1939    *Les épîtres catholique: La seconde épître de Saint Pierre, les épîtres de saint Jean, l'épître de saint Jude*. Paris: Gabalda.

Chancey, M. A.
2002    *The Myth of a Gentile Galilee*. Society for New Testament Studies Monograph Series. Cambridge: Cambridge University Press.

Chang, A. D.
1985    "Second Peter 2:1 and the Extent of the Atonement." *Bibliotheca sacra* 142:52–63.

Charles, J. D.
1990    "'Those' and 'These': The Use of the Old Testament in the Epistle of Jude." *Journal for the Study of the New Testament* 38:109–24.
1991a   "Jude's Use of Pseudepigraphical Source-Material as Part of a Literary Strategy." *New Testament Studies* 37:130–45.
1991b   "Literary Artifice in the Epistle of Jude." *Zeitschrift für die neutestamentliche Wissenschaft* 82:106–24.
1993    *Literary Strategy in the Epistle of Jude*. Scranton, PA: University of Scranton Press.
1997    *Virtue amidst Vice: The Catalogue of Virtues in 2 Peter 1*. Journal for the Study of the New Testament: Supplement Series. Sheffield: Sheffield Academic Press.
1998    "The Language and Logic of Virtue in 2 Peter 1:5–7." *Bulletin for Biblical Research* 8:55–73.
2001    "On Angels and Asses: The Moral Paradigm in 2 Peter 2." *Proceedings—Eastern Great Lakes and Midwest Biblical Societies* 21:1–12.
2005    "The Angels under Reserve in 2 Peter and Jude." *Bulletin for Biblical Research* 15:39–48.

Charles, R. H.
1893    *The Book of Enoch*. Oxford: Clarendon.
1896    *The Apocalypse of Baruch*. London: Black.
1897    *The Assumption of Moses*. Translated from the Latin sixth century ms., the unemended text of which is published herewith, together with the text in its restored and critically emended form. London: Black.

1912    *The Book of Enoch or 1 Enoch.* Translated from the editor's Ethiopic text and edited with the introduction, notes and indexes of the first edition wholly recast, enlarged and rewritten. 2nd edition. Oxford: Clarendon.

1913    *The Apocrypha and Pseudepigrapha of the Old Testament.* 2 vols. Oxford: Clarendon.

Charue, A.
1951    *Les épîtres catholiques.* Paris.

Chase, F. H.
1900    "Second Epistle of Peter." Vol. 3 / pp. 796–818 in *A Dictionary of the Bible.* Edited by J. Hastings. New York: Scribners.

Chester, A., and R. P. Martin
1994    *The Theology of the Letters of James, Peter, and Jude.* New Testament Theology. Cambridge: Cambridge University Press.

Chikane, F.
1985    "The Incarnation in the Life of the People in Southern Africa." *Journal of Theology for South Africa* 51:37–50.

Clowney, E. P.
1988    *The Message of 1 Peter.* Leicester, UK: Inter-Varsity.

Collins, J. J.
1974    *The Sibylline Oracles of Egyptian Judaism.* Society of Biblical Literature Dissertation Series. Missoula, MT: Scholars Press.

Conte, G. B.
1986    *The Rhetoric of Imitation: Genre and Poetic Memory in Virgil and Other Latin Poets.* Edited and translated by C. Segal. Ithaca, NY: Cornell University Press.

Conti, M.
1969    "La sophia di 2 Petr. 3.15." *Revue biblique* 17:121–38.

Cooper, W. H.
1940    "The Objective Nature of Prophecy according to II Peter." *Lutheran Quarterly* 13:190–95.

Corley, K. E.
1993    *Private Women, Public Meals: Social Conflict in the Synoptic Tradition.* Peabody, MA: Hendrickson.

Cothenet, E.
1984    *Las cartas de Pedro.* Estella (Navarra): Verbo Divino.

1989    "La tradition selon Jude et 2 Pierre." *New Testament Studies* 35:407–20.

Coughenour, R. A.
1978    "The Woe-Oracles in Ethiopic Enoch." *Journal for the Study of Judaism* 9:192–97.

Countryman, L. W.
1999    "Asceticism or Household Morality: 1 and 2 Peter and Jude." Pp. 371–82 in *Asceticism and the New Testament.* Edited by L. E. Vaage and V. L. Wimbush. New York: Routledge.

Cox, S.
1875    "From Starlight to Sunlight: 2 Peter i.16–20." *Expositor* 1:169–85.

1884    "Lot: 2 Peter II.7, 8." *Expositor* 2:270–80.

Coyle, J. T.
1985    "The Agape-Eucharist Relationship in 1 Corinthians 11." *Grace Theological Journal* 6:411–24.

CPJ     *Corpus papyrorum judaicarum.* Edited by V. Tcherikover. 3 vols. Cambridge, 1957–64.

CPR     *Corpus papyrorum Raineri archeducis Austriae.* Vienna, 1895–.

Craddock, F. B.
1995a   *First and Second Peter and Jude.* Westminster Bible Companion. Louisville: Westminster John Knox.

1995b   *The Message of Second Peter and Jude.* Leicester, UK: Inter-Varsity.

Cranfield, C. E. B.
1950    *The First Epistle of Peter.* London: SCM.

1960    *1 and 2 Peter and Jude: Introduction and Commentary.* London: SCM.

Crehan, J.
1982    "New Light on 2 Peter from the Bodmer Papyrus." *Studia evangelica* 7:145–49.

Cullmann, O.
1953    *Peter: Disciple-Apostle-Martyr.* Translated by F. V. Filson. London: SCM.

Curran, J. T.
1943    "The Teaching of II Peter 1:20." *Theological Studies* 4:347–68.

Dalton, W. J.
1979    "The Interpretation of 1 Peter 3,19 and 4,6: Light from 2 Peter." *Biblica* 60:547–55.

1989    *Christ's Proclamation to the Spirits. A Study of 1 Peter 3:18–4:6.* Analecta biblica. Rome: Pontificio Instituto Biblico.

Danker, F. W.
1962    "2 Peter 3:10 and Psalm of Solomon 17:10." *Zeitschrift für die neutestamentliche Wissenschaft* 53:82–86.

1977    "The Second Letter of Peter." Pp. 81–91 in *Hebrews, James, 1 and 2 Peter, Jude, Revelation.* Edited by R. H. Fuller et al. Philadelphia: Fortress.

1978    "2 Peter 1: A Solemn Decree." *Catholic Biblical Quarterly* 40:64–82.

1982    *Benefactor: Epigraphic Study of a Graeco-Roman and New Testament Semantic Field.* St. Louis: Clayton.

D'Arcais, F.
1967    *Pietro a Roma.* Roma: Edindustria.

Davey, G. R.
1972    "Old Testament Quotations in the Syriac Version of I and II Peter." *Parole de l'orient* 3:353–64.

Davids, P. H.
1990    *The First Epistle of Peter.* New International Commentary on the New Testament. Grand Rapids: Eerdmans.

2006    *The Letters of 2 Peter and Jude.* Pillar New Testament Commentary. Grand Rapids: Eerdmans/Leicester, UK: Apollos.

Davidson, M. J.
1992    *Angels at Qumran: A Comparative Study of 1 Enoch 1–36, 72–108 and Sectarian Writings from Qumran.* Journal for the Study of the Pseudepigrapha: Supplement Series. Sheffield: JSOT Press.

DeGraaf, D.
2005    "Some Doubts about Doubt: The New Testament use of Διακρίνω." *Journal of the Evangelical Theological Society* 48:733–55.

Dehandschutter, B.
1986    "Pseudo-Cyprian, Jude and Enoch: Some Notes on 1 Enoch 1:9." Pp. 114–20 in *Tradition and Re-interpretation in Jewish and Early Christian Literature. Essays in Honour of Jürgen C. H. Lebram.* Edited by J. W. van Henten and H. J. De Jonge. Leiden: Brill.

Deichgräber, R.
1967    *Gotteshymnus und Christushymnus in der frühen Christenheit: Untersuchungen zur Form, Sprache und Stil der frühchristlichen Hymnen.* Studien zur Umwelt des Neuen Testaments. Göttingen: Vandenhoeck & Ruprecht.

Deiros, P. A.
1992    *Santiago y Judas.* Comentario bíblico hispanoamericano. Miami: Caribe.

Deissmann, A.
1901    *Bible Studies.* Translated by A. Grieve. Edinburgh: T&T Clark.

1911    *Light from the Ancient East: The New Testament Illustrated by Recently Discovered Texts of the Graeco-Roman World.* 2nd edition. Translated by L. R. M. Stra-

chan. London: Hodder & Stoughton. Reprinted Grand Rapids: Baker, 1965.

Delaney, J. J.
1978    *Saints for All Seasons.* Garden City, NY: Doubleday.

Demarest, J. T.
1862    *A Commentary on the Second Epistle of the Apostle Peter.* New York: Sheldon.

Dennison, J. T.
1995    "What Should I Read on the Epistle of Jude?" *Kerux* 10:25–31.

deSilva, D. A.
1995    *Despising Shame: Honor Discourse and Community Maintenance in the Epistle to the Hebrews.* Society of Biblical Literature Dissertation Series. Atlanta: Scholars Press.

2000    *Honor, Patronage, Kinship and Purity: Unlocking New Testament Culture.* Downers Grove, IL: InterVarsity.

Desjardins, M.
1987    "The Portrayal of the Dissidents in 2 Peter and Jude: Does It Tell Us More about the 'Godly' Than the 'Ungodly'?" *Journal for the Study of the New Testament* 30:89–102.

Dillenseger, P. J.
1907    "L'authenticité de la II Petri." *Mélanges de la Faculté Orientale de l'Université Saint-Joseph, Beyrouth* 2:173–212.

Dillon, J. M., and A. A. Long (eds.)
1988    *The Question of "Eclecticism."* Berkeley: University of California Press.

Dinkler, E.
1980    "Petrus und Paulus in Rom. Die literarische und archäologische Frage nach den Tropaia tōn Apostolōn." *Gymnasium* 87:1–37.

Dockx, S. I.
1974    "Essai de chronologie pétrinienne." *Recherches de science religieuse* 62:221–41.

1987    "Chronologie zum Leben des Heiligen Petrus." Pp. 85–108 in *Petrusbild in der neueren Forschung.* Edited by C. P. Thiede. Wuppertal: Brockhaus.

Dodds, E. R.
1965    *Pagan and Christian in an Age of Anxiety.* Cambridge: Cambridge University Press.

Donfried, K. P.
1974    *The Setting of Second Clement in Early Christianity.* Novum Testamentum Supplement 38. Leiden: Brill.

Doty, W. G.
1973    *Letters in Primitive Christianity.* Philadelphia: Fortress.

Douglas, M.
1966    *Purity and Danger. An Analysis of the Concepts of Pollution and Taboo.* London: Routledge.

Dschulnigg, P.
1989    "Der Theologische Ort des zweiten Petrusbriefs." *Biblische Zeitschrift* 33:161–77.
1996    *Petrus im Neuen Testament.* Stuttgart: Katholisches Bibelwerk.

Duke, T. H.
1999    "An Exegetical Analysis of 2 Peter 3:9." *Faith and Mission* 16:6–13.

Dunham, D. A.
1983    "An Exegetical Study of 2 Peter 2:18–22." *Bibliotheca sacra* 140:40–54.

Dunn, J. D. G.
1990    *Unity and Diversity in the New Testament: An Inquiry into the Character of Earliest Christianity.* 2nd edition. Philadelphia: Trinity.
1998    *The Theology of Paul the Apostle.* Grand Rapids: Eerdmans.

Dunnett, W. M.
1988    "The Hermeneutics of Jude and 2 Peter: The Use of Ancient Jewish Traditions." *Journal of the Evangelical Theological Society* 31:287–92.

Dupont, J.
1949    *Gnosis: La connaissance religieuse dans les épîtres de saint Paul.* Louvain: Nauwelaerts/Paris: Gabalda.

Dupont-Roc, R.
1994    "Le motif de la création selon 2 Pierre 3." *Revue biblique* 101:95–114.

Durand, A.
1911    "Le sens de II Petri 1,20." *Recherches de science religieuse* 2:187–89.

du Toit, A.
1994    "Vilification as a Pragmatic Device in Early Christian Epistolography." *Biblica* 75:403–12.

Dyson, R. W.
1998    *Augustine: The City of God against the Pagans.* Cambridge: Cambridge University Press.

Easton, B. S.
1932    "New Testament Ethical Lists." *Journal of Biblical Literature* 51:1–12.

Eckert, W. P.
1972    "Jesus und das heutige Judentum; Jesus: Der Jude und erste Christ." Pp. 52–72 in *Jesus von Nazareth.* Mainz: Grunewald.

Edmundson, G.
1913    *The Church of Rome in the First Century.* Bampton Lectures. London: Longmans, Green.

Ehrman, B. D.
1990    "Cephas and Peter." *Journal of Biblical Literature* 109:463–74.

Elliott, J. K.
1981    "The Language and Style of the Concluding Doxology to the Epistle to the Romans." *Zeitschrift für die neutestamentliche Wissenschaft* 72:124–30.
2000    "The Petrine Epistles in the Editio Critica Maior." *Novum Testamentum* 42:328–39.

Elliott, J. H.
1966    *The Elect and the Holy.* Leiden: Brill.
1969    "A Catholic Gospel: Reflections on 'Early Catholicism' in the New Testament." *Catholic Biblical Quarterly* 31:213–23.
1976    "The Rehabilitation of an Exegetical Stepchild: 1 Peter in Recent Research." *Journal of Biblical Literature* 95:243–54.
1980    "Peter, Silvanus and Mark in 1 Peter and Acts: Sociological-Exegetical Perspectives on a Petrine Group in Rome." Pp. 250–67 in *Wort in der Zeit: Festgabe für K. H. Rengstorf.* Edited by W. Haubeck and M. Bachmann. Leiden: Brill.
1981    *A Home for the Homeless.* Philadelphia: Fortress.
1982    *I and II Peter/Jude.* Augsburg Commentary on the New Testament. Minneapolis: Augsburg.
1993    "The Epistle of James in Rhetorical and Social Scientific Perspective: Holiness-Wholeness and Patterns of Replication." *Biblical Theology Bulletin* 23:71–81.
2000    *1 Peter: A New Translation with Introduction and Commentary.* Anchor Bible. New York: Doubleday.

Elliott, J. H., and R. A. Martin
1982    *James, 1–2 Peter, Jude.* Minneapolis: Augsburg.

Elliott, M.
2005    *Faithful Feelings: Emotion in the New Testament.* Leicester, UK: Inter-Varsity.

Ellis, E. E.
1978    *Prophecy and Hermeneutic in Early Christianity.* Tübingen: Mohr.

**Elton, G. E.**
1965    *Simon Peter: A Study of Discipleship.* London: Davies.

**Epp, E. J., and G. D. Fee**
1981    *New Testament Textual Criticism: Its Significance for Exegesis; Essays in Honour of Bruce M. Metzger.* Oxford: Clarendon.

**Epp, E. J., and G. W. MacRae**
1989    *The New Testament and Its Modern Interpreters.* Philadelphia: Fortress.

**Epstein, D. F.**
1987    *Personal Enmity in Roman Politics 218–43 BC.* London and New York: Routledge.

**Epstein, I. (ed.)**
1935–52    *The Babylonian Talmud.* London: Soncino.

**Ernst, C.**
1962    "The Date of II Peter and the Deposit of Faith." *Clergy Review* 47:686–89.

**Eybers, I. H.**
1975    "Aspects of the Background of the Letter of Jude." Pp. 113–23 in *Essays on the General Epistles of the New Testament: Proceedings of the 11th Meeting of Die Nuwe-Testamentiese Werkgemeenskap van Suid-Afrika Held at the University of Stellenbosch from the 20th of April to the 1st of May, 1975.* Edited by W. Nicol et al. Neotestamentica 9. Pretoria: NTWSA.

**Falconer, R. A.**
1902    "Is Second Peter a Genuine Epistle to the Churches of Samaria?" *Expositor* 6/5:459–72; 6/6:47–56, 117–27, 218–27.

**Farkasfalvy, D.**
1985–86    "The Ecclesial Setting and Pseudepigraphy in 2 Peter and Its Role in the Formation of the Canon." *Second Century* 5:3–29.

**Farmer, W. R.**
1985–86    "Some Critical Reflections on Second Peter: A Response to a Paper on 2 Peter by Denis Farkasfalvy." *Second Century* 5:30–46.

**Farmer, W. R., and R. A. Kereszty**
1990    *Peter and Paul in the Church of Rome: The Ecumenical Potential of a Forgotten Perspective.* New York: Paulist.

**Farrar, F. W.**
1882    "Dr. Abbott on the Second Epistle of St. Peter." *Expositor* 3:401–23.

1888    "The Second Epistle of St. Peter and Josephus." *Expositor* 8:58–69.

**Feldmeier, R.**
1983    "Die Darstellung des Petrus in den synoptischen Evangelien." Pp. 267–71 in *Das Evangelium und die Evangelien: Vorträge vom Tübinger Symposium 1982.* Edited by P. Stuhlmacher. Tübingen: Mohr (Siebeck).

**Felten, J.**
1929    *Die zwei Briefe des Hl. Petrus und der Judasbrief.* Regensburg: Manz.

**Ferguson, E.**
1993    *Backgrounds of Early Christianity.* 2nd edition. Grand Rapids: Eerdmans.

2002    "Factors Leading to the Selection and Closure of the New Testament Canon: A Survey of Some Recent Studies." Pp. 294–320 in *The Canon Debate.* Edited by L. M. McDonald and J. A. Sanders. Peabody, MA: Hendrickson.

**Fields, W. W.**
1997    *Sodom and Gomorrah: History and Motif in Biblical Narrative.* Journal for the Study of the Old Testament: Supplement Series. Sheffield: Sheffield Academic Press.

**Fiensy, D. A.**
1995    "The Composition of the Jerusalem Church." Pp. 213–36 in *The Book of Acts in Its Palestinian Setting.* Edited by R. Bauckham. The Book of Acts in Its First Century Setting 4. Grand Rapids: Eerdmans.

**Fink, J.**
1988    *Das Petrusgrab in Rom.* Innsbruck: Tyrolia.

**Fischel, H. A.**
1973    "The Uses of Sorites (Climax, Gradatio) in the Tannaitic Period." *Hebrew Union College Annual* 44:118–51.

**Fitzmyer, J. A.**
1960–61    "The Use of Explicit Old Testament Quotations in Qumran Literature and in the New Testament." *New Testament Studies* 7:297–333.

1974a    "The Bar Cochba Period." Pp. 305–54 in *Essays on the Semitic Background of the New Testament.* Missoula, MT: Society of Biblical Literature.

1974b    "Some Notes on Aramaic Epistolography." *Journal of Biblical Literature* 93:201–25.

1981    *To Advance the Gospel.* New Testament Studies. New York: Crossroad.

**Flanders, H. J.**
1950    "The Relation of Jude to II Peter." ThD diss., Southern Baptist Theological Seminary.

**Flusser, D.**
1969    "Salvation Present and Future." *Numen* 16:139–55.

1979    "Das Erlebnis, ein Jude zu sein." Pp. 15–25 in *Richte unsere Füsse auf den Weg des Friedens: Helmut Gollwitzer zum 70. Geburtstag*. Edited by A. Baudis et al. Munich: Chr Kaiser.

Foerster, W.
1958    "Εὐσέβεια in den Pastoralbriefen." *New Testament Studies* 5:213–18.
1961    "Peter, Second Epistle of." Pp. 757–59 in *Dictionary of the Bible*. Edited by J. Hastings. Revised by F. C. Grant and H. Rowley. New York: Scribners' Sons.

Fornberg, T.
1977    *An Early Church in a Pluralistic Society. A Study of 2 Peter*. Coniectanea biblica: New Testament Series. Lund: Gleerup.

Fossum, J.
1987    "Kyrios Jesus as the Angel of the Lord in Jude 5–7." *New Testament Studies* 33:226–43.

Franco, R.
1962    "Cartas de San Pedro." Vol. 3 / pp. 221–97 in *La Sagrada Escritura: Nuevo Testamento*. Edited by los Profesores de la Compania de Jesús. Madrid: Biblioteca de Autores Cristianos.

Frankenmölle, H.
1990    *1. Petrusbrief, 2. Petrusbrief, Judasbrief*. Neue Echter Bibel, Neues Testament. Würzburg: Echter.

Fransen, I.
1960    "Le Feu de la Gloire (2 Pierre)." *Bible et vie chrétienne* 33:26–33.

Frend, W. H. C.
1965    *Martyrdom and Persecution in the Early Church*. Oxford: Oxford University Press.

Fridrichsen, A.
1947    *The Apostle and His Message*. Uppsala Universitets Årsskrift 3. Uppsala: Lundequistaka Bokhandeln.

Friedlander, A.
1996    "Deutscher Jude oder jüdischer Deutscher." Pp. 55–66 in *Anfang nach dem Ende*. Dusseldorf: Drostle.

Friedlander, G.
1965    *Pirke de Rabbi Eliezer*. 2nd edition. New York: Hermon.

Frisch, H.
1994    "War Petrus eine Frau? Die Geschichte von der Jüngerin Simone." Pp. 97–108 in *Petrus, der Fels des Anstosses*. Edited by R. Niemann. Stuttgart: Kreuz.

Frühwald, W., and H. Hürten
1987    *Christliches Exil und christlicher Widerstand: Ein Symposion an der Katholischen Universitat Eichstatt 1985*. Regensburg: Pustet.

Fuchs, E., and P. Raymond
1988    *La deuxième épître de saint Pierre: L'épître de saint Jude*. Commentaire du Nouveau Testament. Geneva: Labor et Fides.

Fuller, R. H. (ed.)
1977    *Hebrews, James, 1 and 2 Peter, Jude, Revelation*. Philadelphia: Fortress.

Furnish, V. P.
1968    *Theology and Ethics in Paul*. Nashville: Abingdon.

Galbiati, E.
1967    "L'escatologia delle lettere di S. Pietro." Pp. 412–23 in *San Pietro: Atti della XIX Settimana Biblica*. Brescia: Paideia.

García Martínez, F.
1994    *The Dead Sea Scrolls Translated: The Qumran Texts in English*. Leiden: Brill.

Garnsey, P.
1970    *Social Status and Legal Privilege in the Roman Empire*. Oxford: Clarendon.

Gächter, P.
1958    *Petrus und seine Zeit: Neutestamentliche Studien*. Innsbruck: Tyrolia.

Gerdmar, A.
2001    *Rethinking the Judaism-Hellenism Dichotomy: A Historiographical Study of Second Peter and Jude*. Coniectanea biblica: New Testament Series. Stockholm: Almqvist & Wiksell.

Giles, K.
1985    "Apostles before and after Paul." *Churchman* 99:241–56.

Gilmore, M. J.
1999    "2 Peter in Recent Research: A Bibliography." *Journal of the Evangelical Theological Society* 42:673–78.
2001    "Reflections on the Authorship of 2 Peter." *Evangelical Quarterly* 73:291–309.
2002    *The Significance of Parallels between 2 Peter and Other Early Christian Literature*. Atlanta: Society of Biblical Literature.

Glasson, T. F.
1961    *Greek Influence in Jewish Eschatology*. SPCK Biblical Monographs. London: SPCK.

Gnilka, J.
1974    *Neues Testament und Kirche: Für Rudolf Schnackenburg*. Freiburg: Herder.

Goehring, J. E., and C. W. Hedrick
1990    *Gnosticism and the Early Christian World: In Honour of James M. Robinson*. Sonoma, CA: Polebridge.

Goldstein, H. (ed.)
1979    *Gottesverächter und Menschenfeinde? Juden zwischen Jesus und frühchristlicher Kirche*. Dusseldorf: Patmos.

Goppelt, L.
1982    *Typos: The Typological Interpretation of the Old Testament in the New*. Grand Rapids: Eerdmans.

Gow, A. S. F., and D. L. Page
1968    *The Greek Anthology: The Garland of Philip, and Some Contemporary Epigrams*. 2 vols. London: Cambridge University Press.

Grant, M.
1994    *Saint Peter: A Biography*. New York: Scribner.

Green, C., and D. Lucas
1995    *The Message of 2 Peter and Jude*. Leicester, UK: Inter-Varsity.

Green, E. M. B.
1959    *2 Peter Reconsidered*. London: Tyndale.
1987    "Der 2 Petrusbrief neu betrachtet." Pp. 1–50 in *Petrusbild in der neueren Forschung*. Edited by C. P. Thiede. Wuppertal: Brockhaus.

Green, G. L. (E.)
1979    "Theology and Ethics in 1 Peter." PhD diss., University of Aberdeen.
1993    *1 Pedro y 2 Pedro*. Comentario bíblico hispanoamericano. Miami: Caribe.
2001    "'As for Prophecies, They Will Come to an End': 2 Peter, Paul and Plutarch on 'the Obsolescence of Oracles.'" *Journal for the Study of the New Testament* 82:107–22.
2002    *The Letters to the Thessalonians*. Pillar New Testament Commentary. Grand Rapids: Eerdmans/Leicester: Apollos.

Green, M.
1987    *The Second Epistle General of Peter and the General Epistle of Jude*. Tyndale New Testament Commentaries. Leicester, UK: Inter-Varsity/Grand Rapids: Eerdmans.

Greenlee, J. H.
1999    *An Exegetical Summary of Jude*. Dallas: Summer Institute of Linguistics.

Griego, R.
2004    "Living in the Light of His Return: Peter's Response to the False Teachers' Denial of the Parousia in 2 Peter." Unpublished essay, Wheaton College, IL.

Grispino, J. A.
1961    "The Date of II Peter and the Deposit of Faith." *Clergy Review* 46:601–10.

Gross, J.
1938    *La divinisation du chrétien d'après les pères grecs*. Paris: Gabalda.

Grudem, W.
1988    *1 Peter*. Leicester, UK: Inter-Varsity/Grand Rapids: Eerdmans.

Gruen, E. S.
1982    "Greek Pistis and Roman Fides." *Athenaeum* 60:50–68.

Grundmann, W.
1974    *Der Brief des Judas und der zweite Brief des Petrus*. Theologischer Handkommentar zum Neuen Testament. Berlin: Evangelische Verlagsanstalt.

Grunewald, W.
1986    *Das Neue Testament auf Papyrus*, vol. 1: *Die katholischen Briefe*. Berlin: de Gruyter.

Guarducci, M.
1960    *The Tomb of St. Peter: The New Discoveries in the Sacred Grottoes of the Vatican*. New York: Hawthorn.
1983    *Pietro in Vaticano*. Roma: Istituto poligrafico e zecca dello Stato.
1989    *La tomba di San Pietro: Una straordinaria vicenda*. Milano: Rusconi.

Gundry Volf, J. M.
1990    *Paul and Perseverance: Staying in and Falling Away*. Wissenschaftliche Untersuchungen zum Neuen Testament 2.37. Tübingen: Mohr.

Gunther, J. J.
1984    "The Alexandrian Epistle of Jude." *New Testament Studies* 30:549–62.

Guthrie, D.
1990    *New Testament Introduction*. Downers Grove, IL: InterVarsity.

Gutt, E.-A.
2005    E-mail communication.

Haase, W. (ed.)
1988    *Principat, 25.5: Religion (Vorkonstantinisches Christentum: Leben und Umwelt Jesu; Neues Testament [Kanonische Schriften und Apokryphen])*. Berlin: de Gruyter.

Hagner, D. A.
1973    *The Use of the Old and New Testaments in Clement of Rome*. Novum Testamentum Supplement 34. Leiden: Brill.
1995    *Matthew 14–28*. Word Biblical Commentary. Dallas: Word.

Hahn, F.
1981    "Randbemerkungen zum Judasbrief."
        Theologische Zeitschrift 37:209–18.

Hahneman, G. M.
1992    The Muratorian Fragment and the De-
        velopment of the Canon. Oxford: Clar-
        endon.

Hall, S. G.
1987    "Synoptic Transfigurations: Mark 9:2–10
        and Partners." King's Theological Review
        10:41–44.

Hamann, H. P.
1980    James–Jude. Adelaide: Concordia.

Hamilton, V. P.
1990    The Book of Genesis: Chapters 1–17.
        New International Commentary on the
        Old Testament. Grand Rapids: Eerd-
        mans.
1995    The Book of Genesis: Chapters 18–50.
        New International Commentary on the
        Old Testament. Grand Rapids: Eerd-
        mans.

Hamilton, W. (trans.)
1973    Phaedrus and Letters VII and VIII. By
        Plato. London: Penguin.

Harm, H.
1987    "Logic Line in Jude: The Search for Syl-
        logisms in a Hortatory Text." Occasional
        Papers in Translation and Textlinguistics
        1:147–72.

Harrington, D. J.
1973    "The 'Early Catholic' Writings of the
        New Testament: The Church Adjusting to
        World-History." Pp. 97–113 in The Word
        and the World. Edited by R. J. Clifford and
        G. W. MacRae. Cambridge, MA: Weston
        College.

Harrington, H. K.
1993    The Impurity Systems of Qumran and
        the Rabbis: Biblical Foundations. Society
        of Biblical Literature Dissertation Series.
        Atlanta: Scholars.

Harris, H.
1975    The Tübingen School. Oxford: Claren-
        don.

Hartman, L.
1966    Prophecy Interpreted. Coniectanea biblica:
        New Testament Series. Lund: Gleerup.
1967    "Antikrists mirakler." Religion och Bibel
        26:37–63.

Harvey, A. E.
1990    "The Testament of Simeon Peter." Pp.
        339–54 in A Tribute to Geza Vermès: Es-
        says on Jewish and Christian Literature
        and History. Edited by P. R. Davies and

R. T. White. Journal for the Study of the
        Old Testament: Supplement Series 100.
        Sheffield: JSOT Press.

Hassold, W. J.
1952    "'Keep Yourselves in the Love of God': An
        Interpretation of Jude 20, 21." Concordia
        Theological Monthly 23:884–94.

Hastings, J. (ed.)
1898–1904 A Dictionary of the Bible. Edinburgh:
        T&T Clark.
1915    Dictionary of the Apostolic Church. Ed-
        inburgh: T&T Clark.

Hauck, F.
1957    Die Briefe des Jakobus, Petrus, Judas und
        Johannes. Das Neue Testament Deutsch.
        Göttingen: Vandenhoeck & Ruprecht.

Hays, C. M.
2004    "A Fresh Look at Βοσόρ: Textual Criticism
        in 2 Peter 2:15." Filología neotestmentaria
        17:105–09.

Heide, G. Z.
1997    "What Is New about the New Heaven and
        the New Earth? A Theology of Creation
        from Revelation 21 and 2 Peter 3." Journal
        of the Evangelical Theological Society
        40:37–56.

Heiligenthal, R.
1986    "Der Judasbrief: Aspekte der Forschung
        in den letzten Jahrzehnten." Theologische
        Rundschau 51:117–29.
1992a   "Die Weisheitsschrift aus der Kairoer
        Geniza und der Judasbrief: Ein Vergleich
        zwischen einer umstrittenen jüdischen
        und einer judenchristlichen Schrift."
        Zeitschrift für Religions- und Geistesge-
        schichte 44:356–61.
1992b   Zwischen Henoch und Paulus: Studien
        zum theologiegeschichtlichen Ort des
        Judasbriefes. Texte und Arbeiten zum
        neutestamentlichen Zeitalter. Tübingen:
        Francke.

Heitmann, M.
1986    "Jonas Cohn: Philosoph, Pädagoge und
        Jude; Gedanken zum Werdegang und
        Schicksal des Freiburger Neukantianers
        und seiner Philosophie." Pp. 179–99 in
        Juden in der Weimarer Republik. Stutt-
        gart: Burg.

Hengel, M.
1987    "Petrus und die Heidenmission." Pp.
        163–70 in Petrusbild in der neueren For-
        schung. Edited by C. P. Thiede. Wuppertal:
        Brockhaus.
2006    Der unterschätzte Petrus: Zwei Studien.
        Tübingen: Mohr Siebeck.

Henkel, K.
1904     *Der zweite Brief des Apostelfürsten Petrus*. Biblische Studien. Freiburg i.B.: Herder.

Hennecke, E., and W. Schneemelcher
1963     *New Testament Apocrypha*. 2 vols. London: Lutterworth.

Henten, J. W. van, and H. J. De Jonge (eds.)
1986     *Tradition and Re-interpretation in Jewish and Early Christian Literature: Essays in Honour of Jürgen C. H. Lebram*. Leiden: Brill.

Herzer, J.
1998     *Petrus oder Paulus? Studien über das Verhältnis des ersten Petrusbriefes zur paulinischen Tradition*. Tübingen: Mohr Siebeck.

Hiebert, D. E.
1984a     "Selected Studies from 2 Peter, Pt. 1: The Necessary Growth in the Christian Life: An Exposition of 2 Peter 1:5–11." *Bibliotheca sacra* 141:43–54.

1984b     "Selected Studies from 2 Peter, Pt. 2: The Prophetic Foundation for the Christian Life: An Exposition of 2 Peter 1:19–21." *Bibliotheca sacra* 141:158–68.

1984c     "Selected Studies from 2 Peter, Pt. 3: A Portrayal of False Teachers: An Exposition of 2 Peter 2:1–3." *Bibliotheca sacra* 141:255–65.

1984d     "Selected Studies from 2 Peter, Pt. 4: Directives for Living in Dangerous Days: An Exposition of 2 Peter 3:14–18a." *Bibliotheca sacra* 141:330–40.

1985a     "Selected Studies from Jude, Pt. 1: An Exposition of Jude 3–4." *Bibliotheca sacra* 142:142–51.

1985b     "Selected Studies from Jude, Pt. 2: An Exposition of Jude 12–16." *Bibliotheca sacra* 142:238–49.

1985c     "Selected Studies from Jude, Pt. 3: An Exposition of Jude 17–23." *Bibliotheca sacra* 142:355–66.

1989     *Second Peter and Jude: An Expositional Commentary*. Greenville, SC: Unusual Publications.

Hill, C.
2004     *The Johannine Corpus in the Early Church*. Oxford: Oxford University Press.

Hillyer, N.
1992     *1 and 2 Peter, Jude*. New International Biblical Commentary. Peabody, MA: Hendrickson.

Hoerni-Jung, H.
1997     *Unbekannter Petrus: Schlüssel zum Menschsein*. Munich: Kösel.

Hofmann, N. J.
2000     *Die Assumptio Mosis: Studien zur Rezeption massgültiger Überlieferung*. Supplements to the Journal for the Study of Judaism. Leiden: Brill.

Holladay, C. H.
1977     *Theios Anēr in Hellenistic Judaism: A Critique of the Use of This Category in New Testament Christology*. Society of Biblical Literature Dissertation Series. Missoula, MT: Scholars Press.

Holmer, U., and W. de Boor
1979     *Die Briefe des Petrus und der Brief des Judas*. Wuppertaler Studienbibel: Reihe, Neues Testament. Wuppertal: Brockhaus.

Holzmeister, U.
1949     "Vocabularium secundae epistolae S. Petri erroresque quidam de eo divulg ati." *Biblica* 30:339–55.

Horrell, D.
1998     *The Epistles of Peter and Jude*. Epworth Commentaries. London: Epworth.

Horsley, R. A.
1995     *Galilee: History, Politics, People*. Valley Forge, PA: Trinity.

1996     *Archaeology, History, and Society in Galilee: The Social Context of Jesus and the Rabbis*. Valley Forge, PA: Trinity.

Hort, F. J. A.
1898     *The First Epistle of St. Peter I.1–II.17*. London: Macmillan.

Houghton, J. C.
1953     *Kept by the Power of God: An Introduction to the Epistles of James, Peter and Jude*. London: Lutterworth.

Howe, F. R.
2000a     "Christ, the Building Stone, in Peter's Theology." *Bibliotheca sacra* 157:35–43.

2000b     "The Christian Life in Peter's Theology." *Bibliotheca sacra* 157:304–14.

2000c     "The Cross of Christ in Peter's Theology." *Bibliotheca sacra* 157:190–99.

2000d     "God's Grace in Peter's Theology." *Bibliotheca sacra* 157:432–38.

Hunt, A. S., and C. C. Edgar (trans. and eds.)
1959     *Select Paypri*, vol. 1. London: Heinemann/Cambridge, MA: Harvard University Press.

Hupper, W. G.
1980     "Additions to 'A 2 Peter Bibliography.'" *Journal of the Evangelical Theological Society* 23:65–66.

Hurst, D. (trans.)
1985    The Commentary on the Seven Catholic Epistles of Bede the Venerable. Kalamazoo, MI: Cistercian Publications.

Hutchison, H.
1986    "Some Things to Guard Against." Expository Times 97:115–16.

Huther, J. E.
1887    Critical and Exegetical Handbook to the General Epistles of James, Peter, John, and Jude. New York: Funk & Wagnalls.

Hutton, R. R.
1994    "Moses on the Mount of Transfiguration." Hebrew Annual Review 14:99–120.

IDBSup    Interpreter's Dictionary of the Bible. Edited by K. Crim. Nashville: Abingdon, 1976.

Ilan, T.
1996    Jewish Women in Greco-Roman Palestine. Peabody, MA: Hendrickson.

2002    Lexicon of Jewish Names in Late Antiquity, part 1: Palestine 330 BCE–200 CE. Texts and Studies in Ancient Judaism. Tübingen: Mohr Siebeck.

IT    Inscriptiones graecae Epiri, Macedoniae, Thraciae, Scythiae, part 2: Inscriptiones Macedoniae, fascicle 1: Inscriptiones Thessalonicae et viciniae. Edited by C. F. Edson. Berlin: de Gruyter, 1972.

Jacobs, P. E.
1964    "Exegetical-Devotional Study of 2 Peter 1:16–21." Springfielder 28:18–30.

James, M. R.
1912    The Second Epistle General of Peter and the General Epistle of Jude. Cambridge Greek Testament. Cambridge: Cambridge University Press.

1920    The Lost Apocrypha of the Old Testament. London: SPCK/New York: Macmillan.

1971    The Biblical Antiquities of Philo: Now First Translated from the Old Latin Version. Library of Biblical Studies. New York: Ktav.

Jeremias, J.
1966    The Eucharistic Words of Jesus. Translated by Norman Perrin. New York: Scribner.

Johnson, E.
1988    A Semantic and Structural Analysis of 2 Peter. Dallas: Summer Institute of Linguistics.

Johnson, L. T.
1987    "Conflict and Christian Self-Definition." Bible Translator 25:215–19.

1989    "The New Testament's Anti-Jewish Slander and the Conventions of Ancient Polemic." Journal of Biblical Literature 108:419–41.

2001    The First and Second Letters to Timothy. Anchor Bible. New York: Doubleday.

Joubert, S. J.
1988    "Die Judasbrief: 'N simboliese universum in die gedrang." Harvard Theological Studies 44:613–35.

1995    "Persuasion in the Letter of Jude." Journal for the Study of the New Testament 58:75–87.

1997    "'Die einde is hier!' Tekstuele strategie en historiese verstaan in die Judasbrief." Harvard Theological Studies 53:543–56.

1998    "Facing the Past: Transtextual Relationships and Historical Understanding in the Letter of Jude." Biblische Zeitschrift 42:56–70.

Judge, E. A.
1971    "The Decrees of Caesar at Thessalonica." Reformed Theological Review 30:1–7.

Kahmann, J.
1989    "The Second Letter of Peter and the Letter of Jude: Their Mutual Relationship." Pp. 105–21 in The New Testament in Early Christianity: La réception des écrits néotestamentaires dans le christianisme primitif. Edited by J.-M. Sevrin. Louvain: Leuven University Press.

Kaiser, W. C.
1978    "The Single Intent of Scripture." Pp. 123–41 in Evangelical Roots: A Tribute to Wilbur Smith. Edited by K. S. Kantzer. Nashville: Nelson.

Kamlah, E.
1964    Die Form der katalogischen Paränese im Neuen Testament. Tübingen: Mohr Siebeck.

Karrer, M.
1989    "Petrus im paulinischen Gemeindekreis." Zeitschrift für die neutestamentliche Wissenschaft 80:210–31.

Käsemann, E.
1952    "Eine Apologie der urchristlichen Eschatologie." Zeitschrift für Theologie und Kirche 49:272–96.

1969    New Testament Questions of Today. London: SCM.

1982    "An Apologia for Primitive Christian Eschatology." Pp. 169–95 in Essays on New Testament Themes. Philadelphia: Fortress.

**Kee, H. C.**
1968    "The Terminology of Mark's Exorcism Stories." *New Testament Studies* 14:232–46.

**Kelly, J. N. D.**
1969    *A Commentary on the Epistles of Peter and Jude.* Black's New Testament Commentaries. London: Black.

**Kennard, D. W.**
1987    "Petrine Redemption: Its Meaning and Extent." *Journal of the Evangelical Theological Society* 30:399–405.

**Kennedy, G. A.**
1984    *New Testament Interpretation through Rhetorical Criticism.* Chapel Hill: University of North Carolina.

1997    "Historical Survey of Rhetoric." Pp. 3–41 in *Handbook of Classical Rhetoric in the Hellenistic Period, 330 B.C.–A.D. 400.* Edited by S. E. Porter. Leiden: Brill.

**Kern, P. H.**
1998    *Rhetoric and Galatians: Assessing an Approach to Paul's Epistle.* Society for New Testament Studies Monograph Series. Cambridge: Cambridge University Press.

**Kilpatrick, G. D.**
1966    "Land of Egypt in the New Testament." *Journal of Theological Studies* 17:70.

1982    "Agape as Love-Feast in the New Testament." Vol. 1 / pp. 157–62 in *Parola e spirito: Studi in onore di Settimio Cipriani.* Edited by C. C. Marcheselli. Brescia, Italy: Paideia.

**King, M. A.**
1964    "Jude and 1 and 2 Peter: Notes on the Bodmer Manuscript." *Bibliotheca sacra* 121:54–57.

**Kinman, B.**
1995    *Jesus' Entry into Jerusalem in the Context of Lukan Theology and the Politics of His Day.* Arbeiten zur Geschichte des antiken Judentums und des Urchristentums. Leiden: Brill.

**Kirschbaum, E.**
1974    *Die Gräber der Apostelfürsten: St. Peter und St. Paul in Rom.* Frankfurt: Societäts-Verlag.

**Kistemaker, S. J.**
1987    *Exposition of the Epistles of Peter and of the Epistle of Jude.* Grand Rapids: Baker Academic.

**Klein, G.**
1961    *Die zwölf Apostel: Ursprung und Gehalt einer Idee.* Forschungen zur Religion und Literatur des Alten und Neuen Testaments. Göttingen: Vandenhoeck & Ruprecht.

1970    "Der zweite Petrusbrief und das neutestamentliche Kanon." Pp. 109–14 in *Ärgernisse: Konfrontationen mit dem Neuen Testament.* Munich: Kaiser.

**Klijn, A. F. J.**
1984    "Jude 5 to 7." Vol. 1 / pp. 237–44 in *The New Testament Age: Essays in Honor of Bo Reicke.* Edited by W. C. Weinrich. Macon, GA: Mercer University Press.

**Klinger, J.**
1973    "The Second Epistle of Peter: An Essay in Understanding." *St. Vladimir's Theological Quarterly* 17:152–69.

**Klotz, J. W.**
1983    "The Transfiguration of Our Lord, Last Sunday after the Epiphany: 2 Peter 1:16–21." *Concordia Journal* 9:25–26.

**Knight, J.**
1995    *2 Peter and Jude.* New Testament Guides. Sheffield: Sheffield Academic Press.

**Knoch, O.**
1973a    *Die "Testament" des Petrus und Paulus.* Stuttgarter Bibelstudien. Stuttgart: KBW.

1973b    "Das Vermächtnis des Petrus: Der zweite Petrusbrief." Pp. 149–65 in *Wort Gottes in der Zeit: Festschrift Karl Hermann Schelkle zum 65sten Geburtstag dargebracht von Kollegen, Freunden, Schülern.* Edited by H. Feld and J. Nolte. Düsseldorf: Patmos.

1990    *Der erste und zweite Petrusbrief; Der Judasbrief.* Regensburg: Pustet.

1991    "Petrus im Neuen Testament." Pp. 1–52 in *Il primato del vescovo di Roma nel primo millennio: Ricerche e testimonianze; Atti del symposium storico-teologico, Roma, 9–13 Ottobre 1989.* Edited by M. Maccarrone. Vatican City: Vaticana.

**Knopf, R.**
1912    *Die Briefe Petri und Juda.* Göttingen: Vandenhoeck & Ruprecht.

**Koester, C. R.**
2001    *Hebrews.* Anchor Bible. New York: Doubleday.

**Koester, H.**
1982    *Introduction to the New Testament,* vol. 1: *Culture and Religion of the Hellenistic Age*; vol. 2: *History and Literature of Early Christianity.* Philadelphia: Fortress/Berlin: de Gruyter.

**Kolenkow, A. B.**
1975    "The Genre Testament and Forecasts of the Future in the Hellenistic Jewish Milieu." *Journal for the Study of Judaism* 6:57–71.

**Kolp, A. L.**
1982    "Partakers of the Divine Nature: The Use of 2 Peter 1:4 by Athanasius." Vol. 3 / pp. 1018–23 in *Studia patristica* 17. Edited by E. A. Livingstone. Elmsford, NY: Pergamon.

**Kraftchick, S. J.**
2002    *Jude, 2 Peter*. Abingdon New Testament Commentaries. Nashville: Abingdon.

**Kraus, T. J.**
2000    "Παρὰ κυρίῳ, παρὰ κυρίου oder Omit in 2 Petr 2,11: Textkritik und Interpretation vor dem Hintergrund juristischer Diktion und der Verwendung von παρά." *Zeitschrift für die neutestamentliche Wissenschaft* 91:265–73.
2001    *Sprache, Stil und historischer Ort des zweiten Petrusbriefes*. Tübingen: Mohr Siebeck.

**Krodel, G. A.**
1977    "Letter of Jude." Pp. 92–98 in *Hebrews, James, 1 and 2 Peter, Jude, Revelation*. Edited by R. H. Fuller et al. Philadelphia: Fortress.
1995    *The General Letters: Hebrews; 1–2 Peter; Jude; 1, 2, 3 John*. Minneapolis: Augsburg Fortress.

**Kruger, M. A.**
1993    "Toutois in Jude 7." *Neotestamentica* 27:119–32.
1999    "The Authenticity of 2 Peter." *Journal of the Evangelical Theological Society* 42:645–71.

**Kubo, S.**
1965    𝔓⁷² *and Codex Vaticanus*. Salt Lake City: University of Utah.
1976    "Textual Relationships in Jude." Pp. 276–82 in *Studies in New Testament Language and Text: Essays in Honour of George D. Kilpatrick on the Occasion of His Sixty-fifth Birthday*. Edited by J. K. Elliott. Leiden: Brill.
1981    "Jude 22–23: Two-Division Form or Three?" Pp. 239–53 in *New Testament Textual Crticism: Its Significance for Exegesis*. Edited by E. J. Epp and G. D. Fee. Oxford: Clarendon.

**Kugelman, R.**
1980    *James and Jude: New Testament Message*. Wilmington, DE: Michael Glazier.

**Kuhl, E.**
1987    *Die Briefe Petri und Judae*. Göttingen: Vandenhoeck & Ruprecht.

**Kümmel, W. G.**
1975    *Introduction to the New Testament*. Translated by H. C. Kee. 2nd edition. Nashville: Abingdon.

**Kuss, O., and J. Michl**
1977    *Carta a los Hebreos; Cartas católicas*. Barcelona: Herder.

**Ladd, G. E.**
1993    *New Testament Theology*. Edited by D. Hagner. Grand Rapids: Eerdmans.

**Landon, C. H.**
1993    "The Text Jude 4." *Harvard Theological Studies* 49:823–43.
1996    *A Text-Critical Study of the Epistle of Jude*. Journal for the Study of the New Testament: Supplement Series. Sheffield: Sheffield Academic Press.

**Lapham, F.**
2003    *Peter: The Myth, the Man and the Writing*. Journal for the Study of the New Testament: Supplement Series. Sheffield: Sheffield Academic Press.

**Lattimore, R.**
1942    *Themes in Greek and Latin Epitaphs*. Urbana: University of Illinois Press.

**Lea, T. D.**
1988    *1, 2 Peter, Jude*. Grand Rapids: Zondervan.

**Leahy, T. W.**
1972    "Segunda epístola de San Pedro." Vol. 4 / pp. 593–603 in *Comentario Bíblico "San Jerónimo."* Edited by J. A. Fitzmyer, R. E. Brown, and R. E. Murphy. Madrid: Ediciones Cristiandad.

**Leaney, A. R. C.**
1967    *The Letters of Peter and Jude: A Commentary on the First Letter of Peter, a Letter of Jude and the Second Letter of Peter*. Cambridge: Cambridge University Press.

**Lee, E. K.**
1961–62    "Words Denoting 'Pattern' in the New Testament." *New Testament Studies* 8:166–73.

**Lee, M.**
2002    "Greco-Roman Philosophy of Mind and Paul: Passion, Power, and Progress according to the Platonists, the Stoics, and the Epicureans of the Early Imperial Period (1st Century B.C.E.–2nd Century C.E.) and the Ideology of the Epicurean Wise

in Paul's Corinthian Correspondence."
PhD diss., Fuller Seminary.

**Lenhard, H.**
1961    "Ein Beitrag zur Übersetzung von 2 Ptr.
3:10d." *Zeitschrift für die neutestamentliche Wissenschaft* 52:128–29.
1978    "Noch Einmal zu 2 Petr 3.10d." *Zeitschrift
für die neutestamentliche Wissenschaft*
69:136.

**Lenski, R. C. H.**
1945    *The Interpretation of the Epistles of St.
Peter, St. John and St. Jude.* Columbus,
OH: Wartburg.

**Letellier, R. I.**
1995    *Day in Mamre, Night in Sodom: Abraham
and Lot in Genesis 18 and 19.* Biblical
Interpretation Series. Leiden: Brill.

**Levinskaya, I.**
1996    *The Book of Acts in Its Diaspora Setting.*
The Book of Acts in Its First Century Setting 5. Grand Rapids: Eerdmans.

**Lewis, J. P.**
1978    *A Study of the Interpretation of Noah
and the Flood in Jewish and Christian
Literature.* Leiden: Brill.

**Lias, J. J.**
1913    "The Genuineness of the Second Epistle of
St. Peter." *Bibliotheca sacra* 70:599–606.

**Lightfoot, J. B.**
1891    *The Apostolic Fathers.* Edited by J. R.
Harmer. London: Macmillan.

**Lindars, B., and S. S. Smalley**
1973    *Christ and Spirit in the New Testament:
In Honour of Charles Francis Digby
Moule.* Cambridge: Cambridge University Press.

**Lindemann, A.**
1979    *Paulus im ältesten Christentum: Das
Bild des Apostels und die Rezeption der
paulinischen Theologie in der frühchristlichen Literatur bis Marcion.* Beiträge
zur historischen Theologie. Tübingen:
Mohr.

**Livingstone, E. A. (ed.)**
1982    *Studia Patristica 17.* 3 vols. Elmsford, NY:
Pergamon.

**Ljungman, H.**
1964    *Pistis: A Study of Its Presuppositions
and Its Meaning in Pauline Use.* Lund:
Gleerup.

**Lloyd-Jones, D. M.**
1983    *Expository Sermons on 2 Peter.* London:
Banner of Truth.

**Loader, J. A.**
1990    *A Tale of Two Cities: Sodom and Gomorrah in the Old Testament, Early Jewish
and Early Christian Traditions.* Contributions to Biblical Exegesis and Theology.
Kampen: Kok.

**Lombard, H. A.**
1983    "Tendense en aksente in die geskiedenis
van navorsing oor 2 Petrus en Judas."
*Theologia evangelica* 16:74–82.

**Long, A. A., and D. N. Sedley (eds.)**
1987    *The Hellenistic Philosophers.* 2 vols. Cambridge: Cambridge University Press.

**Lønning, I.**
1971    "Tradisjon og skrift: Eksegese av 2. Petr
1,19–21." *Norsk teologisk Tidsskrift*
72:129–54.

**Louw, J.**
1965    "Wat Wordt in 2 Petrus 1:20 Gesteldt?"
*Nederlands theologische tijdschrift*
19:202–12.

**Love, J. P.**
1960    *The First, Second and Third Letters of
John; The Letter of Jude; The Revelation
to John.* Richmond: John Knox.

**Lövestam, E.**
1984    "Eschatologie und Tradition im 2 Petrus-
brief." Vol. 1 / pp. 287–300 in *The New
Testament Age: Essays in Honor of Bo
Reicke.* Edited by W. C. Weinrich. Macon,
GA: Mercer University Press.

**LSJ**    *A Greek-English Lexicon.* By H. G. Liddell,
R. Scott, and H. S. Jones. 9th ed. Oxford:
Clarendon, 1968.

**Lucas, R. C., and C. Green.**
1995    *The Message of 2 Peter and Jude: The
Promise of His Coming.* The Bible Speaks
Today. Leicester, UK: Inter-Varsity.

**Lugo Rodríguez, R. H., and L. E. Vaage**
1997    "'Wait for the Day of God's Coming and
Do What You Can to Hasten It . . .' (2 Pet
3:12): The Non-Pauline Letters as Resis-
tance Literature." Pp. 193–206 in *Sub-
versive Scriptures.* Edited by L. E. Vaage.
Valley Forge, PA: Trinity.

**Lunn, N.**
1998    "Punishment in 2 Peter 2:9." *Notes on
Translation* 12:15–18.

**Luther, M.**
1967    "Sermons on the Second Epistle of St.
Peter." In *Luther's Works,* vol. 30: *The
Catholic Epistles.* Translated by M. H.
Bertram. Edited by J. Pelikan and W. A.
Hansen. St. Louis, MO: Concordia.

1990    *Commentary on Peter and Jude*. Grand Rapids: Kregel.

Lyle, K. R.
1998    *Ethical Admonition in the Epistle of Jude*. New York: Lang.

Lyons, W. J.
2002    *Canon and Exegesis: Canonical Praxis and the Sodom Narrative*. Journal for the Study of the Old Testament: Supplement Series. Sheffield: Sheffield Academic Press.

MacDonald, D. R.
1987    "Aretē." *Iliff Review* 44:39–43.

Magass, W.
1972    "Semiotik einer Ketzerpolemik am Beispiel von Judas 12 F." *Linguística Bíblica* 19:36–47.

Maier, F.
1905    "Ein Beitrag zur Priorität des Judasbriefs." *Theologische Quartalschrift* 87:547–80.
1906    "Die Echtheit des Judas und 2. Petrusbriefs: Eine Antikritik, vornehmlich gegen H. I. Holtzmann." *Zeitschrift für katholische Theologie* 30:693–729.

Makujina, J.
1998    "The 'Trouble' with Lot in 2 Peter: Locating Peter's Source for Lot's Torment." *Westminster Theological Journal* 60:255–69.

Malan, G.
1999    "Die metafoor: 'Dag van die Here' in 2 Petrus en die dood as marginale ervaring." *Harvard Theological Studies* 55:656–70.
2000    "Die unieke nuansering van die dag van die Here in 2 Petrus en die eskatologiese gerigtheid van die dokument." *Harvard Theological Studies* 56:259–72.

Malan, G., and A. G. Van Aarde
1998a   "'N Kennissosiologiese benadering tot die dag van die Here in 2 Petrus." *Harvard Theological Studies* 54:529–43.
1998b   "Rudolf Bultmann se benadering tot die dag van Here in 2 Petrus." *Harvard Theological Studies* 54:652–71.
1999    "Die invloed van die Mediterreense tydsbegrip op die betekenis van die dag van die Here in 2 Petrus." *Harvard Theological Studies* 55:209–20.

Malan, S. C.
1882    *The Book of Adam and Eve, Also Called The Conflict of Adam and Eve*. London: Williams & Norgate.

Malherbe, A. J.
1970    "'Gentle as a Nurse': The Cynic Background to 1 Thess ii." *Novum Testamentum* 12:203–17.
1986    *Moral Exhortation: A Greco-Roman Sourcebook*. Library of Early Christianity. Philadelphia: Westminster.
1988    *Ancient Epistolary Theorists*. Society of Biblical Literature Sources for Biblical Study. Atlanta: Scholars Press.

Malina, B. J.
2001    *The New Testament World: Insights from Cultural Anthropology*. 3rd ed. Louisville: Westminster John Knox.

Malina, B. J., and J. H. Neyrey
1996    *Portraits of Paul: An Archaeology of Ancient Personality*. Louisville: Westminster John Knox.

Mantey, J. R.
1978    "New Testament Facts about the Apostle Peter." *Journal of the Evangelical Theological Society* 21:211–12.

Manton, T.
1984    *The Epistle of Jude: A Practical Commentary; or an Exposition, with Notes, on the Epistle of Jude*. Reprinted, Mobile, AL: R. E. Publications.

Marín, F.
1975    "Apostolicidad de los escritos neotestamentarios." *Estudios eclesiásticos* 50:211–39.

Marshall, I. H.
1969    *Kept by the Power of God*. Minneapolis: Bethany Fellowship.
1974    "'Early Catholicism' in the New Testament." Pp. 217–31 in *New Dimensions in New Testament Study*. Edited by R. M. Longenecker and M. C. Tenney. Grand Rapids: Zondervan.
1991    *1 Peter*. Downers Grove, IL: InterVarsity/Leicester, UK: Inter-Varsity.

Martin, D. B.
1990    *Slavery as Salvation: The Metaphor of Slavery in Pauline Christianity*. New Haven: Yale University Press.

Massaux, E.
1961    "Le texte de l'épitre de Jude du Papyrus Bodmer VII ($\mathfrak{P}^{72}$)." Pp. 108–25 in *Scrinium Lovaniense: Mélanges historiques historische opstellen Étienne van Cauwenbergh*. Edited by J. Vergote. Gembloux: Duculot.

Matera, F. J.
1989    "2 Peter, Jude." Pp. 353–57 in *The Apoc-rypha and the New Testament*. Edited by B. W. Anderson. New York: Scribner's.

Mayhue, R. L.
1991    "The Apostle's Watchword: Day of the Lord." Pp. 239–63 in *New Testament Essays in Honor of Homer A. Kent Jr.* Edited by G. T. Meadors. Winona Lake, IN: BMH Books.

Maynard, A. H.
1984    "The Role of Peter in the Fourth Gospel." *New Testament Studies* 30:531–48.

Mayor, J. B.
1904    "Notes on the Text of the Second Epistle of Peter." *Expositor* 6/10:284–93.
1907    *The Epistle of St. Jude and the Second Epistle of St. Peter: Greek Text with Introduction, Notes and Comments.* New York: Macmillan.

McDonald, L. M.
1995    *The Formation of the Christian Biblical Canon.* Peabody, MA: Hendrickson.

McDonald, L. M., and J. A. Sanders
2002    *The Canon Debate.* Peabody, MA: Hendrickson.

McEleney, N. J.
1974    "The Vice Lists of the Pastoral Epistles." *Catholic Biblical Quarterly* 36:203–19.

McNamara, M.
1960    "The Unity of Second Peter: A Reconsideration." *Scripture* 12:13–19.

McNamara, M., and E. G. Clarke
1995    *Targum Neofiti 1: Numbers; Targum Pseudo-Jonathan: Numbers.* The Aramaic Bible. Edinburgh: T&T Clark.

Meade, D. G.
1987    *Pseudonymity and Canon: An Investigation into the Relationship between Authorship and Authority in Jewish and Earliest Christian Tradition.* Grand Rapids: Eerdmans.

Mees, M.
1968    "Papyrus Bodmer VII ($\mathfrak{P}^{72}$) und die Zitate aus dem Judasbrief bei Clemens von Alexandrian." Pp. 133–41 in *Miscelánea patristica: Homenaje al Ángel C. Vega.* Edited by T. Alonso et al. Madrid: Real Monasterio de El Escorial.

Méhat, A.
1989    *Simon, dit Kèphas: La vie clandestine de l'apôtre Pierre, essai historique.* Paris: Lethielleux.

Meier, J. P.
1999    "Forming the Canon on the Edge of the Canon: 2 Peter 3:8–18." *Mid-Stream* 38:65–70.

Meier, S.
1988    "2 Peter 3:3–7—An Early Jewish and Christian Response to Eschatological Skepticism." *Biblische Zeitschrift* 32:255–57.

Metzger, B. M.
1987    *The Canon of the New Testament: Its Origin, Development, and Significance.* Oxford: Clarendon.
1994    *A Textual Commentary on the Greek New Testament.* 2nd edition. Stuttgart: German Bible Society/New York: United Bible Societies.

Michaels, J. R.
1969    "Second Peter and Jude—Royal Promises." Pp. 346–61 in *The New Testament Speaks.* Edited by W. L. Lane, G. W. Barker, and J. R. Michaels. New York: Harper & Row.
1988    *1 Peter.* Waco: Word.

Michl, J.
1968    *Die katholischen Briefe.* Regensburger Neues Testament. Regensburg: Pustet.

Migne, J.-P. (ed.)
1844–65   Patrologiae cursus completus: Series latina. 221 vols. Paris: Migne.

Miller, R. J.
1996    "Is There Independent Attestation for the Transfiguration in 2 Peter?" *New Testament Studies* 42:620–25.

Milligan, G.
1920–21   "2 Peter III.10." *Expository Times* 32:331.

Mitchell, M. M.
1991    *Paul and the Rhetoric of Reconciliation: An Exegetical Investigation of the Language and Composition of 1 Corinthians.* Hermeneutische Untersuchungen zur Theologie. Tübingen: Mohr.

MM    *The Vocabulary of the Greek Testament.* By J. H. Moulton and G. Milligan. London: Hodder & Stoughton, 1930. Reprinted, Peabody, MA: Hendrickson, 1997.

Moffatt, J.
1928    *The General Epistles: James, Peter and Judas.* Moffat New Testament Commentary. London: Hodder & Stoughton.

Molina Palma, M. A.
1987    "La provisionalidad responsable: El tiempo cristiano en perspectiva escatológica." *Estudios bíblicos* 45:337–46.

**Molland, E.**
1955     "La thèse 'La prophétie n'est jamais venue de la volonté de l'homme' (2 Pierre 1:21) et les Pseudo-Clémentines." *Studia theologica* 9:67–85.

**Moo, D. J.**
1996     *2 Peter and Jude*. NIV Application Commentary. Grand Rapids: Zondervan.

**Morgan, C. W., and R. A. Peterson (eds.)**
2004     *Hell under Fire*. Grand Rapids: Zondervan.

**Morris, L.**
1965     *The Apostolic Preaching of the Cross*. London: Tyndale.

**Moule, C. F. D.**
1959     "Once More, Who Were the Hellenists?" *Expository Times* 70:100–102.

**Moulton, J. H., and W. F. Howard**
1929     *A Grammar of New Testament Greek*, vol. 2: *Accidence and Word Formation*. Edinburgh: T&T Clark.

**Moulton, J. H., and N. Turner**
1963     *A Grammar of New Testament Greek*, vol. 3: *Syntax*. Edinburgh: T&T Clark.
1976     *A Grammar of New Testament Greek*, vol. 4: *Style*. Edinburgh: T&T Clark.

**Mounce, R. H.**
1982     *A Living Hope: A Commentary on 1 and 2 Peter*. Grand Rapids: Eerdmans.

**Mueller, Ê. R.**
1988     *1 Pedro: Introdução e comentário*. São Paulo: Sociedade Religiosa Edições Vida Nova and Associação Religiosa Editora Mundo Cristão.

**Müller, P.**
1998     "Der Judasbrief." *Theologische Rundschau* 63:267–89.

**Munck, J.**
1950     "Discours d'adieu dans le Nouveau Testament et dans la littérature biblique." Pp. 155–70 in *Aux Sources de la Tradition Chrétienne: Mélanges offerts à M. Maurice Goguel, à l'occasion de son soixante-dixième anniversaire*. Edited by O. Cullmann and P. H. Menoud. Neuchatel: Delachaux & Niestlé.

**Muraoka, T.**
2002     *A Greek-English Lexicon of the Septuagint: Chiefly of the Pentateuch and the Twelve Prophets*. Louvain: Peeters.

**Murdock, J.**
1851     *The New Testament: A Literal Translation from the Syriac Peshitta Version*. New York: Carter & Brothers.

**NA²⁷**     *Novum Testamentum Graece*. Edited by [E. and E. Nestle,] B. Aland, et al. 27th revised edition. Stuttgart: Bibelgesellschaft, 1993.

**Neusner, J.**
1962     *A Life of Rabban Yohanan ben Zakkai, ca. 1–80 C.E.* Studia Post-biblica. Leiden: Brill.
1970     *Development of a Legend: Studies on the Traditions concerning Yohanan ben Zakkai*. Studia Post-biblica. Leiden: Brill.
1973     *The Idea of Purity in Ancient Judaism: The Haskell Lectures, 1972–1973*. Studies in Judaism in Late Antiquity. Leiden: Brill.
1985     *Genesis Rabbah*, vol. 1. Atlanta: Scholars Press.
1994     *Introduction to Rabbinic Literature*. New York: Doubleday.

**NewDocs**     *New Documents Illustrating Early Christianity*. Edited by G. H. R. Horsley and S. R. Llewelyn. North Ryde, NSW: Ancient History Documentary Research Centre, Macquarie University, 1981–.

**Newman, B. M., Jr.**
1974     "Some Suggested Restructurings for the New Testament Letter Openings and Closings." *Bible Translator* 25:240–45.

**Newman, R. C.**
1984     "The Ancient Exegesis of Genesis 6:2, 4." *Grace Theological Journal* 5:13–36.

**Neyrey, J. H.**
1977     "The Form and Background of the Polemic in 2 Peter." PhD diss., Yale University.
1980a     "The Apologetic Use of the Transfiguration in 2 Peter 1:16–21." *Catholic Biblical Quarterly* 42:504–19.
1980b     "The Form and Background of the Polemic in 2 Peter." *Journal of Biblical Literature* 99:407–31.
1990     "The Second Epistle of Peter." Pp. 1017–22 in *The New Jerome Biblical Commentary*. Edited by R. E. Brown, J. A. Fitzmyer, and R. E. Murphy. Englewood Cliffs, NJ: Prentice-Hall.
1993     *2 Peter, Jude: A New Translation with Introduction and Commentary*. Anchor Bible. New York: Doubleday.
1996     "Clean/Unclean, Pure/Polluted, and Holy/Profane: The Idea and the System of Purity." Pp. 80–104 in *The Social Sciences and New Testament Interpretation*. Edited by R. Rohrbaugh. Peabody, MA: Hendrickson.
1998     *Honor and Shame in the Gospel of Matthew*. Louisville: Westminster John Knox.

**Nickelsburg, G. W. E.**
1973    *Studies on the Testament of Moses.* Seminar Papers: Septuagint and Cognate Studies. Missoula, MT: Society of Biblical Literature.
1977    "The Apocalyptic Message of 1 Enoch 92–105." *Catholic Biblical Quarterly* 39:309–28.
2001    *1 Enoch: A Commentary on the Book of 1 Enoch,* vol. 1: *Chapters 1–36; 81–108.* Hermeneia. Minneapolis: Fortress.

**Nicol, W.**
1975    *Essays in the General Epistles of the New Testament: 11th Meeting of die Nuwe-Testamentiese Werkgemeenskap van Suid-Afrika, 1975.* Pretoria: Nuwe-Testamentiese Werkgemeenskap van Suid-Afrik.

*NIDNTT*    *New International Dictionary of New Testament Theology.* Edited by C. Brown. 4 vols. Grand Rapids: Zondervan, 1975–85.

*NIDOTTE*    *New International Dictionary of Old Testament Theology and Exegesis.* Edited by W. A. VanGemeren. 5 vols. Grand Rapids: Zondervan, 1997.

**Niemann, R. (ed.)**
1994    *Petrus, der Fels des Anstosses.* Stuttgart: Kreuz.

**Nienhuis, D. R.**
2007    *Not by Paul Alone: The Formation of the Catholic Epistle Collection and the Christian Canon.* Waco: Baylor University Press.

**Noethlichs, K. L.**
2000    "Der Jude Paulus: Ein Tarser und Römer?" Pp. 53–84 in *Rom und das himmlische Jerusalem.* Edited by Raban von Haehling. Darmstadt: Wissenschaftliche Buchgesellschaft.

**Obbink, D. (ed.)**
1995    *Philodemus and Poetry.* New York and Oxford: Oxford University Press.

**O'Brien, P. T.**
1977    *Introductory Thanksgivings in the Letters of Paul.* Novum Testamentum Supplement 49. Leiden: Brill.

*OCD*    *The Oxford Classical Dictionary.* Edited by S. Hornblower and A. Spawforth. 3rd edition. Oxford: Oxford University Press, 1996.

**O'Connor, D. W.**
1969    *Peter in Rome: The Literary, Liturgical, and the Archeological Evidence.* New York: Columbia University Press.

*ODCC*    *The Oxford Dictionary of the Christian Church.* Edited by F. L. Cross and E. A. Livingstone. 3rd edition. Oxford: Oxford University Press, 1997.

**O'Donnell, M. B.**
1999    "The Use of Annotated Corpora for New Testament Discourse Analysis: A Survey of Current Practice and Future Prospects." Pp. 71–117 in *Discourse Analysis and the New Testament.* Edited by J. T. Reed and S. E. Porter. Sheffield: Sheffield Academic Press.

**Ogden, G. S.**
1977    "The 'Better'-Proverb (Tôb-Spruch), Rhetorical Criticism, and Qoheleth." *Journal of Biblical Literature* 96:489–509.

**Oleson, J. P.**
1979    "An Echo of Hesiod's *Theogony* vv. 190–2 in Jude 13." *New Testament Studies* 25:492–503.

**Osburn, C. D.**
1972    "Text of Jude 22–23." *Zeitschrift für die neutestamentliche Wissenschaft* 63:139–44.
1977    "Christological Use of I Enoch I.9 in Jude 14, 15." *New Testament Studies* 23:334–41.
1981    "The Text of Jude 5." *Biblica* 62:107–15.
1985    "1 Enoch 80:2–8 (67:5–7) and Jude 12–13." *Catholic Biblical Quarterly* 47:296–303.
1992    "Discourse Analysis and Jewish Apocalyptic in the Epistle of Jude." Pp. 287–319 in *Linguistics and New Testament Interpretation: Essays on Discourse Analysis.* Edited by D. A. Black and K. Barnwell. Nashville: Broadman.

**Osiek, C., and D. L. Balch**
1997    *Families in the New Testament World: Households and House Churches.* The Family, Religion, and Culture. Louisville: Westminster John Knox.

*OTP*    *The Old Testament Pseudepigrapha.* Edited by J. H. Charlesworth. 2 vols. Garden City, NY: Doubleday, 1983–85.

**Otto, J. K. T. von**
1877    "Haben Barnabas, Justinus und Irenäus den zweiten Petrusbrief (3,8) benützt?" *Zeitschrift für wissenschaftliche Theologie* 20:525–29.

**Overstreet, R. L.**
1980    "A Study of 2 Peter 3:10–13." *Bibliotheca sacra* 137:354–71.

**Owen, J. G.**
1985    *From Simon to Peter.* Welwyn, UK: Evangelical.

**P.Amh.** *The Amherst Papyri, Being an Account of the Greek Papyri in the Collection of the Right Hon. Lord Amherst of Hackney, F.S.A. at Didlington Hall, Norfolk.* Edited by B. P. Grenfell and A. S. Hunt. 2 vols. London, 1900–1901.

**P.Berlin** Berlin papyrus 7927. In Fritz Krebs, *Hermes* 30 (1895): 144–50. And in Herwig Maehler, *Zeitschrift für Papyrologie und Epigraphik* 23 (1976): 1–20.

**P.Cair.Zen.** *Zenon Papyri, Catalogue général des antiquités égyptiennes du Musée du Caire.* Edited by C. C. Edgar. 5 vols. Cairo, 1925–40.

**P.Dura** *The Excavations at Dura-Europos Conducted by Yale University and the French Academy of Inscriptions and Letters,* final report 5.1: *The Parchments and Papyri.* Edited by C. B. Welles, R. O. Fink, and J. F. Gilliam. New Haven: Yale University Press, 1959.

**P.Fay.** *Fayûm Towns and Their Papyri.* Edited by B. P. Grenfell, A. S. Hunt, D. G. Hogarth, and J. G. Milne. London: Egypt Exploration Fund, 1900.

**P.Oxy.** *The Oxyrhynchus Papyri.* Edited by B. P. Grenfell et al. 66 vols. London: Egypt Exploration Society, 1898–1999.

**P.Ryl.** *Catalogue of the Greek and Latin Papyri in the John Rylands Library, Manchester.* Edited by A. S. Hunt et al. 4 vols. Manchester, 1911–52.

**P.Stras.** *Griechische Papyrus der Kaiserlichen Universitäts- und Landesbibliothek zu Strassburg.* Edited by F. Preisigke. 9 vols. Leipzig, 1912–89.

**P.Tebt.** *The Tebtunis Papyri.* Edited by B. P. Grenfell et al. 4 vols. London: Egypt Exploration Society, 1902–76.

**Packer, J. I.**
1979 "A Lamp in a Dark Place: 2 Peter 1:19–21." Pp. 15–30 in *Can We Trust the Bible?* Edited by E. D. Radmacher. Wheaton: Tyndale House.

**Paulsen, H.**
1992 *Der zweite Petrusbrief und der Judasbrief.* Kritisch-exegetischer Kommentar über das Neue Testament. Göttingen: Vandenhoeck & Ruprecht.

**Pearson, B. A.**
1969 "A Reminiscence of Classical Myth at II Peter 2.4." *Greek, Roman, and Byzantine Studies* 10:71–80.
1989 "James, 1–2 Peter, Jude." Pp. 371–406 in *The New Testament and Its Modern Interpreters.* Edited by E. J. Epp and G. W. MacRae. Philadelphia: Fortress.
1990 "The Apocalypse of Peter and Canonical 2 Peter." Pp. 67–74 in *Gnosticism and the Early Christian World.* Edited by J. E. Goehring and C. W. Hedrick. Sonoma, CA: Polebridge.

**Perkins, P.**
1995 *First and Second Peter, James and Jude.* Interpretation. Louisville: John Knox.
1999 "Christ in Jude and 2 Peter." Pp. 155–65 in *Who Do You Say That I Am?* Edited by M. A. Powell and D. R. Bauer. Louisville: Westminster John Knox.
2000 *Peter: Apostle for the Whole Church.* Edinburgh: T&T Clark.

**Pesch, R.**
1980 *Simon-Petrus: Geschichte und geschichtliche Bedeutung des ersten Jüngers Jesu Christi.* Stuttgart: Hiersemann.

**Pfitzner, V. C.**
1967 *Paul and the Agōn Motif: Traditional Athletic Imagery in the Pauline Literature.* Novum Testamentum Supplement 16. Leiden: Brill.

**PGL** *Patristic Greek Lexicon.* Edited by G. W. H. Lampe. Oxford: Clarendon, 1968.

**Picirelli, R. E.**
1975 "The Meaning of 'Epignosis.'" *Evangelical Quarterly* 47:85–93.
1988 "Allusions to 2 Peter in the Apostolic Fathers." *Journal for the Study of the New Testament* 33:57–83.

**Plummer, A.**
1891 *The General Epistles of St. James and St. Jude.* Expositor's Bible. New York: Ketcham.

**Plumptre, E. H.**
1926 *The General Epistles of St. Peter and St. Jude.* Cambridge: Cambridge University Press.

**Porter, S. E.**
1989 *Verbal Aspect in the Greek of the New Testament, with Reference to Tense and Mood.* Studies in Biblical Greek. New York: Lang.
1993 "The Theoretical Justification for Application of Rhetorical Categories to Pauline Epistolary Literature." In *Rhetorica and the New Testament: Essays from the 1992 Heidelberg Conference.* Edited by S. E. Porter and T. H. Olbricht. Sheffield: JSOT Press.
1994 "Jesus and the Use of Greek in Galilee." Pp. 123–54 in *Studying the Historical Jesus.*

Edited by B. Chilton and C. A. Evans. Leiden: Brill.

**Porter, S. E. (ed.)**
1997 *Handbook of Classical Rhetoric in the Hellenistic Period 330 B.C.–A.D. 400.* Leiden: Brill.

**Porter, S. E., and T. H. Olbricht (eds.)**
1993 *Rhetoric and the New Testament.* Journal for the Study of the New Testament: Supplement Series. Sheffield: JSOT Press.
1996 *Rhetoric, Scripture and Theology: Essays from the 1994 Pretoria Conference.* Sheffield: Sheffield Academic Press.

**Powell, M. A., and D. R. Bauer**
1999 *Who Do You Say That I Am? Essays on Christology.* Louisville: Westminster John Knox.

**Pröhle, K.**
1970 "Die Verheissung seines Kommens—2 Petrus 3,1–13." Pp. 40–50 in *Hoffnung ohne Illusion: Referate und Bibelarbeiten.* Edited by H. Zeddies. Berlin: Evangelische Verlagsanstalt.

**Quast, K.**
1989 *Peter and the Beloved Disciple: Figures for a Community in Crisis.* Sheffield: JSOT Press.

**Quinn, J. D.**
1965 "Notes on the Text of the 𝔓⁷² 1 Pt 2:3, 5:14, and 5:9." *Catholic Biblical Quarterly* 27:241–49.

**Radmacher, E. D. (ed.)**
1979 *Can We Trust the Bible?* Wheaton: Tyndale House.

**Rappaport, S.**
1930 "Der gerechte Lot: Bemerkung zu II Ptr. 2,7.8." *Zeitschrift für die neutestamentliche Wissenschaft* 29:299–304.

**Reed, J. T., and R. A. Reese**
1996 "Verbal Aspect, Discourse Prominence, and the Letter of Jude." *Filología neotestamentaria* 9:180–99.

**Reese, R. A.**
2000 *Writing Jude: The Reader, the Text, and the Author.* Biblical Interpretation Series. Leiden: Brill.
2007 *2 Peter and Jude.* Two Horizons New Testament Commentary. Grand Rapids: Eerdmans.

**Reicke, B.**
1964 *The Epistles of James, Peter and Jude.* Anchor Bible. Garden City, NY: Doubleday.

**Reiling, J.**
1971 "The Use of ΨΕΥΔΟΠΡΟΦΗΤΗΣ in the Septuagint, Philo and Josephus." *Novum Testamentum* 13:147–56.

**Renoux, C.**
1992 "L'Assomption de Moïse: D'Origène à la chaîne arménienne sur les Épîtres catholiques." Pp. 239–49 in *Recherches et tradition: Mélanges patristiques offerts à Henri Crouzel.* Edited by André Dupleix. Théologie historique 88. Paris: Beauchesne.
1994 *La chaîne Arménienne sur les Épîtres catholiques,* vol. 4: *La chaîne sur 2–3 Jean et Jude.* Turnhout, Belgium: Brepols.

**Reymond, E. D.**
2001 "Sirach 40,18–27 as 'Tôb-Spruch.'" *Biblica* 82:84–92.

**Rich, J.**
1989 "Patronage and Interstate Relations in the Roman Republic." Pp. 117–35 in *Patronage in Ancient Society.* Edited by A. Wallace-Hadrill. London: Routledge.

**Richard, E.**
2000 *Reading 1 Peter, Jude and 2 Peter: A Literary and Theological Commentary.* Macon, GA: Smyth & Helwys.

**Richards, E. R.**
1991 *The Secretary in the Letters of Paul.* Wissenschaftliche Untersuchungen zum Neuen Testament. Tübingen: Mohr (Siebeck).
2004 *Paul and First-Century Letter Writing: Secretaries, Composition, and Collection.* Downers Grove, IL: InterVarsity.

**Richards, W. L.**
1974 "Textual Criticism on the Greek Text of the Catholic Epistles: A Bibliography." *Andrews University Seminary Studies* 12:103–11.

**Riesner, R.**
1984 "Der zweite Petrus-Brief und die Eschatologie." Pp. 124–43 in *Zukunftserwartung in biblischer Sicht: Beiträge zur Eschatologie; Bericht von 3. Theologischen Studienkonferenz des Arbeitskreises für Evangelikale Theologie.* Edited by G. Maier. Giessen: Brunnen.
1998 *Paul's Early Period: Chronology, Mission Strategy and Theology.* Translated by D. Scott. Grand Rapids: Eerdmans.

**Rinaldi, G.**
1967 "La 'sapienza data' a Paolo (2 Petr. 3.15)." Pp. 395–441 in *San Pietro: Atti della XIX Settimana Biblica, Associazione Biblica Italiana.* Brescia: Paideia.

Roberts, J. W.
1962    "A Note on the Meaning of II Peter 3:10d." *Restoration Quarterly* 6:32–33.

Robinson, J. A., and M. R. James
1892    *The Gospel according to Peter, and the Revelation of Peter.* London: Clay & Sons.

Robinson, J. A. T.
1976    *Redating the New Testament.* Philadelphia: Westminster.

Robinson, M.
1990    "The First and Second Epistles General of Peter." Pp. 305–15 in *Incarnation: Contemporary Writers on the New Testament.* Edited by A. Corn. New York: Viking.

Robson, E. I.
1915    *Studies in the Second Epistle of St. Peter.* Cambridge: Cambridge University Press.

Ross, J. M.
1989    "Church Discipline in Jude 22–34." *Expository Times* 100:297–98.

Rowston, D. J.
1975    "Most Neglected Book in the New Testament." *New Testament Studies* 21:554–63.

Ru, G. de
1969    "De Authenticiteit van II Petrus." *Nederlands theologische tijdschrift* 24:2–12.

Rübenach, B. (ed.)
1981    *Begegnungen mit dem Judentum.* Stuttgart: Kreuz.

Russell, D. A.
1979    "De Imitatione." Pp. 1–16 in *Creative Imitation and Latin Literature.* Edited by A. West and T. Woodman. Cambridge: Cambridge University Press.

Salguero, J.
1965    "Epístolas católicas; Apocalipsis." In *Biblia comentada*, vol 7. Edited by los Profesores de Salamanca. Biblioteca de autores cristianos 249. Madrid: [La Editoral Católica].

Salles, A.
1957    "La diatribe antipauline dans le 'le Roman Pseudo-Clementin' et l'origine des 'Kerygemes de Pierre.'" *Revue biblique* 64:516–51.

Salmon, P.
1951    "Le Texte latin des épîtres de S. Pierre, S. Jean et S. Jude dans le MS 6 de Montpellier." *Journal of Theological Studies* 2:170–77.

Sass, G.
1941    "Zur Bedeutung von δοῦλος bei Paulus." *Zeitschrift für die neutestamentliche Wissenschaft* 40:24–32.

Sasson, J. M.
1978    "Genealogical 'Convention' in Biblical Chronology." *Zeitschrift für die alttestamentliche Wissenschaft* 90:171–85.

Satlow, M. L.
1995    *Tasting the Dish: Rabbinic Rhetorics of Sexuality.* Brown Judaic Studies. Atlanta: Scholars Press.

Sawyer, J. F. A.
1993    *Prophecy and the Biblical Prophets.* Oxford Bible Series. Oxford: Oxford University Press.

Scaggs, R.
2004    *The Pentecostal Commentary on 1 Peter, 2 Peter, Jude.* London and New York: T&T Clark.

Schalit, A.
1989    *Untersuchungen zur Assumptio Mosis.* Arbeiten zur Literatur und Geschichte des hellenistischen Judentums. Leiden: Brill.

Scheidacker, W.
1973    "Der erste und der zweite Petrusbrief." *Die Zeichen der Zeit* 27:271–78.

Schelkle, K. H.
1963a   "Der Judasbrief bei den Kirchenvätern." Pp. 405–16 in *Abraham unser Vater: Juden und Christen im Gespräch über die Bibel; Festschrift für Otto Michel.* Edited by O. Betz and M. Hengel. Leiden: Brill.
1963b   "Spätapostolisches Briefe als frühkatholisches Zeugnis." Pp. 225–32 in *Neutestamentliche Aufsätze: Festschrift für Josef Schmid zum 70. Geburtstag.* Edited by J. Blinzler, O. Kuss, and F. Mussner. Regensburg: Pustet.
1980    *Die Petrusbriefe; der Judasbrief.* Herders theologischer Kommentar zum Neuen Testament. Freiburg: Herder.

Schlatter, A.
1964    *Die Briefe des Petrus, Judas, Jakobus, der Brief an die Hebräer.* Stuttgart: Calwer.

Schlosser, J.
1973    "Les jours de Noé et de Lot: A propos de Luc XVII,26–30." *Revue biblique* 80:13–36.

Schmitz, F.-J.
2003    *Das Verhältnis der koptischen zur griechischen Überlieferung des Neuen Testaments: Dokumentation und Auswertung der Gesamtmaterialien beider Traditionen*

*zum Jakobusbrief und den beiden Petrus-briefen*. Berlin: de Gruyter.

Schneemelcher, W. (ed.)
1991–92    *New Testament Apocrypha*. English translation edited by R. M. Wilson. Revised edition. 2 vols. Cambridge: Clarke/ Louisville: Westminster John Knox.

Schneider, J.
1961    *Die Briefe des Jakobus, Petrus, Judas und Johannes: Die katholischen Briefe*. Das Neue Testament Deutsch. Göttingen: Vandenhoeck & Ruprecht.

Schrage, W.
1973    *Die "katholischen" Briefe: Die Briefe des Jakobus, Petrus, Johannes, und Judas*. Das Neue Testament Deutsch. Göttingen: Vandenhoeck & Ruprecht.
1985    "'Ein Tag ist beim Herrn wie tausend Jahre, und tausend Jahre sind wie ein Tag' (2 Petr 3,8)." Pp. 267–75 in *Glaube und Eschatologie: Festschrift für Werner Georg Kümmel zum 80. Geburtstag*. Edited by E. Grässer and O. Merk. Tübingen: Mohr.

Schreiner, T. R.
1998    *Romans*. Baker Exegetical Commentary on the New Testament. Grand Rapids: Baker Academic.
2003    *1, 2 Peter, Jude*. New American Commentary. Nashville: Broadman & Holman.

Schulman, G.
1990    "The General Epistle of Jude." Pp. 331–45 in *Incarnation: Contemporary Writers on the New Testament*. Edited by A. Corn. New York: Viking.

Schürer, E.
1979    *The History of the Jewish People in the Age of Jesus Christ (175 B.C.–A.D. 135): A New English Version*, vol. 2. Revised and edited by G. Vermès and F. Millar. Edinburgh: T&T Clark.

Schwank, B., and A. Stoger
1969    *The Two Epistles of St. Peter*. Translated by W. Jerman. New Testament for Spiritual Reading. London: Burns & Oates.

Seethaler, P. A.
1985    *1. und 2. Petrusbrief, Judasbrief*. Stuttgarter kleiner Kommentar: Neues Testament. Stuttgart: Katholisches Bibelwerk.
1987    "Kleine Bemerkungen zum Judasbrief." *Biblische Zeitschrift* 31:261–64.

Sellin, G.
1986    "Die Häretiker des Judasbriefes." *Zeitschrift für die neutestamentliche Wissenschaft* 77:206–25.

Selwyn, E. C.
1900    *The Christian Prophets and the Prophetic Apocalypse*. London: Macmillan.

Selwyn, E. G.
1946    *The First Epistle of Peter: The Greek Text with Introduction, Notes and Essays*. London: Macmillan.

Senior, D.
1980    *1 and 2 Peter*. New Testament Message. Wilmington, DE: Michael Glazier.
1987    "The Letters of Jude and 2 Peter." *Bible Translator* 25:209–14.

Senior, D., and D. J. Harrington
2003    *1 Peter, Jude, and 2 Peter*. Sacra Pagina. Collegeville, MN: Liturgical Press.

Sevenster, J. N.
1968    *Do You Know Greek? How Much Greek Could the First Jewish Christians Have Known?* Translated by J. de Bruin. Novum Testamentum Supplement 19. Leiden: Brill.

Shelton, J.-A.
1988    *As the Romans Did: A Sourcebook in Roman Social History*. New York and Oxford: Oxford University Press.

Sickenberger, J.
1911–12    "Engels- oder Teufelslästerer im Judasbriefe (8–10) und im 2 Petrusbriefe (2,10–12)." *Mitteilungen der schlesischen Gesellschaft für Volkskunde* 13–14:621–39.

Sidebottom, E. M.
1967    *James, Jude and 2 Peter*. New Century Bible. London: Nelson.

*SIG*    *Sylloge inscriptionum graecarum*. Edited by W. Dittenberger. 3rd edition. 4 vols. Leipzig: Hirzelium, 1915–24.

Simms, A. E.
1898    "Second Peter and the Apocalypse of Peter." *Expositor* 5/8:460–71.

Skaggs, R.
2003    *The Pentecostal Commentary on 1 and 2 Peter and Jude*. Pentecostal Commentary Series. New York: Sheffield Academic Press.

Skehan, P. W.
1960    "Note on 2 Peter 2:13." *Biblica* 41:69–71.

Slater, W. J. (ed.)
1991    *Dining in a Classical Context*. Ann Arbor: University of Michigan Press.

Smalley, S.
1964    "The Delay of the Parousia." *Journal of Biblical Literature* 83:41–54.

**Smit Sibinga, J.**

1966    "Une citation du Cantique dans la Secunda Petri." *Revue biblique* 73:107–18.

**Smith, D. E.**

2003    *From Symposium to Eucharist: The Banquet in the Early Christian World.* Minneapolis: Fortress.

**Smith, L. D.**

2001    "The Doxas of Jude 8." *Bible Translator* 52:147–48.

**Smith, M.**

1973    *Clement of Alexandria and a Secret Gospel of Mark.* Cambridge, MA: Harvard University Press.

**Smith, T. V.**

1985    *Petrine Controversies in Early Christianity: Attitudes towards Peter in Christian Writings of the First Two Centuries.* Tübingen: Mohr.

**Snyder, G. F.**

1977    "The Tobspruch in the New Testament." *New Testament Studies* 23:117–20.

**Snyder, J. I.**

1979    "A 2 Peter Bibliography." *Journal of the Evangelical Theological Society* 22:265–67.

1986    *The Promise of His Coming: The Eschatology of 2 Peter.* San Mateo, CA: Western Book/Journal Press.

**Soards, M. L.**

1988    "1 Peter, 2 Peter, and Jude as Evidence for a Petrine School." *Aufstieg und Niedergang der römischen Welt* 2.25. 5:3827–49. New York: de Gruyter.

**Soden, H. von**

1892    *Briefe des Petrus.* Handkommentar zum Neuen Testament. Freiburg: Mohr.

1899    *Hebräerbrief, Briefe des Petrus, Jakobus, Judas.* Handkommentar zum Neuen Testament. Freiburg: Mohr.

**Sordi, M.**

1994    "7Q5 e la prima venuta di Pietro a Roma." *Il Nuovo Areopago* 13:51–56.

**Sorg, T.**

1983    "Die Bibel—Grund des Glaubens: Predigt über 2. Petrus 1,16–21." *Theologische Beiträge* 14:162–66.

**Spence, R. M.**

1896–97    "Private Interpretation." *Expository Times* 8:285–86.

**Sperber, D., and D. Wilson**

1995    *Relevance: Communication and Cognition.* 2nd edition. Oxford: Blackwell.

**Spicq, C.**

1965    *Agape in the New Testament.* St. Louis: Herder.

1966    *Les épîtres de Saint Pierre.* Paris: Gabalda.

1975    "La Secunda Petri e la catechesi di una fede adulta." Pp. 117–40 in *Pietro nella Sacra Scrittura.* Edited by M. G. Rosito. Florence: Città di Vita.

**Spitta, F.**

1885    *Der zweite Brief des Petrus und der Brief des Judas.* Halle: Waisenhauses.

1911    "Die Petrusapokalypse und der zweite Petrusbrief." *Zeitschrift für die neutestamentliche Wissenschaft* 12:237–42.

**Stanley, D.**

1980    "Jesus, Savior of Mankind." *Studia missionalia* 29:57–84.

**Starr, J. M.**

2000    *Sharers in the Divine Nature: 2 Peter 1:4 in Its Hellenistic Context.* Coniectanea biblica: New Testament Series. Stockholm: Almquist & Wiksell.

**Stauffer, E.**

1955    *New Testament Theology.* Translated by J. Marsh. London: SCM.

**Stein, R. H.**

1976    "Is the Transfiguration (Mark 9:2–8) a Misplaced Resurrection Account?" *Journal of Biblical Literature* 95:79–95.

**Stibbs, A. M.**

1959    *The First Epistle General of Peter.* Tyndale New Testament Commentary. London: Tyndale.

**Stirewalt, M. L., Jr.**

2003    *Paul, the Letter Writer.* Grand Rapids: Eerdmans.

**Stoger, A.**

1975    *Carta de San Judas; Segunda carta de San Pedro.* Barcelona: Herder.

**Stowers, S. K.**

1986    *Letter Writing in Greco-Roman Antiquity.* Philadelphia: Westminster.

**Str-B**    *Kommentar zum Neuen Testament aus Talmud und Midrasch.* By H. L. Strack and P. Billerbeck. 6 vols. Munich: Beck, 1922–61.

**Strickert, F. M.**

1998    *Bethsaida: Home of the Apostles.* Collegeville, MN: Liturgical Press.

**Strobel, A.**

1961    *Untersuchungen zum eschatologischen Verzögerungsproblem: Auf Grund der spätjüdisch-urchristlichen Geschichte von*

*Habakuk 2,2ff.* Novum Testamentum Supplement 2. Leiden: Brill.

**Sundberg, A. C.**
1973    "Canon Muratori: A Fourth Century List." *Harvard Theological Review* 66:1–41.

**Szewc, E.**
1976    "'Chwaty' w listach Judy i 2 Piotra ('Les Gloires' dans les épîtres de St. Jude et deuxième de St. Pierre)." *Collectanea theologica* [Warsaw] 46:51–60.

**Taatz, I.**
1991    *Frühjüdischen Briefe: Die paulinischen Briefe im Rahmen der offiziellen religiösen Briefe des Frühjudentums.* Göttingen: Vandenhoeck & Ruprecht.

**Talbert, C. H.**
1966    "2 Peter and the Delay of the Parousia." *Vigiliae christianae* 20:137–45.
1986    *Perspectives on 1 Peter.* Macon: Mercer University Press.

**Taylor, V.**
1933–34    "The Message of the Epistles—2 Peter and Jude." *Expository Times* 45:437–41.

*TDNT*    *Theological Dictionary of the New Testament.* Edited by G. Kittel and G. Friedrich. Translated and edited by G. W. Bromiley. 10 vols. Grand Rapids: Eerdmans, 1964–76.

**Testa, P. E.**
1962    "La distruzione del mondo per il fuoco nella 2 ep. di Pietro 3,7.10.13." *Rivista biblica italiana* 10:252–82.

**Theissen, G.**
1978    *The Sociology of Early Palestinian Christianity.* Philadelphia: Fortress.
1982    *The Social Setting of Pauline Christianity.* Edited and translated by J. H. Schütz. Philadelphia: Fortress.

**Thiede, C. P.**
1986a    "A Pagan Reader of 2 Peter: Cosmic Conflagration in 2 Peter 3 and the 'Octavius' of Minucius Felix." *Journal for the Study of the New Testament* 26:79–96.
1986b    *Simon Peter: From Galilee to Rome.* Exeter: Paternoster.
1987    *Das Petrusbild in der neueren Forschung.* Wuppertal: Brockhaus.
1990    "Zweiter Petrusbrief." Vol. 3 / pp. 1171–74 in *Das grosse Bibellexikon.* Edited by H. Burkhardt. Wuppertal: Brockhaus.
1994    "Petrus (Apostel)." Pp. 1550–51 in *Evangelisches Lexikon für Theologie und Gemeinde.* Edited by H. Burkhardt and U. Swarat. Wuppertal: Brockhaus.

**Thiselton, A. C.**
2000    *The First Epistle to the Corinthians: A Commentary on the Greek Text.* New International Greek Testament Commentary. Grand Rapids: Eerdmans/Carlisle, UK: Paternoster.

**Thomas, E.**
2000    *Translator's Notes on 2 Peter.* Dallas: Summer Institute of Linguistics.

**Thorman, D. J.**
1978    "Jude." Pp. 11–20 in *Saints for All Seasons.* Garden City, NY: Doubleday.

**Thurén, L.**
1996    "Style Never Goes out of Fashion: 2 Peter Re-evaluated." Pp. 329–47 in *Rhetoric, Scripture and Theology.* Edited by S. E. Porter and T. H. Olbricht. Sheffield: Sheffield Academic Press.
1997    "Hey Jude! Asking for the Original Situation and Message of a Catholic Epistle." *New Testament Studies* 43:451–65.

**Thümmel, H. G.**
1999    *Die Memorien für Petrus und Paulus in Rom: Die archäologischen Denkmäler und die literarische Tradition.* Berlin: de Gruyter.

**Titrud, K.**
1992    "The Function of Καί in the Greek New Testament and an Application to 2 Peter." Pp. 240–70 in *Linguistics and New Testament Interpretation.* Edited by D. A. Black and K. Barnwell. Nashville: Broadman.

*TLNT*    *Theological Lexicon of the New Testament.* By C. Spicq. Edited and translated by J. D. Ernest. 3 vols. Peabody, MA: Hendrickson, 1994.

**Townsend, M. J.**
1979    "Exit the Agape." *Expository Times* 90:265–67.

**Trapp, M. (ed.)**
2003    *Greek and Latin Letters: An Anthology with Translation.* Cambridge: Cambridge University Press.

**Tromp, J.**
1993    *The Assumption of Moses: A Critical Edition with Commentary.* Studia in Veteris Testamenti Pseudepigrapha. Leiden: Brill.

**Turner, J. D., E. Deibler, and J. L. Turner**
1996    *Jude: A Structural Commentary.* Lewiston, NY: Mellen Biblical Press.

*UBS⁴*    *The Greek New Testament.* Edited by B. Aland et al. 4th revised edition. Stuttgart: Deutsche Bibelgesellschaft and United Bible Societies, 1994.

**Uhlig, S.**
1991    "Textcritical Questions of the Ethiopic New Bible." Pp. 1583–1600 in *Semitic Studies in Honor of Wolf Leslau on the Occasion of His Eighty-fifth Birthday.* Edited by A. S. Kaye. Wiesbaden: Harrassowitz.

**Vaage, L. E., and V. L. Wimbush**
1999    *Asceticism and the New Testament.* New York: Routledge.

**VanBeek, L.**
2000    "1 Enoch among Jews and Christians: A Fringe Connection?" Pp. 93–115 in *Christian-Jewish Relations through the Centuries.* Edited by S. E. Porter and B. W. R. Pearson. Sheffield: Sheffield Academic Press.

**Van den Heever, G.**
1993    "In Purifying Fire: Worldview and 2 Peter 3:10." *Neotestamentica* 27:107–18.

**VanderKam, J. C.**
1984    *Enoch and the Growth of an Apocalyptic Tradition.* Catholic Biblical Quarterly Monograph Series. Washington, DC: Catholic Biblical Association of America.

**VanderKam, J. C., and W. Adler (eds.)**
1996    *The Jewish Apocalyptic Heritage in Early Christianity.* Compendia rerum Iudaicarum ad Novum Testamentum 3.4. Assen, Netherlands: Van Gorcum/Minneapolis: Fortress.

**Vanhoozer, K. J.**
1998    *Is There a Meaning in This Text? The Bible, the Reader, and the Morality of Literary Knowledge.* Grand Rapids: Zondervan.

**Veenker, R. A.**
1986    "Noah, Herald of Righteousness." *Eastern Great Lakes and Midwest Biblical Societies* 6:204–18.

**Vena, O. D.**
1990    "La lucha por la ortodoxia en las comunidades cristianas del 2° siglo." *Revista biblica* 52:1–28.

**Venetz, H.-J.**
1982    "Dealing with Dissenters in the New Testament Communities." Pp. 67–74 in *The Right to Dissent.* New York: Seabury.

**Verheyden, J.**
2003    "The Canon Muratori." Pp. 487–556 in *The Biblical Canons.* Louvain: Leuven University Press.

**Vermès, G.**
1961a    *The Dead Sea Scrolls in English.* Leiden: Brill.
1961b    *Scripture and Tradition in Judaism: Haggadic Studies.* Studia post-biblica. Leiden: Brill.

**Vielhauer, P., and G. Strecker**
1992    "Apocalyptic in Early Christianity." Pp. 569–602 in *The New Testament Apocrypha,* vol. 2: *Writings Relating to the Apostles; Apocalypses and Related Subjects.* Edited by W. Schneemelcher. English translation edited by R. M. Wilson. Revised edition. Cambridge: Clarke/Louisville: Westminster John Knox.

**Vögtle, A.**
1936    *Die Tugend- und Lasterkataloge im Neuen Testament.* Neutestamentliche Abhandlungen. Münster: Aschendorff.
1970    "Die Parousie- und Gerichtsapologetik 2 P 3." Pp. 121–42 in *Das Neue Testament und die Zukunft des Kosmos.* Düsseldorf: Patmos.
1972    "Die Schriftwerdung der apostolischen Paradosis nach 2 Petr. 1,12–15." Pp. 297–305 in *Neues Testament und Geschichte: Historisches Geschehen und Deutung im Neuen Testament; Oscar Cullmann zum 70sten Geburtstag.* Edited by H. Baltensweiler and B. Reicke. Zurich: Theologischer Verlag/Tübingen: Mohr (Siebeck).
1981    "Petrus und Paulus nach dem zweiten Petrusbrief." Pp. 223–39 in *Kontinuität und Einheit: Für Franz Mussner.* Edited by P. G. Müller and W. Stegner. Freiburg: Herder.
1991    "Christo-Logie und Theo-Logie im zweiten Petrusbrief." Pp. 383–98 in *Anfänge der Christologie: Festschrift für Ferdinand Hahn zum 65. Geburtstag.* Edited by C. Breytenbach and H. Paulsen. Göttingen: Vandenhoeck & Ruprecht.
1994    *Der Judasbrief; Der 2. Petrusbrief.* Evangelisch-katholischer Kommentar zum Neuen Testament. Solothurn: Benziger/Düsseldorf: Neukirchen.

**Wall, R. W.**
2001    "The Canonical Function of 2 Peter." *Biblical Interpretation* 9:64–81.

**Wallace, D. B.**
1996    *Greek Grammar beyond the Basics.* Grand Rapids: Zondervan.

**Wallace-Hadrill, A.**
1989    "Patronage in Roman Society: From Republic to Empire." Pp. 63–87 in *Patronage in Ancient Society.* Edited by A. Wallace-Hadrill. London: Routledge.

**Walls, D.**
1999 *1 and 2 Peter; 1, 2, and 3 John; Jude.* Holman New Testament Commentary. Nashville: Broadman & Holman.

**Walsh, J. E.**
1983 *The Bones of St. Peter: The Fascinating Account of the Search for the Apostle's Body.* London: Gollancz.

**Walter, N.**
1994 "Kann man als Jude auch Grieche sein? Erwägungen zur jüdisch-hellenistischen Pseudepigraphie." Pp. 148–63 in *Pursuing the Text: Studies in Honor of Ben Zion Wacholder on the Occasion of His Seventieth Birthday.* Edited by J. C. Reeves and J. Kampen. Journal for the Study of the Old Testament: Supplement Series 184. Sheffield: Sheffield Academic Press.

**Waltner, E., and J. D. Charles**
1999 *1 and 2 Peter, Jude.* Believers Church Bible Commentary. Scottdale, PA: Herald.

**Walton, J.**
2001 *Genesis.* NIV Application Commentary. Grand Rapids: Zondervan.

**Wand, J. W. C.**
1934 *The General Epistles of St. Peter and St. Jude.* London: Methuen.

**Watson, D. F.**
1988 *Invention, Arrangement, and Style: Rhetorical Criticism of Jude and 2 Peter.* Society of Biblical Literature Dissertation Series. Atlanta: Scholars.

**Wehr, L.**
1996 *Petrus und Paulus, Kontrahenten und Partner: Die beiden Apostel im Spiegel des Neuen Testaments, der apostolischen Väter und früher Zeugnisse ihrer Verehrung.* Münster: Aschendorff.

**Weima, J. A. D.**
1994 *Neglected Endings: The Significance of the Pauline Letter Closings.* Journal for the Study of the New Testament: Supplement Series. Sheffield: Sheffield Academic Press.

**Weinrich, W. C. (ed.)**
1984 *The New Testament Age: Essays in Honor of Bo Reicke*, vol 1. Macon, GA: Mercer University Press.

**Weiss, B.**
1866 "Die petrinische Frage: Kritische Untersuchungen. II. Der zweite petrinische Brief." *Theologische Studien zum Antiken Judentum* 39:255–308.

**Wenham, D.**
1987 "Being 'Found' on the Last Day: New Light on 2 Peter 3:10 and 2 Corinthians 5:3." *New Testament Studies* 33:477–79.

**Werdermann, H.**
1913 *Die Irrlehrer des Judas- und 2 Petrusbriefes.* Gutersloh: Bertelsmann.

**West, D., and T. Woodman**
1979 *Creative Imitation and Latin Literature.* Cambridge: Cambridge University Press.

**Westermann, W. L.**
1955 *The Slave Systems of Greek and Roman Antiquity.* Philadelphia: American Philosophical Society.

**Wettstein, J. J.**
1751–52 *Η ΚΑΙΝΗ ΔΙΑΘΗΚΗ. Novum Testamentum Graecum: Editionis receptae cum lectionibus variantibus codicum mss., editionum aliarum, versionum, et patrum nec non commentario pleniore ex scriptoribus veteribus Hebraeis, Graecis et Latinis historiam et vim verborum illustrante, opera et studio Joannis Jacobi Wetstenii.* 2 vols. Amsterdam: Dommeriana.

**Whallon, W.**
1988 "Should We Keep, Omit, or Alter the οἱ in Jude 12?" *New Testament Studies* 34:156–59.

**White, J. L.**
1972 *The Form and Function of the Body of the Greek Letter: A Study of the Letter-Body in the Non-literary Papyri and in Paul the Apostle.* Missoula, MT: Society of Biblical Literature.
1986 *Light from Ancient Letters.* Philadelphia: Fortress.

**Wiarda, T.**
2000 *Peter in the Gospels: Pattern, Personality and Relationship.* Wissenschaftliche Untersuchungen zum Neuen Testament. Tübingen: Mohr Siebeck.

**Wibbing, S.**
1959 *Die Tugend- und Lasterkataloge im Neuen Testament und ihre Traditionsgeschichte unter besonderer Berücksichtigung der Qumran-Texte.* Beihefte zur Zeitschrift für die neutestamentliche Wissenschaft. Berlin: Töpelmann.

**Wicker, J. R.**
1985 "An Analysis of the Use of Noncanonical Literature in Jude and 2 Peter." PhD diss., Southwestern Baptist Theological Seminary.

**Wiese, W.**
1998 "Em defensa da esperança: Uma análise exegética de 2 Pedro 3:1–13." *Vox scripturae* [Brazil] 8:21–32.

**Wifstrand, A.**
1948 "Stylistic Problems in the Epistles of James and Peter." *Studia theologica* 1:170–82.

**Wikgren, A.**

1967 "Some Problems in Jude 5." Pp. 147–52 in *Studies in the History and Text of the New Testament in Honor of Kenneth Willis Clark*. Edited by B. L. Daniels and M. J. Suggs. Salt Lake City: University of Utah Press.

**Wilder, T. L.**

2004 *Pseudonymity, the New Testament, and Deception: An Inquiry into Intention and Reception*. Lanham, MD: University Press of America.

**Willmington, H. L.**

1985 "Peter's Two Epistles." *Fundamentalist Journal* 4:59.

**Wills, L.**

1984 "The Form of the Sermon in Hellenistic Judaism and Early Christianity." *Harvard Theological Review* 77:277–99.

**Wilson, W. E.**

1920–21 "*Heurethēsetai* in 2 Pet. iii.10." *Expository Times* 32:44–45.

**Windisch, H.**

1951 *Die katholischen Briefe*. 3rd edition. Handbuch zum Neuen Testament 15. Tübingen: Mohr.

**Winter, B. W.**

2001 *After Paul Left Corinth: The Influence of Secular Ethics and Social Change*. Grand Rapids: Eerdmans.

2002 *Philo and Paul among the Sophists: Alexandrian and Corinthian Responses to a Julio-Claudian Movement*. Grand Rapids: Eerdmans.

**Winter, S. C.**

1994 "Jude 22–23: A Note on the Text and Translation." *Harvard Theological Review* 87:215–22.

**Wisse, F.**

1972 "The Epistle of Jude in the History of Heresiology." Pp. 133–43 in *Essays on the Nag Hammadi Texts in Honour of Alexander Böhlig*. Edited by M. Krause. Leiden: Brill.

**Wistrand, E.**

1987 *Felicitas Imperatoria*. Studia Graeca et Latina Gothoburgensia 48. Göteborg: Acta Universitatis Gothoburgensis.

**Witherington, B.**

1985 "A Petrine Source in 2 Peter." Pp. 187–92 in *Society of Biblical Literature Seminar Papers* 24. Missoula, MT: Scholars Press.

**Wohlenberg, G.**

1923 *Der erste und zweite Petrusbriefe und der Judasbrief*. 3rd edition. Kommentar zum Neuen Testament 25. Leipzig: Deichert.

**Wolfe, B. P.**

1998 "The Prophets' Understanding or Understanding the Prophets? 2 Peter 1:20 Reconsidered." *Baptist Review of Theology* 8:92–106.

**Wolff, R.**

1960 *A Commentary on the Epistle of Jude*. Grand Rapids: Zondervan.

**Wolters, A.**

1987 "Worldview and Textual Criticism in 2 Peter 3:10." *Westminster Theological Journal* 49:405–13.

1990 "'Partners of the Deity': A Covenantal Reading of 2 Peter 1:4." *Calvin Theological Journal* 25:28–44.

1991 "Postscript to 'Partners of the Deity.'" *Calvin Theological Journal* 26:418–20.

**Wolthuis, T. R.**

1983 "An Analysis of the Book of Jude in Its Historical Context." *Calvin Theological Journal* 18:291.

1987 "Jude and Jewish Traditions." *Calvin Theological Journal* 22:21–45.

1989 "Jude and the Rhetorician: A Dialogue on the Rhetorical Nature of the Epistle of Jude." *Calvin Theological Journal* 24:126–34.

**Wright, N. T.**

1992 *The New Testament and the People of God*. London: SPCK.

**Young, F. M.**

1998 "The Non-Pauline Letters." Pp. 290–304 in *Cambridge Companion to Biblical Interpretation*. Edited by J. Barton. Cambridge: Cambridge University Press.

**Zahn, T.**

1909 *Introduction to the New Testament*. Translated by M. W. Jacobus et al. 3 vols. Edinburgh: T&T Clark.

**Zimmerli, W.**

1933 "Zur Struktur der alttestamentlichen Weisheit." *Zeitschrift für die alttestamentliche Wissenschaft* 51:177–204.

**Zmijewski, J.**

1979 "Apostolische Paradosis und Pseudepigraphie im Neuen Testament: 'Durch Erinnerung wachhalten' (2 Petr 1,13; 3,1)." *Biblische Zeitschrift* 23:161–71.

# Index of Subjects

Abel 90
abounding in virtues 196–97
Abraham 258
Acts of Peter 150
adultery 281–82
advisory type 55
agape feasts 24, 94, 296
aggression 260
Alexandria 5, 7, 10, 11–12, 24
amanuensis 43, 55, 145, 146–47, 219
amen in doxologies 131, 137, 344
Amram 81
ancestors 317–18
ancient world 320–22
angels 19, 24, 25, 105–6, 128.
    See also fallen angels
    as glories 77
    slander of 270–74
animals 20, 85, 274–76, 287–88
annihilation 73, 265
antediluvian world. See ancient world
antinomianism 17, 19–20, 23, 340
Antioch 11
Apocalypse of Peter 142,150
apocalyptic literature 165–66, 251
apostasy 60, 119, 125, 191, 199, 202, 205, 235, 240, 242, 291, 302–3, 342
    of angels 68
    of exodus generation 64
    of heretics 284
apostates 59, 151–52, 156, 300
apostles 8–9, 114, 173, 219

Apostolic Constitutions 3, 4, 29
apostolic prophecy 112, 113–16
apostolic teaching 56, 59, 151, 234, 235, 309, 312–13
apostolic testimony 61, 206, 221, 224, 226, 229, 315
apostolic tradition 19, 26, 75
Aramaic 14
Aramaic letters 49
archangels 82
Aristotle 163, 189–91, 275
arrogance of heretics 20, 84, 109–11, 269, 270, 291, 293–94
ashes 256
Asia Minor 173, 313, 338–39
Assumption (Testament) of Moses 26–27, 29, 31, 32, 79–81
assurance 134
Athanasius 6
athletic imagery 56
Augustine 5, 30–32, 34
authority 76, 131, 135, 136, 173
avarice 20, 91, 244–45, 278
awaiting 123

Balaam 20, 61, 87, 88, 90–91, 269, 277, 283–88, 304
Balak 90–91
banquets 93–94
baptism 199, 321
Barnabas 313
Barsabbas 1
beasts 85, 274–76, 287–88

beloved 38, 47, 51, 52, 119, 178, 309, 325, 337, 341
benefaction 188–90, 202
"better . . . than" proverbs. See Tob-Spruch
blameless 133–34, 337
blasphemy 77, 107, 243–44, 271
blessings 176
blindness 198, 199, 202
boasting 22, 77, 110–11, 294
body and soul 211
bondage of false teachers 299
brothers and sisters in Christ 195, 200
building up 51, 119, 120, 126, 132
burial 82

Cain 20, 61, 87, 88–90, 284
calling 46–48, 200–201
call to remember 63, 112–13, 312–13
canon 26–29, 30, 340
    and pseudepigraphy 149
    and 2 Peter 143
cardinal virtues 190
Carneades 299
Carpocrates 24
Carpocratians 10, 11, 12, 18, 23–25, 95, 296
Cephas 172
chains 250–51
Christian letters 130
Christian liberty 297–98
Christian life 343
Christology
    of Jude 45, 60, 105
    of Peter 344

Chrysippus 299
church
  as brotherhood/sisterhood 200
  corporate growth of 120
Clement 141
Clement of Alexandria 3, 11, 12, 18, 24–25, 27, 142
closing doxology
  of Jude 33–34, 38, 39, 51, 130–37
  of 2 Peter 168, 344
clouds 87, 96, 99, 292
commandment 305, 313
"common salvation" 18
common security 52, 53–54, 131, 134
common-source hypothesis (Jude and 2 Peter) 160
communal meal 15, 281
community 120–22
condemnation 246
conduct 333, 339
confidence 56
construction metaphor 120
consumer mentality 120
consummation 123, 131, 132, 317, 337
contending for the faith 51, 56, 113, 122, 132
conversion 199, 228
corporate solidarity 195
corruption 99, 187–88, 194, 266–67, 275
  of heretics 291, 302
  of Sodom and Gomorrah 260
courage 190, 194
creation 317–18
  renovation of 334
  Stoics on 158
curse 283
cyclicism of Stoicism 323

darkness 70, 87, 98–99, 227–28, 250–51, 293
daughters of men 66
day of judgment 69, 103, 228, 248, 263–65, 308, 323, 324–28
day of the Lord 145, 219–20, 228, 264, 323, 324, 329–30, 333–35
daytime 279
death 213
debauchery 279

deception 245
defects 94, 133, 337
defilement 75–76, 127–28, 267, 301
delay of judgment 156, 245–47, 264, 308, 313, 317, 328
deliberative rhetoric 35, 163
deliverance of righteous 248, 256, 262–63
demiurge 296, 297
denial of judgment 239, 241–42, 248, 264, 271, 308, 312–13
denunciation of heretics 57–60, 269, 276–77, 291. See also vituperatio
desire 109, 128, 156, 193, 294, 295, 299, 308, 314
destruction
  of day of the Lord 334
  of heretics 236, 240–41, 276, 303, 314
  of Sodom and Gomorrah 256
devil 79
devoid of the Spirit 117–18, 119, 121
Didymus of Alexandria 5, 29
digressio 164
diligence 191, 200–201, 336–37
disclosure formula 52, 53, 178
discontent 108–9
disdaining 267–68
disobedience 268
dispute 126
dissuasion 55, 87
divination 74, 91, 156, 158, 212
divine call 46–47
divine judgment 156, 187, 219, 287–88
divine nature 182
  partaking in 186–87, 188, 191, 197
divine power 181–83
divine voice 222–23, 225
division 116–17, 119
dogs 306–7
Domitian 16
doxology 344
dreamers 75
  heretics as 74
dreams 24
drought 292
drunkenness 280

dualism of gnosticism 148, 154, 296, 297
duty 182, 194–95, 202

earth 319–20
earthly 117
earwitnesses 224–25
ecclesiastical office 148
eclecticism of heretics 296, 308, 328
Eclectic movement 157
election 183, 200–201
elements 330, 334
encouragement 55
endurance 191, 194
Enoch 102
enthronement 224
enticement by heretics 281–82, 283, 293–94
entry into kingdom 202–3
Epicurean thought 23, 27, 155–57, 158, 246, 275, 296, 297–99, 308, 327–28
Epicurus 278–79, 298
epideictic rhetoric 35, 163
Epiphanian view (family of Jesus) 4
Epistle of Barnabas 142
epistolography 164
epistulary greeting 43
epistulary sermon 36
epistulary theory 169
errorists in Jude 18, 26
escape, salvation as 295, 300–301
eschatological skepticism 151–52, 154–55, 317
eschatology 40–41, 48, 88, 203
  and ethics 123, 337
  of false teachers 308
Essenes 154
established in the truth 133, 209
eternal chains 69
eternal fire 73
eternal judgment 99, 100, 137
eternal kingdom 185, 203
eternal life 99, 123, 124, 181–82
eternal punishment 85, 250
eternal ruin 202
eternity 137
ethical admonitions 165, 166
ethics
  and eschatological expectation 123
  and judgment 332

Ethiopian Church 28
Eucharist 94
Eusebius 5, 140–41, 143–44
"Evil One" 262
evil shepherds 95
exhortations 38, 119–28, 209, 308, 336–37
exodus 12, 64
    death as 215
exodus generation 61, 62, 93, 108, 248
*exordium* 163, 179
extraordinary 185
eyewitness 220–21, 224

faith
    and confidence 56
    as foundation 126
    as most holy 121
    as sacred tradition 174
    as virtue 191–92, 195
faithfulness 66, 72, 192
fallen angels 26, 32, 61, 62, 66–70, 78, 84, 149–53, 248, 263, 293
falling away 336
falling into sin 202
false apostle 238
false brother 237
false christ 238
false prophets 234, 235, 236–37
false teachers 18, 51, 114, 149, 151–52, 153–59, 205, 234, 235, 236–37, 293, 296, 337
false teaching 96, 206, 238
false witness 238
family letters 52–53
farewell discourse 164–67
fear 270–71
fear of God 20, 95, 127
feasting 93–94, 280–81
final judgment 125, 179, 216, 217, 231, 264, 293, 314
fire 125, 255, 256, 314, 322–23, 329
Firmilian 143
First Enoch 101, 102–5, 239
    absence in 2 Peter 161
    Augustine on 30–32, 34
    canonicity of 26–29
    use by Jude 5
first letter 337
First Peter 309–11
fishing metaphor 282, 295
Flamininus 298
flattery 22, 101, 110–11, 294

flesh 72, 76, 128, 266–67, 294, 295
flood 62, 247, 250, 251, 252–55, 314, 320–21, 334
foam of the sea 97
"follow after" 243, 285
fool 307
forensic rhetoric 35
forgetting 198–99
foundation of the church 120–21, 126
fraternal love 195, 200
freedom 151, 154, 156, 158, 291, 297–99, 316, 338
friendship 38, 111, 169, 195
fruit 96–97, 99
fruit of the Spirit 190
fulfillment 114, 115

Gabriel 81
genealogies 104
generosity 192
Gentiles in Palestine 15
giants 62, 67, 68, 252
gloom 227–28, 293
glory 131, 222
gnostics/gnosticism 10, 17, 23, 25, 118, 147–48, 153–54
God
    attributes of 136–37, 186
    declaration to Jesus at transfiguration 222–24
    glory of 133, 135–36, 183–84, 223
    as judge 83–84
    love of 47–48, 50, 201
    mercy of 264
    patience of 328
    perception of time 324–26, 332
    presence of 133
    promises of 185–86
    sovereign power of 136–37, 181–83
    sustains creation 319–20, 322
    unity of 134
godlessness 108, 116
gospel
    as demand 305
    slander against 244
grace 49, 59–60, 122, 171, 175–76
    misunderstanding of 17–18, 19
great day. *See* day of judgment

Greco-Roman letters, three-part structure of 39, 41, 51
Greco-Roman rhetoric 163
greed 91, 158, 236, 244–45, 282–83, 285–86
Greek language 13–14
Greek text of First Enoch 104
greeting 33, 39, 43, 44, 48–49, 51, 168, 171
growing in grace 343
grumblers 20, 108, 294
guarding 132, 342
gymnasium 283

hapax legomena in 2 Peter 144
hastening of day of the Lord 334
hearing 224
heaven 225, 330
hedonism 26, 278
hell 250–51
Hellenistic Jews 14
Hellenistic letters 33, 49, 168, 171, 176
Hellenistic terminology in 2 Peter 144–45
Helvidian view (family of Jesus) 4
"heresies of destruction" 236
heresy and division 117
heretics 9, 18–20, 40, 43, 51, 150–59
    adversarial role with angels 270–72
    as apostates 59, 60
    as beasts 274–77
    character of 93–99, 108
    controlled by desire 314
    denunciation of 57–60, 91, 269, 276–77. See also *vituperatio*
    destruction of 240–41, 247
    devoid of the Spirit 117–18, 119, 121
    dissatisfaction of 108–9
    distorted teachings of Scripture 340–41
    as flatterers 101
    judgment on 89, 92–93, 99, 265–67, 283
    leadership of 95
    lifestyle of 279–80, 332
    moral corruption of 187–88, 191
    persuasiveness of 125–27, 242–45
    as victims 108

heterodoxy 316
heteropraxis 316
Hieronymian view (family of Jesus) 4
holiness 194, 201, 332
holy mountain 225
holy myriads 106
Holy Spirit
    and inspiration 30
    and prayer 121–22
    and prophecy 233
Homer 162
homilies, letters as 130
honor 174, 189, 222
honorific decrees 179–80, 181, 184, 185, 188
hope 123, 124, 131, 134, 194, 201, 334
    as virtue 191, 194, 195
hubris 116, 274
human will 232–33
humility 173

idleness 197
idolatry 134
ignorance 20, 84–85, 193, 276–77, 318–19
imitatio 144, 152, 161, 162, 272, 312, 315
immorality of heretics 158, 236, 279–80, 337
imperative 120, 122
impiety 59, 107, 108, 118, 263
inclusion and exclusion 203
indicative in doxologies 135
indicative and imperative 122, 189
individualism 120
inspiration of prophecy 232, 233
instinct 20, 85
insult 273–74
irrationality 85, 269, 274–76, 287–88
Israel 84. See also exodus generation
itinerant ministry 8, 20

James 2
    leadership of 15–16
    prominence in early church 46
Jericho 256
Jerome 4, 5, 143, 144–45
Jerusalem, destruction in AD 66–70 17
Jerusalem church 16

Jerusalem Council 338
Jesus Christ
    denial of 112, 240
    divinity of 221
    and exodus 64–65
    family of 2–3, 4, 8
    first coming 220
    as Judge 65
    parousia of 105, 123, 185, 216, 217, 218–20, 221, 231
    resurrection of 154
    taming of 25
joy 134
Judah (patriarch) 1
Judas Iscariot 9
Judas of Damascus 1
Judas the Galilean 1
Jude (apostle) 2–3, 8
    brother of James 2–3, 4, 44, 46
    grandsons of 13, 16
    half brother of Jesus 162
    third bishop of Jerusalem 3
Jude (epistle)
    authenticity of 4–9, 17, 144
    authorship of 1–9
    canonicity of 5–7, 29
    date of writing 17–18
    as "first letter" 310
    genre of 33–38
    as genuine letter 37–38
    Greek style 7
    midrashic exegesis of 13
    original readers 10
    as pseudepigraphic 4–5, 17
    rhetorical strategy 20–21
    structure of 39–42
    typological exegesis in 74, 88
    use of apocryphal literature 5, 7, 9, 12, 26–33, 161
    use of First Enoch 29–32
Jude "son of James" 2
judgment 93, 123–24, 159, 248, 262–65
    on Balaam 91
    on Cain 89–90
    in coming of Christ 106
    delay of 156, 245–47, 264, 308, 313, 317, 328
    deliverance from 253
    on exodus generation 64–66
    on fallen angels 68–70, 248, 249–53, 263
    on flood generation 248
    on heretics 89, 92–93, 99, 124, 265–67, 283, 293
    on Korah 92

on Sodom and Gomorrah 72–73, 248, 255–62
    swiftness of 326
judicial rhetoric 35, 163
justice 107, 190, 253–54, 335

keeping 122, 263–64, 322
kingdom of God 123, 124, 202–3
knowledge 148, 154, 176–77, 183, 193, 301, 343
Korah 20, 61, 62, 87, 88, 92, 284

lamp 228
last days 114, 115
laudatio 20–21
lawlessness 194, 259–62, 342
laziness 197
letter closings 130, 308
letter genre 167–69, 178
libertine lifestyle 14, 23, 154–55, 157, 240
licentiousness 9, 24, 43, 60, 194, 243, 295, 296
life 181–82
    transitory nature of 293
Lord 60, 64–65, 175, 177
"Lord and Savior" 175, 203–4
Lord's Supper 280–81
Lot 70, 248, 255, 257–61
love 48–50, 94
    of God 119–20
    as virtue 191, 195–96
loyalty 182, 194–95
lust 187–88, 266–67, 282, 296, 316
luxury 279

magic 25
majesty 221, 223
    of God 135–36
malcontents 294
manumission 242
martyrdom 194
Master 240–41
meals 93–94
memory 206, 211–12, 213
    and morality 205, 211, 214–15
mercy 18, 48–50, 123–24, 126, 127, 176, 250
messianic rule 224
metaphors 87, 95–100, 227
Methodius 143
Michael (archangel) 77, 79–84, 270, 271

midrash 40–41, 88
might 136
mists driven by the storm 292–93
mockers/mocking 115–16, 308, 315–16, 318
moral character 186, 191, 192, 196
moral entanglement 302
morality and memory 205, 211, 214–15
moral philosophy 208, 211
moral transformation 186–87
Mormons 28
morning star 228–29
mortality 299
Moses 108
    body of 26, 32, 80–82, 271–72
mountain of transfiguration 225
mouths 109–10
Muratorian Fragment 6, 143
myriad 106
mystery religions 220–21
myth 151, 216, 217–18, 220, 225

narratio 163, 164
natural 117
Nephilim 66
netherworld 250
new covenant 184
new creation 253, 334–35
new heaven and new earth 185, 194–95, 219, 258, 323, 329, 332, 333, 334–35
Noah 102, 248, 250, 251, 252–55, 257, 262, 321
novelty 18, 26, 56–57

obedience 122, 123, 284
oil lamp 227–28
Old Testament in 2 Peter 145
ophthalmia 198, 209
oral discourse 34, 36–37, 130, 163–64
order of things 71–72, 77
Origen 5, 7, 11, 143

pagan lifestyle 295
Palestinian Christianity 12–16, 17
paraenesis 55, 168
parousia 220
    delay of 148, 241–42
    denial of 239

partitio 163
passion 193, 302
patience 194
patronage 192
Paul 16
    before the Areopagus 327
    on Christian liberty 297–98
    letters 130–31, 147, 152
    quotation of classic authors 103
    on received tradition 75
    writings twisted by heretics 336, 338–40
peace 39, 48–50, 171, 175–76, 337
peroratio 163
persecution 194
perseverance 194
personal knowledge 177, 183, 193, 301, 343
persuasion 168–69
    of heretics 125–27, 300
pesher interpretation 40–41, 114
Peshitta 5
Peter
    bilingualism of 172
    death of 17, 139, 150, 206, 210–15, 238
    prominence in early church 159
    solidarity with Paul 338–40
Petrine circle 149
Pidgin Greek 7
pigs 307
plagarism 161
plagues of Egypt 256
planets 98
pleasure 157, 266, 269, 278–80, 282
Pliny the Younger 242–43
polytheism 134
postmodern world 25
power 131, 136, 273
praescriptio 171, 175, 180
praise 131
praxis 316
prayer 121–22
Preaching of Peter 150
predictive prophecy 327
present truth 174, 209
present world 136, 321–22, 329, 334
preservation 48, 248, 253
price 20
pride 294
probatio 163

promise/promises 184–85, 316–17, 326, 334–35
prophecy 23, 58, 103, 156, 219, 230
prophetic witness 206, 210, 216, 226–34, 235, 309, 312–13
protection 132, 342
proverbs 291, 303, 306–7
providence 322
    denial of 23, 155–56, 179, 271
prudence 157
pseudepigrapha 26–33, 40, 61, 101, 161
pseudepigraphy 139, 149–50, 238
    testaments as 165, 207
Pseudo-Demetrius 37–38
Pseudo-Libanius 38
pseudoprophets 155
public notice 58
punishment 99
pure understanding 311
purification 199
purity codes 75

Qumran 40–41, 88, 102, 154

rationality 287–88
reading letters aloud 168
reconciliation 337
reefs 94
reliability 192
reminders 63–64, 167, 211, 214, 309, 311. See also call to remember
remnant, salvation of 256
repentance 328–29, 334
rescuing 18, 125–26, 132, 295
resurrection 124
"revelation" of Jesus Christ 145
revelations of the future 165, 166
revenge 273–74
reverence 107, 116, 182, 194
reward of unrighteousness 277–78
rhetorical markers in Jude 39–40
rhetorical theory 34–38, 163–64
"rhetoric of slander." See vituperatio

righteousness 107, 174–75, 263, 335
  of Lot 257–59, 261
  of Noah 253–54
rock 172

sacred tradition 52, 56, 59, 174
sacrificial animals 133
Sadducees 155
salvation 54, 102
savagery 97
Savior 175
schism 127
scoffers 156
Scriptures distorted by heretics 340–41
sea 97
Second Peter
  authenticity of 139–44, 160, 172, 311
  authorship of 139–50
  genre 162–69
  as postapostolic 147–49
  as pseudepigraphic 149–50, 167, 172
  structure of 162–69
  typological interpretation in 243
  use of Jude 6–7, 16, 22–23, 30, 94, 140, 144, 152, 159–62, 272, 291, 310–11, 312
"second thoughts" 310
secretaries 8, 146–47
secret books 102
sedition and disagreement 92
seed-pickers 157
seeing 224
self-control 188, 193–94
self-restraint 60
Seneca 301
separation 117
Septuagint 64
servant 45
"servant of God" 173
Servant Songs 47, 48
seventh from Adam 104
sexual gratification 18, 22, 293–94
sexual immorality 9, 14, 16, 19, 25, 60, 75, 151, 158, 187, 243, 265, 267, 269, 281–83, 295
  of Balaam 91
  of heretics 98, 128

of Sodom and Gomorrah 70–72, 75–76
shame 97–98
Shema 60, 134
Sheol 93
shepherds 87, 95
shortsightedness 198
siblings 195
Silvanus 219
Simeon Peter 150, 172
skepticism 206
  about prophecy 158, 226, 327
  about parousia of Christ 151–52, 153, 235
skeptics 298, 299
slander 79, 82–83, 84–86, 243–44, 276
slandering of angels 270–74
slandering glories 23, 25, 76–77, 79, 84, 270–71
slave of Jesus Christ 16, 44–45
slaves/slavery 44–45, 173, 298
  to sin 151, 297, 299–300
slumber 247
snatching 125, 127
social good 189
Sodom and Gomorrah 61, 62, 70–75, 84, 248, 255–62
sons of God 66–67, 250, 252
sorite 191
soul 261
soulish 20, 117–18
sows 307
speech act theory 21–22
Spirit of God 117–18
spiritual versus earthly 117–18
spots 87, 94, 337
stability 133
stained clothing 127–28
standing 133
stars 99
steadfastness 194
Stoics/Stoicism 158, 194, 275, 298, 323, 327
strength and power 273
stumbling 132, 202
suffering Servant 224
Syrian churches 5, 7, 11

Tartarus 250–51
temperance 190
temporary dwellings 210–11, 213
temptations 127
tent 210–11
Tertullian 5, 26–27, 28

testament 149, 163, 164–67, 178, 207, 342
Testament of Job 165
Testament of Moses. See Assumption (Testament) of Moses
Testaments of the Twelve Patriarchs 165
textual criticism 124
Thaddeus 2–3
theocentricity of Jude 132
theophany 102, 105
"these things" 20, 210, 214, 312
thief 241, 324, 329
Thomas 3, 11
thousand years 325–26
time 131, 136–37, 324–26, 332
Tob-Spruch 303–5
tongues 121
torment 261, 264–65
tradition 19, 56–57
training of body 283
transfiguration 150, 166, 216, 220–26
transgression of boundaries 76, 84
transitio 164
trees 87, 96–97, 99
trial 262–63
Trinity 177
trust 66
truth 209–10, 304
tunic 128
turning back 305
typology 40

unbelief 66
uncleanness 307
unfaithful acts 72
unfruitful 197
ungodly 59, 114, 262
universal judgment 102
unrighteousness 258, 262, 263, 266, 277–78
unstable 295, 342
uprooting 96

vice/vices 73, 95, 187–88, 190, 197
virtue/virtues 56, 182–84, 186, 189–96, 201–2, 213
vituperatio 20–22, 58–60, 84–85, 245, 270, 275, 276, 283, 342
  of heretics 217

of Jude 101, 109
in 2 Peter 151–52, 306
vituperative language 55–56
vocative voice 38

wages of unrighteousness 258, 263, 277–78, 284
walking 284, 304
wandering 284
wandering stars 87, 98–99, 292
warfare 56
Watchers 62, 67, 68, 72, 99, 249–52
waterless springs 292
waters of creation 256, 320
waters of judgment 256, 322

way 284–85
way of life 259, 295, 333
way of righteousness 304–5, 335
way of truth 244
well 292
wilderness generation. *See* exodus generation
wild waves 97, 292
wind 96
wisdom 190, 338
wish-prayer 48–49, 168, 171, 175–76
witnesses 224–25
woe-oracle 87, 88–89

"word of exhortation" 36, 38, 168
word of God 319–20
world
corruption of 187
immorality of 301
immutability of 158, 314, 318
worldly people 117
world to come 321–22
worship, letters used in 130
wrath of God 240, 331
written communication 36

zeal 200

# Index of Authors

Adams, E., 155, 156, 158
Adler, W., 27, 27n23, 28
Albin, C. A., 129
Alexander, T. D., 258
Arav, R., 14n14, 15n15
Aune, D. E., 238

Balch, D. L., 15, 53
Bartchy, S. S., 2, 46, 299
Bauckham, R. J., xi, 2, 3n4, 4, 7, 9n8, 12, 12n11, 13, 13n13, 15n16, 16, 17n17, 23, 25, 29n25, 36, 40, 46, 48, 65, 76, 77, 79, 80n1, 82, 84, 88, 89, 92, 93, 94, 94n3, 97, 99, 103, 104, 105, 121, 126, 129, 139, 140, 141, 142, 144, 146, 148–49, 153, 154, 155, 159, 160, 162, 163, 164, 165, 166, 167, 175, 182, 186, 199, 207, 212, 219, 221, 223, 231, 232–33, 238, 252, 263, 265, 271, 272, 272n2, 276, 289, 297, 303, 312, 317, 318, 323, 325, 341, 342
Bauder, W., 196
Bauernfeind, O., 192
Baum, A. D., 149
BDF (F. Blass, A. Debrunner, and R. W. Funk), 47, 47n5, 48, 55, 71, 83, 85, 114, 120, 135, 175, 180, 182, 196, 208, 214, 219n1, 226, 227, 230, 240, 260, 265, 267, 286, 294, 295, 302, 306, 315, 326
Beale, G. K., 88
Bertram, G., 115, 316
Betz, O., 223

Bigg, C., 6, 11, 15n16, 76, 103, 139, 140, 152, 159, 160, 162, 264, 283, 289, 298, 300, 310, 313, 341
Birdsall, J. N., 124, 129
Black, C. C., 36n29, 168
Black, M., 39n35, 67, 69, 99, 99n4, 102, 105, 105n4, 107, 133, 250, 264
Blomberg, C. L., 221
Bockmuehl, M., 223
Boobyer, G. H., 89, 91, 145, 221, 310
Braumann, G., 55n4, 220
Braun, H., 245, 284
Bray, G., 117, 134, 300, 303
Brensinger, T. L., 289
Brenton, L. C. L., 304
Bruce, F. F., 24, 102
Bryce, G. E., 303
Buchanan, G. W., 88
Buchholz, D. D., 142
Büchsel, F., 106
Bultmann, R., 56, 124, 212
Burton, E. D. W., 114, 313
Busto Saiz, J. R., 40, 40n37, 74

Caird, G. B., 242
Calderone, S., 192
Callan, T., 159, 159n4
Cantinat, J., 40, 74
Carr, W., 76
Caulley, T. S., 154
Cavallin, H. C. C., 153, 155
Chaine, J., 6, 11, 31, 104, 159, 163
Chancey, M. A., 15n15

Charles, J. D., 7, 8, 8n7, 12, 13, 31, 32, 33, 36, 36n28, 40, 58, 74, 77, 84, 103, 139, 149, 165, 189, 190, 191, 193, 195, 199, 207, 298
Charles, R. H., 28, 67, 79, 80, 102, 307
Charlesworth, J. H., 165
Chase, F. H., 140
Chester, A., 149
Clarke, E. G., 92
Collins, C. J., 135
Conte, G. B., 161
Conzelmann, H., 228
Corley, K. E., 15
Coughenour, R. A., 89
Craddock, F. B., 149, 298
Cullmann, O., 172

Dalton, W. J., 28, 67, 252
Danker, F. W., 179, 180, 181, 184, 185, 187, 188, 189, 192, 195, 196, 200, 202, 203, 222, 301
Daube, D., 120
Davids, P. H., xin1, 29n25
DeGraaf, D., 126
Dehandschutter, B., 104
Deichgräber, R., 39n35, 135
Deiros, P. A., 48n6
Deissmann, A., 8, 43, 60, 134, 147, 181, 183, 189, 192, 201, 203, 220, 226, 231, 283
Delling, G., 196, 245, 330
deSilva, D. A., 75, 75n5, 95, 97, 199, 222
Desjardins, M., 22, 25, 154
Dillon, J. M., 157, 296

Donfried, K. P., 141
Doty, W. G., 33, 44, 130n1, 169, 178
Douglas, M., 75n5
du Toit, A., 20, 21, 22, 40n36, 57, 74, 84n3, 85, 110
Dyson, R. W., 30, 31

Easton, B. S., 190
Edgar, C. C., 34n26, 44n1, 44n2
Ehrman, B. D., 172n1
Elliott, J. H., xi, 47, 68, 137, 148, 168, 173, 199, 252
Elliott, J. K., 39n35, 243
Elliott, M., 196
Ellis, E. E., 40, 58, 88
Epstein, D. F., 84, 127, 273, 274
Esser, H.-H., 261

Falkenroth, U., 195
Farkasfalvy, D., 149
Ferguson, E., 57, 82, 141, 199
Fields, W. W., 256, 258
Fiensy, D. A., 14
Finkenrath, G., 245
Fischel, H. A., 191
Fitzer, G., 270
Fitzmyer, J. A., 1n1, 39, 49, 103, 130n1, 171, 172
Foerster, W., 76, 125, 182
Fornberg, T., 23, 148, 153, 154, 159, 159n4, 182, 219, 221, 271n1, 272, 281, 298
Friedrich, G., 184, 185
Fuchs, E., 10, 12n10, 15n16, 29n25, 129, 163, 165
Furnish, V. P., 122

García Martínez, F., 78
Garnsey, P., 176
Gerdmar, A., 12, 37, 141, 145, 154, 155
Gilmore, M. J., 145, 159, 159n4, 161, 252, 271n1, 303, 311, 337
Glasson, T. F., 251
Goppelt, L., 88, 237
Gow, A. S. F., 97
Green, C., 163
Green, E. M. B., 139, 140
Green, G. L. (E.), 9, 67, 74, 122, 127, 139, 156, 159, 213, 221, 242, 327
Green, M., 11, 15n16, 29, 31, 32, 76, 121, 128, 139, 145,

149, 154, 160, 176, 212, 221, 263, 265, 276, 289, 296, 305, 310
Griego, R., xiii, 275
Gruen, E. S., 192
Grundmann, W., 11, 15n16, 108, 123, 148, 159
Gundry Volf, J. M., 199
Gunther, J. J., 11, 12, 24
Günther, W., 59
Gutbrod, W., 261
Guthrie, D., 139, 140, 153, 154

Hafemann, S., 29n25
Hagner, D. A., 141, 317n1, 341
Hahn, H. C., 228, 240
Hahneman, G. M., 143n2
Hamilton, V. P., 70n2, 90n2, 102
Hamilton, W., 167
Harrington, D. J., 29n25, 144, 149, 165, 167, 182, 221, 238, 263, 327, 341
Harrington, H. K., 75n5
Harris, H., 338
Hauck, F., 267, 298, 301
Hays, C. M., xiii, 289, 290
Hillyer, N., 32, 163
Hofius, O., 318
Hofmann, N. J., 79
Holladay, C. H., 186
Horrell, D., 149, 155, 163, 298
Horsley, R. A., 7, 14
Horst, J., 338
Hunt, A. S., 34n26, 44n1, 44n2
Hurst, D., 3, 65, 77, 79, 106, 196, 202, 228

Ilan, T., 1, 14, 172
Isaac, E., 102, 136

James, M. R., 92, 142
Jeremias, J., 94
Johnson, L. T., 20, 21, 21n20, 21n21, 58, 84n3, 110, 150, 217, 245, 270, 283

Kamlah, E., 190
Kasch, W., 319
Käsemann, E., 147–48, 153, 326
Kee, H. C., 83
Kelly, J. N. D., 7, 11, 15n16, 19n19, 22, 23, 76, 93, 94n3, 99, 115, 129, 145, 147, 152, 159, 160, 163, 176, 182, 198, 221, 229, 231, 238, 264,

276, 289, 298, 300, 313, 317, 342, 343
Kennedy, G. A., 34, 163
Kinman, B., 220
Kittel, G., 135, 184
Klijn, A. F. J., 78, 326
Knight, J., 23, 154
Koester, H., 11
Kolenkow, A. B., 165, 166
Kraftchick, S. J., 84, 129, 145, 149, 155, 159, 165, 167, 263, 265, 297, 298, 299, 341
Kraus, T. J., 289
Kruger, M. A., 139, 140
Kubo, S., 124, 128, 129
Kümmel, W. G., 140, 144, 145, 148, 150, 153

Ladd, G. E., 261
Landon, C. H., 129
Lattimore, R., 317
Lee, E. K., 73
Lee, M., 328
Letellier, R. I., 259
Levinskaya, I., 15
Lewis, J. P., 252
Loader, J. A., 71, 255, 260
Long, A. A., 156, 157, 158, 296
Lucas, D., 163
Lunn, N., 264
Lyons, W. J., 71, 71n3, 258

Malherbe, A. J., 37, 38, 38n33, 55, 56, 63, 73, 147, 164, 168, 169, 171, 188, 190, 209, 211, 257, 342
Malina, B. J., 2, 46, 57, 72, 75n5, 126, 190, 192, 199, 222, 267, 273
Marshall, I. H., 148, 199
Martin, D. B., 45
Martin, R. P., 149
Mayor, J. B., 29, 96, 140, 142, 159n4, 162–63, 198, 208, 275, 333
McDonald, L. M., 143n2, 149
McEleney, N. J., 190
McNamara, M., 92
Meade, D. G., 149
Metzger, B. M., 5, 38n34, 65, 78, 128, 130n2, 268, 289
Michaelis, W., 215, 220, 221
Michel, O., 66, 307
Mitchell, M. M., 117, 120
Moberly, W., 66
Moffatt, J., 11, 163

Moo, D. J., 31, 32, 76, 103, 128, 139, 140, 149, 159, 160, 163, 167, 238, 289, 297, 311, 342
Morgan, C. W., 73
Moule, C. F. D., 14
Mounce, R. H., 163
Müller, D., 196
Munck, J., 166
Mundle, W., 224
Muraoka, T., 72
Murdock, J., 5

Neusner, J., 40n38, 41n38, 67, 75n5
Neyrey, J. H., 2, 7, 11, 23, 29n25, 34, 35, 36, 46, 57, 65, 76, 77, 83, 95, 98, 104, 110, 121, 122, 123, 126, 129, 135, 149, 154, 155, 155n3, 156, 159, 161, 163, 165, 167, 174, 175, 176, 177, 179, 182, 187, 190, 192, 194, 199, 219, 221, 222, 226, 245, 271, 271n1, 273, 288, 297, 327, 328–29
Nickelsburg, G. W. E., 27, 28, 29, 67, 68, 79, 80, 89, 89n1, 102, 105n4, 106
Nienhuis, D. R., xi

O'Brien, P. T., 179
Obbink, D., 162
Oepke, A., 220, 240, 280
Ogden, G. S., 303
Olbricht, T. H., 34n27
Oleson, J. P., 7
Osburn, C. D., 65, 78, 99, 104, 105, 124, 129, 160
Osiek, C., 15, 53

Page, D. L., 97
Paulsen, H., 11, 29n25, 104, 149, 159, 163, 165
Perkins, P., 36, 76, 84, 129, 140, 155, 159, 165, 271, 273, 317
Peterson, R. A., 73
Pfitzner, V. C., 56
Picirelli, R. E., 140, 141, 142, 176, 177, 183
Porter, S. E., 8n7, 34n27, 47, 53, 99, 105, 238, 265, 293
Priest, J. F., 80, 109

Raymond, P., 10, 12n10, 15n16, 29n25, 129, 163, 165

Reese, R. A., xin1, 10
Reicke, B., 53, 76, 160, 297
Reiling, J., 237
Rengstorf, K. H., 108, 114, 238, 341
Reymond, E. D., 304
Rich, J., 192
Richard, E., 147, 149, 341
Richards, E. R., 8, 146, 147, 339
Riesner, R., 17n18, 323
Robinson, J. A., 142
Robinson, J. A. T., 139, 140, 150, 160, 310
Rowston, D. J., xi, 29
Russell, D. A., 161, 162

Sanders, J. A., 149
Sass, G., 45
Sasson, J. M., 104
Satlow, M. L., 14
Sawyer, J. F. A., 233
Scaggs, R., 155, 159, 300
Schalit, A., 79
Schelkle, K. H., 11, 76, 129, 140, 145, 147, 148, 153, 159, 163, 176, 229, 276, 317
Schlier, H., 239, 239n1
Schmidt, K., 117
Schneemelcher, W., 142
Schneider, J., 264
Schniewind, J., 184, 185
Schrage, W., 163
Schreiner, T. R., 29n25, 38n34, 130n2, 139, 140, 145, 154, 155, 273, 276, 289, 298, 300, 311, 342
Schrenk, G., 230, 233, 277, 319
Schürer, E., 134
Schweizer, E., 117
Sedley, D. N., 156, 157, 158
Sellin, G., 76
Selter, F., 245
Selwyn, E. G., 120
Senior, D., 29n25, 144, 149, 159, 165, 167, 182, 221, 238, 263, 327, 341
Sevenster, J. N., 7n7
Shelton, J.-A., 182, 190, 280–81
Shutt, R. J. H., 181, 193
Sidebottom, E. M., 23, 159, 312, 313
Slater, W. J., 280
Smith, D. E., 93
Smith, M., 24, 142
Smith, T. V., 154

Snyder, G. F., 303
Sperber, D., 10n9, 177
Spicq, C., 45, 160, 163, 183, 200, 262
Spitta, F., 159
Spittler, R. P., 164, 165, 166
Starr, J. M., 177, 186
Stauffer, E., 52, 166
Stirewalt, M. L., Jr., 37
Stowers, S. K., 8, 38, 38n31, 44, 147, 178
Str-B (H. L. Strack and P. Billerbeck), 91, 233, 334
Strecker, G., 8
Sundberg, A. C., 143n2

Taatz, I., 1n1
Theissen, G., 14
Thiede, C. P., 154, 323
Thiselton, A. C., 117
Thurén, L., 40n36, 57
Trapp, M., 208
Tromp, J., 28, 79, 80, 80n1

VanderKam, J. C., 27, 27n23, 28, 102
Vanhoozer, K. J., 10n9
Verheyden, J., 143n2
Vermès, G., 285
Vielhauer, P., 8
Vögtle, A., 29n25, 104, 128, 149, 154, 163, 190

Wallace-Hadrill, A., 192
Wallace, D. B., 94n3
Waltner, E., 139, 298
Walton, J., 90n2
Wand, J. W. C., 152
Watson, D. F., 34, 35, 36n28, 90, 92, 159n4, 163, 164, 167, 179
Weima, J. A. D., 1n1, 8, 33, 39, 130, 131, 135, 147, 168
West, D., 161
Westermann, W. L., 299
White, J. L., 8, 33, 34n26, 38, 38n32, 44, 52, 53, 55, 130, 130n1, 130n3, 146, 168, 169, 171, 175, 178, 179, 205, 208, 308
Wibbing, S., 190
Wikgren, A., 65, 78
Wilder, T. L., 149
Wills, L., 36n29, 168
Wilson, W. E., 10n9, 177
Winter, B. W., 84, 217, 245
Winter, S. C., 124, 126, 129

Wintermute, O. S., 76, 78
Wisse, F., 272n2
Wistrand, E., 220
Witherington, B., 145

Wolters, A., 186
Woodman, T., 161
Wright, N. T., 47

Zahn, T., 289n5
Zimmerli, W., 303

# Index of Greek Words

ἀγαπητοί 52
ἀδελφοί 200
ἀδικία 59
αἰώνιον βασιλείαν 203
ἀρετή 183
ἀρπάσατε 125
ἀρχή 68
ἀσεβής 59, 182

γάρ 197n2
γνῶσις 176–77, 193

δέ 197n2
δεσπότης 60
δόξα 135, 222
δόξαι 76–77
δοῦλος 45, 173

ἑαυτοὺς ποιμαίνοντες 95
ἐγκράτειαν 193
ἐν θεῷ πατρί 47n5
ἐπίγνωσις 176–77

ἐπιθυμία 187–88
ἐπόπται 220
εὐσέβεια 182, 194

ἡδονή 187–88

ἱμάτιον 128

καιρὸς ἐσχατός 115
κλῆσις 200–201
κλητοί, οἱ 46
κλοπή 161
κύριος 173

λόγος 113n1

μέγιστα 185
μίμησις 161
μυωπάζω 198

παρακαλῶν 55
πειρασμός 263
Πέτρος 172

ῥῆμα 113n1

σπιλάδες 94, 94n3
Συμεών 172
σωτηρία 53–54

τιμή 222

ὑβρίζω 115–16

φθείρονται 85
φθορά 187, 297
φυλάσσω 132

χαίρειν 49
χιτῶνα 128

ψυχικός 117

# Index of Scripture and Other Ancient Writings

Old Testament  389
New Testament  394
Old Testament Apocrypha  406
Old Testament Pseudepigrapha  409
New Testament Apocrypha  411
Rabbinic Writings  411
Targums  411

Nag Hammadi  411
Qumran / Dead Sea Scrolls  411
Papyri  412
Josephus  412
Philo  413
Classical Writers  414
Church Fathers  418

## Old Testament

**Genesis**

1:3–30  319
1:6–10  320
1:9  320
2:2  325
2:2–3  104
2:7  261, 282
3:8  222
4:1–16  90
4:5–6  90
4:8  90
4:17–18  102
5:1–24  104
5:18  102
5:21–24  102
6  67
6:1–2  250
6:1–4  26, 29, 32, 66, 249, 252
6:2  66, 67
6:5  229
6:5–6  254
6:9  102, 254

6:11 LXX  85
6:17  241
6:17 LXX  254
7  321
7:1  254
7:4  254
7:6–7  254
7:10  254
7:17  254
7:21  321
7:22  254
7:23  321
8:4  104
9:11  254
9:15  254
9:28  254
10:1  254
10:32  254
11:10  254
13:8–13  258
15:2  60
15:8  60
16:7  292

18:1–8  258
18:15  240
18:19 LXX  106
18:20  70, 255
18:22–33  70, 258
18:23  107, 254
18:23 LXX  59
18:25  254
18:25 LXX  106
18:28  107
18:28 LXX  59
19:1–3  258
19:1–26  257
19:5  70, 71, 258
19:8  70, 71, 258
19:9  259
19:12–29  70, 255
19:21  110
19:24–25  70
19:28–29  70
19:29  256
19:29 LXX  261
19:30–38  258

20:9  254
24:13  292
24:16  292
24:48  244
27:36 LXX  310
28:12 LXX  74
29:33  172
34:5 LXX  75
36:32  290
37:5  74
38:24 LXX  72
39:10  261
40:5  74
42:7  108
42:30  108
49:3  270

**Exodus**

2:11  200
2:11–12  82
3:5–6  225
3:10  64

6:3 LXX   212
7:4   64
7:5 LXX   64
9:27   107, 254
9:27 LXX   59
9:28   222
10:4   254
10:15 LXX   85
12:15–16   104
12:37   62
12:51   64
12:51 LXX   64
13:3   64
13:3 LXX   64
13:9 LXX   64
13:14 LXX   64
13:16 LXX   64
14:13   54
15:2   54
15:11 LXX   77
15:24   108
15:26   222
16:2   108
16:6 LXX   64
16:7–9   108
16:12   108
17:2–3   108
18:1 LXX   64
18:18   276
19:9   60
20:2   60
20:2 LXX   64
20:10–11   104
20:25 LXX   75
22:7 LXX   330
22:8   330
23:7   107, 254
23:7 LXX   59
25:37   227
28:2   222
28:40   222
28:43 LXX   241
29:46 LXX   64
32:7   64
32:11   64
33:1   64
33:12 LXX   212
34:6–7   328
34:15 LXX   72
36:1–2   339
40:34–35   133, 223

## Leviticus

5:3 LXX   75
11:7   307
11:24 LXX   75

13:3 LXX   75
15:26   199
15:31   199
18   75n5
18:22   71
19:15   110
19:29 LXX   72
20:13   71
21:17–18   279
21:21   279
22:5–7   199
22:16 LXX   241
24:19–20   279

## Numbers

5:3 LXX   75
11:25–29   233
11:29   233
12:7   66
13:33   66
14:2   108
14:11   66, 108
14:11–12   66
14:11–12 LXX   65
14:18   328
14:22   108
14:26–35   66
14:27   108
14:29   108
14:32   108
14:35   108
14:36   108
15:37–41   92, 134
15:41 LXX   64
16   92
16:1–2   92
16:1–3   92
16:2–4   92
16:5   92
16:32–33   92
16:41   108
17:5   108
17:5–10   108
17:6 LXX   108
17:20 LXX   108
17:20–25 LXX   108
22–24   90, 91
22:1–4   90
22:5   288, 289
22:6   91
22:7   285
22:17   285
22:18   285
22:21–35   286
22:23   285
22:28   286, 287

22:30   286, 287, 288
22:31   285
22:31–35   287
22:32   285
22:34   285
23:7   289
23:22 LXX   64
24:3   289
24:11   91
24:13   91
24:14   91, 285
24:15   289
24:17   229
24:25   91, 285
25   91
25:1–5   285
25:9   91
26:9   92
26:9–11   92
26:10   92
26:54 LXX   196
26:64–65   66
27:3   92
31:8   285, 289
31:16   91, 285
33:9   292

## Deuteronomy

1:27 LXX   64
3:24   273
4:3 LXX   266
4:19   284
4:20 LXX   64
4:33   222
4:37   47
5:6 LXX   64
5:15 LXX   64
5:25–26   222
6:4   60
6:4–9   134
6:12 LXX   64
6:14 LXX   266
7:9   66
7:10 LXX   326
7:16   250
8:14 LXX   64
8:15   292
8:17   273
8:19 LXX   266
8:20   222
9:12   64
9:26   64
9:29   64
10:15   47
10:17   110
10:18 LXX   106

11:2   221
11:13–21   134
11:28   284, 285
11:28–29   283
13:1–5   74
13:1–18   284
13:2 LXX   74
13:4   266
13:4 LXX   74, 226
13:5 LXX   64, 266
13:6 LXX   74
13:8   250
13:9 LXX   250
13:11 LXX   64
14:8   307
15:2   195
18:15   223
19:13   250
19:21   250
21:8   64
22:22   330
22:28   330
23:3–6   91
23:4   290
23:5   289
25:1   107, 254
25:1 LXX   59
26:8 LXX   64
27:15–26   137
28:14 LXX   266
28:15   283
28:28–29   198
28:45   283
28:50   110
29:4   261
29:22–24   255
29:24 LXX   64
29:25   64
29:27   283
30:17   284
31:16 LXX   72
32:15   134
32:22   73, 125, 322
32:32   70
32:46   227
33:2   32, 105
33:3 LXX   105n5
33:18 LXX   210
33:21 LXX   106
33:26   223
34:5–6   32
34:6   80, 81

## Joshua

5:14   60
6:24   256

13:22  91
24:9–10  91
24:29  45, 173
24:30 LXX  45n4,
  173

## Judges

1:24–25  202
2:8  45, 173
2:8 LXX  45n4
2:12  72
2:12 LXX  266
2:17 LXX  266
2:19 LXX  266
5:4–5  105
5:14  96
9:33  228
17:10 Theod.  182
20:36–40  256

## 1 Samuel

2:10  330
3:9–10 LXX  45n4
4:10 LXX  210
7:10  330
10:6  233
10:10  233
12:23  284
15:3  250
17:23  307
19:20  233
19:23  233
22:14  66
23:10–11 LXX  45n4
28:6  74
28:15  74
29:6  203

## 2 Samuel

4:6  247
5:2  95
7:7  95
7:23  64
7:27–28 LXX  45n4
22:20  223
23:2  233
23:4  228

## 1 Kings

1:33  173
1:36  137
1:41  46
1:49  46

4:7 LXX  190
4:29  339
5:1 LXX  190
8:10–11  133, 223
8:28 LXX  45n4
8:36 LXX  212
8:51  64
11:10 LXX  266
11:38 LXX  45n4
13:30  88
18:5  292
18:36 LXX  45n4
20:19 LXX  307
21:19  307
22:13 LXX  226
22:22–23  237
22:38 LXX  307

## 2 Kings

5:1  110
10:23  173
11:16  202
13:2 LXX  266
18:12  45, 173
18:12 LXX  45n4
18:34  316
19:4  243
19:6  243
19:15  134
19:19  134
19:22  243
21:8  45
21:8 LXX  45n4
23:11  202

## 1 Chronicles

1:1–3  104
1:43  290
12:22  273
16:36  137
17:21  64
29:11  39n35, 273
29:29  227

## 2 Chronicles

6:27 LXX  212
9:29  227
12:15  227
18:21–22  237
19:7  110
19:9 LXX  127
26:5 LXX  127
32:32  230

32:33  222
36:16 LXX  115, 316

## Ezra

4:24  246
5:1  230
6:14  230
10:18  330

## Nehemiah

5:9 LXX  127
5:13  137
9:30  233
10:29  173
10:30 LXX  173
13:2  91

## Esther

1:8  233
3:7  261
5:1  220
7:5  270

## Job

5:1  105
7:21  199
9:2  274
9:7  228
13:7  294
13:10  110
15:15  105
21:18  292
22:8  110
24:2  125
24:9  125
24:12–13 LXX  304
24:13 LXX  304
25:3  105
32:21–22  110
34:19  110
34:23  220
37:22  222
38:1  292
38:9  292
40:9  330
40:10  222
41:24  251
42:17 LXX  290

## Psalms

1:1  115, 254, 315
1:5  254
1:6  254

2  224, 225
2:6  224, 225
2:7  224, 225
2:8–9  224
2:9  226
2:11 LXX  127
3:4  225
3:5 LXX  225
5:7  127
5:8 LXX  127
7:11  241
7:12 LXX  241
7:12–16  328
8:5  222
8:6 LXX  222
10:5 LXX  59, 107,
  254
11:5  107, 254
13:1 LXX  229
14:1  229
14:1 LXX  210, 225
15:1  210, 225
18:12 LXX  45n4
19:13  45n4
22:16  307
22:20  307
23:1  95
23:2 LXX  320
23:5 LXX  134
24:2  320
24:5  134
24:5 LXX  134
25:5  134
26:8  133, 223
26:9 LXX  134
26:11 LXX  284
27:9  134
27:11  284
28:1 LXX  222
29:1  222
29:5 LXX  214
30:4  214
31:8 LXX  89, 285
32:6 LXX  319
32:8  89, 285
32:16 LXX  273
33:6  319
33:16  273
35:1 LXX  173
35:16  115, 315
36  173
36:7 LXX  286
36:16 LXX  303
36:38 LXX  254
37:7  286
37:13 LXX  294
37:16  303

37:38   254
38:12   294
40:14 LXX   137
41:4 LXX   316
41:11 LXX   316
41:13   137
42:3   316
42:3 LXX   225
42:10   316
43:2 LXX   253
43:3   225
44:1   253
47:2 LXX   225
47:4   201
48:1   225
51:7 LXX   210
52:5   210
54:20 LXX   136
55:19   136
57:11 LXX   254
58:10   254
61:3 LXX   134
61:7 LXX   134
62:2   134
62:6   134
63:1   293
64:6 LXX   134
65:5   134
68:17   105
70:19   221
70:21 LXX   196
71:18 LXX   134
71:19 LXX   137
71:21   196
72:18   134
72:19   137
74:20   228
77:22 LXX   66
77:50 LXX   250
78:9 LXX   134
78:10 LXX   316
78:21–31   66
78:22   66
78:50   250
78:68   47, 201
79:9   134
79:10   316
79:13   95
80:14 LXX   89, 285
81:13   89, 285
82:5   228
85:10 LXX   134
86:10   134
86:15   328
89:4 LXX   325, 326
89:5   105
89:7   105

90:3   325
90:4   325, 326
90:5–11   325
90:10   325
90:12   325
93:4 LXX   294
94:1 LXX   134
94:4   294
95:1   134
95:7   95
95:7 LXX   222
95:11–12 LXX   134
96:7   222
96:8 LXX   134
96:11 LXX   228
96:11–12   134
97:8   134
97:11   228
98:9 LXX   225
99:9   225
100:3   95
100:6 LXX   89, 285
101:6   89, 285
102:4 LXX   187
103:4   187
103:8   328
103:32 LXX   270
104:32   270
105:21 LXX   64
106:16–18   92
106:21   64
106:25–26   66
108:28 LXX   45n4
109:28   45n4
112:4   228
113:10 LXX   316
115:2   316
115:7 LXX   45n4
116:16   45n4
118:23 LXX   45n4
118:30 LXX   244
118:105 LXX   227
118:125 LXX   45n4
118:140 LXX   45n4
118:176 LXX   284
119:23   45n4
119:30   244
119:105   227
119:176   284
120:3–4 LXX   247
120:8 LXX   203
121:3–4   247
121:8   203
132:3   29
133:1 LXX   173
134:1   173
134:1 LXX   173

135:1   173
142:5 LXX   253
142:12 LXX   45n4
143:5   253
143:8 LXX   294
143:11 LXX   294
143:12   45n4
144:7 LXX   214
144:8   294
144:11   294
145:7   214
145:8 LXX   198
146:8   198
147:9 LXX   212
147:20   212
148:5   319

**Proverbs**

1:1 LXX   306
1:15   285
1:15 LXX   89
1:16   212
1:22   115, 315
1:27   256
2:5 LXX   177
2:6   339
2:13   285
2:13 LXX   89
2:16   284
2:17   69
3:14   303
3:33   283
4:18–19   228
4:20   227
5:1   227
6:10   247
6:34 LXX   264
8:11   303
8:19   303
8:20 LXX   304
9:7–8   115, 315
10:7 LXX   214
10:16   107
10:16 LXX   59
10:20   107
10:20 LXX   59
10:24–25   107
10:24–25 LXX   59
10:28   107
10:28 LXX   59
10:30   107, 254
10:30 LXX   59
10:32   107
10:32 LXX   59
12:28 LXX   304
13:1   115, 315

14:6   115, 315
14:26 LXX   127
15:16 LXX   95
15:16–17   303
16:8   303
16:17 LXX   304
16:19   303
16:31 LXX   304
16:32   303
17:1   303
17:23 LXX   304
18:5   110
18:21   182
19:1   303
19:25   115, 315
19:27   69
19:29   115, 315
21:9   303
21:16   284
21:16 LXX   304
21:18   261
21:19   303
21:21 LXX   304
21:24 LXX   270
23:17 LXX   127
23:29   88
24:33   247
25:7   303
25:13   66
25:14   96
25:24   303
26:11   306, 307
27:5   303
28:6   303
28:12   254
28:18   285
28:18 LXX   89
29:25   60

**Ecclesiastes**

1:5   228
3:16–17   107
3:16–17 LXX   59
10:16   279
12:3   246

**Song of Songs**

1:8 LXX   210
7:6 LXX   279
7:7   279

**Isaiah**

1:9   70
1:10   70
2:2   115

2:3 285
2:3 LXX 89
2:4 312
2:5 228
3:1 60
3:4 LXX 115
3:9 70
5:1–30 88
5:7 LXX 106
5:11 279
5:18–20 313
5:20 228
5:27 247
6:3 60
6:9 261
8:2 66
8:9 300
9:7 335
9:14 LXX 110
9:15 110
10:33 60
11:4–5 335
11:9 225
13:6 228, 329
13:9 228, 329
13:15 300
13:19 70
15:1 312
17:1 312
19:16 LXX 127
21:3 261
24:3 276
24:3 LXX 187
25:1 253
25:9 134
29:6 73, 125, 322, 330
29:18 261, 292
30:27 73, 125, 322
30:30 73, 125, 322
30:31 300
30:33 73, 125, 322
32:16–19 335
33:1 300
33:3 330
33:7 127
33:14 73, 125, 322
34:4 329
34:8 264
34:8–10 255
35:7 292
37:16 134
37:20 134
37:26 253
40:8 312
40:10 LXX 106
41:1 312

41:8 LXX 47
41:9 48, 183, 201
41:9–10 48
42:1 48, 201, 224
42:6 47, 48, 183, 201
42:8 183
42:8 LXX 183
42:12 183
42:12 LXX 183
42:19 LXX 173
42:21 183
43:1 47
43:4 48
43:18 253
44:2 LXX 47, 48
44:3 293
44:6 134
44:8–20 134
45:3–4 47
46:5–13 134
46:13 LXX 326
48:12 47, 48, 183, 201
48:15 48, 183, 201
49:1 47, 48
49:8 48
51:2 47, 183, 201
51:2 LXX 47
51:6 329
52:5 243
52:5 LXX 243
53:6 224, 284
54:6 47, 48
54:17 300
55:7 69
56:1 LXX 106
56:7 225
56:10 247
57:13 225
58:10 228
59:7 212
60:1 229
60:21 335
60:22 334
61:1 233
63:7 183
64:1–3 105
65:2 LXX 266
65:17 334
66:2 271
66:5 271
66:15–16 73, 125, 322
66:16 330
66:22 334
66:24 73, 125, 322

## Jeremiah

1:1 312
1:10 96
2:13 293
2:17 285
3:20 LXX 76
4:10 60
4:24 270–71
5:12–24 313
5:14 312
5:21 261
5:24 229
6:13 237
6:19 227
7:5 LXX 106
13:9 85
13:14 250
13:17 95
14:3 292
14:13–16 232
14:14–15 237
16:20 134
17:15 316
19:3 254
20:1 LXX 226
22:13–17 88
22:18 88
23:1–4 88
23:14 70
23:16 232
23:16 LXX 226
23:21–22 232
23:25 LXX 74
23:25–26 237
23:26 232
23:31 232, 247
23:32 237
25:3 312
25:4 45
25:13 103
25:30 330
25:32 292
27:9 74
27:24 LXX 330
30:7 69
31:1 300
32:30 LXX 226
32:32 LXX 292
33:7–8 237
33:11 237
33:16 237
34:9 237
34:9 LXX 74
34:15 237
35:1 237
36:1 237

36:8 237
39:18 66
39:21 64
49:18 70
50:24 330
50:40 70

## Lamentations

4:6 70

## Ezekiel

5:11 250
7:4 250
7:6 LXX 250
7:8 LXX 250
7:9 250
9:3 77
10:4 77
10:5 222
10:18 77
10:22 77
11:8 254
12:2 261
12:21–25 317
13:2–9 232
13:5 228, 329
13:9 237
13:17 232
16:52 LXX 85
20:30 LXX 72
22:28 237
28:7 241
28:14 225
30:3 228, 329
33:31 301
33:31–32 312
34 95
34:2 95
34:8–10 95
34:10 LXX 95
34:18–19 95
34:31 95
38:21–23 256

## Daniel

1:17 74
2:23–26 LXX 212
2:28–29 115
2:28–30 LXX 212
2:37 222
2:44 85
2:45 115
3:25 187
3:27 284

3:28 LXX 241
3:31 LXX 241
3:92 LXX 187
4:1 49
4:1 Theod. 176
4:3 203
4:17 136
4:30 222
4:37 LXX 176
6:21 LXX 45n4
6:25 49
6:26 168
6:26 Theod. 176
7:8 96, 109, 294
7:10 105, 106
7:14 85, 203
7:20 109, 294
7:23–27 270
7:27 LXX 203
9:10 222
9:15 LXX 64
10:11 271
10:13 81
10:14 115
10:21 81, 272
10:21 Theod. 81
12:1 81, 272
12:1 Theod. 81
12:2 124

**Hosea**

1:2 195
1:2 LXX 72
2:1 200
2:7 LXX 72
2:23 48
2:25 MT 48
2:25 LXX 48
3:5 115
4:1 LXX 177
4:12 LXX 72
4:13 LXX 72

5:3 LXX 72
6:6 LXX 177
8:7 256
9:7 LXX 233
9:9 LXX 85
10:13 66
13:4 64
13:15 241
14:9 284
14:10 LXX 284

**Joel**

1:15 228, 329
2:1 225, 228, 329
2:2 292, 293
2:11 228, 329
2:12–13 328
2:13 328
2:17 316
2:21–32 228, 329
2:28 74, 233
2:30 73, 125, 322
3:1 LXX 74, 233
3:2 312
3:12 312
3:14 228, 329
3:16 330
3:17 225
3:18 228, 329
4:17 LXX 225

**Amos**

1:3–2:3 256
3:7 45
4:11 70, 125
4:13 292
5:9 241
5:18 228, 329
5:20 228, 329
6:1–3 88
9:10 313

**Obadiah**

15–21 228, 329
16 225

**Jonah**

1:9 LXX 45n4
2:7 LXX 187
4:2 328

**Micah**

1:2–5 105
1:4 330, 334
2:10 276
2:10 LXX 187
4:1 115
4:3 312
6:5 289
7:10 316
7:14 334

**Nahum**

1:3 328
1:6 73, 125, 322, 330
3:18 247

**Habakkuk**

2:3 326
2:6–20 88
2:18 66
3:1–19 105

**Zephaniah**

1:7 228, 329
1:14 69, 228, 329
1:15 292, 293
1:18 73, 125, 322, 330
2:4 96

2:9 70
3:4 LXX 233
3:8 73, 125, 322
3:11 225

**Haggai**

1:7 229
1:12 222

**Zechariah**

3 126
3:1 81
3:1–2 32, 81
3:2 81, 83, 125, 126
3:4 126, 127
4:6 233, 273
6:15 222
7:12 233
8:3 225
12:2 LXX 106
12:4 288
13:2 LXX 237
14:1 228, 329
14:1 LXX 106
14:1–21 228, 329
14:5 105

**Malachi**

2:5 LXX 127
2:17 223, 313, 316
3:1 LXX 106
3:2 330
3:13 107
3:19 LXX 330
3:20 229
4:1 73, 125, 322, 330
4:5 69, 228, 329

# New Testament

**Matthew**

1:2–3 1
1:20 74
1:24 211
2:6 1, 237
2:12–13 74
2:19–22 74
3:8 329
3:10 96

3:17 223
4:5 121
4:16 99
4:17 225
4:18 172
4:20 243, 285
4:21 47, 183, 201
4:22 243, 285
5:18 329

5:19 305
5:20 203
5:21 253
5:25 241
5:28 109, 281
5:33 253
5:40 128
5:43–48 196
6:9 200

6:10 203, 334
6:13 132, 137, 203, 262
6:19–20 322
6:23 99
6:24 267
6:33 229, 315
7:6 307
7:11 262

7:13    240
7:15    237
7:15–23    238
7:17–19    96
7:21    203
7:21–27    203
8:6    261
8:12    98, 293
8:27    333
8:29    261
9:3    77, 243, 271
9:13    123
9:15    210
10:2    172
10:2–3    46
10:3    2, 4
10:4    1
10:10    128, 340
10:14–15    71
10:15    70, 264
10:17    250
10:23    317
10:28    93, 132
10:32–33    60, 240
11:3    333
11:4    260
11:12    125, 203
11:13    103
11:21    58
11:22    264
11:23    70
11:24    70, 264
11:26    202
12:7    123
12:18    48, 201
12:29    125
12:33    96
12:36    107, 197, 264
12:41–42    256
12:42    339
12:43–45    302
12:46    2
13:13–17    261
13:14    230
13:14–15    224
13:17    224
13:19    125
13:22    197
13:39    271
13:40    99
13:41    106, 271
13:49    271
13:55    2, 4, 44, 46
13:57    44
14:3    213
14:24    261
15:2–3    56

15:3    305
15:6    56
15:7    103
15:8    237
15:14    198
15:19    238
16:16    172
16:16–18    172
16:17    46
16:17–18    172
16:23    232
16:25–26    261
16:27    271
16:27–28    221
16:28    226, 317
17:1    225
17:1–5    139, 220
17:3    150
17:4    150
17:5    150, 223
17:9    225
18:3    203
18:7    253, 254
18:8    73, 99
18:10    267
18:12–13    284
18:15    106
18:15–20    126
19:16    124
19:17    305
19:23–24    203
19:29    124
20:3    197
20:4    210
20:6    197
20:13    277
20:18    256
20:19    115
21:5    287
21:21    126
21:25    225
21:32    304
21:33    120n1
21:41    93
22:1–14    46
22:13    98, 293
23:8    195
23:13    203
23:13–36    89
23:16–17    198
23:19    198
23:23    123, 192
23:24    198
23:29    120n1
23:30    317
23:32    317
23:33    83

24:3    219
24:6    208
24:11    114, 237
24:11–13    242
24:14    334
24:23–24    114
24:24    237, 238
24:25    113, 312
24:27    219
24:29–30    317
24:30    219
24:31    271
24:34    317
24:35    329
24:36    329
24:37    219
24:39    219
24:43–44    329
24:50    333
25:1–13    148
25:1–46    317
25:5    247
25:11    340
25:30    98, 293
25:31    106, 271
25:40    210
25:41    73, 99
25:45    210
25:46    124, 264
26:14    1
26:17–30    94
26:25    1
26:42    310
26:47    1, 237
26:56    230
26:59    238
26:60    238
26:65    77, 243, 271
26:65–66    83
26:70    60
26:72    60
26:75    113
27:3    1, 256
27:29    115
27:31    115
27:36    69, 264
27:37    83
27:41    115
27:52    317
27:53    121
27:54    69, 264
27:64    98, 295, 302
28:5    271
28:7    241

**Mark**

1:11    223, 225
1:15    203, 225
1:24    93
1:44    199
2:13–17    14
2:14    243, 285
2:17    47, 183, 201
3:16    172
3:18    3, 4
3:19    1
3:21    44
3:29    83
3:32    2
3:32–35    195
4:12    224, 261
4:19    109, 188, 197, 280
4:22    330
4:37    292
4:38    211
4:39    211
5:7    261
5:33    271
6:3    2, 4, 44, 46
6:9    128
7:3    56
7:5    56
7:6    103, 237
7:8    232
7:8–9    56
7:22    60, 243, 245
7:24    318
7:37    227
8:18    261
8:33    232
8:38    106
8:38–9:1    221
9:1    203, 219, 317
9:2    225
9:2–7    139, 220
9:7    223, 309
9:9    225
9:32    113
9:34    82
9:47    203
10:6    318
10:15    203
10:17    124
10:23–25    203
10:30    124
10:33    256
10:34    115
11:22    191
11:23    126
12:6    309

12:14   232
12:24   284
12:27   284
12:36   233
12:40   246
13:1   333
13:5–6   114
13:9   250
13:19   318
13:21–22   114
13:22   237, 238
13:23   113, 312
13:26   219
13:27   106
13:30   317
13:31   329
13:32–37   329, 332
14:10   1
14:12–26   94
14:43   1
14:58   120n1
14:63   128
14:64   256
14:68   60
14:70   60
14:72   113
15:8   208
15:20   115
15:40   4
15:43   123, 270

## Luke

1:2   220
1:6   133
1:9   174
1:13   271
1:17   237
1:21   333
1:29   333
1:30   271
1:38   113, 133
1:39   1
1:44   134
1:47   134
1:50   123
1:51   136
1:55   317
1:56   305
1:58   123
1:67   233
1:69   54
1:70   312
1:77   54
1:78   123, 229
1:79   99, 293
1:80   343

2:8   132
2:9–10   271
2:20   224
2:22   199
2:25   123
2:29   60, 113
2:38   123
2:40   343
2:45   305
2:52   232
3:8   329
3:9   96
3:11   128
3:22   223, 225
3:30   1
3:33–34   1
3:37–38   104
4:16   130
4:21   40
4:34   93
5:8   172
5:14   199
6:14   172
6:16   1, 2, 3
6:23   317
6:26   237, 317
6:29   128
6:43–44   96
7:22   224
7:25   279
7:39   333
8:3   14
8:10   261
8:14   278, 280
8:23   292
8:24   211
8:28   261
8:29   132
8:40   333
8:45   240
8:47   271, 318
9:3   128
9:8   253
9:19   253
9:26–27   221
9:28   225
9:28–35   139, 220
9:31   215
9:34–35   223
9:35   223
9:37   225
9:43   221
9:45   113
10:7   340
10:12   70
10:13   58
10:24   224, 260

10:25   124
10:37   123
11:4   262
11:13   262
11:20   203
11:21   132
11:24–26   302
11:31   339
11:31–32   256
11:42–52   89
11:49   226
12:5   136
12:9   60
12:15   245, 342
12:18   120n1
12:21   322
12:35–40   148
12:36   123
12:36–38   123
12:39–40   329
12:41–48   45
12:45   229, 317
12:46   333
12:47–48   304
12:54   96
12:57   210
14:7–14   46
14:8–11   94
14:9   98
14:15–24   46
14:18   55
15:2   123
15:18   225
15:21   225
15:22   241
16:13   267
16:17   329
16:19–31   264
16:21   307
16:25   182
17:6   96
17:22–37   257
17:27   254
17:29–30   70
17:30   257
18:17   203
18:18   124
18:25   203
18:30   124
18:34   113
19:9   54
20:47   246
21:12   250
21:15   339
21:19   194
21:27   219
21:33   329

22:3   1
22:7–23   94
22:15   109
22:29–30   203
22:32   209
22:47   1
22:48   1
22:57   60
22:61   113
22:63   115
22:71   224
23:4   330
23:11   115
23:17   55
24:8   113
24:27   230, 340
24:32   340
24:39   128
24:45   340

## John

1:1   175
1:1–3   319
1:14   210
1:18   175
1:20   240
1:37   243, 285
1:42   172
2:6   199
2:19   333
3:5   203
3:15–16   124
3:16   66, 94, 196, 328
3:19   99, 228
3:20   106, 128
3:21   201, 330
3:25   199
3:27   225
3:32   224
3:34   234
3:36   124
4:6   292
4:13–14   293
4:14   99
4:20   317, 318
4:42   224, 253, 254
4:52   104
4:54   310
5:24   124
5:35   227
5:37   224
5:39   124, 340
5:44   134
6:15   125
6:31   317
6:40   124

6:41   108
6:43   108
6:47   124
6:51   99
6:54   124
6:58   99
6:60   108
6:61   108
6:68   172, 182
6:71   1
7:3   2, 44
7:5   2, 44
7:10   2
7:17   231, 234
7:32   108
7:37   69
7:37–39   293
8:12   253, 254
8:19   316
8:20   113
8:31–36   298
8:34   299, 300
8:56   65
9:5   253, 254
9:24   310
9:40–41   198
10:12   125
10:28   66, 99, 124, 328
10:28–29   125
10:33   83
11:11–13   317
11:29   241
11:40   133
11:50   237
12:4   1
12:28   225
12:41   65, 223
13–16   207
13:2   1
13:6   172
13:9   172
13:15   257
13:24   172
13:26   1
13:29   1
13:34   305
13:34–35   305
13:36   172
13:38   60
14:6   210
14:15   305
14:21   305
14:22   2
14:28   273
15:10   305
15:12   305

15:15   219
16:8   106
17:3   134
17:5   319
17:11–12   48, 122
17:12   66, 132, 240, 328
17:26   219
18:2–3   1
18:5   1
18:10   172
18:15   172
18:25   60, 172
18:27   60
18:29   222, 232, 274
18:35   203
18:38   330, 337
19:4   330, 337
19:6   337
19:23   128
19:24   174
19:25   4
19:31   69
20:2   172
20:6   172
20:9   230
20:28   175
21:2   172
21:3   172
21:7   172
21:14   310
21:15   95
21:16   95
21:17   95
21:18–19   139, 150, 212
21:22   243, 285
21:22–23   317

Acts

1:7   136, 329
1:13   2, 3
1:14   2, 2n3, 44
1:16   1, 113, 233, 312
1:17   174
1:18   278
1:25   1
2:5–11   14
2:14   113
2:15   279
2:16   40, 103
2:17   74, 115, 315
2:17–18   233
2:19   73, 125, 322, 330
2:20   69, 228, 329

2:28   219
2:31   128
2:33   185
2:37   340
2:46   134
3:5   333
3:6   196
3:13   317
3:19–21   334
3:21   312
3:23   237
3:25   317
3:26   229, 315
4:10   237
4:12   54
4:16   240
4:19   210
4:20   224
4:24   60
4:36–37   14
4:37   196
5:1   14
5:17   239
5:20   182
5:28   241
5:34   185
5:37   1
6:1   14, 108
6:7   56, 191
6:9   14
6:10   339
6:11   83, 224
6:14   224
7:2   223
7:8   202
7:13   310
7:17   237
7:25   54
7:26   277
7:33   121
7:35   240
7:46   210
7:47   120n1
7:51   208
7:53   19, 77
7:55   133, 223
8:3   250
8:7   117
8:25   305
8:27–30   168
8:32   230, 287
8:33   182
9:11   1
9:31   120
9:36   201
10   15
10:2   201

10:5   172
10:15   310
10:20   126
10:24   333
10:33   227
10:36   50
10:42   106
10:44   113
11:9   225
11:16   113
11:17   60
11:28   134, 208
12:4   132
12:5   69, 264
12:12–17   14
12:17   2, 2n3
12:22   222, 232
13   36
13:1   14
13:6   237
13:10   284, 285
13:13   305
13:15   36, 130
13:23   185
13:26   54
13:27   130
13:28   330, 337
13:36   317
13:47   54
14:2   241
14:14   114, 313
14:15–17   134
14:16   89
14:22   203, 209, 282
15:5   239
15:7   253
15:7–12   338
15:9   199
15:13   2, 46
15:14   150, 172, 177, 237
15:21   130, 253
15:22   1
15:23   49
15:25   309
15:26   60
15:27   1
15:30–31   36
15:32   1, 209, 312
15:40   59, 176
15:41   209
16:6   288
16:6–7   212
16:9–10   74
16:10   211
16:16   117
16:17   45n4, 284

16:23   69, 264
17:18   157, 296, 327
17:24–31   134
17:28   31, 103
17:30–31   328
17:31   106, 327
18:9   74
18:10   237
18:23   209
18:25   284
18:26   284
19:6   233
19:9   284
19:13   117
19:19   106
19:20   136
19:23   284
19:23–27   134
19:27   221
19:37   77, 243, 271
19:40   286
20:17–38   166
20:21   329
20:28   95
20:28–29   95
20:29–30   114
21:10–11   212
21:18   2
21:25   342
22:4   250, 284
22:11   223
22:14–15   224
22:16   199
22:20   132
23:3   286
23:9   330
23:10   125
23:21   123
23:26   49
23:35   132
24:5   239
24:11   317
24:14   284
24:15   123, 208
24:17   201
24:20   337
24:22   284
24:25   193
25:7   222, 232, 274
25:18   83, 222
26:2   338
26:5   239
26:6   316
26:11   243–44
26:17   237
26:18   99, 228
26:20   329

26:26   318
27   97
27:10   208
27:34   54
27:41   333
27:43   288
28:6   333
28:7   196
28:16   132
28:17   237
28:22   239
28:25   233
28:26   261
28:26–27   224
28:31   60

## Romans

1:1   45, 47, 173
1:2   121, 230, 340
1:4   60
1:6   47
1:7   47, 49, 56, 60, 175, 309
1:8–15   179
1:13   288, 340
1:16   54, 229, 315
1:16–17   175
1:18   59n7, 210, 263
1:18–23   264
1:20–21   177
1:21   228
1:23   133
1:24   9, 109
1:25   135, 137
1:26–27   275
1:27   98, 295
1:29   245
1:29–31   117
2:1   256
2:2–3   246
2:4   267, 338
2:7   124, 194, 222
2:8   210
2:10   50, 222
2:12   66, 328
2:13   274
2:15   229
2:16   106
2:19   99, 198, 228
2:24   77, 243, 244, 271
2:28   128
2:29   232
3:3   192
3:7   133

3:8   18, 77, 243, 246, 271, 340
3:12   201
3:19   253, 254
3:21–26   175
3:21–27   340
3:23   133
3:24   59, 175
3:30   134
4:5   59n7, 191
4:7   261
4:9   191
4:11–13   191
4:15   340
4:16   191, 201
4:17   183
4:19–20   191
4:20   126, 316
5:1   50, 60, 176, 337
5:1–5   190, 191, 195
5:2   133, 203
5:3–5   191, 194
5:6   59n7
5:6–8   196
5:7   197n2, 270
5:7–8   48, 201
5:10   54, 176
5:11   60
5:13   253, 254
5:15   59, 175
5:16   246
5:19   197
5:20   196, 340
5:20–21   176
5:21   60
6:1   9, 18, 60, 196
6:1–14   199
6:4   182
6:5–23   298
6:6   230, 315
6:12   9
6:15   9
6:15–23   297
6:16   299, 300
6:17   56
7:1   210
7:3   281–82
7:7–8   109, 188
7:12   305
7:18   128, 266
7:25   128, 266
8:1   340
8:4–7   128, 266
8:6   50
8:9   117
8:15   200, 302
8:15–16   121

8:17–18   203
8:19–21   335
8:19–22   187
8:21   187
8:26–27   121
8:28   47
8:30   47, 183, 201
8:34   256
8:38   182
9:3   200
9:5   137, 175
9:6–13   47
9:8   185, 316
9:11   47, 201
9:12   183
9:22   240, 338
9:22–23   219
9:23   123
9:25   48, 237
9:29   70, 113, 312
10:10   54
10:18   113
11:1–2   237
11:5   201
11:8   261
11:13   210
11:20   133
11:21   250
11:26   59n7
11:28   48, 201
11:36   39, 130, 131n5, 137
12:1   55
12:10   195
12:17   133n6
12:19   52
13:1–7   160
13:2   246
13:3   201
13:6   189
13:11   54
13:12   99, 213, 228, 332
13:13   9, 60, 243, 279
14:15   93
14:17   50, 203
14:23   126
15:2   120
15:4   58, 312
15:8   185, 316
15:9   123
15:10   237
15:15   208
15:16   135
15:18   83, 270
15:20   120
15:31   260

16:2    123
16:7    114, 313
16:17    117
16:22    8
16:25    132, 133, 209
16:25–26    38n34, 130n2
16:25–27    38, 131n5
16:26    219, 226, 230
16:27    134, 135, 137

## 1 Corinthians

1:2    47, 56
1:3    49, 175
1:8    201, 329
1:9    47, 183, 201
1:10    55, 117
1:11    212
1:12    172
1:18    54, 66, 328
1:21–24    54
1:24    47
1:25    232
1:27–28    253, 254
1:29    133n6
2:3    127
2:3–5    339
2:5    232
2:6–7    339
2:7    136
2:11    232
2:14    117
3:10    120, 339
3:12    120, 185
3:13    330
3:14    120
3:17    85, 276
3:22    172, 182
4:13    243
4:14    309
4:17    309
4:20    203
5:1    244
5:1–5    126
5:5    228, 329
5:8    311
5:9    310
6:1    83, 270
6:8    277
6:9    203
6:9–10    190, 335
6:9–11    199, 243
6:12    18, 340
6:15–20    243
6:19    118
6:20    241

7:1    53
7:5    302
7:9    193, 303
7:20–24    298
7:22    241
7:23    241
7:37    55
7:37–38    227
7:39    210
8:1    120
8:4–6    134
8:5    60
8:11    66
9:1    114
9:5    2, 13, 16, 44, 172, 340
9:7    95
9:15    208
9:16    55
9:25    193
10:1–13    73
10:4    65
10:5    66
10:10    108
10:11    115
10:13    132, 263
10:14    52, 309
10:18    186
10:19–21    93
10:23    18, 120
10:27    46, 201
10:30    271
11:2    56
11:17–34    94, 280
11:18    117
11:19    239
11:22    267
11:23    56
11:32    256
12–14    212
12:3    219
12:10    230
12:13    45, 173
13:6    210
13:13    191, 196
14:3–5    120
14:4    121
14:12    120
14:14–15    121
14:16    137
14:25    202, 330
14:26    120
14:29    75
14:37    305
15:1    133, 219
15:1–8    9
15:3    56

15:3–4    340
15:5    114, 172, 313
15:6    317
15:7    2, 16, 114, 313
15:8    150
15:15    238
15:17–19    328
15:18    66, 317
15:20    317
15:23    219, 241, 334
15:23–24    220
15:32    150
15:33    31, 85, 103
15:42    187, 299
15:44    117
15:46    117
15:46–49    117
15:50    187, 203, 299
15:51    106, 317
15:58    52, 332
16:2    322
16:13    194
16:21    8, 43

## 2 Corinthians

1:1    56, 338
1:2    49, 175
1:3–4    179
1:6    194
1:7    186–87, 201
1:10    260, 262
1:14    323, 329
1:15–22    185
1:20    316
1:21    201
1:24    133
2:15    66
2:17    133, 234, 311
3:14–15    130
4:4    198
4:6    229
4:11    208
4:13    118
4:15    196
5:1    210
5:2    69
5:3–4    213
5:4    210
5:5    189
5:8    213
5:17    106
6:3–10    150
6:4    194
6:6–7    190
6:8    98
6:10    208

6:14    99, 228, 261
6:17    199
7:1    52, 127, 185, 199
7:2    85
7:3    113
7:11    53
8:1    59, 176, 219
8:5    229, 315
8:7    59, 176, 196
8:18    338
8:21    133n6
8:22    338
8:23    313, 338
9:1    209
9:5    210, 338
9:7    55
9:10    190
10:8    120
10:12    83
11:3    85
11:10    210
11:13    238
11:16–28    150
11:21    270
11:23    288
11:25–26    97
11:26    237
11:31    135
12:13    340
12:14    322
12:19    52, 120
12:21    9, 60, 243
13:2    113, 310
13:10    120

## Galatians

1:1    2, 45, 232
1:3    49, 175
1:5    39, 130, 131n5, 137
1:6    47, 59, 183, 201
1:9    113
1:10    45
1:11    219
1:11–2:14    150
1:13    259
1:15    47, 183, 201
1:17    305
1:18    172
1:19    44, 313
1:20    133n6
1:23    56, 191
2:4    237, 241
2:5    210
2:7–8    172
2:7–10    338

2:9   2, 46, 59, 172,
   176, 339
2:10   189, 200
2:11   172
2:11–21   338
2:12   2, 46
2:14   172, 210
2:17   337
2:18   302
3:1   58
3:2   56
3:5   56, 190
3:8   340
3:10   283
3:13   283
3:14   185
3:17   185, 316
3:19   19, 77
3:20   134
3:21   185, 316
3:22   340
3:28   45
4:1   210
4:3   330
4:4   115
4:6   121, 200
4:13   128
4:14   263
5:1   302
5:4   342
5:5–6   191, 195
5:8   47, 183, 201
5:10   246
5:13   128, 266, 297,
   298, 340
5:16–17   109, 188
5:19   60, 243
5:19–21   117, 190,
   243
5:20   117, 239
5:21   113, 203
5:22   192, 196
5:22–23   197
5:22–26   190
5:23   193
5:24   128, 241, 266
6:1   127, 128
6:8   187, 299
6:10   200, 266
6:11   8, 43, 147, 208
6:16   123

## Ephesians

1:1   56, 339
1:2   49, 175
1:3–6   179
1:4   48, 133, 201
1:5   201
1:9   219
1:13   54, 210
1:17   177, 223
1:18   201
1:19   136, 273
1:21   76, 267
2:3   109, 283, 295
2:3–4   123
2:4   94, 123
2:8   59, 175–76
2:20   120, 226
2:21   120
3:3   219
3:5   219, 233, 312
3:6   185
3:10   219
3:17   133
3:20   132
3:20–21   39, 130,
   131n5
3:21   137
4:1   47, 55, 183, 201
4:1–16   117
4:2   196
4:3   9, 50, 122, 200
4:4   47, 183, 201
4:5   56, 192
4:11   312, 313
4:11–12   95
4:11–16   120
4:12   120
4:13   177
4:14   96, 98, 295, 342
4:16   120
4:17–19   243
4:18   182, 228
4:19   9, 60, 245, 295
4:21   210
4:22   85, 213, 259,
   295
4:24   210
4:25   213
4:29   120
5:1   309
5:3   245
5:5   190, 199, 203,
   230, 315
5:8   228, 283
5:11   99, 106, 197,
   228
5:11–13   332
5:13   330
5:21   127
5:21–6:9   160
5:26   199
5:27   128, 133, 279
6:1   210
6:2   305
6:7   234
6:8   45, 173
6:10   136
6:11   133
6:12   99
6:13–14   133
6:14–17   190
6:15   50
6:18   121
6:19   219
6:21   219, 338
6:22   189

## Philippians

1:1   45, 56, 173
1:2   49, 175
1:3–11   179
1:6   48, 329
1:7   210
1:10   329
1:14   270
1:19   54
1:20   182, 311
1:22   219
1:23   109, 213
1:28   240
2:12   52
2:15   133
2:16   182, 329
2:25   210, 313, 338
2:28   302
2:29   123
3:2   307
3:6   133
3:9   337
3:14   201
3:19   98, 240
4:1   52
4:2   55
4:3   340
4:5   332
4:6   219
4:8   190, 192
4:12   262
4:14   227
4:17   196
4:20   39, 130, 131n5,
   137
4:22   266

## Colossians

1:1   338
1:2   49, 56, 175
1:3–14   179
1:4–5   191, 195
1:5–6   210
1:6   317
1:8   212
1:9   317
1:10   177, 343
1:11   136, 194
1:13   99, 203, 228,
   260, 262
1:16   76, 267, 305
1:17   133, 319
1:22   133
1:27   203, 219
1:28   339
2:1   128
2:7   120
2:8   56, 330
2:11–13   199
2:19   190
2:20   330
2:22   187
2:23   128, 266
3:1   173
3:5   190, 245, 295
3:8   190, 213
3:11   45
3:12   48, 201
3:12–14   190
3:15   47, 183, 201
3:16   202
3:18–4:2   160
3:25   277
4:5   332
4:7   219, 338
4:8   189
4:9   219
4:12   45, 133, 173
4:16   36, 130, 214,
   310, 339
4:18   8, 43

## 1 Thessalonians

1:1   49, 175, 313
1:2–11   179
1:3   60, 191, 194,
   195, 196
1:4   48
1:5   63
1:9–10   123, 329
1:10   260, 262
2:1   63
2:2   63
2:3   98, 295, 342
2:5   63, 91, 245, 278

2:5–6   110, 245
2:6   114
2:7   313
2:9   209, 211
2:11   63
2:12   47, 183, 184, 201
2:13   232
2:16   288
2:17   109, 200
2:19   219, 334
3:1–5   242
3:2   55, 282, 338
3:3–4   63
3:4   113, 211
3:6   209
3:12   196
3:13   106, 133, 209, 219, 282
4:1   55, 200, 211
4:2   329
4:3–8   243
4:4   262
4:5   109, 295
4:6   113
4:7   201
4:9   195, 209
4:9–10   196
4:10   196
4:11   69
4:13–14   317
4:15   219, 334
4:16   82
4:17   125, 202
5:1   209
5:1–2   211
5:1–11   329, 332
5:2   63, 220, 323, 331
5:3   54n1
5:4–5   99
5:4–6   329
5:7   279
5:8   191, 195
5:9   54, 60
5:11   55, 120
5:13   196
5:14   126
5:19–22   75, 212
5:20   230
5:20–22   238
5:23   48, 122, 133, 219
5:23–24   201
5:24   47, 183
5:27   36, 130, 168, 214

**2 Thessalonians**

1:2   49, 175
1:3   196
1:3–4   191
1:4   192, 194
1:5   203
1:5–9   220
1:6   210
1:6–10   329
1:7   106, 219, 271, 273
1:7–8   330
1:8   73, 125, 322
1:9   203
1:9–10   203
2:1   219, 334
2:1–12   220
2:2   75, 212, 228, 238, 323, 329
2:2–3   340
2:3   240, 242
2:5   75
2:10   66, 280
2:11   98, 295
2:12–13   210
2:13   54
2:13–14   183, 200
2:14   47, 184, 201, 203
2:15   9, 75
2:16   59, 176
2:16–17   133
2:17   282
3:2   260, 262
3:2–3   262–63
3:3   132, 133, 209, 282
3:5   211
3:6   56
3:6–15   126
3:10   211
3:12   55
3:15   127, 338
3:17   8, 43, 147

**1 Timothy**

1:1   134
1:2   49, 123
1:4   218, 227
1:6   294
1:9   59n7, 261
1:13   274
1:17   39, 130, 131n5, 134, 135, 137, 222
1:18   230

1:19   56
1:20   250
2:1   229, 315
2:3   134
2:4   328
2:5   134
2:7   192, 254
3:2–3   190
3:5   262
4:1   56, 98, 117, 242
4:1–3   114, 115, 315
4:3   288, 305
4:7   218, 283
4:8   185
4:10   134
4:12   196, 259, 267
4:13   130, 168
5:12   246
5:13   197
5:18   340
5:20   106
5:21   133n6
5:22   122
6:1   244
6:1–2   60, 240
6:2   267
6:5   91, 278
6:9   109, 188, 263
6:11   190, 191, 194, 196
6:12   47, 183, 201
6:13   133n6
6:14   122, 337
6:16   131n5, 135, 136, 137
6:17   136, 182, 202
6:21   56

**2 Timothy**

1:1   182
1:2   49, 123
1:9   47, 48, 136, 183, 201
1:11   254
1:12   132, 253
1:15   149
1:16–18   123
2:4   302
2:12   240
2:14   133n6
2:15   200, 210
2:16   59n7
2:16–17   149, 238
2:16–18   239
2:17–18   340
2:18   149

2:19   92
2:21   60
2:22   196
2:24   45
2:25   149
3:1   115, 230, 315
3:1–5   114
3:1–9   115, 239, 315
3:2   274
3:2–5   238
3:2–9   149
3:3   193
3:5   149
3:8   73
3:10   191, 196
3:11   260, 262
3:12   319
3:13   238, 239
3:16   230, 233, 340
4:1   106, 133n6, 203
4:1–2   332
4:1–18   166
4:2   106
4:3–4   114, 149, 238, 239
4:4   218
4:7   122, 192
4:9   200
4:10   136
4:15   342
4:17–18   260, 263
4:18   39, 130, 131n5, 137, 203, 344
4:21   200

**Titus**

1:1   45, 173
1:2   124, 136
1:3   134
1:4   49, 175
1:7   270
1:7–8   190
1:9   106
1:10   294
1:11   91, 278
1:12   31, 103, 197
1:13   106
1:14   218, 227
1:15   9
1:16   60, 240
2:2   194, 196
2:5   244
2:9   60
2:10   134, 192
2:12   59n7, 109, 136
2:13   123, 175

2:14   199, 261
2:15   106
3:1–2   190
3:2   77, 243, 271
3:3   109, 188, 278, 295
3:3–5   123
3:5   123, 199
3:6   202
3:7   124
3:9–10   117
3:10   310
3:12   200
3:14   197

## Philemon

1   338
3   49, 175
4–6   179
18   277, 278
19   8, 43
23–25   34

## Hebrews

1:1   58, 58n6, 317
1:2   115, 315
1:3   136, 199, 223, 319
1:8   203
1:8–9   175
1:9   128, 261
2:1   227
2:2   77, 201
2:7   222
2:9   222
2:14   136
2:15   127
3:1   201
3:7   233
3:8   263
3:10   208, 284
3:16–19   66
3:18–19   66
4:1   185
4:7   113
4:9   237
4:11   200, 257
4:13   133n6
5:7   132
5:12   302
5:14   283
6:1   191, 329
6:2   99
6:4   57, 64, 228
6:4–8   302

6:6   302
6:8   283
6:9   52
6:10   196
6:12   185
6:13   273, 316
6:15   185
6:17   185
6:19   201, 226
7:14   1
7:27   55
8:6   185
8:7   133, 310
8:8   1
8:10   237
9:2   121
9:10   128
9:14   133, 199
9:15   47, 183, 185, 201
9:17   201
9:19   305
9:26   115
9:26–28   57
9:28   310
10:2   64
10:9   310
10:15–16   233
10:17   261
10:22   199
10:22–24   191, 195
10:23   316
10:26   302
10:27   83
10:32   228
10:34   123
10:36   185, 316
10:36–37   148, 317
10:39   240, 261
11:3   319
11:4–33   191
11:4–38   73
11:5   102
11:7   54, 256
11:11   316
11:26   65
11:35   123
11:38   284
12:1   194, 213
12:2   98
12:11   283
12:15   59
12:22   106
12:23   106
13:1   195
13:2   318
13:4   185

13:7   259
13:9   96
13:15   135
13:18   319
13:20   95
13:21   131n5, 137

## James

1:1   2, 16, 44, 45, 46, 60, 173
1:2   263, 338
1:3–4   194
1:6   126
1:8   141
1:13–16   263
1:14   282
1:14–15   109
1:15   9
1:16   52
1:18   210
1:19   52, 241
1:21   213
1:27   122, 337
2:4   126
2:5   52
2:8   227
2:10   122, 202
2:13   123, 201
2:19   227
2:20   197
3:1   246
3:2   202
3:6   128, 197
3:10   283
3:11   292
3:13   259
3:15   117
3:17   123
3:17–18   190
4:1   278
4:3   278
4:4   197
4:6   59
4:8   141, 199
4:10   133n6
4:12   66, 93, 106, 132
4:14   182, 295
4:17   262
5:3   115, 315
5:7   185
5:7–8   148, 219, 317
5:8–9   332
5:10   257
5:11   194
5:18   302
5:19   210, 284

5:20   295

## 1 Peter

1:1   168, 173, 242, 338
1:1–2   168
1:2   49, 59, 175, 176, 337
1:3   60, 123
1:4   48
1:4–5   48, 122
1:5   48, 54, 115, 219
1:6   134, 151, 263, 295
1:7   185, 219, 222, 337
1:9   145, 282
1:10   59, 103, 343
1:10–11   54, 230, 311, 312
1:10–12   115
1:11   233
1:12   219, 310, 311
1:13   219, 311
1:13–17   332
1:14   9, 109, 188, 283, 295
1:15   47, 183, 201, 259
1:17   95, 127, 200
1:18   259, 311
1:19   133, 185, 337
1:20   115
1:21   191
1:21–22   191, 195
1:22   195, 196, 282
1:23   113n1
1:25   113n1
2:1   213
2:2   310, 343
2:5   120, 135
2:6   340
2:7   120
2:9   47, 99, 183, 198, 201, 228
2:9–10   237
2:11   52, 55, 109, 188, 282, 309, 338
2:12   151, 220, 259
2:13–17   160
2:14   91
2:15   151, 244
2:16   298
2:17   200
2:18   127
2:18–3:7   160

2:19–20   244, 343
2:20   151
2:21   201
2:22   337
2:24   254
2:25   95, 284
3:1   259
3:1–2   259
3:2   127, 220
3:4   133n6
3:6   151
3:7   343
3:9   201
3:11   201
3:13–17   244
3:13–22   151
3:14   254
3:15   208
3:16   259
3:17   303
3:18   57, 60
3:18–22   28, 67, 321
3:19–20   252
3:20   252, 255, 261, 282, 338
3:21   213, 321
4:1   151
4:2   232
4:2–3   9
4:3   60, 109, 117, 190, 243, 295, 316
4:3–4   244
4:4   77, 83, 243, 271
4:5   106
4:7   332
4:8   196, 263
4:10   343
4:10–11   120
4:11   131n5, 135, 137, 190
4:12   52, 263, 309, 338
4:12–19   151, 244
4:13   134, 219
4:18   59n7
4:19   282
5:1   55, 150, 187, 212, 219
5:2   95
5:2–3   95
5:4   95
5:5   343
5:9   200
5:10   47, 133, 183, 184, 201, 209, 282, 295, 343
5:10–11   39, 130

5:11   131n5, 135, 137
5:12   8, 55, 59, 133, 145, 146, 176, 219, 338, 343
5:14   337

## 2 Peter

1   159, 160
1:1   45, 139, 150, 168, 169, 171, 172, 173, 177, 192, 203, 206, 253, 257, 263, 335, 343
1:1–2   163, 169, 171, 180, 204, 344
1:2   49, 59, 145, 148, 154, 168, 169, 171, 175, 177, 183, 203, 267, 301, 304, 337, 343
1:2–3   148, 153, 154, 193
1:3   23, 47, 145, 148, 154, 168, 176, 177, 181, 182, 183, 185, 186, 192, 194, 197, 201, 262, 301, 304, 333, 344
1:3–4   145, 169, 179, 180, 181, 188, 191, 192, 195, 202, 214
1:3–11   164, 165, 169, 179, 208, 213, 214, 333
1:3–15   163, 179
1:3–3:17   169
1:3–3:18   169, 178
1:4   109, 180, 184, 185, 186, 187, 191, 194, 197, 208n1, 210, 214, 253, 267, 276, 295, 297, 299, 300, 301, 316, 317, 335
1:5   53, 151, 154, 176, 178, 180, 188, 189, 191, 197, 202, 213
1:5–6   148, 153, 343
1:5–7   187, 191, 196, 198, 201, 213, 214, 343
1:5–9   176, 179
1:5–10   202
1:5–11   169, 180, 188

1:6   145, 154, 176, 188, 191, 193
1:6–7   190, 262, 333
1:6–3:13   164
1:7   145, 191, 195, 200
1:8   23, 60, 145, 148, 153, 154, 175, 176, 177, 191, 193, 196, 197, 197n2, 198, 199, 203, 267, 301, 304
1:8–9   201
1:8–10   205, 208n1, 214
1:9   151, 191, 196, 197, 197n2, 199, 202, 209, 307
1:10   151, 178, 195, 199, 202, 213, 226, 263, 337, 338, 342
1:10–11   179
1:10–12   199
1:11   145, 175, 185, 189, 190, 192, 197, 202, 203, 226, 239, 267, 301, 313, 343
1:12   148, 167, 174, 205, 206, 207, 208, 208n1, 210, 211, 213, 230, 238, 244, 282, 310, 311, 312, 343
1:12–13   205, 214
1:12–15   149, 150, 165, 166, 167, 169, 178, 205, 206, 207, 218, 241, 309, 312
1:12–21   169, 206, 235
1:12–2:22   169, 205
1:13   145, 205, 206, 210, 211, 213, 279, 311, 338
1:13–14   206, 208
1:14   139, 150, 175, 193, 203, 211, 241, 267
1:14–15   210
1:15   151, 178, 200, 205, 206, 208, 208n1, 210, 211, 213, 238, 311, 337
1:16   23, 145, 174, 175, 203, 206, 216, 217, 219, 221, 222, 224, 225, 243, 245,

267, 285, 310, 316, 334
1:16–17   150
1:16–18   150, 166, 169, 174, 205, 206, 210, 216, 217, 226, 229, 235, 312
1:16–21   155, 169, 206, 216, 219, 234, 240, 309
1:16–2:10   163
1:17   133, 185, 219, 221, 223, 224, 225, 227, 259, 337, 338, 344
1:17–18   139, 220, 222, 232
1:18   142, 216, 221, 222, 223, 224
1:18–21   210
1:19   178, 201, 216, 229, 232, 283, 323, 344
1:19–20   229, 234, 315
1:19–21   153, 155, 156, 166, 169, 205, 206, 216, 226, 234, 235, 236, 312, 313
1:19–2:3   149
1:20   216, 227, 230, 231, 232, 314, 341
1:20–21   152, 206, 236, 237, 340
1:21   xi, 202, 222, 230, 231, 232
2   6, 159, 192
2:1   19, 60, 142, 151, 152, 153, 154, 155, 156, 158, 159, 174, 195, 198, 199, 202, 205, 206, 227, 234, 235, 236, 238, 239, 240, 241, 247, 254, 267, 284, 288, 300, 302, 303, 307, 321, 323, 341
2:1–3   149, 152, 165, 169, 194, 205, 235, 236, 238, 248, 312, 342
2:1–22   169, 235
2:1–3:3   152, 160, 162
2:1–3:13   158
2:2   60, 142, 151, 152, 158, 159, 194,

195, 210, 218, 236,
242, 245, 260, 282,
285, 295, 304
2:2–3   91, 278, 282
2:3   151, 152, 156,
158, 159, 199, 235,
236, 239, 240, 241,
244, 246, 282, 283,
318, 319, 321, 323,
341
2:4   62, 68, 70, 98,
159, 169, 248, 249,
250, 251, 252, 253,
255, 262, 263, 264,
268, 293, 322
2:4–8   248, 252, 266,
269
2:4–9   62
2:4–10   169, 195,
205, 235, 248
2:5   62, 132, 169,
175, 241, 248, 250,
251, 252, 255, 257,
260, 262, 263, 268,
295, 321, 334, 335,
342
2:5–6   59n7, 256,
262, 323
2:5–7   182, 262, 263,
335
2:5–9   259
2:6   59n7, 70, 73,
159, 224, 248, 252,
255, 257, 262, 268,
322
2:6–8   62
2:6–10   169, 248, 255
2:7   60, 71, 194, 243,
253, 257, 262, 263,
282, 295, 333, 342
2:7–8   248, 255, 256,
257, 262, 263
2:7–10   141
2:8   194, 232, 259,
260, 263
2:9   48, 156, 159,
195, 203, 228, 248,
251, 253, 256, 257,
258, 260, 262, 263,
265, 266, 267, 269,
293, 295, 322, 323
2:9–10   248
2:10   76, 77, 109,
151, 152, 153, 159,
187, 194, 243, 262,
265, 266, 269, 270,
271, 272, 274, 276,

277, 282, 294, 295,
297, 301, 316, 344
2:10–11   76, 148, 161
2:10–16   169, 205,
235, 269, 291
2:10–22   149, 163,
164, 238
2:11   159, 203, 222,
232, 267, 270, 271,
277, 284, 288
2:12   77, 84, 85, 159,
187, 193, 194, 239,
243, 271, 274, 276,
288, 297, 299, 300,
340
2:12–13   194
2:12–14   333
2:13   94, 128, 133,
149, 151, 152, 153,
156, 157, 159, 187,
210, 217, 238, 258,
263, 277, 281, 282,
284, 285, 289, 295,
296, 337, 338, 342
2:13–14   158, 296
2:13–16   155, 263
2:14   151, 152, 194,
195, 202, 238, 240,
241, 242, 243, 281,
282, 286, 289, 294,
295, 311, 328, 340,
342
2:14–15   278, 284
2:14–16   245
2:15   89, 91, 142,
151, 158, 159, 218,
240, 241, 243, 244,
258, 263, 277, 278,
283, 288, 289, 290,
304
2:15–16   155, 227,
283, 292, 297
2:16   155, 286, 294
2:17   70, 96, 98, 159,
227, 251, 264, 292,
293, 300, 322
2:17–18   291
2:17–20   205, 235
2:17–22   169, 198,
199, 205, 235, 269,
291
2:18   60, 76, 98, 151,
152, 159, 187, 191,
194, 195, 199, 202,
259, 260, 266, 267,
277, 282, 286, 293,
295, 297, 299, 300,

301, 307, 311, 316,
328, 342
2:18–19   152, 194,
240, 243, 260, 282
2:18–22   195, 240,
241, 242, 333
2:19   23, 142, 148,
151, 152, 153, 154,
156, 158, 187, 194,
238, 266, 276, 291,
293, 297, 300, 302,
316, 338, 340, 341
2:20   145, 148, 151,
153, 154, 175, 176,
177, 187, 193, 199,
203, 204, 208n1,
253, 267, 291, 295,
300, 303, 307, 313,
343
2:20–22   151, 158,
205, 206, 235, 241,
299
2:21   142, 151, 158,
175, 244, 254, 257,
263, 291, 301, 302,
303, 304, 306, 307,
333, 335
2:22   145, 194, 199,
299, 306
3   159, 160
3:1   52, 139, 145,
150, 168, 173, 178,
211, 214, 219, 242,
309, 310, 311, 312,
325, 337, 338, 341
3:1–2   149, 155, 159,
164, 167, 169, 178,
226, 308, 309, 314
3:1–4   165, 217
3:1–10   23
3:1–13   163, 257
3:1–18   169, 308
3:2   112, 113, 134,
147, 155, 174, 175,
203, 204, 219, 230,
267, 301, 305, 309,
311, 315, 343
3:2–3   8, 114, 160,
342
3:2–4   113, 227, 229,
231
3:3   109, 115, 159,
187, 194, 205, 216,
229, 238, 243, 266,
267, 270, 295, 308,
314, 316, 341, 342

3:3–4   116, 149, 151,
152, 153, 154, 216,
231, 235, 239, 271,
297, 311, 341
3:3–7   169, 203, 265,
308, 314, 324
3:3–9   240
3:3–10   151, 153,
274, 312
3:3–13   226
3:4   141, 141n1, 145,
147, 151, 152, 155,
156, 157, 184, 185,
219, 224, 229, 245,
246, 247, 308, 314,
316, 317n1, 318,
320, 324, 325, 326,
333, 340
3:4–5   198, 216
3:5   199, 314, 318,
321, 322, 325, 340
3:5–6   308
3:5–7   155, 238, 239,
247, 253, 255, 256,
264, 318, 329
3:5–10   316, 317
3:6   247, 314, 320,
321, 322, 328, 334
3:7   48, 59n7, 73,
125, 228, 240, 241,
247, 251, 263, 264,
293, 308, 314, 319,
320, 321, 322, 324,
326, 330, 332, 333,
334, 341
3:8   52, 142, 143,
145, 178, 199, 203,
309, 318, 324, 325,
337, 338, 341
3:8–9   185, 264, 332
3:8–10   170, 241,
242, 246, 267, 308,
318, 324
3:9   151, 156, 184,
185, 203, 210, 247,
316, 317, 324, 327,
328, 329, 334, 337,
338
3:10   73, 125, 145,
156, 203, 228, 239,
240, 264, 314, 322,
323, 324, 326, 328,
329, 330, 331, 332,
334, 335, 337, 344
3:10–11   318, 329
3:10–12   322, 333,
334, 336, 338

3:10–13   203, 220,
  247, 264
3:11   178, 203,
  208n1, 259, 262,
  265, 322, 325, 332,
  335
3:11–13   159, 170,
  194, 308, 332, 336
3:11–18   241
3:12   203, 217, 219,
  228, 239, 264, 316,
  323, 326, 329, 330,
  333, 339, 344
3:12–13   332, 337
3:13   175, 184, 185,
  254, 258, 263, 316,
  317, 322, 326, 329,
  333, 336, 337, 338,
  339, 344
3:13–14   333
3:14   52, 159, 178,
  195, 200, 203,
  208n1, 213, 279,
  309, 325, 330, 336,
  337, 338, 339, 341
3:14–18   164, 170,
  308, 336, 343
3:15   xii, 175, 195,
  203, 210, 267, 301,
  313, 325, 331, 336,
  337, 338, 339
3:15–16   139, 152,
  153, 154, 231, 238,
  297, 329, 336
3:16   141, 147,
  208n1, 229, 240,
  241, 247, 321, 323,
  336, 338, 339, 341,
  342
3:17   52, 98, 151,
  178, 191, 194, 195,
  202, 253, 260, 263,
  282, 286, 295, 309,
  325, 336, 338, 341,
  342
3:18   38, 59, 136,
  145, 148, 153, 154,
  159, 168, 169, 170,
  175, 176, 193, 196,
  203, 204, 228, 241,
  267, 301, 313, 336,
  343, 344
4:13   145
5:1   145

## 1 John

1:1–3   224
1:5   224
1:6   99, 201
1:7   199
2:3–5   122
2:7   52
2:7–8   305
2:11   198
2:16   281
2:16–17   9, 109
2:18   114
2:18–19   117
2:21   209
2:22   114
2:22–23   240
2:25   185
2:28   332, 334, 337
2:29   201
3:2   52
3:7   201
3:10   201
3:11–15   90
3:15   124
3:20   273
3:21   52
3:22   122
3:22–24   305
3:24   122
4:1   52, 237
4:1–3   75, 212, 238
4:4   273
4:6   98, 295, 342
4:7   52
4:7–12   196
4:8   196
4:10   94
4:11   52
4:16   94
4:17   195, 264
4:19   196
5:1   94
5:3   122
5:9   232
5:20   175

## 2 John

3   49, 59, 123
4   210
7   98
10   222

## 3 John

2   49

3–4   210
6   227

## Jude

1   12, 16, 41, 43, 46,
  50, 122, 144, 173,
  200
1–2   33, 35, 39,
  41, 43
1–3   51
2   6n6, 41, 43, 48,
  123, 129, 175, 176
3   9, 17, 18, 33, 35,
  37, 38, 40, 41, 43,
  51, 52, 53, 54, 57,
  58, 59, 64, 112,
  113, 119, 121, 122,
  131, 132, 134, 174,
  192, 305, 338
3–4   38, 39, 41, 51,
  52, 53, 56, 63, 75,
  134
3–23   41, 51
4   9, 14, 18, 19, 20,
  22, 23, 25, 31, 35,
  39, 41, 49, 50, 55,
  56, 57, 59, 63, 64,
  68, 70, 74, 76, 91,
  92, 93, 98, 105,
  107, 108, 112, 113,
  116, 122, 123, 126,
  129, 131, 132, 135,
  136, 153, 159, 176,
  177, 239, 240, 243,
  246, 254, 260, 295,
  340, 343
4–8   19, 109, 128
4–15   134
5   8, 12, 20, 33, 41,
  51, 62, 63, 64, 65,
  69, 74, 77, 84, 92,
  93, 108, 112, 122,
  167, 208, 237, 310,
  321, 328
5–6   32, 72
5–7   9, 22, 40, 41,
  42, 51, 58, 61, 63,
  74, 76, 77, 79, 87,
  93, 96, 101, 103,
  129, 252
5–8   41, 61, 62, 84,
  248, 250, 255
5–10   35
5–16   35, 58, 126,
  132

5–19   41, 51, 61, 112,
  119
5–23   36
5:7   112
6   5, 24, 26, 32, 48,
  62, 66, 69, 71, 72,
  74, 78, 84, 99, 101,
  122, 123, 159, 249,
  251, 252, 263, 322
6–7   72
6–8   14
7   33, 57, 62, 69, 70,
  73, 74, 76, 84, 122,
  123, 159, 255, 257,
  260, 261, 265, 266,
  295, 322
7–8   9, 128, 265
8   11, 19, 20, 22, 23,
  25, 40, 41, 42, 51,
  57, 60, 61, 62, 63,
  64, 66, 68, 72, 74,
  77, 79, 83, 84, 86,
  91, 92, 93, 101,
  108, 116, 129, 133,
  153, 159, 243, 266,
  267, 270, 271, 291,
  295
8–9   161
8–10   20, 22
9   12, 13, 26, 27, 28,
  31, 32, 40, 41, 42,
  51, 61, 74, 79, 81,
  85, 86, 93, 101,
  103, 112, 125, 126,
  127, 159, 270, 271,
  272
9–10   42, 61, 77,
  79, 87
10   20, 40, 41, 42,
  51, 57, 61, 62, 74,
  79, 83, 84, 85, 86,
  93, 101, 108, 116,
  118, 159, 243, 275,
  276, 291
10–12   269
10–15   58
11   19, 20, 32, 33,
  40, 41, 42, 51, 58,
  61, 66, 74, 87, 88,
  89n1, 93, 95, 98,
  101, 103, 109, 110,
  112, 123, 129, 155,
  159, 277, 284, 285,
  321, 328
11–12   87, 128
11–13   35, 42, 61, 87

12   11, 14, 19, 20, 22, 25, 40, 50, 51, 57, 84, 93, 95, 97, 99, 108, 109, 116, 159, 197, 277, 279, 292
12–13   41, 42, 51, 61, 62, 74, 87, 88, 93, 97, 101, 291
13   11, 19, 20, 24, 48, 68, 70, 87, 91, 95, 97, 99, 123, 137, 159, 264, 292, 322
14   31, 33, 40, 57, 61, 103, 115, 132
14–15   5, 9, 12, 26, 29, 31, 32, 41, 42, 51, 58, 59, 61, 67, 68, 74, 100, 101, 104, 112, 161, 249
14–16   35, 40, 42, 61, 101, 116
15   20, 59, 83, 106, 108, 110, 111, 116, 123, 282, 286
15–16   20
16   9, 11, 14, 19, 20, 22, 24, 40, 41, 42, 51, 57, 60, 61, 62, 68, 74, 77, 84, 91, 93, 101, 108, 111, 112, 116, 128, 159, 266, 267, 291, 294, 295, 316
16–17   40, 51
17   8, 11, 17, 19, 20, 33, 38, 40, 41, 51, 52, 60, 105, 112, 119, 159, 173, 265, 312, 315
17–18   8, 9, 32, 40, 41, 42, 51, 61, 74, 103, 111, 112, 132, 160, 238
17–19   40, 42, 58, 61, 112
17–23   35
18   8, 9, 17, 19, 20, 22, 59, 60, 68, 77, 91, 107, 109, 114,

128, 159, 267, 295, 315, 316
19   11, 20, 23, 40, 41, 42, 47, 50, 51, 57, 61, 62, 74, 84, 93, 108, 112, 116, 118, 119, 120, 121, 122, 127, 153, 291
19–20   40, 51
19–23   90
20   20, 38, 40, 51, 52, 56, 112, 117, 119, 122
20–21   18, 20, 42, 56, 113, 119, 125, 132
20–23   37, 38, 39, 41, 42, 51, 55, 113, 119
21   48, 50, 60, 64, 105, 120, 122, 123, 127, 189
21–22   22
22   18
22–23   20, 42, 50, 56, 64, 75n4, 102, 113, 116, 119, 122, 123, 124, 128, 132
23   18, 19, 22, 50, 60, 68, 76, 91, 95, 125, 267, 295
24   20, 102, 131, 135, 159, 202, 253, 337, 342
24–25   xi, 20, 29, 33, 35, 39, 39n35, 41, 42, 51, 130, 130–31, 131n5
25   6, 39n35, 60, 105, 131, 132, 134, 159, 175, 183, 344

## Revelation

1:1   45
1:4   49, 59, 175
1:5–6   131n5, 344
1:6   135, 136, 137, 203
1:7   106
2:2   191

2:2–3   194
2:6   128
2:11   97, 277
2:13–14   155
2:16   241
2:19   190
3:2   209, 337
3:3   329
3:10   263
3:11   241
3:17   198
3:18   98
4:9   222
4:11   219, 222
5:5   1
5:9   241
5:11   106
5:12   219, 273
5:12–13   222
5:13   131n5, 135, 136, 137
6:10   60, 106
6:15   45
6:17   69
7:2   271
7:5   1
7:12   131n5, 135, 137, 222, 273
8:1   104
8:2   271
8:6   271
8:10   292
8:13   89, 271
9:5   261
9:15   271
9:17–18   73, 125, 322
9:18   330
10:4   225
10:7   104
10:8   225
11:10   261
11:14   241
11:15   203
12:7   81, 82, 272
12:7–9   81
12:12   89
12:17   122
13:16   45
14:3–4   241

14:5   133, 330
14:7   292
14:10   261
14:12   122
14:13   225
15:8   133, 223
16:4   292
16:8   73, 125, 322
16:13   237
16:14   69, 334
16:15   98, 329
17:4   185
17:8   240
17:11   240
17:13   219
17:14   47
18:1   77
18:4   225
18:8   330
18:10   83, 89
18:12   185
18:16   89, 185
18:19   89
18:20   226
18:23   227
19:2   85
19:18   45
19:20   237
20:2–7   326
20:6   97
20:9   73, 125, 322
20:10   237, 261
20:11   329, 335
20:14   97
21:1   329, 335
21:2   121
21:8   97, 190
21:11   185, 223
21:19   185
21:23   223
21:26   222
21:27   335
22:7   241
22:11   201, 277
22:12   241
22:15   190, 307, 335
22:20   241
22:21   59

# Old Testament Apocrypha

## Additions to Esther

15:2   220

## Baruch

1:18   222
1:21   222

1:21 LXX   226
2:11   64
2:11 LXX   64
4:1   285

4:9–10   254
4:13   285
4:13 LXX   89
4:14   254

4:26   125
4:29   254

## 1 Esdras

1:28   227
1:47 LXX   226
2:26   246
8:24   264
9:6   271
9:47   137

## 2 Esdras

2:8   70
3:28–33   328
4:26   334
4:38–39   328
5:1–13   242
6:38   319
6:42   320
6:43   319
7:106   70
7:132–34   328
8:21   105
8:23   334
12:10   231
12:31–33   106
12:42   227
14:8–9   166
14:27–36   164

## Judith

2:11   250
5:3   273
9:11   134
12:2 LXX   190
13:16   301
13:20   137
14:13   270

## Letter of Jeremiah

3   104

## 1 Maccabees

1:11   317
1:13–14 LXX   266
1:63 LXX   75
2:21   285
3:19   273
4:43   199
4:50   227
5:25   290

5:36   290
5:51 LXX   96
6:22 LXX   106
7:7   264
7:11   227
8:30   239
11:37   225
13:50   301
14:10 LXX   190
14:21   222

## 2 Maccabees

1:1   200
1:28   261
2:3   55n4
2:7   123
2:16   199
3:3 LXX   190
3:34   221
3:39   220
4:2   270
4:43   267
4:49 LXX   190
5:15   121
5:16   222
5:17   60
5:20   60
5:25   246
5:27   253
6:12   55n4
6:14   264
6:23   259
6:28   257
7:5   55n4
7:9   124
7:13   261
7:17   261
7:21   55n4, 211
7:24   59, 59n8
7:35   220
7:37   134
7:38   254
8:11   73, 208
8:15   223
8:16   55n4
8:18   132
8:33   278, 289
9:6   261
9:16 LXX   190
9:26   55n4
9:28   274
10:6   210
10:24   300
10:36   274
11:27   223
12:7 LXX   96

12:22   220
12:42   55n4
13:14   55n4
15:2   220
15:3   220
15:8   55n4
15:10   211
15:12   192, 223
15:13   223
15:14   195
15:17   55n4
15:22   60

## 3 Maccabees

1:4   55n4
2:2   259
2:4   62, 252, 254, 321
2:4–7   62
2:5   62, 70, 252
2:6–7   62
2:9   223
2:13   259
2:21   220
2:24   83
2:26   243
3:26   264
5:12   260
5:15   211
5:36   55n4
5:47   256
6:1   192
6:26   260
6:29   134
6:30 LXX   190
6:32   134
6:40 LXX   190
7:3   264
7:5   97
7:14   264
7:16   134
7:18 LXX   190
7:22   221
7:23   137

## 4 Maccabees

1:2   192
1:10   192
1:11   194
1:16–17   232
1:20–21   278
1:22   278
1:24   278
1:25   278
1:28   278
1:30   192

1:32   117
1:33   278
2:11   286
2:12   264
4:3   322
4:10   271
4:13   232
4:19   286
4:26   268
5:13   286
5:23   278
5:34   193
6:10–11   261
6:35   278
7:6 LXX   75
7:9   194
7:18   128, 266
8:6   264
8:8   280
8:17   55n4
8:27   261
9:30   194
9:31   278
10:1   55n4
10:9   192
10:15   73
12:6   55n4
12:12   73
12:13   330
13:19–14:1   195
13:23   195
13:24   192
13:26   195
14:1   195
15:3   124
15:31–32   254
16:24   55n4
17:4   194
17:12   194
17:23   194, 257
18:5   264
18:24   137

## Prayer of Azariah

5   241
8   241
22   134

## Sirach

1:27   192
2:1   263
2:10   253
3:9   96
3:16   274
5:7   261

6:7   263
8:8   306
9:2–9   14
9:16 LXX   127
11:22   212
11:27   279
11:31   280
11:33   280
13:21   209
14:9   244
14:16   279
15:11–20   263
16:5–6   62
16:6   62
16:7   28, 62, 253
16:7–8   252
16:7–10   62
16:8   62, 250
16:8–10   71
16:9   62
16:10   62
16:21–23   317
16:24   227
17:8   221
17:10   221
17:13   221
17:25   69
18:4   221
18:9–10   326
18:10   344
18:26   212
18:30 LXX   266
18:32   279
20:24   280
22:10   247
23:23   196
24:3   292
27:3 LXX   127
27:5   263
27:7   263
31:8   133
33:22   303
33:28   246
34:1–7   74
35:14–26   326
35:18 LXX   106
35:19 LXX   326

35:22   326
36:1   60
36:7   221
36:7 LXX   334
36:10   334
37:11   197
37:18   182
37:29   279
38:23   215
40:10   254
40:18–27   303
40:19   133
40:26 LXX   127
41:9–10   283
42:21   221
43:5   319
43:5–26   319
43:15   221
43:22   292
43:26   319
43:33   339
44:16   102, 257
44:17   254
44:18   254
45:4   192
45:18   92
45:18–19   92
45:23 LXX   127
45:24   221
46:7   108
46:7–8   108
46:10 LXX   266
46:11 LXX   72
48:1 LXX   226
48:3   319
48:6   62
48:9   292
48:12   292
49:7 LXX   96
49:8   77
49:14   102
50:26   84
51:1   134

Susanna

54   333

Tobit

1:3   244, 285
1:3 LXX   89, 304
1:18 LXX   264
2:6   230
4:5   285
4:10   99, 293
4:14   259
8:8   137
8:17   60
10:1   261
10:13 LXX   309
12:15   82, 272
13:14 LXX   108
14:3–11   164
14:10   99, 293

Wisdom of Solomon

1:6   274
1:8   294, 318
2:4   292, 293
2:22   278
3:1–4   264
3:2   215
4:1 LXX   214
4:3–4   96
4:10–15   102
4:16   107, 254
4:16 LXX   59
4:19 LXX   214
5:6   228, 244, 284
5:6 LXX   304
5:14   292
5:23   292
6:17–20   191
6:18   201
7:2   278
7:6   215
7:7   339
7:15   339
7:17   330
7:25   311
8:3   60
8:7   192

8:8   253
8:10   222
8:13 LXX   214
9:1   319
9:8   225
9:15   210
10:3   90
10:6   257
10:6–9   71
10:8   318
10:17   278
11:1   312
11:5   264
11:8   264
11:9   261
11:21   198
11:23   328
12:10   328
12:12–15   264
12:16–18   273
12:17   273
12:18   198
12:24   98, 284, 295
12:27   240
13:10   253
14:1   97
14:5   197
14:12   187
14:15   57
14:25   187
14:26   60, 243, 267
14:29   277
16:4   261
16:16   240
17:3   318
17:20 LXX   99, 293
17:21   99, 293
18:5   254
18:11   73
19:11   279
19:14   71
19:17   257
19:18   330

# Old Testament Pseudepigrapha

**Ahiqar**

8.15 307

**Apocalypse of Abraham**

32.1 104

**Apocalypse of Elijah**

1.13 114

**Assumption of Moses**

7.9 109, 294
11.5–7 80

**2 Baruch**

6.8 115, 315
9.5 82
20.1–2 334
21.19–21 328
24.1–2 328
32.6 334
41.3 242
41.5 115, 315
42.4 242
44.12 335
48.10 105
48.12–13 326
55.8 106
56.10–16 67, 78
56.12 68
57.2 335
77–86 164
78–86 165, 167
78.2 168
83.1 334
85.8–9 328
86 37

**1 Enoch**

1 102
1–36 27, 27n23
1.2 103
1.3–4 105
1.4 273
1.5 67
1.6 334

1.6–7 73, 103, 125, 322
1.7 106
1.8 28, 102, 123
1.9 26, 31, 59, 101, 102, 104, 105, 107, 108
5.4 107, 107n6, 109, 294
5.8–9 335
6–12 26, 27, 67, 249
6–16 252
6.1–2 67, 250
6.2 67
7.1–8.3 27
9.1 82, 272
9.1–11 274
10.6 69, 106
10.7 67
10.9 67
10.13 69
10.15 67, 106
10.16 335
10.20–22 335
10.22 301
12.3–6 67
12.4 67, 68, 72
12.4–5 28
13.4–7 28
13.10 67
14.1 67
14.3 67
14.4 67
14.5 68, 69, 70
15.2 28
15.3 68, 69
15.7 68
16.2 67
16.3 69
17.5–6 99, 293
18.14–15 99
18.14–16 99n4
20.1–8 82, 272
20.2 82, 251, 272
20.5 81
20.5–6 82
21.3–6 99n4
21.10 69
22.1–11 264
22.11 69, 264
24.6 82
27.2 107, 107n6
27.4 123
32.3 223

37–71 27n23
37.1 104
38.2 335
40.2 102
40.9 82, 124, 272
45.4–5 335
52.6 73, 125, 322
54.6 81, 82, 272
58.3 124
60.8 104
61.1 267
61.10 76
63.6 99, 293
65.11 102
68.1 102
71.3 82, 102
71.8–9 82, 272
71.13 82, 272
72–78 27n23
72.1 334
80 99
80.2 99
80.3 99
80.6 99
83–90 27n23
89 28
90.26 242
91–104 164
91–108 27n23
91.1–19 166
91.16 329, 334
91.18–19 335
93.2 77
93.3 104
93.9 242
95.5 89n1
97.10 250
98.5 83
99.6 27
99.14 317
102.3 223
102.10 256
104.4 134
104.13 134

**2 Enoch**

20.1 76, 267
22.6 [A] 82
22.6 [B] 82
22.7 77
33.1–2 325
47.5 320
65.8 335

**4 Ezra**

see 2 Esdras under OT Apocrypha

**Joseph and Aseneth**

12.8 125

**Jubilees**

1.29 334
2.5–7 320
2.7 320
4.15 27, 78
4.16–25 102
4.22 68, 78
4.30 325
5.1–2 67, 78, 252
5.1–13 27
5.2 68
5.3–5 252
5.6 252
7.20 254
7.20–21 75, 267
7.20–39 27, 254
7.34 254
7.39 104
8.1–4 27
10.1–5 68
10.1–14 27
10.5 67
16.5–6 75
16.5–9 71
20.5–6 71
21–22 164
35 164
36.1–18 164

**Letter of Aristeas**

16 220
20 139
120 203
130 259
141–66 75, 267
144–61 75n5
154 319
155 230
155–57 181
187 132
216 259
222 85
277–78 193

## Life of Adam and Eve

25–29  165
49.3  125, 322

## Martyrdom and Ascension of Isaiah

3.16  82, 272
9.23 [Latin]  82, 272
9.32  77
11.32  223

## Odes of Solomon

2.15  134
7.45  134
9.47  134
9.49  221
11.23  197

## Psalms of Solomon

2.18  110
3.6  134
4.1  286
4.2  107, 256
4.6  187
4.12  286
6.5  127
8.9  286
9.5  274
13.11  124
13.11–12  124
14.9–10  123, 124
15.4  73, 125, 322
15.12  264
15.12–13  124
15.13  124
16.1  247
17.3  134
17.20  286
17.25  106, 335
17.34  127
17.36  335
17.40  127
17.45  123
18.7–9  127

18.10  316
18.11  109, 127

## Pseudo-Philo

### Liber antiquitatum biblicarum

16.1  92
16.3  93
18.2  288
18.7  285
18.12–14  285
18.13–14  91
19.1–5  164
24.1–5  164
28.3–4  164
28.5–10  165
33  165
57.2  92

## Sibylline Oracles

1.98–103  251
1.125  254
1.128–29  254
1.147–98  254
2.165–69  114
2.196–213  73, 125, 322
2.303  251
3.75–92  330
3.80–93  125, 322
3.288  132
3.409  333
3.580  174n2
3.778  97
4.43  70, 98, 293
4.171–82  125, 322
4.186  251
5.124  256
5.155–61  125, 322
5.177  260
5.206–13  125, 322
5.211–12  334
5.379  293

## Testament of Abraham

1.3  82
1.4–7 [A]  81

1.6  82
19.4 [A]  81

## Testament of Asher

2.7  128
5.2  124
6.5  261

## Testament of Benjamin

5.3  228
6.3  279
6.5  311
7.3–5  90
8.2–3  267
9.1  71

## Testament of Dan

3.4  85
4.2  211

## Testament of Issachar

6.1  115, 315
6.2  218, 243, 285

## Testament of Job

33.4  256, 329

## Testament of Joseph

3.4  279
10.1  194

## Testament of Judah

19.4  128, 266
23.1–2  243

## Testament of Levi

3.4  223
4.1  334
6.9  259
14.6  71
17.8  267
18.5  77, 134
18.14  134
19.1  228

## Testament of Moses

7.4  279
7.9  109, 294
11.5–7  80

## Testament of Naphtali

2.7–10  228
3.3  218, 243, 285
3.4  62, 71
3.4–5  62, 72, 252
3.5  62, 67, 78
4.1  71
8.8  193

## Testament of Reuben

5.1–6  68
5.5  264, 322
5.6  78

## Testament of Solomon

8.6  76, 267

## Testament of Zebulun

1.2  227
9.7  128, 266
10.3  73

# New Testament Apocrypha

| Acts of Peter | Apocalypse of Peter | Infancy Gospel of James | Pseudo-Clement |
|---|---|---|---|
| 35 212 | 14 212 | 9.8 4 | *Homilies* |
| | 22–23 142 | | 3.53 223 |

# Rabbinic Writings

| Babylonian Talmud | *Yoma* | Lamentations Rabbah | *Soṭah* |
|---|---|---|---|
| | 86b 334 | | 9.15 191 |
| *Baba Batra* | Ecclesiastes Rabbah | prologue 24 233 | Numbers Rabbah |
| 58a 225 | | | |
| *Baba Meṣiʿa* | 1.1.1 233 | Mishnah | 10.5 257 |
| 59b 225 | | *'Abot* | 13.20 233 |
| *Berakot* | Genesis Rabbah | 1.1 191 | 14.19 225 |
| 4b 233 | | 5.14 285 | 18.2 92 |
| *Sanhedrin* | 19.8 325 | *Berakot* | 18.3 92 |
| 11b 168 | 22.1 325 | 5.5 114 | |
| 97b 334 | 26.5 67, 258 | *Sanhedrin* | Song Rabbah |
| 98a 334 | 30.7 254 | 10.3 62 | 1.1.9 233 |
| 105b 289 | 50.4 259 | | |
| | 50.11 258, 259 | | |

# Targums

| Isaiah | Neofiti | Onqelos | on Num. 22:30 287, 288 |
|---|---|---|---|
| on 42:1 224 | on Gen 6:2 66–67 | on Gen. 6:2 66 | on Num. 24:14 91, 285 |
| | on Num. 16:1–3 92 | | |
| Jonathan | on Num. 22:30 288 | Pseudo-Jonathan | on Num. 24:25 91, 285 |
| on Deut. 34:6 80 | on Num. 26:9 92 | on Num. 16:1–2 92 | on Num. 26:9 92 |
| on Mic. 7:14 334 | | on Num. 22:5 288 | on Num. 31:8 285 |
| | | | on Deut. 34:6 81 |

# Nag Hammadi

On the Origin of the World

100.10–14 320n3

# Qumran / Dead Sea Scrolls

| CD | 2.17–3.1 67, 78 | 2.18–21 62 | 6.11 115, 315 |
|---|---|---|---|
| 2.17 62 | 2.17–3.12 62 | 3.1–12 62 | |
| | 2.18 67, 68 | 4.4 47 | |

411

**1QapGen**

2.1 67

**1QH**

3.19–36 125
10.8 77
11.19–36 322

**1QM**

9.14–15 82, 272
13.15 228

15.9 228
17.6–8 81

**1QpHab**

2.5–6 114
7.5–14 326

**1QS**

1.9–10 228
2.15 73
3.13–4.14 228
4.9–11 191

5.13 73, 267
6.10 200
6.22 200

**1QSa**

1.1 115, 315
2.1 47
2.11 47

**4QʻAmram**

1.10–14 81

**4QFlor**

10–14 224

**4QpsJub (4Q227)**

4 67

**11QpsZion (11Q5)**

22.13 77

# Papyri

**Amherst**

II.3334 286

**Berlin**

7927.8 218, 243, 285

*BGU*

2.596.10 94

*CPJ*

16, l. 8 38n32

**Dura-Europos**

16 b7 174

**Fayûm**

19.10 214

*IT*

n. 67 134

**Oxyrhynchus**

938.3 246
2787, 14–15 37

**Rylands**

2.144 83

**Strassburg**

1.24.15 276
I.416 286

**Tebtunis**

1.33.18 53
I 34, l. 13f. 38n32
3.769.74 53

**Zenon at Cairo**

I 59018, l. 8 38n32
V 59804, l. 10f. 38n32

# Josephus

*Against Apion*

1.11 §59 84, 244
1.26 §232 186
1.31 §282 199
1.33 §296 261
2.2 §26 84, 276
2.4 §37 84, 276
2.8 §89 84, 244
2.11 §130 84, 276
2.13 §142 84, 198, 276
2.16 §156 226
2.16 §168 221
2.19 §175 130
2.24 §194 73
2.24 §202 299
2.29 §213 85, 275
2.33 §240 251

*Jewish Antiquities*

proem 4 §22 218, 243, 285
proem 4 §23 186
proem 4 §24 221
1.1.1 §§194–95 71
1.2.1 §§52–53 90
1.2.1–2 §§52–66 90
1.2.1 §61 90
1.2.3 §70 73, 125, 322
1.3.1 §73 67, 78
1.3.1 §74 254
1.3.7 §96 322
1.3.8 §99 73
2.2.4 §17 312
2.5.6 §86 341
2.6.7 §130 83
2.6.9 §163 198

2.9.1 §202 198
2.9.2 §207 268
2.15.5 §329 268
2.112.1 §267 222
3.1.4 §15 283
3.1.4 §16 268
3.5.2 §80 220
3.5.3 §85 268
3.8.5 §203 220
3.12.2 §279 133
4.2.2–3 §§14–23 92
4.2.4 §26 195
4.6.2 §104 91, 288
4.6.3 §§109–10 287
4.6.6 §§126–30 91, 285
4.6.6 §130 109
4.6.6–9 §§126–40 91, 285
4.6.8 §137 91

4.6.12 §151 243
4.7.29 §274 110
4.7.45–47 §§309–19 165
4.8.2 §189 215
4.8.2 §§215 268
4.8.2 §§217 268
4.8.23 §248 83
4.8.44 §304 198
5.1.26 §109 136
5.5.3 §205 292
6.5.3 §80 267
6.7.4 §142 268
6.7.4 §147 268
6.11.9 §238 125
7.4.1 §75 202
7.6.2 §124 259
8.8.5 §235 193
8.9.1 §241 227
8.10.2 §251 262

8.10.2 §252  243
8.13.8 §§358–59  244
9.3.3 §55  220
9.8.5 §173  268
9.8.6 §182  223
10.7.2 §103  115
10.9.2 §162  85
10.10.2 §193  279
10.11.6 §262  275
10.11.7 §263  136
10.11.7 §266  222
11.4.2 §79  120
11.4.9 §117  83
11.5.1 §130  268
11.6.12 §279  227
11.8.4 §324  189
12.2.3 §29  110
12.2.12 §99  85
12.2.15 §118  222
12.4.6 §191  340

12.5.4 §253  120
12.9.1 §357  268
13.3.1 §63  214
13.8.2 §242  223
13.10.6 §297  57, 317
15.5.3 §136  77
15.10.1 §347  202–3
16.4.3 §115  121
16.7.1 §181  53
16.8.4 §244  246
16.9.3 §290  55
16.10.1 §301  279
17.3.2 §54  183
17.5.6 §130  183
17.5.8 §142  223
17.11.2 §313  257
18.1.1 §§1–10  1
18.1.6 §23  1
18.4.6 §107  83
18.6.9 §214  136

19.4.6 §273  68
20.5.40 §112  243
20.9.1 §199  270
20.9.2 §204  189

### Jewish War

1.3.1 §71  174
1.21.13 §430  117
1.24.1 §468  57
2.9.2 §171  240
2.9.6 §181  211
2.15.1 §313  259
2.17.8 §433  1
2.17.10 §455  301
3.10.2 §475  270
4.2.3 §103  217
4.3.7 §154  226
4.5.2 §323  75, 267
4.8.4 §§483–84  71

5.3.4 §120  282
5.5.5 §220  202
5.13.7 §566  92–93
6.1.4 §32  333
6.2.1 §103  72–73
6.2.1 §109  113, 312
6.2.10 §172  270
7.6.4 §190  53
7.8.1 §264  260
7.10.2 §421  282

### The Life

4 §18  254
32 §158  274
34 §171  55
35 §177  245
62 §320  274
65 §337  245

# Philo

### On Agriculture

30 §133  215
32 §144  307
34 §156  54
40 §177  132

### Allegorical Interpretation

2.17 §§69–70  288
3.6 §18  215
3.9 §30  85, 275
3.14 §43  226
3.34 §106  328

### On the Change of Names

8 §60  133
36 §197  194
37 §203  288

### On the Cherubim

2.35 §127  330

### On the Confusion of Tongues

2 §5  121
27 §141  294

### On the Decalogue

11 §49  229
21 §104  186

### On Dreams

1.1 §2  233
1.43 §256  183
2.2 §8  120
2.2 §11  133, 209
2.20 §140  245

### On Drunkenness

18 §75  222
48 §199  132
53 §223  256

### On the Embassy to Gaius

1 §6  265
7 §49  251
12 §87  195
14 §103  251
18 §120  21n21
19 §131  21n21
19–20 §§131–32  85
20 §132  21n21
25 §162  21n21
43 §338  53

### On the Eternity of the World

5 §19  158
5 §§22–24  158
6 §§26–27  158
8 §§39–40  158
14 §70.1  56
16–17 §§83–88  158
17 §88  158

### On Giants

7 §30  121

### On the Life of Abraham

22 §112  240
25 §129  265
26 §133  71
28 §144  186
36 §206  240

### On the Life of Joseph

5 §26  283
38 §222  270
41 §247  274

### On the Life of Moses

1.16 §§92–94  217
1.16–17 §96  256
1.24 §139  270
1.38 §210  233
1.48 §264  288
1.48 §§264–65  91, 288
1.48 §§266–68  285
1.49 §272  287
1.50 §276  288
1.50 §277  288
1.51 §281  231
1.51 §283  233
1.52 §286  231
1.53 §293  288
1.54–55 §§295–304  91, 285
1.56 §305  60n9, 243
2.3 §14  226
2.10 §§57–58  257
2.14 §69  233
2.17 §84  230
2.37 §198  260
2.39 §212  245
2.39 §§215–16  130
2.46 §250  233
2.48 §264  233
2.49 §273  233
2.51 §291  80

### On the Migration of Abraham

3 §16  214

### On Planting

28 §117  226
34 §151  239

### On the Posterity of Cain

11 §38  90

### Questions and Answers on Genesis

1 §92  78
3 §10  231, 232

### On Rewards and Punishments

4 §25  282
20 §121  244
20 §126  260
26 §152  251

### On the Sacrifices of Cain and Abel

5 §27  191
5 §32  117, 191
16 §62  322
21 §76  218

### On Sobriety

11  280
13 §68  226

### On the Special Laws

1.8 §45  77
1.29 §148  307
1.38 §209  183
1.56 §307  136, 265
2.14 §54  240
2.43 §240  279
2.46 §255  60, 240
3.5 §27  280
4.8 §49  231

### That Every Good Person Is Free

22 §159  282

### That God Is Unchangeable

28 §132  203
30 §143  128, 266
34 §156  322

### That the Worse Attacks the Better

10 §32  90
20–21 §§71–72  157
21 §73  157
21 §78  90
23 §83  181
27 §§101–3  194
27 §102  299

### On the Virtues

12 §76  215n2
12 §77  215
26 §142.1  56

### Who Is the Heir?

12 §58  319
14 §69  233
34 §166  265
52 §259  231, 232

# Classical Writers

### Aelius Aristides

*Platonic Discourses*
307.9–10  270

### Aeschines

*Speeches*
1.12  187

### Aeschylus

*Agamemnon*
39  319
*Persians*
839  70, 98, 293
*Prometheus Bound*
301  220
622–24  304
750–51  303

### Apollodorus

*Library and Epitome*
1.1.2  251

### Appian

*Bella civilia*
1.3.26.12  213
1.71  113, 312
3.75  227
5.19  226

### Aristides

*Orations*
1.3–5  319
23.31  120

### Aristophanes

*Plutus*
1001  58n6
*Thesmophoriazusae*
528–30  306

### Aristotle

*Colors*
3.793A  227
*History of Animals*
535A–536B  287
593A  275

600A  275
608B.10  109
618A  287
*Metaphysics*
998A.20–30  330
*Meteorology*
28  98
31  98
33  292
35  292
342B  98
346B  292
*Nicomachean Ethics*
3.6.3  95, 98
7.1.1–7.11.5  193
7.1.6  193
1127A  110, 111
1161B  45
*Politics*
2.1262B.23  309
1290B  117
1335B  213
*Rhetoric*
1.2.1  34
1.3.3–4  35, 163
1.4–10  35, 163

1.5.4  222
2.2.5–6  274
2.6.2  98
2.6.3–8  98
2.6.13  98
2.6.13–14  98
2.8.2  123
3.12.1  37, 164
3.12.6  35
3.14–19  163n5
1366B  190
1378B  116
1385B  123
1414A  214

### Arrian

*Anabasis*
3.10.2  110
6.22.8  302
6.29.1  68
8.11.1  222

## Artemidorus Daldianus

*The Interpretation of Dreams*
2.25  338
4.11  338

## Athenaeus

*Deipnosophistae*
2.36  83n2
12.546E  296
546F  157

## Augustus

*Res gestae*
6  57

## Catullus

*Poems*
5.4–6  317

## Cicero

*Pro Caelio*
47  279
*On Divination*
1.5.9  212
1.6.12  74
1.18.34  74
*On Ends*
1.29–33  157
1.37–39  157
*Epistulae ad Atticum*
3.15  146
8.14.1  37, 164
9.10.1  37, 164
11.2  146
11.5  146
12.53  37, 164
*Epistulae ad familiares*
5.20  147
16.4.3  146
16.10.2  146
16.11.1  146
*On Fate*
10.23  299
11.23  299
17.40  299
18.41–19.45  299

*De inventione rhetorica*
1.1–19  163n5
2.66  182
*De legibus*
1.7.23  191
*On the Nature of the Gods*
1.116  182
2.118  323
*De officiis*
3.24.92–3.25.95  184
*Orator*
6.21  36
26.91  36
*Partitiones oratoriae*
27  163n5
*De senectute*
13.45  280

## Demetrius

*De elocutione*
223  37, 164
226  37, 164
228  37, 164
229  37, 164
231  37, 164
234  37, 164

## Demosthenes

*Epistles*
2.21  304n2
*Speeches*
21.165  309

## Dio Cassius

*Roman History*
56.25.5–6  212

## Dio Chrysostom

*Orations*
3.97  93
4.33  21n20
4.37  21n20
4.38  21n20
4.116  222
8.36  217
11.14  21n20
12.12  21n20
12.28  186

12.29  186
17  244
17.1–11  63
17.2  63, 113
17.3–5  209
17.4  197
17.6–7  245
17.7  197
17.16  91, 245, 278
23.11  21n20
31.95  181
32.10–11  244–45
32.11  91, 111, 278
32.30  21n20
33.4–5  21n20
35.1  91, 245, 278
44.10  222
49.9  278
54.1  21n20, 217
55.7  21n20
70.10  21n20
77/78.27  21n20

## Diodorus Siculus

*Library of History*
1.14.3  260
1.25.4  218
1.83.8  189
1.96.5  239
2.29.4  226
2.45.2  183
3.44.2  121
3.53.1  68
3.59.1  299
3.67.2  83
4.2.6  262
4.8.4  218
5.23.1–2  218
5.31.4  186
5.62.1  299
11.6.3  259
12.16.2  304n2
12.41.4  239
12.45.1  210
13.97.7  222, 232
15.10.2  37, 130n4
15.33.1  202
15.58.1  76
17.24.2  68
18.34.4  189
18.60.4  212
19.71.3  280
23.15.2  214
37.2.5  54

## Diogenes Laertius

*Lives and Opinions of Eminent Philosophers*
2.12  157
2.136  133, 209
6.102  330
7.110  187
7.111  123
7.134  323
7.137  323
9.13  340
10.18  214
10.73–74  156
10.133  156, 299
10.137  85
10.145  128, 266

## Diogenes of Oenoanda

*Inscription*
frg. 6  318
frg. 8  318

## Dionysius of Halicarnassus

*Antiquitates romanae*
4.24.6  279
4.28.2  270
5.62.4  183
10.54.1  190
*On Literary Composition*
16  161

## Epicharmus

*Fragments*
148  191

## Epictetus

*Discourses*
1.4.10  115, 315
1.9.24  259
1.22.13  259
1.26.3  283
2.15.8  120, 121
2.17.26  127
2.18.27  283

2.22.35 261
3.12 283
3.21.13 254
3.22.13 127
3.22.39–40 298
3.22.48 298
3.22.69 302
3.22.70 254
3.23.6 130n4
4.1 298
4.1.4 127
4.1.29 275
4.4.38 215
4.6.1–5 127
*Enchiridion*
33.8 243
48.3 350

## Epicurus

*Key Doctrines*
3–4 157
8–10 157
*Letter to Herodotus*
38 318
*Letter to Menoeceus*
10.128 278
127–32 157
132 157
134 298
*Sententiae Vaticanae*
33 296
67 299
77 299

## Euripides

*Bacchanals*
199 268
218 245
*Helen*
622 306
*Hercules*
735–39 305
1243–44 294
*Hippolytus*
436 310
966–69 302
1416 70, 98, 293
*Ion*
132 45n4
309 45n4
1157–58 228

## Gellius

*Attic Nights*
3.5.2 281

## Gennadius Scholarius

*Grammatica*
2.467.34 198

## Heraclitus

*Homeric Allegories*
20–26 323
53 307

## Herodotus

*Histories*
1.15 214
1.53 113, 312
1.68 245
1.79 65
2.55 287
2.57 287
3.52.5 304
4.134 115, 315
4.204 261
9.101 202
9.101.2 306

## Hesiod

*Theogony*
617–25 250
715–25 250
718–19 251
729–31 251
*Works and Days*
242 254

## Hierocles

*On Duties*
4.27.20 195
4.27.202 195

## Homer

*Iliad*
2.102–8 191
6.209 318
6.401 309
8.13–14 250
9.524 58n6
9.537 319
11.241 317
15.191 251
19.404–10 287
21.56 70, 98, 251, 293
*Odyssey*
2.365 309
3.272 319
4.817 309
8.245 317
11.55 70, 98, 293
11.57 251
20.356 70, 98, 293

## Horace

*Art*
131 161
131–36 161, 272

## Iamblichus

*Vita Pythagorica*
17.76.2 279

## Isocrates

*Archidamus*
6.95 267
*Ad Demonicum*
9 112
21 283
32 280
*Ad Nicoclem*
10–11 283
*De pace*
34 282
39 54
*Panathenaicus*
8 108–9
*Panegyricus*
85.6 54n1
*Philippus*
69 54n1

## Juvenal

*Satires*
1.141 275
5 93, 94, 280

## Lucian

*Alexander the False Prophet*
54 340
*Dialogues of the Dead*
16.2 306, 306n4
18.1 306
*Fisherman*
48 282
*Icaromenippus*
30 278
*Nigrinus*
4 298
*Phalaris*
2.5 289
*Timon*
13 109
55 109
*Vitarum auctio*
18 198

## Lucretius

*On the Nature of Things*
1.225–37 318
2.251–93 299
2.1170–74 157
3.338–50 157
5.146–49 156
5.146–52 327
5.826–36 157

## Marcus Aurelius

*Meditations*
2.3 108
5.9 132

## Musonius Rufus

*Fragments*
12 243
17 190

## Nicander

*Theriaca*
795 276

# Ovid

*Amores*
1.4 281
1.4.1–70 280
1.4.15–20 281
*Art of Love*
1.229–52 281
*Metamorphoses*
1.253–61 323

# Pausanius

*Description of Greece*
7.10.4 53
8.52.6 183
10.32.12 45n4
10.32.13 46

# Petronius

*Satyricon*
26.6–78.8 280

# Philostratus

*De gymnastica*
42.14–19 197
*Vitae sophistarum*
2.550.21 254

# Plato

*Gorgias*
507B 194
*Greater Hippias*
281C 267
*Laws*
3.691E 181
729E 121
736E 120
814E 302
*Letters*
323C 37
*Phaedo*
66A 311
81C 311
82E 188
*Phaedrus*
265B 96
275C–D 167

*Philebus*
16C 57
*Protagoras*
323E 263
*Republic*
7.530A 319
10.13–16 166
614B–21D 166
*Timaeus*
26E 218

# Plautus

*Menaechmi*
571–79 192

# Pliny the Elder

*Natural History*
8.81.219 275

# Pliny the Younger

*Epistles*
10.96 302
10.96.6 242
10.96.9–10 242

# Plotinus

*Enneads*
6.7.13 284

# Plutarch

*Agis and Cleomenes*
3.1 57, 244
16.1 244
*Alcibiades*
22.3 220
*Alexander*
22.4.5 275
*Brutus*
27.6 68
*De cohibenda ira*
461B 109
*Conjugalia praecepta*
144C–D 243
*Demetrius*
1.6 73

*On Divine Vengeance*
563B–68 166
*Fabius Maximus*
23.2.3 56
*De fraterno amore*
478E–F 195
479D 195
482E–F 195
*Moralia*
12E 197
25C 340
49B 110
49C 110
131A 91, 111, 245, 278
216B 57
266F–276A 222
328D 239
362B 227
486B 222
493C–D 275
493D 85, 275
525A–B 109
528E 281
528E–F 281
548C 327
549B 327
551C–52D 328
567F 222
604A 98
706A 85
706B 281
712C 187, 299
875C 330
1087B 266
1087B–D 128
1096C 128, 266
1098D 266
1119B 110, 294
1124C 217
*Nicias*
9.3 319
*De Pythiae oraculis*
402B 327
*De sera numinis vindicta*
548C 155, 156
548C–D 246
549B 156
*Solon*
12.3 267
*Themistocles*
30.1 319

*Theseus*
1.2–3 218
*Timoleon*
6.1 96
238 96
*Titus Flamininus*
9.5 298
10.3–5 298

# Polyaenus

*Stratagems in War*
6.7.2 301

# Polybius

*Universal History*
1.6.5 243
1.18.11 189
2.7.8 239
2.22.11 82, 126
3.38.3 218
3.63.2 239
3.82.8 110
3.111.10 185
4.17.4 282
4.21.3 270
4.82.1 259
5.28.9 243
5.41.3 83
6.56.12 239
18.28.1 185
21.29.12 189
24.11.3 302
36.16.6 301
38.18.2 83

# Propertius

*Elegies*
3.8 280

# Pseudo-Aristotle

*De mundo*
6.2 319
*Virtues and Vices*
1250B.15 188
1251A 263

# Pseudo-Callisthenes

*Alexander Romance*
2.1.5 231

**Pseudo-Longinus**

*On the Sublime*

4.5 281
13 161
14 161

**Pseudo-Lucian**

*The Cynic*
17 109

**Pseudo-Plutarch**

*Pro nobilitate*
21 227

**Pseudo-Zonaras**

*Lexicon*
711.11 198
1380.2 198

**Quintilian**

*Institutio oratoria*
2.4.20 21
2.4.22 22
2.15.34 34
3.7.15 190
3.9.5 35
4.1.5 35
4.2.1 35
4.5.1 35
5.Pr.5 35
6.1.1 35
9.4.23–25 87
9.4.25 87
10.2 161
10.2.14 162
12.10.58 35

**Quintus Smyrnaeus**

*Posthomerica*
2.612 70, 98, 293
2.619 70, 98, 293

**Seneca**

*De beneficiis*
3.38.2 200
*Epistulae morales*
40.1 43, 44
67.10 194
75.1 37
75.18 298, 301
85.2 191
94.21 211
94.25–26 230
95.65 191

**Seneca the Elder**

*Suasoriae*
3.7 161

**Sextus Empiricus**

*Outlines of Pyrrhonism*
1.56 307

**Sophocles**

*Ajax*
664–65 306
*Electra*
509 317

**Strabo**

*Geography*
11.5.3 218
11.6.2 218
5.1.9 218
6.1.9 287
9.3.12 218

**Suda**

*Lexicon*
1065.1 198

**Suetonius**

*Divus Titus*
3.2 146
*Nero*
16.2 244

**Tacitus**

*Agricola*
1.4 97
*Annals*
15.44.2–8 244
*Histories*
5.5 14

**Theophrastus**

*Characters*
17.1 108
29.6 306

**Thucydides**

*History of the Peloponnesian War*
1.32.1 226
1.70.3 270

2.17.2 306
2.54.3 214
2.60.2–7 54n1

**Timaeus**

*Sicilian History*
4.5 281

**Varro**

*On Agriculture*
1.17.1 45

**Xenophon**

*Agesilaus*
5.1 302
*Anabasis*
3.2.32 54
6.1.23 287
7.7.36 198, 209
*Cynegeticus*
13.5 218
*Cyropaedia*
2.3.9–10 85
7.5.64 276
8.4.6 198
8.8.27 59, 107
*Hellenica*
2.4.20 254
4.1.30 280
7.1.39 37
*Memorabilia*
1.2.55 55n4
1.5.4–5 193
2.1.4 282
4.7.5 98
*Symposium*
4.42 198

# Church Fathers

**Adamantius**

*De recta in Deum fide*
58.1 299

**Apostolic Constitutions**

6.16.3 29
7.46 3

**Augustine**

*City of God*
15.23 3, 5, 30
18.38 3, 5, 30, 33
*Heresies*
7 24n22, 296n1

**Barnabas**

15.4 142, 325
16.5 28

**1 Clement**

intro. 49
4.7 90

6.4 97
7.6 254
9.4 254
9–12 73
11 141
23.3 141, 141n1, 147
23.3–4 317n1
51.4 93
59.3 220
65.2 6n6, 38, 130

## 2 Clement

2.4 341
2.6 209
11.2 58, 141, 141n1,
  147
11.2–4 317n1
13.3 218
13.4 341
15.1 193
16.3 334
19.1 37

## Clement of Alexandria

*Comments on the Epistle of Jude*
in toto 77
1–4 3
*Exhortation to the Greeks*
10.92.4 307
*Fragments from Cassiodorus*
in toto 27
*Letter to Theodorus*
1.3 12
1.7 12, 142
*Selections from the Prophets*
53.4 27
*Stromata*
3.2 18, 24, 24n22
3.2.10 24
3.2.11 11, 12, 25
3.20 296n1
6.8.65 129
7.17 146

## Didache

4.1 76
10.6 330
11 238
11.5–6 91, 278
11.8–12 75
11.12 91, 278
16.3 114

## Diognetus

6.8 211
12.9 38, 130

## Epiphanius

*Panarion*
27 296n1
27.1–28.1 24n22
30.14 24n22, 296n1
32.3–7 24n22, 296n1
66.20.1–2 3

## Eusbeius

*Ecclesiastical History*
1.7.11 16
1.7.14 13
1.13.10 3, 11
2.23.25 5
3.3.1 140
3.3.2 141
3.3.4 141
3.11 16
3.11.1 16
3.19.1–3.20.1 16
3.19.1–3.20.8 13
3.20.1 16
3.20.5–6 16
3.20.7 16
3.20.8 13, 16
3.25.3 5, 141, 143
3.32.5–6 13
3.39.15 146
4.5.3 3
4.7.9–11 24n22,
  296n1
6.13.6 5
6.14.1 5, 142
6.25.8 143

## Firmilian of Caesarea

*Epistles*
75.6 143

## Gelasius Cyzicenus

*Historia Ecclesiastica*
2.17.17 80

## Hippolytus

*Refutation of All Heresies*
7.2 24n22
70.32–33 296n1

## Ignatius

*Letter to the Ephesians*
6.2 239
*Letter to the Trallians*
6.1 239

## Irenaaeus

*Against Heresies*
1.25 24n22, 296n1
1.25.2 24
1.25.3 24
2.31–32 24n22
2.31–33 296n1
4.16.2 28
5.23.2 142, 325
5.28.3 325

## Jerome

*Commentary on Ezekiel*
18 129
*Epistles*
53.9 143
120.11 143, 146
*Homilies*
45 29
*Lives of Illustrious Men*
4 3, 5, 29

## John Chrysostom

*Homilies on First Thessalonians*
9 279

## Justin Martyr

*Dialogue with Trypho*
29.1 223

## Lactantius

*The Divine Institutes*
3.17 156, 279

## Leo the Great

*Sermon*
27.3 303

## Martyrdom of Polycarp

intro. 49
11.1 303
22.3 38, 130

## Muratorian Canon

66–67 6
68–69 6

## Origen

*Commentary on John*
5.3 143
19.6 5
*Commentary on Matthew*
10.17 3, 4, 5, 7
*Commentary on Romans*
3.6 5
*Homilies on Numbers*
6.676 143
*On Opposing Powers*
3.2 3

*De principiis*
3.2.1 80

## Polycarp

*Letter to the
Philippians*
greeting 6n6
7.2 238

## Shepherd
## of Hermas

*Mandates*
4.3.3 212

6.2.5 279
8.3 279
9.9 96–97
12.2.1 279
*Similitudes*
5.4.1 212
5.6.1 76
6.2.6–7 302
6.5.5 279
8.9.4 212
9.9.3 261
9.14.4 340
9.17.5 302
9.20.4 212
9.23.5 239

9.26.6 212
9.28.7 250

## Tatian

*Address
to the Greeks*
12.4 280

## Tertullian

*The Apparel
of Women*
1.2 27
1.3 3, 5, 26–27

*Idolatry*
4 27
*Prescription against
Heretics*
3 24n22
*The Soul*
23 24n22, 296n1
35 24n22, 296n1
*The Veiling
of Virgins*
7 27